Microsoft Office 2000 User Specialist Study Guide

Microsoft® Office 2000 User Specialist Study Guide

Gini Courter
Annette Marquis

San Francisco • Paris • Düsseldorf • Soest • London

Associate Publisher: Amy Romanoff
Contracts and Licensing Manager: Kristine O'Callaghan
Acquisitions & Developmental Editor: Sherry Bonelli
Editor: Elizabeth Hurley-Clevenger
Project Editor: Colleen Strand
Technical Editor: Scott Warmbrand
Electronic Publishing Specialist: Robin Kibby
Project Team Leader: Lisa Reardon
Proofreaders: Kathy Drasky and Elaine Lewinnek
Indexer: Lynnzee Elze
Companion CD: Ginger Warner
Cover Designer: Design Site
Cover Illustrator/Photographer: Jack D. Meyers, Design Site

Library of Congress Card Number: 99-65194
ISBN: 0-7821-2574-3

Manufactured in the United States of America

10 9 8 7 6 5

To all those pioneering souls who have already become Microsoft Office User Specialists.

Acknowledgements

A book with so much material and covering so many topics is always an amazing undertaking, especially in an age where some of the people working on the project may communicate only through e-mail. It's incredible what can be accomplished without the telephone or face-to-face meetings! However, without the personal touch of our acquisitions and developmental editor, Sherry Bonelli, we could not do the work that we do. Sherry always makes us feel loved and appreciated and that makes all the difference.

Colleen Strand, our project editor, was given the somewhat dubious honor of getting her project editor feet wet with us on this project. We hope that we didn't make her too crazy, as we provided her with an introduction to the Sybex production process and the Courter/Marquis style. Good luck with future projects and thanks for diving right into the melee.

Our editor, Elizabeth Hurley-Clevenger, provided valuable suggestions and corrections to make our writing better. Thanks, Elizabeth, for working so feverishly to get everything in on schedule. Our technical editor, Scott Warmbrand, checked and tested the material to make sure it all worked the way we said it did. We especially appreciated the additional "trainer eyes" he brought to the project.

We also want to extend our thanks to the Production group: Lisa Reardon, the Project Team Leader, for managing the book through the entire Production process, Electronic Publishing Specialist Robin Kibby, who laid out the pages so beautifully, and Kathy Drasky and Elaine Lewinnek, who proofread them to make sure we didn't miss anything. You all are fabulous!

Our special thanks goes to Karla Browning who contributed so much to this book through her work as reviser. She bailed us out of a number of time crunches, tackled new material when asked and worked hard to get the CD-ROM in shape before leaving on vacation. We cannot ever express our appreciation for your quality work and your willingness to pitch in whenever and wherever we need you. You are an incredible member of the TRIAD team. Thanks, Karla.

Contents at a Glance

Table of Contents

Introduction

Microsoft Office 2000 User Specialist Study Guide is designed to prepare you for the Microsoft Office User Specialist exams and, in the process, make you a more knowledgeable Office user. Most Office users use less than 15% of the programs' features—they learn what they need to know to accomplish a particular task. Chances are, however, that the methods they use are neither the most efficient or the most effective. Hidden in the menus and toolbars throughout Office is an incredible array of tools designed to help you produce every type of document from a simple letter to an entire Web site. Knowing how to delve more deeply into the available features is what sets a competent user apart from the rest. By the time you finish this book, you will be well equipped to impress your colleagues (and maybe even your employer) with your ability to tackle any project with confidence and skill.

About This Book

This book is a study guide organized around the MOUS objectives published by Microsoft. The Appendix gives you more information about the MOUS exams and what you need to do to prepare. Also in the Appendix, you'll find a comprehensive list of MOUS objectives (skill sets and activities) you need to know to pass the MOUS exams. It's a good idea to start by reviewing the objectives for both the Core and Expert exams so you know what you are aiming for. This book covers each of the activities listed in the guidelines.

Visit the Microsoft Certification site, `www.mous.net`, to get the most current information about the MOUS exam guidelines.

The certification map included with the objectives guides you to the page number where each activity is presented. Every objective is covered somewhere in the book, but you'll find that they are not all presented in order. Why? As experienced trainers who work with beginning and advanced students on a regular basis, we are confident that you'll find it easier to learn the required skills in the order presented here. We have grouped together skills that are shared among the Office applications so that you can learn those once and then focus on those skills that are unique to the application you are studying. In order for you to develop a solid grasp of the fundamentals, we have included the most commonly used skills first. More advanced skills build on these basics and by the time you get to them, you'll be ready. After you have finished learning each skill in a particular application, you can then go back through the list of objectives in order and make sure you are comfortable completing each of the required activities.

To prepare for an exam, work through one application and one chapter at a time. At the beginning of each section related to a specific MOUS activity, you'll find a heading that looks like this, representing the objective number listed in Appendix A.

Objective W2000.1.6

Not all sections relate to specific objectives. We included some additional topics that we think it is important for you to know even if you will not be tested on them (isn't that just like a teacher!). These topics help to round out your understanding of a specific objective and give you the background you need to move ahead.

Throughout the chapter, you'll find summaries of the steps to accomplishing the tasks described in the previous section. Use summaries like the one shown here to review your knowledge and to practice the steps involved in completing a task:

Creating a Numbered or Bulleted List

1. If the text you want to number is already entered, highlight the paragraphs to be numbered, and click the Numbering or Bullets button to number or bullet each paragraph.

   OR

1. To automatically number text as you type, type the number 1 and a period, space once, then enter your text for item 1. For bullets, begin with an asterisk and a space.
2. Press Enter. Word will automatically number the next item 2 and press the Numbering button on the Personal toolbar, or bullet the next item and press the Bullets button.
3. Continue entering text and pressing the Enter key to create numbered or bulleted points.
4. When you are finished creating the list, press Enter twice to turn automatic numbering or bullets off.

After each major topic or group of topics, you will find a *Hands On* section. Each will give you a chance to apply what you've learned. If you can complete these exercises *without* help from the book, you should be in pretty good shape for the exam. Just like the example here, we've included the objectives the exercises relate to so you can refer to the text if you need assistance:

Hands On: Objectives W2000.3.16, 3.5, E.2.2, 3.10 and E.1.2

1. Open an existing document, or create a new document, that is at least three pages long. Save the document before proceeding.
   a) Add a header that contains the name of the document and the date to all but the first page.
   b) Insert a centered page number. Do not number the first page.
   c) Save the document under a different name and then print it.
2. Manually hyphenate an existing document.
3. Create a footer for the odd pages and a different footer for the even pages of a document.
4. Modify the footers you created in Step 3 by adding the date to them.
5. Select a paragraph that has a page break in the middle of it. Set text flow options so the page does not break in the middle of the paragraph.

Notes, Tips, and Warnings

Throughout the book you'll find additional comments about the material in the form of notes, tips, and warnings.

Notes provide additional information about a topic.

Tips offer another way of doing something or a shortcut to completing a particular task.

Warnings suggest possible problems you may encounter when completing a task or things to look out for along the way.

We hope you'll find that each of these extra comments helps you to understand Office 2000 more fully so that you can apply your skills to even more complex Office 2000 applications.

Additional Help on the Web

Although we recommend that you create your own documents to practice the skills in this book, most of the documents used as examples are available on the CD-ROM and for download at `www.Sybex.com`. If you get stuck on how to set up a particular worksheet, we hope these examples will help you figure it out. We have also included additional practice exercises and important links to other resources to help you prepare for the MOUS exams. We hope these additional materials will make your preparation even easier.

A Final Check

When you complete an entire chapter, review the objectives once again and see if there are any topics that you are uncertain about. Go back and review those sections in the text and try the Hands On exercises a second time using different documents. If you're still having difficulty, make a note of it and go on to the next topic. Working on related topics sometimes causes the topic with which you're struggling to fall into place.

When you've finished all the topics, you're ready to take the MOUS exam. Do the best you can—you can always take it again if you find that the first attempt was only a practice round.

We'd Love to Hear From You!

We've provided you with a variety of tools to help you on your path to certification. We hope that you'll find them useful, challenging and fun as you improve your Microsoft Office skills. If you'd like to let us know about your experiences with this book and with taking the exams, we'd love to hear from you. Good luck!

Annette Marquis and Gini Courter
Sybex, Inc.
1151 Marina Village Parkway
Alameda, CA 94501
e-mail: authors@triadconsulting.com

CHAPTER 1

Working in Office 2000

Today's software tools provide many challenges, but they also provide even greater opportunities to show off your skills: impress your supervisor and your customers and earn the respect—and envy—of your coworkers. Microsoft Office 2000 is a toolkit jam-packed with powerful tools. Whether you work for a multinational corporation or run your own small business, Microsoft's Office 2000 top-of-the-line tools will help you upgrade your existing skills so you can work smarter and more efficiently. With Office 2000 you can manage your busy calendar, track important contacts, make sound financial projections, produce impressive proposals, create dynamite presentations, and establish and maintain a sensational presence on the World Wide Web.

This chapter will familiarize you with the basic features in Office 2000, including recognizing parts of the application window and the entering and editing of text. If you've used Office 95 or Office 97, a lot of this will be old territory but you should still work quickly through the chapter, particularly if you came to Windows 95/98 from Windows 3.1 or the Mac. The newer 32-bit versions of Windows (Windows 95, Windows 98, and Windows NT), which we'll simply refer to as Windows throughout this book, and Office 2000 have some subtle time-savers, like the ability to manage files in standard dialog boxes. So whatever your prior experience, we recommend that you skim "*Working in Office 2000*;" you're sure to pick up one or two new concepts that you'll use over and over.

Mastering Office Professional

Microsoft Office 2000 Premium Edition features some of the most popular and powerful software programs around. The suite includes 32-bit versions of eight applications:

- Word: word processor
- Excel: spreadsheet
- Access: database
- PowerPoint: presentation software
- Outlook: desktop information manager
- Publisher: design and layout software
- FrontPage: Web site design and management tool
- PhotoDraw: graphics and photo-editing tool

These are the latest, most powerful versions of Microsoft's award-winning office productivity tools. If you have worked with prior releases of these products, you'll just need to learn some new and improved techniques for the Office 2000 editions. Office 2000 programs support better integration than ever before: between applications, between yourself and other users, and with the Web. All the applications include the Office Assistant, an active Help feature that offers time-saving advice to help you work more efficiently.

Although Office 2000 now includes Publisher in its suite of tools, Microsoft Office User Specialist Certification does not include Publisher skills, so those topics are not covered in this book. For information on working in Publisher, see *Microsoft Office 2000: No Experience Required*, Sybex, Inc.

Office 2000 Premium Edition also includes a number of smaller tools, such as:

- WordArt: a text-graphics program
- The Clip Gallery: an archive of clip art, sounds, and video

Office also features applets that are available within all the major applications, so you can add line art, graphic representations of numeric data, or a text-based logo to any Office document.

The Office 2000 components are amazing tools, and mastering them can be a challenge. But this mastery provides greater opportunities for you to earn the respect of your supervisor, customers, and coworkers.

Exploring Common Features in Office

One of the best things about Office 2000 software is that each application has several useful features in common. If you want to save a letter in Word, a table in Access, or a spreadsheet in Excel, the Save button not only looks the same but it is also located in approximately the same place. This section explores some of Office's universal, commonly used features to give you a general introduction. You'll get more detailed, application-specific information as you work through skills in this book.

Launching the Shortcut Bar and New Office Documents

Typical of Windows applications, you have more than one way to get the job done. You can start using Office 2000 three ways: clicking a New Document button on the Office Shortcut bar, using the Start menu to open a New Office Document, or navigating through the Programs menu to open the actual Office application. The Microsoft Office Shortcut bar does not automatically appear the first time you use Windows after installation. To open it, click the Start button and choose Programs ➢ Microsoft Office Tools ➢ Microsoft Office Shortcut Bar. You are asked if you want to have the Shortcut bar open automatically when you launch Windows, appearing in its default position along the right side of the screen.

As with all of Office's toolbars, you can position the Shortcut Bar anywhere you like on your screen: on the left or right, along the top or bottom, or as a free-floating palette of tools. Simply "grab" the bar by clicking and holding on the gray line at the top/beginning of the toolbar and reposition the mouse to the new location.

The Office Shortcut bar opens vertically by default. You can click and drag it against any edge of the screen, or drag it out to make it a free-floating palette.

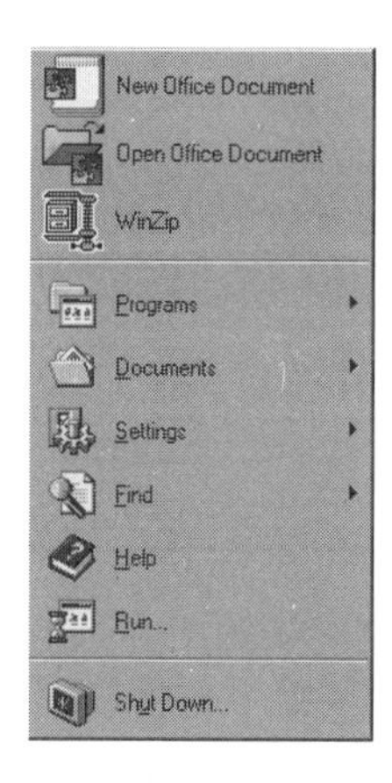

The Shortcut Bar is, obviously, the easiest way to launch any of the Office 2000 applications. If you elect not to show the Shortcut bar on your desktop, try one of these other two ways to open a new document or an Office application. Click the Windows Start button to open the Start menu.

Choose New Office Document or Open Office Document (to retrieve files you've already created) from the top of the Start menu. For brand-new, blank documents, Office 2000 presents you with a host of choices via the New Office Document dialog box—everything from memos and legal briefs to spreadsheets and Web pages are represented there. If all else fails, or if you prefer to launch the application and then open a document, choose Programs from the Start menu. The Office 2000 programs appear as individual choices on the Programs menu. Click any program to launch it.

Using the Office 2000 Interface

The Office 2000 applications share a common user interface. This means, for example, that once you're familiar with the *application window* in Excel (see Figure 1.1), getting around in the application window in Word will be a piece of cake. Likewise, you'll notice a lot of other similarities between the applications. Working in Windows applications is like déjà vu; you will see certain features and tools again and again.

At the top of each application window is a *title bar* that contains three buttons: Minimize, Maximize (or Restore), and Close. Use these buttons to change the size of your window or to close the window itself. When you're working in an application, you'll usually want to maximize it. Before you switch to something else, minimizing the first application frees up system resources, making more memory available to the active application. When a window is maximized, the Restore button is displayed.

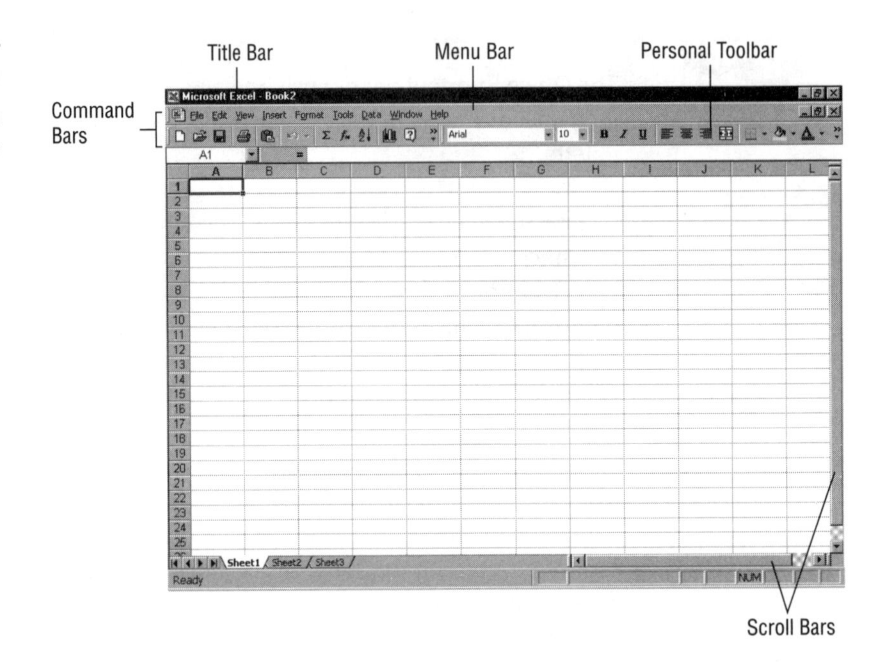

FIGURE 1.1
Excel application window

When it is restored, the Maximize button is displayed. Even with the application window maximized, the Windows Taskbar shows all open applications, so you can easily switch between open Office 2000 applications by clicking an application's Taskbar button. Clicking the Close button on the title bar closes the application, returning you to the Windows desktop or to another open application.

The Document Window

In each application, your work area is known as the *Document window.* Here you're surrounded by the tools you need to get the job done (see Figure 1.1): *scroll bars* to move the display, a status bar to keep you informed of an operation's progress, and the *command bars* at the top of the screen to access all the program's features. You can see two types of command bars: menu bars and toolbars. The menu bar organizes the features into categories: File, Edit, Help, etc. Clicking on any of the categories opens up a list of related features for you to choose from. Many of the menu bar options open dialog boxes which allow you to set several options at once, each related to the feature you choose—all the print options, all the font settings, etc.

Toolbars are the command bars with graphical buttons located below the menu bar. Toolbars make many of the most commonly used features only one click away. Use toolbars when you want a shortcut to a common feature and the menu bar when you want to see *all* the options related to a feature.

In Office 2000, the Standard and Formatting toolbars of previous versions, share one row to conserve space in the document window. If, in this personal toolbar, the button you want to use is not available, click the down arrow to the right of either toolbar and choose the button from the list. This button replaces a less frequently used button from your toolbar.

Office 2000 menus are also personalized to the features you use most commonly. If a pull-down menu has more than a handful of commands, Microsoft has "folded" up the less commonly used features. When you see a set of small, double arrows at the bottom of a pull-down menu, select them to reveal all the menu commands, or wait a few seconds, and the menu "unfolds"—you don't even need to click the mouse.

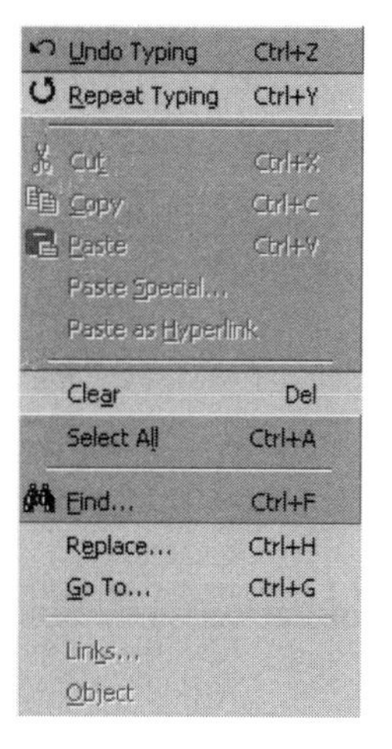

FIGURE 1.2
Word Edit menu with all the available commands showing

If the Personal toolbars option does not suit you, you can display full menus and view the complete Standard and Formatting toolbars on separate rows by choosing View ➢ Toolbars ➢ Customize and clearing the first three checkboxes on the Options tab.

Accessing Commands

And if toolbars and menu bars aren't enough, you can execute commands from one of the many context-sensitive shortcut menus or by using shortcut keys. In order to satisfy many different user's working styles, Microsoft Office usually offers several ways to execute any given command. For example, to copy selected text in any application, you can:

- Click the Copy button on the Standard toolbar.
- Choose Edit ➢ Copy from the menu bar.

- Right-click on the selected text; then choose Copy from the free-floating shortcut menu.

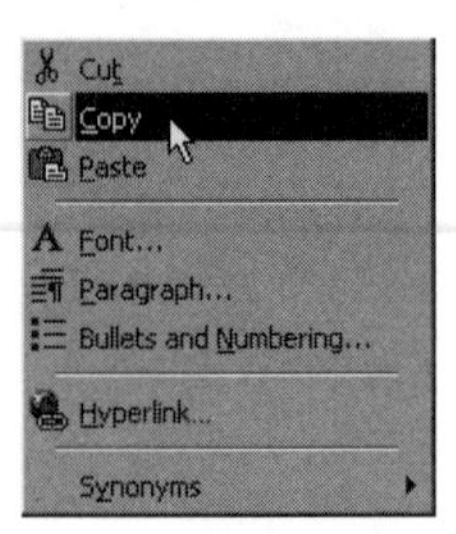

- Hold **Ctrl** and press **C**.

Notice that the Copy button and the keyboard shortcut are both shown on the Copy menu selection, so you can use the menu bar to help you identify quicker ways to access features you commonly use. *ScreenTips* provide additional help with commands. If you're uncertain about which toolbar button to use, point to the button and hover for a moment; a ScreenTip appears, showing the button's name.

The Office Assistant

Objectives W2000.4.9, XL2000.2.8, PP2000.8.4, OI2000.4.1, AC2000.2.1

The *Office Assistant* is Microsoft's help interface for Office 2000. The Office Assistant (see Figure 1.3) crosses all applications and provides help for specific features of each application. You can choose from several Assistants in the Assistant shortcut menu. (Right-click the Office Assistant and click Choose Assistant.) Each has its own "personality," including Rocky the power puppy, Mother Nature symbolized as a globe, and an animated Genius with a definite resemblance to Albert Einstein.

FIGURE 1.3

Office Assistant Clippit offering help

The Office Assistant lives within the application window and displays tips that guide you to better ways to complete a task. The Assistant offers help the first time you work with a feature or if you have difficulty with a task. Sometimes the offer is subtle—Clippit blinks, Rocky wags his tail, or the Genius produces a light bulb. Sometimes the Assistant can be entertaining; in Office 2000 the Assistant icon changes shape during certain basic tasks like saving or running SpellCheck. Offers of help can be a bit more intrusive. If, for example, you open a Wizard, the Office Assistant may pop up to ask if you'd like help with the feature.

After you've worked with Office 2000 for a few days, you might decide that you'd like a little less help from your eager Assistant. To change the Assistant's options, right-click on the Assistant, and then choose Options from the shortcut menu to open the Office Assistant dialog box. Click the Options tab to display the Options page, shown in Figure 1.4.

All the Office 2000 programs share the Office Assistant. Any options you change affect the Assistant in all the Office programs, so if you need an increased level of assistance with Excel, you get the same increased level of assistance with Word.

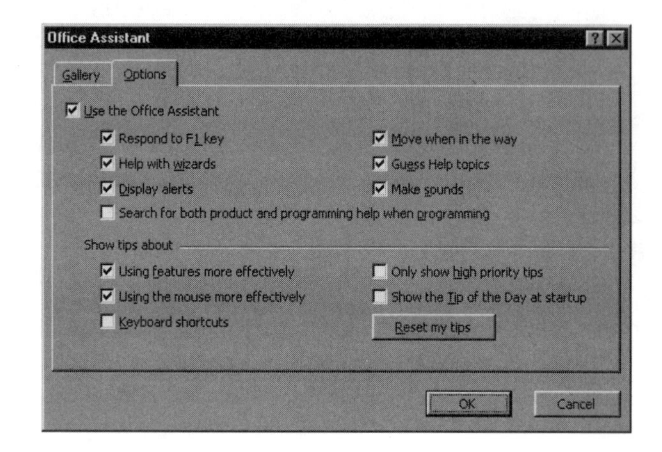

FIGURE 1.4 Office Assistant dialog box

When you're ready to go it alone, you can close the Assistant window to return it to the Standard toolbar. If you start to get lonely, just click the Office Assistant button to invite the Assistant back into your office.

For help with any dialog box in Office 2000, click the dialog box Help button (with the question mark), then click on the dialog box control you want help with.

Hands On: *Objectives W2000.4.9, XL2000.2.8, PP2000.8.4, OI2000.4.1, AC2000.2.1*

1. Browse the Gallery of Office Assistants and choose one you like:
   a) Set up the Office Assistant's options for the level of help you need.
   b) Hide the Office Assistant.
   c) Retrieve the Office Assistant.
2. Use the Office Assistant to look for help on the Office Assistant:
   a) Review the Help topics available.
   b) Choose one topic and explore the Help files on that topic.
   c) Close the Help window.

Working with Files

One of the great things about Office 2000 is that the dialog boxes used for common file functions are similar in all the applications. In this section, we'll look at the common features of the dialog boxes; features specific to an application are covered in the skills for that application.

Creating Something New

You can easily create new documents from the Windows Start menu. Selecting New Office Document opens the New Office Document dialog box, shown in Figure 1.5. Each tab contains *templates* for a number of similar documents. Some of the templates (for example, the Fax templates) include text, graphics, or other content. Blank document templates for all the applications—a blank template for an Access database, Word document, Excel worksheet, PowerPoint presentation, and a Web page and an e-mail message—are found on the General page of the New Office Document dialog box.

To open an application, simply double-click any document in the dialog box.

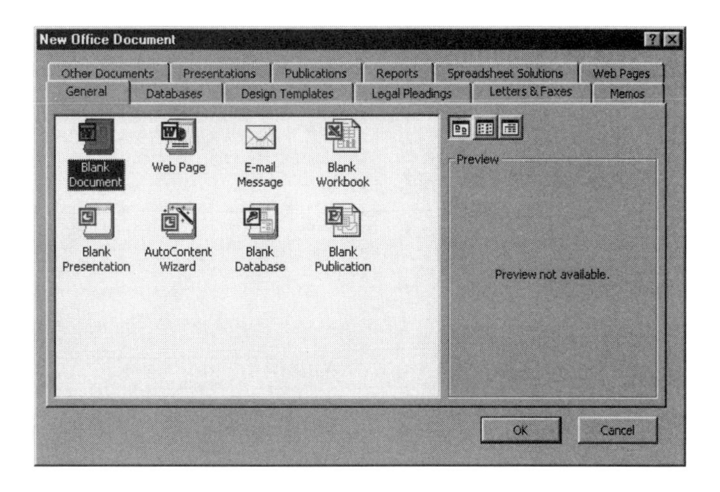

FIGURE 1.5
New Office Document dialog box

If you're already in an application, you have two ways to create a new document.

Objectives W2000.4.7 and XL2000.2.5

Click the New button on the Standard toolbar to open a new blank document in the active application. If you want a new template instead of a blank document, choose File ➢ New from the menu bar to open the New Office Document dialog box with templates appropriate for the active application.

Saving a File

Objectives W2000.4.1, XL2000.2.1, PP2000.8.1

When you're finished working with a document or have completed a sizable amount of work and want to store it before continuing, choose File ➢ Save from the menu bar, or click the Save button on the Standard toolbar to open the Save As dialog box, shown in Figure 1.6.

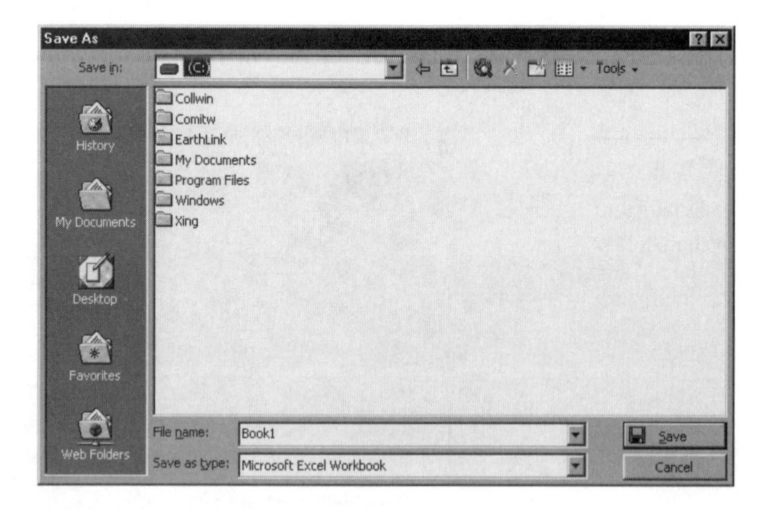

FIGURE 1.6 Excel Save As dialog box

The dialog box opens to your default *folder* (directory), but clicking in the Save In text box opens a drop-down list of accessible drives, as shown in Figure 1.7. Select a drive, and the folders on the drive are displayed in the pane below the list.

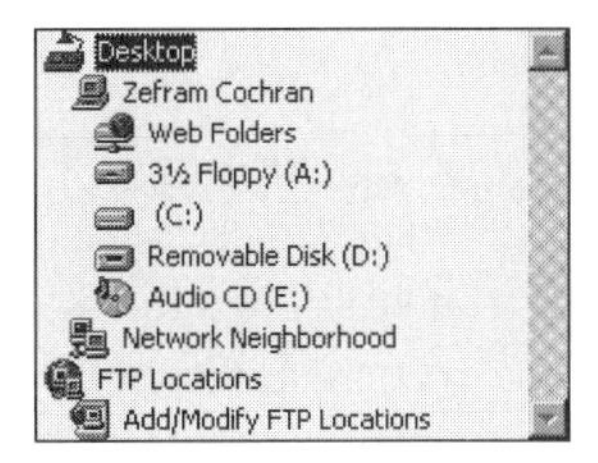

FIGURE 1.7
Save In drop-down list

Double-clicking any folder opens it so that you can view the files and folders that it contains. When you have located the proper drive and folder, enter a filename in the File Name text box at the bottom of the dialog box. With 32 bit versions of Windows, filenames can be up to 256 characters long, use uppercase and lowercase letters, and contain spaces. They can't contain punctuation other than underscores, hyphens, and exclamation points. And unlike filenames on the Macintosh, they are not case-sensitive; 'MY FILE' and 'My File' are the same filename. Make sure the name of the current drive or folder appears in the Save In text box, then click the Save button to save the file.

All the Office 2000 program dialog boxes locate documents based on file *extension*—the three characters following a period in a filename. For example, Word documents have the .doc extension. Don't create your own extensions or change the extensions of existing documents. If you do, the Office 2000 applications will have trouble finding your files—and that means so will you!

Creating a New Folder

Objectives W2000.4.4 and XL2000.2.4

When you're saving a file, you may decide to create a new folder to house it. Click File ➢ Save as you would normally do to begin the Save process. Use the Save In drop down list to navigate to the drive or folder within which you want to create the new folder. Click the New Folder button on the toolbar in the Save As dialog box. Type the name for the folder (no punctuation) and press enter. Be sure to select the new folder with a double-click before you name the file and click Save.

Using Save As

Objectives W2000.4.3, XL2000.2.2, PP2000.8.2

After you've saved a file once, clicking Save re-saves the file without opening the dialog box. If you want to save a previously saved file with a new name, or save it in another location, choose File ➢ Save As from the menu bar to open the Save As dialog box. The Save As feature is particularly useful if you are using an existing document to create a new document and you want to keep both the original *and* the revised document intact.

If you share files with people using other programs, or older versions of Office programs, they may not be able to open your Office 2000 files. You can, however, save your file in a format they can open. In the Save As dialog box, scroll through the Save As Type drop-down list and select an appropriate file format. The Save As Type drop-down list from Word is shown in Figure 1.8.

FIGURE 1.8 Use the Save As Type drop-down list to save a file in a different file format

Closing a File

To remove a document from the document window, choose File ➢ Close or click the Close button on the right end of the menu bar, directly below the application window's Close button. Word 2000 now uses a single document interface, so each new document you open has its own button on the taskbar. Activate the one you want by clicking it, then use the Close button on the title bar to close that document. If you have opened more than one document window, you won't see a Close button on the menu bar. You can click the Close button on the title bar to close the active document. If you close a document that has been changed since it was last saved, you are prompted to save your changes.

Sending Files Using E-mail

Objectives W2000.4.10, XL2000.2.7, PP2000.1.10

Every Office 2000 application—Word, Excel, PowerPoint, Outlook, Access, and Publisher—has two new standard features to help you send files via e-mail. You can either send your file as an e-mail message, or you can attach it to an existing e-mail message, by simply choosing one File menu option.

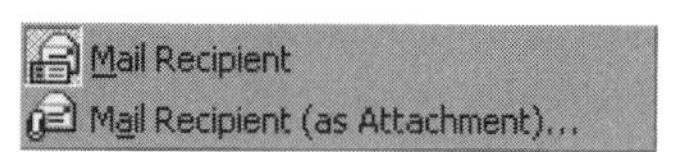

To send a document as an e-mail message, open it in the appropriate Office application and choose File ➢ Send To ➢ Mail Recipient. A space appears at the top of the document where you can fill in the e-mail address(es) and send it on its way.

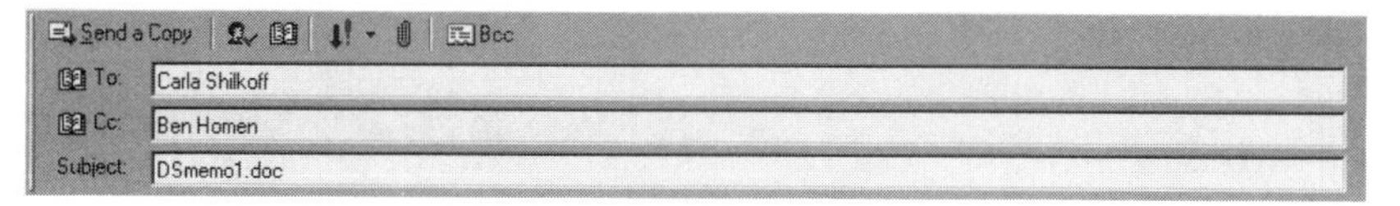

If you prefer to send the document as an attachment, choose File ➢ Send To ➢ Mail Recipient (As Attachment). A separate e-mail window appears, showing the document as an icon in a window at the bottom, with space for you to type a message before you send it out.

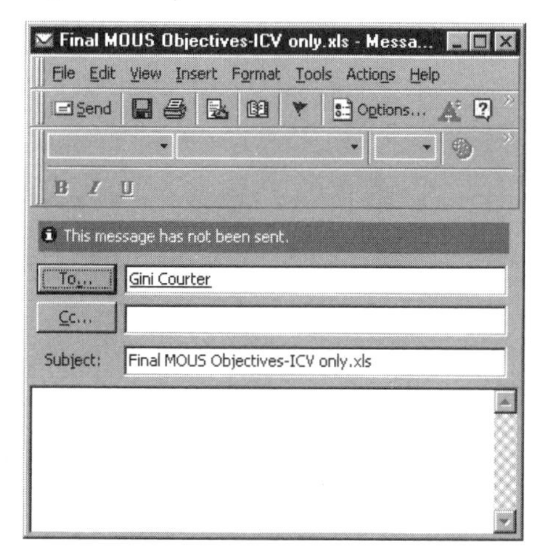

Opening an Existing File

Objectives W2000.4.2 and XL2000.2.3

You can open an existing Office 2000 document in three ways. If the document was created recently, click the Windows Start button and open the Documents menu. If the document appears there, you're in luck—you can open it directly from the menu.

If the document doesn't appear on the Documents menu, choose Open Office Document from the Start menu, and Office opens an Open Office Document dialog box. Use the Look In drop-down list to locate the folder that contains the file.

If you're already working in PowerPoint, for example, and want to open an existing presentation, click the Open button on the Standard toolbar to open the Open dialog box, shown in Figure 1.9.

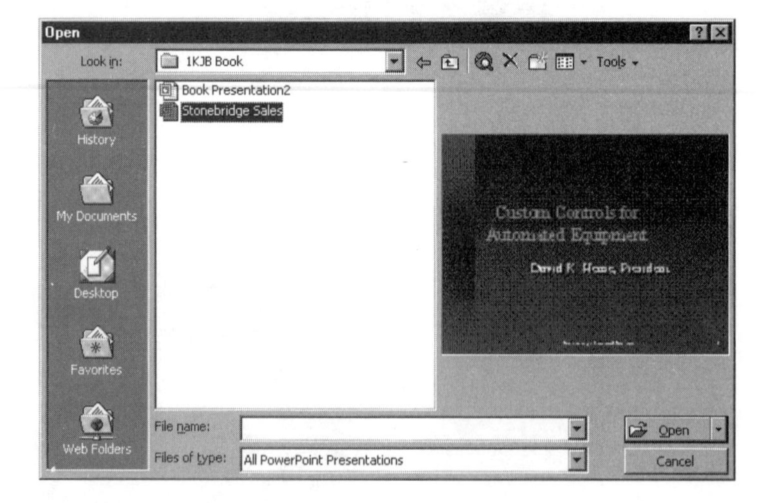

FIGURE 1.9 PowerPoint Open dialog box

This Open dialog box is just like the Open Existing Document dialog box, but it is filtered to only show PowerPoint files. Use the Look In drop-down list to locate the proper folder and file.

Converting Files from Other Formats

Office 2000 applications open files created in other applications and earlier versions of Office. However, Access and Publisher use different file formats than those used in previous versions, so the application has to create a converted copy of the file before it can be opened. For instance, Access 2000 opens a database created in Access 2 or Access 97, but it tells you to convert the database, as shown in Figure 1.10. If you choose not to convert the database, you won't be able to change the database's structure, but you will still be able to use the database.

FIGURE 1.10 Access Conversion prompt

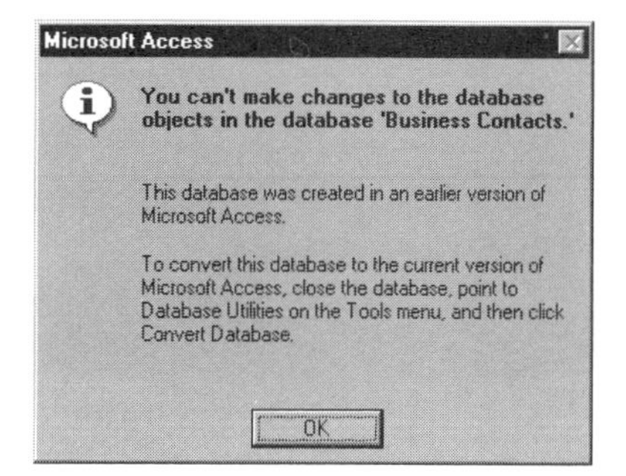

Word, Excel, and PowerPoint documents created in versions prior to Office 97 do not need to be converted to make use of all of the Office 2000 enhancements. When you save a document created in a version prior to Office 97, you are asked if you want to convert the file to the current format.

Print Preview and Printing

Objectives W2000.3.2 and XL2000.4.1

Every Office 2000 application except PowerPoint and Publisher allows you to preview a document before printing. Click the Print Preview button on the Standard toolbar to open the preview window. The preview windows themselves vary in each application.

To print a document, choose File ➢ Print from the menu bar to open the Print dialog box, shown in Figure 1.11. While each application's Print dialog box is slightly different, all allow you to select a printer, choose a number of copies, and specify what should be printed. Clicking the Options button at the bottom of the dialog box opens an Options page where you can select print quality and other settings. Application-specific Print settings are discussed in the skills for each program.

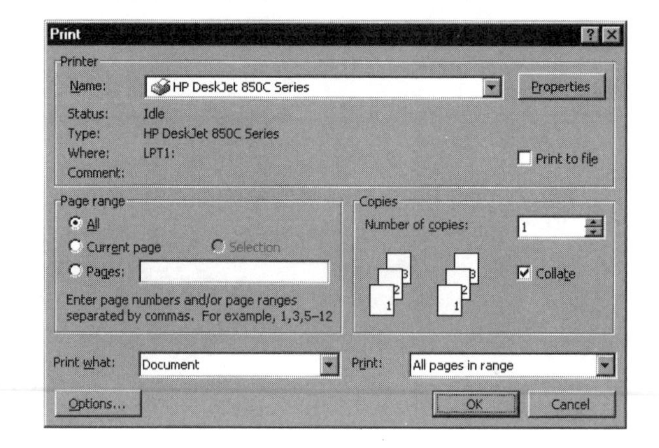

FIGURE 1.11 Word's Print dialog box

To immediately send a document to the printer using the default print options (and without opening a dialog box), click the Print button on the Standard toolbar. The Print button is convenient in most of the applications, but is problematic in PowerPoint, where the default print settings are full-page pictures of each slide in a presentation. What a way to tie up a printer!

Editing in Office 2000

Many editing features are shared among Office 2000 applications. Each application may have a quicker or easier way of editing in particular circumstances, but in this section, you'll learn those features that work no matter where you are or what you're doing.

The Insertion Point

The *insertion point*, or *cursor*, is the flashing vertical bar that shows where the next character you type will appear. You can see the blinking insertion point, shown in Figure 1.12, as soon as you open a document or form. The only exception is Excel, where the insertion point only appears after you begin typing.

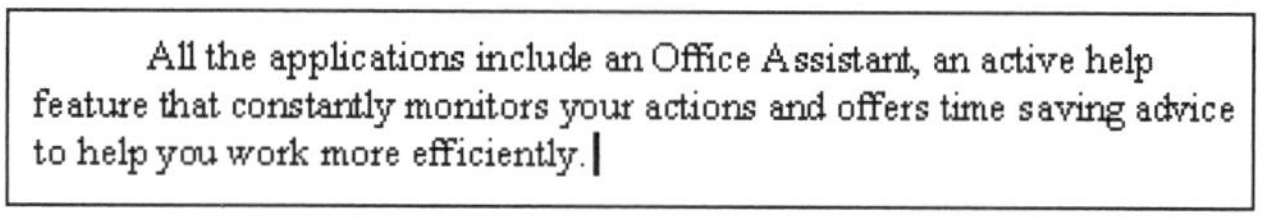

All the applications include an Office Assistant, an active help feature that constantly monitors your actions and offers time saving advice to help you work more efficiently.|

FIGURE 1.12
The insertion point moves to the right as new text is added.

When you move the mouse pointer into an area where you can enter or edit text, the pointer changes to an I-beam. To edit existing text, move the insertion point by moving the I-beam to the text that you want to edit. Click and the insertion point jumps to the new position. Then you can type new text, or delete existing text, at the insertion point.

Hands On: *Objectives W2000.3.2, W2000.4.1-4.3, W2000.4.7, XL2000.2.1-2.3, XL2000.4.1, PP2000.8.1, and PP2000.8.2*

1. Start Word and type a short sentence into a blank document.
   a) Save this file to the My Documents folder and name it *Practice 1*.
   b) Add another sentence to *Practice 1* and use the Save As command to create another document. Name this file *Practice 2*, and save it to My Documents also. Close both documents and then close Word.
2. Retrieve *Practice 2* using the Documents menu.
3. Retrieve *Practice 1* using the Open button on the toolbar.
4. Close *Practice 2* then add another short sentence to *Practice 1*. Use Save As to create another document named Practice 3.

5. Start Excel, type the word "Hello," and press Enter. (You can see your text in the first cell.)
   a) Save this file to the My Documents folder under a name you can remember.
   b) Proceed through steps 1b, and 2-4 using Excel to create the files and naming files and folders as you wish.
6. Use Print Preview to see how your Excel and Word files will look when printed.
7. Create a new document by clicking File ➢ New and choosing one of the available templates. Follow the instructions in the template to customize the template. Save it as you would any other document.

Correcting Mistakes

Helping you to correct mistakes is one of the many things Office 2000 does exceptionally well. In its simplest form, Office lets you erase existing text manually. At its most powerful, Office can automatically correct the words you most commonly misspell.

Backspace and Delete

Most people are familiar with using the Backspace and Delete keys on the keyboard to delete text, but you're not alone if you confuse when to use which one:

- Backspace (represented by a left-pointed arrow on the keyboard) erases one character to the *left* of the insertion point.
- Delete erases one character to the *right* of the insertion point.

Use whichever is more convenient for you, based on where the insertion point is.

Undo and Redo

Objectives W2000.1.1 and XL2000.1.1

Office 2000 is exceptionally forgiving. The Undo button on the Standard toolbar lets you reverse an action or a whole series of actions you have taken.

The Undo button dims when you have reached the last action you can undo. Click the drop-down arrow next to the Undo button and scroll down the history to reverse multiple actions in one step.

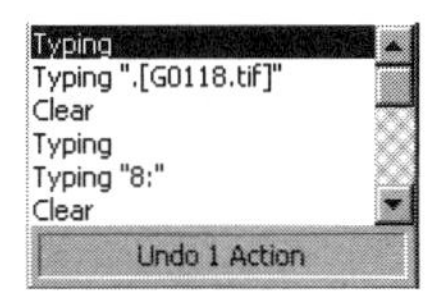

If you change your mind again, clicking the Redo button reverses the last Undo. In Office 2000, you can use the Undo and Redo histories to reverse multiple actions in all the applications. Each application, though, has its own rules about how far you can undo, so it's a good idea to review that information in the specific application.

Overtype and Insert Modes

Objective W2000.1.8

The default-editing mode in Office 2000 is Insert: if you enter new text in the middle of existing text, the original text moves to the right to accommodate it. Overtype mode replaces existing text with the newly entered text. To toggle between Insert and Overtype modes, press the Insert key on the keyboard.

A Quick Look at Spelling

Objectives W2000.1.3, XL2000.5.6, PP2000.3.1

No matter how many spelling tests you may have failed in elementary school, you can still produce documents that are free of spelling errors. The Spelling feature is available in all Office 2000 applications including e-mail created in Outlook. Word and PowerPoint flag misspelled words as you type by placing a wavy red line underneath possible misspellings.

mispelled

All you have to do is right-click on a flagged word to open the Spell It shortcut menu, which lists suggestions for the proper spelling. Click on the correct spelling, choose to Ignore the word, or have Office add the spelling to your custom dictionary—a good idea with names you use a lot. That way Spell It won't flag the name the next time you use it.

In the other applications, you have to ask Office to check your spelling by clicking the Spelling button on the Standard toolbar. Office reviews your document, flags possible misspelled words and, depending on the application, opens the Spelling dialog box or the Spelling and Grammar dialog box.

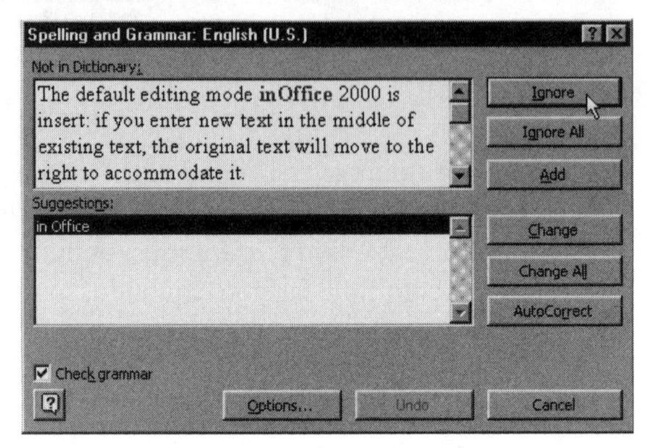

The Spelling and Grammar dialog box gives you all the same options as the Spell It pop-up menu and a few additional ones. Here you can choose to Ignore All occurrences of the word or to Change All occurrences to the correct spelling. You can also enter the correct spelling. All the Office applications share a custom dictionary, so words you add in one application aren't flagged in others.

Grammar checking is not available in Excel, Outlook, and Access.

Automatic Fixes for Common Errors

Objective W2000.1.16

Most Office 2000 applications access a shared feature called AutoCorrect. With AutoCorrect you can build your own list of common misspellings. When Office encounters one of those words, it automatically fixes it for you. Some words, such as "adn" and "teh" are already in the list. As you correct misspelled words, you can add them to the AutoCorrect list. AutoCorrect is one of the options in both the Spell It pop-up menu and the Spelling and Grammar dialog box. You can also access it from Tools ➢ AutoCorrect.

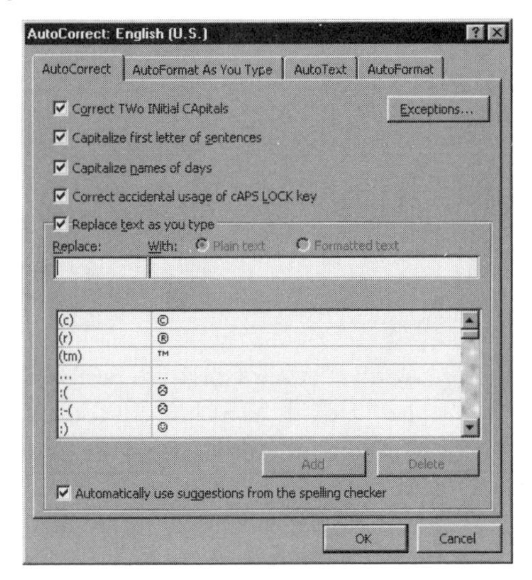

Once you add a word to the AutoCorrect list, you never have to worry about correcting the spelling error again. Also, AutoCorrect can recognize and replace common combinations of symbols like the copyright symbol © and the "smilicon" ☺ now popular online. A couple of words of caution though:

- Be sure to verify you are adding a correctly spelled word to the Auto-Correct list.
- Don't add words that mean something else when you spell them differently. For example, if you commonly reverse the "r" and the "o" in "from", don't add this error to the AutoCorrect list, or every time you want to type "form" AutoCorrect automatically changes the word to "from."

AutoCorrect also gives you a number of options that you can leave on or turn off based on your personal preferences, such as correcting two initial capitals and capitalizing the names of days. Choose Tools ➢ AutoCorrect to open the AutoCorrect dialog box. If you want to turn AutoCorrect off entirely, click to remove the checkmark in front of Replace Text As You Type. The Exceptions button provides you with two options. You can add abbreviations that you type regularly, so that AutoCorrect doesn't automatically capitalize the next word after the period. You can also add words that require two initial caps, so it doesn't automatically change them. The Auto-Correct Exceptions dialog box from Word is shown in Figure 1.13.

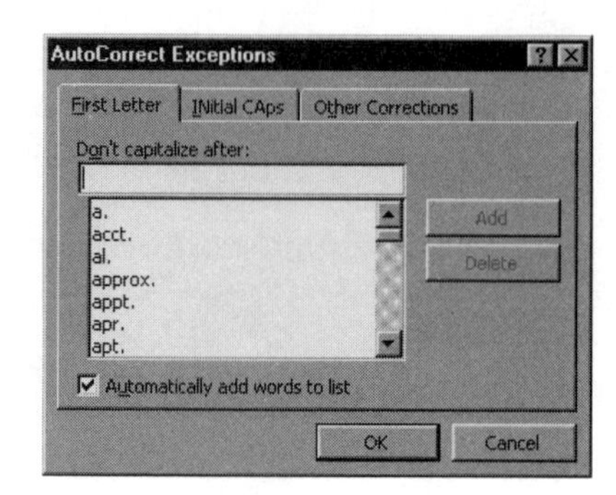

FIGURE 1.13 AutoCorrect Exceptions

Although AutoCorrect is designed to prevent typing and spelling errors, it is also valuable as a shortcut tool. You can enter words that you type regularly into your AutoCorrect list to save yourself time and keystrokes—long company names, for example, or legal or medical terminology. Just enter a code that you will recognize, such as USA, and AutoCorrect expands it for you into United States of America. However, if you think you will ever want to use the abbreviation without expanding it, enter a slash (/) or some other character in front of the abbreviation (/USA). Then you can choose whether to have AutoCorrect supply the long form (by typing /USA) or use the abbreviation (by typing USA without the slash).

Hands On: Objectives W2000.1.1, W2000.1.3, W2000.1.8, W2000.1.16, XL2000.1.1, XL2000.5.6, and PP2000.3.1

1. Open a new blank document and type a three-sentence paragraph of sample text. Include several proper nouns like your boss's name and company address. Intentionally make at least three spelling errors.
   a) Run the spelling checker and fix your spelling mistakes. Add the proper nouns to the custom dictionary.
   b) Create an AutoCorrect entry for your company's name.
2. Click in the middle of the paragraph you just typed and press the Insert key to change to overstrike mode. (You learned this in Chapter 1.)
   a) Type a short sentence. Note how characters disappear as you type. Press Insert again to return to Insert mode.
   b) Click Undo enough times to replace the text you just overtyped, then click Undo an extra time. Click Redo to cancel out the extra Undo.

3. Click at the bottom of the paragraph and type another sentence. Use the Repeat command to insert the same text into your document twice more. Close without saving.
4. Create and store an AutoText entry for your return address, including formatting, to be used on personal correspondence.

Selecting, Moving, and Copying

Whether you are correcting mistakes or shuffling your whole document around, the first step is knowing how to select text. Once text is selected, it can be moved, copied, deleted, aligned, or re-sized.

Selecting Text

Each application has its own shortcuts to selecting. However, no matter where you are, you can always drag to select—even in a dialog box. To select by dragging, move the insertion point to the beginning or the end of the desired text string, hold down the mouse button, and move in the desired direction. In Excel, you can drag the Cell Selection Pointer, a thick cross, to select several cells at once. (More about selecting in Excel in Chapter 5.)

Selected text changes to reverse video—the opposite color from the rest of the text. To unselect text, click anywhere in the document.

Selected text is automatically deleted if you press any key on the keyboard. If you accidentally delete text in a document, click Undo. Undo won't work in dialog boxes.

Moving and Copying Text

Objectives W2000.1.9, XL2000.1.7, PP2000.3.8, AC2000.5.1

Now that you can select text, you can move and copy text in any of the Office applications; for example, you could move text to rearrange sentences in a Word document or topics in a PowerPoint presentation. When you *move* a selection, the original is deleted and placed in the new location. *Copying* text leaves the original in place, and creates a copy in the new location.

You can move text by cutting it from its current location and pasting it in a new location. When you cut a block of text, it is deleted from your document and copied to the *Clipboard*. Copying text moves a copy of the text to the Clipboard without deleting the original. The Clipboard is part of the computer's memory set aside and managed by Windows. The Clipboard can hold only one piece of information at a time, but that piece of information can be text, a graphic, or even a video clip.

Moving or Copying Text

1. Select the text you want to move or copy.

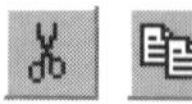

2. Click the Cut or Copy button on the Standard toolbar.
3. Move the insertion point where you want the text to appear.

4. Click the Paste button.

All the moving and copying techniques work with pictures or other objects just as they do with text. See the chapters on each individual application for more detailed information on moving and copying text and objects.

Cut, Copy, and Paste are standard Windows functions, and as a result they have corresponding shortcut keys that you can use even if menu and toolbar options are not available. Select the text or object and press **Ctrl+X** to cut, **Ctrl+C** to copy, or **Ctrl+V** to paste.

Pasting Multiple Items

A new feature of Office 2000 is Collect and Paste, which lets you copy up to 12 items and save them to a temporary Clipboard where you can select and paste them all at once. This makes it easier to move several items from one place to another, without forcing you to scroll up and down or split the screen.

To select items for collecting and pasting, choose your items in order by pressing Edit ➢ Copy or Edit ➢ Cut, and the Clipboard toolbar appears. After you move to the new location in the document where you want to paste the items, select them one by one from the Clipboard by clicking them and pressing Ctrl+V.

Hands On: Objectives W2000.1.9, XL2000.1.7, PP2000.3.8, AC2000.5.1

1. Start a new Word document and type a five-sentence paragraph of sample text.
   a) Select some text, then deselect it.
2. Select the fourth sentence.
   a) Use Cut and Paste to move the sentence to the beginning of the paragraph.
   b) Select two more sentences and copy each to the clipboard.
   c) Paste each sentence back into your document in the opposite order you copied them. Close this document without saving.
3. Open one of the Excel documents you've created in a previous exercise.
   a) Select several cells by dragging over them.
   b) Use Copy/Paste to display the cell contents in two places on your worksheet.

Adding Pizzazz

One of the primary benefits of using Windows applications is the ease with which you can give your documents a professional appearance. The right combination of fonts, font styles, sizes, and attributes can make your words or numbers jump right off the page.

Fonts and Font Styles

Objectives W2000.1.1, W2000.1.2, and XL2000.3.1

Selecting the right font can be the difference between a professional-looking document and an amateur effort that's tedious to read. Fonts are managed by Windows, which means that a font available in one application is available in all Windows applications. You can access fonts and many of their font attributes right from the Formatting toolbar. Excel's Formatting toolbar is shown in Figure 1.14.

FIGURE 1.14

Excel's Formatting toolbar

To change the font, select some text then click the drop-down arrow next to the font name. Choose a font from the list. Either Times New Roman or Arial is the default font, depending on the application. All Windows True Type fonts (designated by the TT in front of them) are scaleable, which means that you can make them any size by entering the desired size in the Font Size text box. Of course, you can also select from the sizes listed in the drop-down list.

To turn on Bold, Italics, or Underline, click the corresponding button on the toolbar. Remember that you must select existing text before you can change the font or font style.

For all of the available font options, choose Format ➢ Font, or in Excel choose Format ➢ Cells, and click the Font tab to open the Font dialog box.

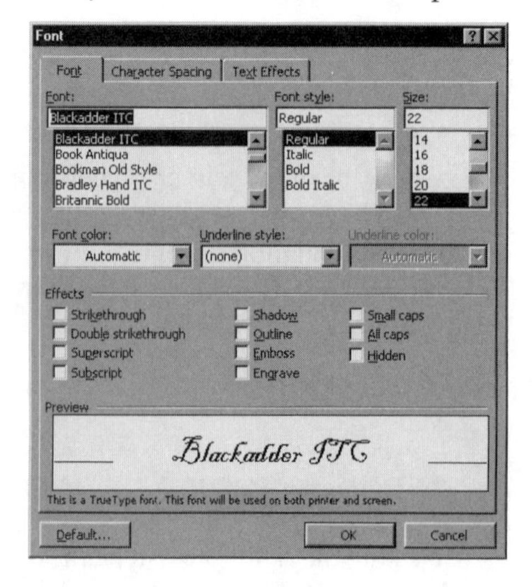

Here you can see what the fonts look like in the Preview window. You can also choose from several underline options, although the options differ depending on the application. For example, you can choose a Wave underline style in Word and a Double Accounting underline style in Excel. You can also apply a number of different effects to your text such as Strikethrough, Superscript, and Subscript. Word and PowerPoint also have effects such as Shadow and Emboss.

With all the color printers around today, being able to add colors to text is an important feature. Font Color is available from most toolbars as well as from the Font dialog box. There are also many new fancy, decorative fonts available in Office 2000, a few of which are shown in Figure 1.15.

This is Blackadder ITC.

THIS IS CASTELLAR.

This is Jokerman.

This is Lucida Calligraphy.

This is Ravie.

FIGURE 1.15

Some new decorative fonts shown in Word

Copying Existing Formats

Objectives W2000.1.10, XI2000.3.6, PP2000.3.9

Once you have formatted the text just the way you like it, there is no need to re-create it for other text that you want formatted the same way. You can easily copy that format to other text in your document using the Format Painter.

Select the text with the format you want to copy and click the Format Painter button on the Standard toolbar. Your mouse pointer changes shape to an I-beam with a paintbrush next to it. (In Excel, the pointer becomes a thick cross with a paintbrush next to it.)

Drag the Format Painter I-beam over some existing text, and it is reformatted to look just like the text you copied. Once you've applied the format, the Format Painter turn offs automatically. If you need to copy the formatting more than once, select the text you want to copy and double-click (instead of single-clicking) the Format Painter button. When you are finished, click the Format Painter button again to turn it off.

The Format Painter not only copies fonts and font attributes but other formatting such as line spacing, bullets, borders and shading, and indents. In Excel, the Format Painter copies number formats too.

Hands On: *Objectives W2000.1.2, W2000.1.10, XL2000.3.1, Xl2000.3.6, and PP2000.3.9*

1. Start a new Word document and type a list of your five favorite holidays.
   - a) Select the first holiday and make it bold.
   - b) Select the second holiday and make it 20 point.
   - c) Select the third holiday. Italicize and underline it.
   - d) Select the fourth holiday and use the Font dialog box to make it 14 point Arial blue.
   - e) Use the format painter to copy the formatting on the fourth holiday to all the others. Close this document without saving.
2. Open an existing Excel Worksheet.
   - a) Select a cell with text in it and format the cell as 20 point Times New Roman Bold.
   - b) Select another cell with text. Italicize and underline it.
   - c) Select one of your formatted cells and use the Format Painter to copy its formatting to another cell.

CHAPTER

2

Mastering the Basics of Word

Whether you're a new or seasoned Word user, Word 2000 has all the features you'll need to create professional-looking documents. Word 2000 is loaded with helpful, time-saving features that allow you to focus on the content of your documents rather than on how to use the software. In this chapter, we'll begin with Word features that are inherited from Office, such as the Office Assistant, Spelling, and AutoText. Then you'll learn more editing techniques you can apply to your Word documents, such as how to align paragraphs, create bulleted and numbered lists, navigate complex documents, work with additional language tools, and print files.

Selecting, Moving, and Copying in Word 2000

Whether you are correcting a few mistakes or rearranging your entire document, the first step in any kind of document formatting is selecting text. Once text is selected, it can be moved, copied, deleted, aligned, or formatted.

Selecting Text

You can always drag to select text—even in a dialog box. To select by dragging, move the insertion point to the beginning or the end of the desired text string, hold down the mouse button, and move in the desired direction. Selected text changes to reverse video—the opposite color from text that isn't selected. To unselect text, click anywhere in the document.

Selecting text doesn't have to by dragging; there are a number of ways to select text. You can use any of these methods, but some methods are easier in certain situations. For example, if you've ever used drag to select text over multiple pages, you have already experienced the terrors of an out-of-control accelerated mouse pointer. On the other hand, if you choose another method to select such as Shift-select (see Table 2.1 below), you can select large amounts of text smoothly.

TABLE 2.1: Selecting Text in Word

To select:	Do this:
A word	Double-click anywhere in the word.
A sentence	Hold Ctrl and click anywhere in the sentence.
A paragraph	Triple-click anywhere in the paragraph, or move the pointer into the left margin so the pointer changes to a right-pointing arrow, then double-click.
Single line	Move the pointer into the left margin. When the pointer changes to a right-pointing arrow, point to the desired line and click.
Entire document	Choose Edit ➢ Select All from the menu bar, or hold Ctrl and click the left margin, or Ctrl+A (keyboard shortcut) or triple-click the left margin.
Multiple lines	Move the pointer to the left margin. With the right-pointing arrow, point to the first desired line and click. Without releasing the mouse button, drag to select additional lines.
Multiple words, lines, or sentences	Move the I-beam into the first word, hold the mouse button, drag to the last word, and release.
Multiple words, lines, or sentences using Shift-select	Click the first word, and then release the mouse button. Move the I-beam to the last word, hold Shift, and click. Everything between the two clicks is selected.

If you begin entering text when other text is selected, the selected text is deleted and the text you enter will replace it. This is an easy way to replace one word or phrase with another. It also works when you don't want it to—for example, when you forget you still have text selected from a previous action. When you are finished working with selected text, click somewhere in the document to remove the selection.

Moving and Copying Text with Cut, Copy, and Paste

Objective W2000.1.9

Now that you know how to select text, you can move and copy text. When you *move* a selection, the selected text is deleted and placed in the new location. *Copying* text leaves the selected text in place and creates a copy in the new location.

You move text by cutting it from its current location and pasting it in a new location. When you cut a block of text, it is deleted from your document and copied to the *Clipboard.* Copying text moves a copy of the text to the Clipboard without deleting the original. The Clipboard is part of the computer's memory set aside and managed by Windows. The Clipboard can hold only one piece of information at a time, but that piece of information can be text, a graphic, or even a video clip. And as you'll see in *Pasting Multiple Items* below, Office has its own clipboard that can hold up to a dozen items. Moving or copying text is a four step process: select, click Cut or Copy, move the insertion point, and paste.

Moving and Copying Text

1. Select the text you want to move or copy.

2. Click the Cut or Copy button on the Standard toolbar,

   OR choose Edit ➢ Cut or Edit ➢ Copy from the menu,

   OR right-click within your selected text and choose Cut or Copy from the shortcut menu.

3. Move the insertion point where you want to place the text.

4. Click the Paste button,

   OR choose Edit ➢ Paste from the menu,

   OR if you like using the shortcut menu, you can combine Steps 3 and 4 by right-clicking where you want to place the text and choosing Paste from the shortcut menu.

All the moving and copying techniques work with pictures or other objects just as they do with text. When you're working with pictures and other graphics, you'll want to know about using Paste Special for object linking and embedding. You'll find more information on linking and embedding Word objects, in Chapter 5.

Cut, Copy, and Paste are standard Windows functions that have corresponding shortcut keys you can use even if menu and toolbar options are not available. Select the text or object and press Ctrl+X to cut, Ctrl+C to copy, or Ctrl+V to paste.

Copying and Moving Text Using Drag-and-Drop

You'll find it easy to move and copy text short distances using a method called *drag-and-drop*. Drag-and-drop works best when you can see both the *source*, the location of original text, and the *destination* (the place you want the moved or copied text to appear).

Moving Text Using Drag-and-Drop

1. Identify the text you want to move and its destination.
2. Select the text.
3. Drag the text to its new location while holding down the right mouse button. Drop the selection into position by releasing the mouse button.
4. Select Move Here from the shortcut menu.

Use these techniques to move or copy text from one location to another in a single document and move or copy text between documents. If you want to work with more than one document, open both documents, and choose Window ➢ Arrange All to see both documents. (When you want to work on just one of the documents again, click the Maximize button on the document's title bar.)

Copying Text Using Drag-and-Drop

1. Identify the text you want to copy and its destination.
2. Select the text.
3. Drag it to its new location while holding down the right mouse button. Drop the text into position by releasing the mouse button.
4. Select Copy Here from the shortcut menu.

You can also use the left mouse button to drag and drop text, but you don't get the shortcut menu. Instead, the text is moved to the new location with no questions asked. If you want to copy text with the left mouse button, you must hold down the Ctrl key while dropping the text. It's easy to forget to hold down Ctrl or accidentally release Ctrl before the text is dropped, so it is good to get in the habit of dragging with the right mouse button.

Pasting Multiple Items

A new feature of Office 2000 is Collect and Paste, which lets you copy up to 12 items to a temporary Clipboard where you can select and paste them all at once (see Figure 2.1). This makes it easier to move several items from one place to another without forcing you to scroll back and forth through the document.

FIGURE 2.1
The Collect and Paste Clipboard

Cut or copy your items in the order you'll want to paste them in using Edit ➢ Copy, or Edit ➢ Cut, and the Clipboard toolbar appears. After you move to the new location in the document where you want to paste the items, paste them one by one from the Office Clipboard by clicking each icon and clicking Paste. Choose Paste All to paste the entire contents of the Office Clipboard at the insertion point.

Collect and Paste is a feature of Office 2000. In non-Office applications, you'll still use the Windows clipboard, which can only hold one item at a time.

Hands On: Objectives W2000.1.1 and 1.9

1. Start a new blank document and type a five-sentence paragraph of sample text.

   a) Select a word, then deselect it.

   b) Select the entire paragraph two separate times. Use two different methods to select a paragraph of text.

2. Select the fourth sentence.
   a) Use Cut and Paste to move the sentence to the beginning of the paragraph.
   b) Select two more sentences and copy each to the clipboard.
   c) Paste each sentence back into your document in the opposite order you copied them. Close this document without saving.
3. Enter two paragraphs of at least three sentences each in a new document. Experiment with the text selection techniques you learned until you feel comfortable using them.
4. Start a new document and enter the following text:

```
This is the third sentence of Doc 1.
This is the first sentence of Doc 2.
This is the fourth sentence of Doc 2.
This is the first sentence of Doc 1.
```

5. Save the text as *Doc 1*.
6. Start another new document and enter the following text:

```
This is the third sentence of Doc 2.
This is the fourth sentence of Doc 1.
This is the second sentence of Doc 1.
This is the second sentence of Doc 2.
```

7. Save the text as *Doc 2*.
8. Using drag-and-drop techniques, rearrange the sentences so they appear in the correct order in the proper document. (With both documents open, choose Window Ø Arrange All to see both documents at once.)
9. Close both documents without saving changes, and then open them and start again. This time use Cut and Paste to move the sentences. Which method did you prefer?

Using the Office Proofing Tools

In Chapter 1, we introduced you to the Spelling features of Office 2000. Word explands on those tools by adding a grammar component.

Checking Your Grammar

Objective W2000.1.5

Word's Grammar feature evaluates sentence structure and word usage to determine if you may be making grammatical errors. Word 2000 identifies possible errors on the fly and suggests how you could rewrite the text to make it grammatically correct. In Figure 2.2, Grammar identifies a sentence written in passive voice and makes a suggestion about how the sentence could be reworded to give it more punch.

FIGURE 2.2 Word's Grammar Checker

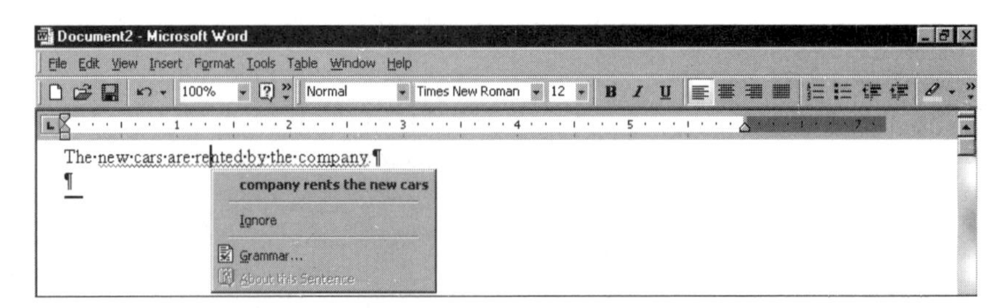

To use Grammar, right-click any word or phrase that has a wavy green line under it. Grammar gives you four options:

- Make one or more suggested corrections
- Leave the text alone
- Open the Grammar dialog box
- Get some additional information about this grammatical issue

Click the About This Sentence button to read some reference information about this particular grammatical problem.

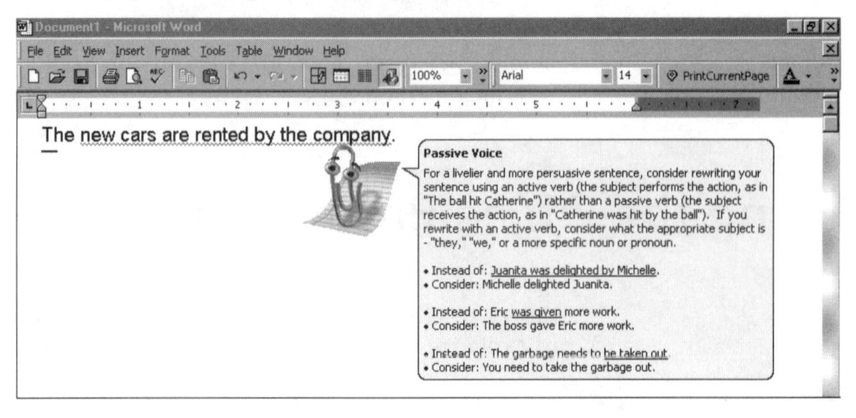

Checking Spelling and Grammar on the Fly

1. Right-click any words that have a wavy line underneath them and choose the correct word or grammar correction from the list.
2. Add words to the Spelling dictionary by clicking the Add button.
3. To see why text was flagged for a grammatical error, click the About This Sentence button.

If you would prefer to wait until you have finished entering and editing text to check the spelling and grammar, you can turn off the Automatic Spelling and Grammar option. Choose Tools ➢ Options ➢ Spelling and Grammar and clear the Check Spelling As You Type and the Check Grammar As You Type check boxes.

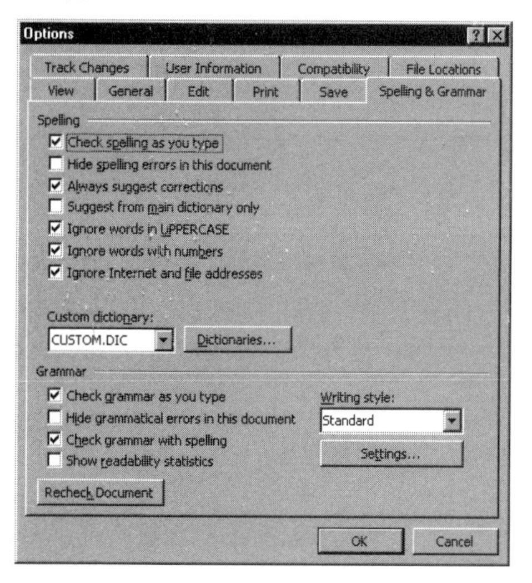

When you are ready to check your entire document for spelling and grammatical errors, click the Spelling and Grammar button on the Standard toolbar. Word will review the document and stop at any misspelled words or grammatical questions. You can choose to accept or ignore the suggestions. Click Next Sentence to resume the process. If you would prefer not to check the grammar, clear the Check Grammar check box.

Although Word's Grammar feature is a dramatic step forward in electronic proofreading, it regularly makes recommendations to fix text that is already correct or misses sentences that are obviously wrong. If you are uncertain, check another grammar reference.

Checking Spelling and Grammar Using the Toolbar

1. Click the Spelling and Grammar button on the Standard toolbar.
2. Accept or ignore any suggested corrections.
3. Click Next Sentence to resume checking.
4. Click Add to add the word to the dictionary.
5. Click Change All or Ignore All to change or ignore all occurrences in the current document.
6. Click the Check Grammar check box to turn off grammar checking.

Spelling and Grammar recognizes more than 80 languages in addition to English. If you type a paragraph in English and then another in Spanish within the same document, Word 2000 will automatically detect the language and use the appropriate spelling and grammar dictionaries.

To check spelling and grammar in a language other than English, first install the languages you want to use from the Office 2000 Language Pack and install the correct keyboard layout in the Windows Control Panel. In Word Help, search for Multilanguage for information on system requirements for each language.

Using the Thesaurus

Objective W2000.1.4

The thesaurus offers assistance only when called upon. It's there to help you find more descriptive, entertaining, or precise words.

To quickly find a synonym, right-click a word in your document and choose Synonyms from the shortcut menu.

Using the Thesaurus

1. Click the word you want to look up and choose Tools ➢ Language ➢ Thesaurus to open the Thesaurus dialog box, shown in Figure 2.3.
2. Click words in the Meanings column that best represent your context to see synonyms for them. Double-click to get a list of words that have the same or similar meaning.
3. Enter a new word to look up in the Replace with Synonym text box.
4. To review previously looked up words, select from the drop-down list under Looked Up.

FIGURE 2.3
Thesaurus dialog box

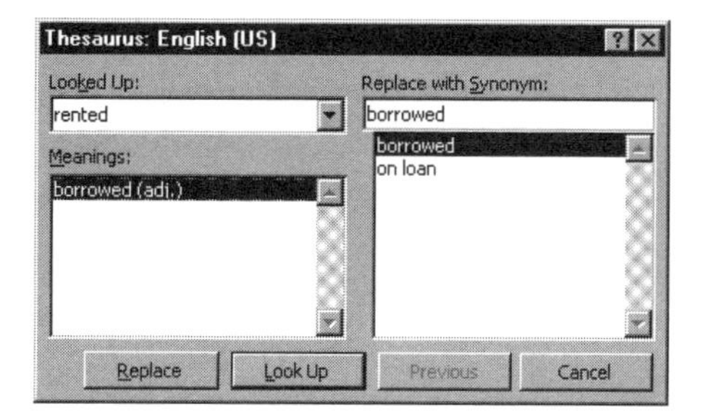

Hands On: *Objectives W2000.1.3, 1.4, and 1.5*

1. Start a new document, enter the following text, and then use the Thesaurus (and a bit of humor if you wish) to improve it:

   ```
   Wanted: Fun companion for good times. Any age over 18 is
   fine. Must be interesting. Should be cute. Big or small,
   give me a call at 800-555-0000 or send a good picture to
   Nice Person, 555 Pining Away Lane, Seattle, WA.
   ```

2. Open a document that contains misspellings. If you don't have any Word 2000 documents with errors (or if you want to pretend that you don't), you can enter the text below in a new document.

   ```
   Every year, several employes are given a specail bonus at
   holiday time. Employees who have done exceptoinal jobs are
   given cars to drive for the next year. The new cars are
   rented by the company. The current years cars have to be
   ```

```
returned and are sold to other employees at a discounted
rate. The holiday program coresponds to the annual awards
banquet where many employees are given awards for there
performance.
```

3. Run spelling and grammar check on the text above (or the document you opened).
4. Close all open documents, saving changes if you wish.

Doing More with Text

Although many font features are shared by all the Office 2000 applications, Word has some additional font tools that can give your text an even more distinctive look

To view all of the available font options, choose Format ➢ Font to open the Font dialog box (see Figure 2.4).

FIGURE 2.4

Font dialog box

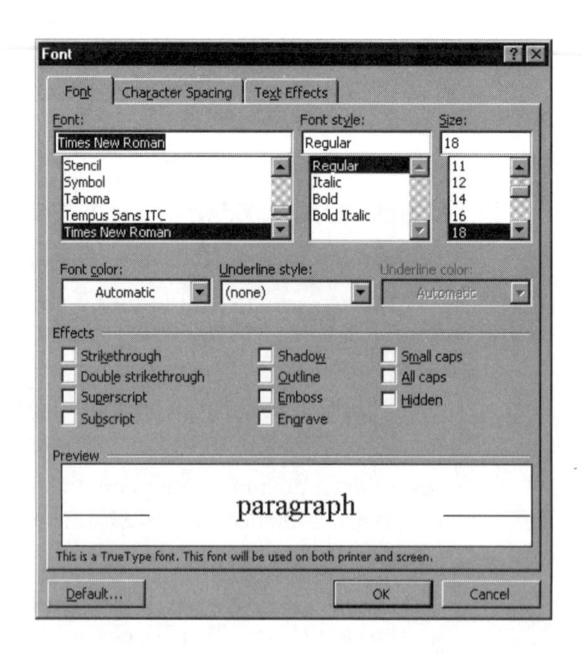

The Font dialog box has three page tabs: Font, Character Spacing, and Text Effects. The Preview window on the Font page lets you see what a font looks like as you apply other options like Font Size, Style, Color, and effects.

Special Text Effects

Objective W2000.1.13

There are eleven effects that you can apply from the Font tab in the Font dialog box. You can use Strikethrough and Double-strikethrough to show proposed deletions in a contract or bylaws. Use Superscript and Subscript to place special characters in formulas (H^{2}0) and footnotes (as in Miller$_{1}$). Shadow, Outline, Emboss, and Engrave stylize the text so that it stands out, as shown in Figure 2.5.

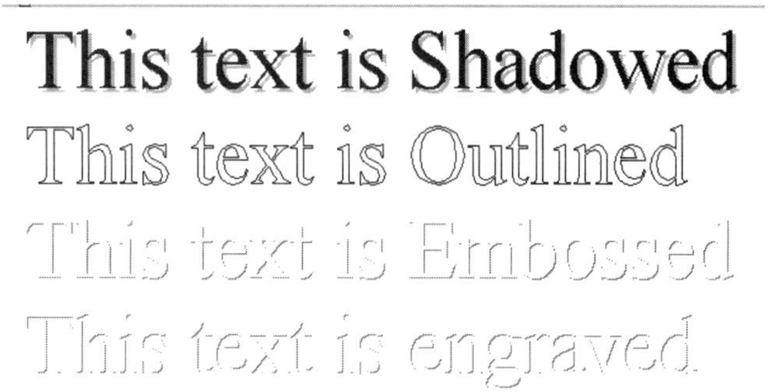

FIGURE 2.5
Text effects in Word

This text is Shadowed
This text is Outlined
This text is Embossed
This text is engraved

Small Caps and All Caps are typically used in stylized documents such as letterheads or business cards. The Small Caps effect converts lowercase letters to smaller versions of the capital letters. To use Small Caps, enter all the text in lowercase and then apply the Small Caps effect.

Hidden text doesn't print and can only be seen when Show/Hide is enabled. This effect was much more commonly applied when there weren't other, more effective ways such as Comments (see Chapter 4) to include non-printing, invisible document notes.

Rather than manually marking revised text with Strikethrough, you can use Word 2000's powerful Track Changes feature. Word also has an automatic footnoting system. Both features are discussed in Chapter 4.

With the preponderance of inexpensive color printers, being able to add colors to text is an important feature. Font Color is available from the

Formatting toolbar as well as in the Font dialog box. There are also many fancy, decorative fonts available in Office 2000, a few of which are shown here.

This is Blackadder ITC.

THIS IS CASTELLAR.

This is Jokerman.

This is Lucida Calligraphy.

This is Ravie.

Character Spacing

Objective W2000.2.3

Use character spacing to adjust the distance between characters. For example, you can spread a title such as *Memorandum* across a page without having to space two or three times between characters.

M E M O R A N D U M

Character spacing is commonly used in advanced desktop publishing when you want to size and scale characters precisely. Select the text you wish to adjust and click Format ➢ Font ➢ Character Spacing. Use the Scaling control if you want specify a percentage for the amount of horizontal space your text currently covers. Word will increase or decrease the between letter spacing accordingly. Use the Spacing control if you'd like to specify the point distance between letters in your selected text. Adjust position to move selected text up or down a certain amount of space.

Kerning is also a feature of desktop publishing used with True Type fonts. Kerning adjusts spacing between certain letter combinations so that letters appear to be more evenly spaced. Enable Kerning by clicking the check box in front of that option then selecting a minimum point size for Word to kern.

Text Effects

On the Text Effects tab of the Font dialog box you'll find six options designed for documents that will be read on-screen. They cause your text to blink, sparkle, or shimmer: Blinking Background, Las Vegas Lights, Marching Black Ants, Marching Red Ants, Shimmer, and Sparkle Text. To apply one of these special effects, select the text you want to animate, choose Format ➢ Font ➢ Text Effects, and select one of the six options. To turn the special effect off, select the text again, open the Font dialog box to the Text Effects tab and select None from the list of options. A word of advice: if you're going to apply animation, use it sparingly and don't apply it until you are done editing document text. Overdone, it is annoying, and animated documents use more computer resources, slowing down your system.

Highlighting Text for a Distinct Look

Objective W2000.1.7

If you are creating a document and want to call someone's attention to a particular part of your text, you can *highlight* it so it stands out for review. This is the computer equivalent of using a highlighter pen on the printout: if you have a color printer, the text will appear highlighted when printed. (Don't overlook the value of highlighting sections of text as a self-reminder.) Select the text you want to highlight and click the drop-down arrow next to the Highlight button to choose and apply a highlight color. The button will save the last chosen pen color, so if you want to use the same color again, just click directly on the Highlight button.

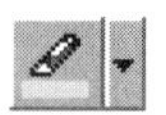

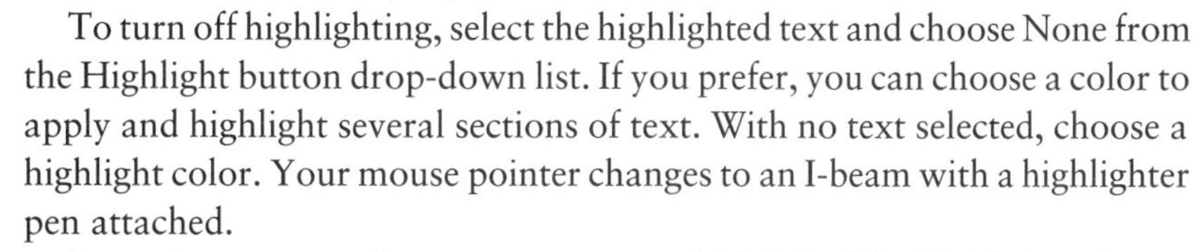

To turn off highlighting, select the highlighted text and choose None from the Highlight button drop-down list. If you prefer, you can choose a color to apply and highlight several sections of text. With no text selected, choose a highlight color. Your mouse pointer changes to an I-beam with a highlighter pen attached.

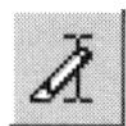

Drag the pen over the text you want to highlight. The highlight pointer will remain active until you click the Highlight button again to turn it off.

Applying Text Enhancements

1. Select the text you want to enhance.
2. Change font, font size, bold, italics, underline, and text color from the Formatting toolbar.

Applying Text Enhancements *(continued)*

3. Choose Format ➢ Font to open the Font dialog box for more advanced features.
4. Click any of the Effects to turn them on, or clear the check box to turn them off.
5. Click the Character Spacing tab to adjust the settings to expand or condense the characters.
6. Click the Text Effects tab to select from the list of animation options.
7. To highlight text, click the Highlight button and drag it over the text you want to highlight.

Hands On: Objectives W2000.1.2, 1.7, 1.10, 1.11, 1.13, and 2.3

1. Start a new blank document and type a list of your five favorite holidays.
   a) Select the first holiday and make it **bold**.
   b) Select the second holiday and make it 20 pt.
   c) Select the third holiday. *Italicize and underline* it.
   d) Select the fourth holiday and use the Font dialog box to make it 14-pt. Arial blue.
   e) Use the format painter to copy the formatting on the fourth holiday to all the others. Close this document without saving.
2. Enter several lines of text. Highlight a sentence yellow; highlight another lime green. Remove the highlight.
3. Select another sentence and apply Marching Red Ants to it. Remove the effect.
4. Select a word and make it embossed.

5. Type the following and format for superscripts, subscripts and other text effects as shown:

   $H_2 0$

   xy^3

   H_2SO_4

   THIS IS AN EXAMPLE OF SMALL CAPS.

   The last word of this sentence is formatted for double strikethrough.

6. Select the small caps example from Exercise 5 above. Adjust character spacing to Expanded by 1.2 ps.

Adding Numbers, Symbols, and the Date and Time

When you know how to use some of Word's special formatting features, you can easily create bulleted and numbered lists that have a professional look. Using the Symbol dialog box, you can insert everything from a happy face to the sign for infinity, and you can use Word's date and time features to add the date to a document even if, at the moment, you don't know what month it is.

Numbering and Bullets

Objective W2000.2.2

We live in a world of list makers (even if you ignore late-night talk show hosts), and Word 2000 makes it easy to create bulleted and numbered lists. If you begin a list with a number, Word will number following paragraphs when you press Enter. Begin with an asterisk and Word will bullet each paragraph.

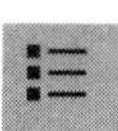

To apply numbers to existing text, select the paragraphs and click the Numbering button on the Formatting toolbar. Use the Bullets button to bullet existing paragraphs of text.

Creating a Numbered or Bulleted List

1. If the text you want to number is already entered, highlight the paragraphs to be numbered, and click the Numbering or Bullets button to number or bullet each paragraph.

   OR

1. To automatically number text as you type, type the "1" and a period, space once, and then enter text for item 1. For bullets, begin with an asterisk and a space.
2. Press Enter. Word will automatically number the next item "2" and press the Numbering button on the Formatting toolbar, or bullet the next item and press the Bullets button.
3. Continue entering text and pressing the Enter key to create numbered or bulleted points.
4. When you are finished creating the list, press Enter twice to turn automatic numbering or bullets off.

You can also begin numbering by clicking the Numbering button at the beginning of your first paragraph. If you want to use letters rather than numbers in automatic numbering, type "A" rather than "1" to begin. Word will number the second and succeeding paragraphs B, C, D, and so on. If you number your first paragraph "I", Word will use Roman numerals to number your paragraphs.

Word automatically turns on numbering when you type a paragraph that begins with a number or letter followed by a period, a space and other text; a period, a tab, and other text; or a tab and other text. You can get out of autonumbering mode by pressing Enter twice after your last numbered item. Since the Numbering button works as a toggle, you can easily convert numbered paragraphs to regular paragraphs by selecting them and clicking the Numbering button.

If automatic numbering or bullets do not work when you follow the steps above, choose Tools > AutoCorrect to open the AutoCorrect dialog box. Make sure that Automatic Bulleted Lists is checked under AutoFormat and Automatic Bulleted Lists and Automatic Numbered Lists are checked under AutoFormat As You Type.

Modifying the Bullet or Number Format

When you use the Bullets and Numbering features, Word supplies a standard, round bullet and leaves a default amount of space between the bullet or number and the text that follows. You can choose a different bullet character, number format, or spacing before entering your list, or you can modify the format of an existing list. If the bulleted or numbered list has already been entered, select the paragraphs you want to change. To change formats, choose Format ➢ Bullets and Numbering to open the Bullets and Numbering dialog box, shown in Figure 2.6.

FIGURE 2.6

The Bullets and Numbering dialog box

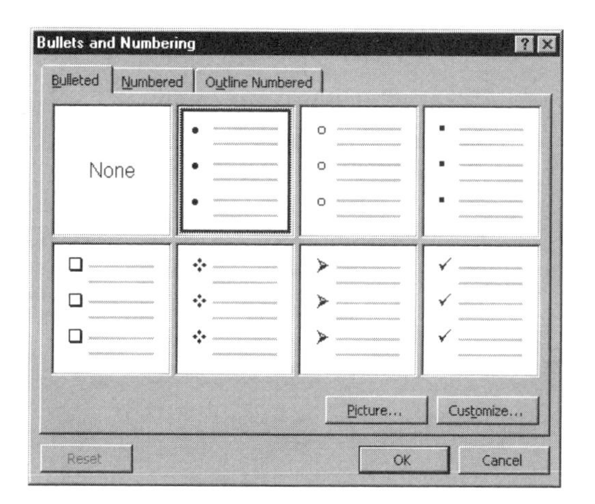

Click the Bulleted, Numbered, or Outline Numbered tab. The dialog box displays seven styles for bulleted text, seven styles for numbered lists, and seven styles for outline numbering. You can simply select any of the styles shown.

See Chapter 3 for information about outlines and outline numbering.

But you aren't limited to the styles shown in the samples. Select the Bulleted tab, and click the Customize button to open the Customize Bulleted List dialog box, as shown in Figure 2.7. (The Customize button is dimmed if None is selected.)

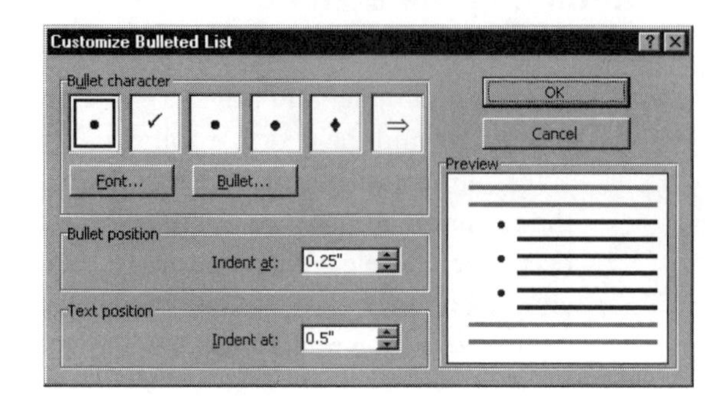

FIGURE 2.7 The Customize Bulleted List dialog box

Here you can change the bullet's font by clicking the Font button to open the Font dialog box. You can replace any of the bullet characters that appear here to create your own list of favorites. Click one of the bullet characters you don't want to use at this time to select it for replacement. Click the Bullet button to open the Symbol dialog box, shown in Figure 2.8.

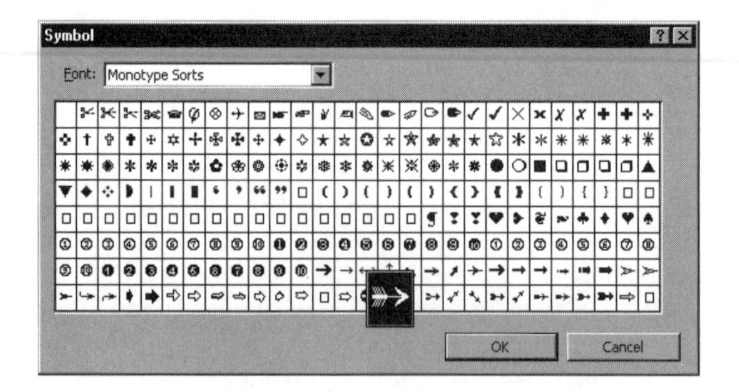

FIGURE 2.8 Symbol dialog box

The Symbol Font drop-down list contains symbol and display fonts. Choose a font or symbol set from the list, and the characters in the symbol set will be displayed in the *character map* below the drop-down. Any of the individual characters shown can be used as a bullet character. Click any character and then click OK to replace the selected bullet character with the symbol you've chosen. You will then be able to select the new symbol from the Bullet Character samples.

If you share documents with others, be sure to select bullets from frequently used fonts or symbol sets (that can also be installed on their computers), or the bullets will be changed when they open your documents. Symbol, Monotype Sorts, and Wingdings are common symbol sets.

The Bullet Position control lets you change the position of the bullet relative to the left margin. The Text Position control adjusts the position of text relative to the bullet. As you modify the Bullet and Text Position settings, the Preview will change to reflect your modifications.

If you want to use a picture instead of a symbol or character, click the Picture button in the Bullets and Numbering dialog box to open the Insert Picture dialog box, and make a selection.

The Customize Numbered List dialog box, shown in Figure 2.9, works much the same as Customized Bulleted List but there are a few important differences. Here, you can enter a number format such as "Chapter 1," "Section 1," or even "____ 1" to create a check-off list. Choose a style from the Number Style drop-down list. You can also have the numbering start at a number other than 1. To change the alignment of the number in the area before the text, click the Number Position drop-down list and choose between Left, Center, and Right.

FIGURE 2.9
Customize Numbered List dialog box

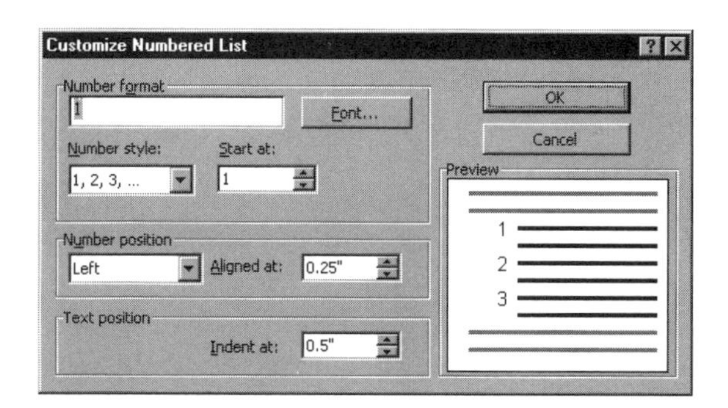

Customizing Number and Bullet Formats

1. Select the list whose numbering or bullet style you want to change.
2. Choose Format ➢ Bullets and Numbering.
3. Make sure the tab you want (Numbered or Bulleted) is displayed.

Customizing Number and Bullet Formats *(continued)*

4. Click a number, letter, or bullet format. To choose a different format, click Customize.
5. Enter a number format, or choose to change the bullet character by clicking the Bullet button. If numbering, enter the starting number if it is other than 1.
6. Adjust the Bullet or Number Position and the Text Position as desired.
7. Click OK to save your changes and return to your document.

To remove numbers and bullets from text, select the bulleted or numbered list, and then click the Bullets or Numbering button on the toolbar to turn bullets or numbering off.

Creating Special Characters

Objective W2000.1.15

Many symbols used regularly in business documents aren't on the standard keyboard. Word 2000 makes many of these common symbols available to you with simple keystrokes, and others are available by choosing Insert ➢ Symbol.

Choose Insert ➢ Symbol and select the Symbols tab to open the symbol character map, shown earlier in Figure 2.8. Select the Special Characters tab, shown below.

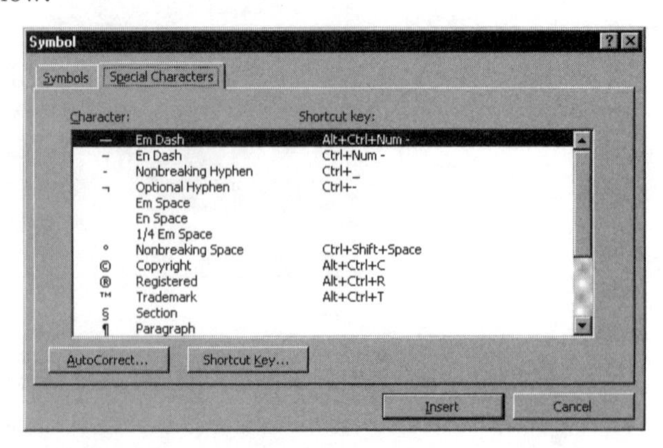

- Choose from the symbol font sets or special characters shown, and then click the Insert button to insert the symbol into your document.

If you need the symbol more than once, copy and paste it to the other locations. The AutoCorrect method suggested for abbreviations in Chapter 1 can also be applied to create special characters and symbols such as ©, ☹ and ➔. To add a symbol to the AutoCorrect list, select the symbol and click the AutoCorrect button or choose Tools ➢ AutoCorrect. Enter a character string that will automatically be replaced with the desired symbol—enter (p) for ¶, for example. Make sure it is a character string you don't use in other situations, or you will find it replaced with the symbol every time you type it.

Using Special Characters

1. Choose Insert ➢ Symbol.
2. Choose a symbol from the font symbol sets shown in the character map on the Symbol page or from the list on the Special Characters page.
3. Add regularly used symbols to the AutoCorrect list by clicking AutoCorrect and entering a text string in the Replace text box.

Inserting the Date and Time

Objective W2000.1.14

Word 2000 has 17 different formats you can choose from when inserting the current date and/or time, so the format you want is probably among them. Choose Insert ➢ Date and Time to open the Date and Time dialog box.

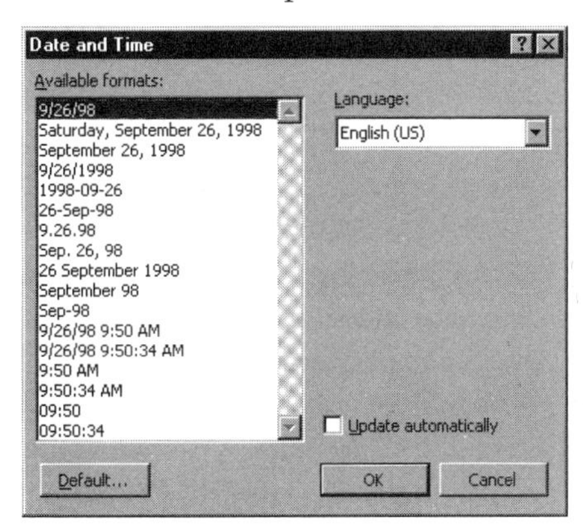

Select a format from the list. If you would like to automatically update the field to the current date and time every time you open the document, click the Update Automatically check box. This inserts date and time as a field rather than as text. A *field* serves as a placeholder which is replaced with current data. (Be careful not to use this option when the date on a document is important to mark a paper trail.) A Date and Time field is most useful when a document is in draft form and you want to know when it was last worked on, or when a memo or notice is regularly printed and mailed and should always have the current date. The Date and Time field is only updated when you print the document, re-open the document, or right-click the field and choose Update Field. Go to Print Preview to see the changed date and time. When you return to the document, the date and time will be updated.

Inserting the Date and Time

1. Choose Insert ➢ Date and Time.
2. Select the desired Date and Time format.
3. Click the Update Automatically check box if you want to insert Date and Time as a field.
4. Click OK to insert the date and time into your document.

Hands On: *Objectives W2000.1.14, 1.15, and 2.2*

1. Enter a list of at least 10 things you have to do this week.
   a) Select the list and turn on Numbering. Select the list again and turn on Bullets.
   b) Change the bullet characters to some other symbol, such as a right-pointed arrow.
2. Type a new list below the To Do list that includes things you need to buy or errands you need to run. Start by entering a "1", a period, and a space. When you press Enter after the first item, a "2" should appear, and a tab should be automatically inserted after each of the two numbers. If Automatic Numbering is not turned on, go to Format ➢ AutoFormat to open the AutoFormat dialog box. Click Options to open the AutoCorrect dialog box, click the AutoFormat As You Type tab, and make sure Automatic Bulleted Lists and Automatic Numbered Lists are checked.

3. On a new blank line, choose Insert ➢ Symbol and insert a symbol or special character that you might use often. Add it to the AutoCorrect list so you can type a few characters and have them replaced with the symbol. After you have entered it, type the characters and see if AutoCorrect changes them to your symbol.

In the same document:

a) Use Ctrl+Home to move to the top of your document. Choose Insert ➢ Date and Time to add the date and time to your document in a format that includes the time. Enable Update Automatically.

b) Below the Date and Time field, choose Insert ➢ Date and Time again but do not enable Update Automatically. Save and close the document. Wait a couple of minutes and reopen the document. Switch to Print Preview and zoom in on the date and time. The first time will reflect the current time, and the second time should still reflect the time the field was originally entered.

Aligning and Formatting Paragraphs

In addition to formatting text or characters, skilled Word users must know how to format lines and paragraphs of text. In this section, you'll learn how to use indents and tabs and to control how text flows on the page.

Aligning Text

Objective W2000.2.1

Word has four ways (see Figure 2.10) to align text: left, center, right, and full (justify).

To align text, position the insertion point anywhere in the paragraph and click one of the alignment buttons on the Formatting toolbar.

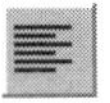   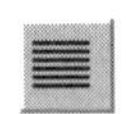

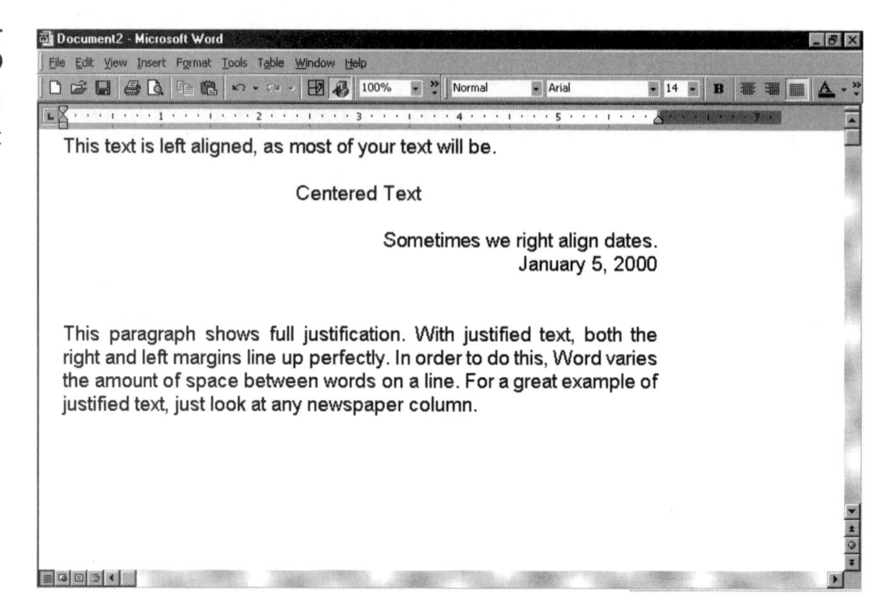

FIGURE 2.10 Aligning paragraph text

Using Indentation Options

Objective W2000.2.5

Word offers three ways to access the paragraph-indenting features: the Formatting toolbar, the ruler, and the Paragraph dialog box.

You'll find the easiest method to change indents on the Formatting toolbar. Click anywhere in the paragraph you want to indent or select multiple paragraphs, and click the Decrease Indent button to reduce the left indent by 1/2 inch. Click the Increase Indent button to extend the indent by 1/2 inch.

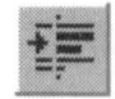

Creating Indents Using the Ruler

The second method of indenting paragraphs—using the ruler—can take a little work to master, but it's a very visual way to set left, right, hanging, and dual indents. You can use the ruler to set tabs as well as indents and left and right margins in Page Layout view.

If you prefer to do most of your work without the ruler, turn the ruler off by choosing View ➢ Ruler to remove the check. To make the ruler temporarily visible, point to the narrow gray line under the command bars and the ruler will reappear. As soon as the pointer moves back to your document, the ruler will slide back under the command bars.

There are four indent markers on the ruler, shown in Figure 2.11:

- A *first line indent* works the same as pressing Tab on the keyboard.
- A *hanging indent* (sometimes called an outdent) "hangs" the remaining lines in a paragraph to the right of the first line when this marker is positioned to the right of the first line indent marker.
- A *left indent* sets a paragraph off from the rest of the text by moving all lines in from the left margin.
- A *right indent* moves text in from the right margin and is typically combined with a left indent to make a *dual indent*. Dual indents are used most commonly to set off block quotations.

FIGURE 2.11

Indent markers on the Ruler

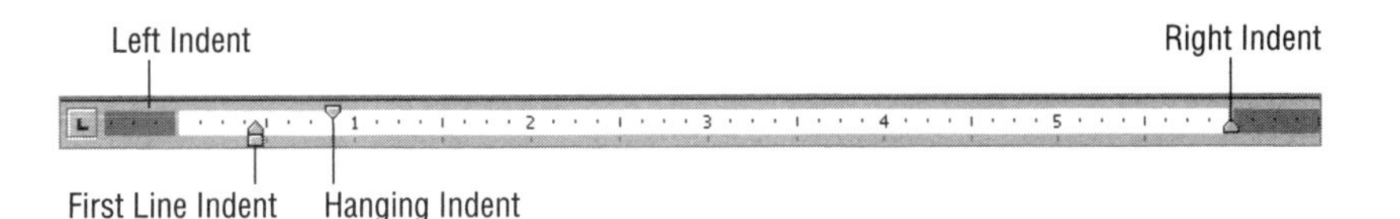

To change the indents for existing text, select the paragraph or paragraphs you want to indent and drag the indent marker on the ruler to the desired location. Moving the first line or the hanging indent marker indents or outdents the first line of each paragraph. Moving the left or right indent marker indents all lines of each paragraph.

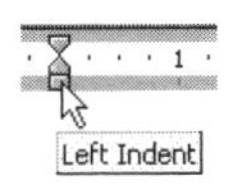

If you forget which marker is which, point to any of them for a moment and view the ScreenTip. You can use the ruler to set indents before entering text. Position the insertion point where you plan to enter the new text. The indents will apply to all newly entered text until you change the indent settings.

Indenting Using the Toolbar and Ruler

1. Click in the paragraph you want to indent, and click the Increase Indent button or the Decrease Indent button on the Formatting toolbar.
2. To use the ruler: change to Normal view and turn on the ruler if it is not already visible (choose View ➢ Ruler).
3. Select the text you want to indent.
4. Drag the First Line Indent marker to the right to indent the first line in a paragraph.
5. Drag the Hanging Indent marker to the right to indent all but the first line in a paragraph.
6. Drag the Left Indent marker to indent all the selected text.
7. Drag the Right Indent marker to indent the selected text from the right margin.

If you select paragraphs that do not share the same indent settings, one or all of the indent markers on the ruler will be dimmed. Click the dimmed marker(s) to make the indent settings the same for all the selected paragraphs.

Indenting Using the Paragraph Dialog Box

The third way to set indents is by using the Paragraph dialog box, shown in Figure 2.12. To access the dialog box, choose Format ➢ Paragraph or right-click and choose Paragraph from the shortcut menu.

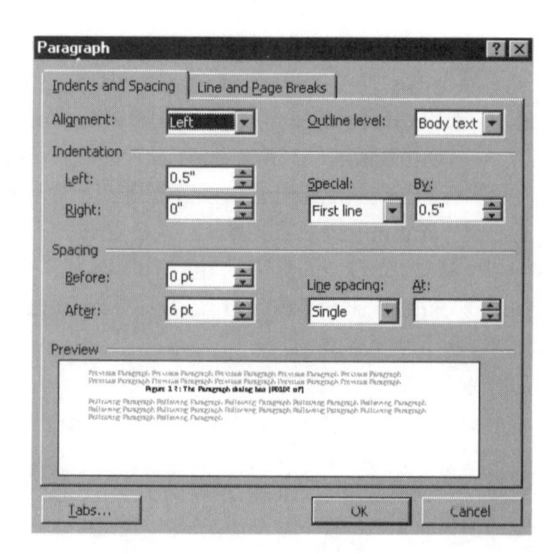

FIGURE 2.12 The Paragraph dialog box

On the Indents and Spacing tab, click the up and down arrows next to the Left and Right text boxes (called *spin boxes* because you can "spin" through the options), or enter decimal numbers directly in the text boxes. In the Special control, you can select First Line or Hanging to indent or outdent the first line of the paragraphs by 1/2 inch. If you want the indent to be more or less than 0.5 inch, enter the special indent value in the By control.

Indenting Using the Paragraph Dialog Box

1. Select the text you want to indent and open the Paragraph dialog box (choose Format ➢ Paragraph or right-click and choose Paragraph).
2. Use the spin box controls to change the Left and Right indent settings.
3. Click the Special drop-down arrow to select First Line or Hanging indent.
4. Click OK to close the Paragraph dialog box and see your changes.

Setting Line Spacing Options

Objective W2000.2.3

Word 2000 provides six options for adjusting *line spacing* of the vertical distance between lines of text.

Single: Enough room to comfortably display the largest character on a line.

1.5 lines: One-and-a-half single lines.

Double: Twice as much room as single spacing.

At Least: A minimum line spacing for the selection.

Exactly: Makes all lines evenly spaced regardless of the size of the fonts or graphics included in those lines.

Multiple: Used to enter line spacing other than single, 1.5, and double.

To change the line spacing for existing text, select the paragraphs you want to change. Open the Paragraph dialog box (choose Format ➢ Paragraph or right-click and select Paragraph from the shortcut menu), and click the drop-down list to select from the line-spacing options:

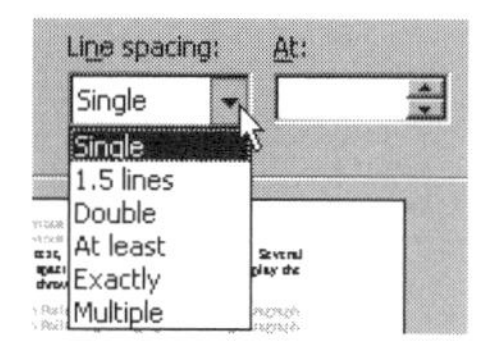

At Least and Exactly require you to enter a point size in the At text box. Multiple requires you to enter the amount by which to multiply. For example, you can triple-space selected paragraphs by choosing Multiple and then entering 3 in the At control.

Setting Line Spacing

1. Select the text whose line spacing you want to change.
2. Choose Format ➢ Paragraph to open the Paragraph dialog box. Click the Indents and Spacing tab if the page is not visible.
3. Click the Line Spacing drop-down list to select the desired line spacing.
4. If you are choosing At Least, Exactly, or Multiple, enter a number in the At control.
5. Click OK to return to the document and review the changes.

To see all the formatting that is applied to a paragraph, choose Help ➢ What's This? and click the paragraph. You'll get an information box, such as the one shown below, that displays paragraph and font formatting related to the paragraph. Choose Help ➢ What's This? again to turn it off.

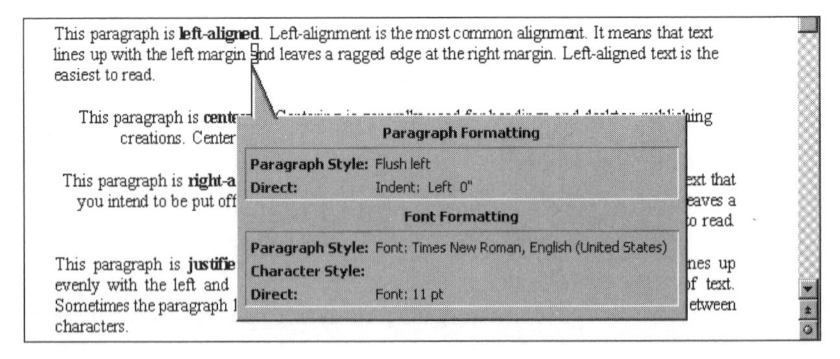

Using Tabs

Objective W2000.2.6

Tab stops are markers set by default at half-inch intervals across the width of the document. Pressing the Tab key moves the cursor from one tab stop to the next. One of the most common uses of a tab is to indent the first line of a paragraph.

Tabs are also used to create *parallel columns*, vertically aligning text within a document. You can change the tab-stop settings by using the ruler or the Tabs dialog box. Setting the stops includes choosing the alignment type and location for each tab stop you want to use. Figure 2.13 shows the five basic types of tab stops:

Left: The default type. Text appears to the right of the tab stop.

Center: Text is automatically adjusted to the left and the right of the tab stop until it is centered under the tab stop.

Right: Text appears to the left of the tab stop.

Decimal: Used for numeric entries. Text lines up with the decimal point.

Bar: Inserts a vertical line in your document at the tab stop. In earlier versions of Word, the Bar tab was used to create a vertical separator for columns. With Word 2000, you can do this automatically when you set up columns.

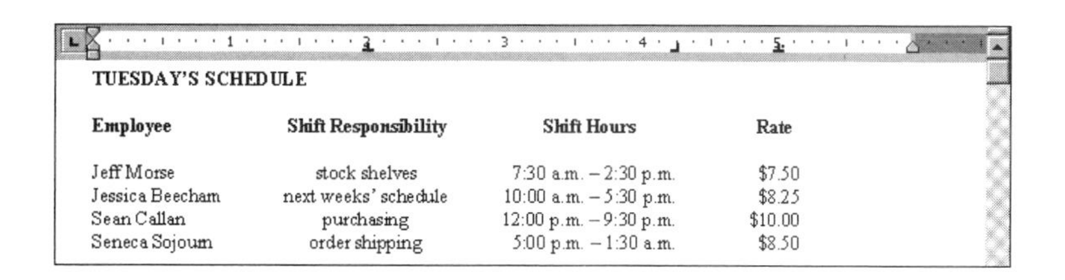

TUESDAY'S SCHEDULE

Employee	Shift Responsibility	Shift Hours	Rate
Jeff Morse	stock shelves	7:30 a.m. – 2:30 p.m.	$7.50
Jessica Beecham	next weeks' schedule	10:00 a.m. – 5:30 p.m.	$8.25
Sean Callan	purchasing	12:00 p.m. – 9:30 p.m.	$10.00
Seneca Sojourn	order shipping	5:00 p.m. – 1:30 a.m.	$8.50

FIGURE 2.13 Four of the five types of tab stops were used to align these columns.

Setting Tab Stops Using the Ruler

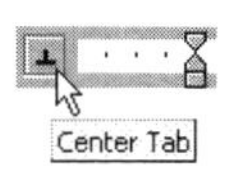

At the left end of the ruler in Print Layout view is a Tab Selection button that allows you to select the type of tab you want to set. By default it is set on Left Tab. Click the button to toggle through the five tab choices.

Once you have chosen the type of tab you want to set, click the ruler to set a tab. The tab-stop marker appears, and all the tabs to the left of the marker are deleted. If you want to move the tab stop, click the marker and drag it to a new location on the ruler.

If you want the tab stops to apply to existing text, be sure to select the text first—before clicking the ruler. Unless you select the entire document or the last paragraph in the document, the tab stops will only apply to the selected paragraph(s). You can, however, set the tab stops for a blank document before you start entering text, and then the tab stops can be used throughout the document. To clear a tab stop, point to the tab stop and simply drag it off the ruler.

Setting Tabs Using the Ruler

1. Click the Tab button at the left end of the ruler to toggle through the five tab choices.
2. Click the ruler to set the tab stops—all the default tab stops to the left of the new tabs are deleted.
3. Drag the tab-stop marker on the ruler to change the tab position.
4. Drag the tab-stop marker off the ruler to remove the tab stop.

If you're using tabs to create parallel columns, you may not be using the most efficient tool. In most situations, it is easier to create parallel columns using Word's Tables feature. See Chapter 3 for information regarding tables.

Setting Tab Stops and Leaders Using the Tabs Dialog Box

Objective W2000.2.8

You can also create tab stops using the Tabs dialog box. Make sure the insertion point is located where you want the new tab stops to begin. (If the text you want to format is already entered, select it.) Access the Tabs dialog box, shown in Figure 2.14, by choosing Format ➢ Tabs.

FIGURE 2.14 The Tabs dialog box

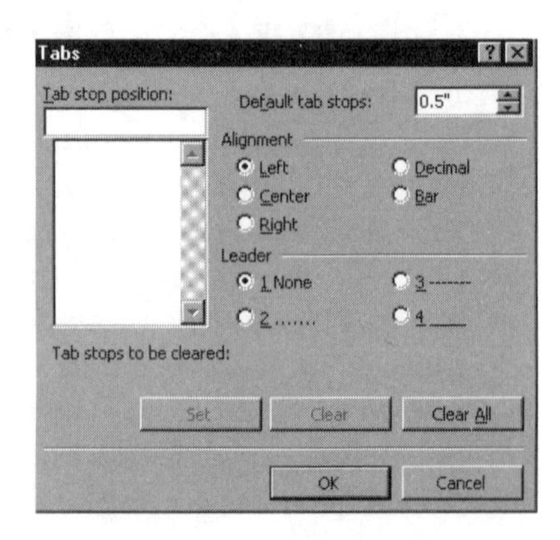

In the Tab Stop Position text box, type the location for the tab stop you want to create. In the Alignment control, choose how you want text to align at the tab stop. The Leader control lets you select a *leader* to lead the reader's eye across the text. The leader (see Figure 2.15) precedes the tabbed text.

FIGURE 2.15

Tab stops and leaders

Vacation Schedule by Month

Frank.. May
Rebecca.. June
Sherry... June
Janis .... July
James .... August
Richard... August

When you have set the position, type, and leader (if you wish) for the tab stop, click the Set button. The new tab stop will be added to the tab-stop list. Repeat these steps to set any other tab stops.

You can also use the dialog box to change an existing tab stop. Select the tab stop from the list below the Tab Stop Position control. Change the Alignment and Leader options; then click Set. To remove an existing tab stop, select it from the list and click the Clear button. Clicking Clear All removes all the tab stops you added, reverting to the default tab settings. When you are done setting tab stops, click OK to close the Tabs dialog box.

Setting Tabs and Leaders Using the Tabs Dialog Box

1. Open the Tabs dialog box by choosing Format ➢ Tabs.
2. Type a decimal value in the Tab Stop Position text box.
3. Select an alignment style and, optionally, a leader style.
4. Click OK.
5. Enter text, pressing tab between each column.

To see where tabs have been typed in existing text, click the Show/Hide Paragraph Marks button on the Standard toolbar. You'll see a right-pointed arrow to indicate a tab.

TUESDAY'S·SCHEDULE¶

¶

Employee →	**Shift·Responsibility** →	**Shift·Hours** →	**Rate¶**
¶			
Jeff·Morse →	stock·shelves →	7:30·a.m.·–·2:30·p.m. →	$7.50¶
Jessica·Beecham →	next·weeks'·schedule →	10:00·a.m.·–·5:30·p.m. →	$8.25¶
Sean·Callan →	purchasing →	12:00·p.m.·–·9:30·p.m. →	$10.00¶
Seneca·Sojourn →	order·shipping →	5:00·p.m.·–·1:30·a.m. →	$8.50¶

Hands On: Objectives W2000.1.14, 1.15, 2.2, 2.3, 2.5, 2.6, and 2.8

1. In a new document, set tabs to enter the text below in parallel columns. Set a right tab for the times and center the number of weeks. Save the document as *Class Schedule*.

Class	Day	Time	Weeks
Access	Monday	1 p.m.–3 p.m.	10
Excel	Tuesday	11 a.m.–2 p.m.	7
FrontPage	Friday	8 a.m.–4 p.m.	2
PowerPoint	Monday	5 p.m.–7 p.m.	4
Outlook	Saturday	9 a.m.–5 p.m.	1
Word	Thursday	7 a.m.–10 a.m.	7

2. In a new document, enter the following text and format each paragraph as described in the paragraph.

   A first line indent works the same as pressing the Tab key on the keyboard. Single-line spacing provides enough room to comfortably display the largest character on a line.

   A hanging indent (sometimes called an outdent) "hangs" the first line of a paragraph to the left of the remaining lines. Double spacing provides twice as much room between lines of text as single spacing.

   A left indent sets a paragraph off from the rest of the text by moving all lines in from the left margin. Line spacing of 1.5 leaves one-and-a-half single lines between each line of text.

   A right indent moves text in from the right margin and is typically combined with a left indent to make a dual indent. Dual indents, like the dual indent used in this paragraph, are used most commonly to set off block quotations. Multiple line spacing is used to specify the number of lines: in this paragraph, 3 lines.

3. In a new document, set a left tab at 0.5, a center tab at 2, a right tab at 4.25, and decimal tab at 5. Then enter the schedule information shown in the text above or similar text of your own.

   Select the line of column headings and change the tab stop for Shift Hours to a Center tab and the tab stop for Rate to a Right tab. Move both tabs so the headings line up appropriately with the columns.

4. Press Ctrl+Home to navigate to the top of your document. Press enter twice to leave some space, then insert a heading above the text you entered in Exercise 3. Change the heading to right-aligned, then change it to centered.
5. Select the text from Step 4 and set the line spacing to 1.5. Experiment with justification using the text you previously entered in Exercise 2. Do you prefer left-aligned or justified?

Replacing and Checking Text

As you create documents in Word, you may want to use the same text in another document or correct an error that occurs several times. Word 2000 offers several features to help you replace and check text—including grammar—efficiently. There's even a thesaurus to help you find that perfectly descriptive word or phrase.

Creating and Applying Frequently Used Text

Objective W2000.1.16

Word has two features that let you easily insert frequently used text and graphics. The first option, AutoCorrect, was covered earlier in this chapter. The second feature, *AutoText*, is particular to Word. It allows you to store formatted text or graphics, even entire paragraphs, and then recall them with a few keystrokes.

To create an AutoText entry, select the text you want to store as AutoText. To include the text's format, such as font and font style, before selecting, click the Show/Hide Paragraph Marks button on the Standard toolbar and make sure you include the paragraph mark in the selection. Choose Insert ➢ AutoText ➢ New to create the entry (see Figure 2.16). You will be prompted to give the entry a name; make it short and easy to remember, but at least four characters long. To insert the AutoText in a document, type the name you assigned to the entry and press the F3 key.

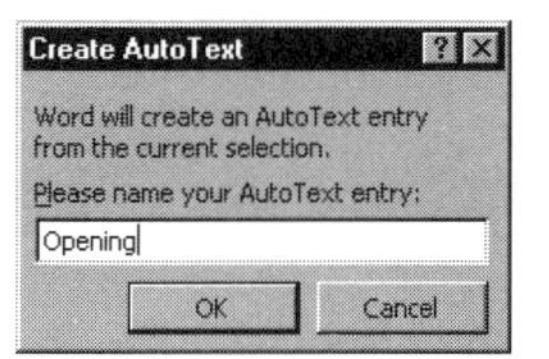

FIGURE 2.16
Creating AutoText

Word provides a number of canned AutoText entries that you can access from the Insert ➢ AutoText menu.

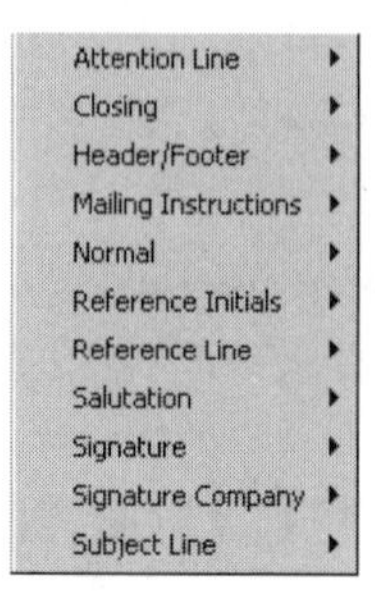

Just choose a category, and then select the entry you want to insert into your document.

If you're inserting a lot of AutoText into a document, you can turn on the AutoText toolbar by choosing View ➢ Toolbars ➢ AutoText. The toolbar's All Entries drop-down menu is the same as the menu bar's AutoText menu.

Delete AutoText entries in the AutoText dialog box (choose Insert ➢ AutoText ➢ AutoText) by selecting the entry you want to delete and clicking the Delete button.

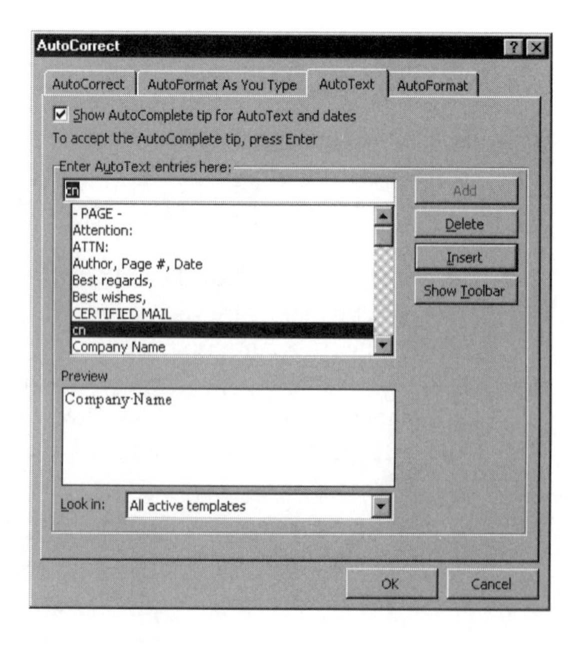

Creating, Inserting, and Deleting AutoText

1. Select the text to include in the AutoText. To include formatting, click the Show/Hide Paragraph Marks button and select the text, including the paragraph mark.
2. Choose Insert ➢ AutoText ➢ New. Then name the AutoText.
3. To insert the AutoText within a document, type the entry's name and press the F3 key.
4. To delete an AutoText entry, click the AutoText button on the toolbar to open the AutoText dialog box. Select the AutoText entry and click the Delete button.

Finding and Replacing Text

Objective W2000.1.12

When you are working in a long document, one of the fastest ways to make repetitive changes to a document is through Find and Replace. Find helps you locate a *text string*, and Replace substitutes new text for the existing string.

Using Find

To locate a word or phrase, click the Select Browse Object button and choose Find, or choose Edit ➢ Find from the menu. Click the More button to see all available options in the Find and Replace dialog box, shown in Figure 2.17.

Enter the text you want to locate in the Find What text box. You can have Word search the entire document (All), or for faster searching, just search above (Up) or below (Down) the insertion point. You can also search for words that are in the same case as you entered (Match Case).

Objective W2000E.2.5

To specify a particular format, or to find special characters or non-printing elements such as paragraph marks and spaces, click the Format or the Special buttons at the bottom of the dialog box. Choose the type of format, such as Font, and then identify the specific format (for example, Times New Roman)

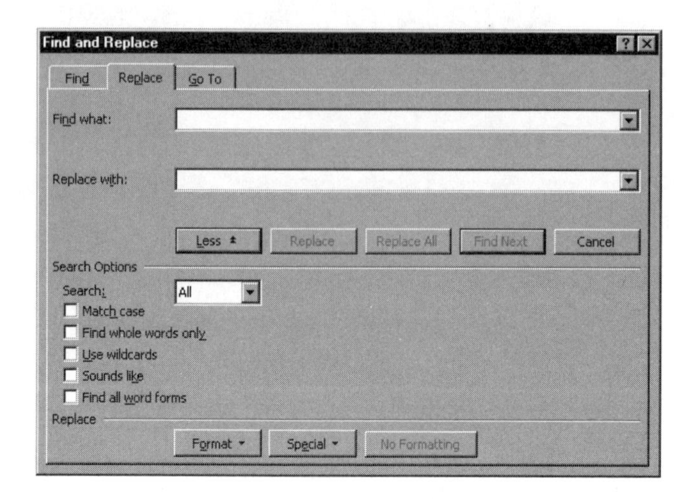

FIGURE 2.17
Find and Replace dialog box

you want to search for. If it's a special or non-printing character you want, click the Special button and then choose the character from the list of choices. Using this option, you can, for example, search for every place you entered two hard returns after a paragraph or every section break.

When you have entered your Search options, click the Find Next button to identify the first occurrence of the text string. You can then close the Find dialog box and use the blue browse buttons at the bottom of the vertical scroll bar to move to previous or next occurrences of the string.

Using Replace

Replace allows you to replace one or all occurrences of a word or phrase with different text. Let's say you just finished a lengthy proposal for a client and you realize you've misspelled their company name throughout. Sure, you could correct each misspelling individually, but why? Click Edit ➢ Replace, and Word opens the Replace tab of the Find and Replace dialog box. Type the incorrectly spelled company name in the Find What field, and the correctly spelled company name in the Replace With field. Click Replace All, and Word does the work for you.

Use Replace with the Format and Special buttons to replace every place you used Times New Roman 12 pt. font, for example, with Comic Sans 14 pt., or every occurrence of two paragraph marks with one.

Finding and Replacing Text

1. Click Select Browse Object button or choose Edit ➢ Find to open the Find dialog box.
2. Enter the characters you want to search for in the Find What text box. Click Find Next.
3. Close the Find dialog box and click the Next Find/Go To button at the bottom of the vertical scroll bar. Browse each of the occurrences of the text string.
4. To replace text, open the Find dialog box again and click the Replace tab.
5. Enter the text string you want to search for in the Find What text box and the characters you want to replace it with in the Replace With text box.
6. Click Replace All to complete the replace operation in one step. If you want to review each replacement, choose Replace. Click Find Next to locate the next occurrence. You may need to reposition the dialog box to see the text. Click Replace until you have made all the replacements.

Getting into Print

Although we are transmitting more and more documents electronically these days, we still print a lot of documents. In this section, we'll look at your printing options. We'll also discuss how to print envelopes and labels, a handy feature for home and office work.

Using Print Preview

Objective W2000.3.2

Previewing your document before printing it gives you the chance to see how the pages break and whether there are any layout problems that will make the document look less than its best.

To open the Print Preview dialog box, click the Print Preview button on the Standard toolbar or choose File ➢ Print Preview.

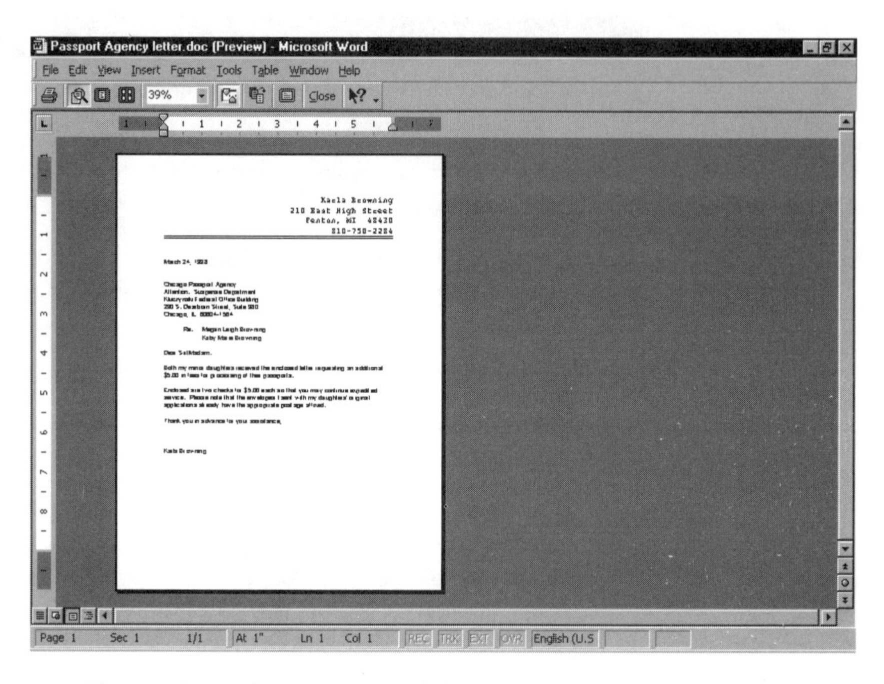

Table 2.2 shows the options available in Print Preview.

TABLE 2.2: Options in Print Preview

Button	Button Name	Placeholder
	Print	Prints the document.
	Magnify	When pressed, click the document to zoom in or out. Inactivate to edit the document.
	One Page	Shows only one page of the document.
	Multiple Page	Shows a maximum of six pages at one time.
50%	Zoom	Changes the magnification level.

TABLE 2.2: Options in Print Preview *(continued)*

Button	Button Name	Placeholder
	View Ruler	Turns the vertical and horizontal rulers on and off.
	Shrink to Fit	Reduces the document by one page to prevent spill-over.
	Full Screen	Turns full screen mode on.
Close	Close	Closes Print Preview.
	Context- Sensitive Help	Click Help, and then click any button within Print Preview to activate Help about that button.

Inserting Page Breaks

Objective W2000.1.6

Word paginates documents automatically—when text exceeds the length of a page, Word moves to the next page by inserting a soft page break. After you've previewed your document, you might decide you want a page to break earlier, say at the end of a cover page or just before a new topic. To insert a *hard page break* that forces the page to break at the insertion point's current location, press Ctrl+Enter.

Changing Page Orientation and Paper Size

Objective W2000.3.6

If you think that your document would look better in *landscape* orientation (11 × 8.5) than *portrait* (8.5 × 11), you can change the orientation in Page

Setup. Choose File ➢ Page Setup ➢ Paper Size or double-click the gray frame at the top of the ruler to open the dialog box.

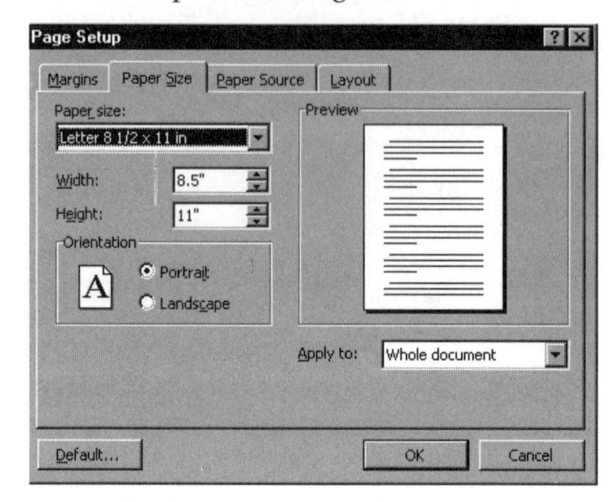

You can also change to another paper size entirely, including a custom size for nonstandard forms such as note cards or half-sheets. If you choose custom size, enter the dimensions for height and width.

Objective W2000.3.16

If you want to apply a page-size change to only part of your document, position the insertion point at the beginning of the page you want to change, go to Page Setup, change the paper size, and choose This Point Forward in the Apply To control. To apply the change to a single page and not all the pages that follow it, move the insertion point to the end of the last page with this formatting, select This Point Forward, and change back to the original paper size.

Changing Page Orientation and Paper Size

1. To change page orientation for the entire document, choose File ➢ Page Setup ➢ Paper Size.
2. Click the Portrait or Landscape Orientation option.
3. To change paper size, click the Paper Size drop-down list and select an option. If you choose Custom, enter the dimensions of the paper in the Height and Width text boxes.
4. To change page orientation for only part of a document, choose This Point Forward in the Apply To text box.

Aligning Text Vertically

Objective W2000.3.11

After you have the page orientation and paper size set, you may want to create a title page for your document. One easy way to do this is to enter the text you want on the title page, and then center text vertically on the page between the top and bottom margins. To activate this feature, position the insertion point on the page you want to align. Choose File ➢ Page Setup and click the Layout tab. Under Vertical Alignment, you will find four options. Choose one and click OK.

Top: The default setting, text lines up with the top margin.

Center: Text on the page is centered between the top and bottom margins.

Justified: Text is spread out so that each line is the same distance apart with the top line at the top margin and the bottom line at the bottom margin.

Bottom: Text lines up with the bottom margin.

Aligning Text Vertically

1. Click the page that contains the text you want to align.
2. Choose File ➢ Page Setup ➢ Layout and choose Top, Center, Justified, or Bottom from the Vertical Alignment drop-down list. Click OK.

Setting Margins

Objective W2000.3.7

Word's default *margins*, the white space between text and the edge of the paper the text will be printed on, are 1 inch on the top and bottom and 1.25 inches on the left and right sides of the page. To change margins, use the Margins page of the Page Setup dialog box, shown in Figure 2.18 and set the following options:

- Top, Bottom, Left, and Right spin box controls set the amount of white space on the four edges of the document.
- The *gutter margin* is used to add additional space to a document that will be bound.

- The *mirror margin* feature helps you format margins for back-to-back printing.
- The default for the Apply To control is Whole Document. You can, however, change margins from the insertion point forward for the rest of a document by choosing This Point Forward from the Apply To drop-down list.

FIGURE 2.18

Page Setup dialog box, Margins tab

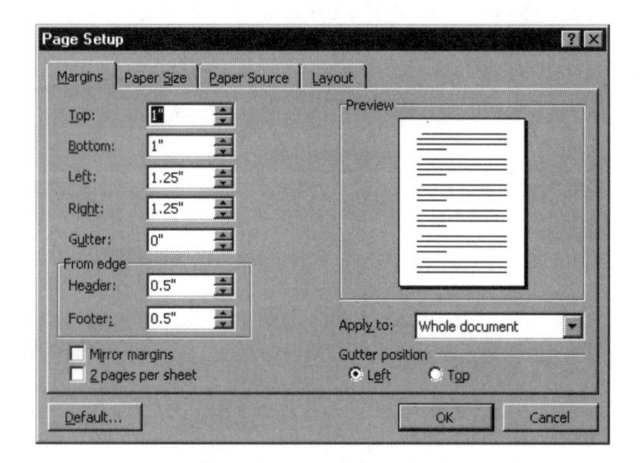

Changing Document Margins

1. Position the insertion point where you want the margin changes to take effect.
2. Choose File ➢ Page Setup to open the Page Setup dialog box, and click the Margins tab.
3. Click the Mirror margins check box to activate mirror margins, if desired.
4. Use the spin box arrows or type in the text boxes to increase or decrease the margins.
5. Click OK to return to the document.

If you prefer, you can change margins using the vertical and horizontal rulers in Print Preview or in Print Layout view. Point to the margin line on the ruler and the pointer changes to a double-headed arrow. When you hold down the mouse button, a dotted line extends through the document, showing the location of the margin. Drag the dotted line in the desired direction to adjust the margin.

Printing Options

Objective W2000.3.1

If you click the Print button on the Standard toolbar, Word uses the current print options. By default, one copy of the document is sent to the Windows default printer. If you want to change the print settings, choose File ➢ Print to open the Print dialog box.

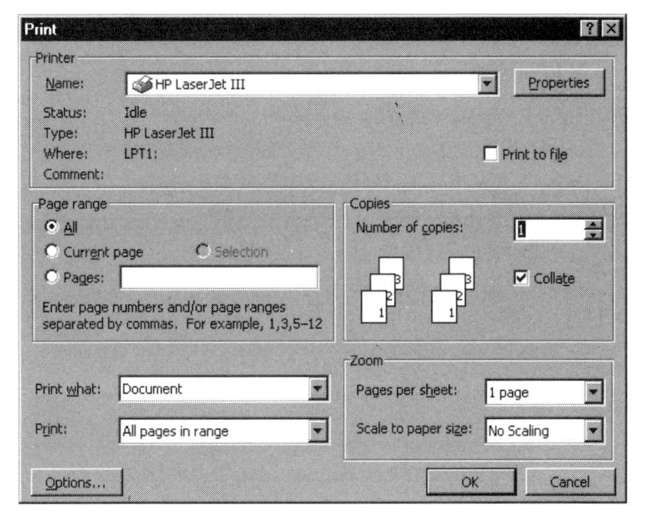

In the Print dialog box, you can:

- Choose another printer
- Print only designated pages of a document, including current page, a range of pages, or selected text
- Choose to print the document properties (who created it, when it was created, how many words, characters, and so on) or other lists such as AutoText entries
- Indicate in the Print text box whether to print just even pages, just odd pages, or both
- Specify the number of copies and have them collated (pages 1, 2, 3 for each copy rather than all copies of page 1, then all copies of page 2, etc.)
- Print to a file so someone without Word 2000 can print the document

Set the print options the way you want them and click Print to send the document to the printer.

You can also print 2, 4, 6, 8, or 16 pages to a sheet. In the Zoom section of the Print dialog box, select the number of pages from the Pages per Sheet drop-down list, and select the paper size from the Scale to Paper Size drop-down list.

Creating and Printing Envelopes and Labels

Objective W2000.3.14

One of the time-saving features of Office 2000 is its ability to maintain address books that are shared among the applications. (See *Mastering Microsoft Outlook 2000*—also from Sybex—for information about Outlook address books.) Combine that with Word's Envelopes and Labels feature, and it has never been easier to prepare documents for mailing. Even if you're not using an address book, Word makes it a snap to produce envelopes and mailing labels.

Creating and Printing an Envelope

1. If you are writing a letter, enter the name and address you want on the envelope as the inside address in the letter.
2. Choose Tools ➢ Envelopes and Labels and choose the Envelopes tab, shown in Figure 2.19.
3. The Name and Address you entered should appear in the Delivery Address box. If it does not, close the dialog box, copy the name and address, reopen the dialog box, and use Ctrl+V or Shift+Ins to paste it.
4. Choose to enter or omit a return address.
5. Click the Options button to open the Envelope Options dialog box.
6. Click the Envelopes Options tab to set envelope options such as envelope size, delivery point bar code, and fonts.
7. Click the Printing Options tab to set printing options such as feed method and the printer tray that contains the envelope, and click OK.
8. Click the Print button to send the envelope to the printer.

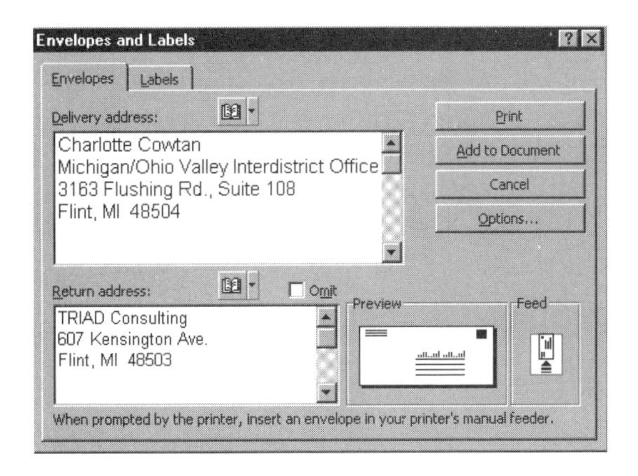

FIGURE 2.19
Envelopes page of the Envelopes and Labels dialog box

If you want your return address to appear as the default in the Envelopes and Labels dialog box, choose Tools ➢ Options ➢ User Information and enter your mailing address.

The Labels feature gives you the option to print one label or a full page of the same label. (See Chapter 4 for information about creating individualized labels for different people.) Click the Labels tab of the Envelopes and Labels dialog box (choose Tools ➢ Envelopes and Labels to get you there).

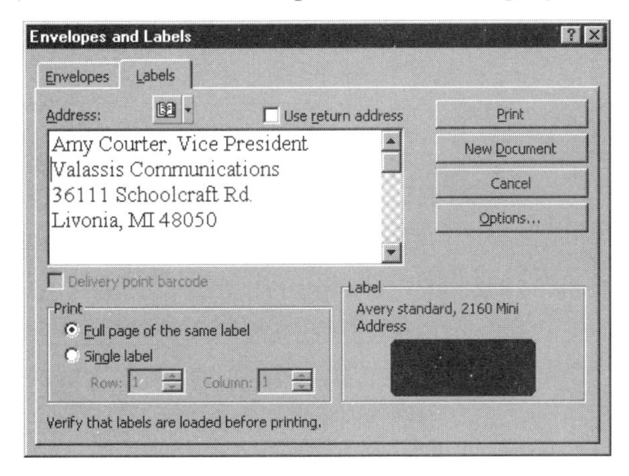

Choose whether you would like a full page of the same label or a single label. You can even specify which row and column to print on so you can use up those partial sheets of labels left over from other printing jobs. If you want to print a full page of return address labels, click the Use Return Address check box.

The default label is Avery standard, 2160 Mini Address. If this is not the kind of label you use, click the Options buttons to select a different label.

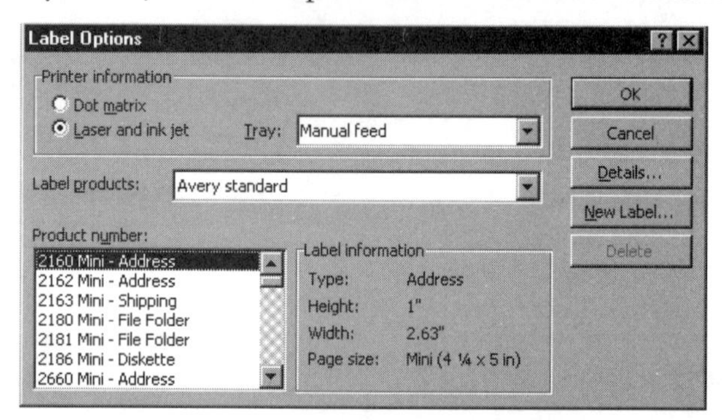

Choose the product and product number you want to use from the list provided. Click the Details button to see the actual measurements and layout of the labels you have selected or the New Label button to design custom labels. Click OK to close either page and OK again to return to the Envelopes and Labels dialog box.

You can now print the labels. If you are creating return address labels or labels that you want to save, click the New Document button to paste the labels into a new document. Save the document before sending the labels to the printer. In the future, to print more of the same labels, you can open the label document and print it without having to recreate the labels.

Creating and Printing Labels

1. Choose Tools ➢ Envelopes and Labels ➢ Labels.
2. Enter any changes to the Address box. Click Use Return Address if you want to create return address labels.
3. Check if you want to print a Full Page of the Same Label or a Single Label.
4. Click the Options button to select a different label product or to change the printer information.

Creating and Printing Labels *(continued)*

5. Click the Details or New Label buttons to adjust the dimensions of the labels selected.
6. Close the New Label or Details pages and the Labels Options pages by clicking OK or Cancel.
7. Click the Print button to send the labels to the printer or the New Document button to create a label document that can be saved for re-use.

Hands On: *Objectives W2000.1.6, 1.12, 3.1, 3.2, 3.6, 3.7, 3.11, 3.14, and 3.16*

1. Open an existing Word document and change the margins to 1 inch each for the top, bottom, left and right.
   - a) Insert a hard page break at the end of the document and type a short sentence on your new page. Apply a portrait orientation to the new page.
   - b) Insert another hard page break at the beginning of the document. Create a title page for this document with your name and today's date (inserted as a field).
   - c) Vertically align the text on the title page only.
   - d) View your document in Print Preview, two pages at a time. Close the preview.
   - e) Navigate to Page 1 of your document (the Title page) and print just that page.
   - f) Print the rest of the document (without the title page).
   - g) Close this document without saving your changes.
2. Create and print an envelope that includes your return address.
3. Create a full page of return labels for yourself. Create and save a new document containing the labels.
4. Type a letter and create an envelope for it that you add to your document. Preview it in Print Preview before printing it.

5. Type the following text in a new Word document. (You may have saved this text from an earlier exercise. If so, open it.) Then use Find and Replace to change all occurrences of "car" to "automobile."

```
Every year, several employees are given special bonuses at
holiday time. Employees who have done exceptional jobs are
given cars to drive for the next year. The new cars are
rented by the company. The current year's cars have to be
returned and are sold to other employees at a discounted
rate. The holiday program corresponds to the annual awards
banquet, where many employees are given awards for their
performance.
```

CHAPTER 3

Applying Advanced Formatting Techniques

When you're comfortable with the basics, you'll soon find yourself looking for ways to enhance the appearance of text. Word features such as tables, columns, outlines, and templates become important as you move beyond simply typing text that wraps at the margin. In this chapter, you will learn to format pages and set text flow options. You'll be impressed with the styles, templates, and shortcuts available in Word, and you'll learn to use Word's advanced formatting tools to create eye-catching documents.

Formatting Pages

Page numbers, headers, and footers make a lengthy document easier to follow. Word 2000 can help you with everything from automatically numbering the pages to inserting different headers and footers on odd and even pages. You can also adjust hyphenation and other text flow options to make sure your final document looks its best.

Formatting Sections

Objective W2000.3.16

Word 2000 organizes the formatting for documents in sections. A section is a part of a document that has a specified number of columns and that uses a common set of margins, page orientation, headers and footers, and sequence of page numbers. Word automatically inserts section breaks when you:

- Format text as columns (see Working With Columns later in this chapter)
- Change Page Setup options and indicate that you want the changes to apply from This Point Forward

You will want to manually insert a section break to apply different page size or header and footer formatting within a document.

Section breaks can be seen in Normal view by default and in other views by clicking the Show/Hide button on the Standard toolbar to view non-printing characters. Breaks appear as double-dotted lines with the words "Section Break" and the type of break in them.

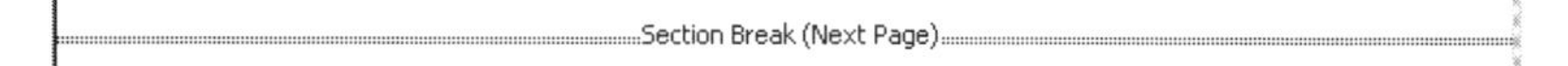

Inserting and Deleting Section Breaks

1. Move the insertion point to where you'd like the break and choose Insert ➢ Break.
2. Choose where you'd like the next section to begin by selecting one of the four section options in the Break dialog box.
3. Switch to Normal view to see the section breaks in your document, or click the Show/Hide button on the Standard toolbar.
4. To delete a section break, select it and press the Delete key.

Creating and Modifying Page Numbers

Objective W2000.3.5 and 3.9

Whether or not you have inserted section breaks, you may want a simple way to automatically number the pages. Nothing could be more effortless than Word's Page Numbering feature. Choose Insert ➢ Page Numbers to open the Page Numbers dialog box, shown in Figure 3.1.

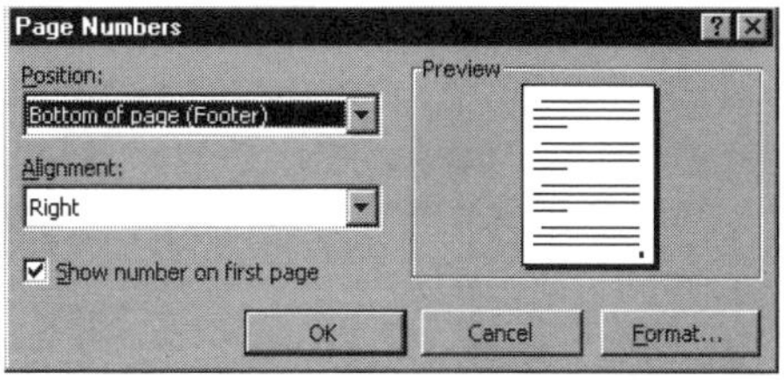

FIGURE 3.1 Page Numbers dialog box

You have four options:

Position—Bottom of Page or Top of Page

Alignment—Left, Center, Right, Inside, or Outside (use Inside or Outside when you have enabled mirror margins in Page Setup)

Show Number on First Page—Toggle on or off

Format—Opens the Page Number Format dialog box:

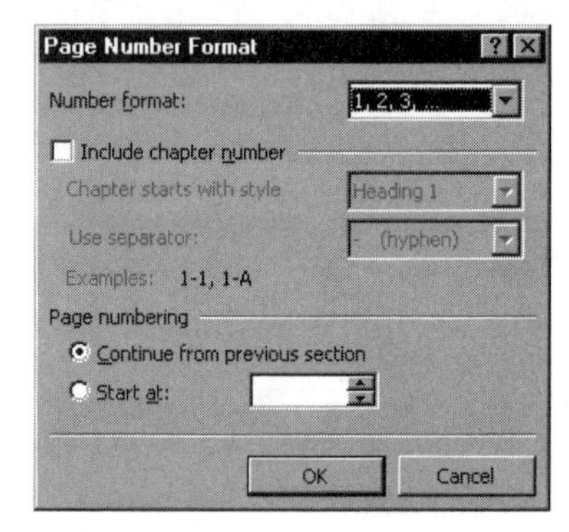

The Page Number Format dialog box allows you to choose a numbering style such as "A, B, C" or "1, 2, 3," and to include a chapter number, if you desire. You could, for example, click the Include Chapter Number check box to show 1–1 as the chapter and page number. If you would like to start your page numbering at a number other than 1, enter a number in the Start At text box. Once you have made your formatting choices, click OK to return to the Page Numbers dialog box and OK again to insert the page numbers. To view the page numbers, switch to Print Layout view or Print Preview.

Setting Up Different Page Numbering

Objective W2000E.2.2

If your document has more than one section, you can set up different page numbering for each section. Position the insertion point on the first page of the document (which is the beginning of the first section) and add page numbering. Then move the insertion point to the first page of the *second* section, and choose Insert ➢ Page Numbers again. Click Format to set up the formatting for this section's numbering. If you want the page numbering to continue from the first section, choose that option in the Page Number Format dialog box. Repeat the process for any additional sections. If you want to remove page numbers, you need to edit the header or footer where the page number appears (see below).

Creating Headers and Footers

Objective W2000.3.10

Page numbers are certainly useful, but you'll probably also want to include other information on each page—All Rights Reserved, your name, or the name of your company, for example. For this type of information, use the Header and Footer feature. Headers and footers are placed in the top and bottom margins. To insert a header or footer, choose View ➢ Header and Footer. The existing document text is immediately dimmed and the Header text box at the top of your document opens. A floating Header and Footer toolbar, like the one shown in Figure 3.2, also opens.

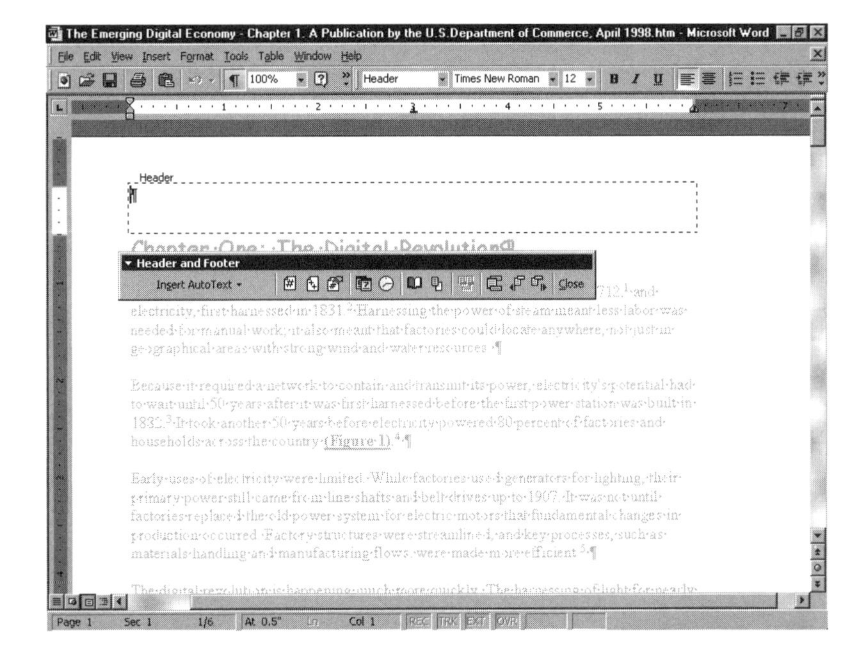

FIGURE 3.2 Header and Footer view

Enter the text you want to appear in the Header text box. Use the toolbar buttons to create and modify the headers and footers. In Table 3.1, each button is defined for you.

TABLE 3.1: Header Footer Toolbar Button

Button	Button Name	Placeholder
 Insert AutoText	Insert AutoText	Provides drop-down list of AutoText entries
	Insert Page Number	Inserts page number placeholder
	Insert Number of Pages	Inserts placeholder for total number of pages
	Format Page Number	Opens Page Number Format dialog box
	Insert Date	Inserts placeholder for date
	Insert Time	Inserts placeholder for time
	Page Setup	Opens Layout page of Page Setup dialog box
	Show/Hide Document Text	Makes document text visible or invisible while working with background
	Same As Previous	Makes header or footer the same as in previous section
	Switch Between Header and Footer	Changes view between header and footer text box
	Show Previous	Moves to previous section's header
	Show Next	Moves to next section's header
 Close	Close Header and Footer	Closes Header and Footer view

Whether you are creating headers, footers, or both, the process is the same. Just move to the header or footer you want to add or edit. Use the Switch between Header and Footer and Show Previous/Show Next buttons to navigate between the headers and footers in each section of your document.

To suppress the header or footer on the first page, choose the Different First Page option from the Layout tab of the Page Setup dialog box and leave the header or footer blank.

Taking Care of Loose Ends

Before you print the final version of a document, you should clean up dangling words, bad line and page breaks, and extra spaces that detract from the appearance of your document. You can clean up these loose ends in three ways:

Hyphenation corrects spaces at the ends of lines where long words wrap to the beginning of the next line.

Non-breaking Spaces keeps text strings together that shouldn't be broken over two lines.

Text Flow Options keeps paragraphs or lines of paragraphs together that currently break across two pages.

Make sure you have done all your editing and formatting before attempting any of this final cleanup. When you add, delete, or reformat text, you have to clean up the document all over again.

Handling Line Breaks

Word includes options for automatically and manually hyphenating your documents. To have Word automatically hyphenate your document, choose Tools ➢ Language ➢ Hyphenation and click the Automatically Hyphenate Document check box.

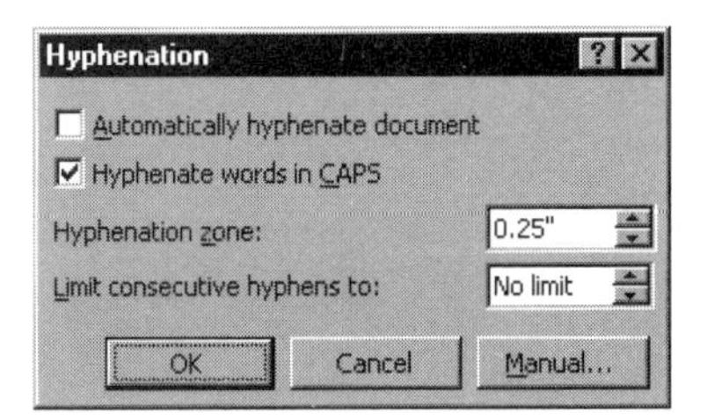

If you want to prevent a word or phrase that contains a hyphen (such as a phone number) from breaking at the end of a line, you can insert a *non-breaking hyphen* by holding down Ctrl+Shift when you enter the hyphen. To enter an *optional hyphen*, a hyphen that breaks a word or a phrase at the designated place if it occurs at the end of a line, hold down Ctrl when you enter the hyphen.

Non-breaking Spaces Occasionally, you might have a text string, such as an address, that should not be separated at the end of a line. You can protect this string by inserting non-breaking spaces instead of regular spaces within the text string. Similar to a non-breaking hyphen, text connected with *non-breaking spaces* will move to the next line rather then breaking between lines. To insert a non-breaking space, hold Ctrl and Shift when you press the spacebar.

Handling Page Breaks

Objective W2000E.1.2

Word 2000 offers a number of other ways to keep text together. One of these options, with the tacky name *Widow/Orphan Control*, is on by default. This feature prevents the first line of a paragraph from being left alone at the bottom of the page (an orphan) or the last line of a paragraph from appearing by itself at the top of a new page (a widow). You can turn off Widow/Orphan Control in the Line and Page Breaks dialog box (choose Format ➢ Paragraph ➢ Line and Page Breaks).

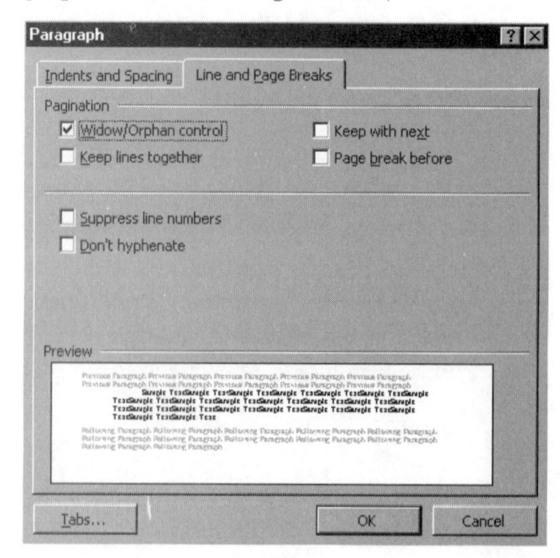

If you want to keep specific lines or paragraphs of text together, first select the text and then open the dialog box.

Adjusting Line and Page Breaks

1. Choose Format ➢ Paragraph ➢ Line and Page Breaks to turn text flow options on or off for Widow/Orphan Control, Keep Lines Together, Keep with Next, and Page Break Before.
2. Press Ctrl+Shift+hyphen to insert a non-breaking hyphen.
3. Press Ctrl+hyphen to insert an optional hyphen.
4. Press Ctrl+Shift+spacebar to insert a non-breaking space.

Hands On: Objectives W2000.3.5, 3.10, 3.16, E.1.2, and E.2.2

1. Open an existing document, or create a new document that is at least three pages long. Save the document before proceeding.
   a) Add a header that contains the name of the document and the date to all but the first page.
   b) Insert a centered page number. Do not number the first page.
   c) Save the document under a different name and then print it.
2. Manually hyphenate an existing document.
3. Create a footer for the odd pages and a different footer for the even pages of a document.
4. Modify the footers you created in Step 3 by adding the date to them.
5. Select a paragraph that has a page break in the middle of it. Set text flow options so the page does not break in the middle of the paragraph.

Working with Columns

Some kinds of information are most effectively presented in tabular or newspaper columns. Tabular parallel columns, discussed later in this chapter, display corresponding text in columns (like a phone book). With *newspaper columns*, text flows from the bottom of one column to the top of the next. If you create newsletters, flyers, reports, announcements, or other types of publications, you'll probably use Word's newspaper columns feature quite a bit.

Working with Newspaper Columns

Working with columns requires a little advance-design work. You'll find it is often easier to enter document text into a single column and then convert the text into multiple columns. Because of the space between the columns, one page of text takes up more than a page when poured into two or more columns. As a result, you may have to go back and edit text to get it to fit on a prescribed number of pages. However, by first focusing on your writing and then switching your attention to the design issues, you'll very likely end up with a higher quality product in the long run.

Entering and Editing Text in Columns

Objectives W2000.3.12 and E.2.7

To work with columns, switch to Print Layout view so you can actually see the columns as they will appear on the page. Although you can format columns in Normal view, you won't be able to see the results.

Creating Columns

1. To create columns from exisiting text, switch to Print Layout view. Select the text you want to change to columns.
2. Click the Columns button on the Standard toolbar and drag to select the number of columns you want.

OR

1. To set up columns and then enter text, switch to Print Layout view.
2. Click the Columns button on the Standard toolbar and drag to select the number of columns you want.
3. Enter text into the column. To make equal columns, like those in Figure 3.3, move the insertion point to the end of the text and insert a continuous section break Insert ➢ Break ➢ Continuous.
4. To enter a title that spans the columns, enter the title at the beginning of the first column. Select the title, click the Columns button, and select one column.

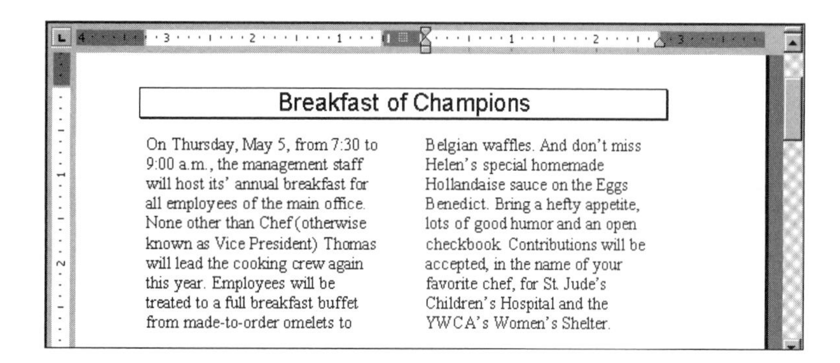

FIGURE 3.3
Text in columns

Revising Column Structure

Objective W2000.3.13

Word provides you with several options for changing the number of columns in your document, the column width, and the white space in the gutter between columns.

If you decide you want to change the number of columns in your document, move the insertion point into the columns section, click the Columns button, and drag to select the new number of columns. To revert to a single column, choose one column or switch to normal view and delete the section breaks.

When you create columns with the Columns button, Word makes all the columns the same width. If you want columns of differing widths, drag the Move Columns marker on the horizontal ruler.

To change the white space in the gutter between the columns, drag the Left and Right Margin markers on the inside of the columns.

Using the Columns Dialog Box

To establish columns of a specific width or to lock columns so they will remain equally wide, use the Columns dialog box (Format ➢ Columns), shown in Figure 3.4. Choose One, Two, or Three from the Preset options; the Equal Column Width check box will be selected automatically. Choose Left or Right from the Presets if you want two columns of unequal size. You can create up to 10 columns using the Number of Columns spin box. Enter the column width and the spacing between columns if you would like settings different from the defaults. Click the Line Between check box to have Word insert vertical lines between each of the columns.

FIGURE 3.4

Columns dialog box

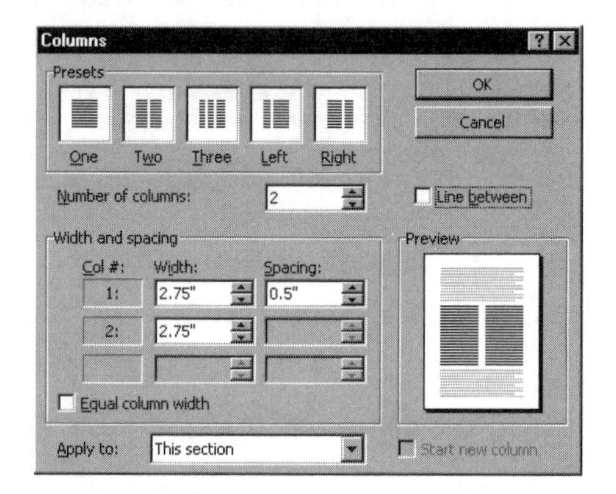

Keeping Text Together in Columns

All the tools you use to keep page text together, including non-breaking spaces, non-breaking hyphens, and Lines and Spacing options, work with columns. Word's Columns dialog box provides you with one other option for controlling where text breaks between columns. Move the insertion point to the beginning of the text you want to reposition in the next column and choose Format ➢ Columns to open the Columns dialog box. Change the Apply To control to This Point Forward and enable the Start New Column check box to insert an End of Section marker and move the text to the next column.

Restructuring Columns

1. To add or delete columns, click anywhere in the columns section of your document and click the Columns button. Drag to select the desired number of columns.
2. Drag the Move Columns marker on the ruler to change column width and to move columns left or right.
3. Drag the Left or Right Margin markers on the ruler to change the white space between columns.

Restructuring Columns *(continued)*

4. Open the Columns dialog box (choose Format ➢ Columns), shown in Figure 3.4, to create as many as 10 columns, to lock columns so they are of equal width, to insert a line between columns, or to enter exact measurements for column widths and spacing.

5. To move text into the next column, move the insertion point in front of the text you want to move. Open the Columns dialog box and choose This Point Forward in the Apply To control. Click the Start New Column check box to move the text to the next column.

Hands On: Objectives W2000.3.12, 3.13, and E.2.7

1. Open an existing document, or create a new document that contains several paragraphs of text.

   a) Create a new document and format it for two columns. Enter two paragraphs of text. Balance the column length by inserting a continuous section break.

   b) Use the ruler to change the column widths, making the first column wider than the second.

   c) Add a line between the columns.

   d) Add a title that spans both columns. Save the document as *Working with Columns*.

   e) Move the last sentence that begins in the first column to the second column by using Keeping Text Together options.

2. In the same document:

   a) Change *Working with Columns*, or another document with columns, back to a single column. (You may have to delete additional section breaks—switch to Normal view to see them.)

   b) Use the Presets in the Columns dialog box to change the text to three columns of equal width.

   c) Add another paragraph of text to the end of the section.

Constructing High-Quality Tables

Although you can use tabs to present information in parallel columns, it is far easier to use Word's powerful Tables features. With tables, every block of text can be easily formatted, edited, deleted, and moved around without affecting the remainder of the text. Tables are one of the most versatile tools in the Word 2000 toolkit.

Creating and Revising Tables

Objective W2000.5.1

You create tables in Word 2000 in three ways: using the Insert Table button, using the Insert Table dialog box, and using the Draw Table button.

To use the Insert Table button, click the button and drag the number of columns and rows you want in your table.

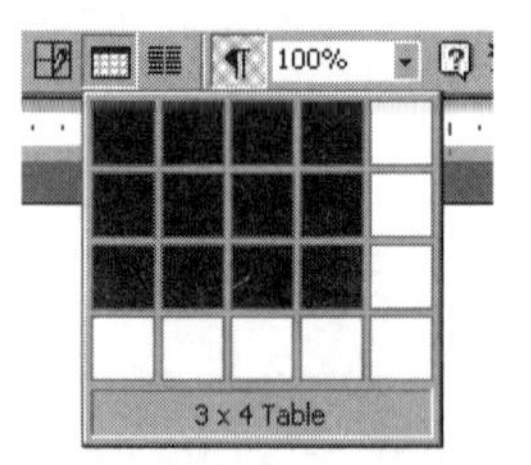

When you release the mouse button, a blank table appears in your document.

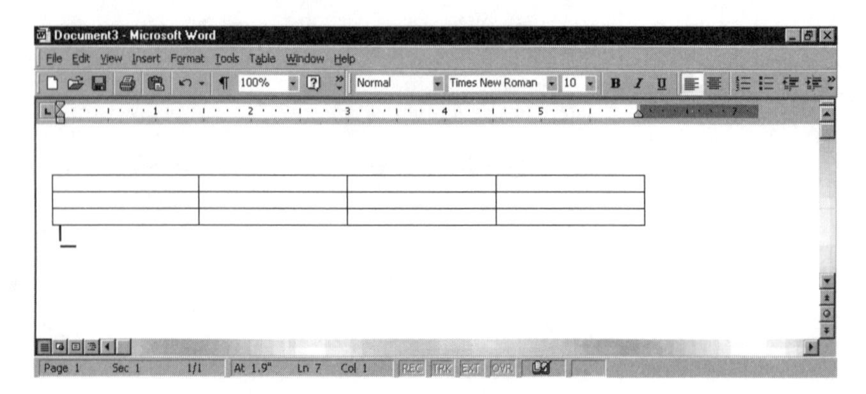

To create a table using the Insert Table dialog box, choose Table ➢ Insert ➢ Table. Enter the number of rows, columns, and column widths in the appropriate controls. When you create a table, it's easiest if you determine the number of columns you're going to need before you start. You can always add columns later, but it may mean changing the widths of the other columns to accommodate them. Adding rows, on the other hand, is as simple as pressing Tab at the end of a row. To create a table that is as wide as your page, leave the Fixed Column Width setting on Auto. When you've entered all the settings, click OK to create the table.

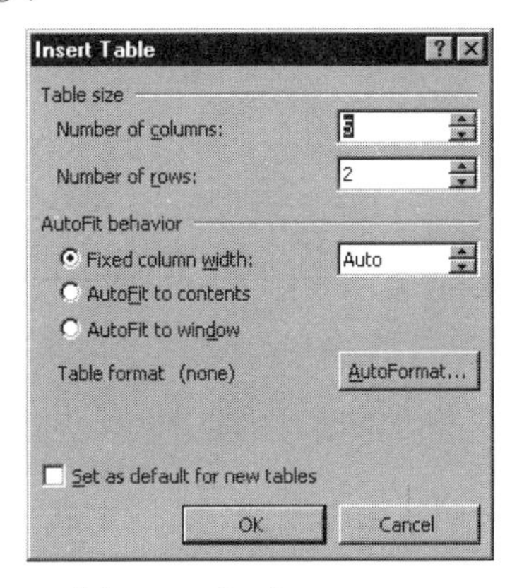

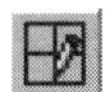

You can also draw a table exactly the way you want it to appear. Clicking the Tables and Borders button on the Standard toolbar opens the Tables and Borders toolbar; the mouse pointer will change to a pencil. Drag the pencil to create a rectangle about the size of the table you want.

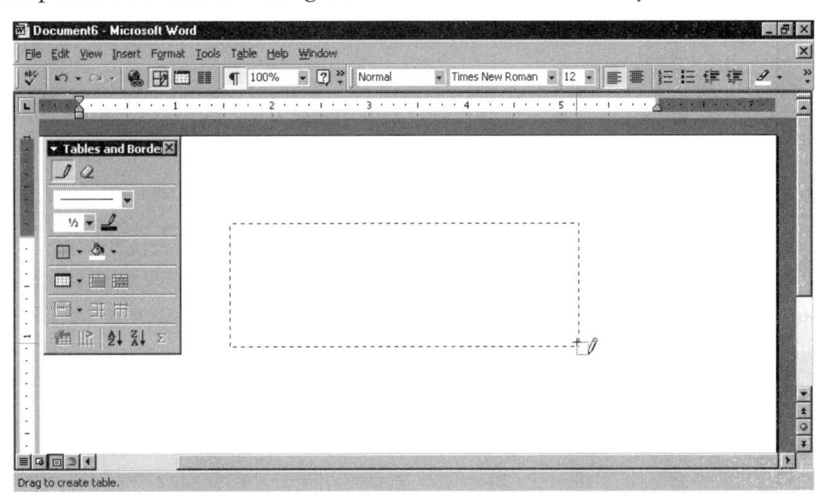

When you release the mouse button, the outside border of the table appears in your document. Use the pencil again to draw in column and row borders.

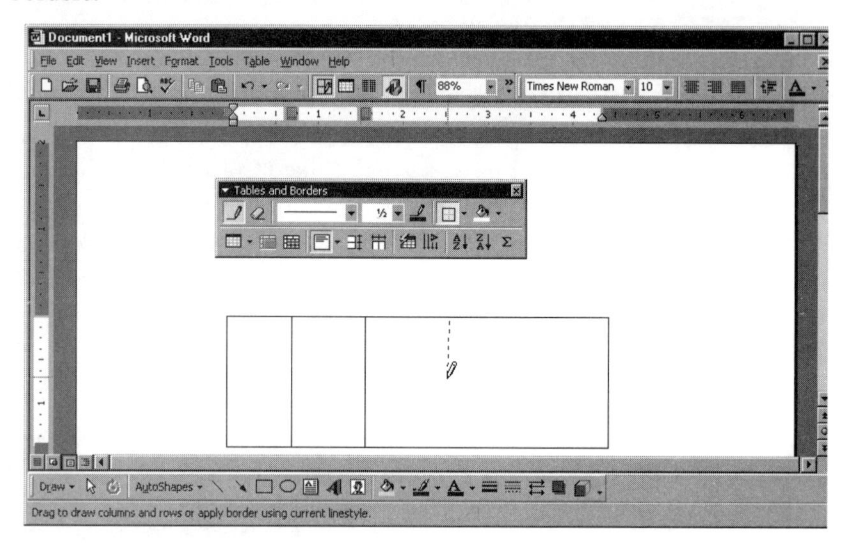

Entering and Editing Text

Once you have created a table, you enter text by clicking in any *cell* (the intersection of a column and row). Use the Tab key or the Right Arrow key on the keyboard to move to the next cell to the right. Shift+Tab or the Left Arrow key will move one cell to the left. The Up and Down arrow keys will move the insertion point to the cell below or above the current cell.

If you created your table by drawing it, click the Draw Table button on the Tables and Borders toolbar or close the toolbar to change the pointer back from a pencil to that old familiar I-beam so you can begin typing.

Table 3.2 shows how to select portions of a table.

TABLE 3.2: Selecting in Tables

To Select	Action
A cell	Triple-click in cell, or click the right-pointed, solid-black arrow inside a cell.
A row	Move mouse to left margin, point to the row, and click.

TABLE 3.2: Selecting in Tables *(continued)*

To Select	Action
Multiple rows	Select first row, hold down mouse button, and drag down the desired number of rows.
A column	Move the mouse above a column. It will change to a downward pointed arrow. Click. *OR* Hold down Alt key and click column.
Multiple columns	Select first column, hold down mouse button, and drag the desired number of columns. *OR* For contiguous columns, select first column (any method), and then hold down Shift and select last column (any method).
Entire table	Choose Table ➢ Select Table. *OR* Hold down Alt key and double-click. *OR* Click the Move icon (the 4-headed arrow) that appears to the upper right of a table when you click anywhere inside it.

Formatting Text in Tables

Each table cell can be formatted separately. Whatever you can do to a paragraph, you can do to the text within a cell. Use the Standard toolbar or the Format menu to apply fonts, font effects, alignment, bullets and numbering, and indents and spacing to the text in a table.

The Tables and Borders toolbar also provides some additional formatting options unique to tables.

The default alignment is top left of the cell. Click the drop-down arrow next to the alignment button on the Tables and Borders toolbar to see other choices. Click one of the nine alignment options to place text exactly where you want it in a cell.

Rotating Text in Tables

Objective W2000.5.5

When you really want to draw attention to your text, rotate it so it is no longer running in the traditional direction across the page. With Word's Text Direction feature, you can rotate text in a table so it runs vertically, facing either right or left. Select the cell or group of cells that contain the text you want to rotate.

Then click the Change Text Direction button on the Tables and Borders toolbar. The button is a toggle button, which means the first click rotates the text so it is facing left, the second click flips it so it faces right, and the third click returns it to the tried-and-true horizontal.

As the text rotates, so do some of the buttons on the Formatting and Tables and Borders toolbars. The alignment buttons, Numbering, Bullets, and Text Direction all change to match the rotation of the text.

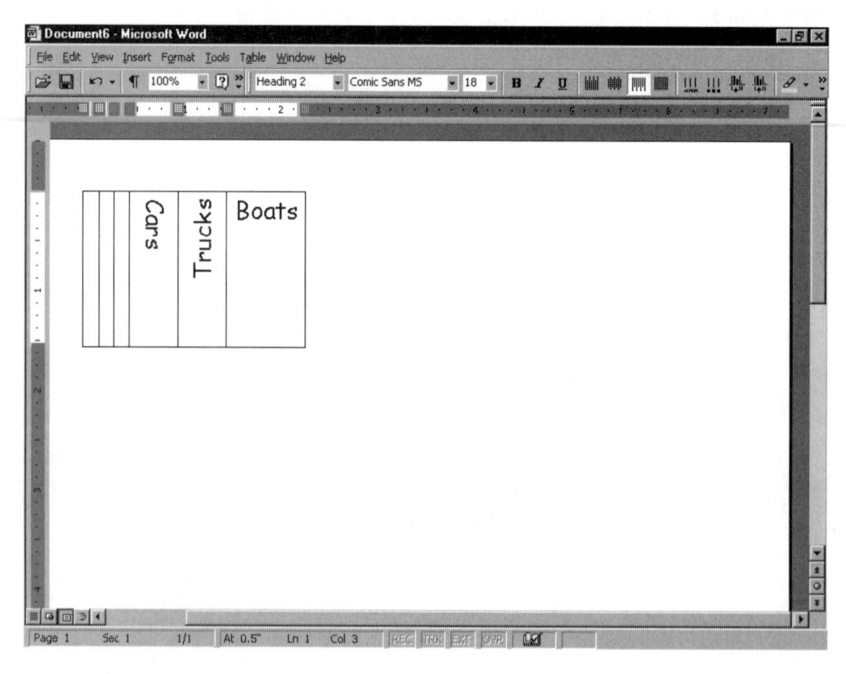

Even the I-beam and the insertion point rotate, so editing can be a little disconcerting at first, but it's technically no different from horizontal editing. The main thing to remember is that you have to drag the mouse vertically to select text. Once you've gotten the hang of that, you're all set.

Entering, Editing, and Positioning Text in Tables

1. Click any cell and begin typing. Use the Tab key to move one cell to the right, Shift+Tab to move to the left, and arrow keys to move up and down or left and right.
2. Apply any character or paragraph formatting options to the text. Each cell is treated as a paragraph.
3. Click one of the alignment buttons on the Tables and Borders toolbar to reposition text within a cell.
4. Click the Change Text Direction button on the Tables and Borders toolbar to rotate text vertically.

Modifying Table Structure

You can easily modify tables. You can add or delete rows and columns, change column and row widths, and merge and split cells without upsetting the rest of the table text.

Adding and Deleting Rows and Columns

Objective W2000.5.3

To add a row at the end of a table, simply move to the last cell in the table and press Tab. If you want to insert rows in the middle of the table, select the number of rows you want to insert and choose Table ➢ Insert ➢ Rows Above or Table ➢ Insert ➢ Rows Below, or right-click and choose Insert Rows from the shortcut menu. Word will insert the rows ahead of the first selected row.

To delete rows, select the rows you want to delete. Choose Table ➢ Delete ➢ Rows, or right-click and choose Delete Rows from the shortcut menu. If you select a cell rather than an entire row, choose Table ➢ Delete ➢ Cells, which opens the Delete Cells dialog box.

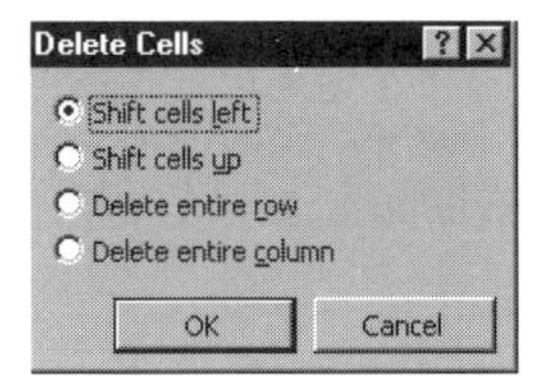

You can choose to delete the current cell and shift the remaining cells left or up. If you want to delete a whole row or column, choose Delete Entire Row or Delete Entire Column.

Inserting columns works the same way as inserting rows. New rows and new columns are the same width as the ones you select to create them, so you may have to adjust the widths of newly inserted columns if they no longer fit the width of the page.

To insert a column at the end of a table, click the last column and then choose Table ➢ Insert ➢ Columns to the Right. To insert a column at the beginning of the table, click the first column, and then choose Table ➢ Insert ➢ Columns to the Left.

Changing Column and Cell Widths

Objective W2000.5.4

The easiest way to adjust a column or a row is to move the insertion point to the border between the row or column. The insertion point will change to a double-headed arrow, allowing you to drag the border in either direction.

1	2	3	4	5
A	B	C	D	E
F	G	H	I	J
K	L	M	O	P
Q	R	S	T	U
V	W	X	Y	Z

If you drag with a cell selected, you're only changing the width for that cell. To be certain, you can, of course, select the entire column or row before dragging.

At times you may want to make all the columns the same width or all rows the same height (for example, when creating a calendar). Select the columns or rows you want to be the same width or height and choose Table ➢ AutoFit ➢ Distribute Columns Evenly or Table ➢ AutoFit ➢ Distribute Rows Evenly, and Word will do the work for you. The Tables and Borders toolbar also has buttons to distribute rows and columns evenly.

You can make another quick adjustment after you enter all the text in your table. Select the columns you want to adjust and choose Table ➢ AutoFit ➢ AutoFit to Contents to automatically adjust the width of the columns to the widest entry.

You can also enter exact height and width measurements for columns and rows. Choose Table ➢ Table Properties to open the Table Properties dialog box. To adjust the width of a column, select the Column tab, as shown in Figure 3.5, and change the measurement in the Preferred Width spin box. Click the Previous Column or Next Column button to adjust the measurement of the previous or next column.

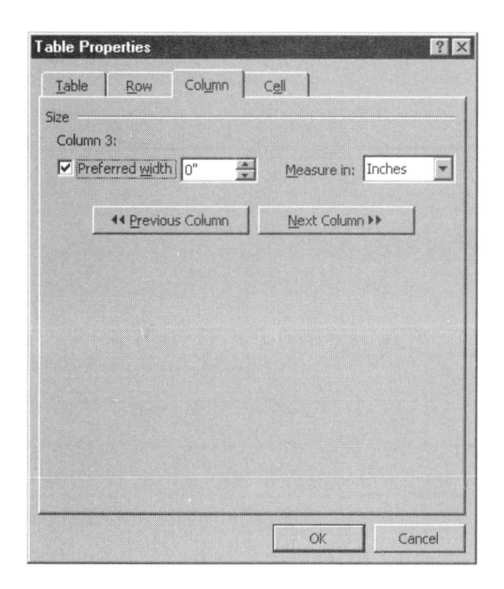

FIGURE 3.5

The Table Properties dialog box, with the Column tab selected

To adjust the height of a row, select the Row tab in the Table Properties dialog box, as shown in Figure 3.6, and change the measurement in the Specify Height spin box.

The Row tab offers some other important options. In the Row Height Is box, select At Least if you want the rows to maintain a minimum height regardless of what is in them. Select Exactly when you want to designate a row height that doesn't change. This is useful when you are creating calendars, for example, and you want the row height to stay the same regardless of the contents.

Click the Previous Row or Next Row button to adjust the height and other characteristics of the previous or next row.

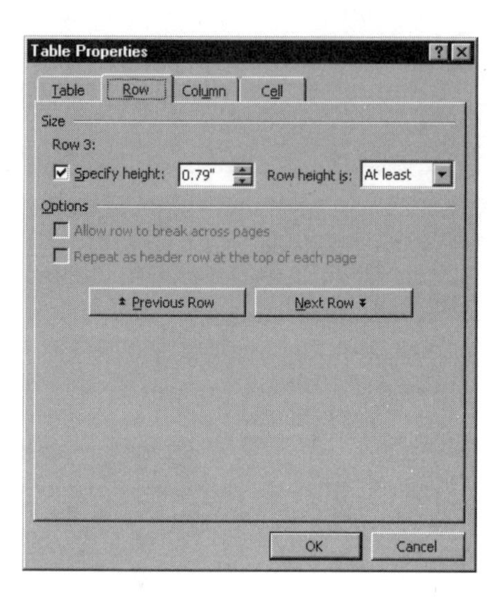

FIGURE 3.6
The Table Properties dialog box, with the Row tab selected

Merging and Splitting Cells

Objective W2000.5.4

It doesn't take much work with tables to discover that you don't want the same number of cells in every row or column. You might want to put a title in a single cell that spans the top of the table. Or you might be creating a form, such as the order form shown in Figure 3.7, and want fewer columns for the totals. When you want to make one cell from two or more cells, you *merge* the cells. *Split* cells to separate a single cell into multiple cells.

FIGURE 3.7
An order form with merged cells

<table>
<tr><th colspan="4">Order Form</th></tr>
<tr><th>Item</th><th>Price</th><th>Quantity</th><th>Total</th></tr>
<tr><td></td><td></td><td></td><td></td></tr>
<tr><td></td><td></td><td></td><td></td></tr>
<tr><td></td><td></td><td></td><td></td></tr>
<tr><td colspan="3" align="right">Subtotal</td><td></td></tr>
<tr><td colspan="3" align="right">Sales Tax</td><td></td></tr>
<tr><td colspan="3" align="right">Total</td><td></td></tr>
</table>

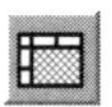

To merge cells, simply select the cells you want to merge and Choose Tables ➢ Merge Cells, or click the Merge Cells button on the Tables and Borders toolbar.

If you prefer the visual approach, you can use the Eraser on the Tables and Borders toolbar to erase the border between cells you want to merge. Drag the Eraser horizontally to merge rows or vertically to merge columns.

Use the Draw Table pencil from the Tables and Borders toolbar to split cells, or choose Table ➢ Split Cells or click the Split Cells button to open the Split Cells dialog box.

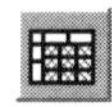

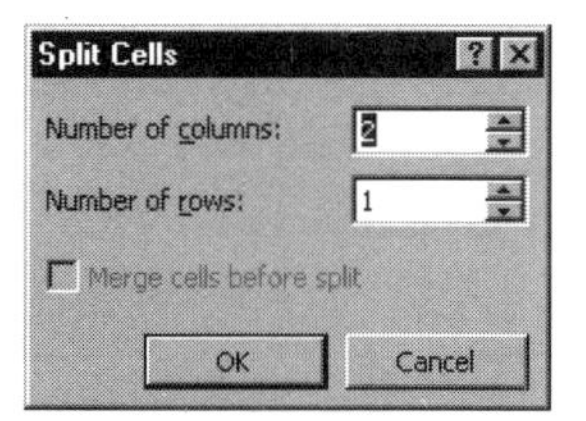

Use the dialog box's spin box controls to enter the number of columns and rows you would like to divide the selected cell(s) into. Enable the Merge Cells Before Split check box if you want to apply the new rows and columns settings to several selected cells. This is one way to quickly reconfigure your table. For example, if you selected a 3×3 table, you could convert it to a 4×3 table by entering 4 columns, 3 rows in the split cells dialog box and enabling the Merge Cells Before Split feature. You can wind up with a real mess if you've already entered text in your table, so be careful. It's best to reserve this feature for empty tables that need reconfiguring.

Modifying Table Structure

1. Insert rows at the end of a table by clicking in the last cell and pressing Tab. Insert rows in the middle of the table by selecting the number of rows you want to insert and choosing Table ➢ Insert ➢ Rows Above or Table ➢ Insert ➢ Rows Below.
2. Delete rows by selecting the rows you want to delete and choosing Table ➢ Delete ➢ Rows.
3. Insert columns by selecting the number of columns you want to insert and selecting Table ➢ Insert ➢ Columns to the Left or Table ➢ Insert ➢ Columns to the Right.

Modifying Table Structure *(continued)*

4. Change the width of columns by pointing to the cell border and dragging the border with the column-adjustment pointer.
5. Merge cells by selecting the cells you want to merge and choosing Table ➢ Merge Cells or by clicking the Merge Cells button.
6. Split cells by dragging the Draw Table button in the cell you want to split. You can also select a cell and click the Split Cells button on the Tables and Borders toolbar if you want to enter the number of rows and columns in the Split Cells dialog box.

Formatting Tables

Before you print your table, you might want to put some finishing touches on it to give it that polished, professional look. Word 2000 offers both automatic and manual table formatting options to add and remove borders, change border types, and add colors and shading.

Using AutoFormat

AutoFormat provides you with a number of formats you can apply in one easy step. Click anywhere in your table and choose Table ➢ Table AutoFormat to open the Table AutoFormat dialog box shown in Figure 3.8.

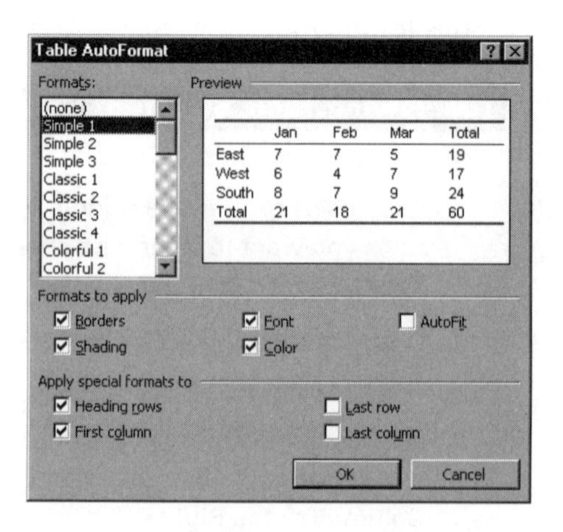

FIGURE 3.8
AutoFormat dialog box

AutoFormat applies borders, shading, fonts, and colors. Most of the formats include special formatting for the header row, last row, and first and last columns since these often contain titles or summary information. Turn checkmarks on or off to indicate which formatting options you want to apply. Choosing any of the formats will give you a preview of the format. Click OK when you want to apply the selected format to your table. If you're not satisfied, click Undo, or choose Table AutoFormat again and select a different format. To unapply an AutoFormat, open the Table AutoFormat dialog box and choose None from the scroll list.

Adding Your Own Borders and Shading

Objective W2000.5.2

You don't have to settle for the pre-designed AutoFormats. You can adjust AutoFormats manually or start from scratch, whichever you prefer. Either way, you'll want to turn on the Tables and Borders toolbar before you begin formatting.

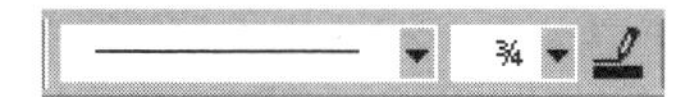

The Line Style, Line Weight, and Border Color buttons all relate to the cell borders. Click the drop-down arrow next to Line Style or Line Weight to select from the list of choices available. Clicking the Border Color button opens a color menu. Select a color and use the pencil pointer to draw over borders you want to color. Make sure you draw over the entire length of the border, or the color will not be applied. All three buttons are dynamic, which means your most recent choice appears on the button to make it easy to reapply.

To apply a border, select the cells you want to apply a border to, select the Line Style, Line Weight, and Border Color you want to apply, and click the Borders button to open a drop-down menu.

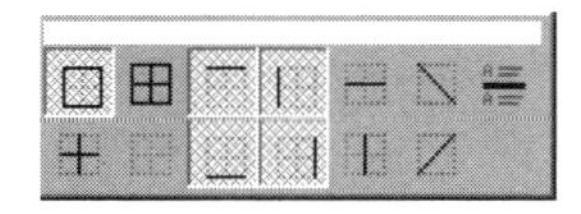

Click the type of border you want to apply.

Click the Shading Color button down arrow to open a menu of shading colors, including various shades of gray. If you are applying a lot of different borders and shading to your table, you can pull the menus off the toolbar so they float on the surface of your document.

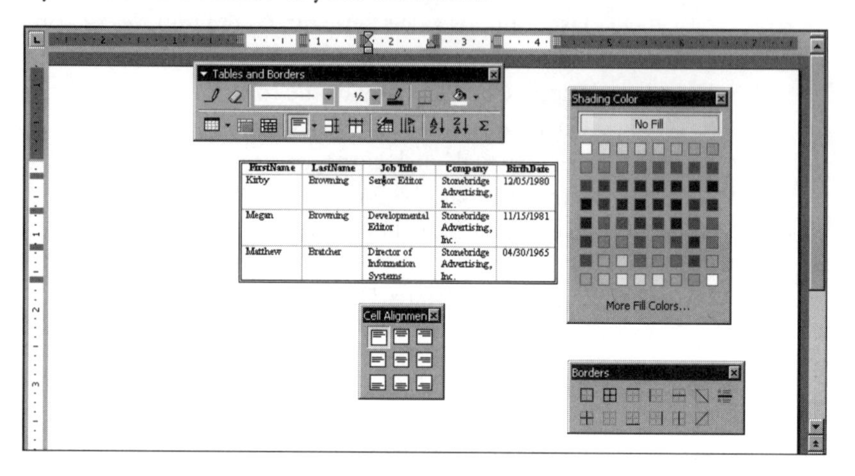

You can then apply as many borders or shades as you want without having to open the menus each time. To float the menus, click the drop-down arrow to open the menu. Point to the gray bar at the top of the menu; the bar will turn the same color as your Windows title bars. Drag the menu into the document. When you're finished with the menu, just click its Close button.

Objectives W2000.2.4, E.1.1, and E.2.1

Borders and Shading are not limited to use in tables. You can apply to any paragraph of text the same skills you just learned. Just select one or more paragraphs and click the Tables and Borders button, or choose Format ➢ Borders and Shading.

To apply a border to the entire page or a section of a document, click the Page Borders tab. Choose the type of border you want to apply and click the Apply To down arrow to specify the whole document or section. Click the Art button to add fancy graphic borders to the page.

If you're having trouble getting a page border to print correctly, click the Options button on the Page Borders tab of the Borders and Shading dialog box and adjust the margins accordingly.

Centering Tables Horizontally

If you've adjusted the column widths in your table, it may no longer extend across the entire width of the page. In Word 2000, you can center the table between the left and right margins by selecting the entire table and clicking the Center button on the Formatting toolbar.

Performing Calculations in a Word Table

Objective W2000E.3.2

There will almost certainly be times when you want to add, multiply, average, or otherwise calculate numbers in a table. Word 2000 provides the tools necessary to "do the math!" Figure 3. 9 shows an example of a table with a simple sum.

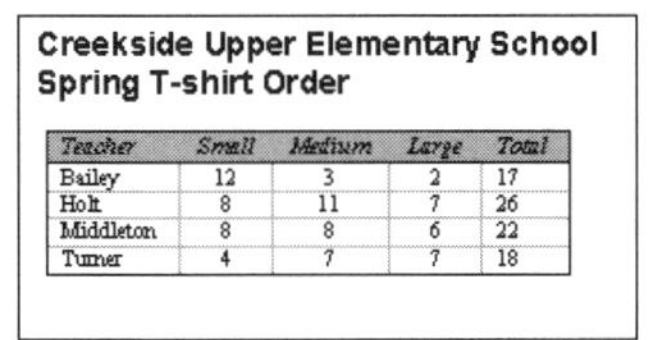

Creekside Upper Elementary School
Spring T-shirt Order

Teacher	*Small*	*Medium*	*Large*	*Total*
Bailey	12	3	2	17
Holt	8	11	7	26
Middleton	8	8	6	22
Turner	4	7	7	18

FIGURE 3.9
Table with a Sum

Including Calculations in a Word Table

1. Position the insertion point in the cell where you want the result to appear.
2. Click Table ➢ Formula.
3. Modify the fields in the Formula dialog box to reflect the actual calculation you want to perform. For example, if the Formula field is set to =SUM(ABOVE) and you want to sum the numbers to the left (as we did in Figure 3.9), simply select "ABOVE" and overtype it with "LEFT."
4. If you want a function other than SUM, use the Paste Function drop-down list to choose another, such as AVERAGE, COUNT or IF.
5. Enter a format for the numbers in the Number Format box. For example, to display two non-significant zeros behind the decimal point (i.e., 22 displays as 22.00) choose 0.00 from the list.
6. Repeat the procedure for each cell that requires a calculation. If you change the numbers included in the formula, select the calculated field and press F9 to update it.

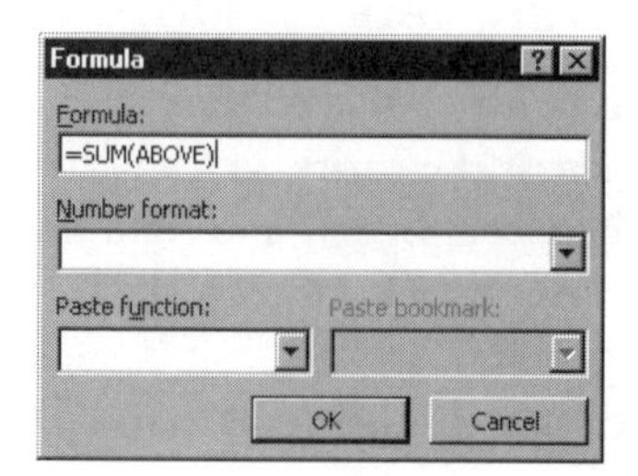

Although it is possible to include calculations in Word tables, the Word Help file on formulas suggests that if you know how to use Excel, embedding all or part of a worksheet is often easier than using formulas in a Word table. We certainly agree. To learn more about embedding an Excel worksheet, see Chapter 5.

Hands On: *Objectives W2000.5.1, 5.2, 5.3, 5.4, and 5.51*

1. Open a new document:

   a) Change the Page Orientation to Landscape. Using the Draw Table feature, insert a seven-column, six-row table to create a calendar for the current month.

   b) Select the columns and click Distribute Columns Evenly. Enter the names of the days of the week in the first row of the table. Center the day names horizontally and vertically. Change the font and font size as appropriate.

   c) Insert a new row at the top of the table. Merge the cells in the row and enter the current month and year using a large font size. Center the text vertically and horizontally. Shade the row.

   d) Enter and right-align dates for the month in the appropriate cells of the table.

   e) Drag the last row so it is just above the bottom margin. Select the date rows and choose Distribute Rows Evenly to make them all the same size.

f) Change the outside border to a thicker, more decorative border. Change the bottom border under the title to a different border type.

g) Identify two important dates in the month and shade them.

h) Insert a document title and an introductory paragraph of text *above* the table. (Press Ctrl+Home to move to the top of the document and press Enter to create blank lines above the table.) Insert a border around the title and apply shading to it.

i) Experiment with rotating text in your table.

2. Duplicate the table shown in Figure 3.9, including its formulas. Or create a table that shows information related to a project you are working on. Use Borders and Shading to make the table attractive and at least one formula to perform a calculation.

Working Smarter with Word

One of the things computers are supposed to prevent is repeating the same tasks over and over again, and Word 2000 does its share of prevention. Learning to use styles and templates may take a bit of practice, but once they become part of your routine, you'll wonder how you lived without them.

You've Got Style

Word's Styles feature lets you save existing formats and apply them to other text. Styles can include fonts, sizes, font attributes, alignment, character spacing, paragraph spacing, bullets and numbering, borders, indenting, and just about any other formatting you can think of. Once you've created a style, all you have to do to apply the style is select it from a list. But the major benefit of styles is that if you change a style, all the text using that style is automatically changed, too—much easier than adjusting the font size on 25 subheadings.

Getting to Know Styles

Objective W2000.3.15

When you open a new Word document, at the beginning of the Formatting toolbar you'll find a list of default styles available for your use.

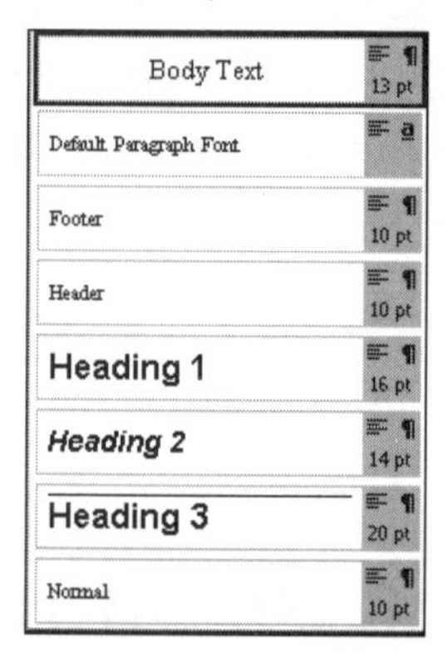

To use any of the default styles, click the drop-down arrow next to Normal and select the style you want to apply. You can apply a style before entering text, or you can apply it to selected text. You'll notice the items on the list are formatted to show the style.

Applying Styles

1. Click the Styles drop-down arrow on the Personal toolbar and choose a style from the list.
2. To apply a style to existing text, select the text, and then choose the style.

To automatically apply heading styles 1 through 9 as you are creating a document, choose Tools ➢ AutoCorrect to open the AutoCorrect dialog box. Click the AutoFormat As You Type tab, and in the Apply As You Type section, click the Headings check box. To automatically apply heading styles 1 through 9 when AutoFormatting a document, click the AutoFormat tab in the AutoCorrect dialog box, and in the Apply section, click the Headings check box.

A Style All Your Own

Objective W2000E.2.4

Once you start working with styles, it won't be long before you're dissatisfied with the basic selection and want to create your own styles. Not a problem. Simply format a paragraph the way you would like the style to appear and click in the Style text box. Type the name of your style and press Enter. The newly created style in Figure 3.10 is 26-pt. bold, italic, Comic Sans MS, centered, with a shadow border.

FIGURE 3.10

A newly created style

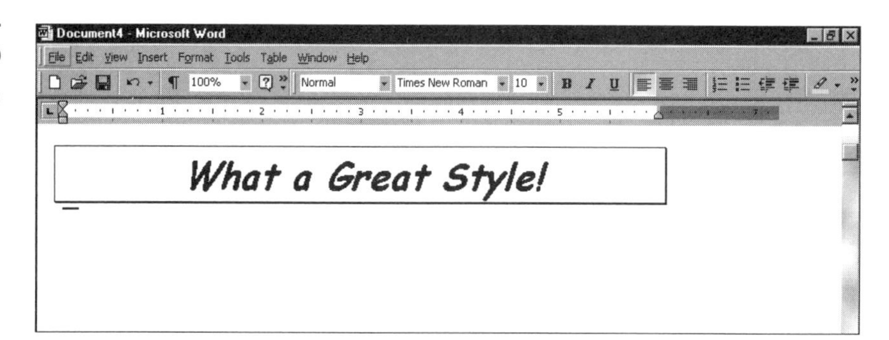

Now when you look at the drop-down list, the new style appears on the list and illustrates what it looks like.

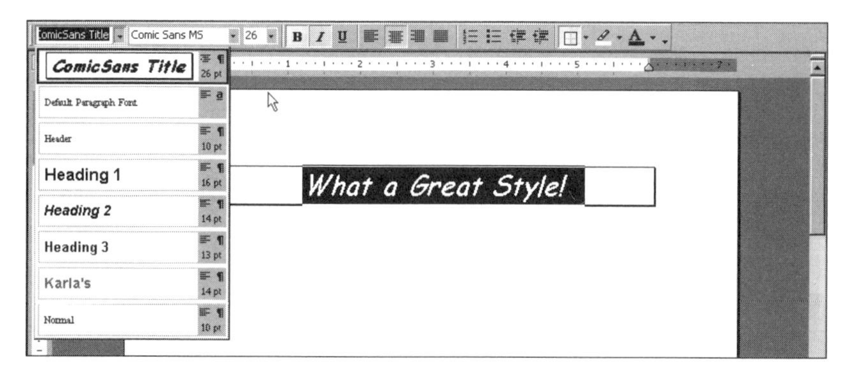

To apply the style to other text, select the text and select the style from the list.

Redefining Styles

After you've created and applied a style, you may decide that you don't like the font or you need some extra spacing between paragraphs. It's in situations like this that styles really shine. You can redefine the style, and it will automatically change all the text formatted in that style throughout the entire document. To change a style, select a paragraph that uses the style and make the desired changes. While the paragraph is still selected, click in the Styles text box, and rather than typing in a new name, just press Enter. The Modify Style dialog box appears, which gives you two choices: Do you want to update the style to reflect the changes you made to this selection, or do you want to cancel the changes you made and reapply the prior formatting?

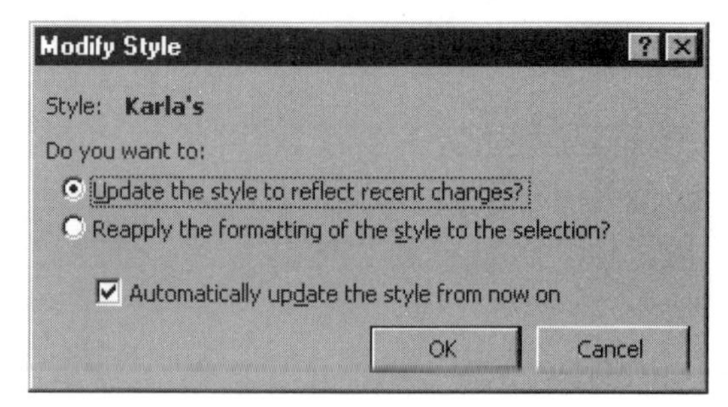

This dialog box also allows you to automatically update the style if you make future changes to text where the style is applied. It's safer to ignore this check box because you're not warned when your formatting changes will affect a style.

Some styles include spacing before or after a paragraph. If you want to change the amount of spacing included in a style, select a sample paragraph, choose Format ➢ Paragraph, and on the Indents and Spacing page, adjust Spacing Before and After. When you've made the changes, redefine the style.

Creating and Redefining Styles

1. Format a paragraph with the options you would like contained in the style.
2. Click in the Style text box and type a name for the new style; press Enter.
3. Select another paragraph and choose the new style from the drop-down list.
4. To redefine a style, select a paragraph and change the formatting. Click in the Style text box and press Enter.
5. Choose Update the Style to Reflect Recent Changes.

If you create a style you would like to have available whenever you create documents, you can assign the style to the Normal template, which opens every time you create a new blank document. Choose Format ➢ Style, select the style from the list, and choose Modify. Click the Add to Template check box. Now every time you create a new blank document, your style will be available.

To delete a style from the Normal template, choose Format ➢ Style, select the style from the list, and choose Organizer to open the Style Organizer. Choose the style or styles in the To NORMAL.DOT list and click the Delete button, then choose Yes; to delete several selected styles without further prompting, click Yes to All. Click Close to close the Style Organizer. Remember, though, that any and all documents based on the style will be reformatted to another style, so you should never delete a style that has been used in existing documents.

You cannot delete any of Word's built-in styles.

Hands On: Objective W2000.3.15 and E.2.4

1. Open an existing document that contains a title and several subheadings. If you'd prefer to create a new document, enter a title at the top of the document, enter a heading, and type a paragraph.

   a) Enter at least two more paragraphs, including headings above each one.

   b) Select the title and apply the Heading 1 style to it.

   c) Select the first heading and apply the Heading 2 style. Use the Format Painter to apply the Heading 2 style to other similar headings (see Chapter 2 for information about the Format Painter).

   d) If you have subheadings, apply the Heading 3 style to them.

   e) Redefine the Heading 2 style, using a different font and other formatting options and update the style to reflect these changes.

   f) Create a new paragraph style for the body text of your document.

   g) Apply the new style to each of the body text paragraphs.

Creating Outlines in Word

You may remember an outline as that horrible thing you had create in school before your teacher would accept an assigned paper. Just trying to figure out which Roman numeral came next could be enough to spoil a good topic. You'll be happy to know that's not the kind of outline we're talking about here. In Word 2000, you can use heading styles (see the previous section) to view the major topics covered in your document—without having to scroll through pages and pages of text. You can collapse and expand heading levels to see more or less of your document at one time, making it a lot easier to ensure you've covered the essential subject matter. You can even print a collapsed outline of your completed document to use as a summary.

Creating an Outline

When you create an outline in Word 2000, you create the document's headings and subheadings in Outline view. After the outline is finished, you enter body text in Normal, Print Layout, or Web Layout view. If you're starting a new document, click the Outline View button on the horizontal scroll bar. The Outlining toolbar appears and the default style is set to Heading 1. To begin the outline, enter your first heading and press Enter. You can choose to enter all your first-level headings and then go back and enter lower level headings, or you can switch back and forth between them. Heading 1 does not actually refer to the first heading but to the first *level* of headings. You can have several level-1 headings in your document. To move down a level to Heading 2, press Tab. There are nine outlining heading levels you can use, as shown in Figure 3.11. If you want to change to a higher heading level, press Shift+Tab.

Promoting and Demoting Headings

When you want to change the level of an existing heading, you *promote* or *demote* it to move it to a higher or lower level. Select the heading as you would select a line. If you'd like to promote or demote a heading and any subheadings underneath it, point to the *outline symbol* (plus, minus, or square) in front of the heading, and click using the four-headed arrow (a plus means a heading has subheadings; a minus means that it does not) to select the entire section.

FIGURE 3.11
Outlining heading levels

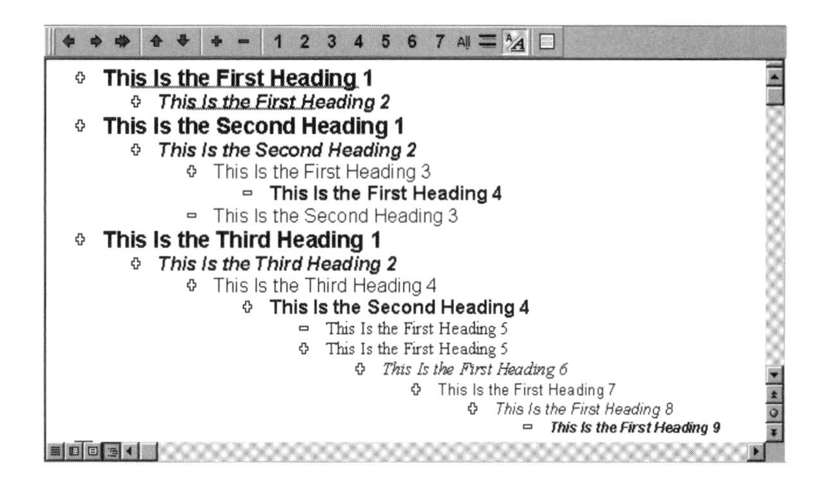

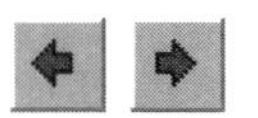

With the text selected, click the Promote or Demote button on the Outlining toolbar.

You can demote headings to body text by clicking the Demote to Body Text button.

Creating an Outline

1. Click the Outline View button to switch to Outline view.
2. Enter a level-1 heading (Heading 1). Press Enter.
3. Press Tab to move to a lower heading level; press Shift+Tab to return to a higher level.
4. Select a single heading by clicking the left margin; select a whole section by clicking the plus or minus sign in front of the section.
5. To promote and demote selected text, click the Promote and Demote buttons.

Viewing and Printing Selected Levels

Once you have entered your outline, you can display at one time as many levels as you would like. Click any of the seven Show Heading buttons on the Outlining toolbar to *collapse* the outline, which, in effect, hides all lower levels. For example, if you click Show Heading 3, headings 4 and above and body text will not be displayed.

When some outline levels aren't displayed, the squiggly line tells you there are hidden levels.

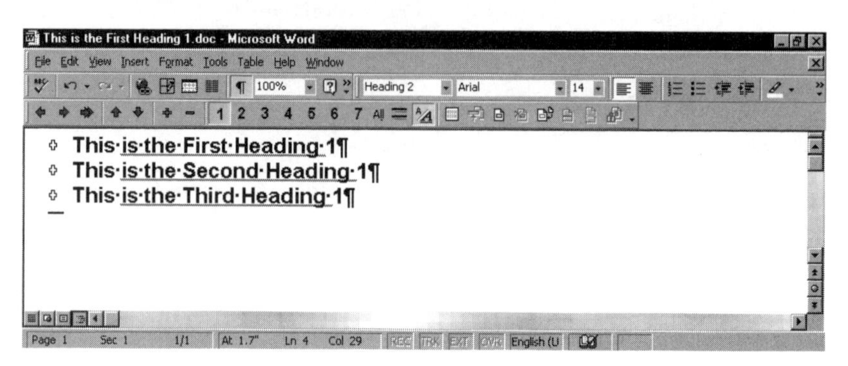

All

Click the All button to *expand* the outline and see all levels again.

If you want to focus on a particular point, you can collapse lower levels and then expand just the one you want to see. Click the Show Heading 1 button to collapse the outline. Move the mouse pointer to the left margin and select the heading you want to expand.

Click the Expand button to expand one level at a time, or double-click the plus sign next to the heading to expand all levels in the section.

Click the Collapse button to collapse one level at a time.

One of the great things about Outline view is that you can print the entire outline or any portion of it. Collapse or expand the outline so it shows just what you want to print, and then click the Print button. Print Preview will still show the entire outline. Don't worry about it. Only the expanded sections and headings will actually print.

Heading styles are directly supported in Outline view. Even if you didn't originally create a document in Outline view, as long as you used heading styles you can use the outlining features.

After you've created your outline, switch to Normal, Web Layout, or Print Layout view and enter body text under each heading, as shown in Figure 3.12. Just click to the right of the heading you want to write about, press Enter, and type the text. If you decide you are not satisfied with the outline, you can switch back to Outline view at any time and rearrange it.

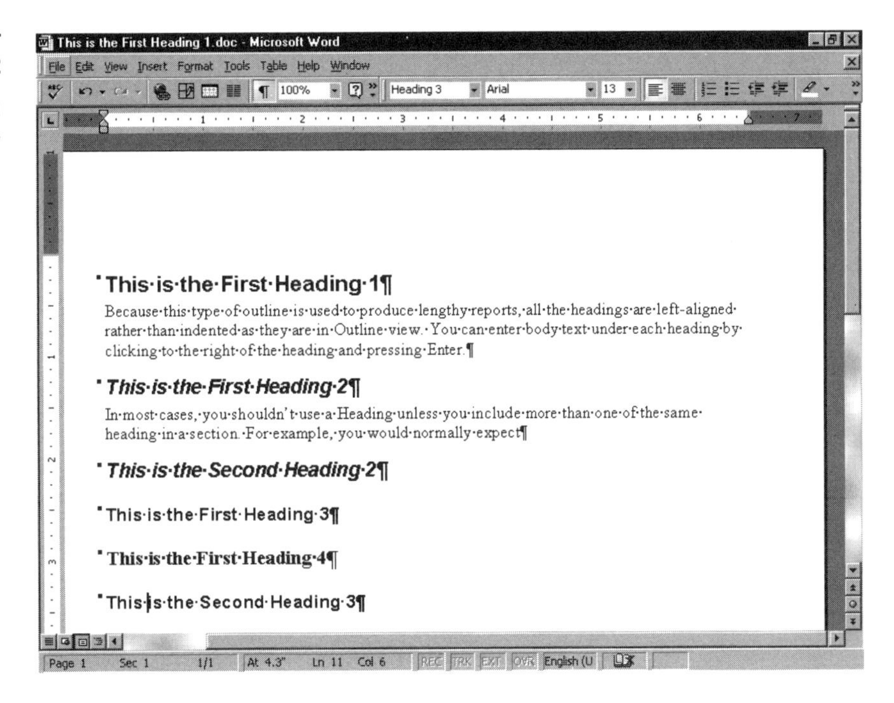

FIGURE 3.12 Entering body text in Print Layout view

Viewing and Printing Selected Portions of an Outline

1. Click any of the Show Heading buttons to hide headings below that level.
2. Click Show All to see the entire document.
3. Double-click the outline symbol to expand or collapse a section.
4. To print an outline, expand or collapse as desired and click Print.

Navigating with the Document Map

You can use the Document Map feature to navigate through a long document with relative ease, no matter what view you are in. Choose View ➢ Document Map in any view to open a frame, like the one shown in Figure 3.13, which contains all the headings. Just click a heading to move to that section.

Unlike Outlining, the Document Map doesn't affect printing, so you can't use it to print parts of the document.

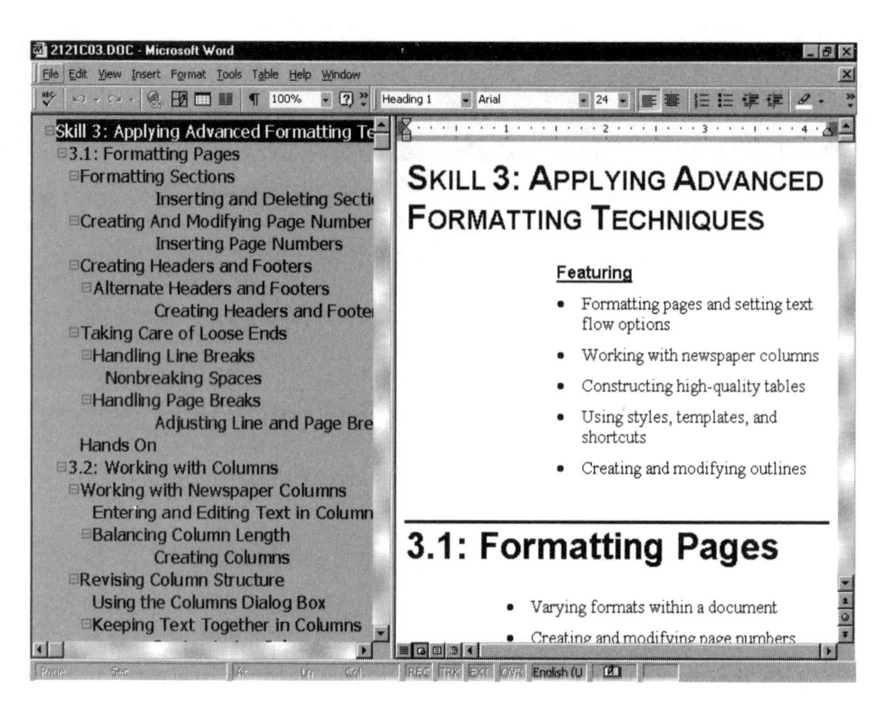

FIGURE 3.13
Navigating with the Document Map

Modifying an Outline

Not only can you collapse and expand an outline, you can select a section of the outline and move it to another location. In Outline view, click the plus sign in front of the section, then drag it toward its new location. A horizontal line will appear. Drag-and-drop the line to move the section.

You can use the Move Up and Move Down buttons on the Outlining toolbar, but make sure you click the button enough times to drop the section into the right spot. It's easy to rearrange your document in ways that you didn't anticipate—another reason that it's always a good idea to save before major rearranging.

Numbering an Outline

Objective W2000.2.7

Numbering headings in an outline is a snap! Just select the Outline and click Format ➢ Bullets and Numbering to open the Bullets and Numbering dialog box. Click the Outline Numbered tab and select one of the choices for Headings or click Customize to create your own.

See Chapter 2 for additional information about customized bulleted and numbered lists.

Modifying an Outline

1. Select the section you want to move by clicking its outline symbol.
2. Drag the section to its new location and drop it when the horizontal line is where you want the text.
3. Apply numbering to your outline by selecting it and clicking Format ➢ Bullets and Numbering. On the Outline Numbered tab, select a style that supports headings or click Customize to create your own.

Hands On: Objective W2000.2.7 (Exercise 9 only)

1. Create an outline on any topic with several heading levels similar to the one shown in Figure 3.11, or open a document that includes heading levels and switch to Outline view.
2. Collapse the outline to show only Heading 1.
3. Double-click an outline symbol to expand the subordinate text.
4. Demote two headings on the outline. Promote them back again or promote two other headings.
5. Expand the entire outline.
6. Switch to Normal view and enter body text under at least two of the headings.
7. Turn on the Document Map and navigate through your document.
8. Switch back to Outline view and move one heading and its subordinate text to another location.
9. Number your outline.

Using Templates

Objective W2000.4.7

Every document is based on a template. A *template* is a collection of document formatting options and content that is available when you create a new document. (The Normal, or standard, template also includes your AutoText entries, macros, toolbars, custom menu settings, and shortcut keys.) To help make your work easier, Word 2000 includes additional templates for preformatted documents and template *Wizards* that walk you through a series of steps to customize a preformatted document.

When you choose File ➢ New from within Word or New Office Document from the Windows Start menu, you are presented with a choice of templates. Figure 3.14 shows the Letters & Faxes page of the New dialog box within Word. The available templates list depends on how Word was installed and whether any new templates have been created on your computer.

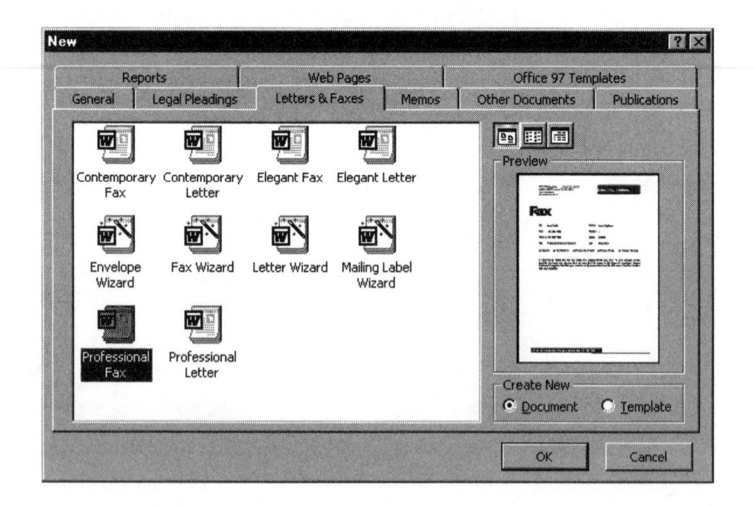

FIGURE 3.14 Letters & Faxes tab of the New dialog box

Any file with a `.dot` extension is a document template. Selections with `.wiz` are template Wizards. Select any template to see a preview in the preview window. (Templates created by other users often can't be previewed.) When you have selected a template you want to use, click OK.

Templates include placeholders where you can insert your text. They also generally include instructions to help you use the template. In the template shown in Figure 3.15, you can insert personalized text and then resave the template, so you can use it again without re-entering your company or personal information.

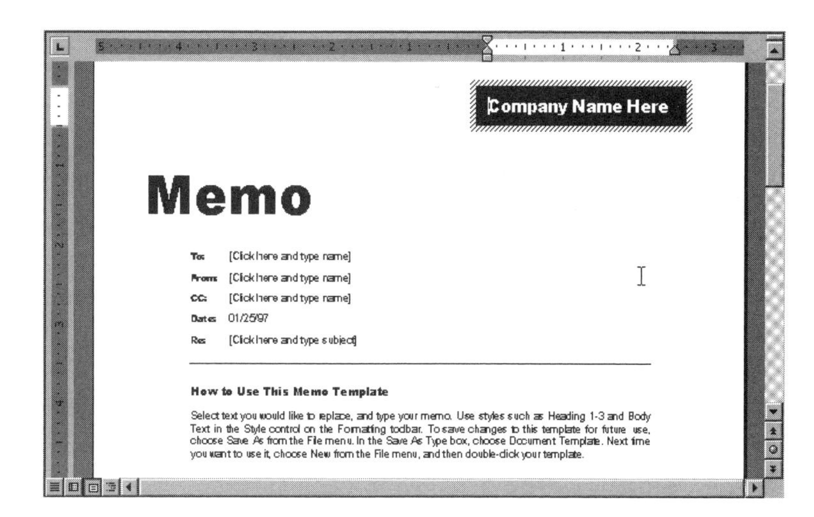

FIGURE 3.15 Professional Memo template

When you save a document created from a template, you must give it a name just like any other new document. If you want to re-use the revised document as a template for future documents, or if you've created a document from scratch that you want to use as a template, click the Save As Type drop-down arrow in the Save As dialog box and choose Document Template (`*.dot`).

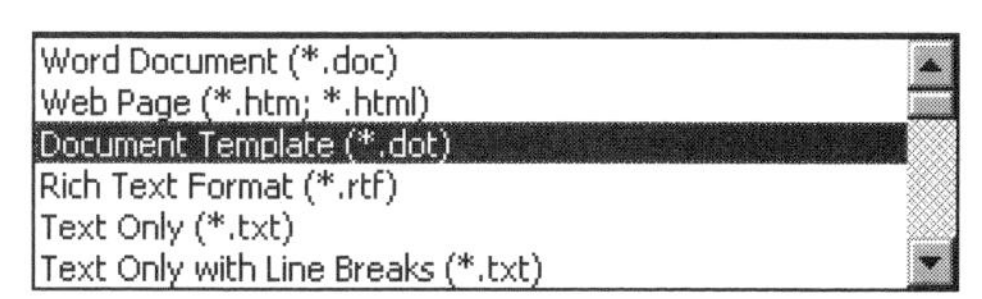

Selecting Document Template opens the Templates folder. If you wish, you can save your template in one of the existing folders. Enter a descriptive name for your template in the File Name control and save the template. Your template will now appear in the File ➢ New dialog box under the appropriate category or the General tab.

Setting a Default File Location for Workgroup Templates

Objective W2000E.7.5

Workgroup templates are templates that are shared by your entire workgroup. Your network administrator should create the workgroup folder and control what templates are saved there. If a workgroup templates folder is available on your network, you can identify the default file location so you can access the shared templates.

Setting the Default File Location for Workgroup Templates

1. Choose Tools ➢ Options and click the File Locations Tab.
2. Select Workgroup Templates and click the Modify button.
3. Browse to the correct file location given to you by your workgroup administrator and when you find it, click OK.
4. Click Close to save the workgroup templates location.

If you are saving a regular document and the Save As dialog box *forces* you to save the document as a template, you may have a version of a Word macro virus on your system. You should immediately run a virus scan using virus protection software that can detect the Word Concept and other macro viruses. Visit the Microsoft Web site at `http://www.microsoft.com` for more information about macro viruses.

Using Wizards

Objective W2000.4.5

Wizards are helpful guides that walk you step-by-step through the process of creating a document. Click File ➢ New to see the Wizards (and Templates) in the New dialog box shown in Figure 3.14. Select a Wizard and click OK. Figure 3.16 shows the first step of the Memo Wizard.

The Start step of any Wizard lists the steps you will follow in a vertical list on the left and briefly describes the purpose of the Wizard below the title on

FIGURE 3.16
First step of the Memo Wizard

the right. Your job is to read the instructions at each step, make choices as they are offered, and click Next to proceed. Some Wizard steps, like the one shown in Figure 3.17, require that you type information that will be placed in your document later. You can return to any step of the Wizard and change your options by clicking the Back button. When you're through with all the steps, click Finish and Word incorporates your choices into a document. You may have further editing to do once the document is on screen. Proceed as you would with any Word document, saving the changes when you're done.

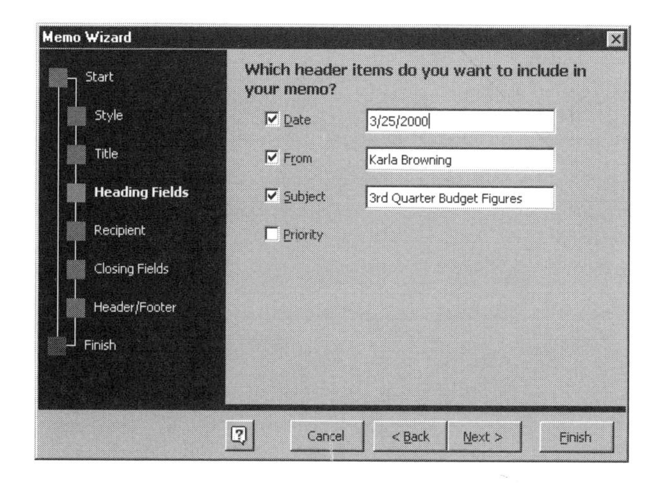

FIGURE 3.17
Heading Fields step of the Memo Wizard

Hands On: Objective W2000.4.5 and 4.7

1. Create a Fax Cover Sheet using one of the Templates in the New dialog box.
   a) Overwrite the placeholders with your own text.
   b) Print the document if you wish.
   c) Delete all the information you typed except for your company information, and then save the cover sheet as a template.
2. Use the Memo Wizard or another Wizard to create a document you can use for a project you're working on. Edit and save the document as necessary once the Wizard finishes.

4

Working with Complex Documents

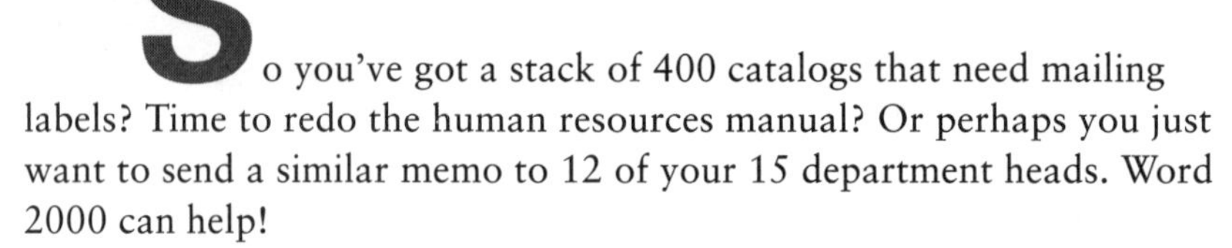

So you've got a stack of 400 catalogs that need mailing labels? Time to redo the human resources manual? Or perhaps you just want to send a similar memo to 12 of your 15 department heads. Word 2000 can help!

Whether the job is large or small, increasing your Word 2000 expertise is a sure way to know you're making the best use of your precious time and resources. Effectively using advanced features such as mail merge, table of contents, and workgroup editing will set you apart from the crowd and give you a storehouse of tools to organize even the most unmanageable project.

Managing Data in Word

Word is more than just a word processor, it is a tool for managing information. Using Word, you can enter, sort, and search through lists of data: names, addresses, and items in an inventory. You can merge data lists with other Word documents and print labels, envelopes, and form letters. In this section, you will learn to create and sort lists. You'll also learn how to produce form letters, labels, and other merged documents in the Creating Customized Merge Documents section.

Understanding Mail Merge

The ability to store lists—personal or business contacts, members of groups or clubs, videotapes, CDs, or books—puts extra power in your hands. Using Word, you can access data stored in:

- a file created using Word
- a file created with other Microsoft Office products

- an external file created using other software

The file that contains a list of information is called a *data source*. (The term *database* also refers to this kind of file.) You can easily sort the information in the data source or use the data source to create labels or envelopes. Create a *main document* that refers to the information in the data source, and you can *merge* the main document with the data source to create personalized letters, labels, or other documents. In summary, you'll need two files to complete a merge: the data source and the main merge document.

Creating a New Data Source in Word

Objective W2000E.5.2

The Mail Merge Helper helps you create data sources and produce merged documents. Before you can get to the step where you're setting up the data, however, you have to do some preliminary work. Open the Mail Merge Helper by choosing Tools ➢ Mail Merge. Begin by clicking the Create button (see Figure 4.1) and selecting the type of document you will create using your data source. Although Word asks you to specify a type of document, your choice at this point doesn't preclude creating another type of main document later.

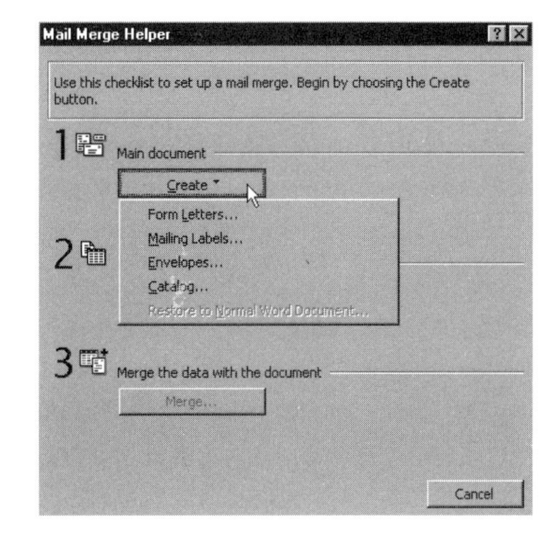

FIGURE 4.1
The Mail Merge Helper

After you select the type of main document you want to create, Word asks if you want to use the active (open) document or a new document for your main document.

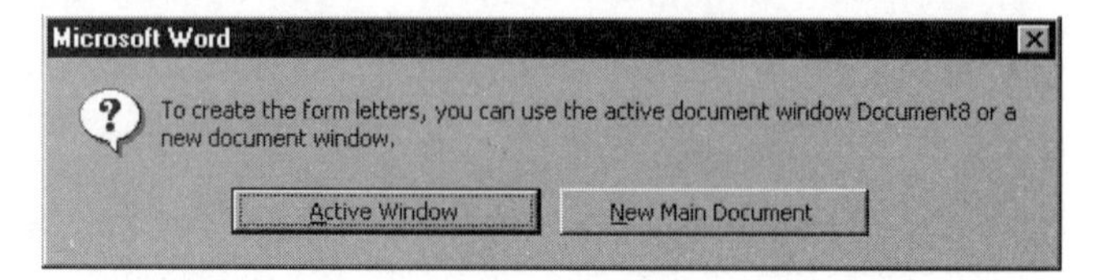

Choose Active Window if the open document is blank or if you've already opened a previously saved document to modify it for use with this merge; if you have any other document open, choose New Main Document.

Now that Word has the preliminary information it needs for the merge, you can proceed to the data step. Click the Get Data button, and then choose Create Data Source from the list to open the Create Data Source dialog box. (The other Get Data options are discussed later in the chapter.) Your goal at this step is to choose the categories for your data. The Create Data Source dialog box, shown in Figure 4.2, comes with a list of *field names* (categories of data) commonly used in mail merges. Scroll the list to find field names you may want to use.

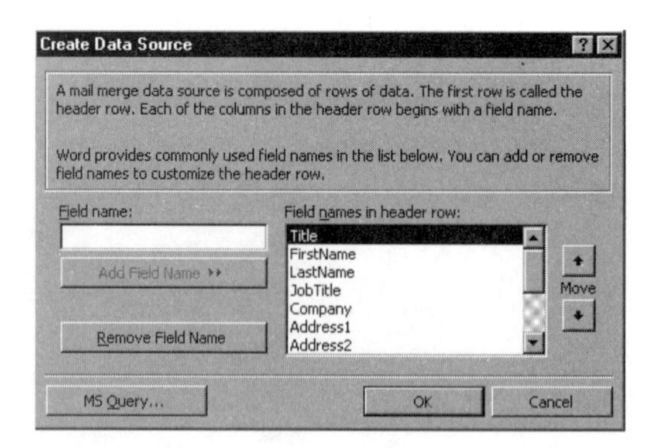

FIGURE 4.2
Create Data Source dialog box

Field names must:

- Be unique—no two fields can have the same name.
- Have less than 40 characters—Word doesn't support larger field names but other programs, like Excel, do.
- Begin with a letter rather than a number—`Supervisor1` and `Supervisor2` are OK; `1Supervisor` and `2Supervisor` are not.

Field names must not:

- Contain spaces—you can separate words with an underscore (First_Name), but we suggest omitting the underscore and simply capitalizing the first letter of each word (FirstName).
- Contain any characters that you can't put in filenames, such as periods, commas, colons, semicolons, slashes, and backslashes—that means you can't use Audit3/15/2000, but you can use Audit3_15_2000 or Audit03152000.

The way you set up your data source can have lasting consequences, so it's a good idea to put some thought into it at the start. Chances are you'll want to use this data to create many different types of main documents. If you create one field called "Name," you probably won't run into any problems using the data for mailing labels. But what if you want to send a letter? You can never begin the letter with "Dear Mr. Hadley" or "Dear Susan" if you've combined first and last name data into one field.

Similarly, you can never sort your mailing labels by zip code if you've entered city, state, and zip into one field. In general, you'll want to enter data into the smallest discreet units that make sense. StreetAddress can usually include the whole field, 123 Ridge Road, unless you do mailings where you determine recipients by their street names. (Example: Your data contains addresses for everyone in Chesterfield Township, but you want to mail ONLY to people who live on Ridge Road.) And don't forget fields you might want later like CourtesyTitle (Mr., Mrs., Ms.), Suffix (Jr., Sr., III), and JobTitle (Account Executive, Vice President of Human Resources). If you are creating several data source files, it's helpful to use the same field names in each data source. For example, if you use FirstName in one data source, don't use FNAME or First in other source files. If you use the same field names, you'll often be able to use the same main documents with different data source files, rather than creating new main documents.

In the Create Data Source dialog box, all the field names in the list are included in the data source by default. To remove a field name from the list, select it, then click the Remove Field Name button. To add a field name to the list, type the name in the Field Name control, and click the Add Field Name button. If you enter an illegal field name (for example, a name that contains a space or that already appears on the list), the Add Field Name button will be disabled to prevent you from adding the illegal name. Use the Move Up and Move Down buttons to the right of the fields list to arrange the field names in the order you'll be using to enter the actual data.

After you enter and arrange all the field names, click OK. You will be prompted to save the data source file. When you save the file, Word will remind you that the file contains no records and will ask whether you want to edit the data source or edit the main document. At this point, you can begin entering information in the data source file by choosing Edit the Data Source.

When you save a data source file, it's a good idea to name the document so that it is easily identifiable as a data source file. You might want to begin all your data source filenames with Data: for example, `Data-Employees`.

Entering Records

Click the Edit Data Source button to open the Data Form dialog box (see Figure 4.3). Enter the information for each field in your first record. When you are ready to enter another record, click the Add New button or press Enter. You can add other records any time you need to, so you don't have to enter all 10,000 employees right now, but can add as many as you wish.

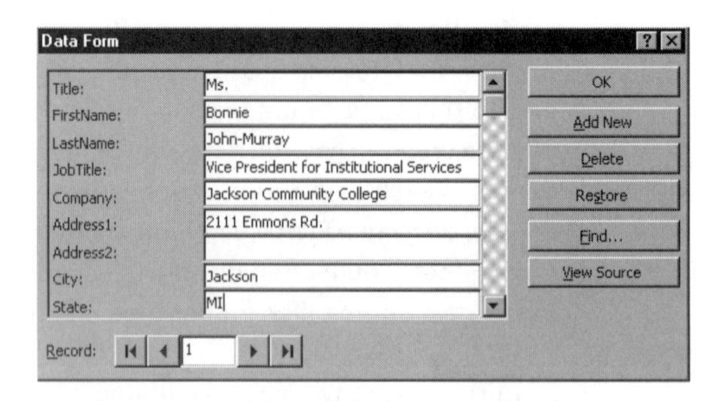

FIGURE 4.3 Data Form dialog box to enter records

When you are finished, you can view all the records by clicking the View Source button. If you have 31 or fewer field names, Word places your document in a table. With 32 or more field names, the data source is displayed in columnar form.

Creating and Entering Records in a Data Source File

1. Choose Tools ➢ Mail Merge.
2. Choose Create and select a type of main document.
3. Indicate whether you want to use the active window as the main document or to create a new document.
4. Click Get Data, and then choose Create Data Source.
5. Review the list of suggested field names in the Create Data Source dialog box; delete field names you don't want.
6. Add new field names by entering them in the Field Name text box and clicking Add Field Name.
7. Use the Move arrows to arrange your fields in the desired order.
8. Click OK when you are finished entering field names and are ready to save the file.
9. Enter a filename for the data source file in the Save As dialog box. Click Save.
10. To begin entering data, choose Edit Data Source when the Option dialog box is presented.
11. Enter records in the Data Form dialog box, pressing Tab between each field and Enter at the end of a record.
12. When you are finished entering records, click OK to go to the Main Document, or click View Source to go directly to the data table.

Editing Records and Managing Fields

When the active file is a data source file, Word automatically displays a Database toolbar.

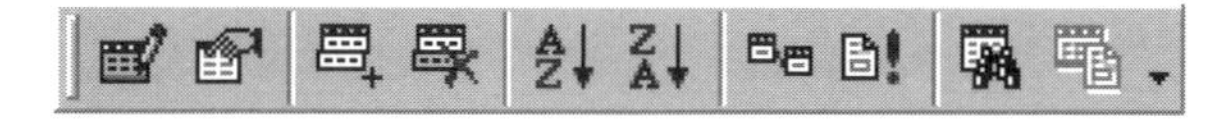

From the toolbar, you can conveniently access tools you will use to manage the data source. You can enter new records, edit, or delete records in the data source just as you would in any table.

To add a new record to the end of your data source, click the Add New Record button on the Database toolbar, or press Tab in the last cell of the table.

To delete a record, move the insertion point within the record you want to delete; then click the Delete Record button on the Database toolbar. Be careful not to delete the first row that contains the field names. If you do, you will have to recreate it to use this file as a data source.

After you chose the field names in the Create Data Source dialog box, you were prompted to save the data file. However, the file you saved was field names only—no data! Remember to resave the file often when you're entering data so that the records themselves are saved.

To add, remove, or rename fields in your data source, click the Manage Fields button to open the Manage Fields dialog box.

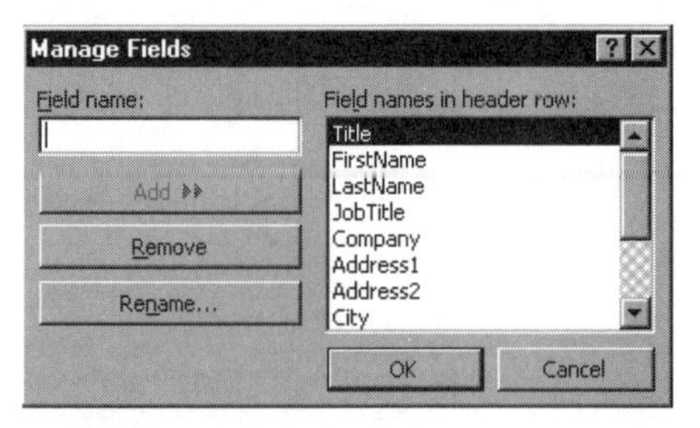

If you prefer to enter or view records using the data form, click the Data Form button on the toolbar to reopen the Data Form dialog box.

You can convert an existing table to a data source by deleting text that precedes the table in the document, deleting any blank rows in the table itself, and renaming column headers so that they follow field name conventions. Word 2000 will recognize a document that meets these requirements as a data source. To use other database options with your table, choose View ➢ Toolbars to turn on the Database toolbar.

Editing Records and Managing Fields in Data Source View

1. Click the View Source button in the Data Form dialog box.
2. Click the Add New Record button to move to an empty row.
3. Click a record you want to delete and click the Delete Record button.
4. Make editing changes just as you would in any other table.
5. Choose Manage Fields to add, remove, or rename fields in the data source.
6. Click the Data Form button to reopen the Data Form dialog box.

Sorting It Out

Objective W2000E.5.3

You can organize your data source by sorting it on any field: last name, zip code, or any other field that you find useful. Records can be sorted in *ascending order* (A to Z, or 0 to 9) or in *descending order* (Z to A, or 9 to 0).

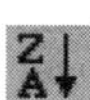

To sort the records in the data source, place the insertion point anywhere in the column you want to sort by. Click the Sort Ascending or Sort Descending button on the Database toolbar to sort the records in the order you specified.

Sorting a Data Source

1. Open a data source document in Data Source view.
2. Move the insertion point to the column that you want to sort by.
3. Click the Sort Ascending or Sort Descending button on the Database toolbar.

Sorting Lists, Paragraphs, and Tables

Objective W2000E.1.3

You can sort any list in Word, whether or not it's a data source. You can sort regular tables, bulleted lists, and even ordinary paragraphs. First, select what you want to sort. Choose Table ➢ Sort from the menu bar to open the Sort dialog box.

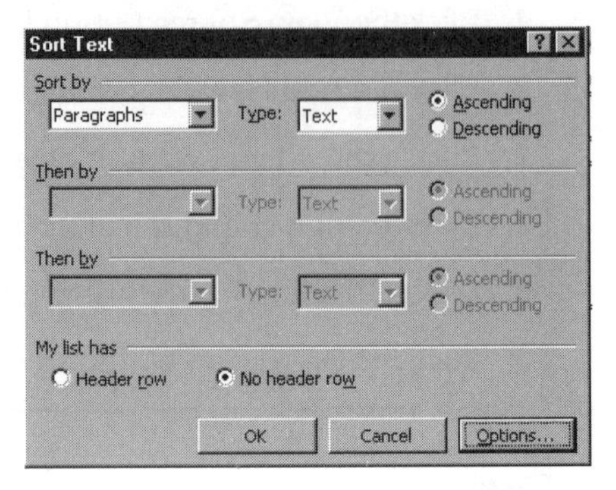

If you've clicked a table or data source, the Sort By drop-down list shows you a list of field names based on the header row of the table. If you've selected a bulleted list or several paragraphs of text, the Sort By list only gives you two options: Paragraphs and Field 1. Choose Paragraphs to sort by the first word in each paragraph, or Field 1 to sort by the first field or tabular column. Choose whether the type of data you want to sort is text, numbers, or dates, and select ascending or descending order. If you are sorting data in a table or data source, you can indicate up to three sort levels. If your table has a header row, mark the Header Row button. When you have entered all the sort criteria, click OK to process the sort.

It's a good idea to save your document before you sort, and always check your data immediately after a sort to make sure it sorted correctly. If it did not, click Undo, or close the document without saving and reopen your saved copy.

Sorting Lists, Tables, and Paragraphs

1. Select the data you want to sort.
2. Choose Table ➢ Sort.
3. Enter what you want to sort by, the type of data you are sorting, and the sort order (ascending or descending).
4. If you're sorting a table, enter additional sort levels, if desired, and indicate if there is a header row.
5. Click OK to process the sort.

Hands On: *Objectives E.5.2, E.5.3, and E.1.3*

1. Create a data source file that contains information about your friends and family.

   a) Include fields that will give maximum flexibility in retrieving the data. The file should contain the following information: name, address, phone number, birth date, spouse/significant other's name, other.

   b) Enter at least 10 records. Leave fields blank if you do not have the information.

   c) Sort alphabetically by last name.

2. Open a document that contains a table.

   a) Convert the table to a data source. Resave the document under a different name.

   b) Switch to the Data Form dialog box (choose View ➢ Toolbars ➢ Database and click the Data Form button) and enter at least five new records.

   c) Sort the records alphabetically.

3. Open or create a document with a bulleted list and sort the list in descending order. Sort it again in ascending order.

Creating Customized Merge Documents

Whether you want to send a letter to 5 people or 500, you can use Word 2000 to personalize each one and create mailing labels or envelopes. You've heard about mail merge, and you may even have used it, but it's never been more foolproof than it is in Word 2000. And don't let the term *mail merge* limit your thinking: You can use mail merge to create telephone directories, birthday lists, nametags, you name it!

Creating a Main Merge Document

Objective W2000E.5.1

Before you can create a main document, you must have the data source in place. This can be a data source file you created in Word, an Excel list, an Access table or query, or a delimited text file you import from some other application. Create or identify your data source before proceeding with this section (review the previous section if you need help creating a data source).

After you've created a Word data source or identified a data source created in Excel, Access, or as a delimited text file in some other application, open the Mail Merge Helper (choose Tools ➢ Mail Merge) and click Create to create a main document. You have four choices of main documents.

Form Letters or reports you want to personalize

Mailing Labels, any other kind of label such as nametags, videotape or disk labels, or file folder labels

Envelopes fed directly into your printer

Catalogs of data such as phone lists or membership directories—any data you want listed consecutively rather than on separate pages

Word will ask if you want to use the current document or begin in a new document window. If the current window is empty, you can choose either option. If the current window contains a document into which you want to insert mail merge codes, choose Active Window. In all other cases, you should begin in a new window. Word again displays the Mail Merge Helper. Click the Get Data button and choose Open Data Source. In the Open Data Source dialog box, select the data source to use with the main document you are creating. After the data source is confirmed, Word will return to the main document and open a dialog box to remind you that the main document has no merge fields, so you cannot merge the main document and data source yet. Choose Edit Main Document to open the Mail Merge toolbar and begin creating the main document.

A main document contains two kinds of text: *regular text* and *variable text*. Regular text will be the same in each version of the merged document—like the body text within a letter. Variable text is represented by a *merge*

field. Merge fields take the place of text that will be different in each merged document—for example, the recipient's name and address.

In the main document, enter, edit, and format regular text as you would in any Word document. Insert a merge field where you want text from the data source to appear in your final, merged document: Place the insertion point where you want the merge field to appear, then click the Insert Merge Field button on the Mail Merge toolbar to display the list of field names from the data source.

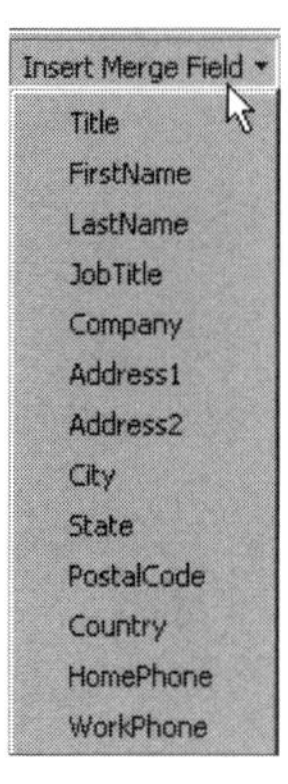

Choose the field name from the list, and Word inserts the merge field, as shown in Figure 4.4.

FIGURE 4.4

Main document with merge codes

August 29, 1999

«Title» «FirstName» «LastName»
«JobTitle»
«Company»
«Address1»
«Address2»
«City», «State» «PostalCode»

Dear «Title» «LastName»:

We are excited about the prospect of working with you on the Web-based economic development program in your region. We believe that the use of an intranet to communicate with businesses in your communities is a critical part of your overall strategy and are looking forward to developing an attractive, easy-to-navigate Web site full of valuable information for all those involved. Int*net technology is moving so fast that every day there are new tools available to make your visions a reality. We will be submitting a proposal to you by the end of next week, and we can then meet to discuss the project in more detail.

Again, thanks for the opportunity, and we'll look forward to hearing from you.

Sincerely,

Annette Marquis Gini Courter

As soon as you've set up the main document the way you want it, you'll want to save it for use in future merges. When you use an existing main document, open the main document before you start the Mail Merge Helper. When you are prompted by the Helper to use the active document or to create a new main document, choose the active document.

When you save a merge document, it's a good idea to indicate the type of document somewhere in the filename. We suggest you begin main documents with the word Main and when appropriate, the name of the data source it is linked to (`Main-Acknowledgment Letter to Clients`), so you can identify your main documents easily.

Creating a Main Document

1. Identify the data source file you want to use with this main document. Create and save a new one if necessary.
2. Start a new document or open a document you wish to convert to a main merge document, then choose Tools ➢ Mail Merge from the menu bar.
3. Choose Create and then select the type of main document that you want to create.
4. Indicate whether you want to use the document in the active window or to create a new main document.
5. Choose Get Data under Data Source to open an existing data source file (the one you identified in step 1 above).
6. Click Edit Main Document to enter the regular text in the main document.
7. Move the insertion point to the position where you want data from the data source to appear. Click Insert Merge Field and select field names from the list to insert merge fields at the desired positions.
8. Save the main document.

Previewing the Merged Document

You've almost done it! When the main document and data source are merged, Word will generate a separate document or listing (if you are setting up a catalog) for each record in the data source based on the layout of the main document.

To see what the first merge document will look like, click the View Merged Data button on the Mail Merge toolbar. The toolbar includes a set of *navigation buttons* that you can use to move to the first record, previous record, next record, or last record. You can preview all the merged documents using the navigation buttons.

Click again on the View Merged Data button to return to the main document.

Merging Documents

Objective W2000E.5.4

You have created a main document and specified a data source. If everything looked okay when you previewed the merge results, you are ready for the actual merge. If the main document is not active, activate the main document window. The Mail Merge toolbar gives you a number of options, depending on how confident you are that everything is set the way you want it.

The most daring choice is Merge to Printer. Choose this option *only* if you have previewed your merge and everything is in perfect order. (Check that nobody has left purple and green paper in the printer!)

A much more conservative choice is Merge to New Document. Word will conduct the merge and create a new document with the results. This gives you the intermediate step of viewing the actual results of the merge before printing it. Once the merge is printed, there is no reason to save the merge results. If you need to print it again at a later date, you'll want to do the merge again, in case you've updated any of the records in the data source.

Your final option is to use the Merge dialog box, shown in Figure 4.5. Click the Merge button on the toolbar to open it.

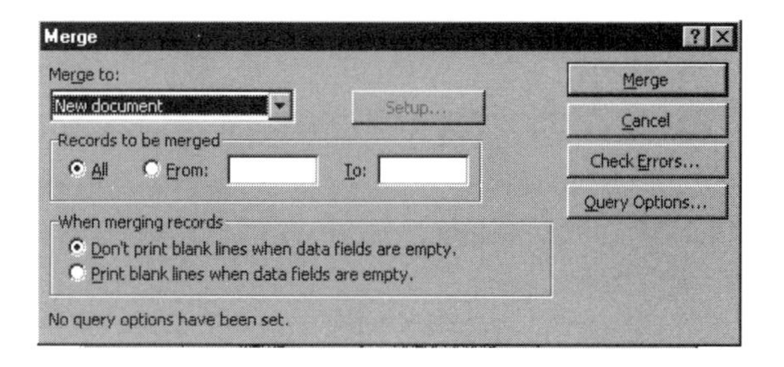

FIGURE 4.5 Merge dialog box

Here, you can choose to merge to a new document, a printer, an e-mail, or a fax, and you can specify only a portion of the records to merge. If you want Word to ignore blank fields (for instance, Address2 for records without a suite number), indicate that by checking the appropriate box.

Merging from an Alternate Data

Objective W2000E.5.6

If your data is kept in another application, an Excel Spreadsheet or an Outlook Address book for example, you can easily merge it with a main document in Word. Open the Mail Merge Helper and proceed as you would with any merge. At the Get Data step, choose Open Data Source (if your data is in Excel, Access, or another database application) or choose Use Address Book to retrieve data from Outlook.

If you're attaching to an Excel or Access data source, you'll see the Open Data Source dialog box. Navigate to the drive and the folder that contains the data file, change the Files of Type drop-down to indicate the type of file you're looking for, select it, and then click Open. With an Excel data source, you will be prompted to choose whether to use the Entire Spreadsheet or a named range you've created in the worksheet. Proceed with creating the main document as you normally would.

Excel is a powerful tool for managing non-relational databases. The *Microsoft Office User Certification Specialist Study Guide for Excel 2000,* also from Sybex, is an excellent resource to learn the application.

When you attach to an Outlook address book, you may be prompted to select a profile from a list. Once you complete this step, the Outlook fields are available to you from the Insert Merge Field drop-down list on the Mail Merge toolbar.

Specifying Records to Merge

Suppose you have a list of names and addresses and only want to send letters to people in a certain zip code or state. You can *filter* records based on criteria that you establish. After you select your data source and main document, click the Merge button to open the Merge dialog box. In the database world, a *query* is a tool used to select a group of records that meet specific criteria. Click the Query Options button to open the Filter Records page of the Query Options dialog box, shown in Figure 4.6.

FIGURE 4.6

Query Options dialog box

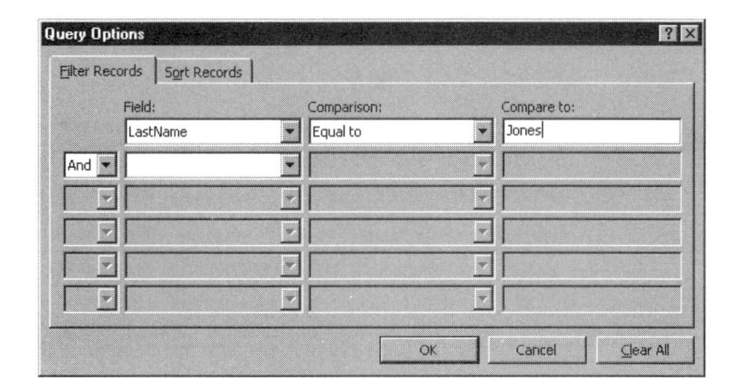

In the Field drop-down list, select the field you want to use to select records. If, for example, you want to merge records with zip code 48439, choose the PostalCode field. To send letters to all the customers whose last name is Jones, choose LastName. In the Compare To control (at the far right of the dialog box), enter the text string you are looking for in the selected field: **48439** or **Jones**. The comparison box lets you determine how the records in the data source are compared to the text string.

Using And and Or

Once you enter a Compare To text string, the word *And* appears in the drop-down to the left of the second row of the Query Options dialog box. You can enter multiple query criteria and select, for example, the records for people in California where the data source doesn't list a zip code. The single most confusing thing about writing queries is knowing when to use And and when to use Or. If you can master this, you qualify as an expert query writer!

Choosing And means both comparisons must be true for a match. If you enter the Field, Comparison, and Compare To information in the example given above, choosing And will select all records where the State is California *and* the PostalCode field in the data source is blank. Records for people from Arkansas, Oregon, or Massachusetts will not be selected. Records for people living in California with a zip code will not be selected. Choosing Or means a match will be found if either comparison is true. In this case, *all* Californians will be selected, as well as anyone from any other state who doesn't have a zip code listed in the data source.

Use Or when you want to select two possible values for the same field. If you select records where State is equal to California *and* State is equal to Nevada, no records will be selected (since no single record includes both states). Choosing Or will select records for both states.

Use And when you want to select records from a numeric range. For example, you might want to send an advertisement to all families with annual incomes between $25,000 and $40,000. In this example, you select Income Greater Than 25000 And Income Less Than 40000. If you used Or, all records would be selected, as every level of income is either less than 40000 or more than 25000.

Here's a general rule for troubleshooting queries: If you expected some records to be selected but none were, you probably used And when you should have used Or. If you got a lot more records than you expected, you probably used Or when you should have used And.

Sorting Records

Objective W2000E.5.3

After you select your merge criteria, you can also choose how you want your data sorted by clicking the Sort Records tab in the Query Options dialog box. Use the skills you learned in the previous section to set the sort criteria. When you've finished setting your query options, click OK, and you're ready to merge.

Selecting and Sorting Records to Merge

1. Choose the Merge button from the Mail Merge toolbar.
2. Click Query Options to open the Query Options dialog box.
3. Select the field you want to use to select (filter) records.
4. Choose a comparison criterion.

Selecting and Sorting Records to Merge *(continued)*

5. Enter the text string you are looking for in the Compare To control.
6. Enter other desired query criteria by selecting And or Or and then selecting the criteria.
7. Click the Sort tab to sort the resulting merged document.
8. Select the desired sort fields and indicate whether you want the records to be sorted in ascending or descending order.
9. Choose OK to return to the Merge dialog box.
10. Preview the merge, if you wish, by clicking the View Merged Data button on the Mail Merge Toolbar. Click Merge to begin the merge.

Creating Catalogs and Lists

A *catalog* main document is used to create lists; each record is listed directly under the previous record on the same page. You might use the catalog option to create, for instance, an employee phone directory. Word doesn't shine its brightest with catalogs. However, if you know how to work around the awkwardness of Word's catalog merge, it's still the most convenient way to present a list of the records in a data source.

When you choose Catalog as the main document type from the Mail Merge Helper, in the main document, you can either create a table to hold the merge field codes or use tabs to separate the codes. We encourage you to use a table; it produces consistent results with the least amount of hassle. Enter any text you want to appear with each *record* of the data source, but don't include other surrounding text. If, for example, you want a heading to appear above the records in the list, *don't* enter it now or your merged document will include a heading, a record, another heading, another record, and so forth.

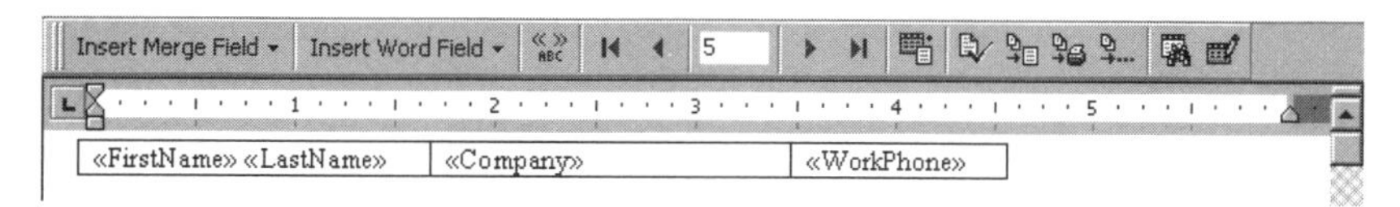

You can click the View Merged Data button to see each individual record as it will appear in the merged document, but you have to actually do the merge to see them all together. You can sort or select records before merging using the Query Options.

After you merge the data source and main document, you can add titles, column headings, and any other information to the merged document before you print it. Merged catalogs are the exception to the suggestion that you not save merge results. If you have to add a lot of heading and title information after the merge, you may want to save it for future reference.

Using the Catalog Merge Feature

1. Choose Tools ➢ Mail Merge.
2. Create or open a main document and a data source. Select Catalog as the main document type.
3. Edit the main document to include any text you want to appear with each record and insert the field codes in the desired positions. Generally, you'll want this information in a table; however, you should not insert column headings at this point.
4. Preview the merge, using View Merged Data to see individual records in the merge.
5. Run the merge, setting query options to select and sort records as desired. Once you run the merge, you should see all records.
6. Add any additional text, headings, or titles to complete the document before printing.
7. Save the merge results document.

Creating Envelopes and Labels

Objective W2000E.5.5

Labels and envelopes are two other types of main documents. Word can merge to various sizes of envelopes: standard, business, note card, and other sizes. If your printer can print on envelopes and labels, you can create them in Word. (You must also know how to load the envelopes and labels. If you're not sure, consult your printer manual.)

To create labels, open the Mail Merge helper and choose Mailing Labels from the Create Main Document drop-down list. After you select a data source, a dialog box will appear. Click the Set Up Main Document button.

The Label Options dialog box opens (see Figure 4.7), offering you a choice of label sizes. You can select Avery, Formtec, Maco, and a host of other labels by choosing a brand from the Label Products list and scrolling through the list below it to select the number printed on the box. You may have to set the dimensions for other brands of labels not included on the Label Products list, but many other brands have the corresponding Avery number printed somewhere on the box.

FIGURE 4.7

Label Options dialog box

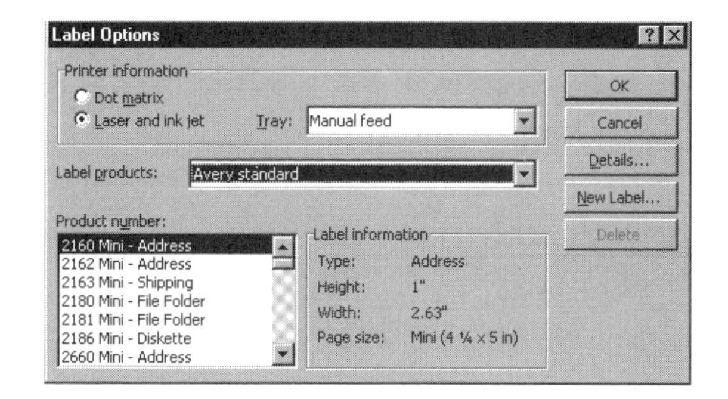

After you select a label, click the OK button to open the Create Labels dialog box (See Figure 4.8).

FIGURE 4.8

Create Labels dialog box

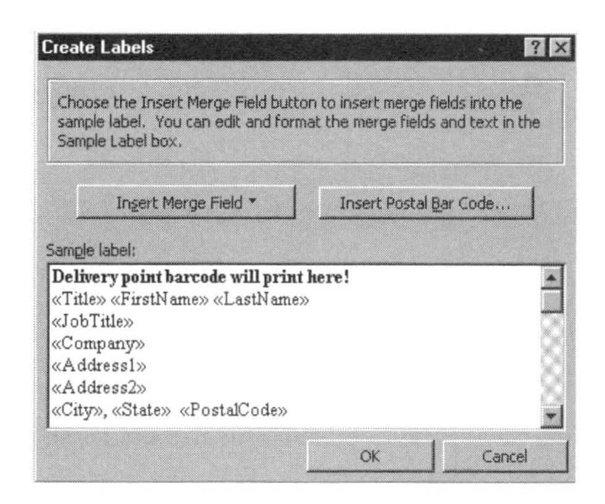

The Sample Label pane is like the main document window. Click the Insert Merge Field button to insert merge code fields in the label. Enter any other text from the keyboard. If you want to print a delivery point barcode to help out the post office, click Insert Postal Bar Code and identify which field holds the zip code and which is your main address field.

You won't find buttons to format in this dialog box, but you can right-click selected text and use the formatting options on the shortcut menu. Click OK to close the Create Labels Dialog box and return to the Mail Merge Helper. Close the Mail Merge Helper and preview your labels before printing them. If you can't see all the needed text, it's easier to re-create the labels from scratch rather than editing them.

If you want to save the label document, you can close the Mail Merge Helper and save the main document, or you can wait until after you have merged the labels. Include the word *Labels* (instead of *Main*) at the beginning of the filename.

Creating Envelopes

Follow the same initial steps for envelopes that you did when you were creating labels. When you click the Create button in the Mail Merge Helper, choose Envelopes rather than Mailing Labels. Select the Envelope Size from the list provided. (You even have options for how to format your envelope; click one of the Font buttons to see them.) Choose OK to proceed to the Envelope Address dialog box. Insert Merge Field names just as you did in the Create Labels dialog box. When you close the Envelope Address dialog box, Word will return you to the Mail Merge Helper so you can merge envelopes.

Creating Labels Using Mail Merge

1. Choose Tools ➢ Mail Merge.
2. Click Create and Choose Mailing Labels as the document type.
3. Click GetData and choose a data source.
4. Click Set Up Main Document to open the Label Options dialog box.
5. Select a label brand from the Label Products list, then scroll down the list of label options and select the label type that you want to use. Click OK.
6. Enter field codes as desired.
7. Select the field codes you have entered and right-click to change the formatting of the text.

Creating Labels Using Mail Merge *(continued)*

8. Click Insert Postal Bar Code to create a bar code on each label.
9. Click OK when you are finished setting up the label to see the main document.
10. Preview the labels to make sure all the lines print on each label.

Troubleshooting Merge Problems

There are three basic reasons for merge problems:

- Document incompatibility
- Problems with the data source
- Problems with the main document

Document incompatibility means that either the data source or the main document isn't a valid Word mail merge file. A dialog box will appear telling you that the main document has no merge codes or that the data source is invalid. Examine the file in question. If it is a data file, make sure it has field names, that there is no extra text at the beginning of the file, and that the data is in a table or is properly delimited. If the problem is the main document, open it and check to make sure you have selected the correct file and that it has merge field codes. (Remember, you must enter merge field codes from the toolbar; you cannot type << before the field name and >> after.) Even if both files seem to be OK, structural problems with individual records (such as missing fields) can cause Word to stop in the middle of a merge.

You can have Word check the data source for omission errors before merging. With the main document active, click the Check for Errors button on the Mail Merge toolbar to open the Checking and Reporting Errors dialog box, shown in Figure 4.9. This is much like checking spelling before printing.

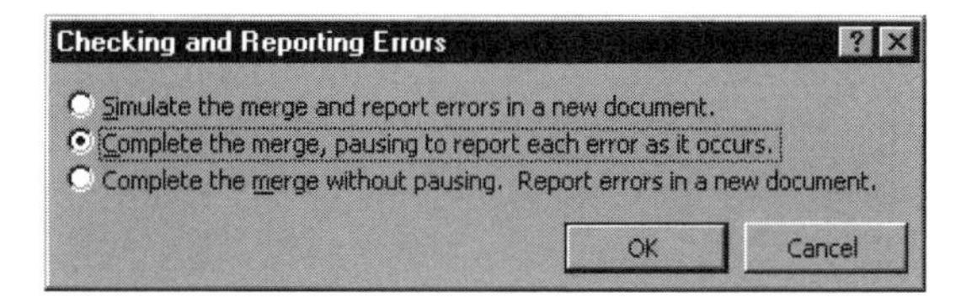

FIGURE 4.9 Checking for data source errors

You can choose to have Word simulate a merge or actually merge the two documents and report errors. If you expect errors, simulation is best. If you don't think there will be errors (always our hope), go ahead and have Word merge; it stops along the way to report any errors it finds. When Word finds an error, a dialog box opens. Depending on the kind of error, you may be allowed to fix the error and then continue merging. If you cannot, note the information provided, and click the OK button to continue finding errors. When Error Checking is complete, close the merged document and fix the data source and/or main document files before merging the documents again.

Even if Word finds no errors and your documents merge, you may still find mistakes in your merged document. There is an easy way to decide if a mistake is in the main document or in the data source:

- If the mistake appears in every merged document, look for the problem in the main document. For example, if there is no space between the first and last names in your merged form letters, you should put a space between the merge codes for FirstName and LastName in the main document. Spelling errors in every merged document should lead you to suspect that you forgot to check the spelling in the main document before merging.
- If a mistake appears in some, but not all, merged documents, the problem is in the data source. If a merged first name is spelled incorrectly in one of the merged letters, it's misspelled in the data source. Close the merged file, open the data source file, and correct the error. Then merge the documents again.

Hands On: Objectives W2000E.5.1, E.5.4, E.5.5, and E.5.6

1. Create a form letter with field codes to represent data in an existing data source file.
    a) Preview the merge to see that everything is correct.
    b) Merge to a new document.
    c) Be sure to save your data source file (if you made any changes to it) and your main document. Discard the merge document without saving changes.

2. Create mailing labels to a select group of people from an existing data source file.
   a) Select only those people on the list who meet certain criteria (from the same zip code, from the same city, name begins with the same letter, and so on).
   b) Sort the records to merge by Last Name.
3. Create a catalog main document using an alternate data source (an Excel spreadsheet or an Outlook address book, for example).
   a) Use a table to hold your fields.
   b) Merge the main document with the data source.
   c) Add a title to the document and header rows to the columns.
   d) Format the table to improve its appearance.
   e) Print the table.

Publishing Online Forms

As more people have computers on their desktops and more computers are networked together, the paperless office is becoming a reality. One way that's happening is through the creation and use of online forms. If you need to create a vacation request form, why go to the trouble of creating the form, printing it, making copies, and distributing them? With an online form, an employee opens the form online, fills it out, and sends it by e-mail to the supervisor, who approves (or disapproves) it and returns the e-mail. It's all over in a matter of minutes—no copies, no lost forms, no missed vacations.

Designing a Form

Objective W2000E.6.4

Because you'll want to use the online form over and over again, you need to create your form as a template. Choose File ➢ New, choose Blank Document from the General tab, click Template from the Create New options at the bottom right of the dialog box, and then click OK.

The new template will open as `Template1`. It's not a bad idea to save it now so you can quickly save changes as you create the form. Since you've identified this as a template, the Save As dialog box opens to the Templates folder and shows the file type as Document Template.

Save the template in one of the existing template folders, or create a new folder for online forms. Creating a new folder in the Templates folder causes it to be displayed as a Tab in the New dialog box. Once you save the new template, it will be available for users to select when they create a new document.

Before you start creating your form, sketch it on paper or use an existing hard-copy form as a model. This gives your online form a better ultimate design and saves you the time and frustration of trying to design the form while you're creating it. Once you have decided on a design, right-click any toolbar and activate the Forms toolbar:

The Forms toolbar includes buttons to insert form fields, to create tables and frames to position questions and prompts on the page, to turn form-field shading on or off, and to protect the form so that users can only enter data where you have placed fields.

The easiest way to lay out the form is by using a table. Tables allow you to place text on different parts of the screen without worrying about user-entered text wrapping to a new line.

Click the Draw Table or Insert Table buttons on the Forms toolbar to create a table. (Feel free to review the Tables section in Chapter 3 if you need a refresher on using these tools.) Figure 4.10 shows an example of an online form that was created using tables. The gridlines and borders have been turned off except for the bottom borders, which form the lines for users' responses.

Figure 4.11 shows the same form with table gridlines turned on. As you can see, rows and columns aren't evenly distributed, and extra cells have been inserted to provide the appropriate spacing for items on the form.

After you enter field names and prompts in the table, you can split cells, merge cells, change borders, and adjust column and row widths as needed. Since the form is to be viewed online, don't forget to add colors, shading, and graphics to really make an impression. For more information about working with graphics, see Chapter 5. See the next section *Adding Field Controls* for more detail on adding fields.

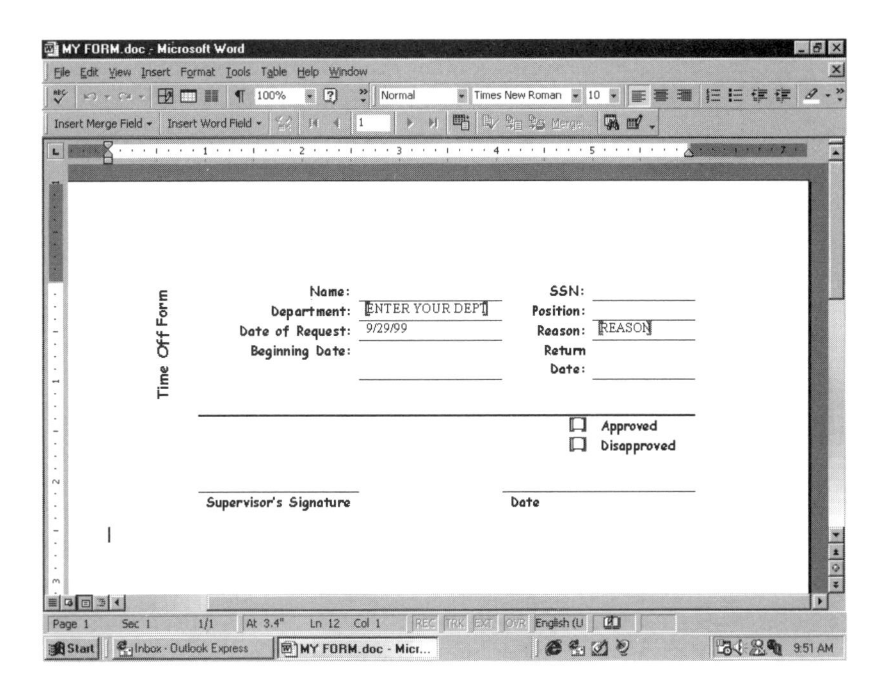

FIGURE 4.10
Online form created using tables

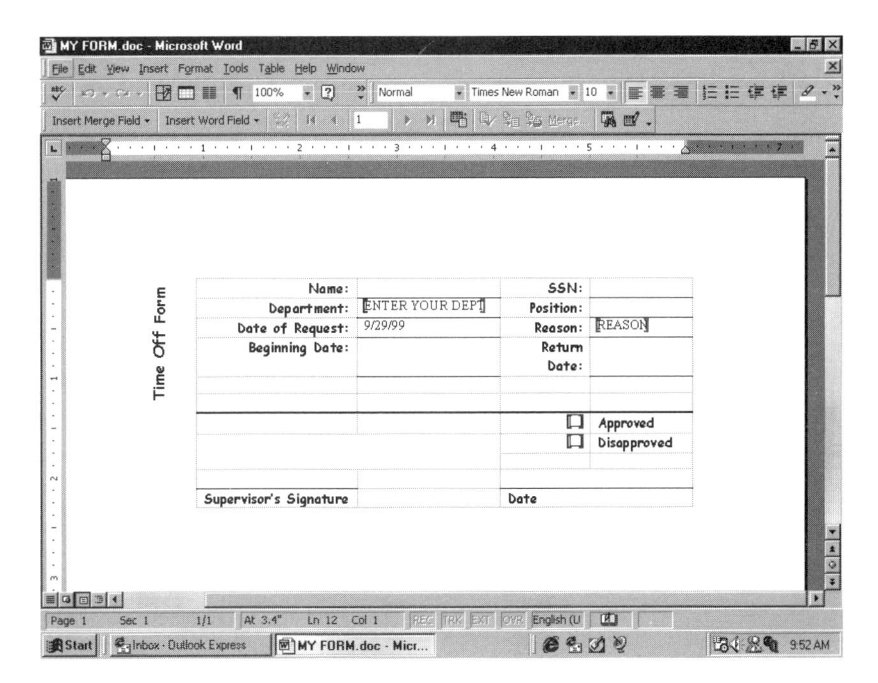

FIGURE 4.11
Online form showing gridlines

Using Frames and Text Boxes

The Forms toolbar has an option for frames, which allow you to place an item precisely at any position on a form. You may want to frame small tables so you can position them easily on the page.

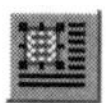

Click the Insert Frame button, drag a rectangle the approximate size of your table, and then insert a table into the frame. You can resize a frame by pointing to one of the black handles around its borders. When the mouse pointer changes to a double-headed arrow, you can drag the handle. To reposition the frame, click the frame to select it, and with the four-headed arrow mouse pointer, drag the frame to a new position.

Insert Frames after you've entered and edited the appropriate fields in the table you're framing.

If it's text you want to position, however, Word's text box feature, found on the Drawing toolbar, is a much more flexible option. With text boxes, you can apply 3-D effects, shadows, fills, and backgrounds, and in addition to changing the orientation of the text, you can flip and rotate the boxes themselves. For more information about text boxes, see Chapter 5.

Designing a Form

1. Open the New dialog box, choose Blank Document, and click Template in the Create New option. Click OK to create a blank template.
2. Choose File ➢ Save As to save the template in the most appropriate template folder. Give the template a descriptive name.
3. Display the Forms toolbar by right-clicking any toolbar and choosing Forms from the list.
4. Design the form using a table for the body of the form. Add bottom borders where appropriate to provide user-response lines.
5. Save the template.

Adding Field Controls

Objective W2000E.6.1 and E.6.5

Once your form is laid out, you must add *fields* or placeholders that other people can use to submit their information. You can access three types of fields from buttons on the Forms toolbar.

Text fields—These are open fields of any length where users can enter text.

Check Box fields—Users can check or clear these boxes to indicate answers.

Drop-down fields—Users choose a response from a list of choices you provide.

When your form is completed and you turn on protection, users will only be able to enter text or choices in the fields. The rest of the document will be off-limits to them.

To insert a field, position your cursor where you would like the field to appear, and then click one of the three form field buttons found on the left end of the toolbar, either Text, Check Box, or Drop-Down.

It's helpful to have the Form Field Shading button turned on while you are creating the form so that you can see where the fields are.

After you enter a field, specify the options you want to apply to the field. Double-click the field to open the appropriate Form Field Options dialog box. The options for text form fields, shown in Figure 4.12, include:

Type—Regular text, number, date, current date, current time, or calculation.

Default Text—If there is a response that users would most commonly give, making it the default means they will only have to enter responses that differ from the default.

Maximum Length—Unlimited or a specified number of characters, which limits the length of user entries.

Text Format—Uppercase, Lowercase, First Capital, or Title Case to format user entries.

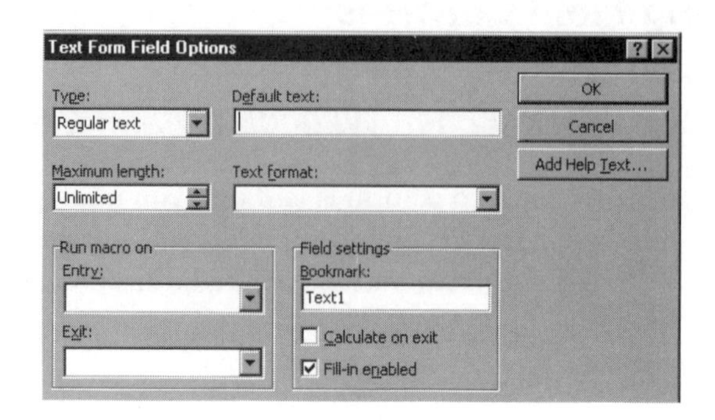

FIGURE 4.12
Text Form Field Options dialog box

You can also run macros on entry into and exit from a field (see Chapter 7 for more information about macros), set bookmarks, or have Word calculate the field on exit. If you want to restrict user access to a field, you can clear the Fill-in Enabled check box.

The Add Help Text option will endear you forever to your users.

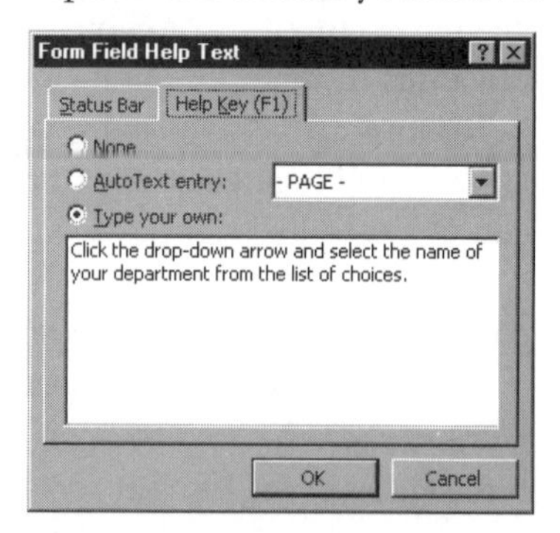

Use this option to add text to the status bar and provide even more detailed instructions when users press the F1 key. Just click Type Your Own and enter whatever text you would like to have appear when the user moves into the field.

The unique options for check box form fields, shown in Figure 4.13, include:

Check Box Size—Choose either Auto (makes your check box the size of the text), or Exactly (lets you designate how large the box will be).

Default Value—Determines whether or not the box is checked when the form opens.

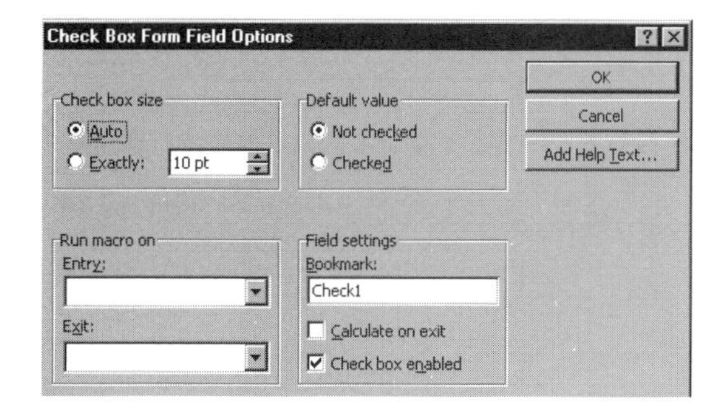

FIGURE 4.13 Check Box Form Field Options dialog box

The only unique option for drop-down form fields, shown in Figure 4.14, is the list of drop-down items, which you must supply. Enter the text in the Drop-Down Item text box and click the Add button. After you create your list, you can use the Move buttons to rearrange the items. Select an item and click Remove to delete or edit an item from the list. Unfortunately, the first item always shows up on the form as if it is the default. The only way around this is to enter a blank item (press the spacebar a few times before you press Add), or to make the first item instructional: `Select your department`. However, if you provide either of these options, you cannot prevent users from selecting these as their choice, so think carefully about this before deciding which way you want to go.

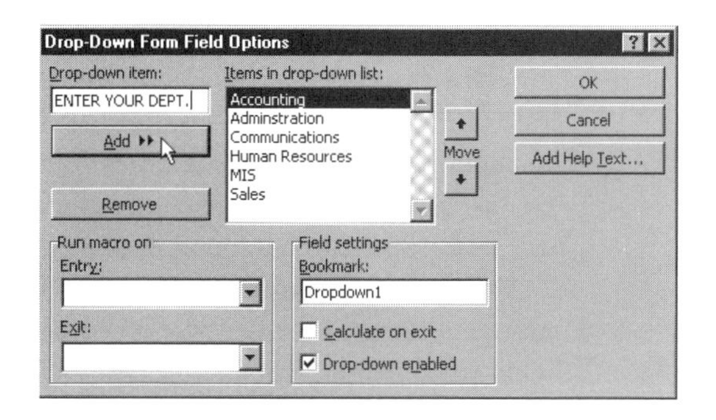

FIGURE 4.14 Drop-Down Form Field Options dialog box

When your form is ready to distribute, you may want to turn off Form Field Shading (click the Form Field Shading button). This is purely optional, but because the shading does not correspond to the actual length of the field, it can give users the wrong impression about how much they should enter in a field.

Adding Form Fields

1. Click the space where you want the field to appear. Click the Text Form Field, Check Box Form Field, or Drop-Down Form Field buttons on the Forms toolbar to insert the field.
2. Double-click the field to edit the form field options.
3. Enter text, check box, and drop-down list options, as appropriate.
4. Click the Add Help Text button to insert your own status bar and F1 Help key instructions into the form.
5. Click OK to save the help instructions and OK again to return to your form.
6. When you are finished setting options in all the fields, you can click the Form Field Shading button to hide the shading, if desired.

Protecting and Using the Form

Your form is almost ready to distribute. One more step will make sure that your template stays intact and that users have access only to the field controls.

After you're sure everything is exactly the way you want it, click the Protect Form button on the Forms toolbar. When you do this, you will no longer have access to most toolbar and menu options. However, you can still save your template, and that's exactly what you want to do next.

When users open a protected form, they will only be able to click the field controls. Pressing Tab and Shift+Tab will move forward and backward through the fields. They will have limited access to toolbars and other options. They can enter their information, send it to the printer, and name and save the document.

After protecting your form, it's always smart to test the form by filling it out to check that the tab order is correct. *Tab order* is the order in which the fields are activated when you press Tab. Depending on how you created the table and positioned the items in it, it may not tab logically through the fields. To correct this, you may have to insert blank cells or reposition items on the form. You may also find that you made a field's length too short or that you didn't include all the options in a drop-down list. Use the form as if you were one of your potential users; if possible, ask a colleague to test the form for you. It's amazing how easy it is to overlook something when you already know what data is expected in a field.

If you need to edit the form, be sure to open the template and not just a copy of the form. To open the template, choose File ➢ Open, change the Files of Type control to Document Templates (`*.dot`), locate the form in the appropriate template folder (the default folder is `C:\Program Files\Microsoft Office\Templates`), and click Open. You can then turn on the Forms toolbar and click the Protect Form button. You will again have free rein to do whatever you want to the form (within reason, of course!).

Protecting and Testing the Form

1. Click the Protect Form button on the Forms toolbar to restrict user access to just the field controls on the form. Resave the form.
2. Open the form as a user would by clicking File ➢ New and choosing it from the dialog box. Test the tab order by pressing Tab through the form and making sure it proceeds in a logical order.
3. Enter data in each field and see what happens if a user enters incorrect data (too much or too little, for example).
4. To edit the form, choose File ➢ Open, change Files of Type to Document Template (*.dot), select the template from the template folders, and click Open.
5. Turn on the Forms toolbar (choose View ➢ Toolbars ➢ Forms) and click the Protect Form button to turn protection off.
6. Correct any tab-order problems by rearranging fields or inserting blank cells in the table.
7. Make additional editing changes as desired, click Protect Form again, and save the template.

Using an Online Form

1. Choose File ➢ New and choose the form from the New dialog box.
2. Press Tab to navigate forward and Shift+Tab to navigate backward through the fields.
3. Save or print the new document as desired.

Hands On: Objectives W2000E.6.1, E.6.4, and E.6.5

1. Design a form similar to the one shown in Figure 4.11. It can be the same form or one of your own design.
   a) Create a new blank template to hold your form.
   b) Enter and format the form title and other information.
   c) Create a table to hold the body of your form. Use each type of field controls where appropriate. Set the options for each control, including length for text fields.
   d) Set the Text format of one of the text fields for Title Case.
   e) Protect, save, and close the form when you have finished designing it.
2. Open the form as if you were a user (choose File ➢ New) and enter data in each field. Note any problems with the form. Close the form without saving changes.
3. Reopen the template and turn off form protection. Make any needed editing changes identified when you tested the form. Turn on protection, save, and retest the form.

Adding References to Your Documents

Adding footnotes, endnotes, tables of contents, indexes, and cross-references makes your documents easy to follow and helps your readers find what they are looking for. When you plan ahead, Word 2000 takes the headache out of these additional touches, providing one more way for your work to stand out.

Adding Footnotes and Endnotes

Objective W2000E.2.8

When you want to provide readers with more information about your topic, Word 2000 gives you options for inserting both *footnotes*, which appear at the bottom of the page, and *endnotes*, which appear at the end of the document. Word automatically numbers the notes for you and calculates how much space footnotes will need at the bottom of the page. Where was this feature when we were typing term papers?

To insert a footnote or an endnote, position the insertion point where you'd like the *reference mark* (footnote or endnote number) to appear and choose Insert ➢ Footnote. The Footnote and Endnote dialog box opens. Select the type of note you want to insert.

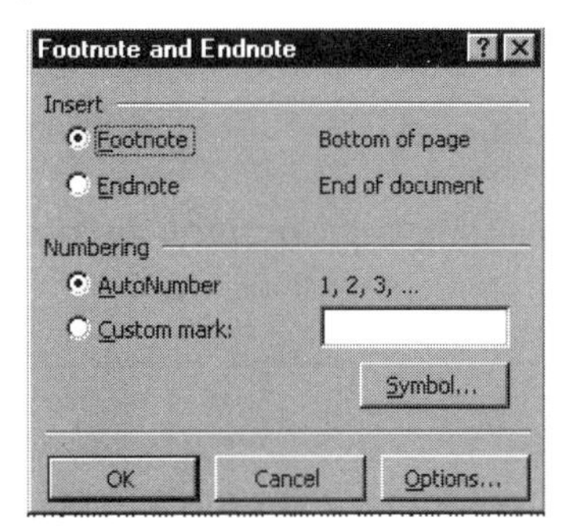

You can choose traditional automatic numbering (1,2,3) or insert a custom mark or symbol. After you make your numbering selection, Word inserts the reference mark and, depending on the current view, either opens a note pane (Normal view) or takes you to the actual location where the note will appear in your document (Print Layout view).

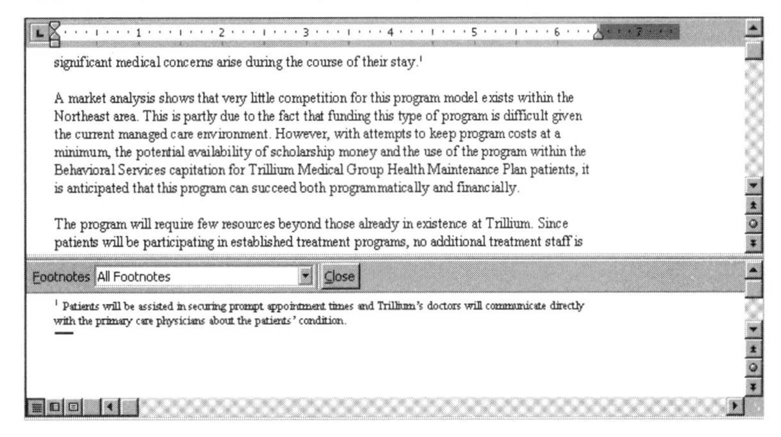

It's much easier to work with notes in Normal view because you can enter your note in the pane and click Close when you are finished. In Print Layout view, you must find your way back to where you inserted the reference mark. In either view, when you want to review your note, all you have to do is point to the reference mark.

The mouse pointer will change to a note, and a moment later, the note will appear.

The Trillium Extended Stay Treatment (TEST) is an innovative, cost-effective program designed
to provide the additional support that patients need when transitioning from residential treatment
to outpatient services. Today, all patients are discharged from residential treatment to return
home as they begin participation in day-treatment or intensi
the Extended Stay Treatment will continue to live at Trilliun
treatment. The primary difference between these patients an
residential program will be the amount of medical care that t
responsible for seeing their primary care physicians in the a
significant medical concerns arise during the course of their stay.

Patients will be assisted in securing prompt appointment times and Trillium's doctors will communicate directly with the primary care physicians about the patients' condition.

Just move the mouse pointer away and the note disappears.

Creating Footnotes and Endnotes

1. Switch to Normal view. Place the insertion point where you want the reference mark to appear.
2. Choose Insert ➢ Footnote.
3. Indicate whether you want automatic numbering or a custom mark. You can type in a custom mark or choose one from the Symbol font sets.
4. Enter your note in the Footnotes or Endnotes box that opens at the bottom of the screen. Click Close when you are finished entering your note.
5. To view the note, point to the reference mark in your document. The note will appear as a yellow ScreenTip.

Revising Footnotes and Endnotes

Now that you have footnotes and endnotes scattered through your text, you may need to edit one of the notes. Just double-click any reference mark in Normal view to open the Footnotes or Endnotes window at the bottom of the screen. All notes of the same type appear in the same window—just scroll to the one you want to edit, make your changes, and click Close.

Deleting Notes

When you want to delete a note entirely, click before or after the reference mark and press the Backspace or Delete key twice—the first time will select the reference mark and the second time will delete both the mark and the note. Subsequent footnotes will automatically be renumbered. Deleting the text inside the note pane or at the bottom or end of the document will not delete the reference mark.

Revising and Deleting Notes

1. To revise a note, double-click any reference mark to open the note pane (in Normal view). Make changes and click Close.
2. To delete a note, select and delete the reference mark in the body of the document.

Using Bookmarks

Objective W2000E.2.3

It's useful to be able to mark a location in the text that you want to return to later, especially when you are working with long documents. This could be a place where you need to insert some additional information before finishing the final draft. Or if your document will be read online, the location could refer to a piece of text you want readers to be able to jump to quickly. Whatever the reason, by inserting bookmarks you can easily move to specific text or objects in a document without having to scroll.

To insert a bookmark, select the text, graphic, table, or other object you want to mark. Choose Insert ➢ Bookmark. The Bookmark dialog box opens so you can name the bookmark. Names must be one word but you can use upper and lower case.

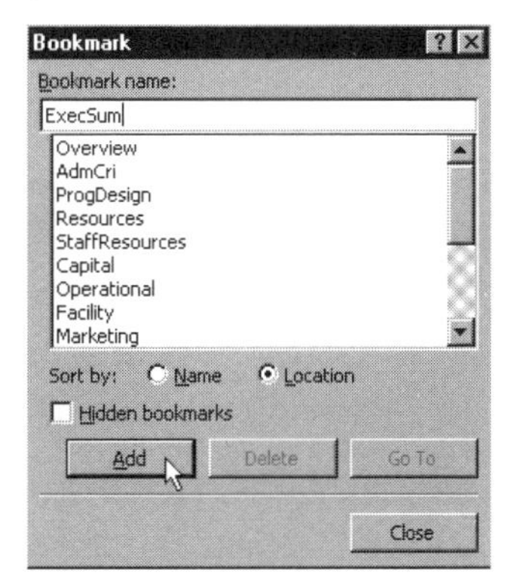

Click Add to add the bookmark and close the dialog box. (You can also delete bookmarks here by selecting the bookmark and clicking Delete.) To find bookmarks easily in the dialog box, sort them alphabetically or by their relative location in the document.

To see the bookmarks in your text, you can either go back to the Bookmark dialog box or choose Tools ➢ Options and click Show Bookmarks on the View page. The bookmarks will be displayed in brackets.

[EXECUTIVE SUMMARY]

The brackets are nonprinting characters, so if you're working a lot with bookmarks, it's handy just to leave them turned on.

When you want to go to a bookmark, choose Go To from the Browse Object menu at the bottom of the vertical scroll bar. Select Bookmarks from the Go To What list, and then click the drop-down arrow next to the Enter Bookmark Name text box to see a list of the bookmarks in your document.

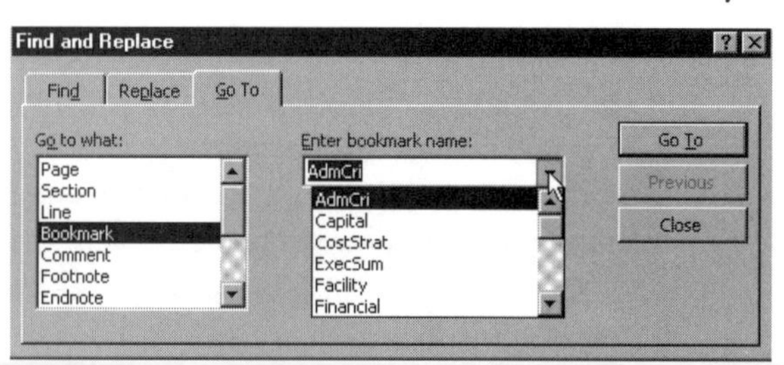

Select the bookmark you want to go to, click Go To and *voilà*, you are there. The Go To dialog box stays open until you close it, so to move to another bookmark, choose it from the list, and click Go To again.

When you close the Go To dialog box, you can use the Browse buttons to move through all your bookmarks.

Inserting, Viewing, and Deleting Bookmarks

1. Select the item you want to bookmark.
2. Choose Insert ➢ Bookmark and either accept the entire selected name or enter another name (names must be one word). Click Add.
3. View all the bookmarks in a document by choosing Tools ➢ Options ➢ View and clicking Show Bookmarks.
4. To jump to a bookmark, open the Browse Object menu, choose Go To, select Bookmark, and choose the bookmark from the Enter Bookmark Name drop-down list. Click Go To.
5. To delete a bookmark, select the bookmark and click Delete.

Creating Cross-References

Objectives W2000.4.8 and E.2.11

There are two reasons to use cross-references: to *refer to* text or objects elsewhere in a document, or to allow users to *move to* referenced text or objects. The traditional cross-reference is the first type and is used to keep references within a document up to date throughout editing. In the text, you might direct a reader to see a paragraph in Chapter 5: `See Employee Benefits for more information`. If the Employee Benefits section is later moved to Chapter 4, you can rest assured that they will still look in the right place, because the cross-reference will be updated when the Employee Benefits section is moved.

The second kind of cross-reference is a hyperlink, commonly used in Internet sites. A *hyperlink* is a connection between two areas of a document or two different documents; users move directly to the Employee Benefits section by clicking the hyperlink. On the Web, hyperlinks are underlined and use a different font color (if they don't stand out, no one knows to click them!). You'll have to format your hyperlinks' font colors and apply underlining. The cross-referencing feature does not do it automatically.

To insert a cross-reference, position your insertion point where you want the reference to appear and type your introductory text. ("For more information on Digital Mastering, see..."). Choose Insert ➢ Cross-Reference to open the Cross-Reference dialog box and identify the text being referred to:

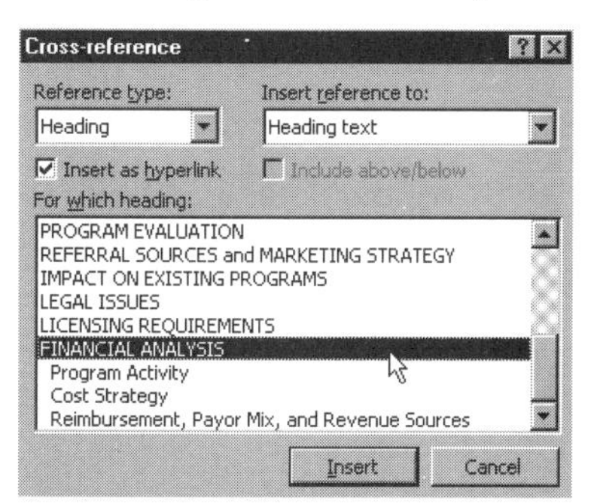

Cross-references can be linked to bookmarks, headings, numbered items, footnotes, endnotes, equations, figures, and tables—and you can choose how the reference will appear in the document. For example, if you want to refer to a heading, you can have the cross-reference indicate the actual text of the heading, the page number where the text is found, or just `see above` or `see below`.

If your document is intended for use online or on-screen, leave the Insert As Hyperlink check box checked. This creates the second, more active kind of cross-reference. When a user points to a hyperlinked cross-reference, the mouse pointer changes to a hand shape, and a ScreenTip appears telling the user where they will go if they click the hyperlink.

Clicking once whisks the user off to the new location and automatically opens the Web toolbar so they can click the Back button to return to their point of origin.

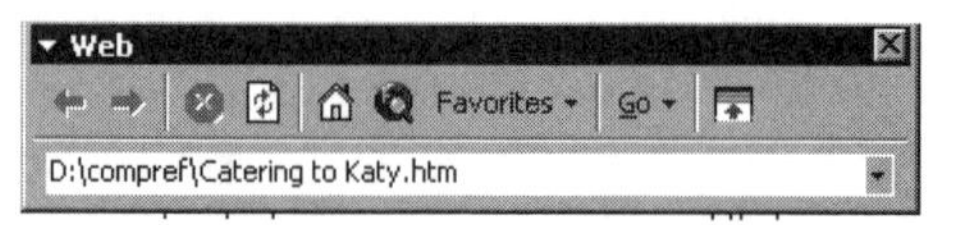

Do *not* use Insert As Hyperlink if you want a traditional, passive reference. If you do, every time you click near the cross-reference to edit surrounding text, you'll end up at the referenced text: an incredibly frustrating experience.

Creating Cross-References

1. Type the text to notify the reader of the cross-reference (**See...**).
2. Choose Insert ➢ Cross-Reference to open the Cross-Reference dialog box.
3. Select the Reference Type: for example, Bookmark.
4. Choose what the reference will refer to (page number, text, numbered item, and so on).
5. Identify the specific reference from the For Which list.
6. If you want the cross-reference to work as a hyperlink, make sure the Insert As Hyperlink box is checked.
7. Click Insert and type a close quote (") after the field that was inserted.

Be careful to not delete an item that is referenced or the link will be broken. If the cross-reference is a hyperlink, Word will take your readers to another location that contains similar text. Users clicking the See Employee Benefits hyperlink could find themselves, for example, on the Termination of Employment page—probably not the message you want to convey.

Indexing for Easy Reference

Objective W2000E.2.12

You can make lengthy documents more user-friendly by creating an index of key words and phrases. Although marking index text is a manual process, Word 2000 automates the creation of the index and will update it on request. When you're ready to mark your first entry, select the text you want to include in the index and press Alt+Shift+X to open the Mark Index Entry dialog box.

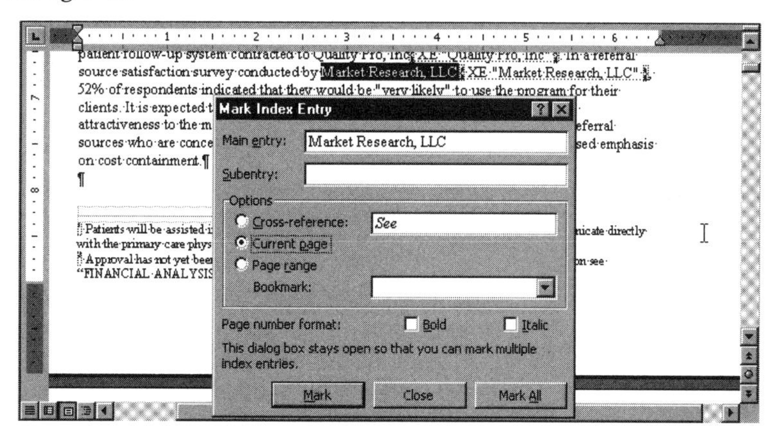

You can accept the selected text as the index entry or edit it any way you prefer. You can also add two subentries. Type the first subentry in the Subentry box, type a colon, and enter the second subentry. Click Mark to mark this specific selection, or Mark All to mark every occurrence of the text string for indexing. The Mark Index Entry dialog box will stay open while you return to your document and select the next text you want to appear in the index. When you click back in the dialog box, the selected text will appear in the Mark Index Entry text box.

If you want this entry to refer to another entry, click Cross-Reference and after the word See, type the name of the other entry, or type the word *also* and the name of the other entry. Because the cross-reference will only occur once in the index, you can Mark but not Mark All cross-references. To include a range of pages in the Index (such as `Formatting Text, 13-17`), you must first select the range and give it a bookmark name. You can then choose Page Range in the Mark Index Entry dialog box and select the name of the bookmark.

Close the Mark Index Entry dialog box when you're through, then move to the last page of your document. Insert a hard page break, then enter a heading for the index. Use a heading style if you want the index heading included in your table of contents later. Press Enter a couple of times to leave some space after the heading, and choose Insert ➢ Index and Tables. The Index and Tables dialog box will open and you can choose how you'd like your index formatted, previewing your choices in the Print Preview pane.

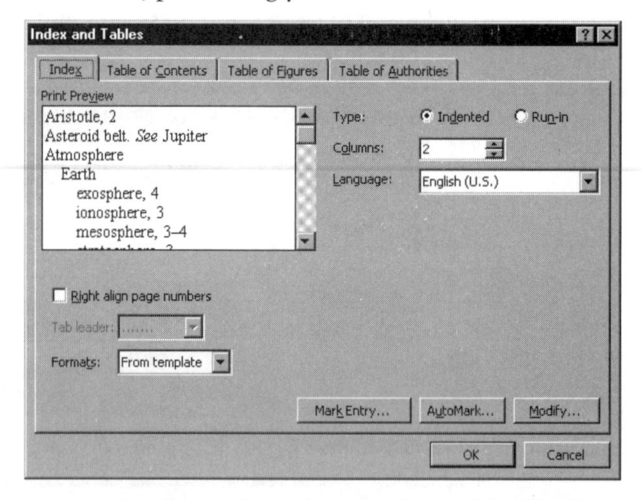

When you've made all your formatting choices, click OK. Your index will be generated automatically at the insertion point.

It's a good idea to go through each entry in the index and make sure it says what you want it to say and that the references are accurate. If you find any errors, you can fix them in the index or in the Index Entry (XE) fields inserted in the document, but any changes made to the index itself will be lost if you regenerate the index. After you make your changes to the XE fields, go to Insert ➢ Index and Tables again to regenerate the index. Word will select the existing index and ask you if you want to replace it.

Creating an Index

1. Select the first text you want to include in the index.
2. Press Alt+Shift+X to open the Mark Index Text dialog box.
3. Type or edit the text in the Main Entry box.
4. Enter subentries in the Subentry box, placing a colon between second- and third-level entries.
5. Choose Mark or Mark All to mark all occurrences of the text in the document.
6. To make additional entries, select the text and click the Mark Index Entry dialog box.
7. To include a cross-reference, choose Cross-Reference from the dialog box and type in the cross-reference text (**See [name of entry]**); choose Mark.
8. To include a range of pages, create a bookmark from the beginning to the end of the range, choose Range of Pages from the Mark Index Entry dialog box, and select the name of the bookmark you created.
9. To generate the index, move to a blank page, insert and format any heading text you want, choose Insert ➢ Index and Tables, and choose the desired formatting options. Click OK to create the index.
10. To regenerate the index, choose Insert ➢ Index and Tables and click OK again or click the index and press the F9 key.

Generating a Table of Contents

Objective W2000E.2.10

After creating an index, a table of contents (TOC) is a breeze: that is, of course, if you used heading styles when you created your document. If you didn't, the breeze just turned into gale-force winds—you need to go back through your document and apply styles to any text you want included in your table of contents.

To create the table of contents, move to the beginning of your document and insert a page break. Move to the blank page and choose Insert ➢ Index and Tables. Click the Table of Contents tab and choose from a number of built-in formats for your TOC.

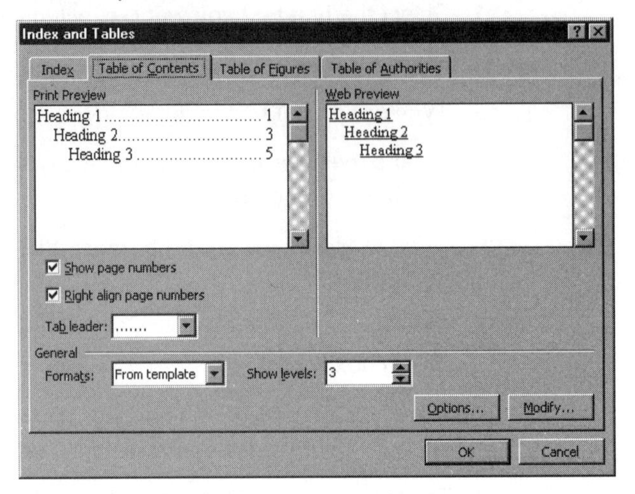

Choose a format and click OK. Add a heading, and your TOC should look something like the one in Figure 4.15.

FIGURE 4.15
Table of Contents

Table of Contents

Modifying a TOC

You can edit directly in the TOC itself. When you click the TOC, it looks like the whole thing is selected, but you can still select text within it and make changes. If you decide that you want fewer heading levels to appear in your TOC, choose Insert ➢ Index and Tables ➢ Table of Contents and decrease the number of heading levels. You can also change the tab leader by selecting a different one from the Tab Leader list. When you click OK, the TOC will regenerate with the requested number of levels. In some documents, you may even want two TOCs—one with all heading levels and one with only the first-level headings.

Creating a Table of Contents

1. Apply heading styles to all the headings you want included in the TOC.
2. Create and move to a blank page at the beginning of the document.
3. Choose Insert ➢ Index and Tables. Click the Table of Contents tab.
4. Choose the format you want for your TOC, the number of heading levels, and the tab leader.
5. Click OK to generate the TOC.
6. Click the TOC and edit or reformat it directly or make changes to the headings in your document; regenerate the TOC by repeating steps 3–5, or by clicking it and pressing F9.

Hands On: Objectives W2000E.2.3, E.2.8, E.2.10, E.2.11, and E.2.12

1. Open an existing document or create a new document that has at least three headings and related paragraphs (be sure to apply Styles to the headings):
   a) Switch to Normal view and add at least two footnotes and two endnotes to the document.
   b) Switch to Print Layout view and view the footnotes and endnotes at the bottom of the page.
   c) Point to one of the footnotes and read the note in the ScreenTip above the footnote marker.
   d) Delete the first footnote and the first endnote.

2. Using the same document you used in the first exercise:
   a) Create a bookmark to the first paragraph.
   b) Create a cross-reference to that bookmark from some later text.
   c) Create a second cross-reference to the second heading.
   d) Test both cross-references.
   e) Use Go To to move to the bookmark you created.
3. Using the same document:
   a) Go through the document and mark index entries for key terms, names, and other important words.
   b) Move to the end of the document, insert a page break, and generate the index.
4. Again in the same document:
   a) Move to the top of the document and insert a blank page for a table of contents.
   b) Generate the table of contents.
   c) Make changes to one or more of your headings and regenerate the TOC.

Working Together on Documents

If you work in a networked office where people collaborate on written projects, Word 2000 offers a number of useful workgroup features. You can track document changes, save multiple versions within a document, and even edit a document simultaneously with your colleagues. This amazing group of features could actually put an end to interoffice squabbling over which *is* the latest version and who had it last.

Creating Master Documents

Objective W2000E.2.9

As a policy manual, personnel handbook, or similar document gets longer, it uses more resources to open, save, or print. It takes forever to scroll down a couple of pages and editing becomes a nightmare. With a little foresight, you can avoid this dilemma by starting with an outline and then dividing the document into various subdocuments. You and others in your workgroup can then work with subdocuments as autonomous entities. However, at any point, you can work with the entire master document, so you can have continuous page numbering, add headers and footers, create a table of contents, attach an index, and insert cross-references—all the stuff that contributes to another kind of nightmare if you try to do it with unrelated documents.

What if you're already 10 chapters into an unruly document? Word 2000 can combine separate documents into one *master document* and divide one long document into several *subdocuments*. So there's no excuse for working with a document that's out of control—the remedy is right at your fingertips.

Creating a New Master Document

To create a new master document from scratch, open a new document, and then click the Outline View button. Word displays the Master Document toolbar to the right of the Outlining toolbar. Create an outline just as you normally would (see Chapter 3) using the same heading level for each section you want subdivided into its own document.

When you have finished creating the outline, select the headings and text you want to split into subdocuments. Click the Create Subdocument button; Word will create individual documents using the first part of the heading text for the document name. The master document will show the subdocuments in a distinct box with a small file document in the upper-left corner.

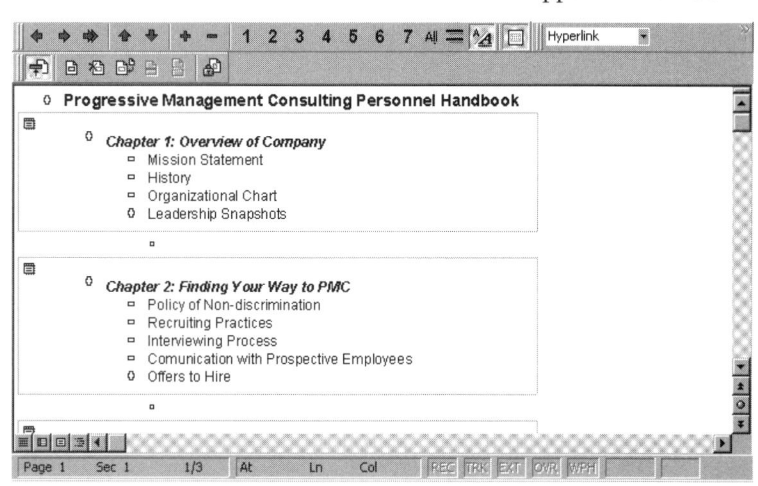

You can double-click any of the document icons to open a subdocument. Any changes you make in the subdocument are reflected in the master document when you save the subdocument.

The primary purpose of creating a master document is to be able to work with discrete sections of the document. It makes sense, then, to collapse the master document so that just the document names are visible. Clicking the Collapse Subdocuments button on the Master Document toolbar will collapse the document, as shown in Figure 4.16. If you want to see all the text in the entire document, click the same button again (it's now the Expand Subdocuments button).

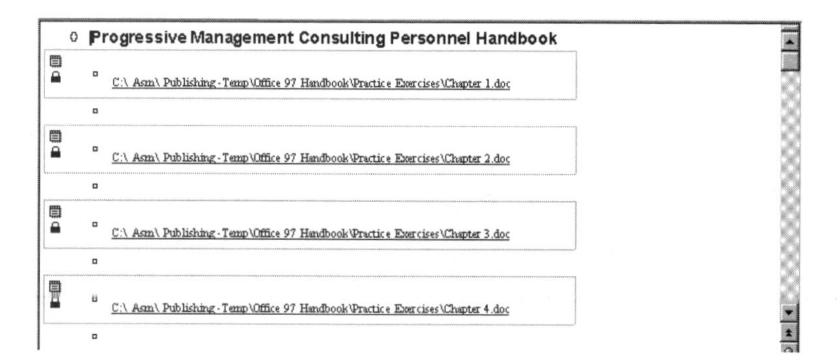

FIGURE 4.16
A Collapsed Master Document

When the master document is collapsed, point to any subdocument and click to open it. When you want to return to the master document, just close and save the changes you made to the subdocument. You'll notice that the link to the subdocument changes color to show that you have already edited that document.

Subdocuments can only be opened for editing by one person at a time—if another person tries to open the same subdocument, they can only open a read-only copy. You can also lock people out from making changes to the master document or any subdocument by expanding the master document, selecting the document or documents you want to lock, and clicking the Lock Document button on the Master Document toolbar. This prevents anyone from making changes after a document is completed.

Creating a Master Document

1. Create a new document and click the Outline View button.
2. Enter the outline for the document, being careful to position each section at the same heading level.
3. Select a heading and text, and then click Create Subdocument from the Master Document toolbar.
4. Double-click any document icon in the top corner of the subdocument to open a subdocument.
5. Click the Collapse Subdocuments button to view only the subdocument names.
6. Select a document and click the Lock Document button to prevent other users from making changes to a subdocument.
7. Save the Master Document.

When the master document is expanded, you can work with it as if it were one document by just switching to Normal or Print Layout view. You can apply page numbering, headers and footers, a table of contents, an index, and references and adjust styles just as you would in a normal document. Just make sure you're in the master document before making any of these changes, or you can easily have a real mess on your hands.

Converting Existing Documents and Making Changes

For a document to be converted to a master document, you must apply heading styles so you can work with it in Outline view. After you have applied heading styles, you can switch to Master Document view and follow the same steps you would to create a new master document. If you have several documents that you want to combine into one master document, you need to first create a new master document with a couple of (temporary, if need be) subdocuments.

After you create the master document, move the insertion point to where you want to insert an existing document and click the Insert Subdocument button on the Master Document toolbar. You'll be taken to the Insert Subdocument dialog box where you can select the document you want to insert.

You can merge two subdocuments into one, split one subdocument into two, delete a subdocument, or convert a subdocument into master document text. Table 4.1 shows you how to accomplish these tasks.

TABLE 4.1: Converting Subdocuments

Task	Action	Click
Merge two subdocuments	Select the two subdocuments	
Split one subdocument	Position insertion point at split point	
Delete a subdocument	Select the subdocument	Press the **Delete** key
Convert a subdocument to master document text	Select the subdocument	

Creating Master Documents from Existing Documents

1. Open the existing document and apply heading styles to the major sections of the document.
2. Click the Outline View button, and click the Create Subdocument button.
3. To insert another document, position the insertion point where you want the document inserted and click the Insert Subdocument button.
4. Save the master document.

Saving Multiple Versions of a Document

Objective W2000E.7.3

Whether you're working with a master document or an isolated document, you can save multiple versions of a document within the document itself and switch back and forth between versions.

To save a version, choose File ➢ Save As, and in the Save As dialog box, click the Tools button. Click Save Versions to open the Save Version dialog box. There you can enter comments describing this version for later reference.

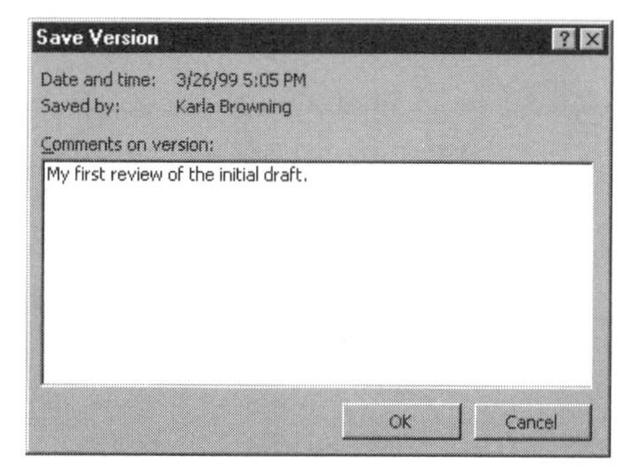

To view or switch between saved versions, choose File ➢ Versions. This dialog box allows you to open a different version, to delete a version that is no longer relevant, and to view comments about a version.

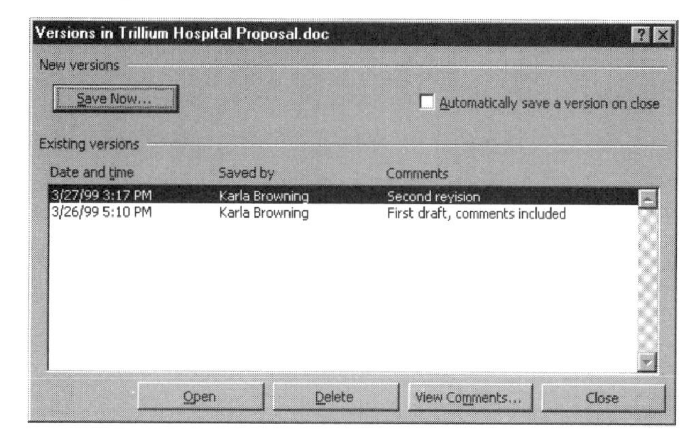

You can enable the Automatically Save a Version on Close check box to assure that a version is preserved every time the document is edited. This option is particularly helpful when the document will be edited by several people consecutively. Although the most recently saved version will open by default, you can always go back to a previous version.

Saving Versions of a Document

1. Click the Save Versions button in the Save As dialog box.
2. Enter Comments about the version you are saving. Click OK.
3. Choose File ➢ Versions to view a list of saved versions, to open or delete versions, to view comments, or to create an automatic version each time the document is closed.

Word 2000 only saves the changes in each version, but this can still result in slowing down your document's performance if there are several versions of a long document that contain lots of editing. If your document becomes too large, open the Versions dialog box and delete versions that you no longer need.

Tracking Changes to a Document

Objective W2000E.7.4

Although saving each version of a document is helpful, it's still difficult to identify where all the changes were made. Word 2000 will track each change to a document and allow you to accept or reject individual revisions or all revisions in one fell swoop. The easiest way to begin tracking changes is to right-click the dimmed option TRK on the status bar.

You can track changes in three ways:

- In the background with no visible queues
- On the screen
- In the printed document

To indicate which option you want, choose Highlight Changes from the pop-up menu. Choose Track Changes While Editing to turn on tracking. Then indicate whether you want the changes visible on the screen or in the printed document.

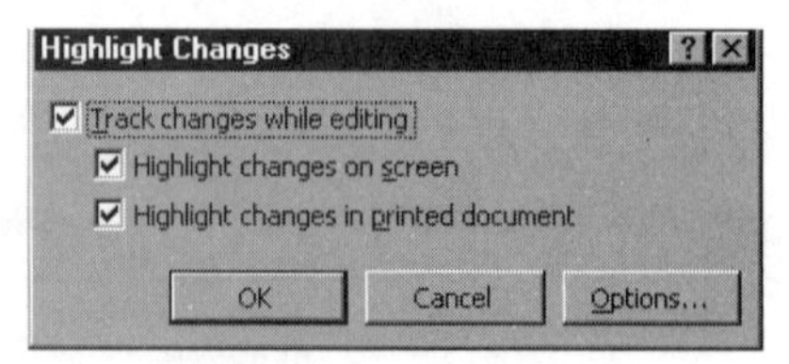

Clear both check boxes if you don't want the changes to be visible in either place. Click OK to close the dialog box and initiate tracking. You'll notice that TRK on the status bar is now enabled. If you choose to have changes visible on the screen, your documents will include a trail of every change. Text you insert will be a different color and will be underlined. Text you delete will be struck through. A vertical line in the margin will indicate lines where text has been changed. Figure 4.17 shows a document that has been edited with Highlight Changes on the Screen turned on.

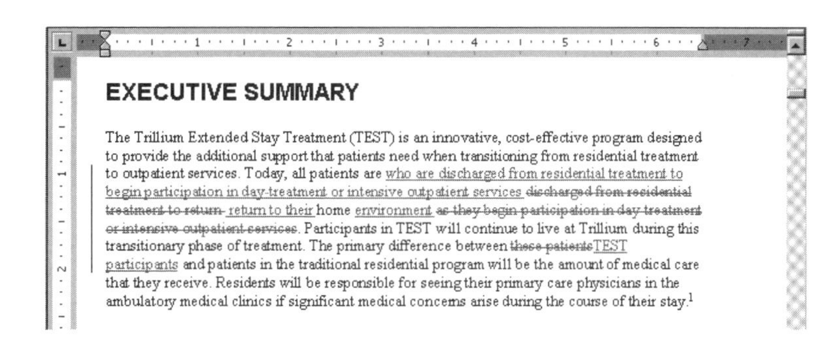

FIGURE 4.17 Tracking changes in a document

As other people open the document, changes they make will appear in different colors (as many 16 authors can work on one document before colors repeat). If you would prefer that all inserted text appear in one color and all deleted text in another, you can set the colors yourself by choosing Options from the pop-up menu or the Highlight Changes dialog box. The Track Changes dialog box lets you set color options for Inserted Text, Deleted Text, Changed Formatting, and Changed Lines.

Tracking Changes to a Document

1. Right-click TRK on the status bar (or choose Tools ➢ Track Changes) and choose Highlight Changes.
2. Click the Track Changes While Editing check box and choose whether to highlight changes on-screen and/or highlight changes in the printed document.
3. Click Options if you want to set a specific color for each type of revision—inserting, deleting, formatting, and borders.
4. When Tracking Changes is turned on, the status bar indicator is black. Double-click it to turn tracking off; double-click it again to turn tracking back on.

Accepting or Rejecting Changes

After a document has been edited, you can accept or reject changes. Right-click the status bar TRK indicator and choose Accept or Reject Changes. The Accept or Reject Changes dialog box allows you to scroll through each individual change and accept or reject them as a group or individually.

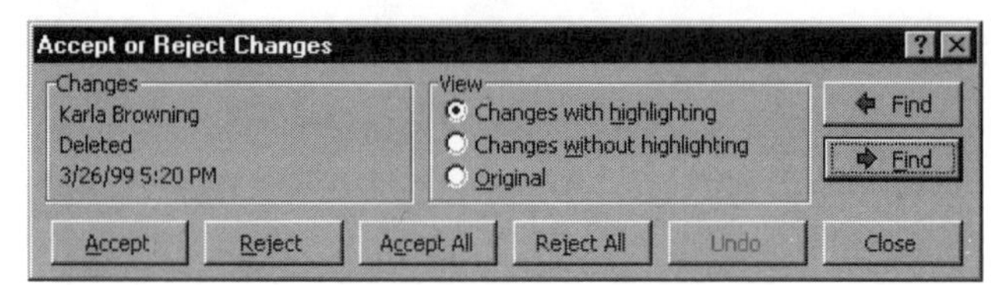

If you want to accept or reject all the changes without reviewing them, click the Accept All or Reject All button. Word will ask if you are certain—click Yes to confirm your choice.

If, on the other hand, you want to review each individual revision, click Find to move through the document. Revisions will be selected one at a time, and you can choose to accept or reject each one. Word starts reviewing where the insertion point is currently located, so if you reach the end of the document without having gone through all the changes, Word will ask if you want to go to the beginning to catch the rest of them. It will also tell you when you have reviewed all the revisions. Click OK and then click Close to close the Accept or Reject dialog box. If you don't want any more marked revisions, make sure you turn off tracking.

Accepting or Rejecting Changes

1. Right-click the status bar Tracking indicator (or choose Tools ➢ Track Changes) and choose Accept or Reject Changes.
2. Click Accept All or Reject All if you don't want to review individual changes.
3. Click Find to review changes one by one. Word will select the change—click the Accept or Reject button and click Find again to move on to the next change.
4. Click Undo to reverse an accept or reject decision that you made.
5. Click Close to exit the Accept and Reject dialog box. Remember to turn off tracking if you do not want further changes tracked.

Inserting Comments

Objective W2000E.7.1

When you're creating or editing a document with others, it's often valuable to be able to make comments that aren't part of the printed document but can be viewed on-screen. Word's Comments feature fits the bill. You can insert comments, view comments from one or all reviewers, and print the comments.

To insert a comment, move the insertion point to where you want to position the comment and choose Insert ➢ Comment. The word immediately preceding the insertion point is highlighted, and your initials and a comment number appear in the text. A comment box then opens at the bottom of the screen.

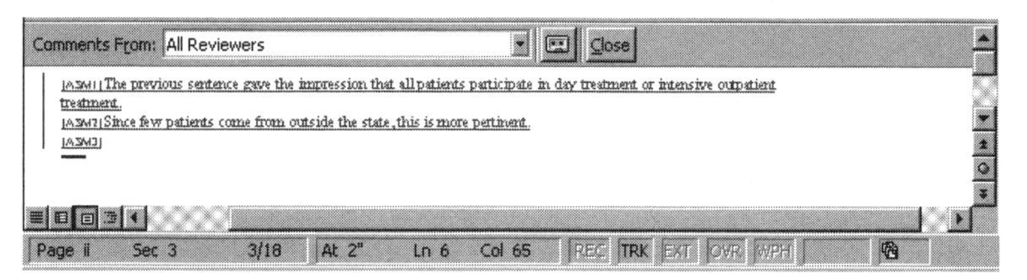

Enter your comment and click Close. To view the comment, just hover over the highlighted word for a second—the insertion point will change to an I-beam with a note attached, and a second later the comment will appear above the text.

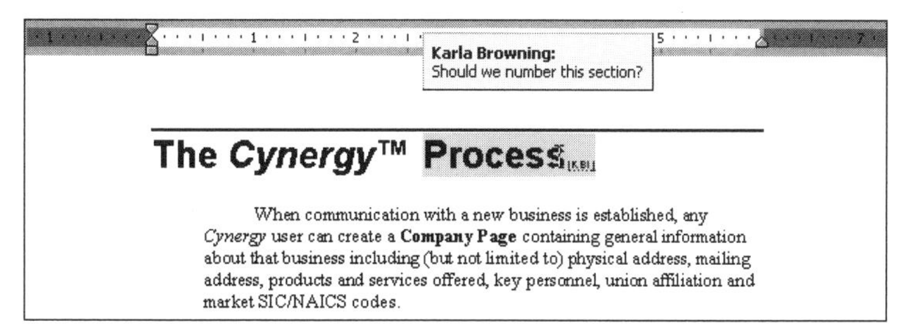

If you're going to be working a lot with comments, turn on the Reviewing toolbar, which includes buttons to insert, edit, and delete a comment and to move to previous and next comments.

Using Comments

1. Click where you want the comment to be inserted and choose Insert ➢ Comment.
2. Type your comment in the Comment box and click Close when you are finished.
3. Point to the comment to view it.
4. Turn on the Reviewing toolbar (choose View ➢ Toolbars ➢ Reviewing) to move between, edit, or delete comments.
5. To print the comments, choose File ➢ Print and choose Comments from the Print What drop-down list.

Protecting Documents

Objective W2000E.7.2

Although you may not think that there is much in your documents that anybody else would want, the sad truth is that your documents could become victims of corporate espionage or of unscrupulous colleagues out to pass your work off as their own. Add to that the risk that some well-meaning but misguided individual might revise one of your documents without your consent, and it's clear that it never hurts to be too careful.

Word 2000 provides several ways to protect your documents. You can:

- Restrict the access of anyone who doesn't have the password to open the document
- Require users to open read-only copies
- Recommend that users open the document as read-only so that, if they make changes, they must save it using a different name
- Prevent changes to a document you route for review, except for comments or tracked changes

To apply document protection, open the Save As dialog box. Click the Tools button and from the drop-down list choose General Options to open the Save dialog box. You can also access this page by choosing Tools ➢ Options and clicking the Save tab.

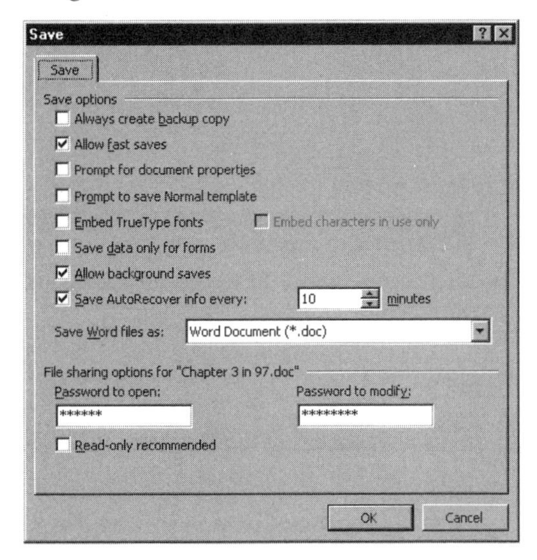

When you enable the Password to Open control, users will be prompted to input the password. Without the password, they will not be able to open the document.

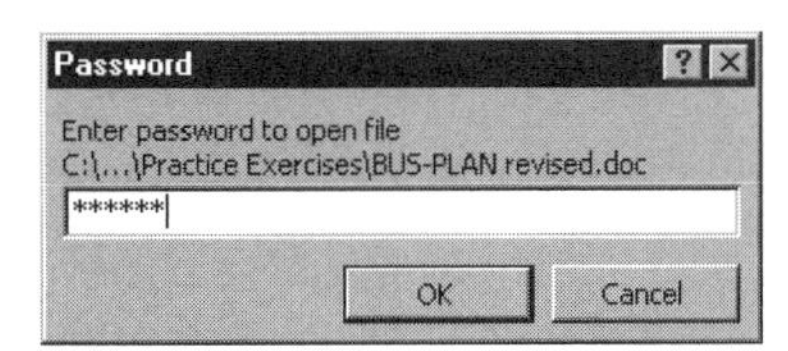

If they know the password, the document will open, and they can modify it and save the changes. If they do not know the password, the document will not open and they are told why.

If you want users to be able to view but not change the original document, enter a Password to Modify. Users who don't know the password can only open the document as read-only and must save any changes under a different name. Click the Read-Only Recommended check box if you want to remind yourself or others that this document should not be modified and that it would be preferable to open it as read-only.

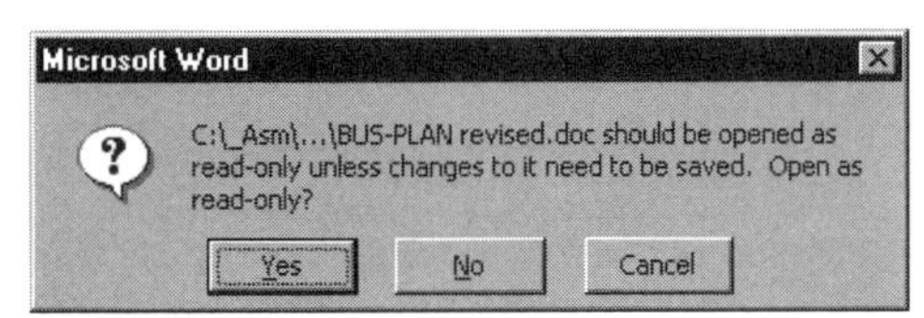

Whichever password option you choose, the password will not be visible on the screen as you type—Word will ask you to reenter the password for verification. Word then gives you a stern warning that password-protected documents cannot be opened if you forget the password. Take this warning seriously. If you forget the password for a document, it's gone for good. To change or delete a password, open the document and reenter or delete the password from the Save dialog box.

Protecting Documents with Passwords

1. In the Save As dialog box, click the Tools button and choose General Options to open the Save dialog box, or choose Tools ➢ Options and click the Save tab.
2. Enter a Password to Open if you want users to be unable to open the document without a password. Click OK and reenter the password to confirm it. Click OK again and save the document.
3. Enter a Password to Modify if you want to allow all users to open the document as read-only but require a password to modify the original document. Click OK and reenter the password to confirm it. Click OK again and save the document.
4. Click the Read-Only Recommended check box if you want to suggest to users that they open the document as read-only to prevent accidental changes to an original document. Click OK and save the document.
5. To change or delete a password, open the document with the password, go to the Save dialog box, and enter a new password or delete the existing one.

Sending a Document via E-mail

Objective W2000.4.10

Office 2000 makes sending a Word document via e-mail as easy as saving a document to a hard drive. You have three options for sending an e-mail message from Word. You can:

- Use Word as your Microsoft Outlook e-mail editor by choosing New ➢ Mail Message from Word's New menu

- Send a Word document from Word as the body of an e-mail message
- Send a document as an attachment by opening the document and choosing File ➢ Send To ➢ Mail Recipient as Attachment

With the first two options, an e-mail header opens at the top of the Word document. In this header, you can fill in To, CC, and Subject boxes, and set message options including importance, voting, tracking, and delivery options. When you are ready to send the message, click the Send or Send a Copy buttons. When you choose the attachment option, an e-mail message form opens with an icon for the document. Complete the e-mail message form and click Send to send the message.

To use Word's e-mail options, you must have an e-mail service such as Outlook, Outlook Express, or Microsoft Exchange set up on your computer and have either a network connection or an Internet service provider.

Hands On: *Objective W2000.4.10*

1. Create a master document using a newly created outline for a project you are working on. Be sure to apply the Heading style to each major topic before creating the subdocuments.
    a) Save the master document and collapse it.
    b) Edit one of the subdocuments, close, and save it. Expand the master document and view the edited document.
    c) Insert a new document into the master document. In the master document, edit and save changes to the inserted document.
    d) Select and delete a subdocument from the master document.
    e) Save and close the master document and any open subdocuments.
2. Open an existing document:
    a) Turn on Track Changes. Make the changes visible on the screen.
    b) Make changes to the document, inserting and deleting text. Save a version of the document. Make additional changes to the document and save another version.

c) Insert a comment and highlight some important text.

d) Choose File ➤ Properties and input Document Summary information describing the document.

e) Protect the document for Tracked Changes or password protect it as Read Only then save another version of the document. Turn on Automatically Save Version on Close.

f) If you're on a network and have names in an address book, prepare a Routing Slip for the document. If possible, send the document to a colleague and ask him or her to make changes and send the document back to you.

g) Open the Versions dialog box and view the Existing Versions. Close the Versions dialog box. Using Accept or Reject Changes, review each change made to the document and accept or reject each as you deem appropriate. Turn off Track Changes and save the final version.

CHAPTER 5

Editing Excel Worksheets

Just as Word is designed to help you work with text, Excel shines when it's working with numbers and data. In this chapter, you'll learn how to enter and edit formulas, to apply worksheet layout and apply other formatting and then how to print your worksheets

Throughout this chapter, we use Excel practice worksheets to illustrate concepts. If you would like to use the practice worksheets, you can create them based on the illustrations in the text, or you can download them from the Sybex Web site: `www.sybex.com`.

Using the Excel 2000 Interface

In Chapter 1, we introduced you to the Office application window. The Excel application window includes the standard title bar and command bars. Below the command bars is a strip that contains the *name box* and the *formula bar*. The Excel status bar displays information about current selections, commands, or operations. The right end of the status bar displays NUM if the keyboard's Num Lock is on.

Workbooks and Worksheets

Objective XL20005.5

In Excel, your work area is known as the *worksheet window*. Here you're surrounded by the tools you need to get the job done: *scroll bars* to move the display, a status bar to keep you informed of an operation's progress, and the *command bars* at the top of the screen to access all the program's features.

FIGURE 5.1
Excel application window

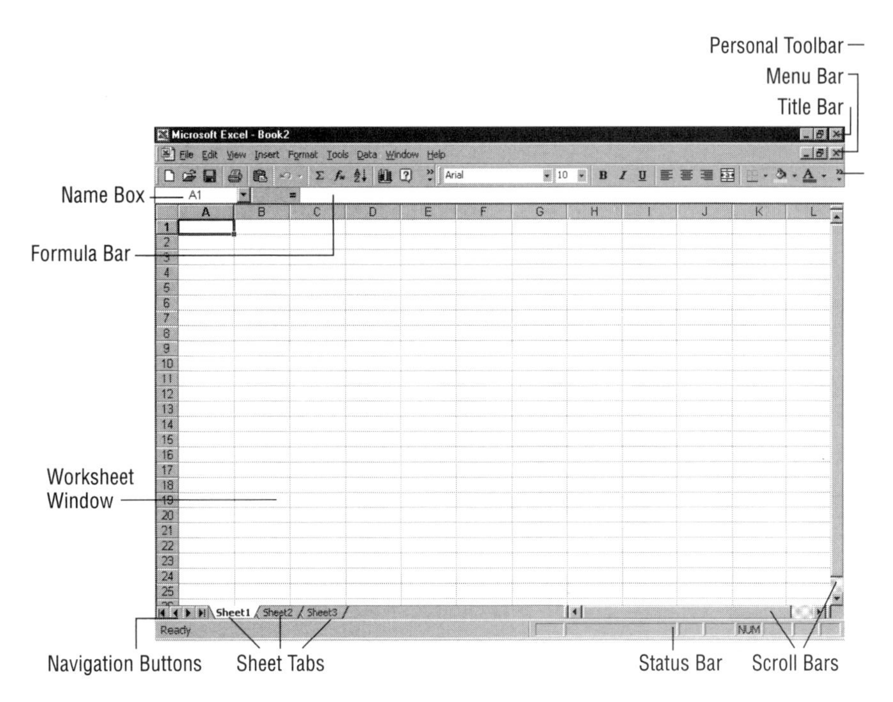

When you launch Excel, the Excel application window opens with a new Excel *workbook*. A workbook is a multi-page Excel document. Each page in the workbook is called a *worksheet*, and the active worksheet is displayed in the document window. At the left end of the horizontal scroll bar are *sheet tabs* and *navigation buttons*. Use the sheet tabs to move to another worksheet and the navigation buttons to scroll the sheet tabs.

Each worksheet is divided into columns, rows, and cells, separated by *gridlines*, as shown in the Payroll worksheet in Figure 5.2. *Columns* are vertical divisions. The first column is column A, and the letter A appears in the *column heading*. The horizontal *rows* are numbered. Each worksheet has 256 columns (A through IV) and 65,536 rows—plenty of room to enter all your numbers!

A *cell* is the intersection of a row and a column. Each cell has a unique address composed of the cell's column and row. For example, the cell in the upper left corner of the worksheet, with the text *Second Hand News* (see Figure 5.2), is cell A1. Even though some of the text appears to run over into cell B1 in the next column, it is really entered in cell A1. The *active cell*, C2 in Figure 5.2, has a box around it called the *cell pointer*, and the headings in the active cell's column (C) and row (2) are outdented or "lit up." When you enter data, it is always placed in the active cell.

FIGURE 5.2

Payroll worksheet

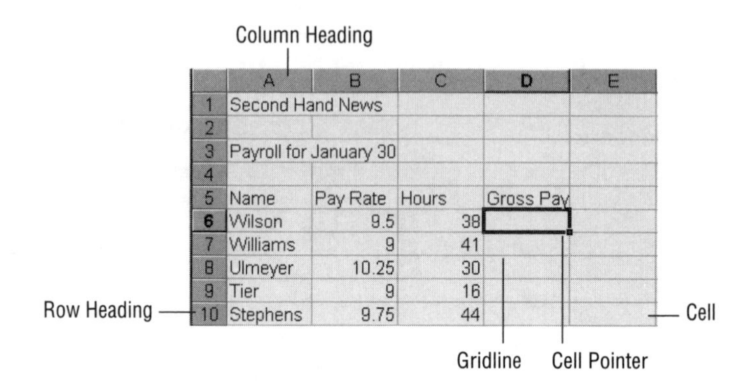

Moving the Cell Pointer

To move the pointer one cell to the left, right, up, or down, use the keyboard arrow keys. Table 5.1 shows other frequently used keyboard commands.

TABLE 5.1: Keystrokes to Move the Cell Pointer

Key(s)	To Move
PgDn	Down one screen
PgUp	Up one screen
Home	To column A in the current row
Ctrl+Home	To cell A1

To activate a cell with the mouse, simply click the cell. If you want to see other areas of the worksheet, use the scroll bars. To scroll up or down one row, click the up or down arrow at the ends of the vertical scroll bar. Use the arrows at either end of the horizontal scroll bar to scroll one column to the left or right. To move up, down, left, or right one window, click the empty space above, below, or to the left or right of the scroll bar's scroll box:

Click here to move over one window.

Column: A

Click here to scroll.

Drag the scroll box to scroll more than a couple of rows or columns. As you drag, a *ScrollTip* shows the location you are scrolling over. Note that scrolling doesn't change the active cell—scrolling lets you view other parts of the worksheet, but the active cell is wherever you left the cell pointer. To scroll large distances, hold the Shift key while dragging the scroll box, and Excel will scroll farther for each movement of the mouse.

Entering and Editing Cell Entries

Objective XL20001.3

You can enter three types of data in a worksheet: numbers, formulas, and text. *Numbers* are values you may want to use in calculations, including dates. Dates are often used in calculations to determine, for example, how many days to charge for an overdue video or how many months of interest you have earned on a deposit. *Formulas* are calculations. *Text* is any entry that isn't a number or a formula. To enter data in a cell, first activate the cell, and then begin typing the data. As soon as you begin entering characters from the keyboard, three things happen: an insertion point appears in the cell, the text you are entering appears in the cell and the formula bar, and the formula bar buttons are activated.

If you make a mistake while you are entering data, click the *Cancel button* (the red X) to discard the entry you were making and turn off the formula bar buttons. You can also cancel an entry by pressing the Esc key on the keyboard. Clicking the *Enter button* (the green checkmark) finishes the entry and turns off the formula bar buttons. Pressing the Enter key on the keyboard is the same as clicking the Enter button, except the Enter key also moves the cell pointer down one cell.

Excel has an *AutoComplete* feature that keeps track of text entered in a column and can complete other entries in the same column. For example, if you have already typed `Jones` in cell A1 and then enter the letter `J` in A2, Excel will automatically fill in `ones` to make `Jones`. If `Jones` is the correct text, simply finish the entry by pressing Enter, moving to another cell, or clicking the Enter button. If it is not correct, just continue entering the correct text to overwrite the AutoComplete entry. AutoComplete resets each time you leave a blank cell in a column.

Selecting Cells

In Excel, at least one cell is always selected: the active cell. A group of cells is called a *range*. To select a range, move to the first cell in the range (check to be sure the mouse pointer is the large cross used for selecting), hold down the mouse button, and drag to the last cell you want to select before releasing the mouse button. To unselect cells, click anywhere in the document.

To select all the cells in a column or row, click on the column heading or row heading. To select multiple columns or rows, select one heading then drag to select the others. When you point to row, or column headers, to select them, be sure that your mouse pointer looks like the fat selection cross as you do this, not a thinner black cross. To select the entire worksheet, click the Select All button, the gray rectangle at the upper left corner of the worksheet above the row headings.

If the cells, columns, or rows you want to select are noncontiguous (not next to each other), select one of the ranges you want to select, and then hold down the Ctrl key while selecting the others.

Correcting Mistakes

You'll find Excel 2000 to be very forgiving. You are able to correct mistakes you just made or mistakes you made several steps ago. When you're working with numbers and formulas, however, it's a good idea to be very cognizant of your actions so you can undo mistakes right away before you've added components that make use of bad data.

Undo and Redo

Objective XL2000.1.1

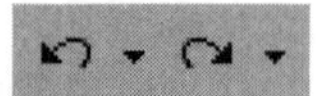

The Undo button on the Standard toolbar lets you reverse an action or a whole series of actions you have taken. The Undo button will dim when you have reached the last action you can undo.

To reverse multiple actions in one step, click the drop-down arrow next to the Undo button and scroll through the history. If you change your mind again, clicking the Redo button reverses the last undo.

Revising Text and Numbers

Objective XL2000.1.4

If you can't undo your mistake, there are two ways you can change an entry in a cell. If you activate the cell and type the new entry, the old entry will be replaced. This is the easiest way to change a number (for example, 15 to 17) or to replace text with a short word.

If the original entry is long and requires only minor adjustment, you might prefer to edit it. To do so, click the cell and edit the entry in the formula bar, or double-click the cell to open it and edit directly in the cell. Use the mouse or the keyboard to edit the entry. When you are finished, you must press Enter or click the Enter button to complete the entry—you can't simply move to a new cell.

Another way to switch into edit mode is to click the cell you want to edit and press the F2 key.

Clearing a Cell

Objective XL2000.1.2

To delete the contents of a cell completely, first activate the cell. Then press the Delete key on the keyboard, or right-click and choose Clear Contents from the shortcut menu.

Don't choose Delete from the Edit menu to clear a cell you've selected—that deletes the entire cell, not just the entry in the cell.

Working with Numbers and Formulas

You already know how to type numbers into a worksheet. However, certain numbers in a spreadsheet must be calculated, and you won't just type those in. You use a *formula* every time you want to perform a calculation in Excel, so you'll appreciate some of the formula features built into Excel 2000. Formulas are what make a spreadsheet a spreadsheet: they are the driving force behind the magic of Excel.

Excel uses standard computer operator symbols for mathematical and logical operators, as shown in Table 5.2.

TABLE 5.2: Mathematical and Logical Operators

Operation	Operator symbol
Addition	+
Subtraction	-
Multiplication	*
Division	/
Exponentiation (to the power of)	^
Precedence (do this operation first)	enclose in ( )
Equal to	=
Not equal to	< >
Greater than	>
Less than	<

Creating Formulas

Objective XL2000.6.2

You can create formulas in a number of ways, but some are more efficient than others. We'll begin with simple formulas that have one math operation. For example, the *Second Hand News* Payroll worksheet shown here needs a formula to multiply Wilson's pay rate by the hours worked in order to calculate his gross pay. You can approach this formula in two different ways. The first method is the highly reliable point-and-click method for which Excel is known.

Payroll for January 30

Name	Pay Rate	Hours	Gross Pay
Wilson	$ 9.50	38	$ 361.00
Williams	$ 9.00	41	$ 369.00
Ulmeyer	$ 10.25	30	$ 307.50
Tier	$ 9.00	16	$ 144.00
Stephens	$ 9.75	44	$ 429.00

Steps: Entering a Point-and-Click Formula

1. Activate the cell where you want the result to appear.
2. Type =.
3. Click the first cell you want to include in the formula.
4. Type an operator (+, -, /, or *).
5. Click the next cell in the formula.
6. Repeat steps 4 and 5 until the entire formula is entered.
7. Finish the entry by pressing Enter or clicking the Enter button on the formula bar.

When you have finished entering the formula, don't just move to another cell—or Excel will include it in the formula!

The other method is the traditional spreadsheet approach: typing in the formula using the cell addresses of each cell you want to include in the formula. This is the least desirable way to create a formula; no matter how well you type, this is the most error-prone method. It's much too easy to glance at the wrong column or row, even when you're working with only a few numbers. When you have thousands of numbers in the middle of a worksheet, the chance of error increases. If you need to reference widely disparate cells, consider naming the cells (see "Naming Ranges" in Chapter 6, *Beyond Excel Basics*) and then referring to the names.

Excel 2000 allows you to use labels in formulas, such as `=pay rate * hours`. To activate this feature, formerly referred to as Natural Language Formulas, choose Tools ➢ Calculations and check the Accept Labels In Formula checkbox.

Whatever formula construction method you use, you can use the *Formula Palette* to view the progress of your formula as it's being constructed. To activate the Formula Palette, click Edit Formula (the = sign button) in the formula bar rather than press the equal (=) key on the keyboard. For more about the Formula Palette, see Chapter 3.

Formulas are dynamic, so the results automatically change each time the numbers in the underlying cells are revised. Typed-in numbers don't change unless they are edited. This is the reason for the first of two very important Excel rules: *Never* do math "in your head" and type the answer in a cell where you or other users would reasonably expect to have a formula calculate the answer. (Read on for very important Excel rule number two.)

Complex Formulas

Complex formulas involve more than one operation. For example, you might have separate columns for hours worked in the first week of a pay period and hours worked in the second. You'll want to add the hours together before multiplying by the pay rate: `= (Hours Week 1 + Hours Week 2) * pay rate`. When you have more than one operation in a formula, you'll need to know about the Order of Operations.

The *Order of Operations* is a short set of rules about how formulas are calculated:

- Formulas are calculated from left to right: `15/3+2` is 7, not 3.
- Multiplication and division are always done before any addition or subtraction. Excel will make two left-to-right passes through the formula. In the formula 15/3+2, for example, Excel will do the division in the first pass. Then it will come back through and add the results of the division (5) to the other number—in this case, 2.

- Any operation in parentheses is calculated first. If you want the hours for the two weeks added together first, just throw a set of parentheses around the addition part of the formula. Note that you never need to include parentheses if you're just doing one operation; they only kick in when you need to tell Excel how to order two or more operations.

Using Autofill to Copy Formulas

Objective XL2000.1.10

Now that you understand formulas, you may be tempted to quickly create all the other gross pay formulas from our payroll example. Don't—there's a much faster way. The formula for each employee's gross pay is the same: `hours * pay rate`. Since you've already created one working formula, all you need to do is to use *Autofill* to fill the series to the other cells.

The square box in the lower-right corner of the cell pointer is called the *fill handle*. As you move the mouse toward the cell pointer, the mouse pointer changes shape to a black cross to let you know that you can use the mouse for a fill operation.

The mouse pointer assumes several shapes as you move it around the worksheet. When the mouse pointer is a large cross, you can use it to activate or select cells.

If you move the mouse toward the border of the active cell, the mouse pointer will change to an arrow. As such, you can use the pointer to move the cell (you'll learn more about moving cells later in this chapter).

You'll want to look at the mouse pointer frequently while working in Excel. A mouse movement of 1/32 of an inch can mean the difference between selecting, moving, and filling a cell.

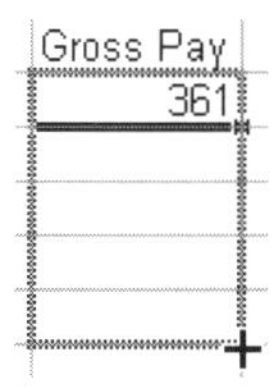

Filling is a kind of copying. Begin by activating the cell that has the formula you want to copy. Move the mouse pointer toward the fill handle until the mouse pointer changes to the fill pointer shape:

Press the mouse button and drag the fill handle down to select the cells you want to copy the formula to. Release the mouse button, and the formula will be filled to the other cells.

Steps: Filling a Formula

1. Select the cell that contains the formula you want to copy to other cells.
2. Drag the fill handle to select the cells where you want the formula copied.
3. Release the fill handle to fill the formula.

A common mistake that users make when they're new to fill operations is to include the wrong cells in the initial selection. At this point in your fill career, if all the selected cells don't include formulas, you've selected incorrectly.

Totaling Columns and Rows

Objective XL2000.6.5

Excel has a one-step method for creating row and column totals using the AutoSum button on the Standard toolbar. Begin by selecting the cells that contain the numbers you want to total; you can include the empty cell that should contain the total in the selection. Then click the AutoSum button. Excel will add a formula to the empty cell (whether or not you selected it) and calculate the total. If you would like a blank row before the totals, simply select two extra cells. Excel always places the total in the last empty cell selected.

If you want to create totals for multiple rows or columns and a grand total, select all the numbers before clicking AutoSum, as shown in the Tickets worksheet in Figure 5.3. In this example, Excel will create formulas in row 9 and column E for each selected row and column. In cell B9, the formula will be `=sum(B5:B8)`, telling Excel to sum (total) the values in the range of cells B5 through B8.

	A	B	C	D	E
1	Vacation Meisters Ticket Sales				
2	First Quarter				
3					
4	Destination	January	February	March	
5	Detroit	17	21	36	
6	Miami	119	101	89	
7	Phoenix	75	77	61	
8	Reno	93	87	90	
9					

FIGURE 5.3 Using AutoSum to total rows and columns

Revising Formulas

Objective XL2000.6.3

There are two reasons why you might want to revise a formula: you entered an incorrect formula, or you've added new data and need to change the formula to reflect the new entries. And there are two ways to revise a formula: you can move to the cell that contains the formula and create a new formula, thus overwriting the original formula, or you can edit the existing formula.

To edit a formula, double-click a cell with a formula to open it for editing. When you do this, Excel paints each cell address or range address in the formula a different color and places a border of the same color around the cell or range. The border is called a *Range Finder.* In this example, B10 in the formula and in the Range Finder around cell B10 are blue, and green is used for C10.

Stephens	9.75	44	=B10*C10

Objective XL2000.6.1

Excel's Range Finder makes it easy to see whether a formula refers to the correct cells. If you want to change the formula reference to C10 so that it refers to another cell, you can use either the keyboard or the Range Finder.

To use the keyboard, select C10 in the formula, and then either click the cell you want to replace it with or type the replacement cell's address. If the formula you're revising uses row labels instead of cell addresses, select the column or row label and type the correct label to replace the original entry.

To use the Range Finder, grab the border of the Range Finder and move it to the correct cell. (You're moving the Range Finder, so the mouse pointer should be an arrow.) If you need to include additional or fewer cells in a range, drag the selection handle at the lower-right corner of the Range Finder to extend or decrease the selection; the pointer will change to a fill pointer. When you are finished editing the formula, press Enter or click the Enter button.

If the cell reference you want to change is a range, the reference will include the first cell in the range, a colon, and the last cell in the range, like this: B10:B15. To revise this reference in a formula, select the entire reference. Then move into the worksheet and drag to select the cells for the new formula, or move and then extend the Range Finder.

Unions and Intersections Unions and intersections are two special types of ranges. A *union* is all the cells in two separate ranges. If you want, for example, to add a group of numbers in C2 though C8 and those in C20 through C28, the ranges would be (C2:C8,C20:C28). By using a comma to separate the two ranges, you're indicating that you want all cells from both ranges.

An *intersection* is just what it sounds like: a place where two ranges come together or overlap. For an intersection, use a blank space instead of a comma. The intersection (C2:C10 A10:J10) refers to just one cell: C10, where the two ranges overlap.

Formatting Numbers

Excel lets you present numbers in a variety of formats. *Formatting* is used to identify numbers as currency or percentages and to make numbers easier to read by aligning decimal points in a column.

When you format a number, you change its appearance, not its numeric value. The default format for numbers, General, doesn't display zeros that don't affect the actual value of the number. For example, if you enter 10.50, 10.5 has the same numeric value, so Excel doesn't display the extra, or *trailing*, zero.

You can format selected cells using the Formatting toolbar, the Format Cells dialog box, or the shortcut menu.

Using the Formatting Toolbar

To format cells with the Formatting toolbar, first select the cells, and then click a button to apply one of the formats shown in Table 5.3.

TABLE 5.3: Numeric Formatting from the Formatting Toolbar

Button	Style	Example
$	Currency	Displays and lines up dollar signs, comma separators, and decimal points: 75.3 as $75.30
%	Percent	Displays number as a percentage: 0.45 as 45%
,	Comma	Same as Currency, but without dollar signs: 12345.6 as 12,345.60
+.0 .00	Increase decimal	Displays one more place after the decimal: .45 as .450
.00 +.0	Decrease decimal	Displays one less place after the decimal: 0.450 as 0.45

The Formatting toolbar is the toolbar displayed on the right side of the Personal toolbar. To see all the buttons on the Formatting toolbar, choose View ➢ Toolbars ➢ Customize. Click the Options tab and clear the Standard And Formatting Toolbars Share One Row checkbox.

Objective XL2000.3.5

If decreasing the number of digits eliminates a nonzero digit, the displayed number will be rounded. For example, if the number 9.45 is displayed with only one decimal place, it will be rounded to 9.5. If you display 9.75 with no digits following the decimal, Excel will display 10.

Formatting affects only the display of a cell, not the cell's contents. To view the contents of a cell, click the cell and look at the formula bar. The number entered in the cell appears in the formula bar exactly as entered regardless of the format that has been applied to the cell.

Steps: Applying Numeric Formats from the Formatting Toolbar

1. Select the cells to be formatted.
2. Click a button on the Formatting toolbar to apply a format to the selected cells.

Using the Format Cells Dialog Box

Objective XL2000E.4.1

Excel has more number formats that you can select from the Format Cells dialog box. To apply a different format, select the cells you want to format. Then open the dialog box: either choose Format ➢ Cells from the menu bar or right-click to open the shortcut menu and choose Format Cells. The Format Cells dialog box has separate pages for Number, Alignment, Font, Border, Patterns, and Protection. The Number page of the Format Cells dialog box is shown in Figure 5.4. If the Number page is not active, click the Number tab.

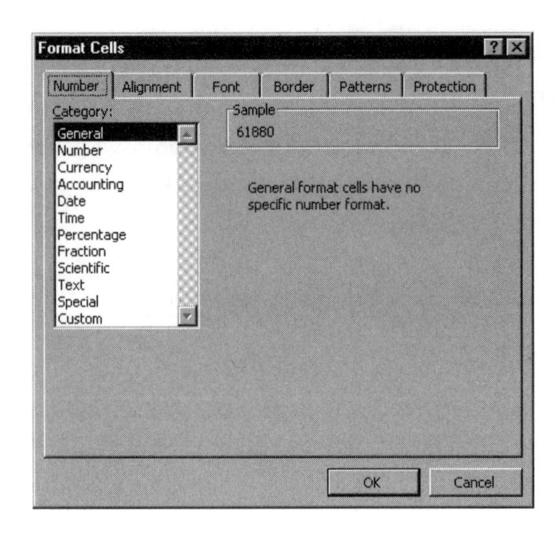

FIGURE 5.4
The Number tab of the Format Cells dialog box

The Number page includes a list of format categories and controls for the number of decimal places, thousands separator, and treatment of negative numbers. Table 5.4 shows the most commonly used categories. To apply a format, first choose a category, and then fill in the other options.

TABLE 5.4: Numeric Formatting in the Format Cells Dialog Box

Category	Description
General	This is the default format.
Number	This category is like General, but you can set decimal places, use a thousands separator, and include negative numbers.
Currency	Numbers are preceded with a dollar sign immediately before the first digit. Zero values are displayed.
Accounting	Dollar signs and decimal points line up. Zero values are shown as dashes.
Percentage	This category is the same as the Percent toolbar button.
Scientific	This category displays numbers in scientific notation: for example, 1.01E+03.

If you point to the button on the Formatting toolbar with the dollar symbol, the ScreenTip indicates it is the Currency Style button. However, when you apply this button's format, Excel applies the Accounting format, with dashes for zeros and the dollar signs lined up. Go figure!

Applying Other Formats

Objective XL2000.1.3 and .3.2

When you click in a cell and type a date, Excel may reformat the date when you press Enter or click away from the date cell. For instance, you type **July 4, 1999** and when you press Enter, Excel converts it to "4-July-99." That's because dates (and numbers) have default formats. If you enter a text string that Excel recognizes as a date, Excel will automatically format it to match the default for dates.

Changing the date format is simple. Select the cell(s) with date(s) and click Format ➢ Cells on the menu to open the Format Cells dialog box. Select the Date category and then select the format you want from the scrollable list box.

In addition to Date and those listed in Table 5.3, the Format Cells dialog box includes five other specialized formatting categories. Date formats are used for dates and times. Use the Time format if you just want to display times without dates. The Fraction category allows you to choose from formats based on either the number of digits to display in the divisor (1, 2, or 3) or the fractional unit (halves, quarters, tenths, and so on). Special and Text both convert a number to text.

Special includes formats for kinds of numbers that aren't really mathematical values: Zip Code, Zip Code + 4, Phone Number, and Social Security Number. You wouldn't want to add or multiply any of these numbers; they are informational labels just like a last name.

Text changes a number to text, so it is no longer a number and can't be used in calculations. This is fine if the number is really a label. For example, you might need to include employee numbers in a worksheet: 8712, 0913, 7639. But how do you get Excel to leave the 0 in employee number 0913? All the regular numeric formats strip off leading zeros. To keep the leading zero in 0913, format the cell for text *before* entering the number. You won't be able to include the employee numbers in a calculation, but you wouldn't want to anyway, so it's no loss.

Unlike the other formatting categories, Special and Text *change the underlying value of the number.* If you format a number with Special or Text, you will no longer be able to use the number in mathematical operations—unless you first reformat the cells with some other format. If you only have a few numbers that need to be treated as text, you can enter them manually. Simply type an apostrophe (') before the number, and Excel treats the number as text.

Custom allows you to select from or make an addition to a list of formats for numbers, dates, and times. (You'll learn more about the Custom category in Chapter 6.)

Steps: Using the Format Cells Dialog Box

1. Select the cells to be formatted.
2. Choose Format ➢ Cells, or right-click and choose Format Cells.
3. Click the Number tab.
4. From the Category list, choose the appropriate formatting category.
5. Set other available options, such as the color of text and the background of cells.
6. Click the OK button to apply the format and to close the dialog box.

Hands On: Objectives XL2000.1.1, 1.2, 1.3, 1.4, 1.10, 3.2, 3.5, 6.1, 6.2, 6.3, 6.5, and E.4.1

1. Open the workbook that contains the Cyclops Proposal Hardware and Software worksheets. If you prefer to use your own worksheet or create one from scratch, you may do so.
   a) Edit any cells where you may have made data entry errors.
   b) Intentionally make a mistake and click Undo to correct it. Enter text in a cell where no text is needed. Select that cell and clear its contents.

c) In the Price columns on the Cyclops worksheets, format the numbers using the Accounting style. Format them for Currency and notice the difference in placement of the dollar ($) sign.

d) Format these same numbers Comma style. What's different about how they're displayed? Increase, then decrease, the number of decimal places being displayed.

e) Experiment with the Percentage format. Why wouldn't you want these prices formatted as percentages?

f) Select and reformat the prices as either Currency or Accounting.

g) Make sure you're on Sheet 1 of the Cyclops workbook (or using similar data) and enter the text **Total Cost** in D4. In D5, enter a formula to calculate Quantity by Price. Fill the formula to the cells below and repeat this step on Sheet 2.

h) Switch to edit mode and examine the formula you entered in the previous step to make sure it is calculating the correct values.

i) Double-click one of the formula cells to view the Range Finder, then click away to turn it off. Save the workbook before closing it.

2. Create or open a worksheet that contains dates and numbers (like the Tickets worksheet in Figure 5.1).

   a) Edit the contents of B4, C4, and D4 so they display specific dates rather than just the months. (Example: Edit B4 to display January 5, 2000 rather than just January).

   b) Experiment with different date formats in cells B4, C4, and D4.

   c) Use AutoSum to total the columns and rows as shown in Figure 5.1. Resave the worksheet before closing it.

Changing Worksheet Layout

As you have seen, the way you initially enter data in a worksheet doesn't necessarily produce the most attractive or useful presentation. You'll almost always want to make adjustments to the layout.

Adjusting Column Width and Row Height

Objective XL2000.3.3

By default, Excel columns are slightly more than eight characters wide. If the data in a worksheet is wider or much narrower than the column, you'll want to adjust the column width so it is wide enough to contain the data, but not so wide that data seems lost. You can adjust column width manually or use AutoFit to fit the column width to the existing data.

To adjust the width of a column manually, begin by pointing to the border at the right side of the column header. The mouse pointer will change to an adjustment tool, shaped like a double-headed arrow. Drag the edge of the column header to the desired width, and then release the button. If you double-click the column header border instead of dragging the border, Excel will AutoFit the column, making the column slightly larger than the widest entry in the column.

You can select several columns and size them all at the same time. By dragging the header border of any selected column, all columns are sized to the same width. Double-clicking the header border of any of the selected columns will size each column individually to fit the data in the column. You can also select the column(s) you want to adjust and select AutoFit from the menu (choose Format ➢ Column ➢ AutoFit Selection).

The second very-important-Excel-rule: *Never* leave blank columns between columns in a worksheet. Blank columns create problems with charts, sorting, and many other advanced features. Instead, adjust column widths to provide adequate space for and between entries.

You can adjust row height the same way you adjust column width. If you move the pointer to the lower edge of a row heading, the pointer will change to an adjustment tool. Double-click to adjust the row height to fit the font size; drag to manually increase or decrease size.

Steps: Adjusting Column Widths

1. Select the column(s) you want to adjust.
2. Position the mouse pointer at the right edge of one of the selected columns' headings. The pointer changes shape to a double-headed arrow.

Steps: Adjusting Column Widths *(continued)*

3. Double-click to have Excel adjust the widths of the selected column to fit the contents of the column.
4. Click anywhere in the worksheet to turn off the selection.
5. To adjust column widths manually, drag the right border of a column's heading to make the column wider or narrower.

Inserting and Deleting Rows and Columns

Objective XL2000.5.1

To insert a column between the current columns A and B, begin by selecting column B. Right-click and select Insert from the shortcut menu, or choose Insert ➢ Columns from the menu bar to insert a column.

To insert multiple columns simultaneously, select more than one column before inserting. For example, you can insert three columns by first selecting B, C, and D. You can insert rows in the same fashion.

To quickly insert a single row or column, select the row or column heading by right-clicking. As soon as the row or column is selected, Excel immediately opens the shortcut menu.

Deleting rows and columns is much like inserting. Begin by selecting one or more rows or columns. To clear the contents but leave the emptied row in place, press the Delete key on your keyboard. To delete the contents *and* remove the row or column, choose Edit ➢ Delete from the menu bar or right-click the row or column heading and choose Delete. When you delete a row or column, all information is deleted, including cells that may not be in the part of the worksheet you can see.

You can use some nifty keystroke combinations to see if there is more data in a row or column. Select an occupied cell, hold Ctrl, and using the arrow keys, press →. The cell pointer moves to the last occupied cell to the right of the original cell. If you press Ctrl+→ again, the cell pointer stops to the left of the first occupied cell. Ctrl+→, Ctrl+↑, and Ctrl+↓ work the same way. Ctrl+End moves you to the outer limit of the used portion of the worksheet: a cell in the last used row and column.

Steps: Inserting and Deleting Rows and Columns

1. Select the row or column where you want the new inserted column to appear.
2. Right-click and choose Insert (or choose Insert ➢ Rows from the menu bar) to insert a row. To insert a column from the menu bar, choose Insert ➢ Columns.
3. To delete a column or row, first select it. Then right-click and choose Delete, or choose Edit ➢ Delete from the menu bar.

Inserting and Deleting Cells

Objective XL2000.1.6

Sometimes you'll need to add or delete cells in part of a worksheet without inserting or deleting entire rows or columns. For example, Figure 5.5 shows a section of a worksheet for a network switchover project. Tasks are listed in columns A–D, and project components (like software) are in column E.

FIGURE 5.5 Network switchover worksheet

	A	B	C	D	E
1	Cyclops Software Division				
2	Windows NT Network Conversion Project				
4	Date	Task	Days	Resource	Project Components
5	10-Mar	Install NT Server 1	1.0	Ken	Windows NT Server
6	10-Mar	Install NT Server 2	1.0	Jody	Windows NT Client - 25
7	11-Mar	Switch sales printers	0.5	Ken	Innoculan Server
8	11-Mar	Switch service printers	0.5	Ken	Carbon Copy
9	12-Mar	Backup CS Sales files	0.3	Jody	
10	12-Mar	Backup CS Service files	0.5	Jody	

If you needed to add some tasks for March 10, you can't insert rows, because it would leave blanks in the components list in column E. Instead, you can insert cells in columns A–D, select the range where new cells should be inserted and then right-click and choose Insert. If you would like to delete cells, you can right-click and choose Delete from the shortcut menu.

When you insert or delete rows and columns, Excel automatically moves the surrounding rows and columns to fill the gap. If you insert or delete cells, Excel needs more instruction to know how to move the surrounding cells, so, depending on which option you choose, the Insert or Delete dialog box opens.

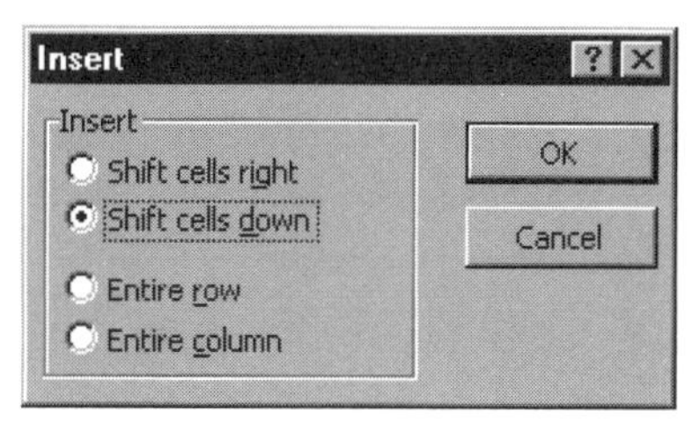

If you choose Shift Cells Down, the cells in the selection and all cells below them in the same columns are shifted down. If you choose Shift Cells Right, cells in the same row(s) are moved to the right. Notice that you can also use this dialog box to insert entire rows or columns.

If you choose Delete from the shortcut menu, the Delete dialog box opens with the same four choices.

Moving and Copying Cell Contents

Objective XL2000.1.7

Basic move and copy techniques in Excel are discussed in Chapter 1. However, there are a few additional tips that make moving and copying in Excel even easier:

- If you paste cells on top of existing data, the existing data will be overwritten, so make sure that there are enough blank cells to accommodate the selection you want to paste. For example, if you want to move the contents of column E to the right of column A without overwriting column B, begin by inserting a blank column between A and B.
- *Cut and paste* and *copy and paste* operate differently in Excel than in other Office 2000 applications. Unless you open the Clipboard toolbar (View ➢ Toolbars ➢ Clipboard; see Chapter 1 for more about the Clipboard toolbar), you can't copy now, do a few other things, and then paste later. You must paste the data immediately; if you don't, the cut (or copy) operation is canceled.

- When you cut a cell in Excel, it is copied to the Clipboard but is not removed from the worksheet until you paste it in its new location by pressing Enter, by clicking the Paste button, or by pressing Ctrl+V.
- When you get ready to paste, just click the first cell, row, or column where you want pasted cells, rows, or columns to appear. If you select more than one cell to paste into, the selected range must be exactly the same size as the range you want to paste, or an error will occur.
- When you cut a selection, you can only paste it once, so you can't use cut to make multiple copies. However, you can *copy* and paste repeatedly. When you press Enter at the end of a paste operation, Excel empties the Clipboard. To paste multiple copies, click the Paste button instead of pressing Enter. This holds the selection in the Clipboard so you can click Paste as many times as you need. Press Enter to place the final pasted copy.
- If you want to move or copy data from one worksheet to another, cut or copy the selection, and then click the sheet tab for the sheet that you want to paste into. Click in the appropriate cell, and then press Enter to paste.
- If you want to move or copy data from one workbook to another, both workbooks must be open. Select and cut or copy the data, and then choose Window from the menu bar and select the destination workbook from the list of open workbooks. Click in the destination cell and press Enter.

Steps: Moving and Copying Cells with Cut/Copy and Paste

1. If there is data below or to the right of the paste area, begin by inserting enough blank cells, rows, or columns for the data you want to move or copy.
2. Select the data you want to move or copy. To move, click the Cut button, choose Edit ➢ Cut, press Ctrl+X, or right-click and select Cut from the shortcut menu. To copy, click the Copy button, choose Edit ➢ Copy, press Ctrl+C, or right-click and select Copy from the shortcut menu.
3. Select the first cell, row, or column where you want to place the moved or copied data.
4. Press Enter to move or copy the data to its new location.

Using Drag-and-Drop

When you're moving or copying cells between worksheets or workbooks, it's easiest to cut or copy and paste. Another method, called *drag-and-drop*, works well when you can see the cells to be copied and their destination on one screen. After you select the cells, move the mouse so that it points to any part of the cell pointer except the fill handle (the mouse pointer will change to an arrow). Hold down the *right* mouse button and drag the cells to their new location. When you release the mouse button, a shortcut menu opens that lets you select whether you want to move or copy the cells.

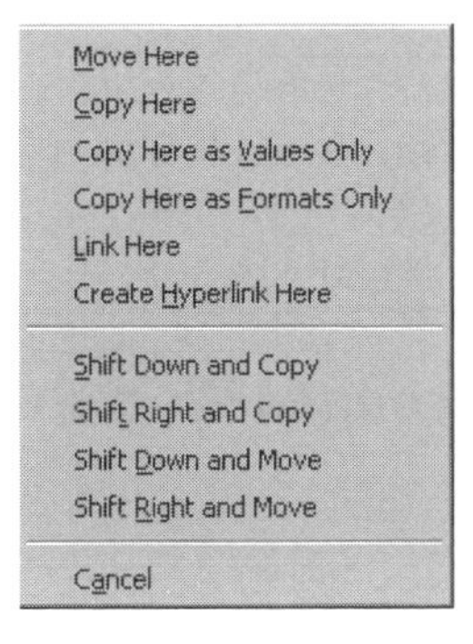

You can also move cells by copying them with the *left* mouse button. To do so, hold the Ctrl key down, drag and drop the selected cells, then release the Ctrl key.

Steps: Moving and Copying Cells with Drag-and-Drop

1. Select the cells, rows, or columns to be moved or copied.
2. Point to any part of the cell pointer. The mouse pointer will change to an arrow shape.
3. To move the selection, drag and drop it in its new location. To copy a selection, hold the Ctrl key while dropping the selection or right-drag and choose Copy Here from the Shorcut menu.

Naming a Worksheet

Objective XL2000.5.7

Because a workbook contains multiple worksheets, it is not always easy to remember which sheet contains what data. Excel allows you to give each worksheet a descriptive name so that you can locate it instantly within the workbook.

Steps: Naming a Worksheet

1. Double-click the sheet tab to select it.
2. Type a new name for the worksheet and press Enter.

Selecting Worksheets

You can move, copy, delete, and enter data in selected worksheets. To select one worksheet, click the sheet tab. To select more than one worksheet, hold the Ctrl key while selecting each worksheet. To select all worksheets in a workbook, right-click any tab and choose Select All Sheets from the shortcut menu.

Using Grouped Worksheets

When more than one worksheet is selected, the worksheets are *grouped*. Data entered into one sheet is entered into all sheets in the group, making it easy to enter the same title on five sheets in the same workbook. However, this also means that you need to remember to immediately *ungroup* worksheets when you are finished entering, moving, or copying common data. Otherwise, entries you make on one worksheet will be made on all worksheets, overwriting the existing entries on the other sheets in the group.

Ungrouping Worksheets

To ungroup worksheets, right-click any grouped worksheet tab and choose Ungroup Sheets from the shortcut menu. Alternatively, click any worksheet in the workbook that is not included in the group.

Steps: Grouping and Ungrouping Worksheets

1. To select one worksheet, click the sheet tab.
2. To select more than one worksheet, hold the Ctrl key while selecting each worksheet.
3. To select all worksheets in a workbook, right-click any tab and choose Select All Sheets from the shortcut menu.
4. To ungroup worksheets, right-click any grouped worksheet tab and choose Ungroup Sheets from the shortcut menu.

Copying and Moving Worksheets

Objective XL2000.5.9

You can copy or move one or more selected worksheets within and between workbooks. You can copy or move a worksheet to a new workbook or to an existing workbook.

To move worksheets within the same workbook, drag the sheet's sheet tab to the new location (marked by a small triangle just above the tab) and drop it:

To copy a worksheet in the same workbook, hold the Ctrl key while dragging. The copy will have the same name as the original sheet, followed by the copy number:

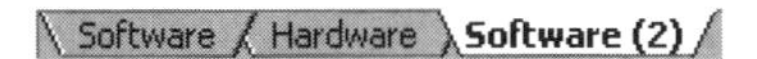

Steps: Copying and Moving Worksheets

1. To move a worksheet within the same workbook, drag the sheet's sheet tab to the new location (marked by the triangle) and drop it. Hold down the Ctrl key while dragging to copy the worksheet.
2. To move or copy between workbooks, select the worksheet you want to copy, then either choose Edit ➢ Move or Copy Sheet from the menu bar. Select the name of the workbook you want to copy the sheet to. Click Create A Copy to copy it, and then click OK.

Inserting and Deleting Worksheets

Objective XL2000.5.8

When you insert a new worksheet into a workbook, it appears to the left of the selected sheet. You can save yourself the trouble of moving it later if you first select the sheet you want to be to the right of the inserted sheet. To insert a new worksheet, choose Insert ➢ Worksheet from the menu bar.

Delete one or more selected sheets by choosing Edit ➢ Delete Sheet from the menu bar, or right-click the sheet(s) and choose Delete from the shortcut menu. When you delete a worksheet, a dialog box will open, asking you to confirm the deletion.

Excel includes three worksheets in every new workbook. If you frequently find yourself adding sheets to workbooks, you might want to increase the default number of sheets in a new book. To do so, select Tools ➢ Options from the menu bar, and change the Sheets In New Workbook setting on the General page of the Options dialog box.

Hiding and Unhiding Rows and Columns

Objective XL2000.5.2

You may find there are times when you want to hide certain rows or columns that contain data you don't want to be visible. For example, you may have a worksheet that you use to enter data into a new column each day. Rather than scrolling over to the column you need for today, you could hide the preceding day's columns and make today's column easily accessible.

To hide rows or columns, select the ones you want to hide and choose Format ➢ Columns/Row ➢ Hide. You know that rows or columns are missing because the row or column headings are not in sequence, as shown here.

	A	D	E	F
23	Beginning Database Design	Advanced Excel Databases		
24	Beginning Access	Beginning Database Design		
25	Advanced Database Design - Client Server Design	Beginning Access		
26	Advanced Access	Advanced Database Design - Client Server		
27	Project Management	Outlook – Workgroup Information Management		
28	*Reporting Tools*			
29	Access Reports and Queries	Intermediate Excel		
30	Beginning Crystal Reports	Beginning Excel or Beginning Impromptu		
31	Advanced Crystal Reports	Beginning Crystal Reports		
32	Beginning Impromptu	Beginning Excel or Beginning Crystal Reports		

You can also hide rows and columns by dragging the column or row headings using the two-headed arrow pointer.

Freezing and Unfreezing Rows and Columns

Objective XL2000.5.3

When you have a large worksheet, it's difficult to navigate around when you can no longer see the row and column labels at the top and left of the worksheet. Excel can help by freezing row and column labels so they stay put while you scroll to see the rest of the data. In this example, notice how column F is next to column A, and row 33 is next to row 1.

	A	F	G	H	I
1	**Vendors**	**May-99**	**Jun-99**	**Jul-99**	**Aug-99**
33	Browning, Karla	1,340	1,984	1,119	3,840
34	Carol A. Fallis, P.C.	-	-	-	-
35	Charlotte Cowtan	-	-	-	-
36	Courter, Gini (Expenses)	2,233	-	-	1,000
37	Creative Printing and Graphics	421	-	-	200
38	Database Advisor	-	-	-	-
39	Federal Express	-	-	-	50
40	Flint Area Chamber of Commerce	-	-	-	-
41	Flint Journal	59	-	-	-

To freeze rows and columns, click in the first cell of the worksheet you do not want frozen. For example, if you clicked in B3, column A and rows 1 and 2 would be frozen. Choose Window ➢ Freeze Panes. To test to see if it works, scroll to see if the columns or rows you wanted to freeze stay in position.

To unfreeze the panes, choose Windows ➢ Unfreeze Panes.

Freezing panes does not affect what rows and columns of a worksheet print. However, hidden rows or columns do not print.

Hands On: *Objectives XL2000.1.6, 1.7, 3.3, 5.1, 5.3, 5.7, 5.8, and 5.9*

1. Practice naming worksheets in your workbooks. Open an existing workbook and rename each of the worksheets.
2. Open an existing workbook that contains a list of names or, if you don't have one, enter five last names in column 1 of a blank worksheet. Use cut and paste to alphabetize a list within a worksheet.

3. In an existing workbook:
   - a) Adjust column widths where needed.
   - b) Insert blank rows between column labels and data.
   - c) Practice moving cells, columns, and rows using cut and paste, copy and paste, and drag-and-drop techniques.
   - d) Name all used worksheets.
   - e) Move worksheets so they are ordered by sheet name.
   - f) Hide columns B and C and row 2. View the worksheet in Print Preview. Close Print Preview and unhide the columns and rows.
   - g) Freeze column and row labels and scroll to see that the frozen columns and rows stay in position.
4. In a new workbook, group all three sheets. Enter and format a title and some data; then ungroup the sheets and enter data on one sheet only.
5. Open a new workbook:
   - a) Name each of the sheets in the workbook by clicking each sheet tab and entering a name; then press Enter.
   - b) Hold Ctrl and select the first two sheets by clicking their sheet tabs.
   - c) Move to cell A1 in the first sheet and enter your name.
   - d) Click the second sheet and notice that your name has also been entered in A1.
   - e) Right-click either grouped sheet and choose Ungroup Sheets to turn off grouping.
   - f) f) Delete the extra sheet in the workbook, then reinsert it.

Other Formatting Options

There are additional ways in which you can enhance the appearance of a worksheet. You can call attention to certain cells by the way text is aligned in them—you can even rotate text!—and you can add borders, fill color, and font colors.

Aligning Text

Objective XL2000.3.4

By default, Excel left-aligns text and right-aligns numbers. You can use the buttons on the Formatting toolbar to override the defaults and align text and numbers at the left, at the center, or at the right within cells.

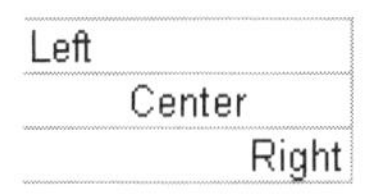

Excel has a fourth alignment called Merge and Center, which *merges* selected cells into one cell and centers the contents of the top-left selected cell across the new merged cell. Worksheet titles are often merged and centered.

To merge and center a title, select the cell containing the title and the cells in the same row for all the used columns in the worksheet; then click the Merge And Center button. Excel only centers the text in the top-left cell of the selection, so if your worksheet's title is in more than one row, merge and center each title row separately.

There are other alignment options that aren't accessible from the toolbar but are set in the Alignment page of the Format Cells dialog box. Some of the more unique alignments, including text rotation, are illustrated in Figure 5.6. The Alignment page of the Format Cells dialog box is shown in Figure 5.7, and its options are discussed in the following four sections.

FIGURE 5.6
Text alignments

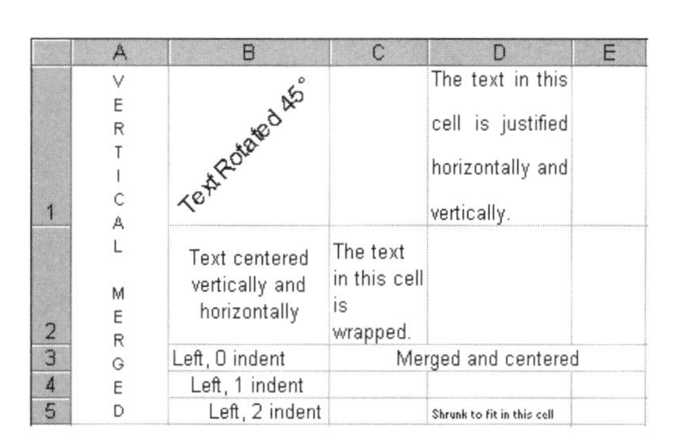

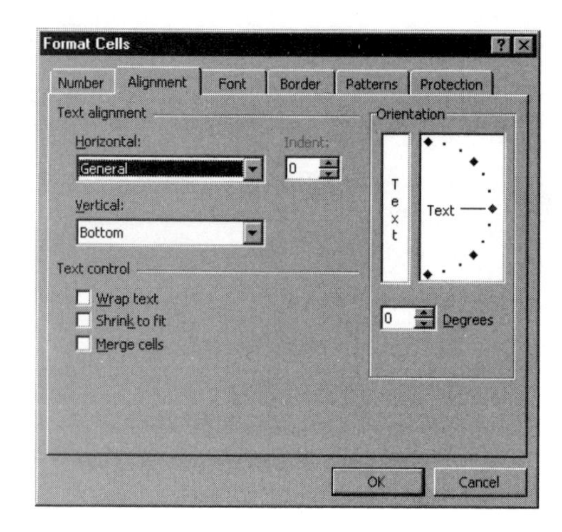

FIGURE 5.7
Alignment page of the Format Cells dialog box

Horizontal Alignment and Indenting

There are seven types of Horizontal alignment:

General is the default alignment: text to the left and numbers to the right.

Left (Indent) aligns the contents of the cell at the cell's left edge, just like the Formatting toolbar button. However, if you choose Left in the dialog box, you can also specify a number of characters to indent in the Indent box.

Center and **Right** are identical to the Formatting toolbar buttons.

Fill "fills" the cell with the current contents by repeating the contents for the width of the cell. If, for example, "-" is the contents of the cell and you choose Fill for the alignment, "--------" will appear in the cell.

Justify wraps the text within the cell and adjusts the spacing within each line so that all lines are as wide as the cell, providing a smooth right edge, like text in a newspaper column.

Center Across Selection is applied to a range of cells. The contents of the leftmost cell are centered across all the cells selected. This is similar to Merge And Center, but it does not merge the cells.

Vertical Alignment

The default Vertical alignment (in the Text Alignment section of the Format Cells dialog box) is Bottom. Top and Center are used to float the contents nearer to the top or middle of the cell. Justify adds space between the lines in a wrapped cell.

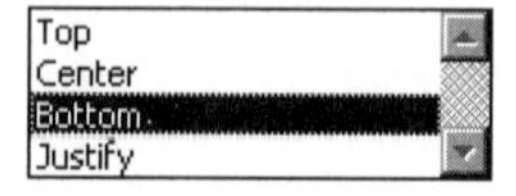

Rotating Text

Use the rotation tools to orient text vertically or to rotate text to a specific orientation. Rotating text lets you create a splashy column or row label. Vertically orient and merge text (see below) to label a group of row labels.

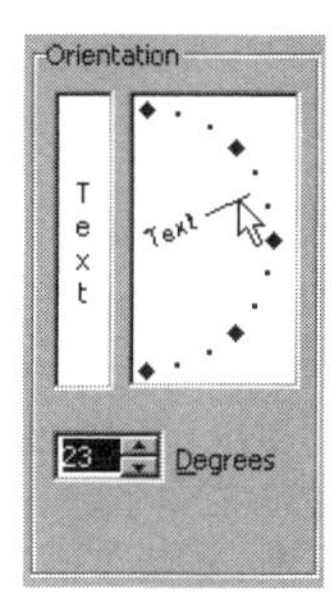

To orient text vertically, in the Orientation section of the Format Cells dialog box, click the box with the vertical word Text in it. To rotate text to another orientation, either use the Degrees spin box or drag the Text indicator in the rotation tool.

Merge, Shrink to Fit, and Wrap Text

Objective XL2000.3.9

If you want a vertical title to cross several rows (such as the label "Vertical Merged" in column A of Figure 5.4), select the title and several additional cells below the title. In the Text Control section of the Format Cells dialog box, check the Merge Cells checkbox to merge the cells.

Also in the Text Control section, Shrink To Fit reduces the size of the type within selected cells so the contents fit. Wrap Text wraps the contents of a cell if it would exceed the cells' boundaries. Both Shrink To Fit and Wrap Text use the current column widths. If you narrow or widen a column after you shrink or wrap a label, you'll need to reshrink or rewrap.

Steps: Aligning Text

1. Select the range of cells to be formatted.
2. Choose Format ➢ Cells from the menu bar or right-click and choose Format from the shortcut menu.
3. Click the Alignment page tab.
4. Choose horizontal, vertical, rotation, merge, and wrap options, and then click OK.

Borders and Color

Objective XL2000.3.8

Effective use of fonts, discussed in Chapter 1, can help make worksheets easier to understand. Borders and color provide further ways to highlight information in a worksheet. A *border* is a line drawn around a cell or group of cells. *Fill color* is used to highlight the background of part of a worksheet; *font color* is applied to text. Even if you don't have access to a color printer, you might still want to use color in worksheets that you or others use frequently. Color distinguishes between similar looking worksheets; for example, the Sales Department's budget could have a blue title, and Production's title could be burgundy.

The Borders, Fill Color, and Font Color buttons are found on the Formatting toolbar. All three buttons are combination buttons that include a menu opened by clicking the drop-down arrow attached to the button.

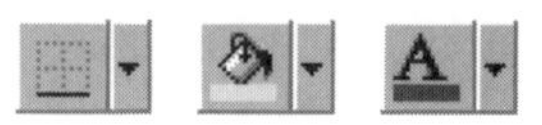

For example, this is the Borders menu.

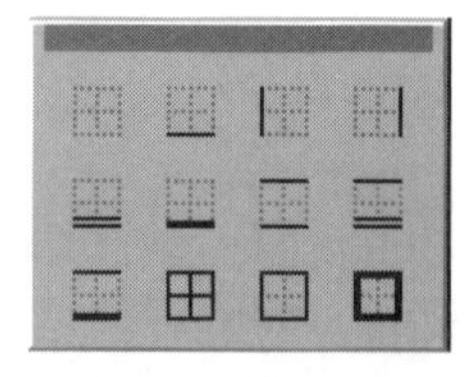

Borders can completely surround a group of cells, surround each cell individually, provide an underline, or double-underline the selected range. Selecting a border from the menu assigns it to the button and applies it to the selected cells. After you assign a border to the button, the next time you click the Border button, the same border style will be applied to your currently active cell or range of cells.

The Fill Color and Font Color buttons also have attached menus and are used the same way.

If you have a lot of borders, colors, or font colors to apply, you can open any or all of the menus as separate windows that float on your worksheet. Open the menu, and then point to the dark gray bar at the top of the menu. The bar will turn the same color as your program title bar; if you hover for a moment, a ScreenTip saying "Drag to make this menu float" will appear.

Drag the menu into the worksheet and release the mouse button. Close the menu with its Close button.

Steps: Adding Borders, Colors, and Font Colors

1. To apply a font color or fill color, select the cells to be formatted. Click the color button's drop-down arrow and select a color from the menu.
2. To add a border, select the cells to be formatted. Click the Borders button's drop-down arrow and select a border from the menu.

If you need to apply several formatting changes to a group of cells, you may find it easier to use the Format Cells dialog box. Click the page tabs to move from page to page and set the desired formats for the selected cells. When you are finished, click OK to apply all the chosen formats to the selection.

Clearing Cell Formats

Objective XL2000.1.9

If you remove the contents of a cell by selecting it and pressing Delete or Backspace, Excel removes the cell contents but does not remove formatting. That means when you delete the contents of a cell that displays a number as a percentage, the next time you type a number in that cell, it will be formatted as a percentage.

To clear formatting from a cell, select it and click Edit ➢ Clear ➢ Formats.

Hands On: *Objectives XL2000.1.9, 3.4, 3.8, and 3.9*

1. Create an "alignment sampler" similar to Figure 5.4.
2. Use alignments, fonts, borders, and colors to format at least two different worksheets.
3. In an existing worksheet, use borders to separate numeric data from totals.
4. Select a cell or range of cells and clear the formatting.

Printing in Excel

Objective XL2000.4.1

Print Preview, Print, Page Setup, and Page Break Preview are interrelated features:

- Print Preview lets you see how each page of the workbook will appear when it is printed.
- Print prints the specified number of copies of selected worksheets or workbooks.
- Page Setup is used to change the margins, print quality, print area, and print features.
- Page Break Preview displays the current page breaks and allows you to adjust them.

Print Preview

Excel 2000 allows you to preview a spreadsheet before printing it. Click the Print Preview button on the Standard toolbar to open the preview window. The preview window displays the current worksheet as it will appear when it is printed, as shown in Figure 5.8.

If the worksheet is wider or longer than one page, the Previous and Next buttons let you move between pages. (If the worksheet fits on one page, these two buttons are disabled.) The preview window's Zoom button toggles between full-page view and a magnified view of the worksheet. The full-page view lets you see the general layout of the page. Use the magnified view to look at specific details.

Adjusting Margins in Print Preview

The Print Preview Margins button displays the current margin settings. Point to any of the margin lines, and the pointer will change to an adjustment tool, as shown in Figure 5.9. Press the mouse button, and the status bar will indicate the name and current setting for the margin. Drag a margin to adjust it.

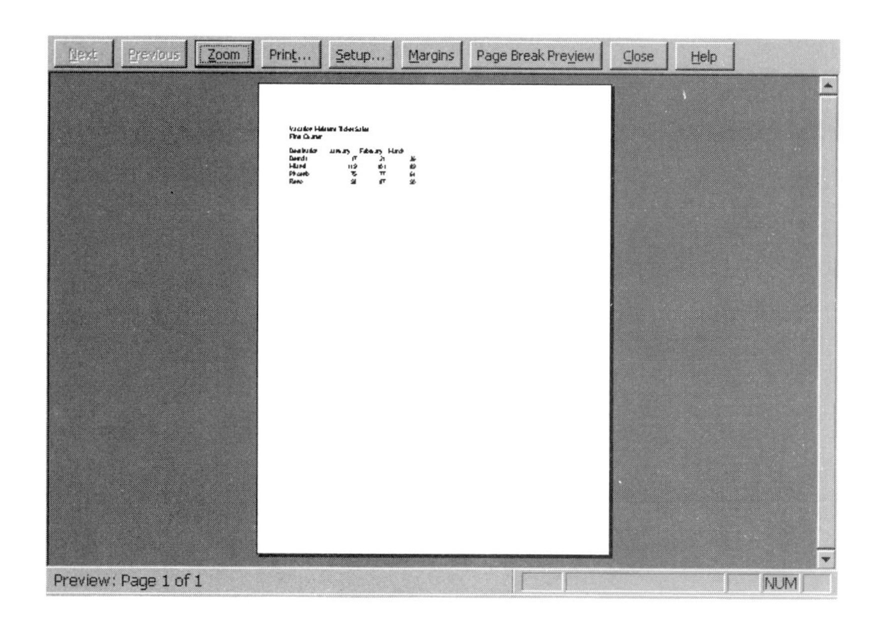

FIGURE 5.8 Excel's Print Preview window

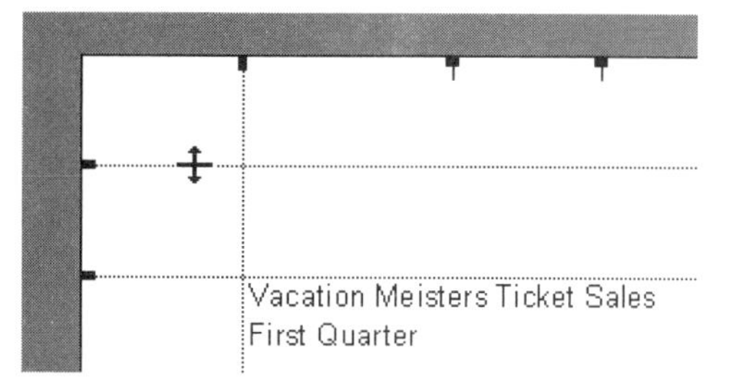

FIGURE 5.9 Adjusting margins in Print Preview

Excel's default margins are 3/4 of an inch on each side, and 1 inch on the top and bottom, with a half-inch header and footer margin. Headers and footers print in the half-inch of space between the header/footer margin and the regular margin. The top and bottom margins define the limits of the printed worksheet, and the header and footer margins define the areas where the header and footer will print. If you use headers and footers, the top and bottom margins need to be inside the header and footer margins, or part of the worksheet will print on top of the header and footer.

Steps: Adjusting Margins in Print Preview

1. Click Print Preview to open the preview window.
2. Click the Margins button to display page margins.
3. Drag the margin you wish to change to its new location.

Printing a Document

To immediately send a document to the printer using the default print options (and without opening a dialog box), click the Print button on the Standard toolbar. This is convenient if you want to print one copy of the active sheet to the default printer.

Changing Print Settings

To choose a printer, to specify what to print, and to set the number of copies, you must use the Print dialog box (see Figure 5.10).

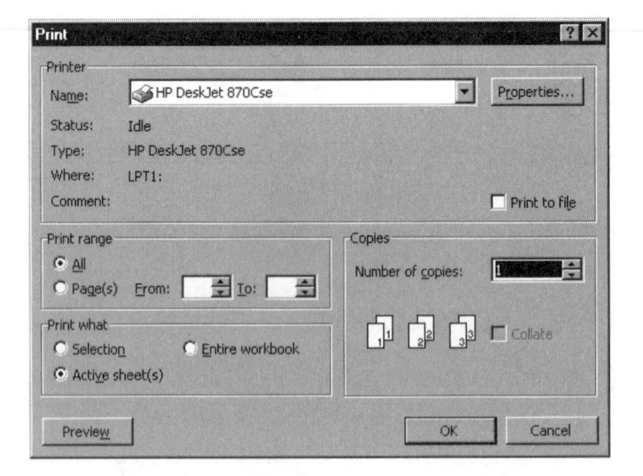

FIGURE 5.10
Excel's Print dialog box

Click the Name drop-down list to select a different printer from the default. Click the Properties button to view or change the printer's settings.

Use the Print Range controls to print some, but not all, of the pages of a multi-page print job and the spin boxes to specify a starting and ending page to print. You cannot specify noncontiguous pages in Excel, so if you want to print pages 1–4 and 6–8, for example, you either have to print twice or choose the cells on those pages and specify them as your print area.

Objective XL2000.4.3

In the Print What section of the Print dialog box, specify which part of the worksheet or workbook you want to print. The Selection option provides another way to override the default print area: select the cells you want to print, and then print the selection. Choose Workbook to print all used worksheets in the active workbook. To print some, but not all worksheets in a workbook, select the sheets before opening the Print dialog box, and then choose Active Sheets.

Use the Number Of Copies spin box to print more than one copy of the selection, worksheet, or workbook. If you are printing multiple copies of more than one page, use the Collate control to print the pages in order. For example, two copies of a three-page worksheet will print 1–2–3, then 1–2–3. With Collate turned off, the same print request will print 1–1, 2–2, and 3–3.

Steps: Changing Print Settings

1. Choose File ➢ Print to open the Print dialog box.
2. Select a printer from the Printer Name drop-down menu.
3. Select what you wish to print: a selection, active worksheets, or the current workbook.
4. Set the number of copies using the Copies spin box, and turn Collate on or off for multi-page print jobs.
5. Specify a page range or leave the default as All.
6. Click OK to print and return to the worksheet.

Printing and Previewing Multiple Worksheets

Objective XL2000E.5.1

To print multiple worksheets from a workbook at one time, hold the Ctrl key while clicking the sheet tabs of the worksheet you want to print. The sheet tabs turn white, indicating that multiple sheets are grouped. When you choose File ➢ Print Preview, click the Next and Previous button to view each sheet. Click Print to print all of the selected sheets.

To ungroup the sheets, click the sheet tab of another sheet in the workbook.

Hands On: Objectives XL2000.4.1, 4.3, and E.5.1

1. Create a new workbook or open an existing workbook.
   a) View the spreadsheet in Print Preview.
   b) Use your mouse to zoom in on a section, then zoom back out.
   c) Print one copy of the spreadsheet on your default printer.
   d) Close Print Preview and return to Excel.
2. Select a portion of your worksheet.
   a) Print just the selected cells to your default printer.
3. Select more than one sheet in a workbook and preview and then print them all.

Changing Page Setup

Objectives XL2000.4.4 and 4.5

To change page setup, choose File ➢ Page Setup from the menu bar to open the Page Setup dialog box. (If you're already in Print Preview, click the Setup button; from Page Break Preview, right-click and choose Page Setup from the shortcut menu.) The Page Setup dialog box splits page layout into four tabbed pages that contain Page, Margins, Header/Footer, and Sheet settings.

Page Settings

Use the Page options of the Page Setup dialog box, shown in Figure 5.11, to set orientation, scaling, paper size, and print quality.

Orientation is the direction of print in relation to the paper it is printed on. Portrait, the default setting, places the short edge of the paper at the top and bottom. If your worksheet is wider than it is long, consider using landscape orientation.

Scaling is used to reduce or enlarge the print. If you simply need to make the print larger, use the Adjust To control and choose a size greater than 100 percent. The Fit To control instructs Excel to reduce a worksheet that exceeds a specific number of pages so it will fit.

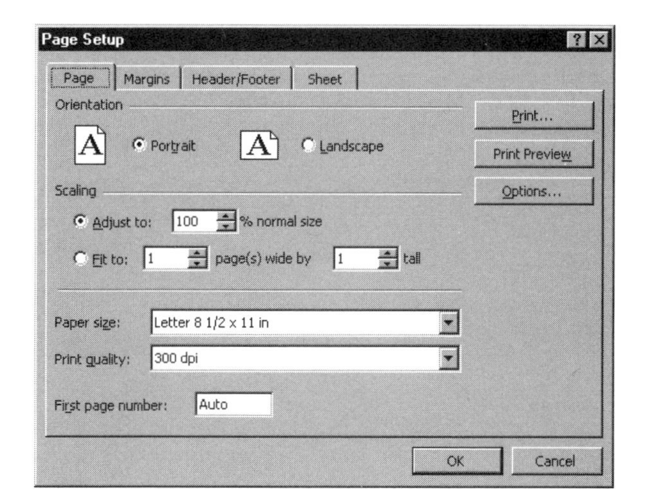

FIGURE 5.11
Page settings in the Page Setup dialog box

Paper Size should be adjusted if you are using a paper size other than the default (for example, legal paper).

Print Quality is measured in dpi: dots per inch. Higher dpi means higher print quality, but there is a trade-off: It takes longer to print at higher dpi.

First Page Number is used to set an initial page number other than 1.

The Options button appears on every page of the Page Setup dialog box. Clicking it opens the Windows property sheet (or the manufacturer's property sheet, if there is one) for the printer that's currently selected.

Steps: Changing Page Settings

1. Open the Page Setup dialog box by choosing File ➢ Page Setup or by clicking the Setup button in the Print Preview window. Click the Page tab.
2. Change settings for Orientation, Scaling, Paper Size, Print Quality, and/or First Page Number.
3. Click OK to apply the settings.

Setting Margins in the Page Setup Dialog Box

Objective XL2000.4.5

The preview in the Margins page of the Page Setup dialog box (see Figure 5.12) displays the margins as dotted lines. You can change the margins here using the spin box controls for each margin. As you change settings on the Margins page, the preview will change to reflect the new margin settings.

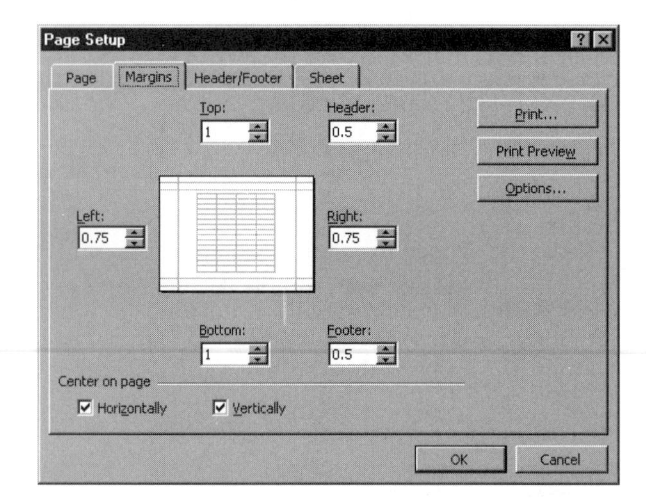

FIGURE 5.12 The Margins page of the Page Setup dialog box

Use the Center On Page controls to center the printed worksheet horizontally between the side margins or vertically between the top and bottom margins.

Steps: Changing Margins in Page Setup

1. In the Page Setup dialog box, select the Margins page.
2. Using the spin box controls, set the top, bottom, left, and right margins.
3. If you are using a header or footer, use the Header and Footer spin boxes to set the distance for the header and footer margins.
4. Use the Center On Page checkboxes to center the printed worksheet.

Headers and Footers

Objective XL2000.4.8

A header appears at the top of each page of a document. Footers are printed at the bottom of the page. Excel's default setting is no header or footer. If you want a header or footer, choose or create it in the Header/Footer page in the Page Setup dialog box, shown in Figure 5.13.

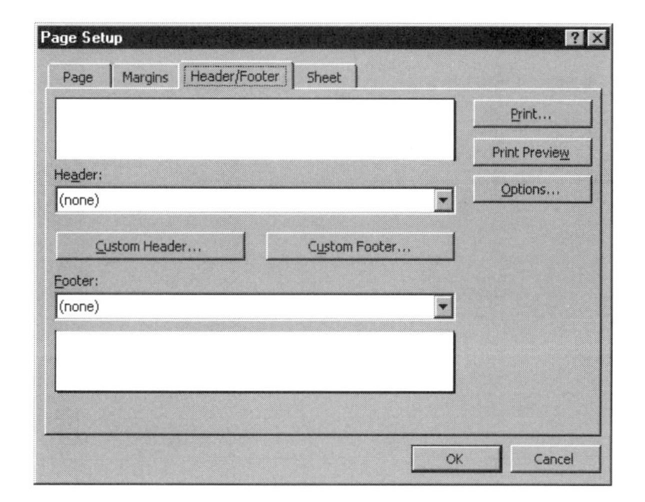

FIGURE 5.13 The Header/Footer page of the Page Setup dialog box

The currently selected header and footer are displayed in the two preview panes. To choose a different pre-designed header, click the Header drop-down list. Choose a footer the same way, using the Footer drop-down list. When you select a different header (or footer), the preview pane will reflect the change.

Creating New Headers and Footers To create a new header, click the Custom Header button to open the Header dialog box, shown in Figure 5.14. The header is separated into three sections: left, center, and right. Click in any section to place information in that portion of the header. You can enter text (like your name) or insert a placeholder from Table 5.5.

When the file is printed, Excel will replace each placeholder with the actual page number, date, time, workbook, or worksheet name.

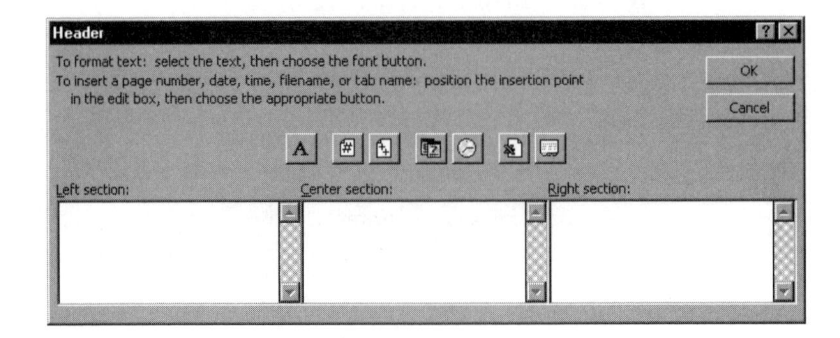

FIGURE 5.14
Header dialog box

TABLE 5.5: Header and Footer Placeholders

Button	Button Name	Placeholder
	Page Number	Current page number
	Total Pages	Total number of pages printed
	Date	Date worksheet was printed
	Time	Time worksheet was printed
	Filename	Name of workbook
	Tab	Name of worksheet

Formatting Header and Footer Text To format header text, including placeholders, select the text and click the Font button to open the Font dialog box. Change the Font, Font Style, Size, Underline, and Effects that you want applied to the text. Click OK to save the font settings and return to the Header dialog box.

When you are finished creating the header, click OK to return to the Header/Footer page of the Page Setup dialog box and add the new header to the drop-down list.

You can open the Header And Footer dialog box directly, rather than going through Page Setup, by selecting View ➢ Header And Footer.

Steps: Selecting and Creating Headers and Footers

1. Choose File ➢ Page Setup from the menu bar.
2. In the Page Setup dialog box, select the Header/Footer page.
3. Click the Header drop-down list and select a header, or click Custom Header to create a header. Click the Footer drop-down arrow and select a footer, or click Custom Footer to create a footer.
4. Press Enter to return to the Page Setup dialog box.

Changing Sheet Settings

The Sheet page (see Figure 5.15) contains settings that relate to the sheet features that will appear in the printed copy, including the print area, repeating rows and columns, and gridlines.

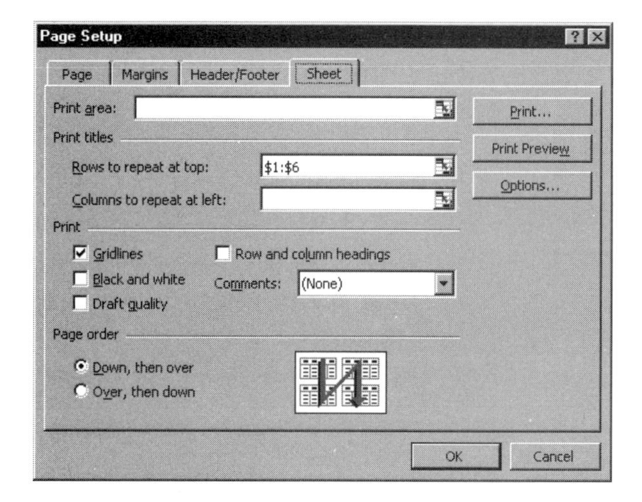

FIGURE 5.15
Sheet settings

The Print Area, Rows To Repeat, and Columns To Repeat controls are only enabled when you open the Page Setup dialog box from the menu (choose File ➢ Page Setup or View ➢ Header And Footer). If you go to Page Setup from Print Preview or the Print dialog box, you won't be able to change these three settings.

Objectives XL2000.4.7 and XL2000.4.9

Print Area By default, Excel prints from the home cell (A1) to the last occupied cell in a worksheet. To specify a different range, type the range in the Print Area text box, or select the print area with the mouse. If the Print Area includes noncontiguous cells, each contiguous range will print on a separate page.

The easiest way to set the Print Area is from the menu bar. Select the cells to be printed, and then choose File ➢ Print Area ➢ Set Print Area from the menu bar. When you want to print the entire worksheet again, choose File ➢ Print Area ➢ Clear Print Area.

Print Titles The options in this section allow you to print column and row labels on each page of the printout. Specify these rows or columns in the Rows To Repeat At Top and Columns To Repeat At Left text boxes. (Excel requires a *range* with a colon for these entries, even if it's only one row or column.)

Gridlines This box determines whether gridlines will be printed but does not affect their display in the worksheet. Turning off the gridlines by clearing the checkbox gives your printed worksheet a cleaner appearance and can make it easier to read. Turn on the gridlines by checking the checkbox.

To turn off screen gridlines, choose Tools ➢ Options and clear the check mark in the Gridlines option on the View page of the Options dialog box.

Black And White If you used colors in the worksheet but won't be printing on a color printer, click this control to speed up the print process.

Draft Quality Checking this box chooses draft mode to print the worksheet without gridlines or graphics.

Row And Column Headings If this box is checked, the row numbers and column letters will be included in the printout. This is a useful feature when you are editing or trying to locate an error in a worksheet.

Page Order This section establishes the order in which multi-page worksheets are printed.

If you find it difficult to select cells with the Page Setup dialog box in the way, click the Collapse Dialog button to minimize the dialog box while you select cells.

Click the Expand Dialog button to return to the Print Setup dialog box.

Steps: Changing Sheet Settings

1. To open the Page Setup dialog box, choose File ➢ Page Setup. Click the Sheet tab.
2. Specify ranges for a print area and rows and columns to be repeated as titles on each printed page by entering them from the keyboard or by using the mouse.
3. Enter option settings in the Print and Page Order sections.
4. Click OK.

You can set Page Setup options for multiple worksheets by grouping (selecting) the worksheets before opening the Page Setup dialog box. Remember to ungroup the worksheets after you've changed the Page Setup.

Using Page Break Preview

Objective XL2000.4.6

Page Break Preview, shown in Figure 5.16, is a view of the worksheet window that shows you what will be printed and the order in which the pages will be printed. To turn on Page Break Preview, click the Page Break Preview button in Print Preview, or choose View ➢ Page Break Preview from the menu bar.

FIGURE 5.16

Page Break Preview

	A	B	C	D	E	F
1	Vacation Meisters Ticket Sales					
2	First Quarter					
3						
4	Destination	January	February	March		
5	Detroit	17	21	36		
6	Miami	119	101	89		
7	Phoenix	75	77	61		
8	Reno	93	87	90		
9						
10						

Page 1

In Page Break Preview, areas that will be printed are white; cells that won't be printed are gray. Each printed page is numbered. You can quickly change the range to be printed by dragging the edge of the page break with your mouse to include or exclude cells.

If a worksheet prints on multiple pages, you can adjust the breaks by dragging the page break. To add a manual page break, select the first column or row you want to appear in the page after the break. Right-click and choose Insert Page Break from the shortcut menu.

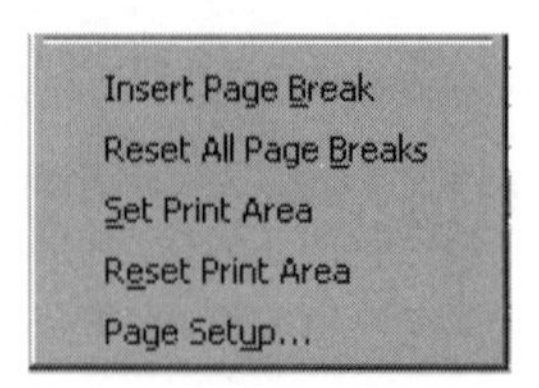

To remove a manual page break, right-click in the row below the horizontal page break or in the column to the right of the vertical page break, and choose Remove Page Break from the shortcut menu. To remove all manual page breaks, right-click any cell and choose Reset All Page Breaks from the shortcut menu. In Page Break Preview, you can also remove a page break by dragging it outside the print area.

To return to Normal view, choose View ➢ Normal from the menu bar. Note that you can also go directly from the worksheet to Page Break Preview from the View menu.

Steps: Previewing and Adjusting Page Breaks

1. From the Print Preview window, click the Page Break Preview button.

   OR

1. From the worksheet window, choose View ➢ Page Break Preview.
2. Using the mouse, drag the page break to extend or limit the range of cells to be printed.
3. Choose View ➢ Normal to close Page Break Preview.

Hands On: *Objectives XL2000.4.4, 4.5, 4.6, 4.7, 4.8, and 4.9*

Open the Cyclops Proposal workbook or another workbook of your choice.

1. In the first worksheet:
   a) Preview the worksheet.
   b) Center the worksheet horizontally and vertically on the page.
   c) Create a header that includes your name, and then create a footer with the current date and time left-justified and the sheet name right-justified.
   d) Preview and print the worksheet.

2. In the second worksheet:

    a) Use Page Break Preview to extend the print area to include two blank columns and one blank row.

    b) Reset the print area to include the entire worksheet.

    c) Change the paper orientation to Landscape.

    d) Change the top margin to 1.5 inches so the worksheet can be placed in a notebook.

    e) Add a horizontal page break so the worksheet prints on at least two pages.

    f) Print the worksheet title and column labels on each page.

    g) Preview and print the worksheet.

CHAPTER 6

Beyond Excel Basics

Once you've mastered the basics of Excel, it's only a matter of time before you need more advanced skills. You'll want to look at ways to graphically display data using Excel charts. Exploring financial and statistical functions might appeal to you, or perhaps you'll seek ways to sort and filter data for more focused reporting. In this chapter, you'll learn how to move beyond simple data entry and calculation into efficient use of Excel's higher-level features.

Working with Relative and Absolute Cell References

Objective XL2000.6.4

When you copy a formula from one cell to another, Excel automatically adjusts each cell reference in the formula. In the last chapter—and indeed, most of the time—this is exactly what you want Excel to do. However, there are exceptions. For example, Vacation Meisters would like to know the percentage of tickets sold for each destination city. To calculate a city's percentage, you would divide the city's total into the grand total for all cities.

To help visualize this process, take a look at Figure 6.1. We've entered a formula in cell G6 to divide the total Detroit tickets (74) into the grand total (866). The formula produces a reasonable answer for Detroit, but the same formula is obviously wrong when filled to the other cities.

FIGURE 6.1
Calculating percentages

	A	B	C	D	E	F	G
1	**Vacation Meisters Ticket Sales**						
2	First Quarter						
3							
4	Destination	January	February	March	Total	Average	Percent of Total
5							
6	Detroit	17	21	36	**74**	25	9%
7	Miami	119	101	89	**309**	103	143%
8	Phoenix	75	77	61	**213**	71	288%
9	Reno	93	87	90	**270**	90	87%
10							
11	Total for Month	**304**	**286**	**276**	**866**		
12	Average for Month	76	72	69	217		
13	Minimum for Month	17	21	36	74		
14	Maximum for Month	119	101	90	309		

So what happened? The formula in G6 was =E6/E11. When it was filled from G6 to G7, Excel changed each cell reference, just as it did with the totals you filled earlier. You can see which cells were referenced in a formula by double-clicking the formula. The formula in G7 was changed to =E7/E12, and the change from E11 to E12 created the problem. Rather than dividing Miami's total into the total for all destinations, it divided it into the average in cell E12. The formulas for Phoenix and Reno have a similar problem.

When you fill this formula, you want E6 to change to E7 (*relative* to the formula's new location), but you don't want E11 to change at all. The reference to E11 should be *absolute*—not changeable. You instruct Excel to not change the reference to E11 by making it an *absolute cell reference*. Absolute cell references are preceded with dollar signs, such as E11. The dollar signs "lock in" the cell reference so Excel doesn't change it if you fill or copy the formula to another cell. The dollar sign in front of the E instructs Excel not to change the column; the dollar sign in front of the 11 locks in the row. As you fill the formula =E6/E11 to the other cities, E6 will change to E7, E8, and E9, but E11 will always be E11.

You create an absolute cell reference in the original formula. If you never intend to fill or copy a formula, you don't need to use absolutes, and absolutes won't fix a formula that doesn't work correctly to begin with. Remember, the original formula in G6 worked just fine. If you are typing the formula, just precede the column and row addresses with a $. You can also create the absolute cell reference using the F4 key, as you will see in steps below.

Creating an Absolute Cell Reference

1. Place the cell pointer where you want the results of the formula to appear.
2. Begin entering the formula. After you enter the address of the cell that contains the absolute value, press the F4 key once to add dollar ($) signs to the row and column of the cell reference.
3. When the formula is complete, press Enter or click the green check mark.
4. Fill the formula to the appropriate cells.

You can also create a *mixed reference*, making a cell address part absolute and part relative, by locking in *either* the column *or* the row. Use mixed references when you want to copy a formula down *and* across and to have a reference change relatively in one direction but not in the other. For example, E$5 will remain E$5 when copied down, because the row reference is absolute, but it can change to F$5, G$5, and so on when copied across, because the column reference is relative.

The Absolute key (F4) is a four-way toggle. The first time you press it, it locks both the column and row: E11. Press again, and only the row is locked: E$11. The third time you press, the column is locked: $E11. Press a fourth time, and both row and column are relative again: E11.

Working with Ranges

Rather than using cell addresses as references, you can apply a *name* to refer to a cell or a range of cells. Names provide multiple benefits:

- Names are more descriptive and easier to remember than cell addresses.
- When a cell moves, the name moves with it.
- You can use a name in place of a cell or range address in a formula or function argument.
- When you copy a formula that uses a named cell, the effect is the same as using an absolute cell reference.

Naming Ranges

Objective XL2000E.6.1

Names can be a maximum of 255 characters and can include letters, numbers, underscores, and periods. The name must begin with either a letter or the underscore character (_), and you cannot use spaces, commas, exclamation points, or other special characters. Names cannot be valid cell addresses; for example, `FY1998` cannot be used as a name, because there's a cell with that address in every Excel worksheet. Names are not case-sensitive: `INTEREST RATE` and `interest rate` are the same name. The traditional naming practice is to exclude spaces and begin each word within the name with an uppercase letter: `InterestRate`. A name can't be repeated within a workbook, so you can't use the same name on two different sheets.

You can name a range in three ways. The easiest is to select the range (which can include noncontiguous cells) and then click in the Name box at the left end of the formula bar. (Click the box, not the drop-down arrow.) Type the name for the range, and then press Enter.

You can also name ranges and change or delete existing range names using the Define Name dialog box, shown in Figure 6.2. The dialog box displays a list of the names already used in the workbook.

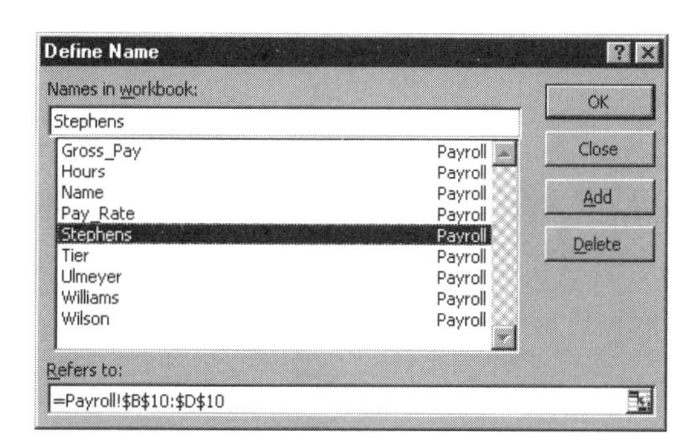

FIGURE 6.2 Excel's Define Name dialog box

Defining, Changing, and Deleting Range Names

1. To define a name, select the range of cells you want to name.
2. Choose Insert ➢ Name ➢ Define from the menu bar.
3. In the Names In Workbook text box, type a valid range name, and then click Add.

Defining, Changing, and Deleting Range Names *(continued)*

4. To change a name, select the name from the Names In Workbook list. Select the name in the Names In Workbook text box, overtype the old name with the new name, and then click Add.
5. To delete a name, select the name from the Names In Workbook list, and then click the Delete button.
6. When you are finished, click OK.

Excel allows you to use a worksheet's row and column labels in formulas (choose Tools ➢ Options and enable Accept Labels In Formulas on the Calculation tab to enable this feature). Use the Create Names dialog box (see Figure 6.3) to *assign* a name to one cell from text in another cell, even if the text is not a row or column label.

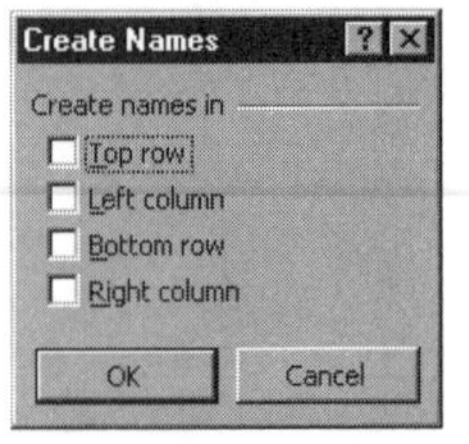

FIGURE 6.3 The Create Names dialog box

Excel edits labels as needed to make them valid names. If the label for a column or row contains spaces, Excel will replace the space with an underscore: `Interest_Rate`. If the cell contents begin with a number, like `8-Mar` or `4 bags`, Excel adds an underscore to the beginning of the name: `_8-Mar` or `_4_bags`. However, Excel does not create a name from a cell that contains *only* a number (like 1998, 78, or 1254.50). Excel will let you go through the motions, but it won't create the name.

Creating Names from a Row or Column of Text

1. Select the range to be named. Include the cells you want to use as names as either the top or bottom row, or the first or last column selected.
2. Choose Insert ➢ Name ➢ Create from the menu bar to open the Create Names dialog box.

Creating Names from a Row or Column of Text *(continued)*

3. In the Create Names In text box, select the row (Top or Bottom) and/or column (Left or Right) that contain the labels you want to use to name the selected range.
4. Click OK to apply the names and close the dialog box.

Using Names

Objective XL2000E.6.2

You can enter a name anywhere a regular cell reference is valid. For example, you can type in the name of a range as an argument for a function: `=SUM(ToHourstals)`. Names also serve a valuable navigation function, particularly in large workbooks and worksheets. To move to and select a named range anywhere in the workbook, click the down arrow in the Name box and select the name from the list.

Hands On: *Objectives XL2000.6.4, E.6.1, and E.6.2*

1. Using the Cyclops Proposal Software worksheet or another worksheet:
   a) Practice naming ranges using both Name ➢ Create and Name ➢ Define.
   b) Move to a named range.
   c) Delete one of the named ranges.
2. Create a mileage worksheet to calculate mileage reimbursement for business travel. In Column A, list the destinations. In Column B, record the number of miles from your office to the destination. In Column C, record the number of miles of the return from the destination to your office.
   a) Use Name ➢ Define to name the cells in Column B; give a different name to the cells in Column C.
   b) Create a formula in Column D to add columns B and C using the named ranges.

3. Using the Cyclops Proposal Software worksheet or another worksheet, use absolute cell references to calculate the Percentage column (percentage of total).
4. In the mileage worksheet you created in Exercise 2,
   a) Enter $.31 in a cell at the top of the worksheet. Name it Rate.
   b) Use absolute cell references and named ranges to create a new column that calculates Rate * TotalMiles.

Understanding Functions

Functions are pre-defined, structured programs that calculate a specific result: a total, an average, the amount of a monthly loan payment, or the geometric mean of a group of numbers, for example. Each function has a specific order, or *syntax*, that must be used for the function to work properly. Functions are formulas, so all functions begin with the = sign. After the = is the *function name*, followed by one or more *arguments* separated by commas and enclosed in parentheses.

```
=SUM(D6:D11)
```

In Chapter 5, when you clicked the AutoSum button, you used the SUM function to total numbers. Excel includes hundreds of other functions that you can use to calculate results used in statistics, finance, engineering, math, and other fields. These functions are grouped into 10 categories, as listed in Table 6.1.

TABLE 6.1: Excel Functions

Category	Examples
Financial	Calculates interest rates, loan payments, depreciation amounts
Date & Time	Returns the current hour, day of week or year, time, or date
Math & Trig	Calculates absolute values, cosines, logarithms
Statistical	Performs common functions used for totals, averages, and high and low numbers in a range; advanced functions for t-tests, Chi tests, deviation

TABLE 6.1: Excel Functions *(continued)*

Category	Examples
Lookup & Reference	Searches for and returns values from a range; creates hyperlinks to network or Internet documents
Database	Calculates values in an Excel database table
Text	Converts text to uppercase or lowercase, trims characters from the right or left end of a text string, concatenates text strings
Logical	Evaluates an expression and returns a value of True or False, used to trigger other actions or formatting
Information	Returns information from Excel or Windows about the current status of a cell, an object, or the environment
Engineering	Included with Office 2000, but must be installed separately from the Analysis Toolpack

You don't have to learn all of Excel's functions, but you should know the common functions and have enough knowledge about others so that you can find them as you need them.

SUM is the only individual function included on the Standard toolbar. You can access all the functions (including SUM) using the Formula Palette.

Entering Functions

Objective XL2000.6.8

Before entering a function, make sure the cell where you want the results to be displayed is activated. Click Edit Formula (the equal sign) in the formula bar to open the Formula Palette. The Name box (to the left of the formula bar) changes to a Function box, displaying the name of the last function that was used (SUM), as shown in Figure 6.4.

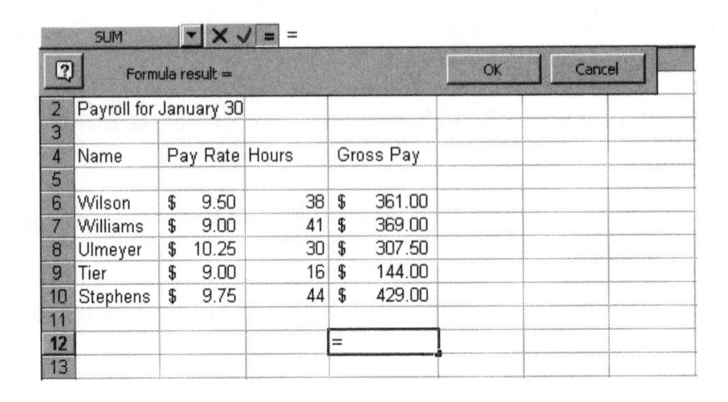

	A	B	C	D
2	Payroll for January 30			
3				
4	Name	Pay Rate	Hours	Gross Pay
5				
6	Wilson	$ 9.50	38	$ 361.00
7	Williams	$ 9.00	41	$ 369.00
8	Ulmeyer	$ 10.25	30	$ 307.50
9	Tier	$ 9.00	16	$ 144.00
10	Stephens	$ 9.75	44	$ 429.00
11				
12				=
13				

FIGURE 6.4

Excel's Formula Palette and Function box

Click the Function drop-down list to choose from recently used functions.

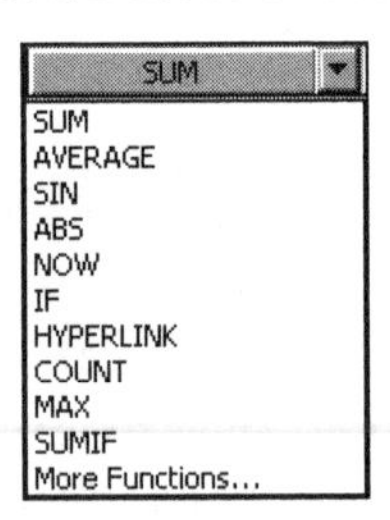

If the function you want is on the list, select it, and Excel moves the function to the formula bar and the Formula Palette. The Formula Palette includes a description of the function and one or more text boxes for the function's arguments, as shown in Figure 6.5.

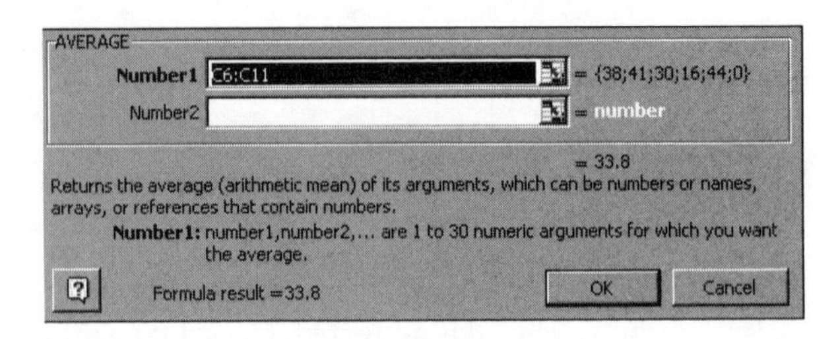

FIGURE 6.5

The Formula Palette (AVERAGE function)

For common functions that use a single range of cells as an argument, Excel "guesses" which numbers you might want to sum or average and places the range in the argument text box. Required arguments are bold, like

Number1 in Figure 6.5. These text boxes must be filled in to successfully use the function.

In Figure 6.5, you can't tell whether the range in the Number1 text box is correct, because the Formula Palette covers the cells. Click the Collapse Dialog button to shrink the Formula Palette.

Confirm that the correct cells are selected or use the mouse to select the correct cells before expanding the palette with the Expand Dialog button. After you have selected all the required arguments, click OK to finish the entry and to close the Formula Palette. As with any formula, the results of the function are displayed in the active cell; the function itself is displayed in the formula bar when the cell is active.

If the function you want is not listed in the Function box, choose More Functions at the bottom of the list to open the Paste Function dialog box, shown in Figure 6.6.

FIGURE 6.6

The Paste Function dialog box

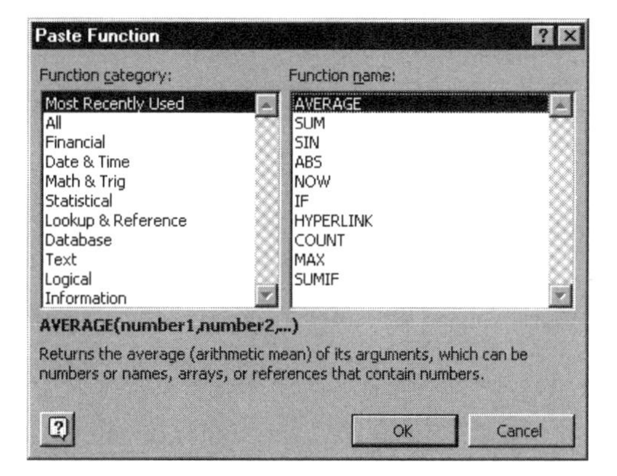

Objective XL2000.6.6

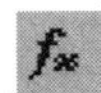

If you're using a function that you rarely use, you can start by opening the Paste Function dialog box by clicking the Paste Function button on the Standard toolbar.

Select a function category from the left pane of the dialog box, and then scroll the right pane and select a function. If you need more information, clicking the Office Assistant button opens the Assistant, which offers help on the selected function. Click the OK button to choose the selected function and to return to the Formula Palette.

Using Functions

1. Activate the cell where you want the result of the function to appear.
2. Click the Edit Formula button on the formula bar.
3. Choose a function from the Function Box drop-down list.

   OR

3. If the function does not appear on the list, choose More Functions to open the Paste Function dialog box. Choose a Category in the left pane and a function from the right pane. Click OK to return to the Formula Palette.
4. In the Formula Palette, select the first argument's text box. Click the Collapse Dialog button to move the dialog box, and then select the cells you want to include in the argument. Click the Expand Dialog button to return to the Formula Palette.
5. Click the OK button to complete the entry.

Hands On: Objectives XL2000.6.6 and 6.8

1. In a new or existing worksheet, use the Formula Palette to enter an AVERAGE function for a range of numbers:
   a) Enter a column of numbers.
   b) Click in the cell where you want the average.
   c) Click the = sign on the Formula Palette and choose Average from the list of available functions.
   d) Enter or select the cells you want to average.
   e) Click OK.
2. Use the Paste Function button on the Standard toolbar to create an average for a range of numbers.

Financial Functions

Excel has more than 50 built-in financial functions, and you don't have to be an accountant to find ways to use them. You can use the financial functions to determine how much your monthly car payments will be, how long you'll be paying off your student loan, or how much you can afford to finance on a new home. If you have a small business, the financial functions give you five ways to calculate depreciation and several tools to manage the profit you invest in various stocks and bonds.

To work with the financial functions, it's helpful to be familiar with the common arguments you encounter. These are the most common:

- FV (future value): What a loan or investment will be worth at a future time when all payments have been made
- NPER (number of periods): The number of months, years, days, or other periods for an investment or loan
- PMT (payment): The amount you periodically receive from an investment or are paid on a loan
- PV (present value): The initial value of an investment or loan
- RATE: The interest rate on a loan; the discount or interest rate on an investment

The amount of a periodic payment, present value, interest rate, and the total number of payments have a fixed relationship to each other. If you know any three of these, you can use one of the Excel financial functions to calculate the fourth:

- NPER: Calculates the number of periods
- PMT: Calculates the payment amount
- PV: Returns the present value for the amount loaned or invested
- RATE: Returns the interest rate

With these four functions, you can determine how much interest you paid on a loan or how much income you would receive from an annuity. The worksheet in Figure 6.7 uses the PMT function to calculate a monthly payment for various present values at an interest rate entered by the user.

When you work with financial functions, you need to make sure that all the arguments in a function are based on the same period: a day, a month, or a year. For example, in Figure 6.7 the payments are monthly payments, but the number of periods and the user-entered interest rate are based on years. In the PMT function arguments, then, NPER has to be multiplied by 12 and Rate divided by 12 so that all the arguments are based on a period of one month, as shown in Figure 6.8. (Pasting the PMT function in a cell opens this dialog box.)

FIGURE 6.7

Loan Payment Calculator worksheet

	A	B	C	D	E	F
1	LOAN PAYMENT CALCULATOR					
2						
3	Enter an interest rate here:		12%			
4						
5	Loan Life (in years)	$5,000.00	$10,000.00	$15,000.00	$20,000.00	$25,000.00
6						
7	1	$444.24	$888.49	$1,332.73	$1,776.98	$2,221.22
8	2	$235.37	$470.73	$706.10	$941.47	$1,176.84
9	3	$166.07	$332.14	$498.21	$664.29	$830.36
10	4	$131.67	$263.34	$395.01	$526.68	$658.35
11	5	$111.22	$222.44	$333.67	$444.89	$556.11
12	6	$97.75	$195.50	$293.25	$391.00	$488.75
13	7	$88.26	$176.53	$264.79	$353.05	$441.32
14	8	$81.26	$162.53	$243.79	$325.06	$406.32
15	9	$75.92	$151.84	$227.76	$303.68	$379.61
16	10	$71.74	$143.47	$215.21	$286.94	$358.68
17						

FIGURE 6.8

When using the PMT function, make sure the payments, number of periods, and the interest rate are based on the same time period.

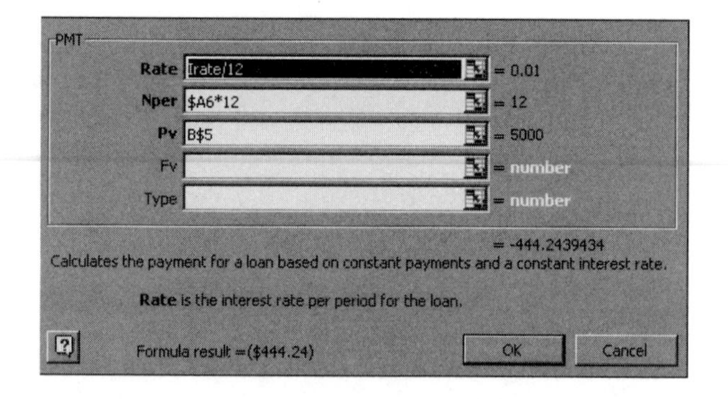

Calculating Payment (PMT) and Future Value (FV)

Objective XL2000.6.10

The Payment (PMT) function calculates the payments on a loan given constant payments and a constant interest rate. For example, if you want to buy a new truck, PMT can tell you how much your monthly payments would be based on the amount of the loan (the price of the truck—minus the down payment or trade-in) and the amount of the interest rate charged by the lender.

To use the PMT function:

1. Click the Paste Function button and choose Financial as the category. Select PMT, and click OK.

2. In the Rate box, enter the Interest Rate of the loan divided by the number of payments in a year (e.g., /12 for monthly payments).

3. In the NPER box, enter the number of payments you plan to make on the loan (e.g., 3 years = 36; 4 years = 48, and so on.)

4. In the PV box, enter the amount of the loan.

5. Click OK to paste the result.

If you enter the interest rate, number of payments, and amount of the loan in the worksheet *before* using the PMT function, click the Collapse Dialog buttons on the Paste Function dialog box to select the cells from the worksheet.

The Future Value (FV) function calculates the future value of an investment based on period, constant payments, and a constant interest rate. Let's say you just paid off the truck you bought four years ago. Rather than buy another truck right away, you decide to save your truck payments and use the money you save as a down payment on a new truck in two years. If your truck payments are $353 per month and you save for 24 months at 3.5 percent interest, FV shows you how much money you'll have to use as a down payment on your new truck.

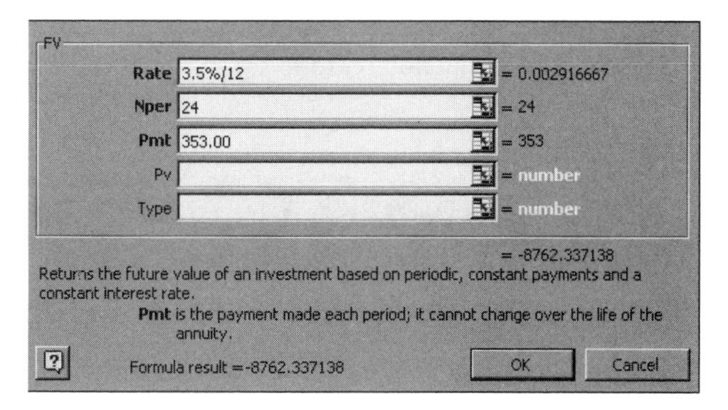

Working with Statistical Tables

Although you may never have a need for many of Excel's Statistics functions, it is in this category where you find everyday statistics functions such as AVERAGE. Other common statistics functions include:

- COUNT: Returns the number of numbers in a selected range

- MEDIAN: Another kind of average; used to calculate the value in the middle of a range
- MODE: Returns the value that occurs most frequently
- MIN: Returns the lowest value in a range
- MAX: Returns the highest value in a range

If you don't have a statistics background, don't worry. All of these functions are useful and easy to understand.

Using COUNT, MEDIAN, MODE, MIN, and MAX

Objective XL2000.6.7

The COUNT function tells you how many numbers are in a selected range. If you have a small worksheet, it's a breeze to glance down column C and say, "Looks like four numbers to me." It's a bit harder with larger worksheets, and the problem is compounded when some cells in a column are blank.

Entering a COUNT, MIN, or MAX function is as simple as the same steps you used when practicing the AVERAGE function in the Hands On earlier in the chapter:

1. Select the cell where you want the answer to go, then click the Paste Function button.
2. Choose COUNT (or MIN or MAX) from the Statistical category in the Paste Function dialog box.
3. Click OK to open the Formula Palette, then enter the range(s) you want Excel to examine.
4. Click OK to close the palette and apply your formula.

AVERAGE returns a value called the *arithmetic mean*—the total of all the values in a range divided by the number of values in the range. But there are two other types of averages: MEDIAN and MODE. MEDIAN tells you which value is the middle value in a range, and MODE tells you which value occurs most frequently, as shown in Figure 6.9. (COUNT is used to calculate the number of survey responses.)

FIGURE 6.9

Functions that return averages

Question 14: How much would you be wiling to pay for this product?	
Survey Number	Response
109871	30
109874	30
109880	40
109881	150
109889	40
109899	30
110001	40
110051	30
110060	33
Number of Responses	9
Mean Average	47
Median	33
Mode	30

The marketing department's survey question is "What is the most you are willing to pay for this product?" The AVERAGE answer is $47, but is it fair to say, "The average person is willing to pay $47 for our product."? No—only one person is willing to pay that much: the person who'll pay up to $150. If the marketing department uses the average, they'll price the product so high that most customers won't buy it.

That's where median MEDIAN and mode MODE come in. The response in the middle (the MEDIAN) is $33. There are as many people willing to pay less than $33 as people willing to pay more than $33, so this might be a good price. You can routinely use MEDIAN to test the AVERAGE. If MEDIAN and AVERAGE values are close to each other, there aren't too many bizarre values (such as the $150 answer) in the range. MODE tells us that more people are willing to pay $30 than any other price—more useful information for the marketing department to know.

Enter arguments for the financial and statistical functions as you would any other function.

Date and Logical Functions

Objective XL2000.6.9

The DATE function provides another way to insert a date in a cell. Enter arguments for year, month, and day (values, formulas, or cell references), and Excel inserts the corresponding date into the selected cell.

Using the NOW function to insert the system date and time is even easier, because it doesn't require any arguments. Choose the NOW function from the Paste Function dialog box, then click OK when the Formula Palette opens. The current date and time are inserted into the selected cell. Be aware, however, that a cell with a NOW function doesn't update automatically. Press F9 to update all NOW cells.

Using the IF Function

Objective XL2000.6.11

Use IF to evaluate whether a value meets a certain condition and display results depending on whether the condition is met. For example, a teacher who keeps her gradebook in Excel maintains a minimum passing score of 65 percent. An IF statement can be set up so that the cell adjacent to each student's score reads *Pass* or *Fail*, depending on whether that student's score is at or above 65 percent. Figure 6.10 shows an example of what this gradebook might look like.

FIGURE 6.10

Gradebook with IF statement

	A	B	C	D	E	F	G	H	I	J	K	L
1				TEAM PROJECTS			TESTS					
2												
3	POSSIBLE POINTS		10	10	5	15	30	40	110			
4												
5	Last Nam	First Nam	Project 1	Project 2	Project 3	Project 4	Midterm	Final	TOTAL POINTS	% GRADE		
6	Adams	Abby	10	9	5	15	29	39	107	100%	Pass	
7	Adams	Adam	5	3	5	7	17	20	57	53%	Fail	
8	Barney	Bill	0	10	4	10	22	33	79	74%	Pass	
9	Charles	Chuckie	10	10	5	15	26	35	101	94%	Pass	
10	Dawson	Denise	9	9	0	13	26	32	89	83%	Pass	
11	Ellis	Eileen	10	10	5	12	28	40	105	98%	Pass	
12	Friendly	Fritz	6	8	5	15	29	40	103	96%	Pass	
13	Gomez	Glen	9	10	5	15	28	40	107	100%	Pass	
14	Hill	Hector	6	8	5	15	25	32	91	85%	Pass	
15	Hill	Helen	10	7	4	13	20	29	83	78%	Pass	
16												
17	Class Averages		7.50	8.40	4.30	13.00	25.00	34.00	92.20	86%		
18												

You'll need three arguments for an IF statement:

- `Logical test` is any value or expression that can be considered True or False. For example, J6<65% is a logical expression; if the value in cell J6 is less than 65 percent, the expression is True. Otherwise, the expression evaluates to False.

- `Value_if_true` is the value that is displayed if `logical_test` is Truc. Using the teacher's example, if the value in `J6` is less than 65 percent, we want the word "Fail" to display, so we would type the word **Fail** as the value of true.
- `Value_if_false` is what displays if `logical_test` is False. In our case, we would enter the word **Pass** to produce the results in Figure 6.10.

Using an IF Function

1. Click in the cell where you want your first value displayed.
2. Click the Paste Function button and choose IF from the Logical category.
3. Enter the expression you want to use as a Llogical test.
4. Enter values for when the expression evaluates to True and False.
5. Click OK to close the Formula Palette.
6. Fill the formula to other cells as needed.

Using Lookup Functions

Objective XL2000E.6.3

Excel's *lookup functions* are used to look up information within an array. An *array* is an Excel database with one column and/or row that contains unique values. The VLOOKUP function searches vertically through the first column of an array until it finds a value. It then looks in a specified column of the value's row and returns the value in that column. VLOOKUP has three required and one optional argument:

- Lookup value: The value Excel searches for in the first column of the array. The lookup value can be a number, text, or a cell reference.
- Table array: The range of cells that contains the array. This can be a named range.
- Column index number: The column number in the array that contains the value that should be returned. The leftmost (first) column is column 1.
- Range lookup: This optional field can either be True or False.

Range lookup requires a bit of explanation. If this argument is False, the array doesn't have to be sorted by the values in the first column, but VLOOKUP will find only exact matches for the lookup value. If you don't enter **False**, this value is assumed to be True; the array must be sorted on the first column in ascending order, and Excel will use the closest match in the column. If the lookup value is larger than the last item in the array, Excel returns the last item. If it is smaller than the first item in the array, Excel returns an error.

Figure 6.11 shows a portion of an inventory worksheet that we'll use as an example. If you're creating an order form for the items in the inventory, you don't have to enter the item's description, cost, or price—you can look these items up in the array. Let's say, for example, that a user will enter an item number in cell `F15`. You can enter a formula in `G15` to look up the description. The formula `=VLOOKUP(F15,A2:F5,2,FALSE)`looks in the array `A2:F5` to find a match for the value in cell `F15` (the lookup value). The range lookup is `False`, so it will only be satisfied by an exact match, which is the behavior we'd like. If the wrong item number is entered, we don't want Excel to return a "close match." When it finds one, it looks in the second column of the array (column index number = `2`) and returns the value: the description of the item.

FIGURE 6.11

Use VLOOKUP to find values in an array like this one.

	A	B	C	D	E	F
1	Part	Desc	Cost	Quantity	Markup	Price
2	23612	Raceway 7 ft section	17.89	5	19%	21.29
3	35781	10BT SOHO 5 port hub	35.22	7	17%	41.21
4	42351	CAT5 Patch Cable 5 ft	3.18	22	17%	3.72
5	98431	Bulk CAT5 PVC	0.18	1200	19%	0.21

You can use the logical and lookup functions together to check first in the Quantity column, then return either the price or notification that an item's quantity is 0: `=IF(VLOOKUP(F15,A2:F5,4,FALSE)>0, VLOOKUP(F15,A2:F5,6,FALSE),"OUT OF STOCK")`.

The HLOOKUP function searches the first row of an array, and has similar arguments: lookup value, table array, row index number, and range lookup. Figure 6.12 shows a portion of a worksheet that includes a ticket cost calculator and a ticket price array. There are three different types of ticket prices: Corporate (C), Educational (E), and Individual (I). This formula in cell `C3` looks up the ticket price based on the lookup value (C, E, or I); the row index number is the number of tickets entered in `C4` plus 1: `=HLOOKUP(C1,B6:D12,C2+1,FALSE)`.

	A	B	C	D	E
1		Ticket Type:	E		
2		Quantity:	2		
3		Price Per Ticket:	=HLOOKUP(C1,B6:D12,C2+1,FALSE)		
4		Total Cost:	45.00		
5					
6		C	E	I	
7	1	20.00	22.50	22.50	
8	2	20.00	22.50	22.50	
9	3	20.00	15.00	22.50	
10	4	20.00	15.00	22.50	
11	5	17.00	15.00	22.50	
12	6	17.00	13.50	20.00	

FIGURE 6.12 HLOOKUP searches a row and then returns a value in the same column.

You can use Excel's horizontal and vertical lookup functions to search for information in any database where the contents of one field are unique, so look for opportunities to use the HLOOKUP and VLOOKUP functions whenever you know one value in an Excel database and have to return other information from the same "record."

Hands On: *Objectives XL2000.6.7, 6.9, 6.10, 6.11, and E.6.3*

1. In this exercise, you'll create and modify the Loan Payment Calculator worksheet shown in Figure 6.7.

   a) Enter the titles and labels shown in Figure 6.7. Apply formatting as indicated in the figure.

   b) Name cell C3 "IRate."

   c) In B7, click the = button to open the Formula Palette. Click the Function drop-down list and choose More Functions. Select the PMT financial function and enter the required arguments, as shown in Figure 6.8. Notice that Rate uses an absolute reference, while NPER and PV are mixed references. NPER should change when filled down rows, but remain unchanged when filled across columns; the opposite is true for PV.

   d) Enter a monthly interest rate in C3 to test the function. The monthly payment amounts will all be negative (because you're sending, not receiving, these payments). Edit the formula to begin =-PMT so that the payment value is positive. Fill the formula in B7 to the other monthly payment cells.

e) Test the worksheet by entering different interest rates and amounts. Notice the changes in the monthly payments.

f) For more practice with the PMT function, rebuild the worksheet so that the periods in column A are months rather than years.

2. Create the worksheet shown in Figure 6.9.

3. Open any worksheet that includes an average.

   a) Calculate the mode, median, min, max and count for the same range as the average.

   b) Practice using the DATE and NOW functions.

   c) Incorporate an IF function into the worksheet.

4. Create the worksheet shown in Figure 6.12 or a similar worksheet using the HLOOKUP function.

5. Create the worksheet shown in Figure 6.11. In another worksheet in the same workbook, create part of an order form that includes space for at least five items. Add lookups to return the description of each item. Use IF and a lookup function to create formulas for each item that returns the price if the quantity in stock is greater than or equal to the quantity ordered. If the quantity ordered is more than the quantity in stock, return the text string "INSUFFICIENT STOCK."

Charting Your Data

Charts are graphical representations of numeric data. Because charts make it easier for users to compare and understand numbers, they have become a popular way to present numeric data. Every chart tells a story. Stories can be simple—"See how our sales have increased"—or complex—"This is how our overhead costs relate to the price of our product." Either way, the story should be readily understandable. If you can't immediately understand what a chart means, it isn't a good chart.

Charts are constructed with *data points*—individual numbers in a worksheet—and *data series*—groups of related data points within a column or row. In the Vacation Meisters Tickets worksheet (see Figure 6.1), each of the numbers is a data point, and each column or row of numbers is a series.

There are many possible sets of data series in this worksheet. One set includes four data series—one for each city's row. Another set includes a data series for each month's column.

The most commonly used charts fall into one of two categories. *Pie Charts* show the relationship between pieces of an entity. The implication is that the pie includes *all* of something: all the tickets sold in a month or all the tickets sold in the first quarter (see Figure 6.13). The pie chart isn't appropriate for illustrating *some* of anything, so if there's not an obvious "all" in the data you're charting, don't use a pie chart.

FIGURE 6.13

Pie chart from the Tickets worksheet

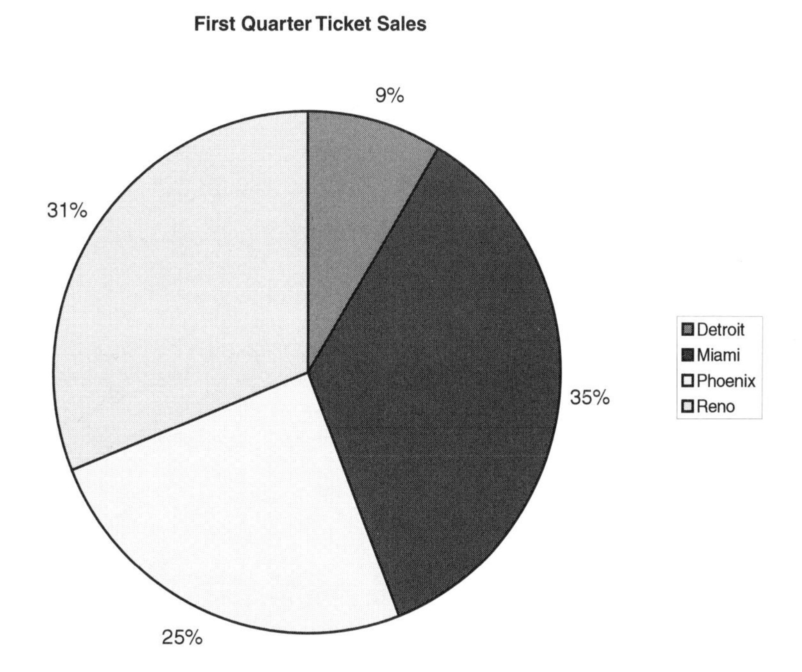

Pie and Series Charts

Series charts allow you to chart more than one data series. This lets you compare the data points in the series, such as January versus February, Reno versus Phoenix, and so on. Series charts are open-ended; there is no requirement that the data shown is all the data for a month or year. There are several types of series charts: line, area, bar, and column. You can give the same set of data a very different look by simply changing the chart type.

Line and Area Charts

Line charts and *area charts* are typically used to show one or more variables (sales, income, price) changing over time. An area chart is simply a line chart with the area below the line filled.

Line and area charts share a common layout. The horizontal line is called the x-axis, and the vertical line is the y-axis (the same x- and y-axes you may have learned about in algebra or geometry class when plotting data points). Line and area charts are available in 2-D versions (as shown in Figure 6.14) or in 3-D versions. (The 3-D version of a line chart is sometimes called a *ribbon chart*.) The series chart in Figure 6.14 is a line chart showing the relationship between ticket sales and each city during the first quarter. Each data series is a city.

FIGURE 6.14

A 2-D line chart[

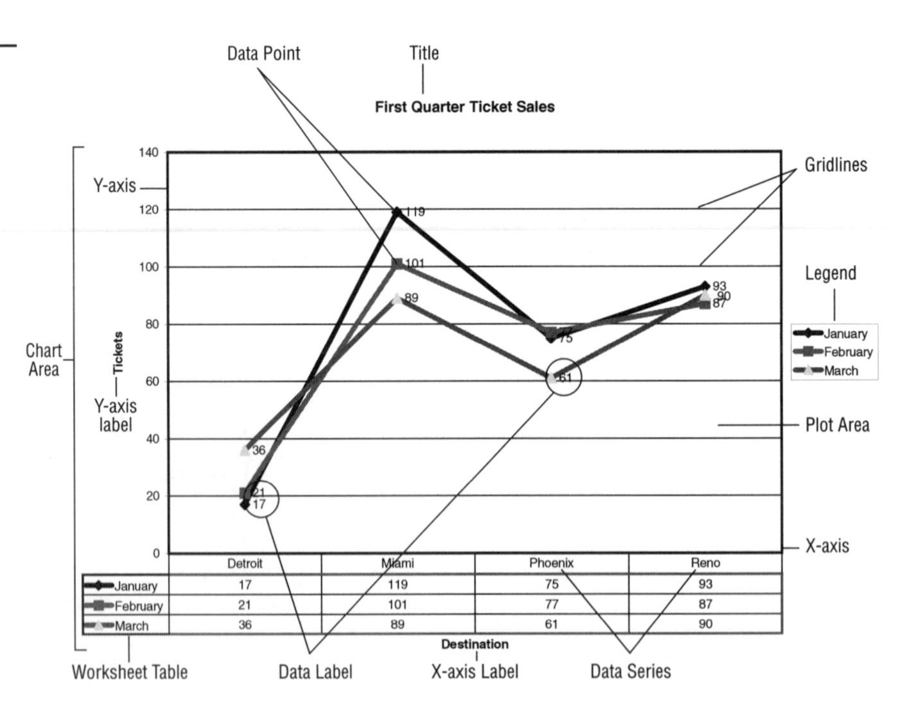

	Detroit	Miami	Phoenix	Reno
January	17	119	75	93
February	21	101	77	87
March	36	89	61	90

Bar and Column Charts

Figure 6.15 shows the same information as the line chart in Figure 6.14, but it is presented as a *bar chart*. Unlike area and line charts, a bar chart's axes are turned 90 degrees, so the x-axis is on the left side. Further, the bars give added substance to the chart. In a line chart, the reader notices the trend up or down in each line and the gaps between the lines. A bar chart makes all ticket sales seem more substantial, but it also makes the difference between destinations even clearer—like why doesn't anyone vacation in Detroit?

FIGURE 6.15
A bar chart

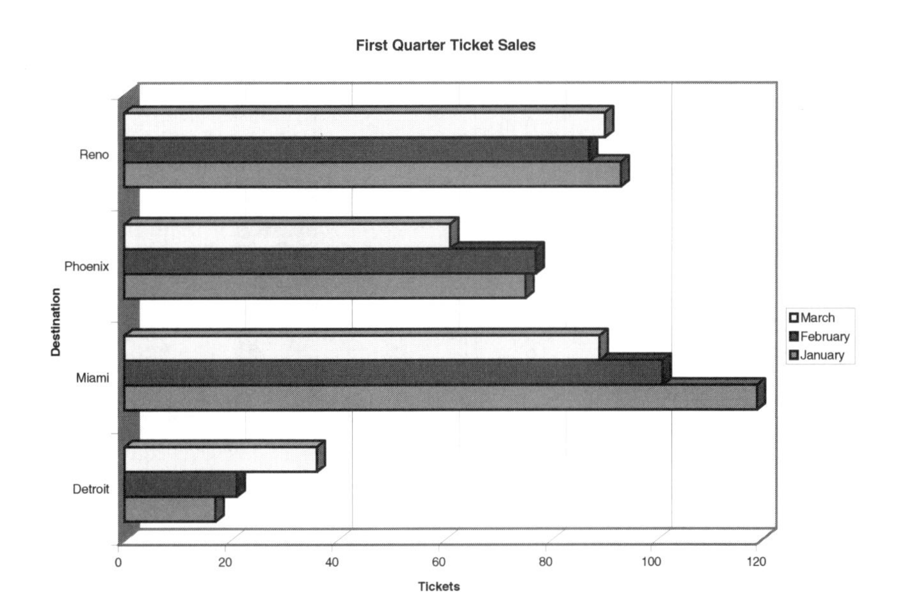

Column charts are the same as bar charts, but with the x-axis at the bottom. There are three-dimensional varieties of bar and column charts, which add depth to the regular chart. Cylinders, cones, and pyramids are variations of a column chart.

Excel also offers another style of bar and column chart—the *stacked chart*. In a stacked chart, parallel data points in each data series are stacked on top of or to the right of each other. Stacking adds another dimension to the chart, since it allows the user to compare sales between as well as within time periods—like providing a column chart and a pie chart for each time period. Figure 6.16 shows a stacked 3-D column chart, using the same data as Figures 6.14 and 6.15.

The 3-D charts have three axes. In a 3-D column chart, the x-axis is on the bottom; the vertical axis is the z-axis; the y-axis goes from front to back, providing the "three-dimensional" depth in the chart.

Don't worry about memorizing which axis is which in each chart type; there are ways to know which is which when you're creating or editing the chart.

FIGURE 6.16
A stacked 3-D column chart

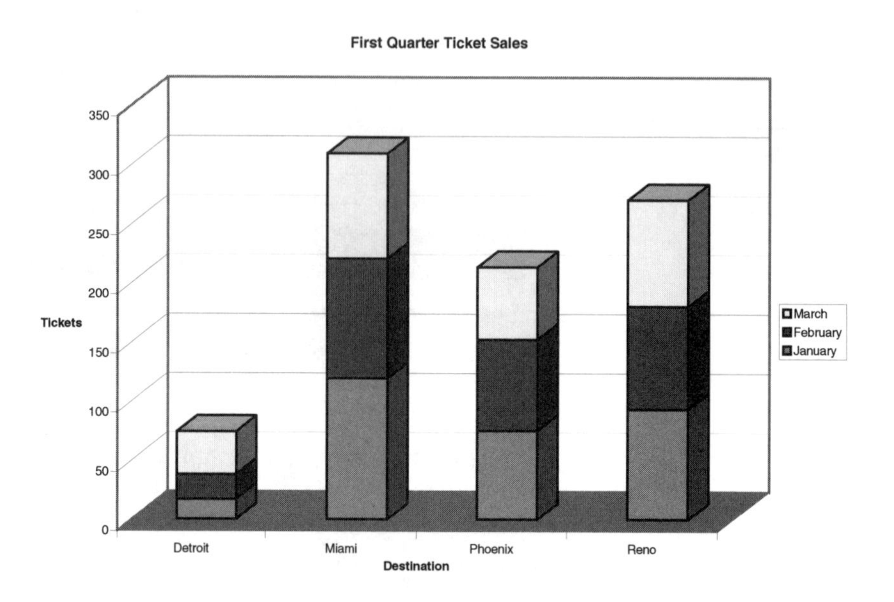

Creating Easy-to-Use Charts

Objective XL2000.7.2

The easiest way to create a chart is by using the Chart Wizard. Begin the charting process by selecting the data to be used in the chart. With the exception of the chart's title, everything that appears in the chart will be selected from entries in the worksheet. Make sure that the ranges you select are symmetrical: If you select four labels in rows 9–12 of column A, select data points from the other columns in rows 9–12. If you select labels in columns A–D of row 5, the data series you select should also be in columns A–D.

If you include blank rows or extra empty columns in your selection, you'll have empty spaces in your chart. Remember that you can hold the Ctrl key to select noncontiguous ranges of data. If you select some cells you don't want to include, press Esc and start again.

When you have your text and numbers selected, click the Chart Wizard button on the Standard toolbar to launch the Chart Wizard. In the first step of the Chart Wizard (see Figure 6.17), choose a chart type in the Chart Type list box. If the type of chart you want isn't listed, check out the chart types on the Custom Types tab.

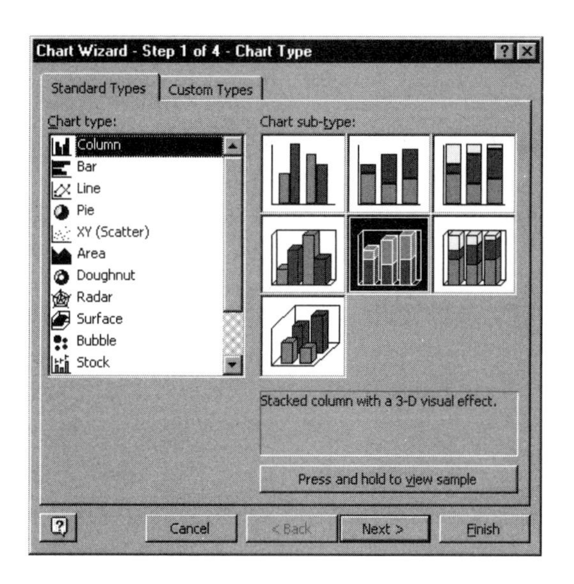

FIGURE 6.17 Step 1 of the Chart Wizard

For more information about a chart type, select the chart type, click the Chart Wizard's Office Assistant button, and choose Help With This Feature. The Assistant will offer to provide a sample of the selected chart.

After choosing a chart type in the left pane, choose a subtype in the right pane. To see a rough sample of the type and subtype using your data, click the Press And Hold To View Sample button in the Chart Wizard. When you've selected a type and a subtype, click Next to continue.

In the second step of the Chart Wizard, shown in Figure 6.18, you have an opportunity to make sure the range you selected is correct. (If it isn't, click the Collapse Dialog button on the right side of the Data Range text box and re-select the proper range before continuing.) Choose how you would like your data to be laid out by selecting Rows or Columns in the Series In option group. The preview will change to reflect the range and series arrangement you specify. Click Next.

In the Chart Wizard's third step, use the tabs to change options for various aspects of the chart:

Titles Enter titles for the chart and axes.

Axes Display or hide axes.

Gridlines Display gridlines and display or hide the third dimension of a 3-D chart.

Legend Display and place a legend.

FIGURE 6.18

Step 2 of the Chart Wizard

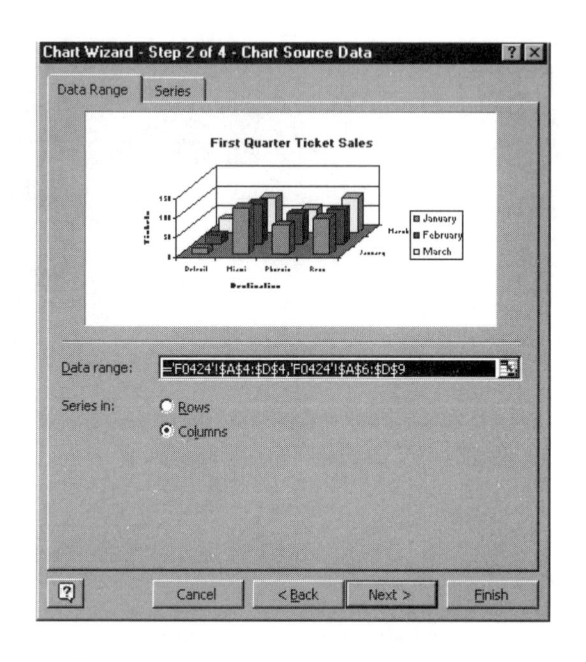

Data Labels Display text or values as data labels.

Data Table Show the selected range from the worksheet as part of the chart.

As you change options, the chart preview will reflect your changes. When you've finished setting options, click Next to continue.

Every chart needs a title. The title provides information that is not already included in the graphical portion of the chart. The chart's picture, legend, and title taken together should answer any questions about the timing, location, or contents of the chart.

In the last step of the Chart Wizard, you can place the chart on the current worksheet or on a new, blank sheet in the same workbook. If the chart is placed on its own sheet, it will print as a full-size, single-page chart whenever it is printed. If you add it to the current worksheet as an object, it will print as part of the worksheet, but it can also be printed separately. Enter a new sheet name, or choose As Object In, and click Finish to create and place the chart.

Don't spend a lot of time deciding whether to place the chart in the current worksheet or in its own worksheet. You can always move a chart object to its own worksheet or make a chart an object in another worksheet. Select the chart or chart object, right-click, and choose Location from the shortcut menu to open the Chart Location dialog box.

Moving and Sizing Chart Objects

If you place a chart as an object in the current worksheet, you might find that you'd like to move or resize the chart—especially if the chart is too small or if it covers part of the worksheet data. If you need to, moving a chart in Excel is a snap!

When the chart is placed in the worksheet, it is selected; it has square *handles* on the corners and sides. If the chart isn't selected, clicking once on the chart selects it. To deselect the chart and return to the worksheet, click once on part of the worksheet that isn't covered by the chart.

Moving and Sizing Charts

1. If the chart isn't selected, click once on the chart to select it.
2. To move the selected chart, point to the chart. Hold down the mouse button until the pointer changes to a four-headed arrow. Drag the outline of the chart to its new location. Release the mouse button to drop the outline and move the chart.
3. To size the chart, move the mouse pointer to one of the handles. Hold down the mouse button and drag the handle to change the size of the chart.

You might want to turn on Page Break Preview when sizing and moving charts to make sure they remain within the boundaries of a page. Page Break Preview isn't an option while a chart is selected, so click anywhere in the worksheet to deselect the chart, and then choose View ➢ Page Break Preview.

Printing Chart Objects

Objective XL2000.7.1

Even if you placed your chart as an object in the current worksheet, you can still print it separately. If the chart is selected when you print, it will print by itself on a full page. If the worksheet is selected, the worksheet prints, including the chart object.

Printing Chart Objects

1. To print a worksheet, including a chart object, activate any worksheet cell before printing.
2. To print a chart object as a full-page chart, select the chart before printing.

Hands On: *Objectives XL2000.7.1 and 7.2*

1. Create any or all of the charts shown in this section. Place at least one chart as an object in the current worksheet.
2. Create a pie chart to illustrate the Cyclops Proposal Software worksheet. Place the chart on the same page as the worksheet. Move and size the chart appropriately, and then print the entire worksheet.
3. Create a series chart to illustrate the Second Hand News Payroll information. Include a data table. Place the chart in a separate worksheet. Print the chart.
4. Select the row and column labels and all the regular numbers (not the formulas) in the Tickets worksheet. Open the Chart Wizard and choose each of the chart types in turn to see how it would present your data.

Editing and Formatting Charts

Creating a chart in Excel is really easy, and often you can use one of Excel's preformatted charts right "out of the box." But you can also customize charts so that they reflect exactly the emphasis and information that you want to convey.

Adding a Data Series

Excel's charting tools allow you to modify charts quickly and easily. You can, for example, create a simple series chart and then add another data series using drag-and-drop. (You can't add individual data points, just data series.)

Adding Data Series to a Chart

1. In the worksheet, select the data series to be added (be sure to select the same number of columns or rows represented in previous data series).
2. Drag the series and drop it in the chart.

Deleting a Data Series

A chart is a collection of graphic objects. To access the objects, select the chart, and then click the object you want to select. The selected object (data point, data series, title, and so on) will have handles. When an object is selected, you can delete or format the object.

Deleting a Data Series from a Chart

1. In the chart, select the data series or any data point in the series.
2. Press the Delete key on the keyboard.

Modifying and Formatting Charts

Objective XL2000.7.3

The *chart area* is a rectangular area within the chart window bounded by the chart border (refer back to Figure 6.14 for an example). Changing the size of the chart window changes the size of the chart area. All objects in a chart must be within the chart area.

The *plot area* is bounded by the axes and contains the columns, lines, wedges, or other objects used to represent the data points. Objects within the plot area have fixed locations and cannot be moved or individually sized. For example, the x-axis labels must be located near the x-axis. You can, however, resize all the objects in the plot area by increasing or decreasing the plot area itself. (There's an exception to this rule; see "Exploding Pies" later in this section.)

Objects outside the plot area and axes can be sized or moved to other locations in the chart area. The title and legend can be placed above, below, or in the plot area.

Any object in a chart can be selected and then formatted or deleted, with the exception of individual data points. Data points can be formatted, but only data *series* can be added or deleted. To select a data point, first select the data series, and then click once on the data point.

Using the Chart Toolbar

Common formatting options are available on the Chart toolbar, as indicated in Table 6.2. To display the Chart toolbar, right-click any toolbar, and click Chart. Select the chart object you want to format from the Chart Objects drop-down list, and then use the toolbar buttons to format the object or the entire chart.

TABLE 6.2: Chart Toolbar Buttons

Button	Button Name	Function
	Format *Object*	Opens the Format dialog box for the selected object.
	Chart Type	The drop-down menu lists chart types; clicking the button applies the type indicated on the button face.
	Legend	Displays or hides the legend.
	Data Table	Displays or hides the data table.
	By Row	Uses the selected worksheet rows as a data series.
	By Column	Uses the selected worksheet columns as data series.
	Angle Text Downward	Angles selected text downward.
	Angle Text Upward	Angles selected text upward.

Double-click an object to open the formatting dialog box for the object. For example, double-clicking any column in a data series opens the Format Data Series dialog box, shown in Figure 6.19.

FIGURE 6.19
Format Data Series dialog box

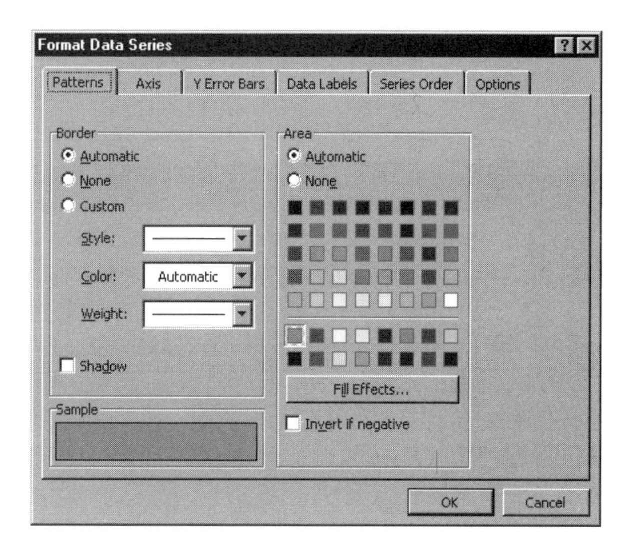

There are five or six pages in this dialog box, and each contains a group of settings for the selected data series. Depending on the chart type, the dialog box may or may not include a tab for Shape, Axis, or Y Error Bars.

Patterns These options are used to set the color and pattern for the series.

Shape This option is only available with 3-D charts when you can choose from a variety of shapes to display the data series.

Axis If the chart has more than one series, this tab allows you to add a second vertical axis at the right end of the plot area scaled to this data series.

Y Error Bars This option adds a graphic display of the standard error; it is used to approximate sampling error when the data in a chart is a statistical sample being applied to a larger population.

Data Labels Use this tab to add a descriptive label or the numeric value for each data point in the series.

Series Order This tab allows you to reorder the series in a chart; this is especially helpful with 3-D charts, in which the selected range is initially charted in reverse order.

Options This tab offers settings for the bar or column overlap, gap, and color variation.

For more information on a specific control within the Data Series dialog box, click the dialog box Help button (?), and then click the control.

Similar options are available when you double-click a selected data point, the plot area, chart area, or other chart object. You can select any object or series, right-click, then select Format from the shortcut menu. Chart Type is always a shortcut menu option, giving you access to all the types and subtypes. If the entire chart is selected, Chart Options appears on the menu.

Inserting and Formatting Titles

If you decide to insert a title, select the chart, right-click, and open the Chart Options dialog box from the shortcut menu to open the Titles page of the dialog box. You can edit or format existing titles (including placeholders) in a selected chart without having to use the Chart Options from the shortcut menu. To change the text in a title, click once to select the title, and then click again to edit the selected text.

To seperate a title into multiple lines, place the insertion point where you want the second line to begin, hold the Ctrl key, and press Enter.

To format a title, double-click the title (or select the title, right-click, and choose Format Title from the shortcut menu) to open the Format Chart Title dialog box. Use the controls in the Patterns, Font, and Alignment pages to format the title as you would format other text.

To change all the fonts used in a chart, double-click in the chart area and change fonts in the Format Chart Area dialog box.

Exploding Pies

If you want to emphasize specific data points in a pie chart, you can *explode* the pie chart by moving one or more pieces of the pie farther from the center (see Figure 6.20). Usually, you'll move one or two individual slices to emphasize specific data points in the chart.

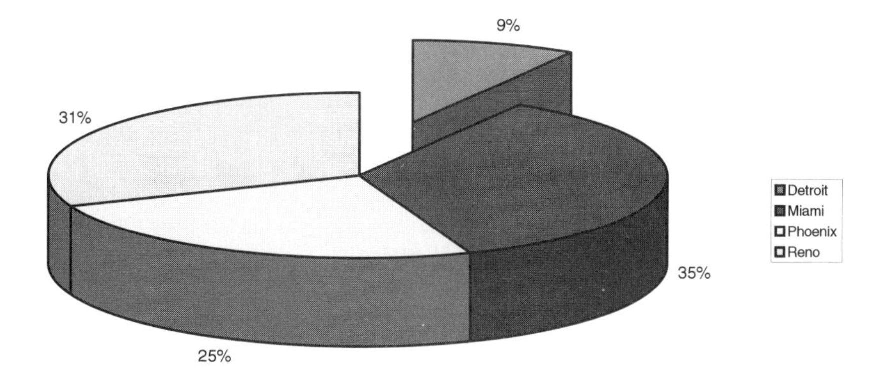

FIGURE 6.20
Exploded pie chart

In Figure 6.20, the Detroit slice has been exploded. Although you can select an exploded pie in the Chart Wizard, the Wizard explodes all slices of the pie or the first slice, depending on which explosion sample you choose. It's easiest to create an unexploded pie of the type you wish and then edit the chart to explode select slices.

If you want to explode all the slices in an existing chart, select the chart, and then select the pie in the plot area. Excel will put handles on the outside edge of each slice of the pie. Drag any slice away from the center to explode all the pie slices.

To explode a single pie slice, first select the chart, and then click the pie to select the data series. With the series selected, click to select the slice you want to explode and drag the slice away from the center.

When you explode all slices in a pie, each slice gets smaller as you increase the space between the slices. If you explode slices individually, the other slices remain centered in the plot area, and the slices don't get smaller.

Hands On: Objective XL2000.7.3

1. Create or open a 2-D pie chart. Change the chart to a 3-D pie. Explode one slice, and change the color and pattern of all the slices.

2. Create or open a series chart object. Move the chart to its own worksheet. Format each series. Edit the text and then format the chart's title (insert a title if it doesn't have one).

Using Custom and Special Formats

You already know how to apply cell formats from the toolbar and the Format Cells dialog box. In this section, you'll kick your skills up a few notches with four tools for specialized formatting: AutoFormat, styles, conditional formatting, and custom formats.

AutoFormatting

Objective XL2000.3.7

Excel's AutoFormat feature includes a number of canned worksheet designs, including formal business, list, and 3-D formats. If you're in a hurry, the predesigned formats allow you to quickly apply a standard format to all or part of a worksheet.

Before you AutoFormat, select the cells to be formatted. This will usually include all the text and numbers in your worksheet, but you might want to apply an AutoFormat to titles or data only. Choose Format ➢ AutoFormat from the menu bar to open the AutoFormat dialog box. Click the Options button to expand the dialog box to display the formatting elements you can apply, as shown in Figure 6.21. For example, you might choose not to apply column widths if you've already adjusted column widths and don't want them changed. As you select formats and turn the Formats To Apply options on and off, the selected thumbnail will change to reflect your choices.

FIGURE 6.21
AutoFormat dialog box

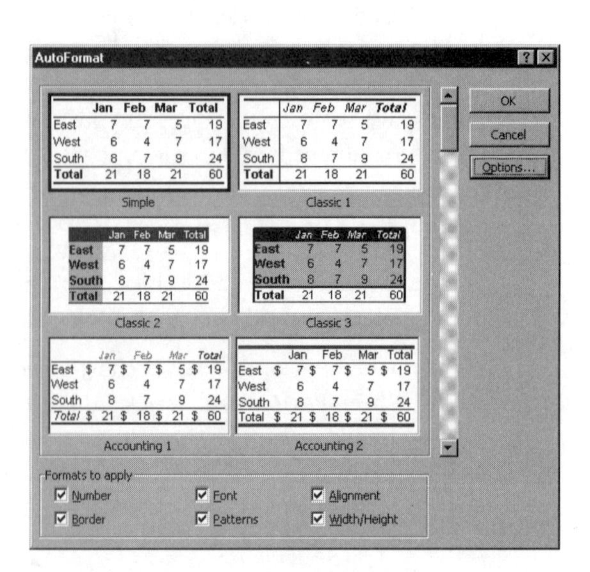

AutoFormatting a Worksheet

1. Select the portion of the worksheet you want to AutoFormat.
2. Choose Format ➢ AutoFormat from the menu bar to open the AutoFormat dialog box.
3. Choose a format.
4. Click the Options button to show Formats To Apply. Deselect any options you don't want to include.
5. Click OK to apply the selected formats.

Working with Styles

Objective XL2000.3.11

AutoFormats are composed of *styles*, specifications about one or more formatting options. Most AutoFormats include several styles: Arial 14-point teal bold for the title; Arial 12-point, accounting format, for the numbers; Arial 12-point bold with a top border for totals.

Creating Your Own Styles

Although you can't create your own AutoFormats, you can create individual styles and apply them to ranges in a worksheet. You can create a style in two ways: from existing formatted entries or by specifying formatting options as you create the style. If the formatting you want to save as a style already exists in the worksheet, select a range that includes the formatting; if not, select a cell that's close to what you want so you'll have less formatting to modify. Choose Format ➢ Style from the menu bar to open the Style dialog box shown in Figure 6.22.

Don't begin creating a style by clicking options. First, enter a descriptive name for the new style in the Style Name text box. As soon as you begin entering the name, previously disabled options will be enabled. Use the check boxes to exclude format settings from the style, or click the Modify button to open the familiar Format Cells dialog box and set other formatting attributes before clicking OK. When you return to the Style dialog box, the Style will include the options you selected in the Format Cells dialog box. Click the Add button to create the style.

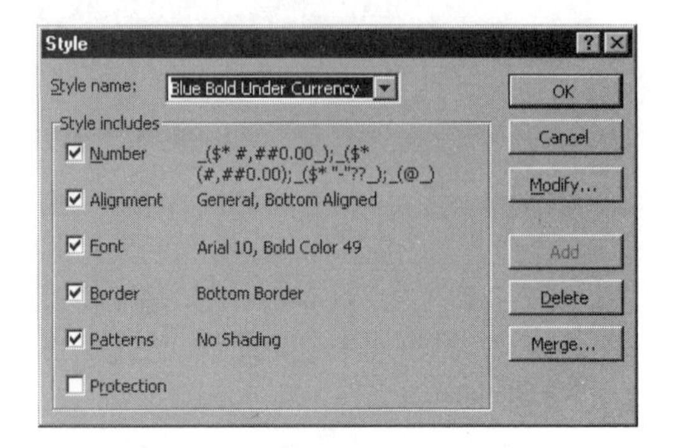

FIGURE 6.22
Style dialog box

Creating a Style

1. Select cells that are the same as, or similar to, the style you want to create.
2. Choose Format ➢ Style from the menu bar to open the Style dialog box.
3. Enter a new name for the style.
4. Use the check boxes to disable formatting features that should not be included in the style.
5. Click the Modify button and change any format options you wish in the Format Cells dialog box. Click OK to close the dialog box.
6. Click the Add button to add the new style. Click Close to close the dialog box, or click OK to apply the style to the current selection and close the Style dialog box.

Using Existing Styles

Applying a style that already exists in a workbook is simple:

1. Select the range you want to format.
2. Choose Format ➢ Style to open the Style dialog box.
3. Choose the style you want from the Style Name drop-down list.
4. Click OK.

If the style you want to apply is in a different workbook, you can merge the style into the current workbook and then apply it:

1. Open the workbook that contains the style.
2. Choose Format ➢ Style to open the Style dialog box.

3. Click the Merge button to open the Merge Styles dialog box.

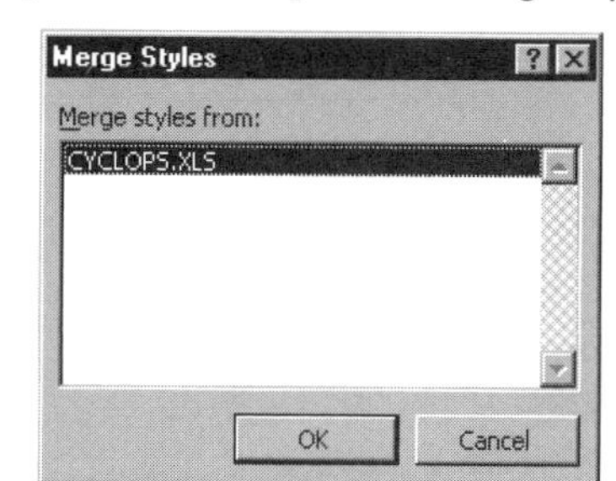

4. Choose the open workbook that contains the styles you want to add to the existing workbook, and then click OK.
5. Choose the merged style from the Style Name drop-down list.

Notice that you don't get to select which styles to merge; you get them all. If you have a style in both workbooks with the same name, Excel will open a dialog box asking if you want to merge these styles, too. If you choose Yes, the styles from the selected workbook will replace styles with the same name in the current workbook. If you choose No, the current styles remain.

Potential conflicts in style names is a good reason to give styles descriptive, rather than functional names.

Deleting and Editing Styles

Styles hang around forever unless you delete them. To delete a style, open the Style dialog box, select the style from the Style Name drop-down list, and click the Delete button.

To change an existing style, choose the style from the Style Name drop-down list. Change any formatting options you wish, and then click the Add button to add the changes to the style.

Conditional Formatting

Objective XL2000E.4.3 and XL2000E.10.1

With *conditional formatting*, you can apply formats to selected cells based on a *condition*. A condition is an expression that, when evaluated, is either true or false. Examples of conditions are: Hourly Rate greater than $10.00, State equal to CA, and Cost between 2000 and 3000.

For any given cell, each of the conditions will either be true or false: the value in the cell either is or is not greater than $10.00, equal to CA, or between 2000 and 3000. You can apply font attributes, borders, or patterns to cells based on whether the condition is true or false. In Figure 6.23, for example, all values greater than 200 are bold and have a border.

FIGURE 6.23

Loan Payment worksheet with conditional formatting

Interest Rate						
10%						
	Amount Borrowed					
Loan Life (Years)	$5,000.00	$10,000.00	$15,000.00	$20,000.00	$25,000.00	
						M
1	$420.14	$840.28	$1,260.42	$1,680.56	$2,100.69	O
2	$210.94	$421.88	$632.82	$843.76	$1,054.71	N
3	$141.21	$282.42	$423.63	$564.84	$706.05	T
4	$106.35	$212.69	$319.04	$425.38	$531.73	H
5	$85.43	$170.86	$256.28	$341.71	$427.14	L
6	$71.48	$142.97	$214.45	$285.94	$357.42	Y
7	$61.52	$123.05	$184.57	$246.10	$307.62	
8	$54.06	$108.11	$162.17	$216.22	$270.28	P
9	$48.25	$96.49	$144.74	$192.99	$241.23	M
10	$43.60	$87.20	$130.80	$174.40	$218.00	T

To apply conditional formatting to a selection, choose Format ➢ Conditional Formatting from the menu bar. The Conditional Formatting dialog box opens (see Figure 6.24).

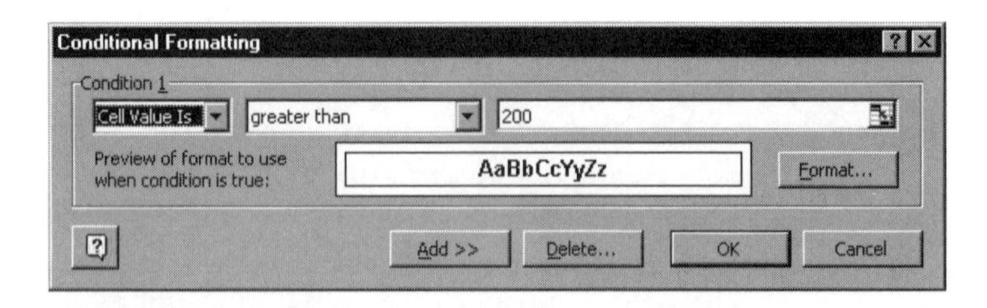

FIGURE 6.24

Conditional Formatting dialog box

From the first drop-down list, choose either Cell Value Is to base the formatting on the value in the cell or Formula Is to base the formatting on a formula that returns a value of true or false. Don't let this confuse you; it doesn't matter whether the cell contains a typed-in value or a formula. If you want the format to be applied based on the number or text that appears in a cell, use Cell Value Is. You'll only use Formula Is with specialized functions such as the Date and Logical functions.

In the second drop-down list, choose one of the conditional operators: Between, Not Between, Equal To, Not Equal To, Greater Than, Less Than, Greater Than Or Equal To, or Less Than Or Equal To. In the condition text box, either type in a constant (such as 200), select a cell in the worksheet, or enter a formula. (There's more about the second and third options in the next section *Using Cell References in Conditions*.)

Now click the Format button to open an abbreviated version of the Format Cells dialog box. Some of the formats are disabled (such as font type and size), so you know you can't use them for conditional formatting. You can, however, pile on borders, shading, and different colors to make cells jump off the page. Choose the format options you want to apply when the condition is true, and then click OK to return to the Conditional Formatting dialog box. Click OK to close the dialog box, and the formats will be applied to the appropriate cells.

What if you want more than one alternate format? For example, you might want to show last month's sales increases in blue and decreases in red. In this case, you need two conditions. Create the first condition in the Conditional Formatting dialog box, and then click the Add button to add another condition.

Using Cell References in Conditions

Objective XL2000.6.4

You can compare the value in a cell to the value in another cell in the worksheet. For example, you might select a cell that shows an average and apply a conditional format to all the numbers that are above average. In this case, each cell you conditionally format will refer to the cell that contains the average, so you'll use an absolute cell reference. Simply click the cell with the average to place the absolute reference in the condition text box.

Using relative references in conditional formats is just as easy. In the section of the Tickets worksheet shown below, February sales that were greater than January sales are bold and shaded.

	A	B	C
1	**Vacation Meisters Ticket Sales**		
2	First Quarter		
3			
4	Destination	January	February
5			
6	Detroit	17	**21**
7	Miami	119	101
8	Phoenix	75	**77**
9	Reno	93	87

To decide what kind of reference to create, think about how you would create a formula for each cell in column C to compare it to the value in column B. Each cell needs its own formula relative to column B, so to create this condition, make sure that you use relative cell references. In this example:

1. Select the cells.
2. Open the Conditional Formatting dialog box and choose Cell Value Is and Greater Than.
3. Click in the conditions text box, then click cell B6. B6 is added as an absolute cell reference: `$B$6`.
4. Use the F4 key to change the reference to a relative reference.

Extending Conditional Formatting You don't have to apply conditional formatting to all the cells in a range at once. You can create conditional formats for one cell and tweak them until they're exactly what you want. Then select the entire range you want to format, including the formatted cell. Choose Format ➢ Conditional Formatting, and the dialog box will open, displaying the format you created. Just click OK, and the format will be adjusted and applied to the other selected cells.

Using Formulas as Conditions

Now add one more flourish: you can compare a cell to a formula. For example, you only want to bold and shade a cell in column C if the value is at least 3 greater than the value in column B. If sales didn't go up by at least three tickets, it's not a substantial enough increase to warrant special formatting. So instead of using the condition `greater than B6`, create the condition `greater than B6+3`. Use formulas like this to format the sales that went up more than 20 percent or individual items that represent more than 5 percent of the total budget.

Conditionally Formatting Cells

1. Select the cells you want to format.
2. Choose Format ➢ Conditional Formatting from the menu bar to open the Conditional Formatting dialog box.
3. Choose Cell Value Is (most of the time) or Formula Is.
4. Select a conditional operator.

Conditionally Formatting Cells *(continued)*

5. In the condition text box, enter a value, cell reference, or formula.
6. Click the Format button. Set up a format for this condition, and click OK.
7. If you have additional conditions or formats, click the Add button and repeat steps 3–6 for each condition.
8. Click OK to close the dialog box and apply conditional formatting.

Using Formatting Codes

Excel includes a huge number of formats, but you might need a particular format that isn't part of the package. You can use codes to create *custom formats* to handle specialized formatting needs. A common use of custom formats is creating formats that include a text string: **10 mpg, $1.75/sq ft, or $3.00/dozen**. You create custom formats in the Format Cells dialog box. But before you open the dialog box, let's look at the codes you'll use to create custom formats.

Codes for Numbers

Objective XL2000E.4.2

Each of the codes shown in Table 6.3 is a placeholder for a digit or a character. You string together a number of placeholders to create a format. If a number has more digits to the right of the decimal than there are placeholders, the number will be rounded so it fits in the number of placeholders. For example, if the format has two placeholders to the right of the decimal, 5.988 will be rounded to 5.99.

Excel differentiates between significant digits and insignificant digits. A *significant digit* is part of a number's "real value." In the value 3.70, the 3 and 7 are significant; the zero is an *insignificant digit*, because removing it doesn't change the real value of the number. Only zeros can be insignificant. Insignificant zeros after the decimal are called trailing zeros. Different placeholders display or hide insignificant zeros.

TABLE 6.3: Number Format Codes

Code	Use	Example
#	Displays significant digits.	###.## formats 3.50 as 3.5 and 3.977 as 3.98
0	Displays all digits; placeholders to the right of the decimal are filled with trailing zeros, if required.	##0.00 formats 3.5 as 3.50 and 57.1 as 57.10
?	Displays significant digits and aligns decimal or slash placeholders.	???.?? aligns decimals and displays 3.50 as 3.5, 57.10 as 57.1, and 3.977 as 3.98
/	Displays a number as a fraction.	# ??/?? displays 7.5 as 7 1/2
,	Thousands separator; this code is also used to format numbers as if they were divided by a thousand or a million.	##,### displays 99999 as 99,999; ##, displays 9,000 as 9; ##,, displays 9,000,000 as 9
( )	Format negative numbers.	(##,###) formats -99999 as (99,999)
-	Places a hyphen in a number.	000-000 formats 123456 as 123-456
" "	Indicates a text string.	###"/per hour" formats 100 as 100/per hour

You can add color to a format. Simply type the name of the color in brackets at the beginning of the format: [BLUE], [GREEN], [RED].

There are a couple of approaches to conditional formatting within a custom format. If you include two formats, separated by a semicolon, Excel uses the first format for positive numbers and the second for negative numbers. For example, the format ##,###; RED]##,### will format negative numbers in red. If you have three sections of format, the third format is used for zero. The format [BLUE]##; [RED]##; [WHITE]## will display blue positive numbers, red negative numbers, and white zeros. On a white background, this makes zeros disappear. A fourth section can be used for text that appears in the cell (see *Codes for Text* below).

You can enter a condition in brackets, followed by the two formats to be used based on whether the condition is true or false. A common use for a conditional custom format is formatting zip codes when some have nine digits and others have five. The condition [>99999] will be true for nine-digit zip codes, so the format [>99999]00000-0000;00000 will format both nine-digit and five-digit zip codes correctly, including leading zeros.

Codes for Dates and Times

Use the format codes shown in Table 6.4 to create date and time formats. The m code is used for both months and minutes. Excel treats the m as a month code unless it appears directly after a code for hours or before a code for seconds.

TABLE 6.4: Date and Time Format Codes

Code	Use	Examples
m	Months as ##	Formats January as 1 and December as 12
mm	Months as 00	Formats January as 01 and December as 12
mmm	Months as three-letter abbreviation	Formats January as Jan
mmmm	Month named spelled out	Formats Jan as January
mmmmm	Month's first letter	Formats January as J and December as D
d	Days as ##	Formats 1 as 1 and 31 as 31
dd	Days as 00	Formats 1 as 01 and 31 as 31
ddd	Days as weekday abbreviation	Formats 1/1/99 as Fri
dddd	Days as weekday	Formats 1/1/99 as Friday
yy	Years as 00	Formats 1999 as 99
yyyy	Years as 0000	Formats 1/1/99 as 1999
h, m, s	Hours, minutes, and seconds as ##	Formats 3 as 3
hh, mm, ss	Hours, minutes, and seconds as 00	Formats 3 as 03
AM/PM	12-hour clock, uppercase	h AM/PM formats 3 as 3 AM
am/pm	12-hour clock, lowercase	hh am/pm formats 3 as 03 am
a/p	12-hour clock, short form	hh:mm a/p formats 3 as 3:00 a

If you don't include one of the versions of am/pm, Excel bases time on the 24-hour clock.

According to Microsoft, Excel 2000 is fully Y2K compliant. Additional date formats for displaying four-digit years have been added. Choose Format ➢ Cells, click the Number tab, and then scroll through the Type list to see them. For more information, go to www.microsoft.com/technet/topics/year2k/default.htm.

Codes for Text

If you want to include text along with a number in a cell, put quotes around the text string or precede the text with a backslash (\ ). If you want to include a format for text entered in a cell, make it the final section in your format. The @ symbol stands for any text typed in the cell, so [BLUE]@ will format text in the cell in blue. (If you just type the format [BLUE], the text won't appear at all, but it would be blue if it did appear!)

If you don't include a text format, text entered in the cell is formatted according to the defaults or the formatting applied with the toolbar and Format Cells dialog box.

Spacing Codes

You'll use spacing codes for two reasons: alignment and filling. In some formats, negative numbers are surrounded by parentheses. If you use parentheses in a custom format, you need to add a space to the end of the positive format that will line up with the right parenthesis in a negative value. (This keeps the decimal points lined up.) To create a one-character space in a format, include an underscore: ##,##0.00_.

You can fill any empty space in a cell by entering an asterisk (*) and then a fill character in the number format. For example, the accounting format begins with an underscore and a dollar sign, followed by an asterisk and a space before the digit placeholders: _$* #,##0.00. This ensures that the dollar sign is one space from the left edge of the cell, and that all the room between the dollar sign and digits is filled with spaces.

Creating a Custom Format

To create a custom format, select the cells to be formatted and open the Format Cells dialog box. When you've decided which format you want to create, you can enter the custom format in the Format Cells dialog box. On the Number page, choose Custom from the Format Type list. The Type list already includes formats. Scroll the list and choose a format similar to the custom format you want to create, and then edit the format, adding or deleting placeholders. Alternatively, you can select the format in the Type text box and begin typing a format from scratch. As you enter a format, the sample will reflect your changes. Click OK to create the format. To delete a custom format, select it from the Type list, and then click the Delete button in the Format Cells dialog box.

Creating a Custom Format

1. Select the cells to be formatted. Choose Format ➢ Cells from the menu bar or right-click and choose Format Cells from the shortcut menu.
2. On the Number page of the Format Cells dialog box, choose Custom from the category list.
3. Enter a format in the Type text box.
4. Click OK to apply the custom format.

Hands On: Objectives XL2000.3.7, 3.11, 6.4, E.4.2, E.4.3, and E.10.1

1. Use AutoFormat to format an existing worksheet.
2. Create conditional formats in an existing worksheet. Create at least one format that includes two or more conditions.
3. In an existing worksheet, create:
   a) A custom format that includes a text string.
   b) A custom format that includes different colors for positive and negative numbers.
   c) A custom format that prints the word "Zero" if the value in a cell is 0.
4. Create a style suitable for header rows or columns. Select some cells in your worksheet and apply the new style.

Tracking Data with Excel

You've worked with Excel's spreadsheet and charting features. In the next two sections, you'll use Excel's database capabilities to create and manage lists. A *database* is a list with a specific structure defined by its *fields*, the categories of information it contains. A telephone directory, for example, is a printout of a computer database whose fields include last name, first name, middle initial, address, and telephone number. An individual listing in the phone book is a *record* in the database, containing a single set of the fields: one phone user's last name, first name, middle initial, address, and telephone number. Each field must have a unique *field name*: LastName, last name, LASTNAME, and LastNameforListing are all possible field names for a field containing last names. In Excel, fields are columns, and each record is an individual row.

The Traverse Tree Sales worksheet (shown in Figure 6.25) is an Excel database. Each field is a separate column. Field names (Month, County, Type, Quantity, and Bundles) are used as column labels. Each individual row is a record.

FIGURE 6.25

The Traverse Tree database

	A	B	C	D	E
1	Traverse Tree Sales				
2	County Cooperative Tree Orders				
3					
4	Month	County	Type	Quantity	Bundles
5	Jan-2000	Genesee	White Pine	37000	74
6	Jan-2000	Oakland	Blue Spruce	22500	45
7	Jan-2000	Oakland	White Pine	15500	31
8	Jan-2000	Oakland	Concolor Fir	13500	27
9	Jan-2000	Genesee	Blue Spruce	12500	25
10	Feb-2000	Oakland	Scotch Pine	11000	22
11	Feb-2000	Genesee	Frazier Fir	6500	13
12	Feb-2000	Lake	Blue Spruce	42500	85
13	Feb-2000	Lake	White Pine	32000	64
14	Mar-2000	Lake	Frazier Fir	14500	29
15	Mar-2000	Kalkaska	Blue Spruce	13500	27
16	Mar-2000	Lake	Concolor Fir	12000	24
17	Mar-2000	Kalkaska	Concolor Fir	10000	20
18	Apr-2000	Kalkaska	Frazier Fir	7500	15
19	Apr-2000	Lake	Blue Spruce	31000	62
20	Apr-2000	Lake	White Pine	26500	53

Microsoft Access is designed specifically to create databases and allows you to create and manage incredibly large numbers of records, limited only by the amount of space on your hard drive. Excel databases are limited to the number of rows in a worksheet: 65,536. Despite these and other limitations, Excel's list management features are powerful tools for creating small databases and manipulating smaller sets of records from larger databases.

Creating a database is as simple as creating any other worksheet, but there are two additional rules for worksheets that you intend to use as databases:

Blank rows Signal the end of a database. *Don't* leave a blank row between column headings and data records. *Do* leave a blank row after all records and before totals, averages, or other summary rows.

Field names At the top of columns. Field names must be in a single cell and unique within a worksheet. Be consistent: label every column.

Any worksheet you've already created can be used as a database, but you might have to delete or add rows or edit column labels to meet these requirements.

Sorting a Database

Objective XL2000E.10.2

Database software must allow you to do two distinct things with data: organize, or *sort*, the data in a specific order (for example, alphabetized by state), and separate, or *filter*, the data to find specific information (for example, all your customers who live in Oregon).

To sort the data in a database, first select any cell in the database (do *not* select the column or only that column will be sorted). Then choose Data ➢ Sort from the menu bar to have Excel select the records in the database and open the Sort dialog box, shown in Figure 6.26.

FIGURE 6.26
Excel's Sort dialog box

Excel will select all cells above, below, to the right, and to the left of the cell you selected until it encounters a blank column and row. Excel will examine the top row of the database and assign it as a record by including it in the selection, or deselect it, assuming it is a row of column headings. The last section of the Sort dialog box lets you correct an incorrect selection by specifying whether you have a header row.

If you didn't select a cell within the database before choosing Data ➢ Sort, Excel will open a dialog box and warn you that there was no list to select. Click the OK button in the dialog box, select a cell in the database, and choose Data ➢ Sort again.

In a telephone book, records are sorted initially by last name. This is called a *primary sort*. What if there is a tie: for example, all the people whose last name is Smith? If you know that lots of your records will have the same entry in the primary sort field, you can do a *secondary sort* on another field, such as first name. And if you have two David Smiths, you can use middle initial as a *tertiary sort*. Note that the secondary and tertiary sorts occur only in case of a tie at a higher level of sorting.

You can sort a maximum of three levels using the Sort dialog box. Records can be sorted in *ascending order* (i.e., A–Z or 0–9) or *descending order* (i.e., Z–A or 9–0).

1. In the Sort By text box, enter or use the drop-down menu to select the field name you want to sort by.
2. Choose a sort order.
3. If some of the records have the same value in the Sort By field, use the first of the two Then By text boxes to select the field you want to sort by when there is a tie in the primary sort field. For databases with many similar records (like the family reunion mailing list), you might want to add a tertiary sort.
4. When you have made all the sort selections, click the OK button to sort the database according to the specifications you entered.

You can sort a database that includes no column headings—just records. However, the drop-down lists in all the database dialog boxes contain the words "Column A," "Column B," and so on rather than the field names.

Sorting Data Using the Menu

1. Select any cell within the database.
2. From the menu bar, choose Data ➢ Sort.
3. In the Sort By drop-down list, select the field you want to sort by.

Sorting Data Using the Menu *(continued)*

4. Use the Then By drop-down lists to select secondary and tertiary sort fields.
5. Click the OK button to sort the database.

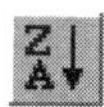

You can also sort a database using the sort buttons on the Standard toolbar. Select a single cell within the *column* you want to sort by. Click the Ascending Sort or Descending Sort button to sort the database. This is an easy way to sort, but it has one major drawback: Excel doesn't allow you to verify that the correct cells have been selected as the database. It's best to sort each database once using the Sort dialog box and ensure that the correct rows and columns have been selected before using the toolbar.

When sorting, it is vital that all the *columns* of a database are included. If some columns are not selected, the selected columns will be sorted, but the unselected columns will not be, thus ruining the integrity of the data by mixing up the records. (Another reason why you never include empty columns in a worksheet.) Always check to be sure that all columns were included before sorting. Click Undo immediately if some columns were omitted in a sort.

Once you know how Excel sorts, you can use the sort buttons to do secondary and tertiary sorts. When Excel sorts the records in a database, it only rearranges records when necessary. If a list is already sorted by city, sorting it by state will create a list sorted first by state, then by city within each state, because the existing city sort will only be rearranged to put the states in order. If you need to sort by more than the three fields allowed in the Sort dialog box, sort the least important field first and work backward through the sort fields to the primary sort field.

Sorting Using the Toolbar

1. Select any cell within the database in the column you want to sort by.
2. Click the Ascending or Descending Sort button.
3. For secondary, tertiary, and other sorts, use the Ascending and Descending Sort buttons to work through the sorts in reverse order.

Filtering a Database

Objectives XL2000E.10.6

Many times you'll want to work with a database *subset*, a group of records in the database. For example, you might want to print all sales records for one salesperson, all the orders from one client, or all the customers who haven't made a purchase this year. A *filter* is used to select records that meet a specific criterion (which you enter to set the filter) and temporarily hide all the other records.

To set up an AutoFilter, select any cell in the database and choose Data ➢ Filter ➢ AutoFilter. Excel reads every record in the database and creates a filter criteria list for each field.

If you have occupied rows above the header row in a database, insert a blank row above the header row or select the entire database before turning on AutoFilter.

Click the drop-down arrow that appears next to each field name (see Figure 6.27) to access the field's criteria list:

All The default criteria setting in each field, meaning that the contents of the field are not being used to limit the records displayed.

Top 10 Used in numeric fields to display the top or bottom ten, five, or any other number or percentage of values.

Custom Prompts you to create a custom filter (see "Creating a Custom Filter" below) for choices that don't appear on the list.

When you apply a filter, all the records not included in the subset are hidden, as shown in Figure 6.28, where the records are being filtered on Lake County. The number of records found and the total number of records in the database are displayed in the status bar. Each record retains its original row number; the row numbers of filtered records appear in blue. The field criteria drop-down arrow for the filtered field turns blue, to show that it is being actively used to filter the database.

FIGURE 6.27
Database with an AutoFilter

	A	B	C	D	E
1	Traverse Tree Sales				
2	County Cooperative Tree Orders				
3					
4	Month	County	Type	Quanti	Bundl
5	Jan-2000	Genesee	White Pine	37000	74
6	Jan-2000	Oakland	Blue Spruce	22500	45
7	Jan-2000	Oakland	White Pine	15500	31
8	Jan-2000	Oakland	Concolor Fir	13500	27
9	Jan-2000	Genesee	Blue Spruce	12500	25
10	Feb-2000	Oakland	Scotch Pine	11000	22
11	Feb-2000	Genesee	Frazier Fir	6500	13
12	Feb-2000	Lake	Blue Spruce	42500	85
13	Feb-2000	Lake	White Pine	32000	64
14	Mar-2000	Lake	Frazier Fir	14500	29
15	Mar-2000	Kalkaska	Blue Spruce	13500	27
16	Mar-2000	Lake	Concolor Fir	12000	24
17	Mar-2000	Kalkaska	Concolor Fir	10000	20
18	Apr-2000	Kalkaska	Frazier Fir	7500	15
19	Apr-2000	Lake	Blue Spruce	31000	62
20	Apr-2000	Lake	White Pine	26500	53

FIGURE 6.28
Filtering a database

	A	B	C	D	E
1	Traverse Tree Sales				
2	County Cooperative Tree Orders				
3					
4	Month	County	Type	Quanti	Bundl
12	Feb-2000	Lake	Blue Spruce	42500	85
13	Feb-2000	Lake	White Pine	32000	64
14	Mar-2000	Lake	Frazier Fir	14500	29
16	Mar-2000	Lake	Concolor Fir	12000	24
19	Apr-2000	Lake	Blue Spruce	31000	62
20	Apr-2000	Lake	White Pine	26500	53
21					

The major advantage to returning a recordset instead of a cellset is that the recordset can be used in any context where a regular ADO recordset is valid. For example, it can be bound to a grid control (as in this example) or even passed back over HTTP via RDS (see Chapter 11). On the other hand, the formatting of the recordset is uninspiring, and the concatenated field names can be difficult to work with. If you're developing an interface that allows people to work with multidimensional data interactively, you're almost certainly better off using cellsets rather than recordsets.

Filter on more than one field to select, for example, all the Scotch Pine sales in Oakland County. Set the criteria using each field's drop-down list. Only records that meet all the criteria you selected will be included in the filtered subset. To redisplay the entire database, change the filter criteria for all filtered fields back to All, or simply choose Data ➢ Filter ➢ Show All. You'll know at a glance that all filters are set to All because the drop-down arrows and the row headings will all be black again.

Sometimes, the field criteria drop-down list has so many entries that it runs off the top or bottom of the screen. You can scroll down to see a list that runs off the bottom. If the list runs off the top, insert several blank rows above the column labels to force the filtered list down the screen.

Applying and Using the AutoFilter

1. Select any cell in the database.
2. Choose Data ➢ Filter ➢ AutoFilter to turn on the filter.
3. Click the drop-down arrow for the field you want to use to filter, and choose a filter from the criteria drop-down list.
4. To see all the records in the database, reset all filter criteria to All.

Using the Top 10 Filter

When you choose Top 10 as your filter criterion, the Top 10 AutoFilter dialog box opens.

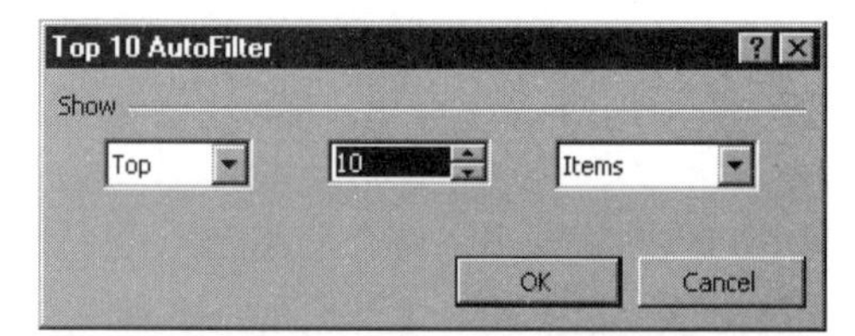

In the first drop-down box, choose Top or Bottom, depending on whether you want to see the highest or lowest values in the database. In the spin box, enter a number larger than 0. In the last drop-down box, choose Items or Percent. To see the top 10 percent of the scores in a column of test scores, choose Top, enter **10**, then choose Percent. The Top 10 filter only works with numbers (including dates and times).

Creating a Custom Filter

When you filter using the drop-down criteria, you are always looking for records that exactly equal specific criteria or fall in a Top 10 criterion. Custom filters give you access to other ways to set criteria:

- All records with fields that are *not* equal to a criterion.
- Records that are greater than or less than a criterion.
- Records that meet one condition or another.

To create a custom filter, choose Custom from the drop-down criteria list to open the Custom AutoFilter dialog box, shown in Figure 6.29.

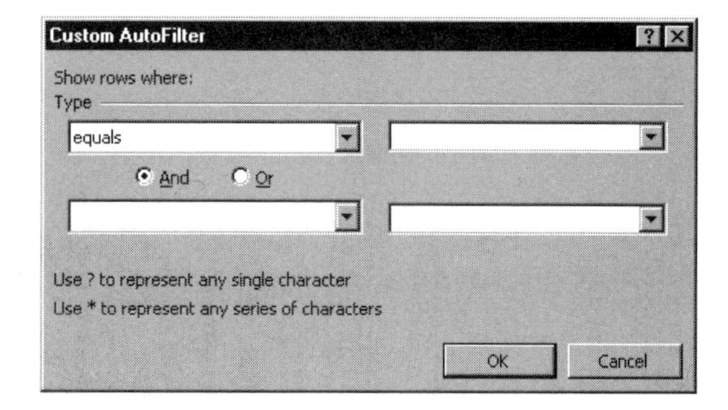

FIGURE 6.29

Custom AutoFilter dialog box

The first drop-down box under Show Rows Where opens a list of operators. The list includes regular logical operators such as Equals and Is Greater Than Or Equal To, but as you scroll the list, you'll notice other operators that allow you to look for entries that do or do not begin with, end with, or contain a string.

The right drop-down list displays the record entries in the field from the field criteria list. To find all records that are *not* in Lake County, choose Not Equal To as the operator and select Lake from the drop-down. You can also enter text in the criteria control. In the bottom of the dialog box, notice that you can use the * and ? wildcards to broaden the search string. To find all orders for Oakland and Ottawa counties, you could:

- Use the wildcard character and search for "`Equals O*`"
- Use the Begins With Type option and search for "`Begins with O`"

Using AND and OR The AND and OR options are used when you want to filter by more than one criterion in a column. AND is used to establish the upper and lower ends of a range and is almost always used with numeric entries: "Quantity is greater than 100 AND Quantity is less than 201" leaves only the quantities between 100 and 201. OR is used to filter by two different criteria: "Lake County OR Oakland County."

If you use AND when you mean OR, you'll often get a *null set*—no records. (There are no sales in Lake County AND Oakland County—it's one or the other.) If you use OR when you mean AND, you'll get all the records. (Every record is either less than 201 OR greater than 100.)

Creating a Custom Filter

1. If the AutoFilter is not turned on, turn it on (choose Data ➢ Filter ➢ AutoFilter). Choose Custom from the Filter Criteria drop-down list to open the Custom AutoFilter dialog box.
2. Set the operator (Type) for the first criterion.
3. Enter or select the first criterion from the drop-down list.
4. Set an operator, and enter or select the second criterion.
5. Set AND for a range; set OR to filter for more than one possible value.
6. Click OK to apply the custom filter.

The filter criteria drop-downs don't appear when you print a database, so there usually isn't a reason to turn the AutoFilter off until you are done working with a database. To turn the AutoFilter off, choose Data ➢ Filter ➢ AutoFilter again.

Working with Filtered Records

You can work with the filtered set of records in a number of ways. If you print the database while it is filtered, only the filtered records will print; this is a quick way to generate reports based on any portion of the information in the Excel database.

Filtering is also useful when you need to create charts using part of the data in the database. Filter the records you want to chart, and then select and chart the information as you would normally.

When you create a chart based on a filter, you need to print the chart before changing the filter criteria. Changing the criteria changes the chart. If you need to create a permanent chart, see the following section on creating a subset database.

Creating a New Database from a Filtered Subset

1. Filter the active database to create a filtered subset.
2. Select the filtered database, including the column labels and any other titles you wish to copy.

Creating a New Database from a Filtered Subset *(continued)*

3. Click the Copy button or choose Edit ➢ Copy.
4. Select the first cell where you want the new database to appear.
5. Press Enter (or click Paste) to paste the database.

Extracting a Subset

Objective XL2000E.10.7

If you prefer, you can create a subset by *extracting* the subset's records from the database using Excel's Advanced Filter. The Advanced Filter requires you to establish a *criteria range* that includes the column labels from your database and one or more criteria that you enter directly below the labels.

The criteria range is the heart of advanced filtering. If the criteria range is incorrect, the extracted data will be wrong—so take your time with this. The column labels must be precisely the same as they are in the database, so begin by copying the column labels to another location in your workbook (a separate worksheet that you name Criteria is good).

Then, on this same worksheet, type the criteria you want to establish. For example, if you want to extract records where the Quantity is over 10000, enter **>10000** in the cell just below the Quantity column label. If you have more than one criterion in a single column (for example, County = Genesee or County = Oakland), use one cell for each criterion.

Month	County	Type	Quantity	Bundles
	Genesee			
	Oakland			

There are two ways to filter for two criteria in separate columns, based on whether you want to use AND or OR. Enter criteria on the same row for an AND condition.

Month	County	Type	Quantity	Bundles
	Genesee		>20000	

Place criteria on separate rows for an OR condition.

Month	County	Type	Quantity	Bundles
	Genesee			
			>20000	

In this example, criteria are established to find quantities over 20,000 in Oakland County or over 10,000 in Lake County.

Month	County	Type	Quantity	Bundles
	Oakland		>20000	
	Lake		>10000	

You can't create this last criterion with an AutoFilter in one pass. You would need to find each county separately. A need to mix AND and OR conditions is one of the two reasons to use an Advanced Filter.

You'll need to refer to the criteria range in the Advanced Filter dialog box, so you might want to name it.

When the criteria range is set, click anywhere in the database and open the Advanced Filter dialog box (choose Data ➢ Filter ➢ Advanced Filter) to see the second reason to use an advanced filter: You can instruct Excel to return only unique records, as shown in Figure 6.30.

FIGURE 6.30 Advanced Filter dialog box

Excel will automatically select your database for the List Range text box. Select the Criteria Range text box and identify your criteria range, including the column labels. Choose whether you want to filter the records in their current location (as AutoFilter does) or extract the records by copying them to another location. If you choose another location, the Copy To text box will be enabled so that you can select the first cell of the range where the filtered records should be copied.

As with any copy operation, just select one cell; if you select a range, it must match exactly the range required by the extracted data. Be sure that there is room in the destination area for the incoming data.

You can enter a cell in any open workbook in the Copy To text box, so you can put the filtered subset of your database in a different workbook or a different worksheet than the original database. If you want to eliminate duplicate records from the filtered list, turn on the Unique Records Only checkbox. Finally, click OK, and Excel will filter in place or extract data as you have indicated.

You have a database with 10,000 records, many of them duplicate records. Don't eliminate the duplicates manually. Set up a criteria range without criteria and use the Unique Records Only option to extract a list without duplicates.

When you use the Advanced Filter to filter in place, the filtered subset will have blue row numbers, just as it does with AutoFilter. To turn the filter off, choose Data ➢ Filter ➢ Show All.

Using the Advanced Filter

1. Copy the database column labels to another location.
2. Enter criteria in the cells directly under the column labels.
3. Select any cell in the database, and choose Data ➢ Filter ➢ Advanced Filter to open the Advanced Filter dialog box.
4. Check to ensure Excel has accurately identified the database range. If not, adjust it in the List Range text box.
5. Enter the criteria range in the Criteria Range list box.
6. Choose the Filter In Place or Copy To option.
7. If you are extracting (copying) the filtered list to another location, enter the upper-left cell of that location in the Copy To text box.
8. Enable or disable the Unique Records Only check box.
9. Click OK to create the filter.

Creating Subtotals

Objective XL2000E.10.5

You can create subtotals based on any field in the database. A *subtotal* is not necessarily a sum: it can be an average, count, minimum, maximum, or other statistical calculation based on a group of records. Before subtotaling, you need to sort the database on the field you want to subtotal. For example, if you want to subtotal each month's orders, first sort by month. Then, select a cell anywhere in the database and choose Data ➢ Subtotals to open the Subtotal dialog box, shown in Figure 6.31.

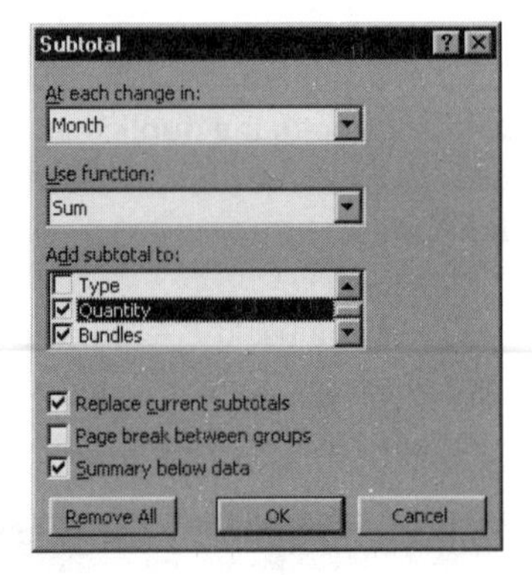

FIGURE 6.31
Subtotal dialog box

In the At Each Change In drop-down list, select the field the database is sorted on. The trigger for Excel to insert a subtotal is a change in this column. If you choose an unsorted field, you'll get a multitude of subtotals (interesting, but useless). Select a type of subtotal from the Use Function drop-down list. In the Add Subtotal To control, select each field you want to subtotal. You can subtotal more than one field at a time, but you have to use the same function: average three fields, sum three fields, and so on.

Enable the Replace Current Subtotals checkbox if you have subtotaled earlier and want to replace the former set with new subtotals. If you want both sets of subtotals to appear (for example, sums and averages), deselect this option.

If you are going to print the worksheet with subtotals and want each subtotaled set of records to print on a separate page, check the Page Break Between Groups checkbox. Selecting Summary Below Data places a summary (grand total, grand average) row at the bottom of the database.

When you have entered the information for subtotals, click the OK button to add subtotals, as shown in Figure 6.32. To remove subtotals from a worksheet, open the Subtotal dialog box again and click the Remove All button.

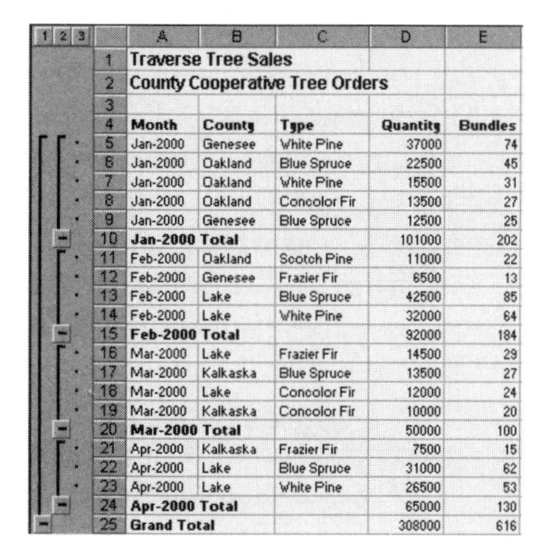

	A	B	C	D	E
1	Traverse Tree Sales				
2	County Cooperative Tree Orders				
3					
4	**Month**	**County**	**Type**	**Quantity**	**Bundles**
5	Jan-2000	Genesee	White Pine	37000	74
6	Jan-2000	Oakland	Blue Spruce	22500	45
7	Jan-2000	Oakland	White Pine	15500	31
8	Jan-2000	Oakland	Concolor Fir	13500	27
9	Jan-2000	Genesee	Blue Spruce	12500	25
10	**Jan-2000 Total**			101000	202
11	Feb-2000	Oakland	Scotch Pine	11000	22
12	Feb-2000	Genesee	Frazier Fir	6500	13
13	Feb-2000	Lake	Blue Spruce	42500	85
14	Feb-2000	Lake	White Pine	32000	64
15	**Feb-2000 Total**			92000	184
16	Mar-2000	Lake	Frazier Fir	14500	29
17	Mar-2000	Kalkaska	Blue Spruce	13500	27
18	Mar-2000	Lake	Concolor Fir	12000	24
19	Mar-2000	Kalkaska	Concolor Fir	10000	20
20	**Mar-2000 Total**			50000	100
21	Apr-2000	Kalkaska	Frazier Fir	7500	15
22	Apr-2000	Lake	Blue Spruce	31000	62
23	Apr-2000	Lake	White Pine	26500	53
24	**Apr-2000 Total**			65000	130
25	**Grand Total**			308000	616

FIGURE 6.32
Traverse Tree Sales subtotals

Creating Subtotals

1. In your database, sort the records on the field you want to trigger the subtotal.
2. Select any cell in the database.
3. Choose Data ➢ Subtotals from the menu bar.
4. Select the sorted field from the At Each Change In drop-down list.
5. Select a type of subtotal.
6. Select the numeric fields to be subtotaled when the value of the At Each Change In field changes.
7. If necessary, change the settings for Replace Current Subtotals, Page Break Between Groups, and Summary Below Data.
8. Click OK to generate subtotals.
9. To remove subtotals, choose Data ➢ Subtotals, and then click Remove All.

Querying a Database

Objective XL2000E.10.8

Combine Excel 2000's database features with the power of Microsoft Query, and you have an analysis and reporting tool for any ODBC-compliant database on your system. *ODBC* (Open Database Connectivity) is an open standard for database access. ODBC was not developed by Microsoft, but is often thought of as a Microsoft standard, because Windows was the first operating system to support ODBC. Access and SQL Server are both ODBC-compliant, as are many other database programs. For example, you may want to retrieve information from an Oracle database and work with it in Excel 2000. To do this, you will use a combination of software:

- Microsoft Query to create a query
- Excel 2000 to open the query
- The ODBC Driver Manager, which is part of Windows
- A specific ODBC driver designed to allow Query to "talk to" the Oracle database
- The Oracle database

The combination of a database and the ODBC driver to connect to it is called a *data source*. Excel 2000 includes ODBC drivers for the following programs:

- dBASE
- Microsoft Access 2000
- Microsoft Excel
- Microsoft SQL Server
- Microsoft SQL Server OLAP Services
- Oracle
- Paradox
- Text database files (for example, comma-delimited files)

To query a database in Excel 2000, you select a data source, then specify the data you want to return to Excel.

Selecting a Data Source

From Excel, choose Data ➢ Get External Data ➢ New Database Query to launch Microsoft Query. Query will display the Choose Data Source dialog box, shown in Figure 6.33. The Databases page of the dialog box shows data sources that have already been created as well as available ODBC drivers you can use to connect to databases and create data sources. The Queries page has a list of saved queries. OLAP Cubes are multidimensional data sources.

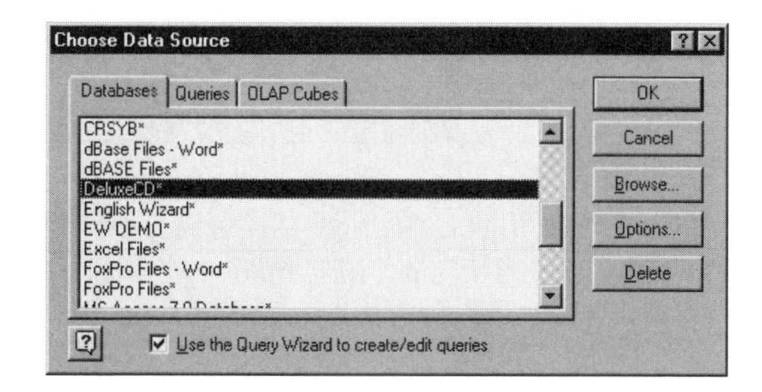

FIGURE 6.33 Select a data source for your query.

If you've created ODBC data sources to use with programs like Seagate Crystal Reports, Cognos Impromptu, or Access 2000, they'll be listed on the Databases page, and you can use them in Excel. If you don't have a data source and need to create one, visit the Sybex Web site (`www.sybex.com`) for instructions on creating a data source. Select your data source, and then click OK to launch the Query Wizard.

Creating Queries with the Query Wizard

The Query Wizard opens with a list of the views (queries), tables, and columns (fields) in your data source. In Figure 6.34, the data source is the Deluxe CD database that is included with Windows 98 and Windows Plus.

The left pane of the Query Wizard works like the Windows Explorer. Tables and views have a plus sign; click the plus sign to display the table's fields. The right pane displays the columns included in your query. Select a view, table, or column, and use the pick buttons to move the selection to the right pane. To display data from the column for a quick reminder of its contents, select a column in the left pane and click the Preview Now button in the dialog box. You can select data from more than one table or view.

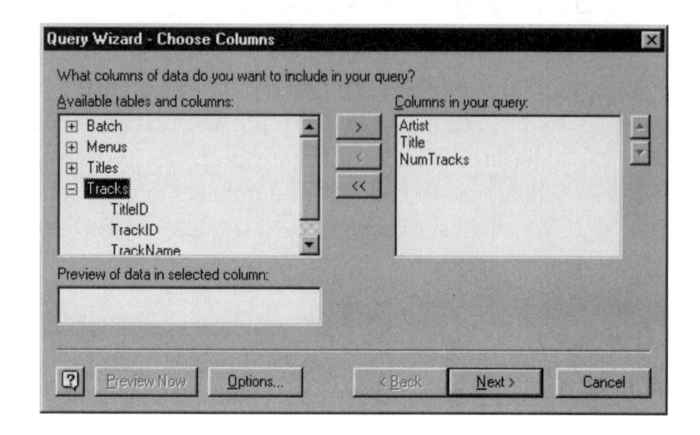

FIGURE 6.34
Select fields or entire tables to include in your query.

When you have finished selecting columns, click the Next button. If you selected columns from more than one table, the Query Wizard will check to see if there are relationships between the tables before proceeding. If any of the tables from which you included columns is not related to the others in the data source, you'll be prompted to leave the Wizard and define the relationships in Microsoft Query. You can Cancel the message and remove some fields from the Query Wizard, or click OK and move into Query so you can indicate the appropriate relationships.

In the next step of the Query Wizard, if you want to restrict the results based on values in specific columns, use the drop-down lists and text boxes to specify filter criteria. Use the AND operator between criteria when all conditions must be met; use OR when any of the conditions should place a record in the query result set. After you've set any filters, click Next.

When setting sort columns, you can set up to three; then click Next. In the final step of the Query Wizard, you can save the query by clicking the Save Query button. (This saves the query so it can be used in another Excel workbook or another program. When you save the current Excel workbook, it will save a copy of the query.) Finally, choose Return The Data To Excel and click Finish. An Excel dialog box will open so you can specify the placement of the results.

Working with Query Results

In Excel, you can use the query result set as you would any Excel data. You can, for example, add formulas, create totals or averages, and chart the information.

When the query results open in Excel, the External Data toolbar also opens. If you want to change the query, click the Edit Query button to launch Microsoft Query and reopen the Query Wizard so you can add or delete tables and columns, or change filters or sort order.

To view the latest data from the data source, click the Refresh Data button on the Query toolbar to rerun your query. The Refresh All button reruns all queries in the current workbook.

Outlining Worksheets

Objective XL2000E.10.3

Outlining makes it easy to focus in on the data within a worksheet that contains multiple levels of detail. For instance, a budget worksheet might have a line item for "4th Quarter Revenue." That line item consists of data from each of the individual sales offices in the East Coast and West Coast regions, and all the detail rolls up into the main line item. Excel's outlining feature allows you to view as much or little of the detail as you want.

When you add subtotals, Excel's outlining feature automatically turns on. Use the level (1, 2, 3, and so on) buttons in the upper-left corner of the worksheet window (see Figure 6.32) to view different levels of the outline. Use the plus and minus buttons to expand or collapse sections of the outline. In Figure 6.32, all sections of the worksheet are expanded. Clicking any one of the minus buttons, such as the one next to April 00 Total, collapses that section of the worksheet.

You can outline any worksheet with formulas. Just choose Data ➢ Group And Outline ➢ AutoOutline to turn the outline on or off.

Using a Data Form

Objective XL2000E.10.4

Data forms provide an easy way to enter or search for data yourself, and a bulletproof way to let a less accomplished user enter data. To open a data form select any cell in a database, and choose Data ➢ Form to open a data form. The first record in the database will be displayed in the data form. A sample data form for Traverse Tree Sales is shown in Figure 6.35.

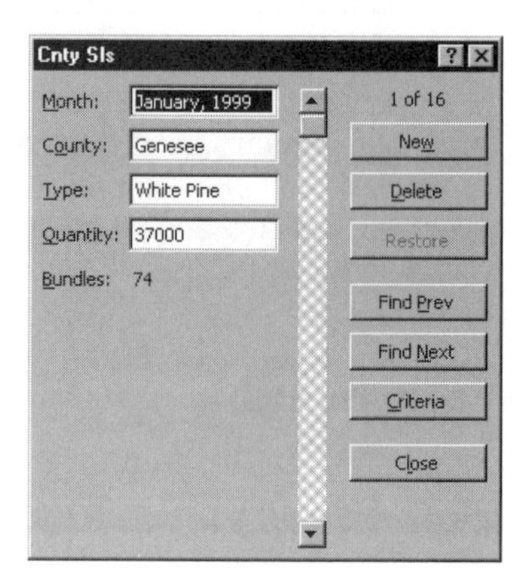

FIGURE 6.35
Traverse Tree Sales data form

Because data forms have a portrait orientation, they're particularly helpful when the columns in your database exceed the width of the screen. Using the form allows you to see all the database fields at once without scrolling horizontally—use the vertical scroll bar or the arrow keys to browse the records. Use the Tab key to move between fields in the form; pressing Enter moves to the next record.

You can change the contents of a field by editing the text box next to the field name. The contents of *calculated fields* (like the Bundles field in Figure 6.35) are displayed without a text box, because you can't edit them. However, if you change a value that a calculated field is based on, Excel will recalculate the field. To discard changes made to a record, click the Restore button before moving to another record.

Adding and Deleting Records

Clicking the New button or scrolling to the last record of the database opens the New Record form. Enter each field in the appropriate text box control. When you have entered information for the last field, press Enter or, if you want to keep entering new records, click the New button again. Press the up arrow or click the scroll bar to close the New dialog box.

To delete the record currently displayed in the data form, click the Delete button. A dialog box appears, warning that the record will be permanently deleted. Pay attention to the warning—clicking Undo will *not* bring the record back. Click the OK button to delete the record's row from the database.

Adding and Deleting Records with a Data Form

1. Select any cell in the database.
2. Choose Data ➢ Form from the menu bar to open the data form.
3. To add a record, click the New button or scroll to the end of the database. Enter the record using the Data Form text box controls. Tab between controls. Press Enter on the last field of a record to open another New Record form. Press the up arrow or scroll the database to close the New Record form.
4. To delete the record displayed in the form, click the Delete button. When prompted, click OK to delete the row that contains the record.

It isn't always more convenient to use the data form. Excel's AutoComplete feature (which fills in the remaining characters if the first few characters you type in a cell match an existing entry in that column) doesn't work with the data form, so you have to type each entry fully. However, when you close the data form, you'll notice that Excel has automatically filled calculated values.

Hands On: Objectives XL2000E.10.2, E.10.3, E.10.4, E.10.5, E.10.6, E.10.7, and E.10.8

1. Open any worksheet that can be used as a database, or create the Traverse Tree Sales worksheet in Figure 6.25. The values in Bundles are formulas (Qty/500). Sort the database:
   a) Using the Sort dialog box
   b) Using the toolbar buttons
   c) By one field
   d) By two fields (primary and secondary sort)

2. Open any worksheet that can be used as a database. Filter the database:
   a) By a value in a field
   b) Using a Top 10 filter in a numeric field
   c) Using a custom filter with the Begins With or Contains type
   d) Using a custom filter and AND or OR
   e) Extract a subset of data based on a criteria you set
3. Open any worksheet that can be used as a database.
   a) Create at least two types of subtotals.
   b) Use the outline buttons to show/hide different levels of the outline.
   c) Remove the subtotals.
4. Create a data form for the worksheet like the Traverse Tree Sales worksheet. Enter at least five records using the form.
5. Query a database created in an application other than Excel. Retrieve all the data from one table.
   a) Edit the query and remove one or more fields from the query.
   b) In Excel, add a calculation or formula that uses the query results. Refresh the query data.

CHAPTER 7

Taking Excel to the Max

Chapter 6 introduced you to several tools for working with data. In this chapter, you'll take Excel one step further with sophisticated analysis using pivot tables and data validation. You'll learn about features that separate casual users from Excel experts, proficiencies that make other users wonder, "How did they *do* that?" After pivot tables, we'll look at other nifty analysis and presentation tools including Goal Seek, Solver, custom views, and the Report Manager. Throughout the chapter, we'll use Excel practice worksheets to illustrate concepts, beginning with the Traverse Tree Sales example from Chapter 6.

Analyzing Data with Pivot Tables

Often when you work with Excel, you use it to support decision making: the data provide a means to an end. Pivot tables are the best tools for analyzing the endless rows and columns in a typical database. A *pivot table* summarizes the columns of information in a database in relationship to each other.

Creating Pivot Tables

Objectives XL2000E.11.3 and E.11.6

The Traverse Tree Sales database shown in Figure 7.1 is a small database, but it would still take time and effort to answer the following questions accurately:

- How many trees of each type were delivered each month?
- How many blue spruces were delivered each month?
- How many white pines were delivered in each county?
- What was the average number of each type of tree sold to Oakland County?

FIGURE 7.1

Traverse Tree Sales database

	A	B	C	D	E
1	**Traverse Tree Sales**				
2	**County Cooperative Tree Orders**				
3					
4	**Month**	**County**	**Type**	**Quantity**	**Bundles**
5	Jan-2000	Genesee	White Pine	37000	74
6	Jan-2000	Oakland	Blue Spruce	22500	45
7	Jan-2000	Oakland	White Pine	15500	31
8	Jan-2000	Oakland	Concolor Fir	13500	27
9	Jan-2000	Genesee	Blue Spruce	12500	25
10	Feb-2000	Oakland	Scotch Pine	11000	22
11	Feb-2000	Genesee	Frazier Fir	6500	13
12	Feb-2000	Lake	Blue Spruce	42500	85
13	Feb-2000	Lake	White Pine	32000	64
14	Mar-2000	Lake	Frazier Fir	14500	29
15	Mar-2000	Kalkaska	Blue Spruce	13500	27
16	Mar-2000	Lake	Concolor Fir	12000	24
17	Mar-2000	Kalkaska	Concolor Fir	10000	20
18	Apr-2000	Kalkaska	Frazier Fir	7500	15
19	Apr-2000	Lake	Blue Spruce	31000	62
20	Apr-2000	Lake	White Pine	26500	53

You could sort the list and then add subtotals to answer any one of these questions. Then, to answer any other question, you would have to sort and subtotal again. A single pivot table helps you answer all the above questions and more, with much less effort than sorting and filtering.

If you have data that resides outside of Excel in an ODBC or OLE DB–compliant database such as Microsoft Access or Oracle, you can create a pivot table by retrieving the data through Microsoft Query. (See Chapter 6 for information on querying databases in Excel 2000.)

Using the PivotTable Wizard

You use a Wizard to create pivot tables in Excel 2000. To launch the PivotTable And PivotChart Wizard, select any cell in a database and choose Data ➢ PivotTable And PivotChart Report. In the first step of the wizard, select a data source: data in a single Excel database, data from an external source such as Microsoft Access, data that you want to consolidate from several worksheets or sources, or an existing pivot table or pivot chart. You also specify whether you want to create a pivot table or a pivot chart with a pivot table.

In the Wizard's second step, verify the range of the database. A flashing line appears around a suggested range of cells. Use the scroll bars to verify that the entire database—including the field names—is selected. If there is no range selected, or if the range is incorrect, select the correct range before clicking the Next button.

Remember that Excel identifies a database as a range of cells bounded by the edge of the worksheet or an empty row or column. If Excel doesn't select the entire database, we encourage you to close the wizard, insert/delete rows and columns to properly define your database area, and then start the wizard again.

In the third step of the Wizard, select a location for the pivot table: a new worksheet or an existing one. If you want to place the pivot table in an existing worksheet, choose the Existing Worksheet option and then select a cell for the upper-left corner of the pivot table.

You'll be able to modify the arrangement of the pivot table's fields after the pivot table is created, but you can set the initial layout in the Wizard. Click the Layout button to open the dialog box shown in Figure 7.2.

FIGURE 7.2

The Layout dialog box of the PivotTable And PivotChart Wizard

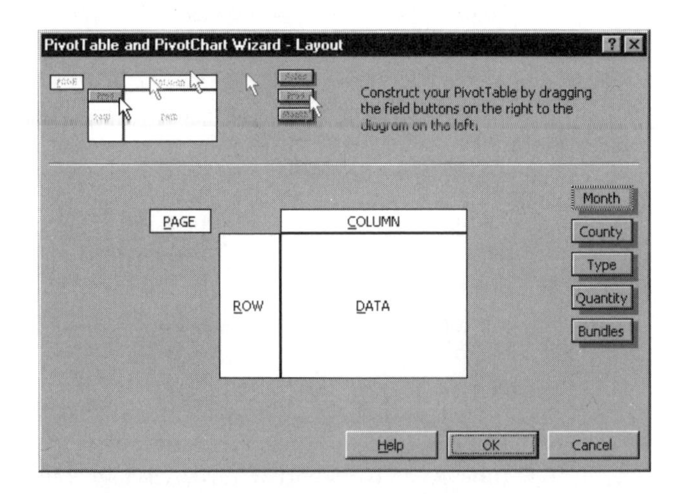

A pivot table contains four areas: the Page number, the Column labels, the Row labels, and the Data. Each area has a corresponding layout area in the Layout dialog box. At the right side of the dialog box is a group of *field buttons*, one for each field name in the database. You design the pivot table layout by dragging the field buttons into one of the four sections of the layout area. The Row, Column, and Data areas must have fields assigned to them; Page is an optional area.

Place fields you want to compare in the Row and Column areas. For example, you might want to compare sales regions by month or by types of trees sold by county. When the table is created, Excel will examine the fields you choose. Each unique entry in a field becomes a row or column heading in the pivot table.

The Page area works like a filter in the completed Pivot table. If you'll need to create separate reports for values in one or more columns (such as a separate report for each department in a company or county in our example), drag those field buttons to the Page area.

Information in the Data area is summarized using the SUM, MIN, MAX, COUNT, or AVERAGE functions, so numeric fields are generally placed in the Data layout area. (With a non-numeric field you can only COUNT the number of entries.) For Traverse Tree Sales, we could place either Quantity, Bundles, or both in the Data area.

As you drop a field button in the Data area, Excel will indicate the type of summary that will be performed. SUM is the default for numeric fields. To change the type of summary, double-click the field button to open the Pivot-Table Field dialog box, then choose a summarization method from the list.

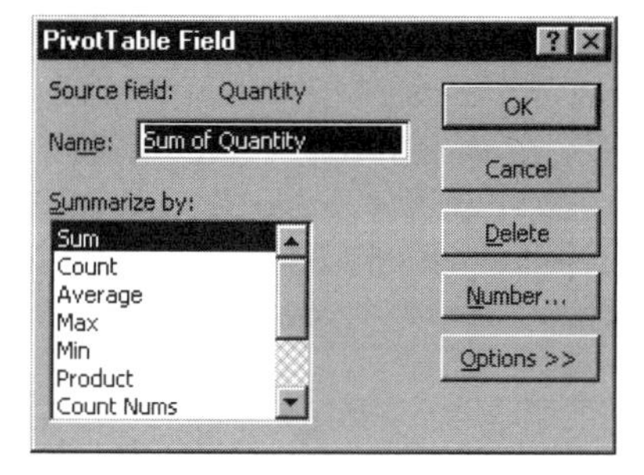

Click the Number button in the PivotTable Field dialog box to format the numbers for this field (the default is General), or wait and format the completed pivot table. Clicking the Options button extends the PivotTable Field dialog box so that you can perform custom calculations (see "Using Custom Calculations" later in this chapter). Click OK to close the dialog box and return to the Layout dialog box. Click OK again to return to the PivotTable And PivotChart Wizard.

Click the Options button in the Wizard to open the PivotTable Options dialog box, shown in Figure 7.3. You can name the pivot table just as you name any other range of cells. If you don't name it, Excel will give it a riveting name such as PivotTable1. For more information about any other option, click the dialog box Help button, and then click the option. When you are finished setting options, click OK to return to the PivotTable And PivotChart Wizard.

Click Finish to close the Wizard and create the PivotTable Report. The pivot table in Figure 7.4 shows the total trees sold by county and month. The PivotTable toolbar will also open.

FIGURE 7.3

Excel's PivotTable Options dialog box

Sum of Quantity	Month				
County	Jan-2000	Feb-2000	Mar-2000	Apr-2000	Grand Total
☑ Genesee	00	6500			56000
☑ Kalkaska			23500	7500	31000
☐ Lake		74500	26500	57500	158500
☐ Oakland	00	11000			62500
	00	92000	50000	65000	308000
OK / Cancel					

FIGURE 7.4

PivotTable Report

Sum of Quantity	Month				
County	Jan-2000	Feb-2000	Mar-2000	Apr-2000	Grand Total
Genesee	49500	6500			56000
Kalkaska			23500	7500	31000
Lake		74500	26500	57500	158500
Oakland	51500	11000			62500
Grand Total	101000	92000	50000	65000	308000

Using the PivotTable Toolbar If the PivotTable toolbar does not appear once your PivotTable Report has been created, turn it on by choosing View ➢ Toolbars ➢ PivotTable. The PivotTable toolbar lets you change the completed table's layout and options.

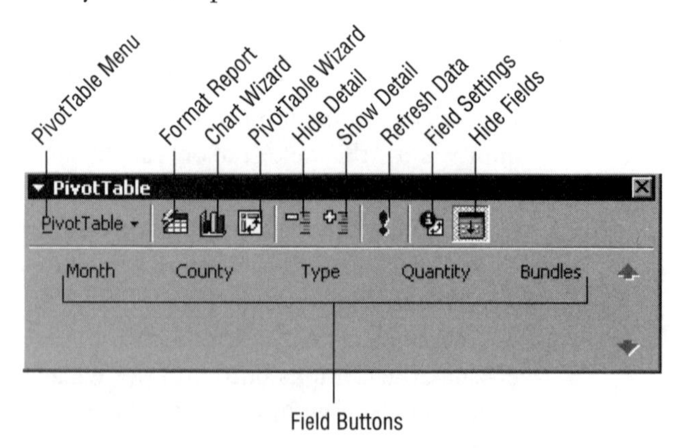

Objective XL2000E.11.1

Format Report displays a group of AutoFormats appropriate for pivot tables. To apply the AutoFormat, select a format sample and click OK.

Clicking the Chart Wizard button creates a PivotTable Chart. If you want to return to the Wizard, just click the PivotTable Wizard toolbar button.

To drill down in the pivot table and reveal the details underlying the data in a cell, select the cell and click the Show Detail button. Excel will extract the details records in another worksheet.

Perhaps the most amazing feature of Excel's implementation of pivot tables is the ability to quickly generate reports for any column of data in the original database. Simply move the field you want to create reports for to the Page area, and then either click the arrow on the PivotTable button and select Show Pages from the menu, or right-click anywhere in the pivot table and choose Show Pages from the shortcut menu. Excel will create a separate pivot table for each value in the field in the Pages area. Check it out—each pivot table appears on its own sheet, and Excel even names them all.

Filtering Pivot Tables If you need to work with some but not all of the values in a field, use the PivotTable Filter feature:

1. Click the arrow attached to the field button in the Row or Column area. 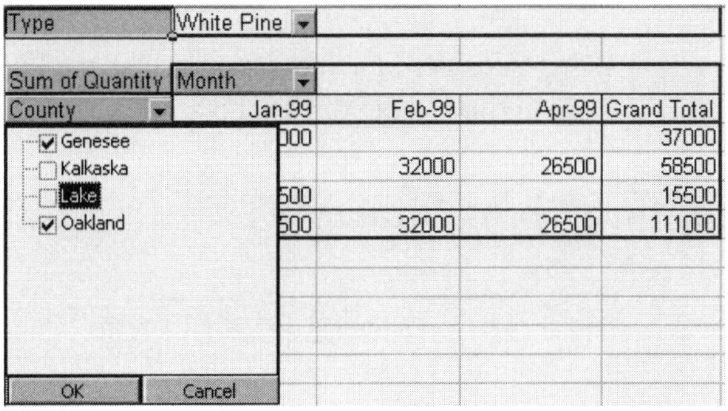
2. Turn values on or off until the values you want to see in the pivot table are enabled.
3. Click OK.

Changing Pivot Table Layout

There are a number of ways to summarize a database. Rather than create a new pivot table, you can change the layout of an existing one. The field buttons you placed in the Page, Column, and Row areas are in the pivot table; change the table by dragging a field button to another area, and Excel will update the table. For example, if you want to view the data in Figure 7.4 by type and date, you can drag the Type button to the Column area and the Month button to the Row area. The pivot table will change to reflect the new layout.

Drag a field button from the PivotTable toolbar and drop it in the table to add a new field. To remove a field from the pivot table, in the Layout dialog box drag the field button out of the pivot table area.

Keeping the PivotTable Up-to-Date A pivot table is dynamically linked to the database used to create the table. If you edit values within the database, simply choose Data ➢ Refresh Data, or click the Refresh Data button on the PivotTable toolbar; Excel will update the pivot table to reflect the database changes.

However, if you add rows or columns to the database, you *cannot* simply refresh the data. You must return to the PivotTable And PivotChart Wizard and identify the new range of records that should be included in the table. If you don't, the pivot table values won't include the added data.

To update the range being used by the pivot table, choose Data ➢ PivotTable And PivotChart Report from the menu bar, or click the PivotTable menu in the toolbar and choose Wizard. The PivotTable Wizard will open at step 3. Reselect the database, or hold Shift and extend the current selection. Click the Finish button to close the PivotTable And PivotChart Wizard and return to the updated pivot table.

Creating Pivot Charts

Objective XL2000E.11.3

Pivot charts can be created at the same time you generate a pivot table or later on after you have studied the pivot table. The default pivot chart type is a simple column chart, but you can change the chart to any of Excel's other chart types, except for the scatter, bubble, and stock charts.

You can rearrange the way the pivot table data fields are displayed on the chart, but the pivot chart will start out with the row fields in the table becoming the *category fields* (horizontal, or x-axis) in the chart. Similarly, the column fields in the table become the *series* (vertical, or y-axis) fields in the chart. Pivot charts also have *page fields*, which are optional.

To create a pivot chart, select any cell in your database, and then choose Data ➢ PivotTable And PivotChart Report. In the first step of the PivotChart Wizard, select PivotChart (With PivotTable) and click Next. In the second Wizard step, check that the data range selected is the right one. If not, select the correct range, then click Next.

If you have already created a pivot table with the selected data range, Excel will ask whether you want to create a chart based on the existing pivot table. If more than one pivot table exists for the data, Excel will prompt you to pick the one you want to use. To quickly create a PivotChart from an existing pivot table, click the PivotChart button on the PivotTable toolbar.

The third and final step in the Wizard asks you where to put the pivot table, if you are creating one along with the chart. You can change the layout and other options here, as described in the "Using the PivotTable Wizard" section. Choose New Worksheet or Existing Worksheet and click Finish.

You will see the blank PivotChart and the PivotTable toolbar with fields from the PivotChart. Drag fields from the toolbar onto the labeled chart areas to create the chart. The fields you drag onto the chart become labels with list buttons. Click these labels to change the data displayed. You can select any of these data display options and click OK to redisplay the chart with your data choice. Use the Chart menu to modify the pivot chart in the same way you would modify a regular Excel chart.

See Chapter 13 to learn how to create interactive pivot charts and tables for the Web.

Creating a Pivot Chart

1. Open the workbook that contains the data you want to chart and choose Select Data ➢ PivotTable And PivotChart Report.
2. Select PivotChart (With PivotTable) and click Next.
3. Make sure the data range selected is the right one. If not, select the correct range.
4. Change the layout and other options, choose New Worksheet or Existing Worksheet, and click Finish.
5. Drag fields from the toolbar onto the labeled chart areas to create the chart.
6. Click the list buttons and make another selection to change data display options. Click OK.

Hands On: Objectives XL2000.11.1, E.11.3, and E.11.6

1. Open any worksheet that contains a database with text or dates in more than one column. (The *Traverse Tree Sales* worksheet shown in Figure 7.1 works very well if you don't have a worksheet already.) Practice using pivot table features by:
   a) Creating a pivot table that uses the SUM function in the data area
   b) Changing the SUM function to AVERAGE or COUNT
   c) Altering the pivot table layout in the worksheet by moving columns and rows
   d) Adding and deleting a column or row
   e) Drilling down through a value
   f) Making separate pivot tables based on a value in a column using Show Pages
   g) Applying an AutoFormat
2. Add one or two new records to the database, then reset the range for the pivot table.
3. Edit a record in the database and note the changes in the pivot tables based on the database.
4. Create a PivotChart using this data or one of your own workbooks.

Error-Proofing Your Workbook

Excel makes numbers look believable—even when results are so incorrect that no one should believe them. You know how to use Excel to create flashy worksheets and reports, complete with pivot tables and charts. But part of creating a worksheet is checking the completed worksheet for errors, before you or other people rely on the results for decision-making.

You can make two kinds of errors when creating a worksheet: *data-entry errors* and *logical errors*. With Excel, you can minimize data entry errors and use the auditing tools to resolve logical errors.

Minimizing Data-Entry Errors

You're entering payroll. You're in a hurry. Instead of entering Richard Steinhoff's 10 hours, you enter 100. When payday rolls around, Rich is a very happy person. You, on the other hand, are not.

A helpful tool called *data validation* allows you to build business rules into your workbook so that grossly incorrect entries result in error messages. *Business rules* are the policies and procedures, formal and informal, that govern how a business operates. Examples of business rules include: no refunds after 30 days; no one ever works more than 80 hours; and all employees must be at least 16 years of age. Validation ensures that the data entered falls within the range allowed by the business rule.

Objective XL2000E.10.9

To create a validation rule, select the cell or range of cells that have the same business rule. Then choose Data ➢ Validation to open the Data Validation dialog box, shown in Figure 7.5. The dialog box has three pages: Settings, Input Message, and Error Alert. The business rule you want to enforce goes on the Settings page. On the Input Message page, you can enter a prompt that lets users know how to enter data in the cell. And on the Error Alert page, you can enter a message that a user will see when invalid data is entered.

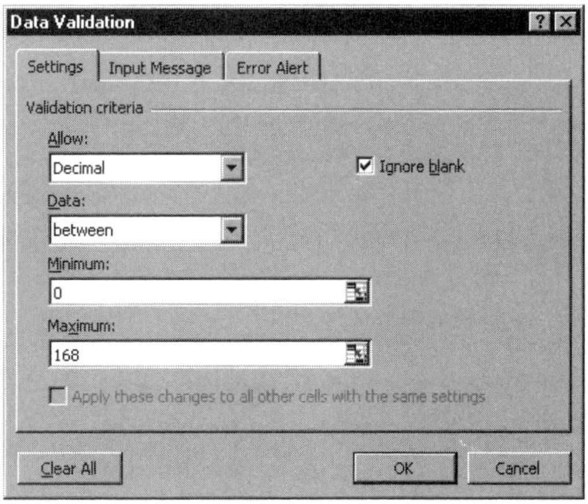

FIGURE 7.5
Excel's Data Validation dialog box

Setting Validation Rules

Let's use the error in entering payroll hours mentioned above as an example for setting validation rules. In the Settings page:

1. Select the type of value that's an acceptable entry for this cell from the Allow drop-down list. There are two possible choices: whole number and decimal. When you select either, additional text box controls will open so you can enter values.
2. If the Ignore Blank check box is checked, the user can leave the cell blank. Uncheck the box if entries are required in all the selected cells.
3. In the Data drop-down list, choose the operator that you need. In Figure 7.5, we used the Between operator, because there is an upper and a lower limit on hours that employees can work.
4. Enter values for the Minimum and Maximum values. No one can work fewer than 0 hours. If no maximum is established in the workplace, you could use 168. It's not possible to work more than 168 hours in a week—that's all there are. Notice that you can use the value in another cell as the minimum or maximum.

Displaying Input Messages

The Input Message page of the Data Validation dialog box lets you display a message (like a ScreenTip) to tell the user how to enter data in the cell. The message is displayed each time a user selects one of the cells in the range. This is great help if you have a number of users working infrequently with this worksheet. However, if the same people use the worksheet over and over, input messages become annoying. If you add a title, it will appear in bold above the message.

Input messages are great additions to worksheets you build for other people to use, even if you don't want to validate the data they enter in a cell. On the Settings page, leave the default Any Value setting, and then enter your message on the Input Message page.

Adding Error Messages

Use the Error Alert page of the Data Validation dialog box to build an error dialog box like those used throughout Excel. Choose one of three styles—Information, Warning, or Stop—based on the severity of the error:

- The Information style is a casual notice.
- A Warning is a bit more severe than Information.

- Stop uses the same icon that users see when an application is about to shut down; it really catches people's attention.

Include an error message and a title if you wish.

You don't have to include an error message; you might prefer to enter data and then have Excel show you all the data that isn't valid. Whether you show error messages is a matter of practicality. If someone else is entering data in the worksheet, you should probably let them know when the data is incorrect so they can immediately find the correct data and enter it. Sometimes, the person entering data isn't in a position to correct it; in that case, you might want to dispense with the error message and handle the validation afterward (see "Using the Auditing Toolbar" below).

Validating Data and Providing Input Messages

1. Select the cells you want to validate.
2. Choose Data ➢ Validation to open the Data Validation dialog box.
3. If you want to set validation rules, on the Settings page, set validation criteria for entries allowed, data, and minimum and/or maximum.
4. If you want to include an input message, enter a message and optional title on the Input Message page. Make sure the Show Input Message When Cell Is Selected check box is checked.
5. If you want to display an error message when invalid data is entered, choose a style and enter an error message and optional title on the Error Alert page. Make sure the Show Error Alert After Invalid Data Is Entered check box is checked.
6. Click OK.
7. Test the input message, validation, and error message by entering invalid data in one of the cells you selected.

Removing Validation or Input Messages

To remove data validation or input messages, select the cells, open the Validation dialog box, and click the Clear All button to clear all three pages of the dialog box.

Resolving Logical Errors

The other kind of error is a logical error: adding rather than subtracting, or multiplying the wrong numbers. Some logical errors violate Excel's rules about how formulas are constructed and result in an *error code* in the cell or an interruption from the Office Assistant. Those errors are the easy ones to catch and correct. But errors that don't violate Excel's internal logic are the really nasty ones, because nothing jumps out and says, "This is wrong!"

If you are familiar with the data, you can check the logic yourself to make sure the results make sense. If you are not conversant with the data, find someone who is and review the worksheet with them before relying on it for critical operations or reporting.

Working with Error Codes

Objective XL2000E.9.2

Excel has eight standard error codes that appear in cells to let you know that a formula requires your attention. The codes, listed in Table 7.1, give you information about what caused the error. The first is the ###### error, which is usually telling you that the data is too wide for the column. This is easy to fix (hardly an error, but you get the idea).

TABLE 7.1: Error Codes

Error Code/Error Name	Cause
#####	**1.** Data is too wide for the cell, or **2.** You subtracted one date from another, and the result is a negative number. Double-check your formula.
#DIV/0 (Division by Zero)	The number or cell reference you divided by is either zero or blank. If you see this in cells you just filled, you need an absolute cell reference in the original formula.
#N/A (Not Available)	**1.** You omitted a required argument in a function, *or* **2.** The cell that contains the argument is blank or doesn't have the kind of entry the function requires.
#NAME	**1.** You misspelled the name of a range or function, *or* **2.** You referred to a name that doesn't exist, *or* **3.** You used text in a formula or format without putting it in quotes, *or* **4.** You left out the colon in a range (B3:D7).
#NULL	You referred to an intersection that doesn't exist by using a space between two ranges in an argument.

TABLE 7.1: Error Codes *(continued)*

Error Code/Error Name	Cause
#NUM	**1.** You used text or a blank cell in an argument that requires a number, *or* **2.** You entered a formula that creates a number too large or too small for Excel to handle.
#REF (Invalid Reference)	You deleted some cells that this formula requires, so the formula can't find the cell that it refers to. You may have deleted some cells by pasting other cells over them.
#VALUE	You entered text when a formula requires a number or a value such as True or False.

Resolving Circular Cell References

If you enter a formula that contains a *circular cell reference*, Excel doesn't just place an error code in the cell; it displays a message box and immediately offers help. A circular cell reference occurs when a formula refers to the cell that it is in. For example, when the formula `=SUM(J15:J20)` is in cell `J20`, Excel tries to add `J20` to itself over and over again. This is called *iteration*. Excel will iterate 100 times; then it will give up and display an error message.

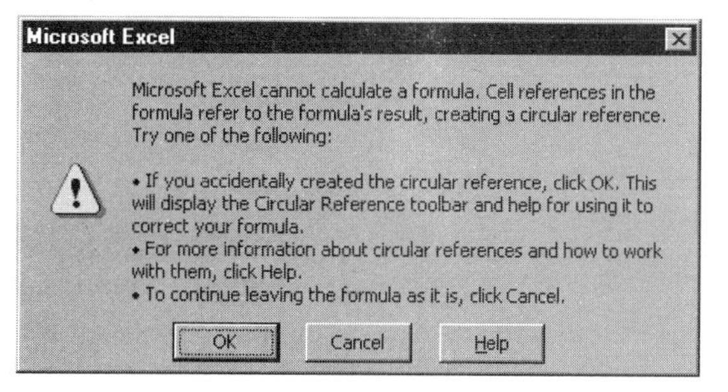

Click OK in the message box, and Help opens with information about circular references. (Help only opens the first time you create a circular reference in a session.) Excel places a blue dot next to the formula that created the circular reference and displays `Circular` and the reference for the offending cell in the status bar. If Help opened, clicking the cell with the circular reference opens the Circular Reference toolbar (or you can turn it on from the View menu).

Objectives XL2000E.9.3 and 9.4

The drop-down list in the Circular Reference toolbar displays the current circular reference; clicking the drop-down list shows all the circular references in open workbooks.

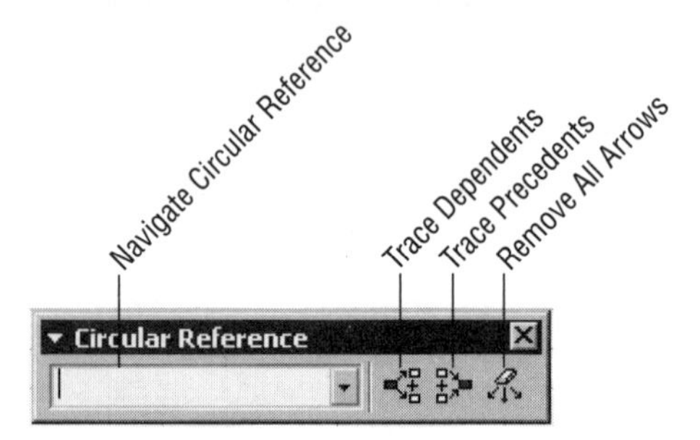

The first two buttons on the toolbar are used to trace dependents and precedents. *Dependents* are cells with formulas that rely on the cell in the drop-down list; *precedents* are the cells that are referred to in this cell's formula. Click the Trace Precedents button, and Excel will show you the precedent cells, as shown in Figure 7.6.

FIGURE 7.6
Tracing precedents

County Cooperative Tree Orders				
Month	**County**	**Type**	**Quantity**	**Bundles**
Jan-2000	Genesee	White Pine	37000	74
Jan-2000	Oakland	Blue Spruce	22500	45
Jan-2000	Oakland	White Pine	15500	31
Jan-2000	Oakland	Concolor Fir	13500	27
Jan-2000	Genesee	Blue Spruce	12500	25
Feb-2000	Oakland	Scotch Pine	11000	22
Feb-2000	Genesee	Frazier Fir	6500	13
Feb-2C			2500	85
Feb-2C			2000	64
Mar-2C			4500	29
Mar-2000	Kalkaska	Blue Spruce	13500	27
Mar-2000	Lake	Concolor Fir	12000	24
Mar-2000	Kalkaska	Concolor Fir	10000	20
Apr-2000	Kalkaska	Frazier Fir	7500	15
Apr-2000	Lake	Blue Spruce	31000	62
Apr-2000	Lake	White Pine	26500	53
				0

The arrow in the Bundles column shows that all the cells in the column, including cell E22, are included in the formula in E22.

Click the Remove All Arrows button, and Excel will turn the arrows off. Then move to the circular reference cell and fix the formula so that it does not include a reference to itself.

Indirect Circular References In the example we've used so far, the circular reference was easy to find, because the formula referred directly to the cell it was stored in. *Indirect circular references* are harder to find. For example, Excel reports a circular reference in J24. When you trace the precedents, the formula in J24 refers to cells E4:E11. So where is the problem? A formula in cells E4:E11 refers to J24 or refers to another cell whose formula refers to J24. This is an indirect circular reference. Just continue clicking the Trace Precedents button, and you'll eventually find a formula that refers to the cell where the circular reference was reported.

Resolving a Circular Reference

1. If the circular reference error dialog box is open, click OK to clear the dialog box and open the Circular Reference toolbar, or open the toolbar (choose View ➢ Toolbars) from the menu bar.
2. Choose the circular reference cell from the drop-down list on the toolbar.
3. Click the Trace Precedents button to see the cells that the formula refers to. Continue clicking Trace Precedents until an arrow points back to the cell with the reference.
4. Fix the formula in the original cell (or, if necessary, in a precedent cell) to remove the circular reference.
5. Click Remove All Arrows, and close the Circular Reference toolbar.

Using the Auditing Toolbar

Objective XL2000E.9.1

The Auditing toolbar is one-stop shopping for error checking in your worksheet. Turn on the toolbar from the Tools menu (not the View menu) by choosing Tools ➢ Auditing ➢ Show Auditing Toolbar.

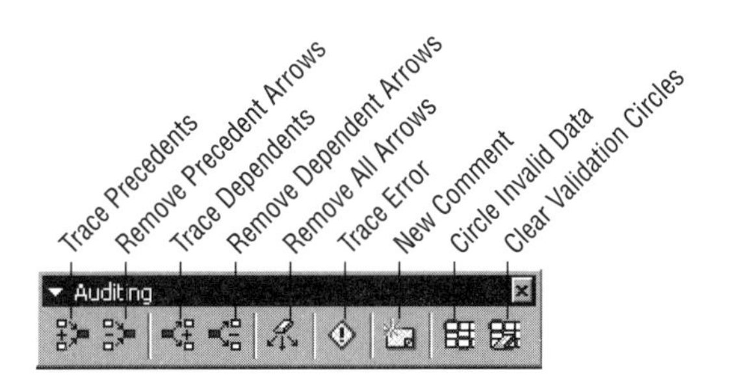

The Auditing toolbar includes tracing tools from the Circular Reference toolbar and a Trace Error tool to check the precedents for cells displaying error codes. Tracing works for DIV/0, but not for many other common errors. When the error is a missing reference or name, for example, the problem is that the formula doesn't have precedents, so there's nothing to trace.

The last three tools on the toolbar work in conjunction with validation rules. Use the Circle Invalid Data button to mark cells with contents that violate established validation rules. If you find invalid entries, insert comments using the New Comment button to note values that need to be corrected. Use the Clear Validation Circles button to hide the circles. (If the entry is corrected so that it's valid, Excel removes the validation circle.)

Hands On: *Objectives XL2000E.9.1, E.9.2, E.9.3, E.9.4, and E.10.9*

1. In any worksheet you're not too attached to, add a formula that includes a circular cell reference. Use the Circular Reference toolbar to view the precedents and resolve the error. Create a DIV/0 error by using a blank cell as the divisor in a formula. Open the Auditing toolbar and trace the error.

2. In any worksheet, add data validation, including input messages and error alerts. Test the validation, messages, and alerts by entering invalid data. When the error alert appears, continue and enter the invalid data. Then use the Circle Invalid Data button on the Auditing toolbar to identify the invalid data.

3. In any worksheet, use the Data Validation dialog box to add several input messages without validating the entries in the cell. Add a comment to another cell. Edit the comment, then Delete it and clear the input messages.

Using and Constructing Templates

Templates are workbook models that you use to create other workbooks. Templates let you quickly construct workbooks that are identical in format, giving your work a consistent look. Excel includes some templates, and you can create others for your personal use or for novice users in your workplace. An Excel template can include text, numbers, formatting, formulas, and all the other features you already use.

When you open a template, a copy is opened—the original template is not altered.

Working with Existing Templates

Objective XL2000E.2.1

Excel includes predesigned workbook templates that you can use or modify. To open a template:

1. Choose File ➢ New from the menu bar to open the New dialog box. (You can't simply click the New button on the Standard toolbar. The New button opens the default template—an empty workbook.)
2. Click the Spreadsheet Solutions tab to view the built-in Excel templates, such as Invoice and Village Software.

Some templates are included in the Typical Excel installation; others have to be custom installed, but they can always be added later.

3. Select the template in the Spreadsheet Solutions window.
4. Click OK.

Entering Data

The Invoice template, shown in Figure 7.7, is a typical template. There are two worksheets in the template: Invoice and Customize Your Invoice. Each template includes a special toolbar. As you use each template, its toolbar is added to the list in the Toolbars dialog box. The Invoice toolbar initially appears as a palette in the worksheet window. You can move the toolbar if you wish.

To view the entire worksheet template, click the Size To Screen button on the Invoice toolbar. Clicking the button again returns the worksheet to its original size.

Cells with a red triangle include comments (also called *CellTips* or *ScreenTips* when they're used as a form of online help) to explain the information you should enter in the cell. To view a comment, move the mouse pointer

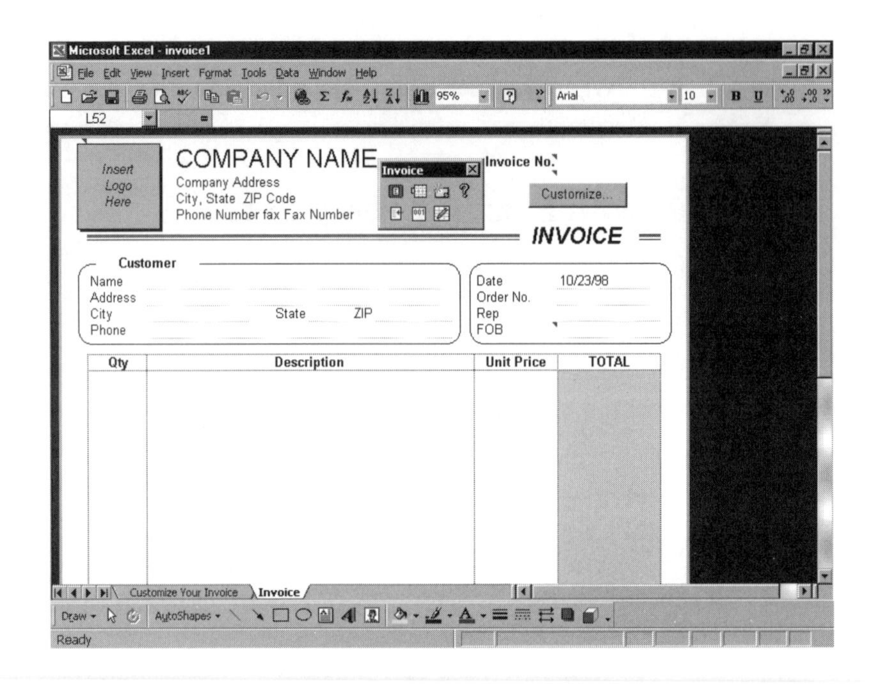

FIGURE 7.7 Excel's Invoice template

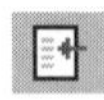

over the cell. You can click the Hide Comments/Display Comments button on the Invoice toolbar to suppress or enable comment display.

Click the New Comment button to add your own comment to the template.

The canned templates include sample data that you can examine as a guide to enter your data. To view the sample data, click the Display Example/Remove Example button on the template's toolbar. To enter data in the template, turn off the example. Activate the cell, and then enter the information.

Cells with a light-blue fill color contain formulas, so don't enter information in shaded cells.

Customizing the Template

Objective XL2000E.2.2

The Invoice sheet includes placeholders for generic title information: the company name, a place for a logo or picture, and so on. To add your personal information, click the Customize button in the Invoice worksheet to move to the Customize Your Invoice worksheet. At the top of the worksheet is a Lock/Save Sheet button. *Locking* a template prevents users from accidentally changing the customized information in this workbook, but it does not alter the template. You can always choose to customize again and unlock the template if you want to change it.

Alternatively, you can save a copy of the template that includes the custom information you entered. It's more convenient to permanently alter the template by saving. To lock or save template changes, click the Lock/Save Sheet button. A dialog box opens so that you can select locking or locking and saving.

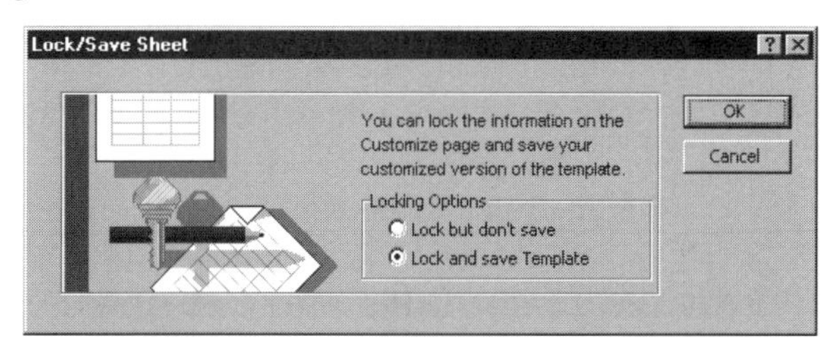

Customizing a Template

1. Activate the Customize worksheet.
2. Enter your custom information as indicated in the worksheet.
3. Click the Lock/Save Sheet button.
4. Choose Lock But Don't Save or Lock And Save Template; then click OK.

Creating a Template

Objective XL2000E.2.3

You can create a template for workbooks that you use frequently. For example, you might use Excel to complete a weekly payroll and put all the payroll worksheets for one month into a separate workbook. Rather than construct a new workbook each month, you can create a monthly payroll template; then, at the beginning of each month, you can create a new workbook from the template. Your template will differ from a regular workbook in three specific ways:

- The completed workbook will be saved as a template (rather than as a workbook).

- The template will contain only the text, formulas, and formatting that remain the same each month.
- The template in the Office 2000 Templates folder or one of its subfolders will include visual formatting clues and comments to assist users.

Adding and Testing Formulas

You can create a template from scratch or base it on an existing workbook. If you're using an existing workbook, first make sure that all the formulas work and that numbers and text are formatted as you want them. Then remove the text and numbers that will be entered each time the template is used. Don't remove formulas—although the results of the formulas change, the formulas remain the same. If you're creating a template from scratch, you'll still need to enter test values, then remove them before saving the template.

Providing User Cues and CellTips

Now, use borders and shading to let users know where they should—and shouldn't—enter text or other information. The Invoice template is a good model.

Objective XL2000E.12.1

Add comments (choose Insert Comment from the shortcut menu) to provide CellTips where users might have questions about data entry. To edit or delete an existing comment, right-click the cell with the comment and choose Edit or Delete from the menu. If you're editing, simply select and overtype the old comment and then click away from it to exit edit mode.

Saving Your Template

Before you save your template, remove any blank worksheets from the workbook to improve its overall appearance. When you're finished formatting the worksheet, choose File ➢ Save As, and save the workbook as a Template type.

Excel templates have the `.xlt` extension, but simply typing the extension does not save the workbook as a template.

When you choose Template as the Save As file type, Excel switches the Save In location to the Template folder. You can create a folder within the Templates folder to hold your personal templates. Other than the General tab, tabs in the New dialog box represent subfolders of the Templates folder that contain Excel templates or workbooks. To automatically open a template every time Excel is launched, save the template in the XLStart folder or in the folder specified as the Alternate Startup File Location on the General tab of Excel's Options dialog box.

Saving a Template

1. Click the Save button or choose File ➢ Save As.
2. In the Save As Type control, choose Template from the drop-down list. The Save In control will change to the default Templates folder.
3. Use the New Folder button to create a new folder if you want to add a tab to the New dialog box. Enter a filename for the template.
4. Click the Save button.

Opening and Editing Your Template

When you choose File ➢ New, your new template will be included on the General page or the specific folder you saved it in. Double-click the template's icon to open a workbook based on your template.

When you or other users use your template to create new workbooks, the template itself will not be altered. To modify a template, open the template from the Templates folder with File ➢ Open rather than File ➢ New. When you are finished editing, save and close the template.

The location of the Templates folder depends on a number of installation options. Use the Find feature on the Start Menu and search for files with the `.xlt` extension if you're having trouble locating the folder.

Hands On: Objectives XL2000E.2.1, E.2.2, E.2.3, and E.12.1

1. Use another of the templates (such as Expenses) included with Excel 2000. Customize the template with your company's information. Save the customized template.

2. Create a template that calculates and totals gross pay, taxes, and net pay for 10 employees based on information entered by the user. Users should enter the following information for each employee: social security number, last name, first name, hourly rate, tax rate (as a percentage), and hours worked.
3. Modify the template in step 2 to allow for payroll deduction of employee contributions to National Public Radio. The deduction amount will be entered with the employee information and deducted from the pay after taxes are calculated. Total the contribution column. Resave the template.

Linking Information

A *link* is a reference to a cell or range in another workbook. Links are commonly used to avoid double-entering workbook information, or to obtain the most current data from a shared data source.

Linking Workbooks

Objective XL2000E.3.2

Suppose that in your company, departments are responsible for their own budgets. As the time to finalize the coming year's budget approaches, each manager is working furiously on his or her budget. The vice president for finance has a master budget that is a roll-up of the department budgets. It's not practical to put all the department worksheets and the master budget in one large workbook, because many people would need to use the workbook at the same time, and only one user needs to work with all the data for the various departments.

What's the practical solution? By linking the workbooks, the changes made by the department managers can be immediately reflected in the vice president's master budget workbook.

Each link establishes a relationship between two workbooks. The vice president's workbook is called the *dependent workbook*, because the value that the VP sees depends on a value in departmental workbook. The department's workbook that contains that value is called the *source workbook*.

Creating a Link

You can create a link in two ways: by using an open workbook or by referring to a workbook on disk. The first method is much easier. It's the same as creating any other reference in a formula, but you need to switch to the source workbook before selecting the cell to reference in the formula.

To create a link to an open workbook:

1. Open the source workbook, then switch to the dependent workbook.
2. Begin entering the formula in the dependent workbook with an equal sign (=).
3. At the point in the formula where you want to include a cell reference from the source workbook, choose Window on the menu bar and select the source workbook.
4. In the source workbook, click the cell that you want to reference to include it in the formula as shown in Figure 7.8.
5. Switch back to the dependent worksheet by pressing Enter.
6. Double-click the cell with the formula and notice that the cell reference includes the workbook and worksheet names as well as the cell address.

FIGURE 7.8 Creating a link

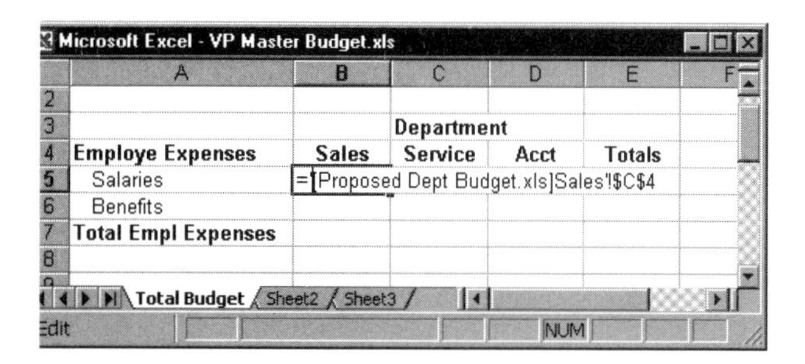

You may prefer to arrange the source and dependent workbooks so that you can see the results cell and the cell to be referenced at the same time. With both workbooks open, choose Window ➢ Arrange to open the Arrange Windows dialog box.

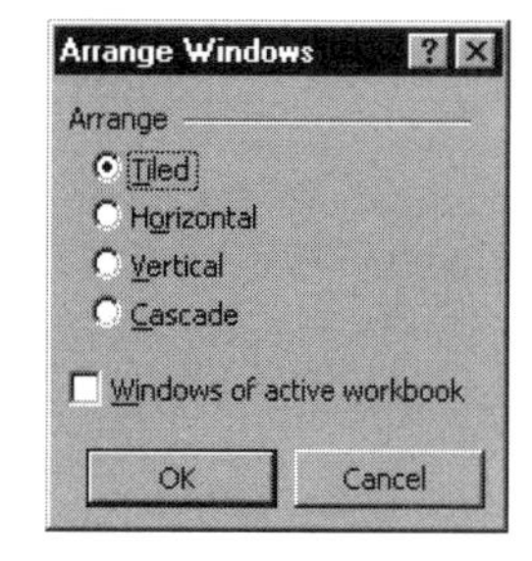

Choose how you want the open workbooks arranged, and then use each workbook window's sizing tool to further size and arrange the windows.

You can also arrange copies of a single workbook so that you can work in two different areas of the workbook in separate windows. First, choose Window ➢ New Window, and then open the Arrange Windows dialog box (Window ➢ Arrange) and arrange the windows.

To link to a workbook that is not open, you must provide all the information that Excel needs to find the source workbook, including the full path. For example, if you want to refer to cell D4 in the Sales sheet of the Proposed Dept Budget workbook, stored in the Sales Management folder on the C drive, the reference would be `'C:\Sales Management\[Proposed Dept Budget.xls]Sales'!D4`. There are many places to make a mistake when typing an entry like this. Try to create links with open source workbooks whenever possible.

Linking with Paste Link

If you simply want to refer to a cell in another workbook (as opposed to using it in a formula), create a link with Copy And Paste Link. To do so, open both workbooks, and then select and copy the cell(s) from the source workbook. Next, activate the destination workbook and choose Edit ➢ Paste Special from the menu bar to open the Paste Special dialog box.

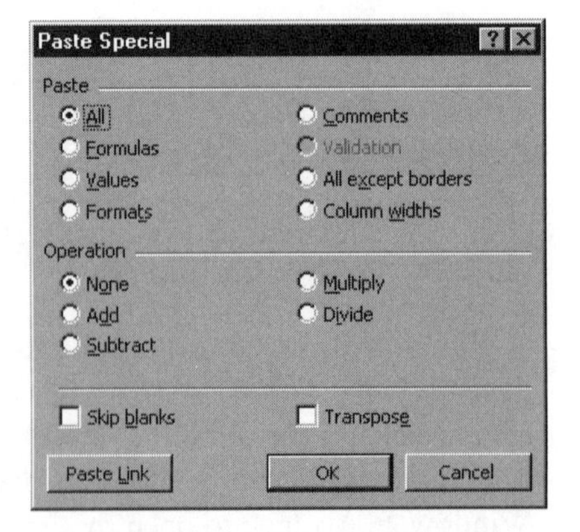

A normal paste simply pastes the formula(s) from the Clipboard, but here you can paste values, formula, formats, and other cell attributes or perform a math operation during the paste.

Once you've made your choices in the Paste Special dialog box, click the Paste Link button, select a destination for the pasted selection, and then press Enter to paste the link to the source workbook.

Updating Links

When you open a dependent workbook and its source workbook is not open, Excel will ask if you want to update the links. If both workbooks are open, changes in the source workbook are automatically updated in the dependent workbook.

If, however, the source workbook can be opened by other users, they could be making changes to the workbook while you are working with the dependent workbook. In this case, the links will not be updated automatically; you have to instruct Excel to update the links:

1. With the dependent workbook open, choose Edit ➢ Links to open the Links dialog box:

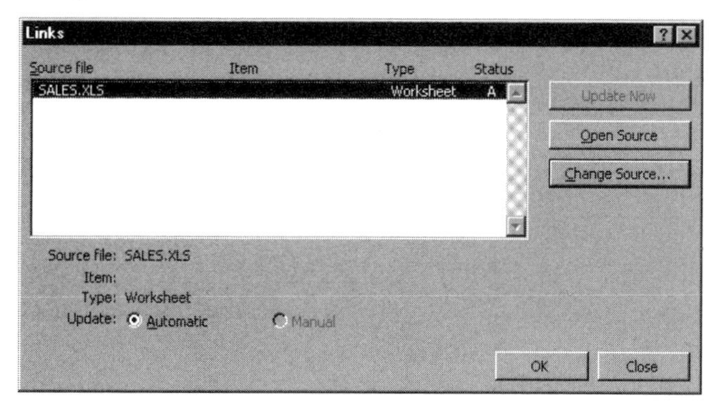

2. From the Source File list, choose the source workbook that you want to update.

3. Click the Update Now button to update the dependent workbook with information from the latest saved version of the source workbook.

References That Span Worksheets

In Excel, you can reference ranges that occur in the same cell or group of cells on two or more worksheets. For example, Figure 7.9 shows the 1st Quarter worksheet for reporting types of media sold at various locations.

FIGURE 7.9
Media Types worksheet

	A	B	C	D	E
1	Media Sales by Location and Type				
2	Sales in Units - 1st Qtr 1999				
3					
4	Location	Disk	CD	Video	Total
5	Temple Street	110	141	67	318
6	Mt. Vernon	45	90	104	239
7	Cambridge	211	300	41	552
8	Milton	351	313	0	664
9		717	844	212	1773
10					

The January, February, and March worksheets have the same layout, and the FirstQuarter worksheet summarizes the figures from the three monthly worksheets. You can total all worksheets at one time with a 3-D cell reference, which can be filled or copied like any other Excel formula.

Creating a 3-D Reference in a Formula

1. Arrange the workbook so the sheets you want to include as a 3-D reference are next to each other.
2. In the results cell, begin constructing the formula.
3. To include the 3-D reference, click the sheet tab of the first sheet of the 3-D range.
4. Hold Shift, and select the last sheet you want to refer to.
5. Select the cell or range of cells to include in the formula.
6. Finish the formula, and press Enter.

Using 3-D Names

You might want to use 3-D names if you're creating a lot of 3-D cell references. For example, if cell B10 in three worksheets is the value for April's salaries, you could name all three cells salaryApr or AprSalary.

Defining 3-D Range Names

1. Arrange the workbook so the sheets that include cells to be named are next to each other. Choose Insert ➢ Name ➢ Define from the menu bar.
2. In the Names In Workbook text box, type the name.

Defining 3-D Range Names *(continued)*

3. In the Refers To text box, delete the existing reference except for the equal sign (=).
4. Click the sheet tab of the first worksheet with a cell you want to include in the named range.
5. Hold Shift and select the sheet tab for the last worksheet to be included.
6. Release Shift and select the cell or range to be named in the last worksheet.
7. Click Add to add the name, and then click OK to close the dialog box.

Using a Workspace

Objective XL2000E.3.1

If you're frequently using a particular group of workbooks together, you can save time opening them by creating a *workspace file*. A workspace file saves information about all open workbooks: their on-screen positions, window sizes, and drive and folder location. When you open a saved workspace file, it opens all the workbooks in the workspace.

Creating a Workspace File

1. Open the workbooks you want to include in the workspace file.
2. Move and resize the workbook windows so they are in the exact position you want them to be when you open the workspace.
3. Click File ➢ Save Workspace.
4. Enter a name and location for the workspace file and click Save.

Make sure you continue to save changes you make to the individual workbooks while working with the workspace file.

Hands On: Objectives XL2000E.3.1 and E.3.2

1. Create the worksheet shown below for the Sales department. Re-create or copy the Sales worksheet to two separate workbooks. Edit the worksheet for the Accounting and Service departments. Save all three workbooks.

	A	B	C	D
1	**Proposed Budget - 1999**			
2				
3	**Employee Expense**	**1998 Budget**	**1998 Actual**	**1999 Proposed**
4	Salaries	147,000	148,540	151,000
5	Benefits	39,690	38,790	40,770
6	**Total Employee Expense**	186,690	187,330	191,770

   a) In a new workbook, create the Budget Summary worksheet shown in Figure 7.8. Use links to refer to the figures in column D of the three departmental workbooks.

   b) Close all four workbooks. Open the Accounting department workbook and change the proposed salaries and benefits for 1999. Close and save the Accounting department workbook.

   c) Open the Budget Summary workbook. Do not update the links. Note the figures for Accounting. Update the links.

   d) Open and arrange all four workbooks.

2. In a new workbook, create at least three periodic worksheets and one total worksheet. Use 3-D cell references to total the periodic worksheets on the total worksheet.

Working with Others in Excel

Excel 2000 was designed to allow multiple users to view and modify a single workbook simultaneously. If you want others to be able to use a workbook while you have it open, you need to share the workbook and ensure that it is stored on a network or shared drive that other users can access.

Sharing Workbooks

Objective XL2000E.12.6

To share a workbook, open the Share Workbook dialog box (choose Tools ➢ Share Workbook).

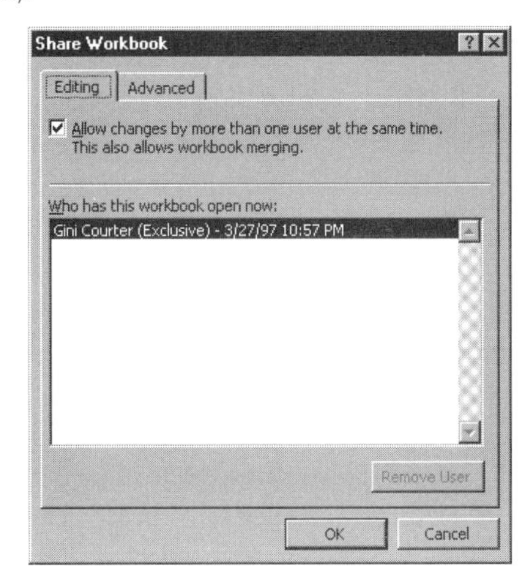

On the Editing page, enable the Allow Changes check box to make the file accessible to other users. Then click the Advanced tab to set options for tracking changes and resolving conflicts.

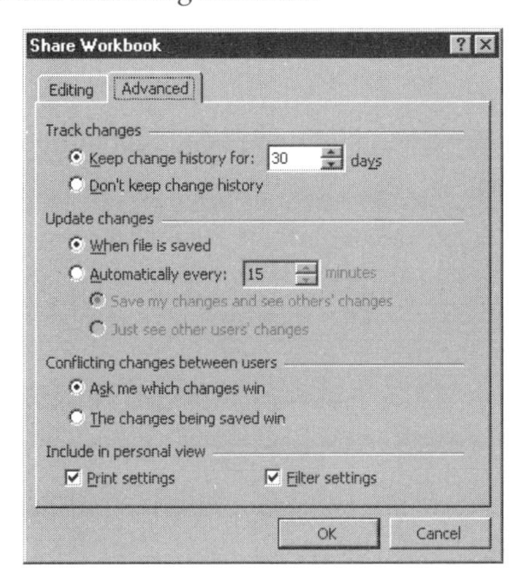

Tracking Changes

Tracking is only available in shared workbooks. If you choose to track changes in a *change history*, select the number of days changes should be kept. (If you intend to distribute copies of the workbook, see "Merging Workbook Changes" below for more about this setting). If you don't want to track changes, tell Excel not to keep a history.

Whether you track changes or not, you need to determine when changes are updated. The default only updates changes When File Is Saved. This means that each time you (or another user) save, Excel will save your changes and update your workbook with changes made by other users. Alternatively, you can choose to have your workbook updated Automatically Every set number of minutes; by choosing the Save My Changes And See Others' Changes option, your changes will be saved when the update occurs. (If you update changes Automatically, other users still won't see your changes until you save; however, they can also choose to see saved changes Automatically rather than waiting until they save.)

When two or more users try to save different changes in the same cell, it causes a conflict. Set the Conflicting Changes Between Users option to indicate how conflicts should be resolved. Excel can prompt you to resolve conflicts, or it can automatically accept your changes.

The Personal view section of the Advanced page contains your print and filter settings for the workbook. These settings do not affect other users' view of the workbook. Use the check boxes to include or exclude these settings when the workbook is saved.

Sharing a Workbook

1. With the workbook open, choose Tools ➢ Share Workbook from the menu bar.
2. On the Editing page, enable Allow Changes By More Than One User.
3. On the Advanced page, set Track Changes, Update Changes, Conflicting Changes, and Personal View options.
4. Click OK to close the dialog box.

When you close the dialog box, Excel will save the workbook as a shared workbook; if you haven't previously saved, the Save As dialog box will open.

Excel tracks workbook users by name. If the name listed in the Editing tab is incorrect, you can change it on the General page of the Options dialog box (choose Tools ➢ Options).

Working in a Shared Workbook

Objective XL2000E.12.5

When Tracking Changes is enabled, each change made is noted in a comment, and changed cells are flagged. For example, if you delete the value in a cell, a triangle appears in the upper-left corner of the cell. When you move the mouse pointer over the cell, a comment tells you who changed the cell, when they changed it, and what the former value in the cell was.

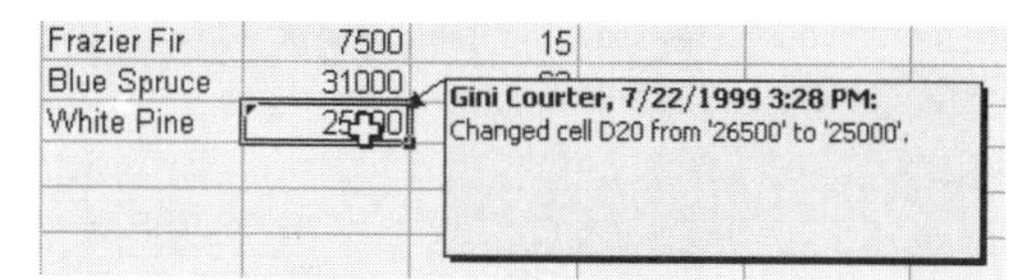

Excel assigns a different color for each user who modifies the workbook, so you can visually inspect the workbook to find all the changes made by one user. Reject a change by right-clicking that change and choosing Reject Change from the shortcut menu.

When you save the workbook, you accept the changes, so the triangles and comments disappear.

Limitations of Shared Workbooks

Some Excel 2000 features aren't available in shared workbooks. For instance, while a workbook is shared, you can't:

- Delete worksheets
- Add or apply conditional formatting and data validation
- Insert or delete ranges of cells (you can still insert and delete individual cells, rows, and columns), charts, hyperlinks, or other objects (including those created with Draw)
- Group or outline data
- Write, change, view, record, or assign macros

Though not available when working in a shared workbook, you can use the features before you share a workbook, or you can temporarily unshare the workbook, make changes, and then turn sharing on again.

See Excel's Online Help for the complete list of limitations of shared workbooks.

Resolving Conflicts

If changes you are saving conflict with changes saved by another user, you'll be prompted to resolve the conflict (unless you changed the Conflicting Changes setting in the Advanced page of the Share Workbook dialog box). The Resolve Conflict dialog box will open automatically. You can review each change individually and accept your change or others' changes, or accept/reject changes in bulk.

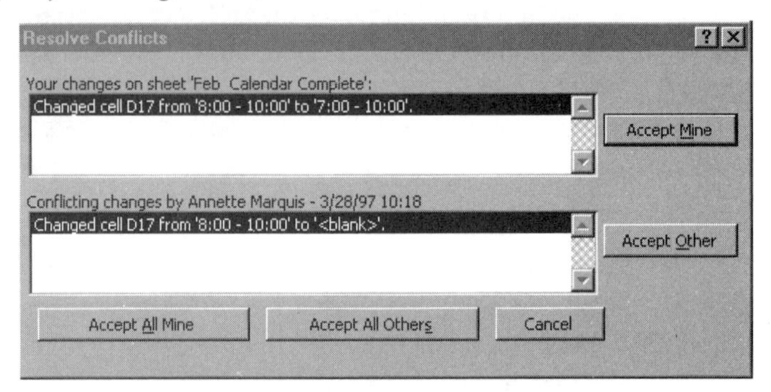

Viewing the Change History

If you have chosen to track changes in a change history, you can examine all the changes saved in a workbook since you turned on the change history. Choose Tools ➢ Track Changes ➢ Highlight Changes to open the Highlight Changes dialog box.

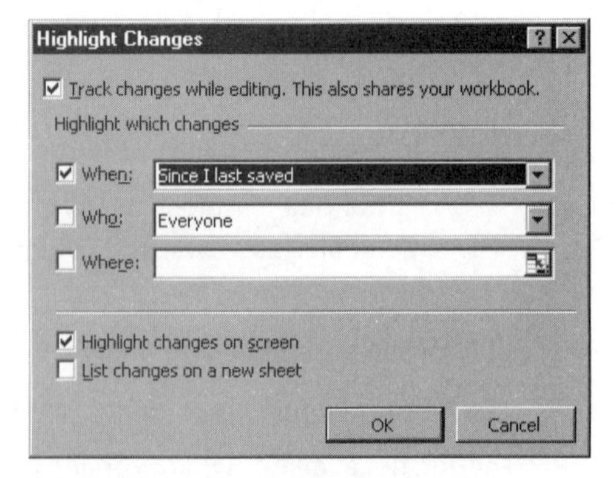

In the dialog box, select the time period for the changes you want to review, and specify the users whose changes you want to see. If you only want to see changes for a particular range or sheet, select the range you want to view. You can view the changes on screen or on a separate worksheet in the workbook.

Viewing the Change History

1. Choose Tools > Track Changes > Highlight Changes.
2. In the Highlight Changes dialog box, set the When, Who, and Where options.
3. Enable or disable viewing on screen or in a separate worksheet.
4. Click OK.

When you view the history on a separate worksheet, you can filter the changes to find changes made by different users or on specific dates, as you would with any Excel database. When you remove a workbook from shared use, the change history is turned off and reset. If you want to keep the changes, select the information on the History worksheet and copy it to another worksheet before unsharing the workbook.

Merging Workbook Changes

Objective XL2000E.12.7

If you want users to be able to make changes independently and then review all changes at once, make and distribute copies of the shared workbook. To create the copies, use Save As and give each copy of the workbook a different name. Then you can merge the copies when users are done with their changes.

You can only merge workbooks that have the same change history, so it's important that none of the users turns off sharing while using the workbook. Also, the history must be complete when you merge the workbooks. If, for example, you set the number of days for the history at 30 days and users keep the workbooks for 32 days, you won't be able to merge the workbooks. Before you make copies of the shared workbook, make sure you set the history to allow enough time for changes and merging. If you're uncertain, set 600 days or an equally ridiculous length of time.

Merging Shared Workbooks

1. Open your copy of the shared workbook that you want to merge changes into.
2. Choose Tools > Merge Workbooks. If you haven't saved your copy of the workbook, you'll be prompted to do so.
3. In the Select Files To Merge Into Current Document dialog box, choose the copy of the shared workbook that has the changes you wish to merge. (Use Ctrl or Shift to select multiple workbooks from one location.) Click OK.

Setting Passwords and Protection

Objective XL2000E.12.4

You can restrict who can view and modify the data in any workbook by setting passwords to open or modify the workbook. To do so:

1. Choose File ➢ Save As and click the Tools button in the Save As dialog box. Choose General Options to open the Save Options dialog box:

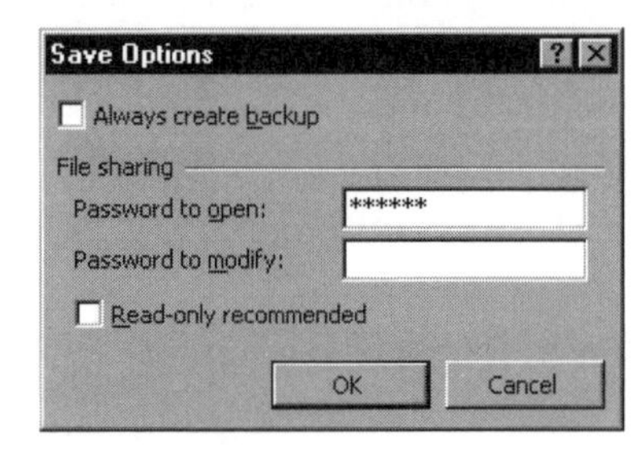

2. Enter passwords that users (including you) must enter to open or modify the workbooks.
3. Click OK to return to the Save As procedure.

Give anyone who should be able to open the file the Password To Open, which they will be prompted to enter when they try to open the file. Users who can supply the Open password are then prompted to enter a second password (the Modify password) or open the file as Read Only. If you forget a password, you won't be able to open/modify the file.

The two-password system lets you control who can change the file. If you want lots of users to be able to look at the file (or save a copy of the file) but reserve modification rights for yourself, use different passwords and distribute only the password that opens the file. If any user who can open the file should be able to modify it, use the same password for Open and Modify passwords.

Deleting or Changing Passwords

Delete a password from a file by changing the Password To Open or Password To Modify field in the Save Options dialog box. Select the asterisks that represent the current password and press Delete if you want to remove the password. If you want to change the password, select the asterisks and type a new password. Retype it, click OK, and then save the workbook. Any user who can modify the workbook can change both passwords.

Using Workbook and Worksheet Protection

Objective XL2000E.12.2

If you don't want to password-protect the workbook file, but you're still concerned about others' errors, consider using Workbook and/or Worksheet Protection. Protection prevents other users from changing or deleting data and other objects in your worksheet or change the structure of the workbook. To enable Protection:

1. Click Tools ➢ Protection ➢ Protect Workbook or Tools ➢ Protection ➢ Protect Sheet.
2. Enable the items you want to protect.
3. Type a password if you want to limit users' ability to unprotect the workbook.
4. Click OK when you're finished.

Remove Protection by clicking Tools ➢ Protection ➢ Unprotect Workbook (or Sheet).

Changing Workbook Properties

Objective XL2000E.12.3

Workbook properties describe the workbook and make it easy to organize and locate specific workbooks. To access the properties for an open workbook, choose File ➢ Properties; the workbook's Properties page opens.

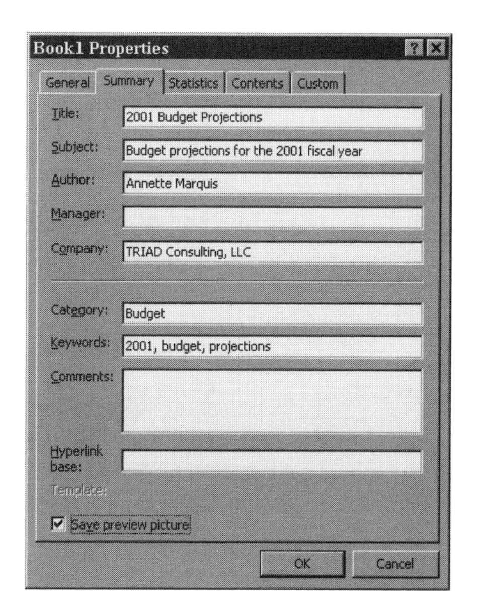

The workbook's Properties dialog box has five tabs:

- General displays type, location, size, MS-DOS name, and attributes of the file.
- Summary is an editable tab that includes such things as title, subject, author, company, category, and keywords.
- Statistics displays when the file was created, modified, accessed, printed, last saved by, revision number, and total editing time.
- Contents displays the workbook name and the names of each sheet in the workbook.
- Custom includes options for entering values for 27 additional properties such as Date Completed, Editor, Owner, Project, Publisher, Purpose, and so on.

You can modify the properties on the Summary and Custom pages. On the Summary page, click in an open text box and enter property information. To add a value for a Custom property:

1. Switch to the Custom tab of the Workbook Properties dialog box.
2. Select the property from the list.
3. Indicate if the Type is Text, Date, Number, Yes or No.
4. Enter the actual value for this property.
5. Click the Add button.

To delete a custom property, select it from the Properties list and click Delete.

Hands On: *Objectives XL2000E.12.2, E.12.3, E.12.4, E.12.5, E.12.6, and E.12.7*

1. Open one of the practice workbooks you've used in this chapter, or use another file with non-critical data.
   - a) Set up the workbook for sharing.
   - b) Apply Open and Modify passwords to the workbook, then resave and close it. Open the workbook and then remove both passwords.
   - c) Turn on Track Changes and use Save As to save the file under a different name. Send the renamed workbook to a colleague and ask her/him to make several changes and send it back to you.

d) In the original shared workbook, make your own changes.

e) Open the workbook your colleague modified and review the changes s/he made. Accept or reject them as desired.

f) Merge the two workbooks, resolving conflicts as necessary.

2. In the same or another workbook, apply Worksheet Protection so you cannot modify cell contents. Test it to make sure it worked, then remove Worksheet Protection.

3. Open the workbook's Properties page and enter a title and subject for the workbook.

a) Add a category and enter some comments.

b) Add values for at least custom properties.

Forecasting and Modeling

If you were going to fly across country for a week of business meetings, chances are you would at least think about checking the weather forecast to find out what type of clothing to pack. And even though the forecast prompted you to pack a raincoat, you wouldn't be too surprised if the snow turned to rain or even sunshine. Regardless of the forecast, no one can personally alter the weather that actually "arrives." Following the forecast does, however, increase the possibility that you will be properly prepared.

Business forecasts—predictions of business factors like product demand, production costs, income, and expenses—are the "weather prediction" for a business unit's future. Like a weather forecast, the business forecast may be less than completely accurate. However, there is one important difference between a weather forecast and a business forecast: while you can't change the weather, managers can monitor the progress a business makes and alter business decisions so that actual performance is more closely related to the forecast.

Forecasts try to *simulate* or predict future behavior of variables like gross profit based on many types of information. A forecast may be based on:

- Historical information, such as last year's earnings
- Judgments or educated guesses by people in a position to help predict future performance, such as managers, client focus groups, and sales staff
- Information about indicators, such as the prices charged by competitors, the local employment level, or the current interest rate

The more sources of information you consider, the more accurate your forecast will be. You might be more likely to trust a weather person who looked at a radar reading than one who simply looked out the window.

There are different ways to construct forecasts. In Excel, forecasting always involves creating a *model*, one or more worksheets that use formulas to show how different variables interrelate. Amortization schedules are an example of a forecasting model. If you enter different values for principal or interest, you can see how the payment amount or length of loan changes. Payroll worksheets are models of the relationships between hours worked, pay rate, gross pay, taxes, and net pay. Inventory worksheets model the interactions of quantity, cost, and total cost.

Forecasting is always based on assumptions. Each model has specific, built-in assumptions, but there are some assumptions common to most models. One general assumption is that the future will be much like the present: the world's financial markets won't fall apart during the life of a loan (pre- or post-Y2K), and you will need to make a loan payment this month, and every month in the future until the loan is paid off. There is also an assumption that a modeled forecast will not be perfect. There will always be some neglected piece of information that ends up being important (like the month that the payment is received late, resulting in a penalty).

Another assumption is that the distant future is more difficult to predict than the near future. (That's why it's difficult to get 50-year mortgages.) No one could have accurately predicted the last four years of stock market prices, or the increasing importance of E-commerce over the past decade. As the time period involved in a forecast increases, the accuracy of the forecast decreases, even if the model was essentially accurate for a shorter time frame.

Building a Business Model

There are several steps involved in building a model and using it to forecast performance:

1. Decide what you need to know from the model.
2. Make explicit assumptions.
3. Define and collect information for the model.
4. Create the model in Excel.
5. Use the model to forecast the future value of variables.
6. Compare real performance to the model and adjust the model (or change actual performance) as necessary.

The amount of effort spent on each step should be based on the importance of the information you intend to obtain from the model. You don't want to spend hours researching and modeling a decision that will save $2.00. But you need to spend sufficient time when you are creating a model to support decision making that involves hundreds of thousands of dollars.

Let's use a fictitious company, the WellBilt Corporation, to look at business modeling. The WellBilt Manufacturing Corporation makes a variety of PC accessories. WellBilt's CD Division makes organizers for compact disks.

What You Need to Know

WellBilt needs to decide how many organizers the CD Division should make each month. You have been put in charge of collecting and modeling the information needed to decide how the CD Division can maximize monthly gross profit.

Model Assumptions

WellBilt assumes that they will be able to market the CD organizers to large computer stores and e-commerce sites as they have in the past. More assumptions will be added as information is collected.

Collecting Information

You will need to collect information on the income generated by organizer sales and the expenses involved in manufacturing the CD organizers. Some of the expenses are *fixed expenses*, expenses that, in the short run, are the same amount no matter how many CD organizers are manufactured. Other expenses (like labor and materials) are *variable expenses*

You talked to the Accounting department and found that the CD Division's fixed expenses are not expected to change from current monthly costs ($80,000 for building mortgage, maintenance, and salaries) in the next year. There are several pieces of variable cost information: hourly employees make $6.00; overtime hours are paid at time and a half. During a month, the current workforce can build 48,000 organizers without working overtime. Each CD organizer takes an hour to make and uses $1.25 in raw materials.

You also spoke with the Marketing department. It has already created an Excel statistical model to determine sales at various prices for the CD Organizer. They have determined that the formula `Price=$20-(Quantity/5000)` expresses the price needed to sell a particular quantity. In other words, the most anyone will spend for a CD organizer is $20. At a price of $19, WellBilt would be able to sell only 5,000 units. For each additional 5,000 units sold,

WellBilt has to drop the price $1. From the Production and Sales managers, you know that WellBilt manufactured and sold 45,000 units this past month.

Creating the Model

You now have enough information to create an Excel model of the basic factors that influence production of CD organizers. (You also have some new assumptions: that the information from Accounting and Marketing is accurate, and that the Marketing model is good for the next year.)

The Accounting department information contains an IF statement: if production is less than or equal to 48,000 units, then the cost of labor is $6 per hour. Hours in excess of 48,000 cost $9 per hour. Since this month's sales were 45,000, let's begin by modeling production of sales of 40,000, 45,000, and 50,000 units, as shown in Figure 7.10.

FIGURE 7.10

CD Division model

	A	B	C	D
1	**WellBilt Manuracturing**			
2	**CD ROM Disk Organizer Production**			
3				
4	**Income**	**High**	**Medium**	**Low**
5	Units Produced & Sold	50,000	45,000	40,000
6	Unit Price	10.00	11.00	12.00
7	**Total Income**	**500,000**	**495,000**	**480,000**
8				
9	**Expense**			
10	Fixed Expense	80,000	80,000	80,000
11	Labor Expense	306,000	270,000	240,000
12	Material Expense	62,500	56,250	50,000
13	**Total Expense**	**448,500**	**406,250**	**370,000**
14				
15	**Gross Profit**	**51,500**	**88,750**	**110,000**

Cells `B6`, `B11`, and `B12` use the following formulas, respectively:

- `=20-(B5/5000)`
- `=IF(B5<48000,B5*6,(48000*6)+(B5-48000)*9)`
- `=1.25*B5`

Total Income is, of course, Unit Price multiplied by Units Produced & Sold. Gross Profit is a subtraction formula: Total Income minus Total Expenses.

The model indicates that lower levels of production produce higher levels of gross profit. Since your model includes the current level of production, you have a way to check accuracy of the model. Is gross profit currently $88,750 a month? If it is not, you know that there is information missing from the model that you need to identify and include. If current gross profit is close to the figure in the model, you can have more confidence in the model's ability to predict gross profit at other levels of production. Remember, though, that the model has a limitation: It's only valid for the three production figures that you included. You can't draw conclusions about the gross profit at other quantities produced and sold without expanding the model.

Using Excel's Forecasting Tools

Excel provides a number of good tools for numerical forecasting. You already know how to use many of these tools: the functions and formulas. For more advanced work, Excel includes specialized forecasting tools called What If tools, used in What If analysis. (Using What If tools is sometimes called *wiffing*, short for "What If"ing.)

Goal Seek

Objective XL2000E.11.2

Use Excel's *Goal Seek* tool when you need to find a specific solution to a formula. Goal Seek is used to calculate backwards—to determine the values necessary to reach a specific goal. Once you have created a worksheet model, you can use Goal Seek to get a specific answer. For example, one of the Well-Bilt managers wants to know how many units must be manufactured and sold to result in gross profits of exactly $100,000 per month. You know the goal, and Goal Seek will help you find the answer.

Goal Seek changes the value of an underlying number (the Quantity Produced & Sold) until the value in the goal cell (Gross Profit) is equal to the goal ($100,000). Excel will begin by trying an upper and lower value for the Quantity Produced. If the goal falls between the initial values, Goal Seek then narrows the value in small increments until the Gross Profit value is within 0.001 of the goal. If the goal value is outside the initial range, Goal Seek will try larger values. Each attempt to meet the goal is called an *iteration*. The default Calculation settings (Tools ➢ Options ➢ Calculation) instruct Excel to try 100 iterations before giving up.

Choose Tools ➢ Goal Seek to open the Goal Seek dialog box.

You must enter references or values in all three controls of the Goal Seek dialog box:

Set Cell The cell (`B15`, gross profit) that will contain the goal result

To Value The goal we're trying to reach (100,000)

By Changing Cell The cell (`B5`) that contains the value that will be incrementally changed to try to reach the goal in the Set Cell control

You can type in the Set Cell and Changing Cell references, or use the mouse to enter the references. The contents of the To Value control must be a number. After you have entered all three pieces of information, click the OK button, and Goal Seek will begin testing different values in the changing cell.

There are two possible results of a Goal Seek operation: the goal can be reached within the number of iterations set in Excel's options, or it cannot. If Goal Seek finds a value that results in the target value you specified, it will let you know in the Goal Seek Status dialog box.

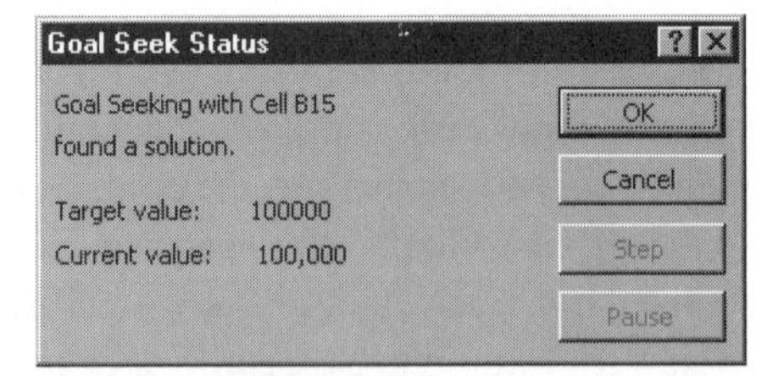

The dialog box indicates both the goal value and Goal Seek's progress in matching the value. In this case, the match is exact. Goal Seek was able to find a value for Quantity Produced & Sold that resulted in a gross profit of exactly $100,000. Clicking the OK button replaces the figures in `B5` and `B15` with the Goal Seek results. Clicking Cancel leaves the original figures in the two cells.

Some problems don't have a solution. Figure 7.11 shows the Goal Seek dialog box when a solution could not be found. The target value entered for Gross Profit was 250,000. Goal Seek has already tried 100 numbers. The last number tried is displayed as the Current Value—a very large negative number. Goal Seek has already tried both positive and negative numbers as large as the Current Value shown in the dialog box.

FIGURE 7.11
Goal Seek:
No Solution

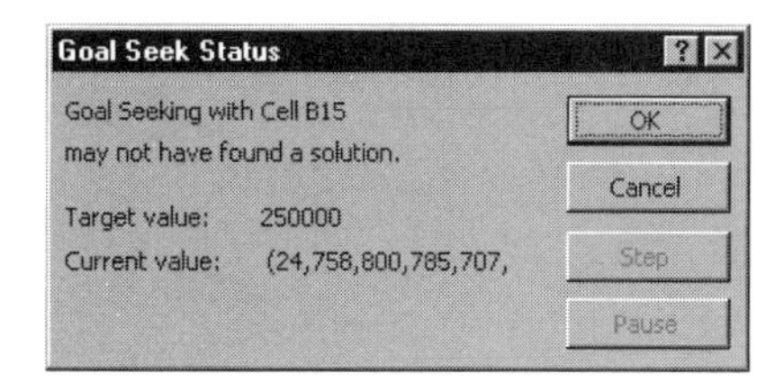

Even when Goal Seek can't find a solution, you know more than you did before: there is no solution. Given the current values for price, fixed expenses, and variable expenses, WellBilt cannot make $250,000 a month from the CD Division no matter how many CD organizers they manufacture. You can click Cancel to discard the value and close the dialog box.

Using Goal Seek

1. Open the workbook that has the figures you want to calculate from.
2. Choose Tools ➢ Goal Seek from the menu.
3. Select a Set Cell where you want the goal value to appear. The cell must contain a formula.
4. Enter the goal value in the To Value control.
5. Enter the value to change in the By Changing Cell control.
6. Click OK to start Goal Seek.
7. To accept the solution, click OK in the Goal Seek Status dialog box to enter the Goal Seek solution. To reject the solution, click Cancel.

Using Solver for Optimization

Objective XL2000E.11.5

Another Excel forecasting tool, *Solver*, is used to find the best or optimal solution. Optimization has many business applications. Solver can be used to find the least expensive solution to a problem, or a solution that maximizes income. Remember that our original assignment was to maximize gross profit. This is a job for Solver. Choose Tools ➢Solver to open the Solver Parameters dialog box, shown in Figure 7.12.

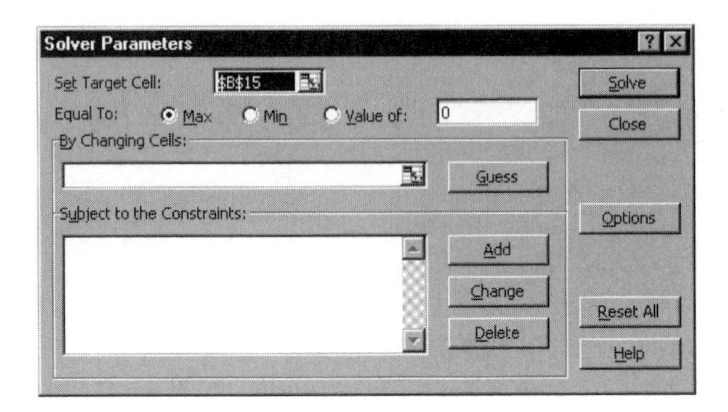

FIGURE 7.12
The Solver dialog box

Solver is an add-in and may not have been installed on your computer. If you don't see Solver on the Tools menu, click Tools ➢ Add-Ins, choose Solver Add-In from the Add-Ins dialog box, and click OK. Excel may prompt you for the Office 2000 CD to install this feature.

Solver's *Target Cell* is the same as Goal Seek's Set Cell—the cell that the final result should appear in. In the Equal To section, choose the Max, Min, or Value option to indicate whether you are looking for the largest or smallest possible number, or a set value (as you did with Goal Seek). As in Goal Seek, the By Changing Cells is the cell that Solver is to change to find the solution. Click the Guess button, and Excel will add cells that contain values reflected in the Target Cell results in the By Changing Cells control. Unlike Goal Seek, Solver can change more than one cell value to create an optimal solution.

In the WellBilt worksheet, Excel will "guess" cells B5 and B10–the only non-formula cells in column B. The value in B10 can't change in our model, so we would need to change to B5 only.

After you have made choices for these three controls, clicking the Solve button instructs Solver to find a solution. Like Goal Seek, Solver will try 100 iterations before reporting that it cannot find a solution. The results of a successful optimization are shown in Figure 7.13.

With Excel 2000, you can save and load Solver models and add constraints that provide upper and lower limits to changing values. See Excel's Online Help for more information on Solver.

FIGURE 7.13
The Solver Results dialog box

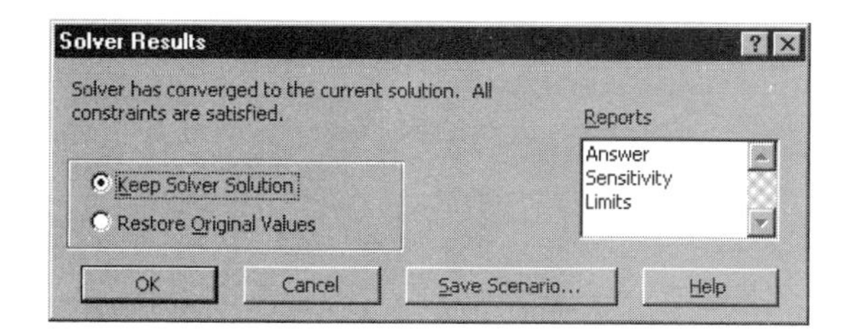

You can choose to place the Solver solution in the worksheet, or restore the original values.

If you choose Keep Solver Solution, the original values will be deleted. You cannot undo this change.

Using Solver

1. Open the worksheet with the data you want to analyze.
2. Choose Tools ➢ Solver to open the Solver dialog box.
3. Select a Target Cell.
4. Choose an Equal To option.
5. Enter the cell to be changed in the By Changing Cells control.
6. Click Solve.
7. Choose Keep Solver Solution (to replace the original values) or Restore Original Values, and then click OK to discard the solution.

Creating Scenarios

Wouldn't it be nice if you could create multiple sets of values to simulate the best case/worst case/most likely case scenarios? Excel has just the tool for this type of "what if" analysis! Create and save different groups of values using Excel's Scenarios feature, then view the results of different scenarios with just a couple of clicks.

Objective XL2000E.11.4

We used Solver to find the maximum gross profit. Given the current assumptions and fixed costs, WellBilt can maximize their gross profits by producing 31,875 CDs at a unit price of $13.63. The Solver solution is shown in column D in Figure 7.14.

FIGURE 7.14

WellBilt data

	A	B	C	D
1	**WellBilt Manuracturing**			
2	**CD ROM Disk Organizer Production**			
3				
4	**Income**	**High**	**Medium**	**Low**
5	Units Produced & Sold	50,000	45,000	31,875
6	Unit Price	10.00	11.00	13.63
7	**Total Income**	**500,000**	**495,000**	**434,297**
8				
9	**Expense**			
10	Fixed Expense	80,000	80,000	80,000
11	Labor Expense	306,000	270,000	191,250
12	Material Expense	62,500	56,250	39,844
13	**Total Expense**	**448,500**	**406,250**	**311,094**
14				
15	**Gross Profit**	**51,500**	**88,750**	**123,203**

Now that we know how good it can get, let's take a look at WellBilt's gross profits in a worst-case scenario. We can create a scenario that projects gross profits for a bad month where production delays cause the Units Produced & Sold to fall to 15,000. It's easiest to begin by clicking in the cell that contains the variable you are changing. Since we're experimenting with Units Produced & Sold, cell `D5` needs to be selected.

Click Tools ➢ Scenarios to open the Scenario Manager. Click the Add button to open the Add Scenarios dialog box:

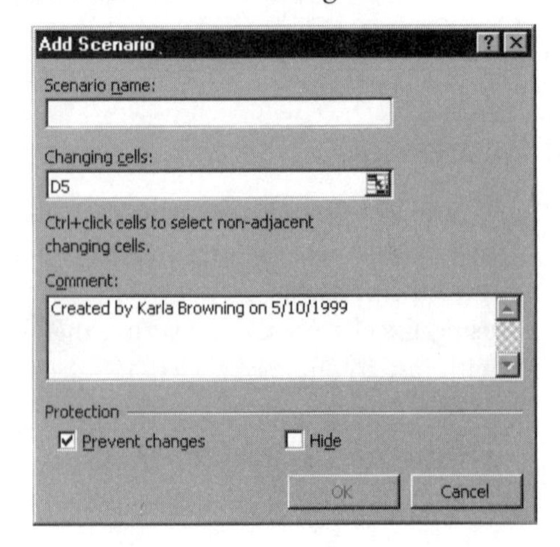

Type a name for the scenario (like Worst Case Production) and then enter the changing cell's address. If you selected the cell in advance, the address is already entered. Enter additional details about the scenario in the Comment field. If you're sharing the workbook with other users, you may choose to protect the scenario by preventing changes or hiding it. Click OK; the Scenario Values dialog box opens:

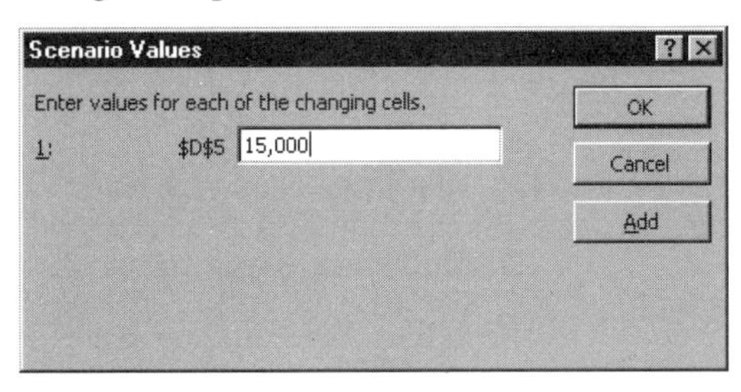

Enter the value that "fits" your scenario. In this example, we entered **15,000**, a number that represents a very low production rate. Click OK to return to the Scenario Manager, and create additional scenarios as needed.

When you're ready to view the results of a particular scenario, open the Scenario Manager if it isn't already open and choose the scenario from the list. Click the Show button to display the scenario results in your worksheet. To display another scenario, choose it from the list and click Show.

Creating and Displaying Multiple Scenarios

1. Click Tools ➢ Scenarios to open the Scenario Manager.
2. Click Add to create a scenario.
3. Type a name for the scenario in the Scenario Name field.
4. Enter the references for the cells that you want to change in the Changing Cells field. Enable protection options if desired.
5. Click OK to proceed to the Scenario Values dialog box. Type the values you want for the changing cells, and then click OK to finish creating the scenario.
6. To create additional scenarios, click Add, and then repeat steps 3–5.
7. When you're ready to view one of your scenarios, choose it from the list in the Scenario Manager dialog box, then click Show.

Creating a View

A *view* is a specification for the appearance of an Excel workbook. You can define custom views for a workbook, allowing you to quickly switch, for example, between a view that includes all the columns in a worksheet and a view with hidden columns that you print for customers. View settings include:

- Size and position of the Excel window and child windows, including split windows
- The hidden/displayed status of each worksheet in the workbook
- The active sheet and active cells when the view is created
- Column widths, zoom ratio, and other display settings

You can specify whether print area and other print settings and hidden rows, hidden columns, and current filter settings should be included in a view.

Creating a Custom View

1. Set print options, hide worksheets, set column widths, zoom, and other display options, and activate the worksheet and cell that should be selected when a user opens the view.
2. Choose View ➢ Custom Views to open the Custom Views dialog box.
3. Click the Add button to add a new view.
4. In the Add View dialog box, enter a name for the view. Choose whether to include the current print settings and hidden rows, columns, and filter settings in your view.
5. Click OK to create the view and add it to the Custom Views dialog box.

To open a view, choose View ➢ Custom Views, select the view in the Custom View dialog box, then click Show.

Using the Report Manager

Objective XL2000E.5.2

The Report Manager, another Excel add-in, creates reports that can include views and scenarios. You create a report by combining sections (worksheet) in the order in which you want them printed. Reports are saved within the workbook.

To create a new report:

1. If you want to use a view and/or scenario in your report, create them first.
2. Choose View ➢ Report Manager to open the Report Manager.

If Report Manager doesn't appear on the View menu, choose Tools ➢ Add-ins and install the Report Manager add-in.

3. Click the Add button to open the Add Report dialog box:

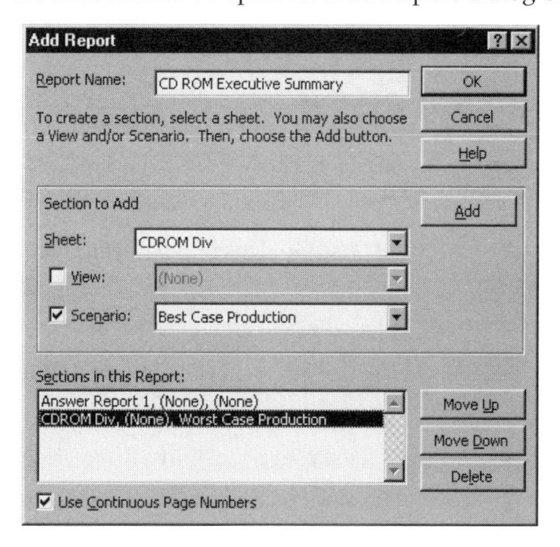

4. Enter a Report Name.
5. Select a sheet (and, optionally, a view and/or scenario within the sheet) to add to the report.

6. Click Add to add the section to the report.
7. Repeat steps 5 and 6 until you're finished adding sections.
8. Use the Move Up, Move Down, and Delete buttons to rearrange the report sections.
9. Enable the Continuous Page Numbering checkbox to print the report with page numbers.
10. Click OK to add the report to the Report Manager.
11. Click OK again to close the Report Manager dialog box.

Printing Reports

To print a report, choose View ➢ Report Manager to open the Report Manager dialog box. Select the report, and then click Print to open the Print Report dialog box. Select the number of copies you wish to print, then click OK.

Deleting and Editing Reports

To delete or edit a report, open the Report Manager and click the Delete or Edit button.

Hands On: Objectives XL2000E.11.2, E.11.4, and E.11.5

1. Recreate the WellBilt data model shown in Figure 7.14 or, alternatively, develop a worksheet model using your own data.
   a) Use Goal Seek to determine unit price and production numbers for a gross profit of $90,000. (Use Ctrl to enter two changing cell values.)
   b) Use Solver to determine maximum gross profit.
   c) Create a best case and worse scenario by changing fixed expenses. View each scenario after you create it.

CHAPTER 8

Creating PowerPoint Presentations

When you make your next presentation—whether it's to demonstrate a product, outline a project, or sell an idea—PowerPoint offers a way to take the focus off you and put it where it belongs—on what you have to say! In this chapter, you'll learn how to create a polished presentation with minimal effort. From outline to slide design, to running the slide show, PowerPoint offers features to enhance your message in a professional way.

Use PowerPoint to create electronic slide shows that can liven up even the most apathetic crowd. If you don't want to give your presentation electronically, you can create vivid overhead transparencies and valuable audience handouts that will rival the most polished presenters. With PowerPoint, you can create presentations that run automatically. Automated presentations are often used as kiosks at trade shows, and such presentations are also seeing increased use on the Internet.

Creating a Basic Presentation

There's no one correct way to begin a presentation. Some people prefer to start with a written outline and work from there. Others prefer to "wing it," creating content as they go. You'll find that PowerPoint incorporates tools geared toward many different work styles. If your presentation is a team effort, PowerPoint offers numerous features for collaboration. In this chapter, you'll be introduced to several methods for beginning and working on presentations. The trick is, as with all Office applications, to find which method works best for you.

No matter how you start, you should think about your audience and plan your presentation so that the audience will receive the message you want to convey. Will it be a small, intimate gathering or a presentation in a large lecture hall? If you're creating a kiosk, will you have a captive audience of people standing in line for a few minutes, or will you have to catch their attention as they pass through a busy hallway? The answers to these questions will guide the choices you make while assembling your presentation.

Creating Your First Presentation

Every PowerPoint presentation consists of a series of *slides*: text or objects displayed on a graphic background, as shown in Figure 8.1. You create your presentation by adding text and objects to slides.

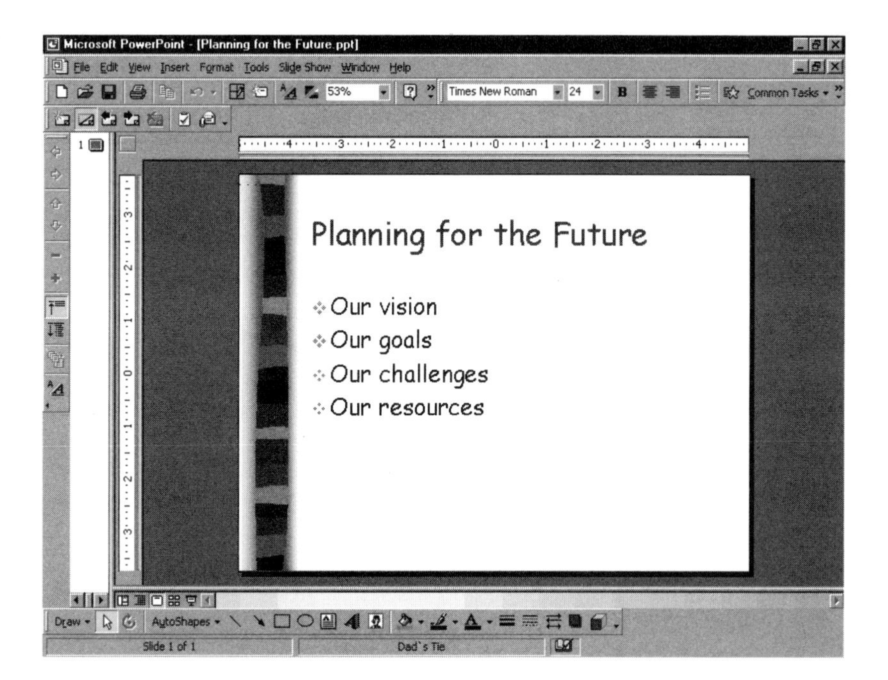

FIGURE 8.1 PowerPoint slide

You'll go through a series of steps for every presentation you create in PowerPoint:

1. Create the presentation, entering and editing text, and rearranging slides.
2. Apply a presentation design. Modify the design if necessary.
3. Format individual slides if you wish.
4. Add objects to the presentation.

5. Apply and modify transitions, animation effects, and links for electronic presentations.
6. Create audience materials and speaker notes.
7. Rehearse and add slide timings.
8. Present the presentation.

When you launch PowerPoint, the PowerPoint dialog box opens.

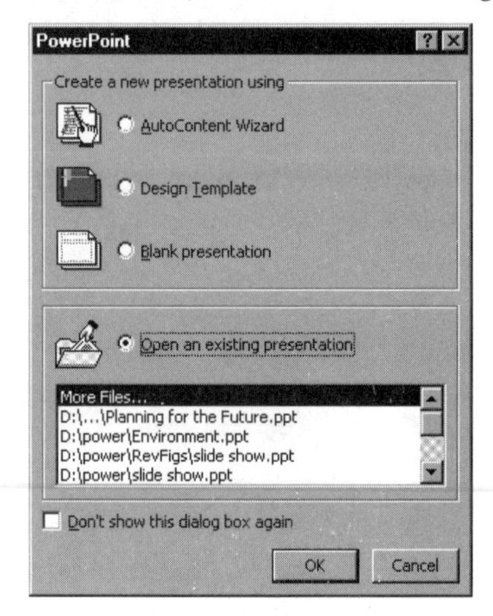

You can create a new presentation or open an existing presentation. To help you become familiar with PowerPoint, you'll create your first presentation using the AutoContent Wizard. The other creation methods are discussed later in the chapter.

Using the AutoContent Wizard

Objective PP2000.1.9

The AutoContent Wizard works like any of the other Wizards in Office 2000. You are taken through a series of steps with additional questions that help design your presentation. In each step, click Next to advance, or click Back to return to a previous step. If you have just launched PowerPoint, choose AutoContent Wizard from the PowerPoint dialog box, and click OK to start the Wizard. If PowerPoint is already running from an earlier presentation, or if you closed the PowerPoint dialog box, choose File ➢ New to open the New Presentation dialog box, and choose the AutoContent Wizard, as shown in Figure 8.2.

FIGURE 8.2

New Presentation dialog box

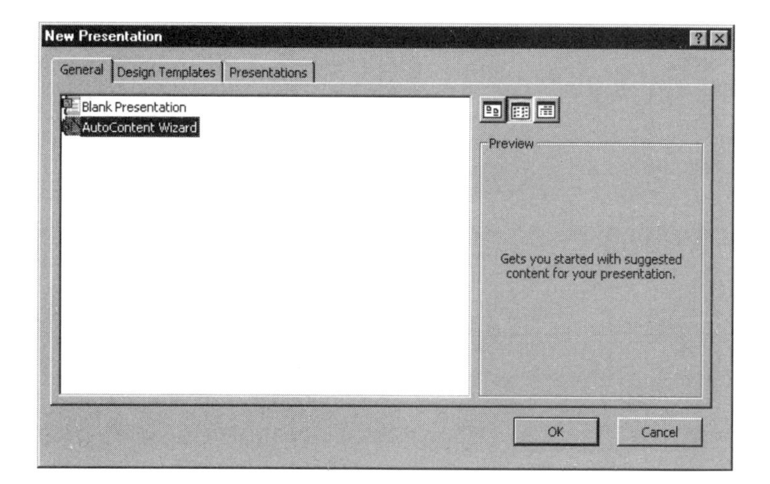

The first step explains the Wizard. In the second step, choose a presentation type. Clicking one of the category buttons (see Figure 8.3) displays a list of types in the list box.

FIGURE 8.3

Choosing a presentation type

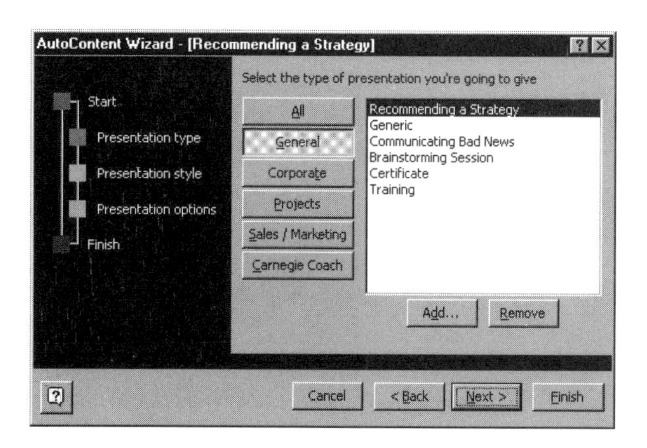

In the third step (see Figure 8.4), specify the type of output you want. The first four output options determine which set of design templates you'll choose from. For example, the On-Screen presentations use color backgrounds; the Color Overhead templates have no backgrounds, but color graphic images.

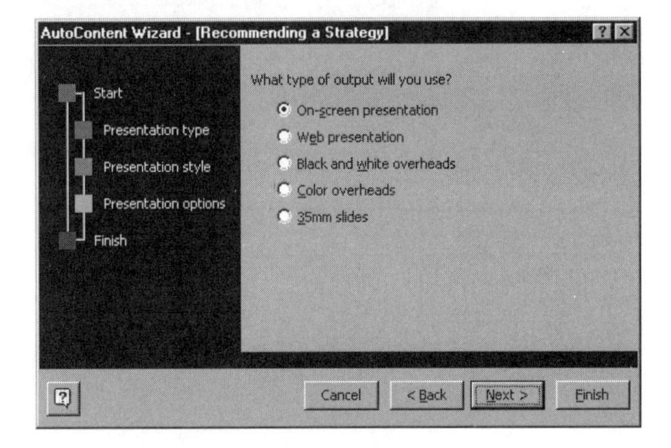

FIGURE 8.4
Presentation output options

In the fourth step, shown in Figure 8.5, supply a title for your presentation, and specify whether it will have a footer. After you enter the presentation options, you're done with the Wizard. Click Next and then click Finish to open the presentation.

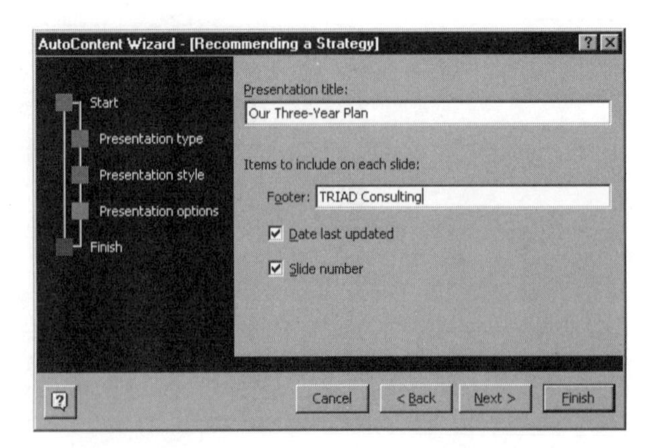

FIGURE 8.5
Presentation options

Using the Auto Content Wizard

1. Choose AutoContent Wizard from the New Presentation dialog box or the PowerPoint dialog box.
2. Click Next to move beyond the first screen.
3. Choose a presentation type from the list provided. Click Next.
4. Specify the type of output. Click Next.
5. Enter a title for your presentation and specify whether you want a footer. Click Next.
6. Click Finish to close the Wizard and open the presentation in Normal view.

Viewing Slides

Objective PP2000.1.4

The PowerPoint window includes a few features that aren't included in other Office 2000 applications. In Figure 8.6, the AutoContent Wizard has just closed and the presentation has been opened in *Normal view*, one of five ways to view a presentation.

Five view buttons appear at the left end of the horizontal scroll bar; the Normal View button is pressed in.

Each view provides a different way to look at and work with your presentation. In Normal view, the presentation text appears in the Outline pane on the left, the slide appears in the Slide pane on the right and an area for notes is visible at the bottom in the Notes pane. You can edit the content of the presentation in either the Outline pane or the Slide pane.

In *Outline view*, which is shown in Figure 8.7, presentation text appears in the main pane on the left, and the slide displays in miniature in the pane on the right. In this view, you can also edit in either pane, but working with the miniature slide is a bit difficult, of course. You can also add notes in Outline view. See the section *Adding Notes to the Notes Pane* later in this chapter for information about how and why you do this. The Outlining toolbar is displayed by default.

FIGURE 8.6
Normal View

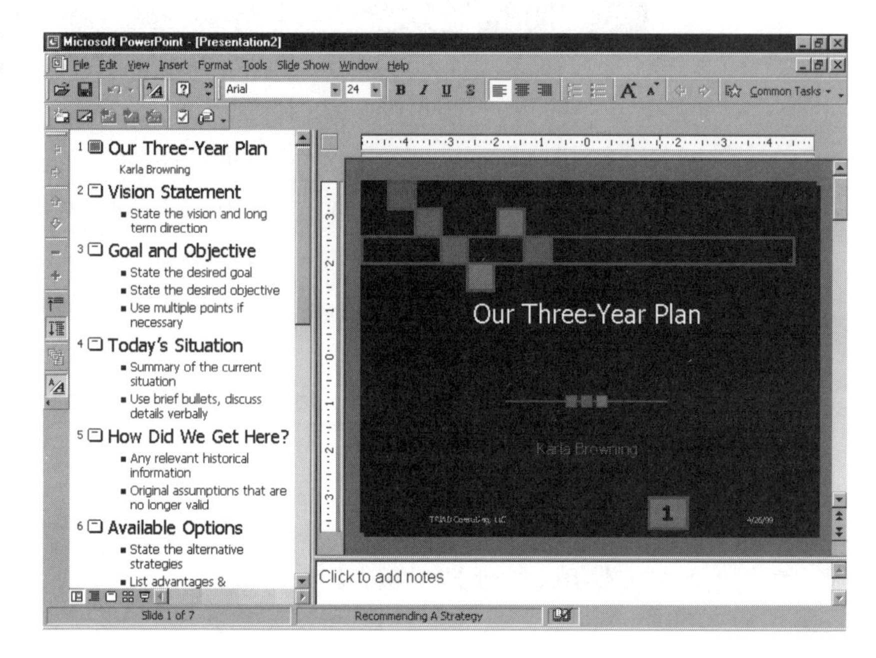

To display a slide, click on its topic in the outline. Use the scroll bars to scroll through the outline.

FIGURE 8.7
Outline View

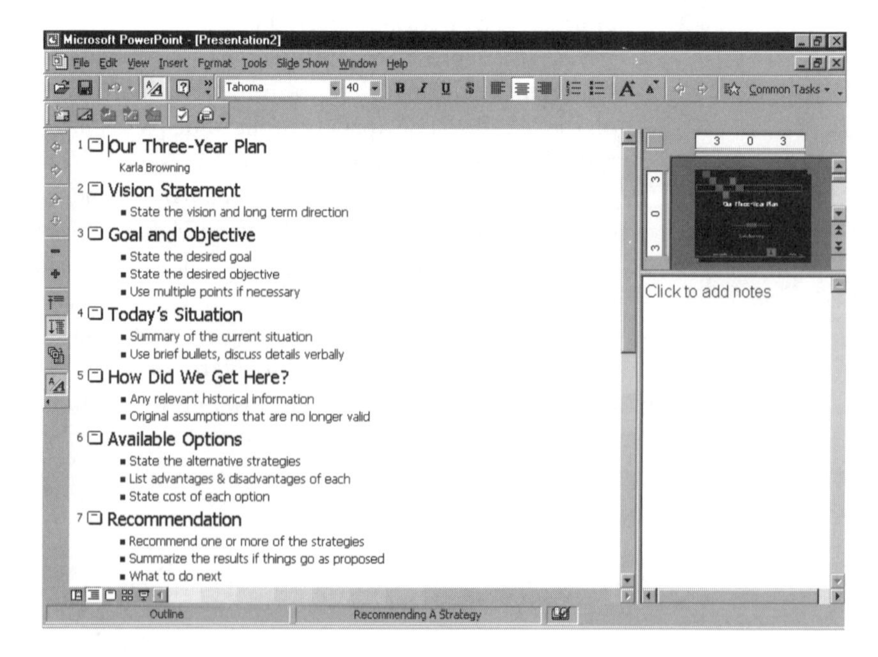

Slide view lets you work with one slide at a time. Click a slide's icon in the left pane to display that slide. You can edit text or place objects on slides and immediately see the impact of your changes and additions. Some users prefer to do all their editing in Slide view.

Slide Sorter view allows you to see a screen full of slides at one time. You can swap slides around, delete slides, and add special effects. You cannot edit text or place objects on slides in this view.

The final button in this group is the *Slide Show view*. Click this button to see how a slide looks in full-screen mode. Once you're in Slide Show view, click the icon in the lower left of the screen and choose from the shortcut menu to go to the next or the previous slide. Press the Esc key on the keyboard if you want to leave the slide show before the last slide.

Objective PP2000.7.1

When you switch from one view to another, the current slide remains current, regardless of view. If you are on slide five in Slide view and switch to Outline view, the fifth slide is selected. Clicking the Slide Show button begins the Slide Show with slide five.

Developing a Presentation

In the early stages of your presentation's development, you probably want to work in Normal view or in Outline view. Each has advantages. In Normal view, you can edit the text in the left pane or the right pane, and you can work with graphical elements in the right pane. In Outline view, you can easily enter and edit text and rearrange bullet points, paragraphs, and slides.

In Outline view or in the Outline pane of Normal view, each slide has a number in the left margin and a slide icon. The slide title is located next to the slide icon. Indented below the title is the body text.

Entering and Editing Text

Objectives PP2000.3.3 and 3.10

You will want to replace the contents of the slides created by the Wizard before making substantial formatting changes. To change the contents, edit text as you would in Word. If you click in the left margin, the cursor changes to a four-headed arrow because you can drag the selected line to move it. There are five levels below the slide title:

1 Slide Title
• Level 1
– Level 2
• Level 3
– Level 4
» Level 5

When you reach the end of a line and press Enter, the next line is on the same level as the previous line; if you position the insertion point at the end of a slide's title and press Enter, you insert a new slide.

Press the Tab key or click the Demote button to move to a lower level. By default, each level below the title is automatically bulleted (except on Slide one). Press Tab or click Demote again, and you are at the second level. Press Enter at the end of a bulleted line to get another line at the same level. Text entered at any level other than the title level is a *point* or a *subpoint.*

To move back a level, either hold Shift and press Tab or click the Promote button. Promoting and demoting works the same whether you're working in the Outline pane or directly on the slide.

You can also promote and demote by placing your mouse on the bullet that precedes the point and dragging right to demote or left to promote.

Checking Spelling

Objective PP2000.3.1

PowerPoint includes two spelling features. To correct spelling as you type, right-click on words with a red wavy underline to see suggested correct spellings. To check the spelling for an entire presentation, click the Spelling button on the Standard toolbar. (For more information on spelling, see Chapter 1.)

Using Find and Replace

Objective PP2000.2.2

Use PowerPoint's Find feature to locate a text string in your presentation. Choose Edit ➢ Find to open the Find dialog box

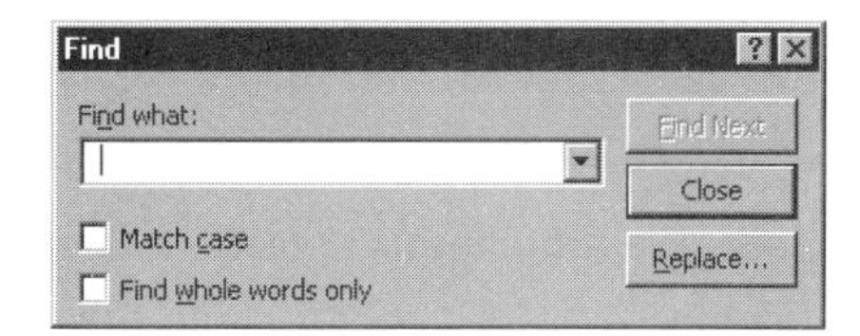

In the Find what text box, enter the text string that you want to find, and then set the Find options. Turn on the Match Case option to find only those text strings in the presentation that exactly match the string you entered. If you entered 'Review,' and turn on Match Case, Find locates 'Review' but not 'review' or 'REVIEW.' To find 'Review' but not 'Reviews,' turn on Whole Words Only.

If you use Find in Normal, Outline, or Slide view, clicking Find Next moves to and selects the next text string that matches the Find what string. In Slide Sorter view, there isn't a Find Next button; instead, the button is Find All. Clicking Find All selects all the slides that contain the Find what string.

You can replace each occurrence of one text string with another. For example, you've created a presentation for the Three Year Project. The Three Year Project has just been renamed Building Sales Partnerships. You can find every occurrence of 'Three Year Project' and change it to 'Building Sales Partnerships.' Choose Edit ➢ Replace, or if the Find dialog box is already open, click the Replace button in the Find dialog box. Enter the string you want to find in Find what and the string you want to replace it with in Replace with.

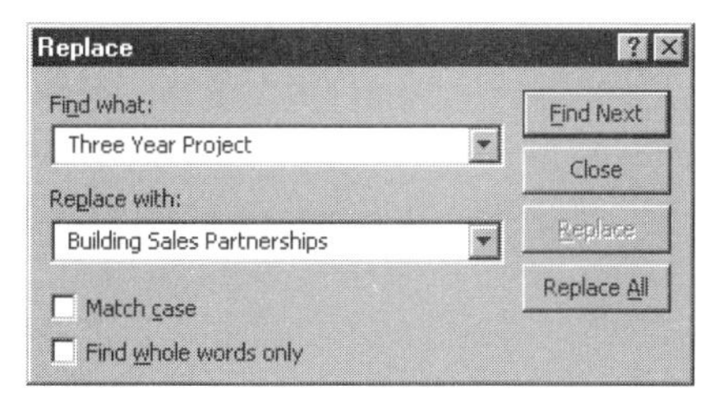

To replace all the occurrences, click Replace All. Or, you can work through the replacements one at a time. To find the next occurrence, click Find Next. Click Replace to make the replacement, and click Find Next to move to the next possible replacement. When you've replaced all occurrences of the text string, a message box appears to let you know that PowerPoint has searched the entire presentation and there aren't any more occurrences of the text string. A similar dialog box opens to let you know if the text string you entered in Find what doesn't appear in the presentation.

Finding or Replacing a Text String

1. Choose Edit ➢ Find from the menu bar to open the Find dialog box.
2. Enter the text you want to locate in the Find what text box.
3. To replace the text, click the Replace button and enter the replacement text string in the Replace With text box.
4. Click Replace All to replace all occurrences of Find What with Replace With.

   OR

4. Click Find Next to find the next occurrence, then click Replace to replace it and Find Next to continue to the next occurrence.

Selecting Text, Lines, and Slides

Select text in PowerPoint just as you do in Word or Excel. Double-click a word, or drag across one or more words to select them. To select a point or title, click the bullet or slide icon or triple-click anywhere in the point or title. If you select a first-level point that has second-level points underneath it, the second-level points are also selected. Selecting the title selects the entire slide.

Moving and Deleting Points and Slides

Objectives PP2000.1.1 and 2.5

To move a point (and all the subpoints underneath it), select the point. If you click a slide's icon, the entire slide—title and any body text—is selected. Place your mouse over the bullet icon and the pointer changes to a four-headed arrow.

Using the four-headed arrow, drag the selection toward its new location, and a horizontal line appears in the outline. Drag-and-drop the horizontal line, and the selected point(s) or slide moves to the new location. You can use this method to move points and subpoints in Normal, Slide, and Outline view. Try it in the Outline pane and directly on the slide. It works the same in both places. If you wish to move an entire slide using this method, you need to work with the Outline portion of the tri-pane window.

Once a slide, point, or subpoint is selected you can delete it by pressing Delete on the keyboard.

Working in Slide View

Some people prefer to work on one slide at a time. Slide view gives you a better feel for how the slide will actually look when complete.

Most slides include two text boxes, one for the title and one for the body text. When you click on the title or body, a frame appears around the text box. You can point to the frame and drag the text box to another location on the slide. To format the text in the box, select the text by clicking or dragging as you would in Outline view or Normal view, and then change formats using the Formatting toolbar or Format menu.

If you're planning on making similar text formatting changes to all your slides, don't make those changes on each individual slide. See *Modifying the Slide Master*, in the next section.

Working in Slide View

1. Click the Slide View button to move to slide view. Click a slide icon to move to the slide that you want to format.
2. Click on the text box for the title or body to select it. Use the handles to re-size the text box. Drag the box to move it to a new location, or click the Delete key to delete the box.
3. Select and format text using the Formatting toolbar or the Format menu.
4. Enter text just as you would in the Outline pane. Promote and demote as needed.

Using the Slide Sorter

Objective PP2000.2.1

In Slide Sorter view, shown in Figure 8.8, you work with entire slides. You can't re-arrange the text *on* a slide, but you can move or copy entire slides.

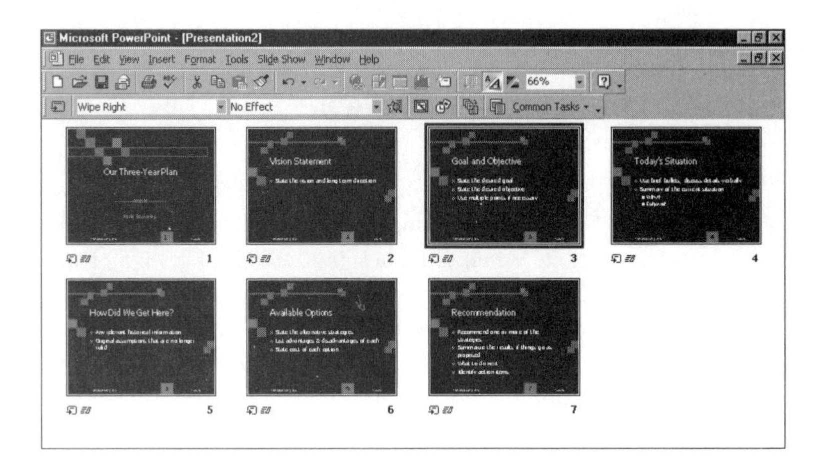

FIGURE 8.8
Slide Sorter view

Click once on a slide to select it, or select multiple slides by holding Ctrl while clicking. A selected slide has a dark border around it, like Slide 3 in Figure 8.8. To move a selected slide, drag the slide toward its new location. A gray vertical line appears. Drag-and-drop to move the line, and the selected slide, to the new location. To copy a slide, hold the Ctrl key on the keyboard while dragging; release Ctrl after dropping the slide in place. To delete slides in Slide Sorter view, select the slides, and then press the Delete key on the keyboard.

In Slide Sorter view, you can't always read the text on a slide. To see just the title, hold Alt and click on the slide. When you release the mouse button, the slide miniature returns to normal.

Moving, Copying, and Deleting Slides in Slide Sorter Views

1. Click once on a slide to select it.
2. Hold Ctrl and click to select additional slides.
3. Press Delete to delete the slides.

   OR

3. Drag selected slides to a new location to move them. Hold Ctrl while releasing the mouse button to copy the slides.

Grayscale Preview

Objective PP2000.6.1

Large presentations with dozens of slides and heavy graphics can be cumbersome to work with. Your system may slow down when dragging slides or switching views. To conserve system resources and work faster, switch to grayscale preview by clicking the Grayscale Preview button on the standard toolbar in Outline, Slide, Normal, or Slide Sorter view. The presentation still shows in color when you switch to Slide Show view because you haven't really changed formatting. You've just given PowerPoint a break from redrawing color backgrounds and objects.

Working with Summary Slides

Objective PP2000E.1.1

You may want your final slide to be a summary of the main points you've made during your presentation. Or, in a very long presentation, you may want several summary slides throughout. There's no need to re-type main points if that text is already contained your slide titles. PowerPoint can automatically pull slide titles for a summary slide.

Creating a Summary Slide

1. Switch to Slide Sorter view and select the slides whose titles you want to use.
2. Click the Summary Slide button on the Slide Sorter toolbar.
3. The new summary slide, with bulleted titles from the selected slides, gets inserted in front of the first selected slide.
4. Drag and drop the summary slide where you want it to be.

Adding Notes to the Notes Pane

Objective PP2000.5.2

You can use the Notes Pane to add speaker notes that you can print and use during a presentation. But you can also use them to keep track of other information about particular slides as you're creating a presentation; data that needs to be verified or alternative information or wording you've considered adding to the slide. You can add notes in three ways:

- In Normal view, simply type your notes in the pane at the bottom right (see Figure 8.6, earlier in this chapter).
- Choose View ➢ Notes Page to open Notes Page view, as shown in Figure 8.9.
- In Slide Show view, right-click to open the shortcut menu, and select Speaker Notes to open the Notes dialog box, as shown in Figure 8.10. Enter your note, and click Close to return to the Slide Show. To check the spelling or format of notes, open Notes Page view.

FIGURE 8.9

Notes Page view

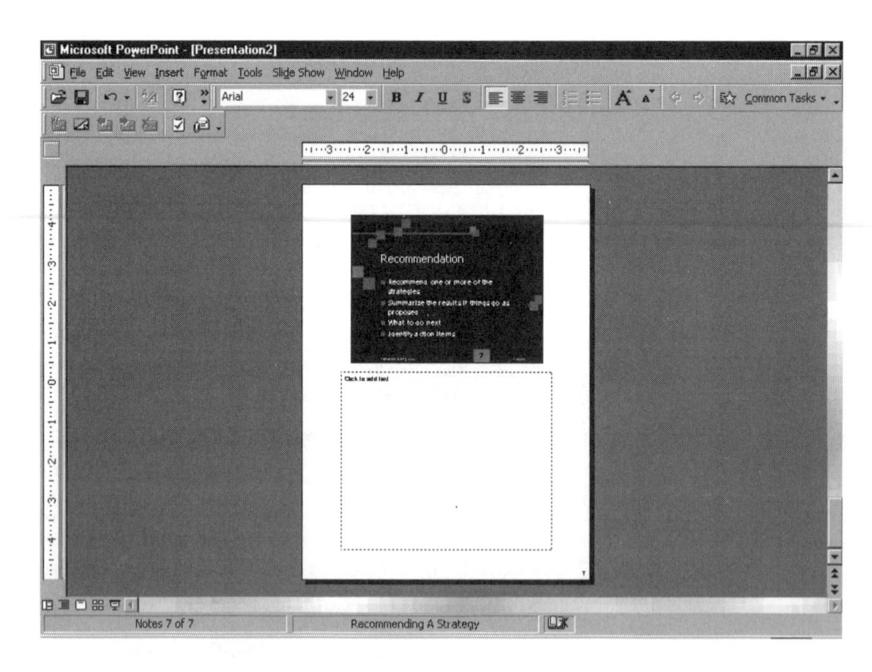

Notes Page view opens with a view of a single page (see Figure 8.9). The slide is at the top of the page; the bottom half of the page is a single text box where you can type your notes.

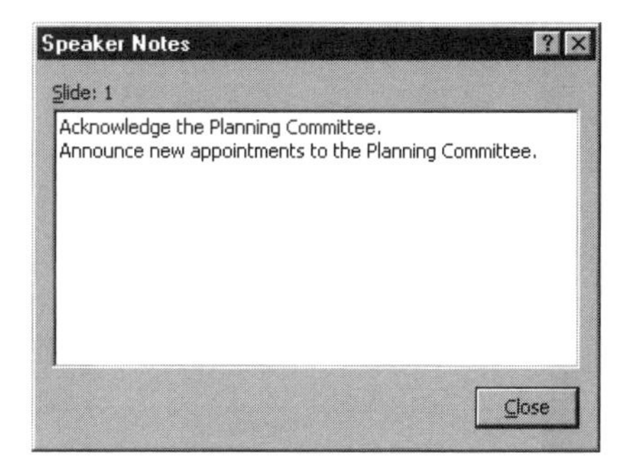

FIGURE 8.10
The Notes dialog box

Change the Zoom percentage so that you can actually see what you're typing, and then click in the text box and enter your notes. When you're finished entering notes for a slide and want to add notes to another slide, navigate to that slide by clicking the Next or Previous Slide buttons at the bottom of the vertical scroll bar.

Adding Notes in Notes Page View

1. Click View ➢ Notes pages to open that view.
2. Adjust your zoom setting, if necessary, to see the notes text box more clearly.
3. Click the text box and type the text for the note on the current slide.
4. Navigate to another slide and enter notes for that slide.

Hands On: Objectives PP2000.1.1, 1.4, 1.9, 2.1, 2.2, 2.5, 3.1, 3.3, 3.10, 5.2, 6.1, 7.1, 8.1, and PD2000E.1.1

1. Use the AutoContent Wizard to create a presentation of your choice.
   - a) Add a note to one of the slides in Notes Page view.
   - b) Move, copy, and delete slides in Slide Sorter view.
   - c) Edit the existing text in Outline view or Normal view to add your own content. Add a new slide with a title and subpoints.
   - d) Add text to a slide in Slide view.

e) Experiment with promoting and demoting bulleted points in the Outline pane and directly on the slide in Normal view.

f) Create a summary slide and move it to the end of the presentation.

g) Switch to Slide Sorter view and preview the presentation in grayscale.

h) View the presentation twice in Slide Show view. Experiment with starting the show on different slides.

2. In Outline view:

   a) Use Find and Replace to locate and change a text string.

   b) Select a slide and move it to a new location using Drag and Drop.

   c) Run spell check.

3. Save the presentation.

Building Presentations

The benefit of the AutoContent Wizard is that it helps you to develop your content. If you've already decided what should be in your presentation, you don't need to use the Wizard. You can create a presentation in other ways:

- Using a design template, which gives you a "look" without burdening you with text to alter or delete
- Borrowing the design from an existing presentation, which is useful if the presentations in your department should share a common design
- "From scratch"—entering your text first, and then applying a design
- Importing and modifying an existing Word outline

You can always apply another design template or presentation design to an existing presentation.

Using Design Templates or Blank Presentations

Objectives PP2000.1.3 and 1.8

You can use the design elements from any presentation or template in a new presentation. To create a presentation using a design template, either choose Design Template in the dialog box that opens when you launch PowerPoint, or choose File ➢ New from the menu bar to open the New Presentation dialog box. Click the Design Templates tab, and select a template. You can see the sample title slide in the Preview area, as shown in Figure 8.11. Double-click a design template or click OK to choose the selected template.

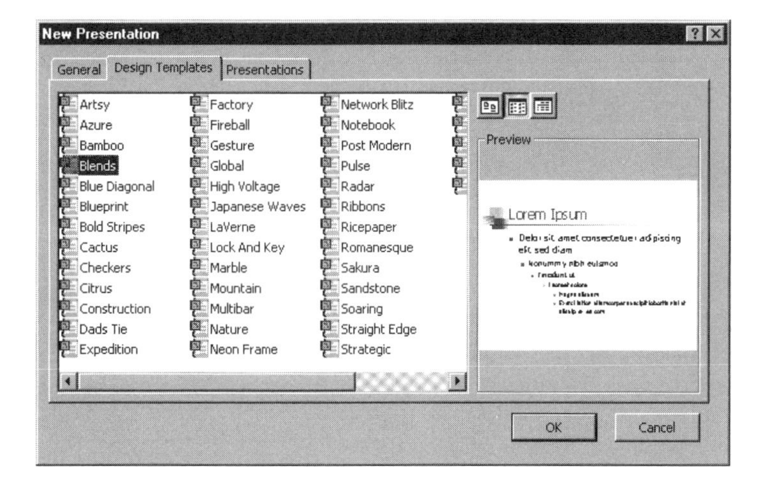

FIGURE 8.11
The Design Templates tab in the New Presentation dialog box

The Presentations tab contains the presentation types, which are the same as those you see in the AutoContent Wizard. Click an icon to see a preview, as shown in Figure 8.12.

The difference between a design template and a presentation type is that the template contains only the design; the presentation type also contains placeholder content.

To create a presentation without a design, choose Blank Presentation when you launch PowerPoint, or choose Blank Presentation from the General tab in the New Presentation dialog box.

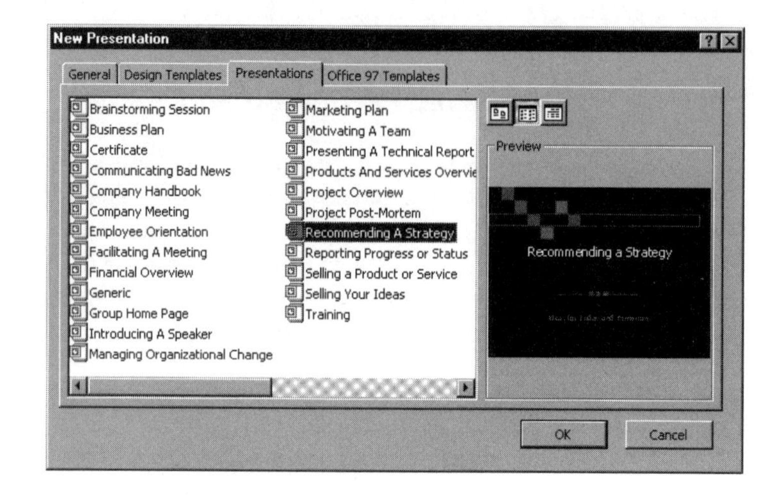

FIGURE 8.12 The Presentations tab in the New Presentation dialog box

Selecting Slide Layouts

If you begin a presentation with a design template, or choose to create a blank presentation, the New Slide dialog box opens, as shown in Figure 8.13.

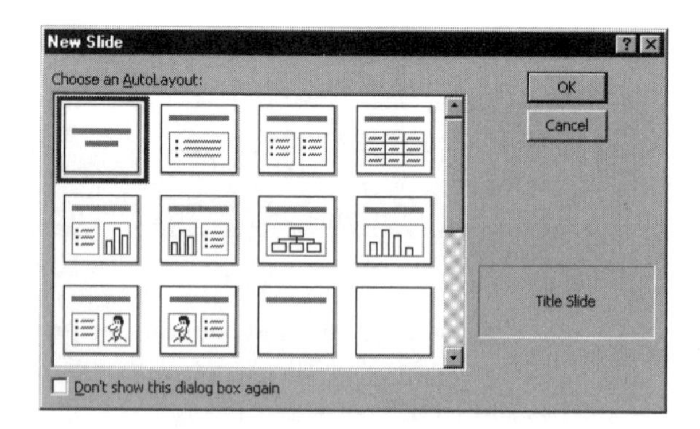

FIGURE 8.13 New Slide dialog box

In the New Slide Dialog box, you select an AutoLayout for each new slide. When you click the thumbnail for the layout, a description appears. No choice that you make in this dialog box is carved in stone; you can always change a slide's layout. Notice that there is a scroll bar in this dialog box; there are other layouts you might want to look at. Select the Title Slide layout for the first slide in the presentation, and click OK. The slide opens in Normal view. (If you prefer, you can switch to Outline view and enter all the text for this slide.)

Enter a title for your presentation and, optionally, a subtitle. You can use the text boxes on the slide, or you can work in the outline pane on the left. To use a text box, simply click inside it, and enter the text you want. Your text also appears, as you type it, in the left pane.

Objective PP2000.1.2

When you finish the first slide, choose New Slide from the Common Tasks toolbar. (Or choose Insert ➢ New Slide from the menu.) This opens the New Slide dialog box again so that you can select a layout for the second slide.

Objective PP2000.2.3

To change the layout of an existing slide or slides, switch to Slide Sorter view and select the slides you want to change. Choose Slide Layout from the Common Tasks menu to re-open the Slide Layout dialog box. Select the layout you want and click OK.

Applying a Design

Objectives PP2000.2.6 and PP2000.E.2.3

If you want to use the design from an existing presentation, begin by choosing any design template or a blank presentation. Then click Apply Design Template in the Common Tasks dialog box or choose Format ➢ Apply Design Template. When the Apply Design Template dialog box opens (see Figure 8.14), set the Look In control to the folder that contains the presentation. Change the Files of Type drop-down list at the bottom of the dialog box to All PowerPoint Files. Select the presentation that has the design you want to use, and click Apply. Use the same method to apply any of the design templates in the Presentations folder to an existing presentation.

FIGURE 8.14

Apply Design Template dialog box

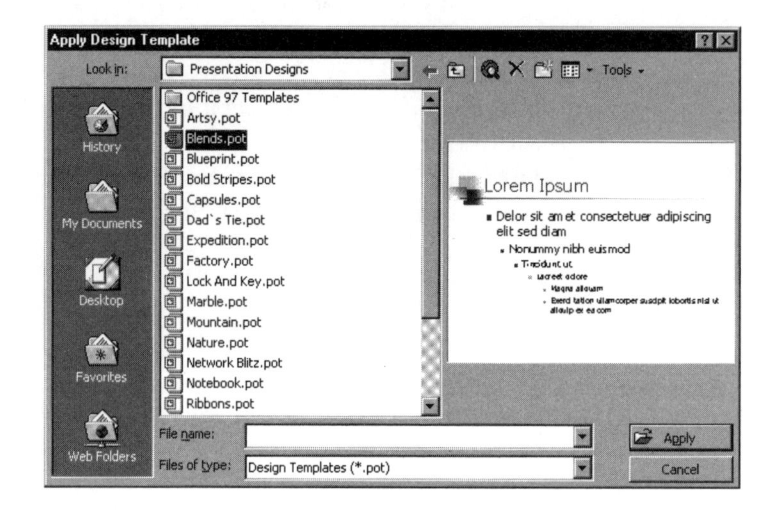

Applying a Design to a Presentation

1. Click Format ➢ Apply Design Template or choose Apply Design Template from the Common Tasks toolbar to open the Apply Design Template dialog box.
2. Select one of the PowerPoint templates in the Presentation Designs folder and click Apply.

   OR

3. If the presentation you want to use is not a template, change the Look In control to the folder where the presentation is stored. Change the Files of Type drop-down control to All PowerPoint files.
4. Select the presentation or design template you want to apply.
5. Click Apply.

Using Slides from an Existing Presentation

Objective PP2000.1.6

Applying a design template from an existing presentation uses its background, fonts, and formatting without any of the content. You can take entire slides from an existing presentation and add them to another presentation using the Slide Finder. Choose Insert ➢ Slides from Files to open the Slide Finder. Click the Browse button and select the file that contains the slides you want to add to your presentation; then click the Display button to add thumbnails of the slides to the Slide Finder, as shown in Figure 8.15.

FIGURE 8.15
Slide Finder

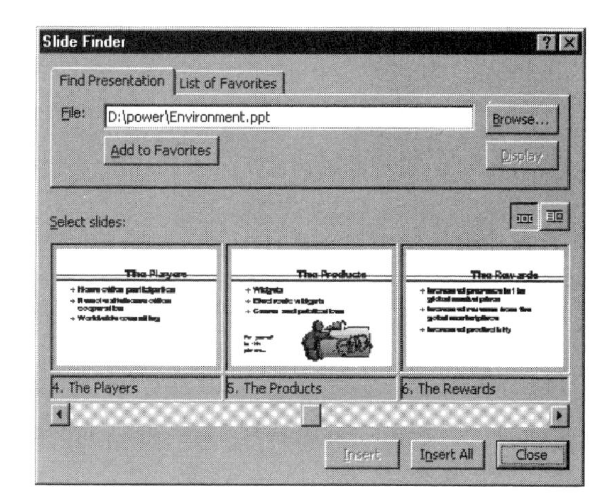

The slides appear with each slide's number and title below the slide. Use the horizontal scroll bar to move through the slides in order. To work more quickly, click the Show Titles button in the dialog box to display a list of slide titles with a single preview pane.

Click the Show Slides button to return to the thumbnails view. Select and then insert the slide or slides you want (hold Shift or Ctrl to select multiple slides). When you insert a slide, the text and any objects (such as a picture or chart) on the slide are imported. The slide's design is *not* imported into the current presentation.

Inserting Slides from Other Presentations

1. Position the insertion point (in Outline view or Normal view) or slide selector (in Slide Sorter view) where you want to insert slides.
2. Choose Insert ➢ Slides from Files to open the Slide Finder.
3. Browse to select the presentation that includes the slides you want to insert. Click Open.

Inserting Slides from Other Presentations *(continued)*

4. Select the slide(s) you want to insert, and then click Insert to place the slides in the current presentation. If you want to insert all the slides, click the Insert All button.
5. The Slide Finder remains open, so you can move to a different location in the active presentation and insert other slides.
6. When you are finished inserting, close the Slide Finder.

Using Word Outlines

Objective PP2000.3.4

You can import a Word outline (see Figure 8.16) to create a PowerPoint presentation. (For more information on Word outlines, see "Chapter 3, Applying Advanced Formatting Techniques".) The outline is inserted into the current presentation, so you can use the outline as the total presentation, or to add content to a presentation you're already working on.

FIGURE 8.16
Word outline

- **Building Sales Partnerships**
  - ***a presentation by the Sales and Marketing Staff***
- **Vision**
  - ***connect directly to clients:***
    - Fax services
    - EDI
- **Goal**
  - ***to create at least three new partnerships this fiscal year***
  - ***generate four new partnerships each of the next three years***
- **Resources Required**
- **Utilization of Existing Staff**

Adding a Word Outline to a Presentation

1. Choose Insert ➢ Slides from Outline from the menu bar.
2. Select the Word document you want to insert.
3. Click Insert.

Hands On: Objectives PP2000.1.2, 1.3, 1.6, 2.3, 2.6, 3.4, and PP2000.E.2.3

1. Create a new presentation based on a design template.
   a) Apply a new design from an existing presentation.
   b) Apply a new design from the PowerPoint design templates.
   c) Insert a slide using the Two Column Text format in the New Slide dialog box. Add text to the slide.
   d) Insert one or more slides from an existing presentation using the Slide Finder.
   e) If you do not have a Word outline, open Word and create a short outline. Insert the outline into the presentation.
2. In Slide Sorter view, select one or more slides and change the layout to a single bulleted list.
3. Save changes to the presentation if you wish.

Modifying Visual Elements

You can customize the visual elements of a presentation in several ways:

- By changing the color scheme
- By editing the Slide Master
- By adding footers
- By replacing or adding a background

Changing the Color Scheme

Objective PP2000E.2.4

It's easiest to choose one of PowerPoint's design templates to establish the primary background for your presentation and then change the background or colors to meet your specific needs. Consider the purpose of your presentation when changing colors. For overheads, the lighter the better. Dark backgrounds work well for on-screen presentations, but if you need to show a presentation with room lights on, choose a light background and dark text. Choosing Format ➢ Slide Color Scheme opens the Color Scheme dialog box, shown in Figure 8.17. (You can't change the color scheme in a blank presentation; you must have already applied a design.)

FIGURE 8.17
Color Scheme dialog box

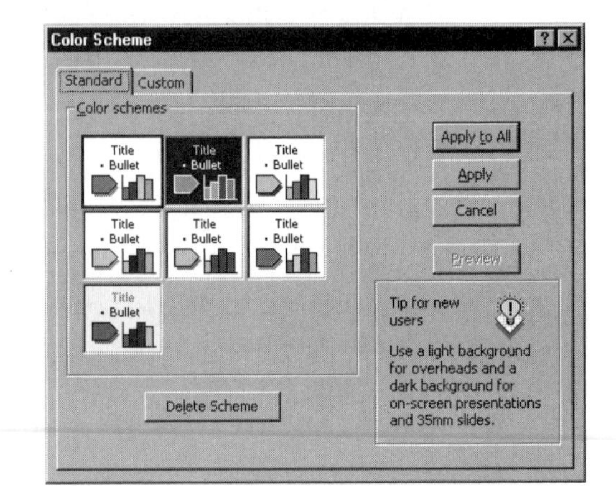

The dialog box has tabs for Standard and Custom color schemes. The standard color schemes include the current color scheme, at least one alternate scheme, and one black-and-white choice. You can choose to apply a scheme to the current slide or to all the slides in the presentation. To see how a slide looks, click the Preview button. (You have to move the dialog box out of the way to see the impact on the slide.) When you're satisfied, click Apply to change the selected slide or slides or Apply to All to change every slide in the presentation.

If you don't like any of the standard schemes, you can create your own. Select the scheme that's closest to what you want and click the Custom tab on the Color Scheme dialog box, shown in Figure 8.18. Select the color you want to change and click the Change Color button to open the Colors dialog box. Choose a color from the array of colors presented, or if you want to mix your own, click the Custom tab, and use the slider bar. If you wish, you can save the color scheme for future use with the current design by adding it to the schemes shown on the Standard tab (see Figure 8.17).

FIGURE 8.18
Custom color schemes

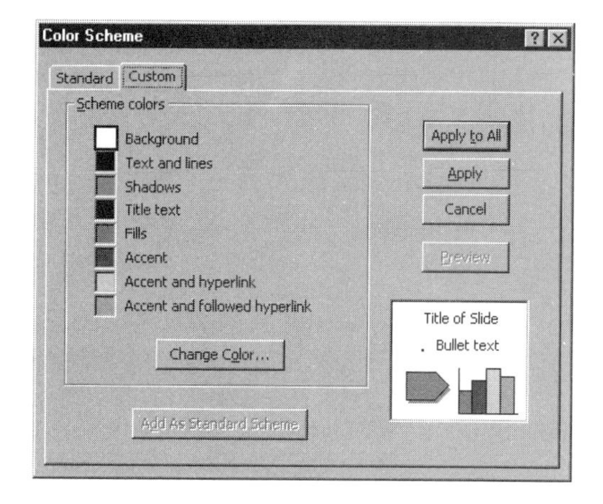

Applying a New Color Scheme

1. Choose Format ➢ Slide Color Scheme to open the Color Scheme dialog box.
2. Click the color scheme you want to apply.
3. To create your own scheme, click the Custom tab to change specific colors in the color scheme. Click the color you want to change and click the Change Color button. Repeat this step for each color you want to change.
4. Choose Preview to see the changes before applying them. Click Apply to or Apply to All to apply the scheme to the current slide or all slides in the presentation.

Modifying the Slide Master

Objective PP2000.2.4

Every design includes a *Slide Master* (see Figure 8.19) that identifies the position of the text and graphic objects, the style of the fonts, the footer elements, and the background for all slides. There is at least one Slide Master for each presentation; some designs include separate Slide and Title Masters. Any change that you make to the Master is reflected in each slide that is based on the Master. For example, if you want a graphic object (a logo perhaps) to appear on every slide, you could attach it to the Master rather than inserting it on each slide. To change the title font for all slides or the font for the bulleted points, make the change on the Master. To open the Master, either choose View ➢ Master ➢ Slide Master or hold the Shift key and click the Slide View button. (The name of the Slide View button changes to Slide Master View when you hold down the Shift key. If you're on Slide 1, the button name changes to Title Master View.)

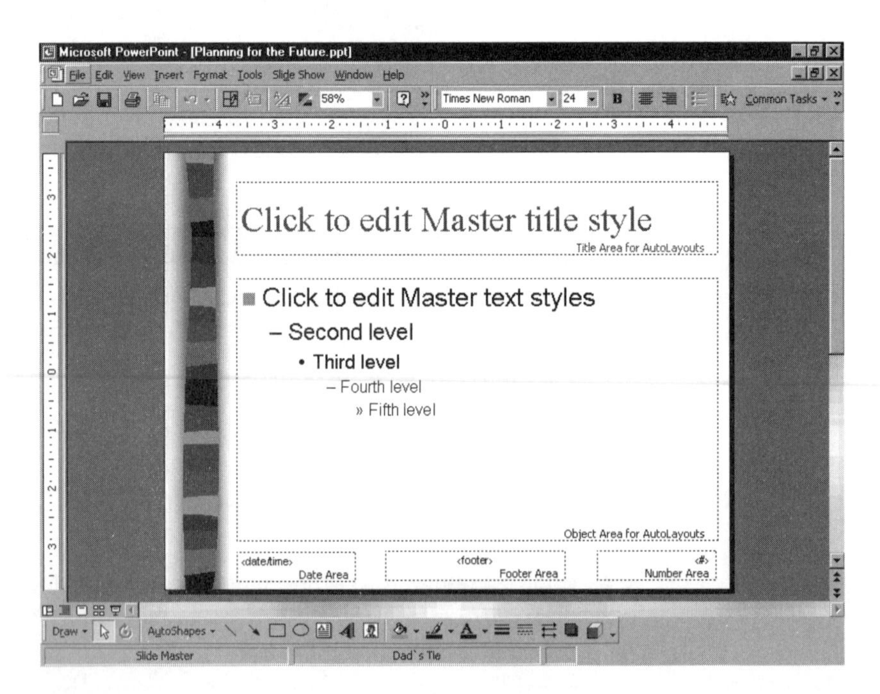

FIGURE 8.19
The Slide Master

Editing a Master Slide

1. Choose View ➢ Master ➢ Slide Master or hold Shift and click the Slide View button to open the Slide Master.
2. On the Master, select the text in any text box to format its contents using the buttons on the Formatting toolbar. Select and move or delete placeholders, including graphic objects and text boxes.

Adding Slide Headers and Footers

Objective PP2000.1.7

Most Slide Masters include a footer area and some also include a header area. You can have a date, slide number, or other header or footer appear on every slide by changing it in the Master. Choose View ➢ Header and Footer from the menu bar to open the dialog box shown in Figure 8.20.

FIGURE 8.20
Header and Footer dialog box

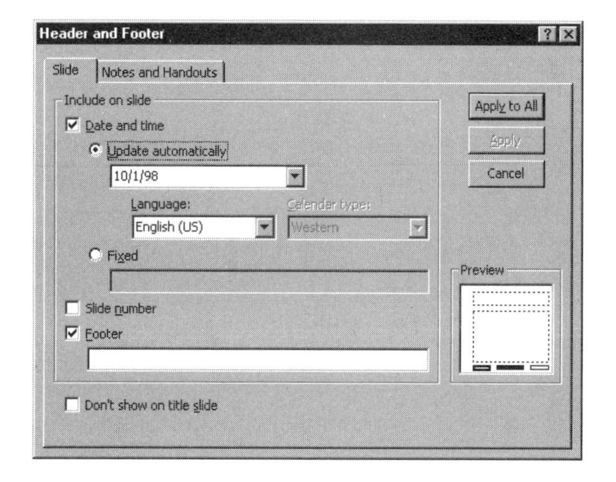

For Date and Time, choose Update Automatically or Fixed to add a changing or fixed date to each slide. Click the Slide Number text box to show the slide number. If you want footer text, click the Footer check box and type the footer in the text box.

Setting Slide Headers and Footers

1. Choose View ➢ Header and Footer to open the Header and Footer dialog box.
2. Turn on items you want displayed on all slides.

Setting Slide Headers and Footers *(continued)*

3. Turn on Don't Show on Title Slide if you don't want the footer to appear on the first slide in the presentation.
4. Choose Apply to apply to the active or selected slide, or choose Apply to All to apply to every slide in the presentation. (If you open the dialog box from the Slide Master, you can only choose Apply to All.)

Customizing the Background

Objective PP2000E.2.6

When you choose to apply a design template, the template includes the color scheme and background color. But the background may have a shaded effect, a pattern, or a texture. A picture or a graphic object may also be part of the background. All these characteristics form the background of the slide. Any text or objects that you place on the slide are positioned on top of the background.

To change the background, choose Format ➢ Background to open the Background dialog box, shown in Figure 8.21. For individual slides, you can choose to Omit Background Graphics from Master. (This means that Master background graphics won't be applied on the selected slide.) By omitting background objects, your slide can retain the same basic appearance as the other slides, but won't detract from other graphics, such as charts, that you might add to the slide. If you omit background graphics, you also omit the footer.

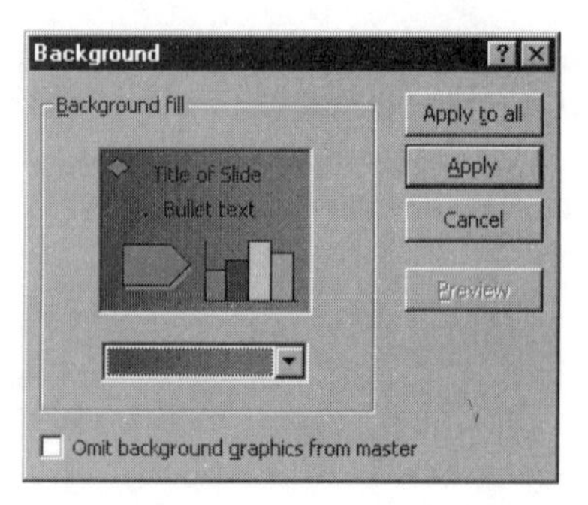

FIGURE 8.21 Background dialog box

To make changes in the background fill, click the drop-down arrow in the Background Fill area of the dialog box to open a drop-down menu of fill choices.

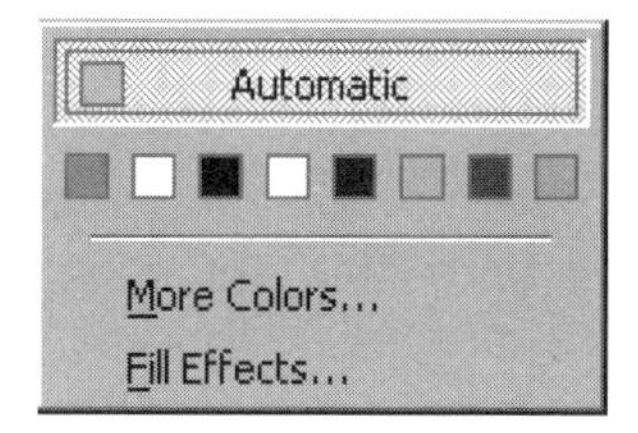

Choosing Automatic fills the background with the default fill color. Selecting a color from the eight color-scheme colors or choosing an Other Color (which opens the Color Picker) changes the background fill color. Choosing Fill Effects opens the Fill Effects dialog box, shown in Figure 8.22.

FIGURE 8.22

Fill Effects dialog box

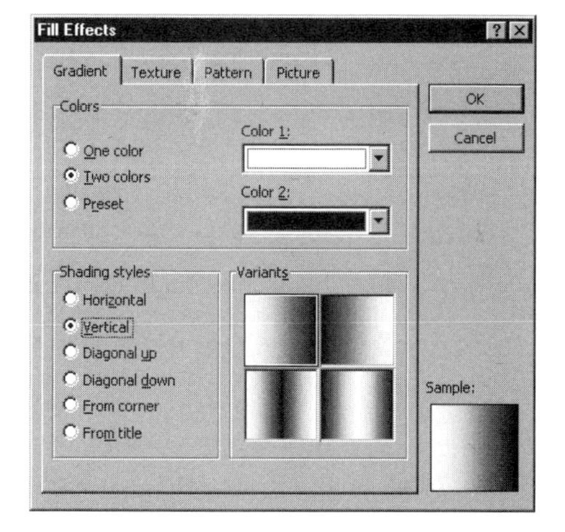

In this dialog box, you can select from four types of fills: Gradients, Textures, Patterns, or Pictures. *Gradients* are shaded color mixes. *Textures* are photo-like fills and *patterns* are repeated elements like diagonal lines, vertical stripes, or boxes. On the *Pictures* page, you use the Browse button to select a picture to apply to a background. PowerPoint supports many different graphic formats, from Windows MetaFiles to JPEGs. Whether you choose a picture or texture, pattern or gradient, it's a good idea to preview the fill before applying it.

Customizing Background Fills

1. Choose Format ➢ Background to open the Custom Background dialog box.
2. Click the Omit Background Graphics from Master check box to remove the background graphics from a particular slide or all the slides.
3. Click the drop-down arrow next to the blank text box to select the fill options that you want to change. Choose from shadowed, patterned, or textured fill, or choose a picture. To return to the original fill, choose Automatic from the drop-down list.

Hands On: Objectives PP2000.1.7, 2.4, and PP2000.E.2.4, 2.6

1. In an existing presentation:
   a) Change the color scheme.
   b) Create and apply a custom color scheme.
   c) Open the Slide Master. Change the font for the slide title.
   d) Add a footer that contains the current date and your name.
   e) Change the Background Fill for the Slide Master.
   f) Change the Fill for a single slide to one of the background textures.
   g) Turn off objects from the Master on a single slide.

Formatting and Checking Text

The design templates that come with PowerPoint were created by professional graphic artists and, therefore, reflect the principles that are commonly applied to the choice of typeface, size, and attributes. You can, however, format text to suit yourself, using the techniques you use in any Windows application. And, as you would with anything you plan to distribute or present, you want to proof spelling, grammar, and style.

Formatting Text

When you format text on individual slides, the formatting takes precedence over formatting from the Slide Master. Even if you apply a new design, formatting applied to individual slides won't change, so you should make sure you are pleased with the design before formatting individual slides. You can apply standard text enhancements that you know from other Windows applications to your PowerPoint slides. Select the text to be formatted, and then change font typeface, size, and attributes using the Formatting toolbar or the Format menu.

Formatting always appears in Slide view. In Outline view and Normal view, you can decide whether to display formatting. The Show Formatting button on the Formatting toolbar toggles between displaying and hiding text formatting.

Two buttons that do not appear in other Office applications are the Increase Font Size and Decrease Font Size buttons. Each click changes the font size in standard increments. The increment increases as font size increases.

Add a shadow to text by clicking the Text Shadow button; change the color of the text by clicking the Font Color button on the Drawing toolbar. When you select the desired text, and then click the down arrow to see the dialog box associated with this button, the colors from the current color scheme are displayed.

Aligning Text

Objective PP2000.3.5

Selected text can be left, center, or right-aligned, or fully justified like in newspaper stories. Left, Center, and Right alignment are options on the Formatting toolbar. Just select your text and click one of the three alignment options. You can't justify text from the toolbar, though. To justify selected text, choose Format ➢ Alignment ➢ Justify from the menu bar.

Replacing Fonts

Objective PP2000.3.2

You use the Replace Font dialog box to substitute one font for another, throughout the presentation. You might choose to replace fonts to change the look of a presentation, but there is a more pressing reason to use the dialog box. If you open a presentation on a computer that doesn't have the presentation's fonts installed, another font is automatically substituted—unless the fonts were embedded in the presentation. And the substitute font doesn't have to be good-looking; occasionally, it isn't even readable. Rather than changing various levels of the Master, you can have PowerPoint change each occurrence of the font.

Replacing Fonts in a Presentation

1. Select a text box that includes the font you want to replace.
2. Choose Format ➢ Replace Fonts to open the Replace Font dialog box.
3. Select a replacement font.
4. Click OK.

Adjusting Line Spacing

In PowerPoint 2000, you can add or subtract space between lines and before or after paragraphs in a text box, much as you add leading in desktop publishing. Rather than entering extra blank lines between points or subpoints, adjust the line spacing. Click Format ➢ Line Spacing from the menu. Adjusting line spacing only applies to the current slide, so if you want to make this adjustment on several slides, switch to Outline view and select the text on multiple slides before opening the Line Spacing dialog box.

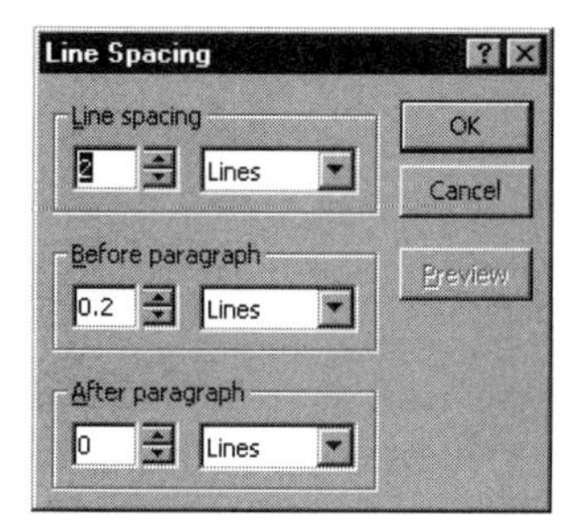

Adjusting Line Spacing

1. In Slide or Outline view, select the text you want to space.
2. Choose Format ➢ Line Spacing to open the Line Spacing dialog box.
3. Set the lines or points (1/72 inch) to be added as Line Spacing (between each line, even within a point or subpoint) or Before or After Paragraph, and then click OK.

Adjusting Tabs and Indents

Objective PP2000E.2.1

The indent distance when you press the Tab key is preset at one-half inch. You can see the default tab stops in Slide view on the ruler.

Changing Default Tabs

1. In Slide view, display the ruler (choose View ➢ Ruler).
2. Select the text that you want to change tabs for.
3. On the ruler, drag the first default tab stop to its new position. All other tab stops adjust so that the distance between each tab stop is the same.

The distances between the left edge of a text box and each level of bulleted text are also preset. When a text box with levels of text is selected, the upper and lower indent markers show on the ruler. Each level of text has its own set of indent markers.

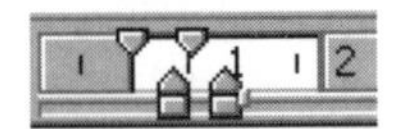

Changing Indentation

1. In Slide view, select the text you want to set indents for.
2. If the ruler isn't displayed, turn it on (choose View ➢ Ruler).
3. Drag the upper indent marker to change the indent for the first line of a paragraph.
4. Drag the lower indent marker to set the indent for other lines in a paragraph.
5. To change the indent for an entire paragraph, drag the square box beneath the lower indent marker to move both the upper and lower markers at the same time.

Checking Presentation Styles

PowerPoint automatically checks your presentation for consistency, style, and punctuation. When it encounters a style violation, a light bulb appears on the slide or next to the Office Assistant. Click the light bulb to review the reason for the flag. Once you decide how you want to handle the style violation, you have to make the changes manually.

The light bulb does not appear if you have turned off the Office Assistant. To turn on the Assistant, click Help ➢Show Office Assistant.

To specify options for style, choose Tools ➢ Options, and in the Options dialog box, select the Spelling and Style tab. Click the Style Options button to open the Style Options dialog box.

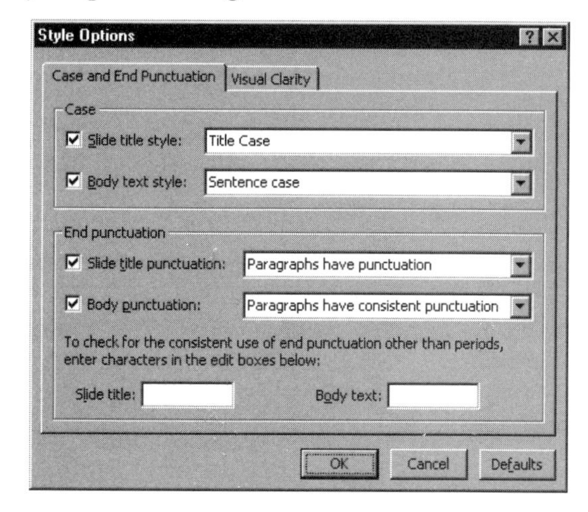

In the Case section, you can have the Checker notify you if some titles or body text don't match the case you select in the Case drop-down lists. Or you can turn off the checking of title and body text case. In the End Punctuation section, you can have the Checker notify you if punctuation is inconsistent with the rules you establish.

On the Visual Clarity tab, shown in Figure 8.23, set options for the maximum number of fonts, minimum font sizes, and number of points per slide that should be included in the presentation.

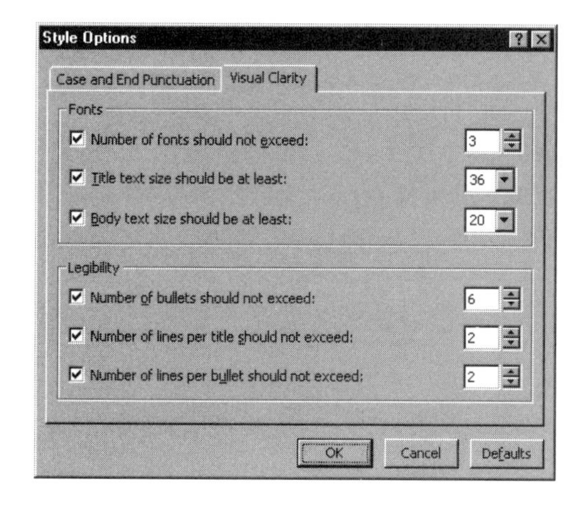

FIGURE 8.23

The Visual Clarity tab in the Style Options dialog box

When the Style checker encounters violation of the style options you set, it notifies you and allows you to correct the error.

Checking Presentation Styles

1. Choose Tools ➢ Options to open the Options dialog box, and select the Spelling and Style tab.
2. Click the Style Options button to open the Style Options dialog box.
3. Review, and if necessary, change the settings on the Case and End Punctuation and Visual Clarity pages. Click OK.

Hands On: *Objectives PP2000.3.2 and 3.5*

1. In an existing presentation:
   a) Change the font and font color to emphasize one word on a slide.
   b) Add a shadow to the title for all slides in the Slide Master.
   c) Replace the all body text font with another font.
2. In an existing presentation:
   a) Change the alignment for titles.
   b) Increase the spacing between the paragraphs in a bulleted list.
   c) Change the indentation and tab stops in the list.
   d) Change the style checking options.
   e) Correct any style violations PowerPoint finds.

Adding Objects

In PowerPoint, each item on a slide is an object, including text, clip art, a table, a chart, a sound, and a video clip. Objects can enhance and enliven your presentation. Remember, however, that slide real estate is limited; you don't want an overwhelming number of elements competing for audience attention.

Inserting Objects

If you want to insert an object, such as clip art or a chart, you'll find it easiest to begin with a slide layout that includes the object. Once you've selected the correct slide layout, just double-click inside the object's frame to be taken to the appropriate application to either insert or create the indicated object.

Inserting Clip Art

Objective PP2000.4.1

If you want to use Clip Art with your presentation, choose Insert ➢ Picture ➢ Clip Art. From there, click the Clip Art button, or select a slide layout with a Clip Art placeholder (see Figure 8.24) and double-click the placeholder.

FIGURE 8.24 Slide Layout with a Clip Art placeholder

The Insert ClipArt dialog box opens, as shown in Figure 8.25. Clip Art is arranged in categories. Click a category, and then locate the thumbnail for the Clip Art you want to insert. Select the picture, then click Insert Clip from the pop-up menu. Figure 8.26 shows this menu and your other choices.

FIGURE 8.25
Inserting Clip Art

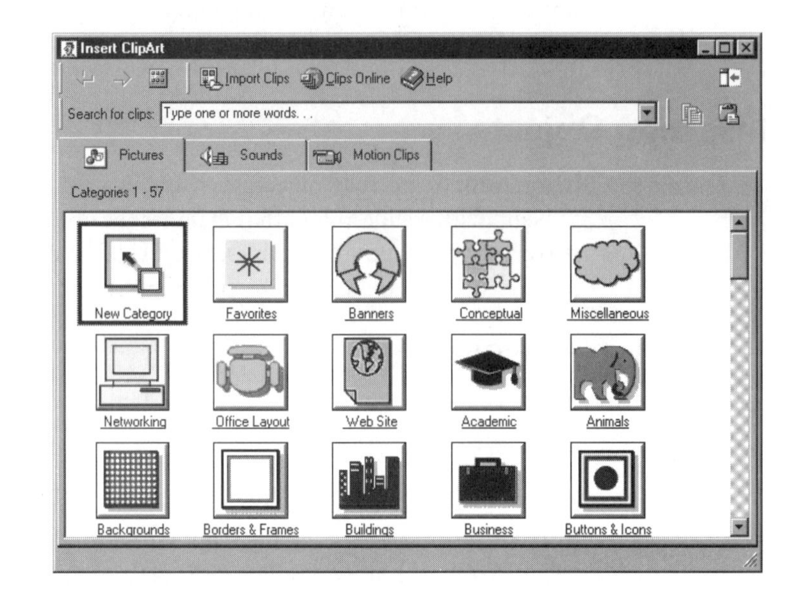

FIGURE 8.26
Pop-up menu

Objectives PP2000.4.5 and PP2000E.2.9

In the slide, click once on the object to select it. When an object is selected, you can drag it to another location on the slide or use the object's handles to resize the object. Delete a selected object by pressing Delete on the keyboard.

Adding Clip Art to a Slide

1. Choose Insert ➢ Picture ➢ Clip Art or double-click a Clip Art placeholder to open the Insert Clip Art dialog box.
2. Select a category, then click the picture you want or choose Keep Looking to see more choices.

Adding Clip Art to a Slide *(continued)*

3. Choose Insert Clip from the popup menu then close the Insert Clip Art dialog box.
4. Move and resize the clip as necessary.

Recoloring a Clip Art Object When you select a Clip Art object, the Picture toolbar automatically opens.

One toolbar button is available only in PowerPoint: the Recolor Picture button. Clicking the button opens the Recolor Picture dialog box, shown in Figure 8.27.

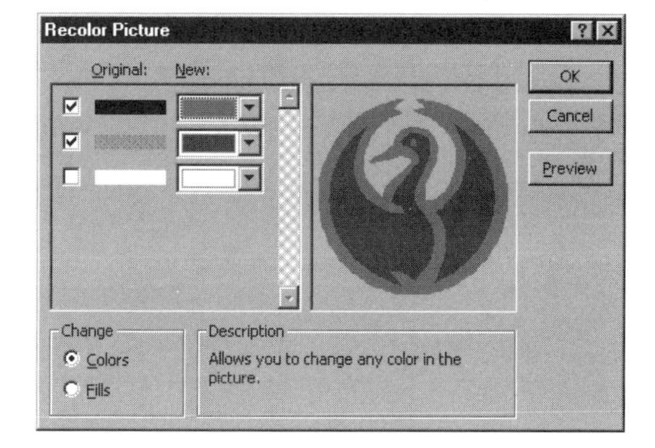

FIGURE 8.27

Recolor Picture dialog box

In the lower left corner of the dialog box is a Change area. Choose Colors, which changes the colors of lines and fills, or Fills, which doesn't affect lines. To change a color, turn on the check box in front of the color you want to change, then select a new color from the corresponding New drop-down list. The sample changes as you recolor different colors and fill in the Clip Art.

If you forget to check the box and simply choose a new color from the drop down list, PowerPoint automatically displays the check mark in front of the old color. This way you can keep track of which elements you've changed.

Recoloring Clip Art

1. In the slide, select the Clip Art object.
2. Click the Recolor Picture button on the Picture toolbar. If the toolbar isn't visible, choose View ➢ Toolbars ➢ Picture.
3. Choose to change Colors or Fills.
4. Check and choose a new color for each color you want to change.
5. Click Preview to preview the changes in the slide; click OK to apply the changes.

Using Animated Pictures

Objective PP2000E.2.7

Animated pictures are just what they sound like – pictures that move. Inserting an animated picture is as easy as inserting any object from the Clip Gallery. Navigate to the slide on which you want to insert the animated picture and click Insert ➢ Picture ➢ Clip Art on the menu. Click the Motion Clips tab of the Insert Picture dialog box and choose a category. Motion clips are .GIF files, the same format as many animated Web pictures. Select the clip you like and insert it just as you would a piece of clip art. You can also preview, categorize, and import animated GIFs like other Clip Gallery objects. Once you've inserted the clip you like, you have to switch to Slide Show view to see the animation.

If you've downloaded an animated GIF from the Web, you can insert it without using the Clip Gallery. Choose Insert ➢ Picture ➢ From File. Locate, select, and open the GIF to place it on a slide. Move and/or re-size the picture as necessary. View its animation in Slide Show view.

You can't use all of the tools on PowerPoint's Picture toolbar to modify the formatting of an animated GIF. (Frequently you can use the Contrast and Brightness buttons, but you can't recolor.) Copy and paste the picture into an animated GIF editing program, make your changes, and copy/paste the edited GIF back on the slide.

Creating Graphical Bullets

Objective PP2000.5.3

Microsoft Office has always offered users the option of choosing bullet characters from the many font sets installed with Windows and Office. But now, you also have the capability to create a bullet character from any picture file, giving you endless possibilities for emphasizing points on slides.

Before you make a change to bullet characters, decide whether you want to make the change on all slides, or just the selected slide. If you wish to make the change for all slides, be sure you are working from the Slide Master. (See *Modifying the Slide Master*, earlier in this chapter.)

Select the text for which you wish to change the bullet character. If you are working on the Slide Master, click in the appropriate level. Then choose Format ➢ Bullets and Numbering. The Bullets and Numbering dialog box opens as shown in Figure 8.28.

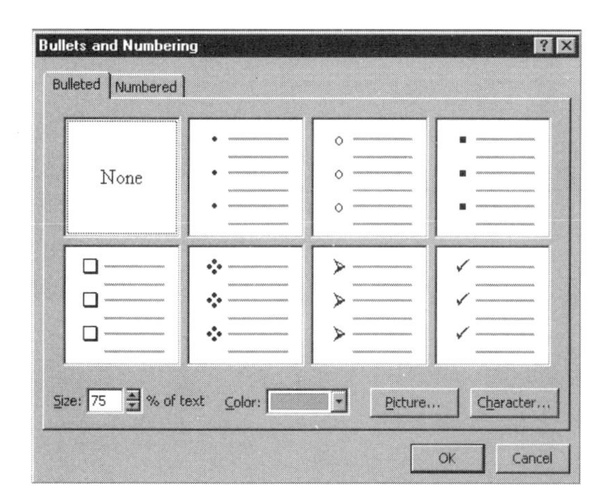

FIGURE 8.28 Use the Bullets and Numbering dialog box to choose or customize bullet characters.

You can select one of the seven bullet types displayed here, or you can change the size and/or color of your bullet character. If you want to see more bullet choices, choose either Character or Picture. Choosing Character takes you to the Bullet dialog box shown in Figure 8.29. Change the Bullets From selection to see another sheet of character choices. Click on a character to see a larger sample, as shown in the figure. Click on the character you wish to use and click OK.

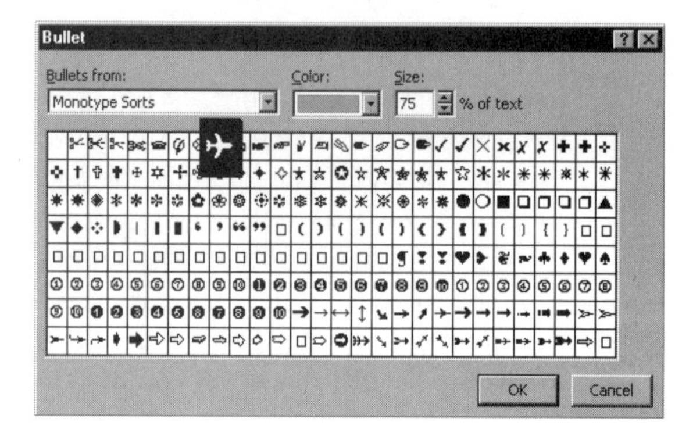

FIGURE 8.29 Previewing a bullet character in the Bullet dialog box

Choosing Picture takes you to the bullet character portion of the Clip Gallery, shown in Figure 8.30. (If you haven't installed the Clip Gallery, choosing Picture takes you to the Insert Picture dialog box.) Choose one of the displayed bullets, click for More Clips, or choose a picture from a file.

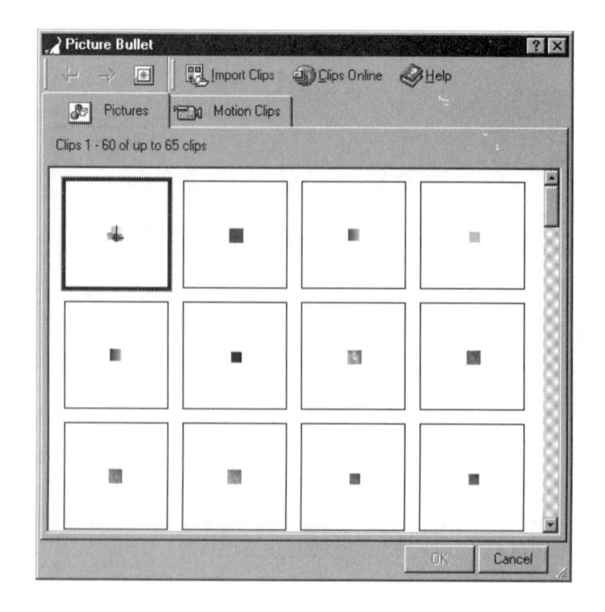

FIGURE 8.30 The Picture Bullet dialog box lets you choose a picture from the Clip Gallery to use as a bullet character.

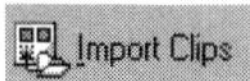

To select a bullet character from a picture file, click the Import Clips button near the top of the dialog box. Choose the drive and folder that contains the file you wish to use, select it, and click Import. The first time you import a picture to use as a bullet it appears on a page by itself. However, the next time you wish to use the same picture bullet, it will appear as a choice among others in the Clip Gallery.

Choosing a Bullet Character

1. Navigate to the slide for which you wish to select a bullet character, or click in the appropriate level on the slide master.
2. Choose Format ➢ Bullets and Numbering from the menu.
3. Select one of the seven choices shown in the Bullets and Numbering dialog box. If you want to see other choices click either the Character button (to choose a symbol from a font set) or the Picture button (to choose a graphical bullet from the Clip Gallery).
4. Select the picture or symbol you wish to use for a character and click OK.
5. Change the point size or color of the bullet character in the Bullets and Numbering dialog box. Click OK to apply it.

Automatic Numbering of Points on Slides

Objective PP2000.5.1

If you prefer to number your paragraphs rather than bullet them, you'll be pleased to see that PowerPoint keeps track of which point you're on! Apply a design template to your presentation (if you haven't already) and open the slide master (View ➢ Master ➢ Slide Master).

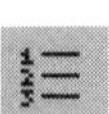

Click in the level you wish to number, then click the Numbering button on the Formatting toolbar. Repeat the procedure for all levels you wish to number. Close the slide master and return to any view. You'll see numbered paragraphs for each level you changed.

PowerPoint, like Word, allows custom formatting of numbers, too. You could, for instance, number Level 1 points in the traditional fashion: 1, 2, 3… and letter Level 2 subpoints like you would in an outline: A, B, C…. On the slide master, click in the level that has numbers you want to customize then choose Format ➢ Bullets and Numbering from the menu. The Bullets and Numbering dialog box opens. Click the Numbering tab to see choices for custom numbering as shown in Figure 8.31.

Choose one of the preset numbering styles, then choose a color, point size, and start at number (or letter). Click OK to apply your custom numbering to

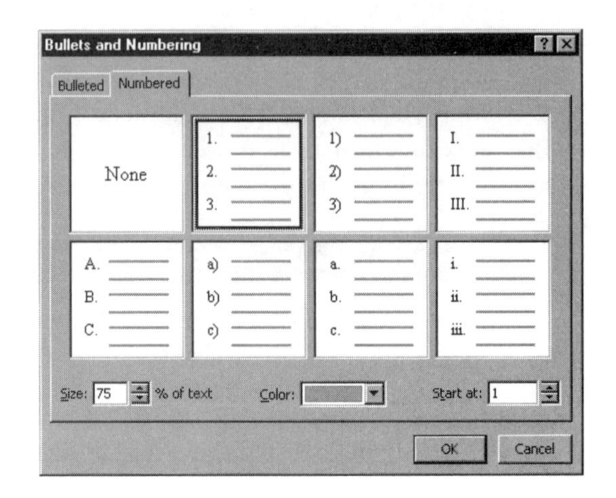

FIGURE 8.31 Bullets and Numbering dialog box

the current level. Click in another level and repeat the procedure to apply a different numbering format. Close the slide master and return to any view to see the changes. When you add points and subpoints to a slide or on the outline, PowerPoint automatically numbers them in sequence with the other points at that level.

If you have used drawing tools to add a text box to a slide, PowerPoint sees it as an object and won't include its numbered paragraph(s) in sequence with the others on the slide. No problem. Just select the paragraph(s) in the drawn text box, open the Bullets and Numbering dialog box and change the Start At number.

Sound and Motion Clips

Objectives PP2000E.4.4 and 4.5

PowerPoint includes sounds and motion clips you can play during your slide shows. Some sounds, like the typewriter or laser sound, are included on the Animation Effects toolbar. Other sounds, music, and motion clips are in the Insert Clip Art dialog box.

Inserting a Sound or Video File

1. Open the slide you want to add an object to.
2. Choose Insert ➢ Movies and Sounds ➢ Sound from Gallery or Movies from Gallery.
3. In the Insert Clip Art dialog box, select the sound or motion clip you want to add. Click Play Clip to preview the selected sound or motion clip.
4. Click Insert Clip to insert the object and place a sound icon or motion clip object on the slide.
5. To play the sound or motion clip, double-click the icon or object.

To insert a sound or motion clip that isn't in the Insert Clip Art dialog box, choose Insert ➢ Movies and Sounds, and then select Movie from File or Sound from File. Locate, select, and open the file.

Inserting Tables from Word

Objectives PP2000.4.6 and PP2000E.4.2

If you've already created a table in Word that you want to use in a presentation, you can copy it in Word and paste it onto a slide. A table any bigger than three columns by four rows is too large to show up clearly on a slide, so keep it simple. If you want to create a Word table in the current presentation, choose Insert ➢ Picture ➢ Microsoft Word Table or choose a Table AutoLayout from the New Slide dialog box and double-click the Table icon on the slide. You are asked how many columns and rows you want:

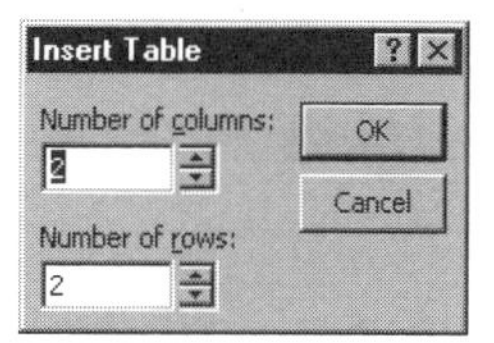

After you select the appropriate number of rows and columns and click OK, PowerPoint displays the Tables and Borders toolbar.

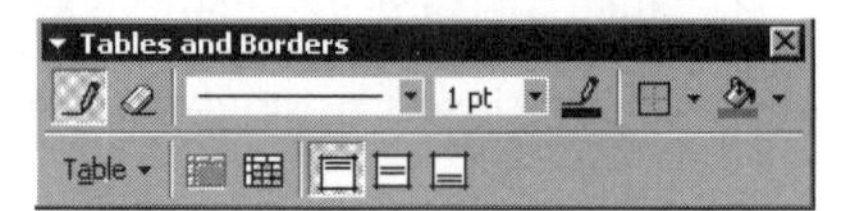

Use the Tables and Borders toolbar and the Table command on the Format menu to create a table just as you would in Word. (For a review of Word's table features, see Chapter 3.)

Objective P2000E.10.5

After you enter the text for the table, click outside the table and the Tables and Borders toolbar closes. You can resize the table using the handles or reposition the table by dragging it to a new location. If you need to edit the table, double-click it, select the text or cells you want to change and type your new data.

Inserting a Word Table

1. Select a Slide AutoLayout that includes a table and double-click the table placeholder, or on any slide choose Insert ➢ Picture ➢ Word Table.
2. Indicate the number of columns and rows that you want and click OK.
3. Enter the text for the table using Word's table features to format or enhance the table.
4. Click outside the table to close the table object. Double-click the table object to edit it.

Creating and Modifying an Organizational Chart

Objectives P2000E.10.3 and 10.4

Organizational charts often show the hierarchy of employees in a company or team members assigned to a project. You can also use an orginizational chart to display a process, much like you would in a flow chart. Slide space is limited, so you want to be selective with the information you want to display. Figure 8.32 shows an example of a slide with an organizational chart.

FIGURE 8.32
Slide with Org Chart

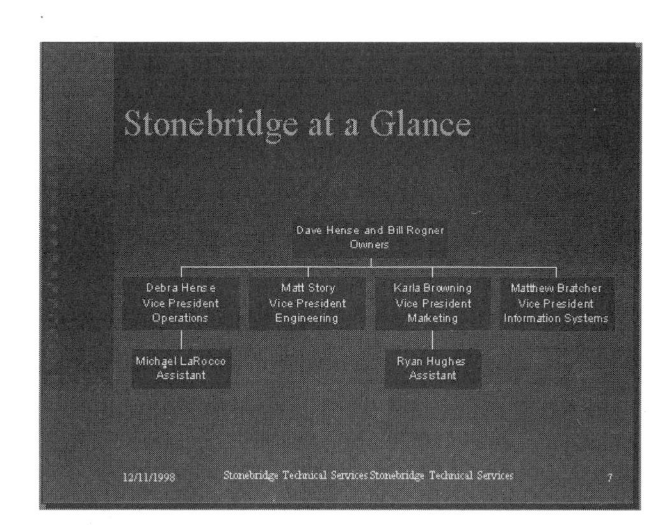

To create an organizational chart, click the New Slide button to open the New Slide dialog box then choose the slide layout that includes an organizational chart. Click in the title text box and type a title for the slide. Then double-click the Organizational Chart icon to launch Microsoft Organizational Chart. You may be prompted to install the program if this is the first time you have used it. The Organizational Chart program runs inside its own window, as shown in Figure 8.33.

FIGURE 8.33
Org Chart Working Window

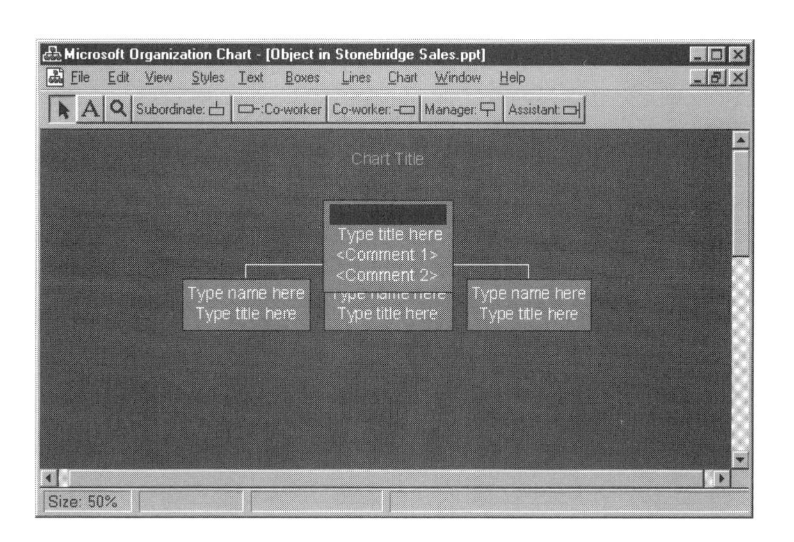

When the Organizational Chart window opens, you are automatically given four boxes: one manager and three subordinates. You are also given the option of including a title for your Organizational Chart. Select the placeholder text and overtype it with the your own information. Delete boxes you don't want by clicking them and pressing Delete on the keyboard.

Before you add a box, decide which level is appropriate for the person whose name appears in the box. Click that level on the toolbar (manager, subordinate, assistant, etc.), then click in the box to which you wish to attach this person. A new box appears with placeholder text to select and overtype.

Choose a particular level or all levels for editing by clicking Edit ➢ Select from the Menu Bar. Change the color, shadow, and border options on selected boxes using the Boxes Menu. Change the thickness and/or color of connecting lines using the Lines Menu. Options for different chart styles and text formatting are also available from the menu.

When you are finished, click the close button on the Microsoft Organizational Chart program window. You are prompted to update the object in your presentation before proceeding. Click Yes to return to the PowerPoint view you were in when you began. If you wish to edit the Organizational Chart at any time, simply double-click the chart to re-launch the program.

Building an Organizational Chart

1. Select a Slide AutoLayout that includes an organizational chart and double-click the organizational chart icon.
2. Select and overtype the placeholder text with your own.
3. Delete unwanted boxes by clicking them then pressing Delete.
4. Add a box by clicking one of the toolbar buttons (manager, subordinate, assistant, etc.) then clicking inside the box to which you wish to attach the new box.
5. Select a level for formatting by clicking the Edit menu and choosing the level you want to edit or All to edit all boxes.
6. Click the Boxes menu to find options to edit borders, shadow, and color of boxes.
7. Click the Lines menu to find options for formatting connecting lines.

Building an Organizational Chart *(continued)*

8. To place the organizational chart on the slide, click the Close button on the Microsoft Organizational Chart window and choose Yes when prompted to update.
9. Double-click the organizational chart at any time to open it for editing.

Hands On: Objectives PP2000.4.1, 4.5, 4.6, 5.1, 5.3, and PP2000E2.7, 4.2, 4.4, 10.3, 10.4, 10.5

1. In a new or existing presentation:
   - a) Insert Clip Art on a single slide.
   - b) Insert Clip Art on the Slide Master. Resize the Clip Art to the size of a small logo and place it in a corner of the slide.
   - c) Recolor the Clip Art on the single slide.
   - d) Insert an animated GIF from the Clip Gallery.
   - e) Insert an existing table from Word.
   - f) Insert a new slide with a table placeholder. Create a three-column, two-row table and format it using the tools on the Tables and Borders toolbar.
   - g) Edit the content of the table you inserted in either Step d or e.
   - h) Create a slide with an organizational chart showing the top three levels of management in your company. Format the borders, text color, and fills as desired.
2. In a new or existing presentation.
   - a) Insert a sound file.
   - b) Test the playback in Slide Show view.
3. In the same presentation:
   - a) Open the Slide Master and apply custom numbering to levels one and two.
   - b) Exit the Slide Master and add a bulleted point to a slide at level one.
   - c) Add a subpoint at level two.
   - d) Open the Slide Master again and apply graphical bullets to level one.

Applying Transitions, Animation Effects, and Linking

An electronic presentation, or Slide Show, is displayed on a computer screen or projected with an LCD projector. Since slides are "changed" by the computer rather than by hand, you can add computerized special effects to a slide show that aren't possible when you use overheads for a presentation. A *transition* is a special effect added to the slide's initial appearance on screen. The slide can appear from the right, dissolve in gradually, or fade through the background of the previous slide. Some of the design templates also include animated features: for example, one of the background objects may streak into place.

Individual slides can include *animation*—different steps used to construct the slide, one placeholder at a time. For example, the slide can appear with a title only, and bulleted points can be added one at a time for emphasis. You can add transitions in Slide Sorter view using the tools on the Slide Sorter toolbar, shown below. While you can add preset text animation in the Slide Sorter, you can't animate other objects, so you generally want to work with animation in Slide view.

Modifying and Adding Transitions

Objective PP2000.5.4

If a presentation doesn't have transitions, each slide simply appears in place of the previous slide—very vanilla. Most of the PowerPoint design templates include transitions, so there is more pizzazz. To change or add transitions, select the slide(s), then choose a transition from the Slide Transition Effects drop-down list.

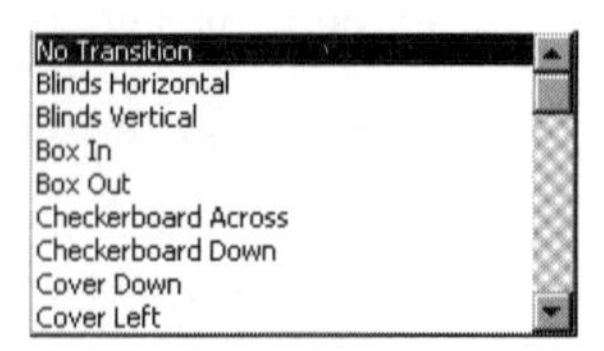

Many of the transitions listed differ only in direction; for example, Cover Up, Cover Down, and Cover Up-Left. When you select a new transition from the list, PowerPoint provides a preview of the transition using the selected slide. (Look fast—it doesn't take long.)

A *transition icon* appears below the lower-left corner of a slide with an assigned transition. Clicking this icon shows the transition again in the slide miniature. Take some time to browse the various types of transitions.

Adding or Changing Transitions

1. In Slide Sorter view, select the slide(s) to transition.
2. Choose a transition from the Slide Transition Effects drop-down list.

Setting Transition Speed and Sound

Each type of transition has a default speed. The default for Wipes, for example, is Fast. You can change the speed for transitions, choose a different transition, or add sound effects to accompany a transition in the Slide Transition dialog box.

Make sure the slides you want to alter are selected; then click the Slide Transition button on the Slide Sorter toolbar to open the Slide Transition dialog box, shown in Figure 8.34.

FIGURE 8.34 Slide Transition dialog box

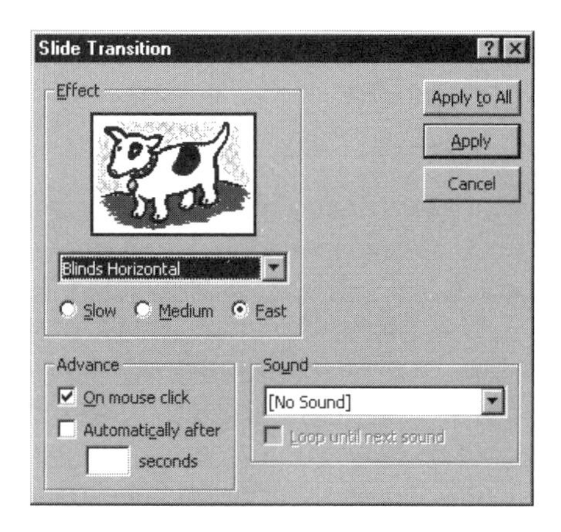

From the Effect drop-down list, select a transition, and then choose one of the Speed options. When you select a transition effect, the preview picture transitions into a key using the effect you selected. If you want to preview the transition again simply click the key. There is a drop-down list of Sounds you can add to a transition. If you assign a sound, you can choose to have the sound loop until another sound is assigned. The last choice on the list, Other Sound, opens a dialog box so that you can select a sound file. PowerPoint uses wave sounds, files with a `.wav` extension. You can find some wave files in the Media subfolder of the Windows folder, but you can purchase CDs of wave files at many computer stores.

The Advance section of the Slide Transition dialog box is for entering timings for automatic slide advances. If your presentation is to run automatically (like those at trade show kiosks) use the Rehearse Timings feature, rather than setting them individually here. (See *Setting Slide Timings* later in this chapter). When you've finished setting options, choose Apply or Apply to All. Once the dialog box is closed you can preview effects, including sound, by clicking the transition icon below the slide in the Slide Sorter.

Changing Transition Speed and Sound

1. In Slide Sorter view, select the slide(s) you want to change.
2. Click the Slide Transition button on the Slide Sorter toolbar to open the Slide Transition dialog box.
3. Choose settings for Effect and Speed (and Sound if you wish).
4. Click Apply or Apply to All.

Adding Animation

Objectives PP2000.5.5 and PP2000E.2.5

Transition effects are used *between* slides; animation effects occur *within* a slide. Each title, bulleted point, or other object on a slide can be added to the slide separately. This allows you to discuss individual points or add illustrations in a particular order during the presentation. In Slide Sorter view, you can apply a group of preset text animation settings. Select the slide or slides, and then choose a type of animation from the Preset Animation drop-down menu.

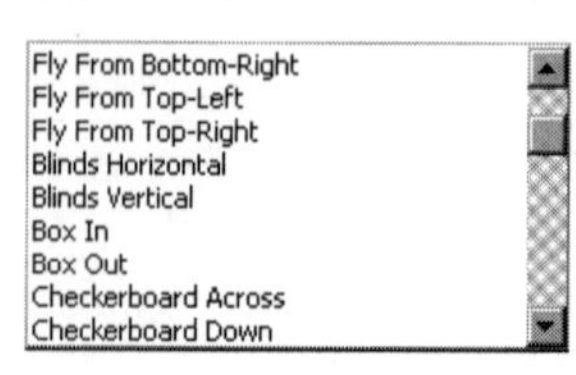

The selected animation is applied to all text (other than the title) in the slide. Preview the animation by clicking the animation icon in Slide Sorter. If you animate body text, moving to Slide Show view opens the slide with the title and any background objects and graphics. Click anywhere, and the first bulleted point is animated. Click again for each point.

Another group of animation effects are available from the context menu. Right-click a selected slide in Slide Sorter view, and choose one of the Preset Animations, which include sound.

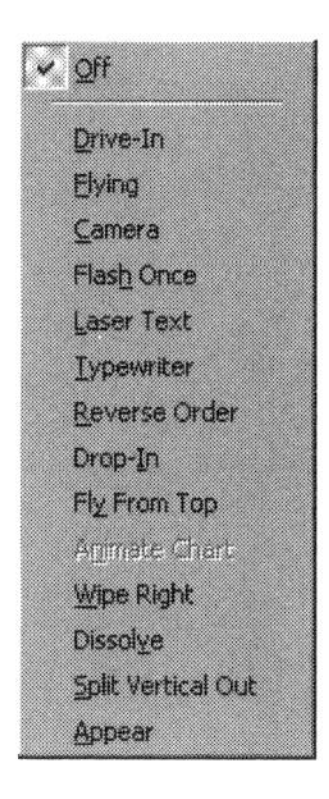

Adding Preset Animation to Slides

1. In Slide Sorter view, select the slide you want to animate.
2. Choose a preset animation from the Preset Animation drop-down menu on the Slide Sorter toolbar.

   OR

2. Right-click a selected slide and choose a Preset Animation from the shortcut menu.

Adding Custom Animation

The Custom Animation tools take sound and motion to new heights in electronic presentations. Use the custom animation tools to add sound and motion to individual graphic elements on a slide.

To open the Animation Effects toolbar, switch to Slide view and click the Animation Effects button on the Formatting toolbar.

To move quickly to Slide view, double-click the slide you want to animate.

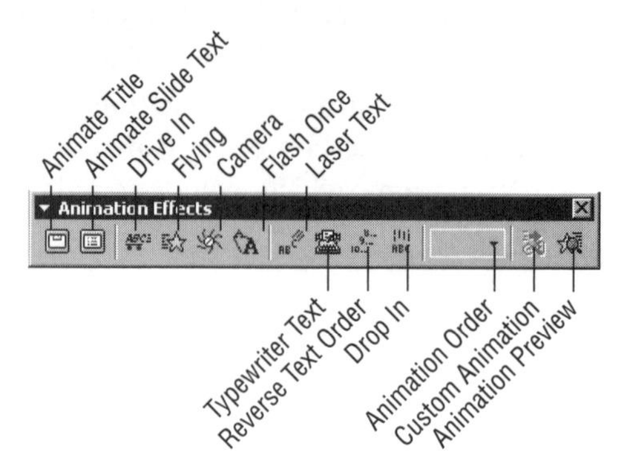

To have the slide title drop in from the top, click the Animate Title button. To see the effect click the Animation Preview button on the Animation Effects toolbar. Your slide opens in Animation Preview, and you see the effect of the animation option you selected.

The other Animation Effects buttons are used for specific graphic elements, including text boxes and objects. Select the object you want to animate, then click one of the eight Animation Effects buttons on the Animation Effects toolbar. After you click an effect button, the object is added to the slide's animation list. When the object is selected, its animation order number appears in the Animation Order drop-down list on the toolbar.

Click the Custom Animation button to open the Custom Animation dialog box, shown in Figure 8.35. Click the Preview button to preview the current animations in order. To rearrange the order select the Order & Timing tab, select an animation in the Animation Order list, and use the Move Up and Move Down arrows. On the Effects tab, shown in Figure 8.36, assign an animation and, if you wish, a sound. The After Animation drop-down allows you to change the color of animated text as the next animation occurs. You can use this in multi-point slides with rather dramatic effect; for example, you can have each point animate as white text, then change to gray when the next point enters, drawing the viewer's attention immediately to the new point. In the Introduce Text drop-down, you can choose to animate a text box by specific levels or all at once.

FIGURE 8.35

The Order & Timing tab of the Custom Animation dialog box

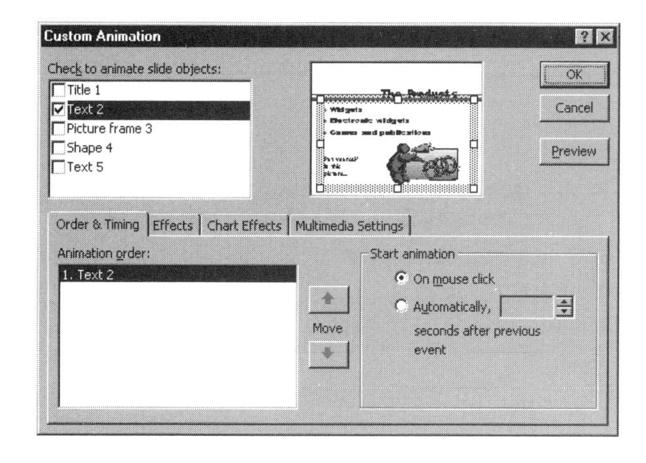

FIGURE 8.36

The Effects tab of the Custom Animation dialog box

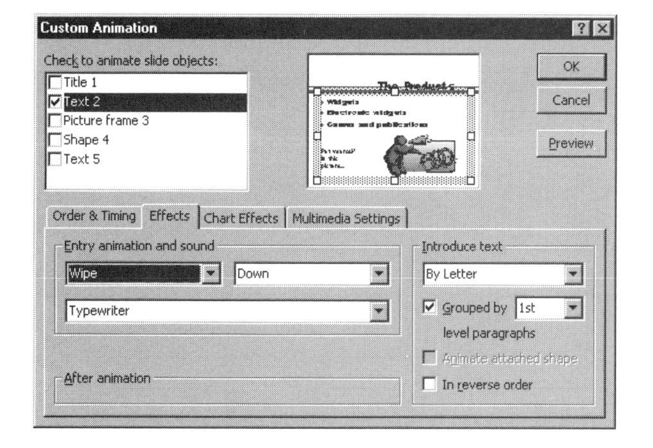

The Check to Animate Slide Objects list shows all the objects on a slide. Those that are checked are animated. The Start Animation options, however, refer to the selected object either in the list or in the Animation Order list on the Order & Timing tab. If you want the animation to proceed without mouse clicks, choose the Automatically option and set a number of seconds that should pass between the end of the previous animation and the beginning of the selected animation.

Chart Effects are disabled unless the selected object is a chart. (See *Creating and Animating Charts* on next page.) You can introduce an entire chart at one time, or you can have chart elements appear by category, by data series, or individually in the Introduce Chart Elements drop-down list. Chart effects let you provide dramatic illustrations of numeric data in your presentation.

The Play Settings are enabled when a sound or video object is selected. If you choose to assign the media an Animation Order, you don't have to click on the object to play it.

Adding Custom Animation Effects

1. View the slide you want to animate in Slide view.
2. Click the Animation Effects button on the Formatting toolbar to open the Animation Effects toolbar.
3. Select preset effects from the toolbar.
4. Click the Custom Animation button to open the Custom Animation dialog box.
5. In the Order & Timing tab, use the Move Up and Move Down buttons to change the Animation Order.
6. Select any item in the Animation Order list, and then use the Effects tab to set custom options.
7. Set animation options for charts on the Chart Effects page.
8. Change media playback settings on the Multimedia Settings tab.
9. Click the Preview button to preview changes.
10. Click OK to apply the custom animation changes.

Creating and Animating Charts

Objective PP2000E.4.3

In Office, there are two programs that create charts: Excel and Microsoft Graph. If you already have a chart in Excel, you can easily copy and embed it or link it to your slide. To embed an Excel chart object, open the Excel file that contains the chart. Select the chart object and click the copy button on the Standard toolbar. Switch to PowerPoint and navigate to the slide where you want to place the chart. Click the Paste button on the Standard toolbar. If you don't have access to Excel, however, Microsoft Graph lets you create charts quickly and easily in PowerPoint.

Creating Charts

Objective P2000E.10.1

To launch Microsoft Graph, click the Insert Chart button on the Standard toolbar or choose Insert ➢ Chart from PowerPoint's menu bar. If a slide already contains a chart, double-clicking that object icon also launches Microsoft Graph for editing.

Objective P2000E.10.2

In Figure 8.37, you can see that Graph contains two windows: a datasheet that includes sample data, and a chart. Replace the labels (text) in the top row and left column with your labels and the values in the remaining cells with your numbers, and you have a basic bar chart. To delete a column or row you don't need, click on its header and press Delete. Close the datasheet at any point to place the chart in your document.

You can re-size and reposition the chart object as you would any other object. You must select the chart to re-size it; a selected chart object has hollow handles. Double-clicking the chart opens the chart object so you can edit the individual objects inside it; when you can edit the chart, the object handles are solid, and you cannot move the chart object. To select the entire object again for moving or sizing, click outside of the chart to close it, then click once on the chart object.

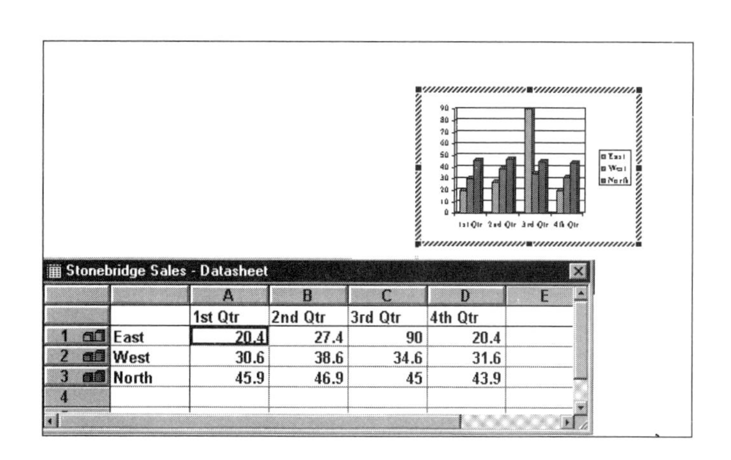

FIGURE 8.37
Inserting a Microsoft Graph 97 Chart object

Using Existing Data If you already have data, don't re-enter it—you can import or copy data into Microsoft Graph. Graph can convert data from Excel, text files, SYLK files, Lotus 1-2-3, and CSV (Comma Separated Files) that can be exported from most spreadsheet and database programs.

To import data from an existing file, start Graph just as you would if you were creating a chart from scratch, choose Edit ➢ Import File on the Graph menu or click the Import File button to open the Import File dialog box. Once you select a file in this typical Windows file window, the Import Data Options dialog box opens so you can select which part of the workbook or worksheet to use. Turn on Overwrite Existing Cells to replace the current data in the Graph datasheet. Turn this option off, and the imported data is appended at the end of the current data in the datasheet.

Copying or Linking Existing Data Use Copy and Paste or Paste Special to use existing data from Word or Excel to create a chart. Select and copy the data in its source application. In Graph, select the first cell where you want the data to appear. Choose the upper-left cell to overwrite the existing data, or select the left cell in an empty row to append the data. Paste the data, or choose Edit ➢ Paste Link from the Graph menu to link the chart to the table or worksheet. (With linking, changes you make to the data in the source application are automatically reflected in the Graph chart.)

If you often work in Excel, you probably create most of your charts there. However, you can choose to create charts from within PowerPoint using Microsoft Graph and have access to most of Excel's formatting features as well.

Creating a Chart Using Microsoft Graph

1. Click the Insert Chart button on the Standard toolbar, double-click a chart object icon on a slide with a chart placeholder, or choose Insert ➢ Chart from PowerPoint's menu bar.

Creating a Chart Using Microsoft Graph *(continued)*

2. Replace the text in the top row and left column with your own labels.
3. Replace the sample numbers with your own. If you have existing data, choose Edit ➢ Import File, select the file that contains the data and choose whether or not or overwrite the current data the click OK.
4. If you prefer to link data so that your Microsoft Graph object updates when the data changes at its source, open the file in its original application. Select and copy the data then click in the first cell of the datasheet in PowerPoint. Choose Edit ➢ Paste Link and overwrite the existing sample data.

Formatting a Chart

Microsoft Graph has its own buttons that append themselves to the Standard toolbar once a chart is created. You have all the features you need to create a great-looking representation of your numerical data. Table 8.1 describes the buttons on the Graph toolbar.

TABLE 8.1: Microsoft Graph Toolbar Buttons

Button	Name	Use
	By Rows	Displays data series by Row. First row of the table provides x-axis labels.
	By Columns	Displays data series by Column. First column of the table provides x-axis labels.
	Data Table	Toggles between showing and hiding data table with Chart.
	Chart Type	Allows you to change to another chart type such as 3-D Pie or Area.
	Category Axis Guidelines	Toggles to show or hide major vertical guidelines on chart.

TABLE 8.1: Microsoft Graph Toolbar Buttons *(continued)*

Button	Name	Use
	Value Axis Guidelines	Toggles to show or hide major horizontal guidelines on chart.
	Legend	Toggles to show or hide legend.
	Drawing	Turns Drawing toolbar off or on.
	Fill Color	Fills the background of the selected chart area.

You can hide the datasheet display using the View Datasheet button on the Graph toolbar. Turning the datasheet off won't prevent you from displaying it with the chart on your slide; you can still use the Data Table button referred to in Table 8.1. However, to edit numbers on the datasheet, you must display it.

With the chart selected, right-click and choose Chart Options to open the Chart Options dialog box. Use the dialog box options to add titles, display minor as well as major gridlines, show and position a legend, display data labels, and include the datasheet as part of the chart object.

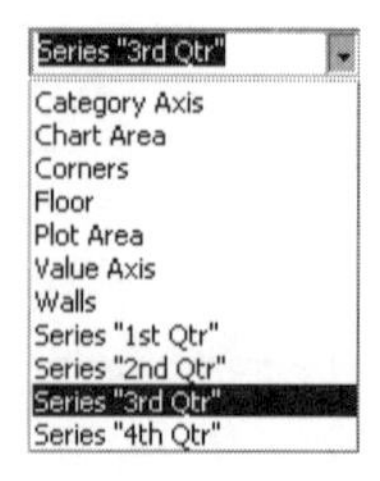

To format an individual chart object (for example, the columns, all the data in a row or column, the chart background, or the legend), select the object in the chart, or choose it from the Chart Objects drop-down list on the toolbar. Then double-click the selected object, right-click, and choose Format [Object Name], or click the Format Object button on the toolbar to open the relevant dialog box. For example, the Format Data Series dialog box is shown in Figure 8.38.

When you select an entire data series for formatting and then double-click an item in the chart to open the formatting dialog box, the formatting is *only* applied to whichever point in the data series you double-clicked on. If you want to apply formatting to the entire data series, select it using any of the methods previously described and then open the Format dialog box using the toolbar button, rather than double-clicking on the chart object.

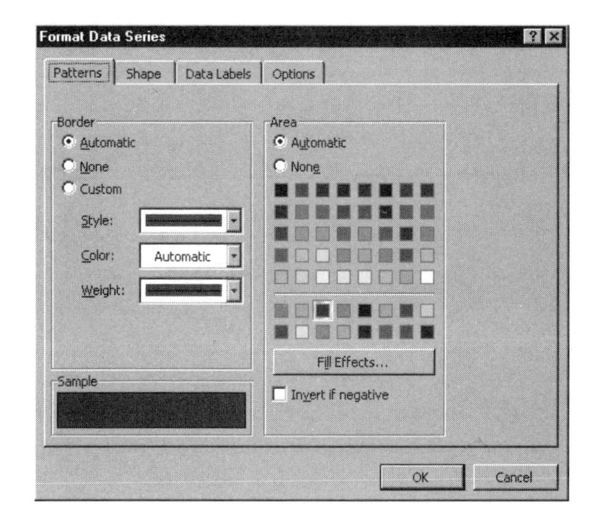

FIGURE 8.38 The Format Data Series dialog box

Several options are available to you when you choose to format individual chart objects:

- Use the Pattern tab of the dialog box to change borders and shading of the selected chart objects.
- Use the Shape tab (when formatting a data series) for changing the shape of bars in your graph.
- You can display values or percents on point in a series using the Data Labels tab.
- Increase the depth of the chart and the space between each category of columns under Options.

When you've made all your choices, click OK.

Animating Charts

Chart animation allows you to provide dramatic illustrations of numeric data in your presentation. During your slide show, you can introduce an entire chart at one time, or have chart elements appear by category, by data series, or individually. Adding the data separately lets you apply emphasis where needed, and it allows your audience to digest one piece of information before you give them another.

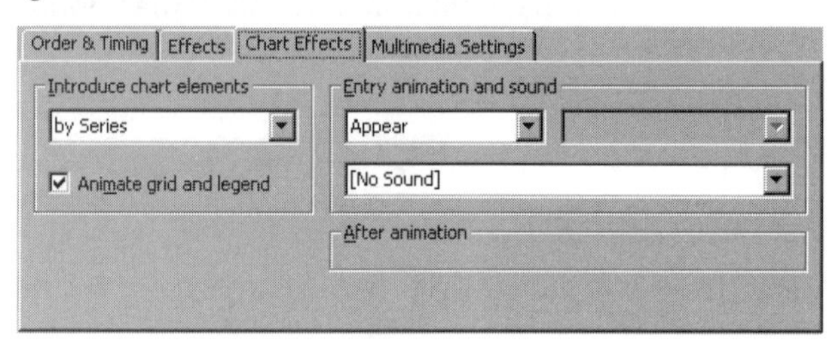

Open the Animation Settings dialog box to the Chart tab. In the Introduce Chart Elements drop-down list, select how you want your chart to appear. Choose By Series to have all bars from a category appear at once. (For example, all four quarters of the West Coast Data appear, then the East Coast, etc.). By Category brings in each group of bars separately (all first quarter, then all second quarter, and so on) By Element in a Series and By Element in a Category work essentially the same as By Element and By Category, respectively. The only difference is that only one bar appears at a time, rather than several bars at once.

Choose an effect from the drop-down list. You may find that if you choose to introduce data any way other than all at once, you can't use the particular effect you want. For instance, you can't have chart elements spiral in by category, but you can have them strip down. Turn on Animate Grid and Legend if you want to apply the effect to those chart elements as well. Assign a sound and an After Animation option if you wish.

Tips for Transitions and Animation

When you give a slide show, you want the audience to remember your presentation's *content*—not just the flashy effects. Use one or two similar transitions throughout the presentation. For example, alternating left and right or top and down transitions of the same type provides variety without irritating your audience. When a presentation has transitions, slides without transitions stand out, so No Transition effectively becomes another type of transition. Sound can be attention-grabbing, but new sound on every slide is too much.

The same tips apply to animation. Choose a small group of animation effects. Text that flies in from the right feels normal because the side we read first enters first. To add emphasis, then, have text enter from the left, top, or bottom.

Presentations with many different animation settings and transition effects require a fair amount of practice to show well. For a perfectly polished presentation, practice on your own until you have memorized which slides animate automatically and which advance on mouse click. Always keep in mind that your goal is to enhance, not overpower the content of your presentation. If it's difficult to memorize your animations during practice, you're probably using too many.

Hands On: Objectives PP2000.5.4, 5.5, and PP2000E.2.5, 10.1, 10.2

1. In a new or existing presentation:
   - a) Select a slide and animate its title.
   - b) Select a slide and animate the bulleted text so that it displays with a Strips effect and dims to another color when you advance to the next bullet.
   - c) Insert a piece of art on the slide you used in Step b. Animate the slide so the art spirals in after the bulleted text.
   - d) Change and preview the animation order.
   - e) Have one animation follow another without a mouse click.
2. In Slide Sorter view apply a Checkerboard Across transition to all your slides.
   - a) Select a slide and change the speed of the transition.
   - b) Apply a sound to another transition and preview it in the Slide Sorter.

3. Insert a new slide with a placeholder for a chart.
    a) Edit the existing labels and data by overwriting them with your own.
    b) Format the chart area with a color or fill that contrasts with the slide background.
    c) Animate the chart to introduce each data series on mouse click.
4. Create a new blank slide and insert an existing Excel chart on it.

Hiding Slides

Objective PP2000E.2.12

Many presentations contain "emergency slides" that are only displayed if certain questions or topics arise during the presentation. Creating, then hiding, a slide gives you some leeway: if the question isn't asked, you don't have to show the slide. If, on the other hand, a member of the audience asks how you plan to raise the $10 million you are talking about spending, you can whip out the hidden slide.

In Slide Sorter view, select the slide you want to hide, and then click the Hide Slide button on the toolbar.

A null symbol appears over the slide's number. To unhide the slide, select it and click the Hide Slide button again.

During the presentation, you can right-click any slide, and choose Go ➢ By Title. Then from the shortcut menu, click the slide number that is in parentheses (parentheses around a slide number indicate that it is hidden). However, the shortcut menu is very intrusive and lets everyone know you had a hidden slide (so they may begin to wonder what *else* you're not sharing). Hyperlinks provide a slicker way to show hidden slides.

During the slide show you can display hidden slides by pressing **H** on the keyboard when you're on the slide that directly precedes the hidden slide. The audience is none the wiser when you use this method, but it assumes you're on Slide 14 when you're ready to show hidden Slide 15.

Adding Links to Other Slides

Objectives PP2000.8.5 and PP2000E.2.8

Hyperlinks, like those used to navigate a Web site, can also be used in PowerPoint presentations. Clicking a hyperlink moves the user from the current slide to another slide, another presentation, or a site on the Internet. To create a hyperlink, select the text that you want to use as a hyperlink. Normally, this text tells the user where they're going to end up: `Click Here to Exit the Presentation` or `Click to View More Options`. You don't want to have `Click Here for Hidden Slide`, so select some existing text that forms a logical jumping-off point. With the text selected, right-click and choose Action Settings from the shortcut menu or choose Slide Show ➢ Action Settings from the menu bar to open the dialog box shown in Figure 8.39.

FIGURE 8.39 Action Settings dialog box

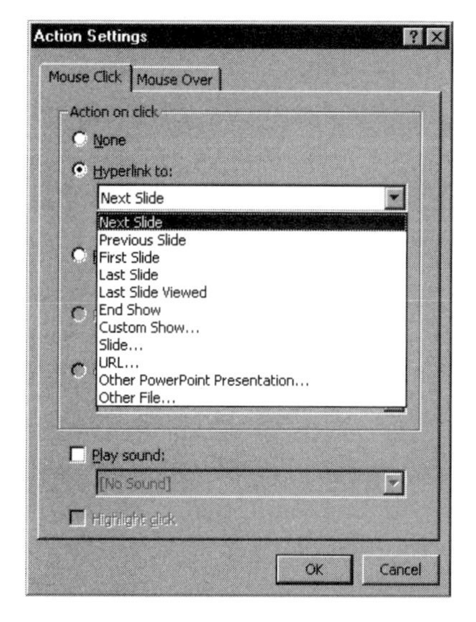

You can activate a hyperlink in two ways: by clicking on it or by moving the mouse over it. Both pages of this dialog box are identical—choose a page based on which mouse action you want to trigger the hyperlink. Click the Hyperlink option, and select the slide you want to link to. Choosing Next

Slide shows the next slide, even if it's hidden. To choose a specific slide, choose Slide from the list to open the Hyperlink to Slide dialog box.

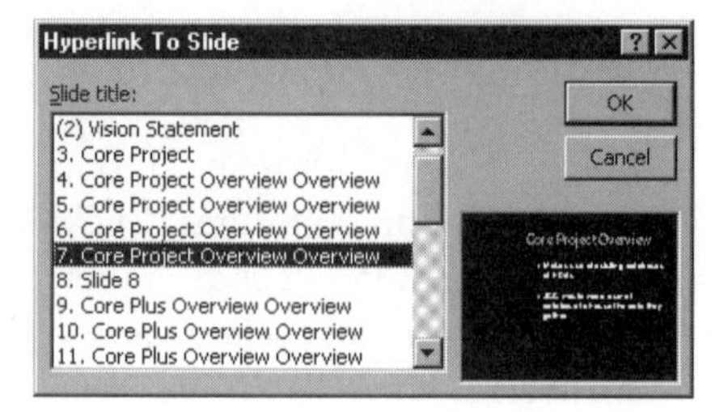

Choose a slide from the list, and then click OK. Click OK in the Action Settings dialog box to create the hyperlink.

Creating a Hyperlink to Another Slide

1. In Slide view, select the text that you want to use as a hyperlink.
2. Choose Slide Show ➢ Action Settings or right-click and choose Action Settings from the shortcut menu.
3. Choose the Hyperlink option. From the Hyperlink drop-down list, select the slide you want to link to. For a specific slide, choose Slide... to open the Hyperlink to Slide dialog box. Select a slide, and then click OK.
4. Choose OK to create the hyperlink.
5. Test the hyperlink in Slide Show view.

When text is turned into a hypertext link, its formatting is changed. The text is underlined, and a contrasting font color is applied. You won't be able to change the color or remove the underlining, but you can apply the same color and underline to surrounding text to make the hyperlink blend in. (Of course, you only want to do this if you're the person running the presentation. Other users won't know it's a hyperlink if it doesn't stand out.)

Creating a Presentation Template

Objective PP2000E.1.3

Companies that have employees regularly using PowerPoint often create templates for different types of presentations. For example, salespeople all use the same general template but customize the outline for the product they're selling. Templates offer a way to ensure that your company's presentations contain the style elements you want them to have: company logo on every slide, consistent background colors, transitions and animations, inclusion of the company mission statement on slide two—you name it!

Start from scratch and create the outline for your template. Include placeholder text on each slide such as "Include three reasons why the client would benefit from the product we're selling" or "Insert a chart showing our market share compared to competitors X, Y, and Z." Apply a design and customize the background as needed. Apply transitions, animations, and other effects. Modify the slide master to include your company logo, if desired.

When you're ready to save, click File ➢ Save As and change the Save As Type control to Design Template (.pot). This changes the Save In location to the Templates folder. Name your template and click Save. To use the template, launch PowerPoint and choose Design Template from the PowerPoint dialog box. You can find the template on the General tab of the New Presentation dialog box.

Hands On: *Objectives PP20008.5, PP2000E.1.3, 2.8, and 2.2*

1. In an existing presentation:
   - a) Hide one or more slides.
   - b) In Slide Show view, display a hidden slide with the shortcut menu.
   - c) Add a hyperlink to the hidden slide.
   - d) In Slide Show view, display the hidden slide by using the hyperlink.
   - e) Create hyperlinks to move to the last slide viewed, the previous slide, a slide that displays data in a chart or table, and then one that enables you to exit the presentation.
   - f) Test the hyperlinks.
2. Start a new presentation and create a template for use in your company.
   - a) Add placeholder text in Outline view.
   - b) Modify the slide master to include graphical bullets of your choice and the company logo in an appropriate place on each slide.
   - c) Apply transitions, animations, and other formatting as desired.
   - d) Save the presentation as a template.

Preparing Handouts

It's often helpful to give your audience paper copies of your slides so that they have something to refer to later. (They might also choose to add their own notes to these handouts.)

Preparing Handouts and Notes

Handouts are pictures of the slides in a presentation, arranged with either two, three, or six slides to a page to give participants a copy of each slide.

The Handout Master

You use the Handout Master to view the handout layouts. Choose View ➢ Master ➢ Handout Master or press Shift and click the Outline View button to open the Master, shown in Figure 8.40.

FIGURE 8.40
Handout Master

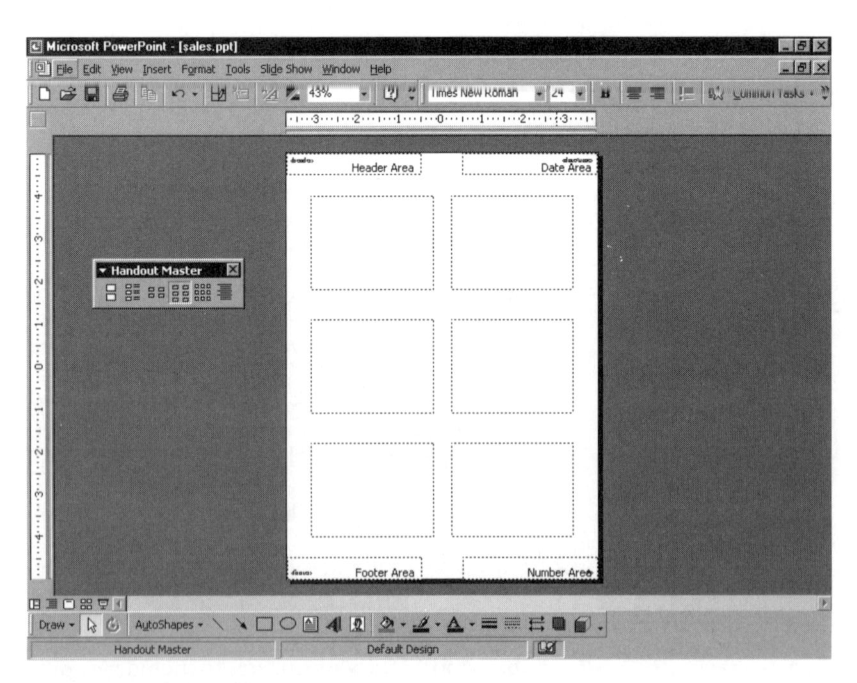

The dotted lines show where slides appear in the layout selected in the Handout Master toolbar. The Handout Master contains areas for the footer, header, and page number. You can click in any of the areas to edit the contents. It's easiest to edit the Master if you change the Zoom ratio to 75% or 100% so you can see the text. Or you can open the Header and Footer dialog box (choose View ➢ Header and Footer) and change settings for any of the areas in the Header and Footer dialog box. The header, footer, number, and date information you enter in the dialog box replaces the appropriate placeholders in the Handout Master when you print handouts.

Changing Output Format

Objective PP2000E.5.3

Slides are generally sized for on-screen shows by default. (An exception would be if you used the AutoContent Wizard to start a presentation and selected Black and White or Color Overheads as your output type.) There may be times, however, when you want to change the type of output you're working with. Let's say you're preparing a packet of supplementary materials for your audience. Wouldn't it be nice to print Slide 1 as a cover for the packet? Easy enough, but the slides are probably set up with a landscape orientation. Printed pages generally require portrait. Change the size and shape of your slides by clicking File ➢ Page Setup from the menu to open the Page Setup dialog box shown in Figure 8.41.

FIGURE 8.41

Page Setup dialog box

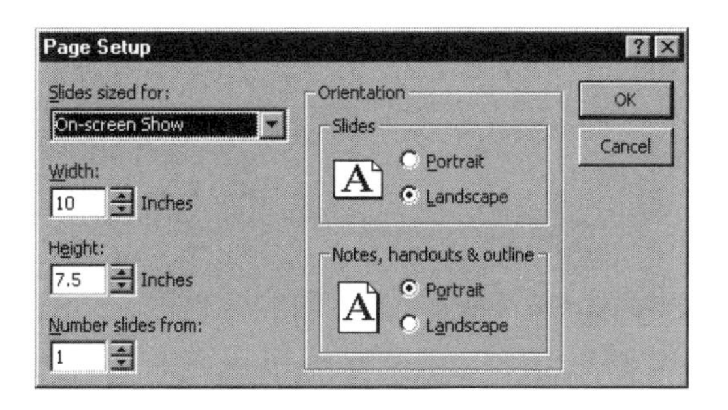

In the Slides Sized For list, select the type of output you need. Select Custom if you want to enter your own dimensions in the Length and Width fields below. Choose an orientation for slides and handouts and choose a different Start At number for slide numbering if desired. Click OK to apply your changes.

Printing in PowerPoint

Clicking the Print button on the Standard toolbar prints the entire presentation in the default setting—usually Slide view. If the slides have a background, this can take up to an hour on an impact printer. In PowerPoint, it's always best to choose File ➢ Print to open the Print dialog box (shown in Figure 8.42) so you can select whether to print slides, handouts, notes, or an outline.

FIGURE 8.42 Print dialog box

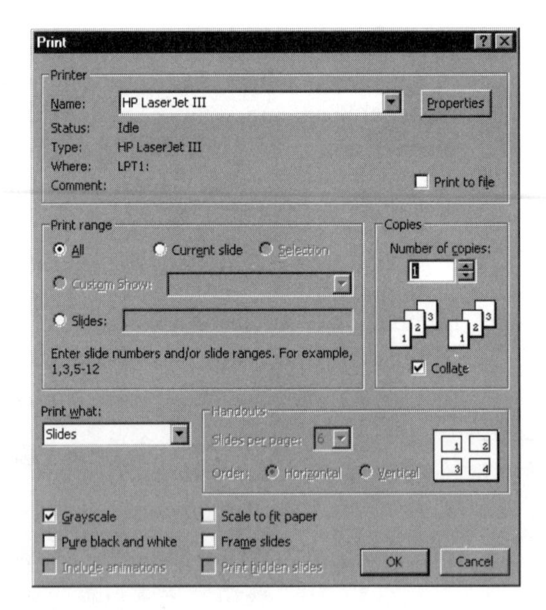

Objectives PP2000.6.2, 6.3, and 6.4

The default print setting is to print all slides. If you just want to print some slides, enter the numbers of the slides in the Slides text box. Choose what you want to print (slides, handouts, an outline, notes pages) in the Print What drop-down. When you choose to print handouts, you have to choose how many slides per page and the order to print them. If you are printing a color presentation on a noncolor printer, click the Grayscale or Black and White control to speed up the printing process. Click the Frame Slides check box to print a simple box around each slide: a good idea if the slides themselves don't include a border. Then click the OK button to print.

Objective PP2000.7.3

To print black-and-white or color transparencies for an overhead projector, simply insert transparency film in your printer, and then print the slides (without animations) using the Print dialog box.

Transparencies look best with clear (white) backgrounds, black text, and occasional splashes of color. Avoid dark backgrounds or graphic-heavy templates more appropriate to on-screen presentations.

Printing in PowerPoint

1. Choose File ➢ Print to open the Print dialog box.
2. In the Print Range area, choose the slides to be printed.
3. In the Print What drop-down list, select whether to print slides, handouts, notes pages, or an outline.
4. Set other print options.
5. Click Print.

Creating Handouts in Word

Objective PP2000E.4.1

You can use the power of Office 2000 integration to create handouts and reports for a PowerPoint presentation in Word. Write-Up transfers the text and/or slides from the current presentation to a Word document, which you can then edit, format, and print. Choose File ➢ Send To ➢ Microsoft Word to open the Write-Up dialog box.

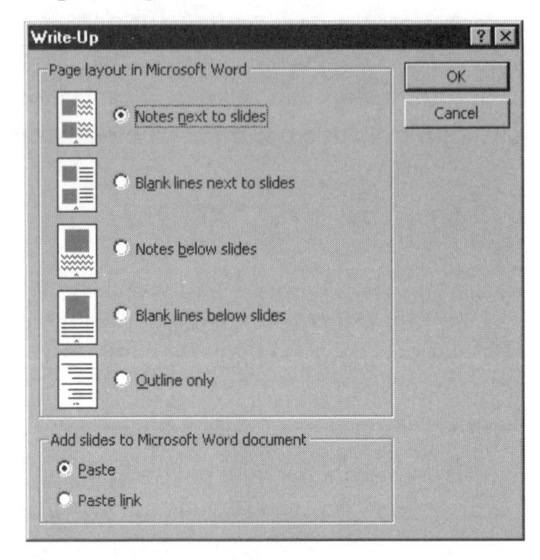

Select how you want the presentation to appear: in one of the four different handout-style layouts or as an outline. Choose whether you want to paste a copy from your presentation or link the Word document to the presentation. If you choose Paste Link, changes to the presentation are updated in the Word document; however, you lose some of the editing flexibility in Word. (See "Chapter 4, Working with Complex Documents" for more on linking.)

When you have selected Page Layout and Paste options, click OK. PowerPoint launches Word and exports your outline or slides. Edit and print the document as you would a Word document. If you sent slides (instead of an outline), don't worry if it takes a few minutes. Each slide is exported as a graphic object, which takes some time.

If you're only transferring an outline, click the Grayscale Preview button on the Standard toolbar before opening the Write-Up dialog box for easier formatting in Word.

Creating PowerPoint Handouts in Word

1. If you intend to "write up" the outline, click the Grayscale Preview button on the Standard toolbar.
2. Choose File ➢ Send To ➢ Microsoft Word to open the Write-Up dialog box.

Creating PowerPoint Handouts in Word *(continued)*

3. Choose a page layout from the Write-Up dialog box.
4. Select Paste Link or Paste.
5. Click OK to launch Word and create the Write-Up document.

Using a PowerPoint Slide as a Graphic

Objective PP2000E.5.1

It's possible you may want to use one slide as a graphic object in a report you were working on in Word. Saving a slide as a graphic is just as easy as saving a presentation. Navigate to the slide you want to use as a graphic and click File ➢ Save As on the menu. In the Save As dialog box, change the Save As Type control to one of the graphic formats (JPEG, BMP, or GIF, for example). Select the drive and folder you want to save the image in, type a file name, and click Save.

Because you are changing the slide format in to a graphic format, you are prompted as to whether you want to export all slides or just the current slide. Click No to export just the current slide to a graphic format. In Word, insert the new graphic file like you would any picture file.

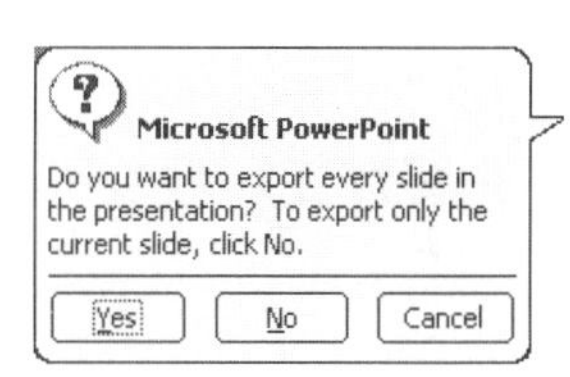

Preparing 35mm Slides and Overhead Transparencies

Objective PP2000E.5.4

If you have a desktop slide printer, you can print your slides as 35mm slides for use in a traditional slide projector. Even if you don't, you can still convert the PowerPoint slides to 35mm. Genigraphics and other service bureaus can take your presentation (or selected slides from it) and convert it to 35mm. To send files to Genigraphics, you use the Genigraphics Wizard. Choose File ➢ Send To ➢ Genigraphics, and the Wizard walks you through packaging the slides. To print black-and-white or color transparencies, simply insert transparency film in your printer, and then print the slides (without animations) using the Print dialog box.

Hands On: Objectives PP2000.6.2, 6.3, 6.4, and PP2000E.4.1, 5.1

1. In an existing presentation:
   a) Add a header and footer for handouts.
   b) Preview the layouts in the Handout Master.
   c) Print handouts with headers and footers.
2. In an existing presentation with notes:
   a) Export the presentation's outline to Word.
   b) Format the outline in Word to create audience handouts.
   c) Export the slides with notes.
   d) Print the outline and handouts in Word.
   e) Save one slide as a graphic and insert it into a Word document.

Taking the Show on the Road

You now have the content, design, formatting, and special effects in place for your presentation. But you're not quite ready for prime time. In this section, we'll look at the remaining tasks that you need to take care of before the curtain goes up.

Setting Slide Timings

Once you have added transitions and animation, you are ready to run through your slides in preparation for the actual presentation. Rehearsal is vital—you'd rather discover problems in private than have them projected to a large audience.

Automated vs. Manual Advance

You can advance an electronic presentation in two ways. If the presentation is designed to run "on its own"—for example, in a booth at a trade show—

you want to advance slides automatically. If your finished presentation will be used to illustrate a verbal presentation, or posted on a company intranet, you will usually prefer to advance slides manually. If you use manual advance, your presentation is essentially completed. You need to rehearse the presentation a few times, making sure that you know how many times to click on each slide to display all the animations.

Setting Automatic Timings

Objective PP2000E.2.13

If you want to use automatic advance, a bit more work is required. You can set slide timings in two ways: through rehearsal, or manually in the Slide Transition dialog box. (You can only enter animation timings by rehearsal.) It's easier to create timings through rehearsal and then alter individual advances manually. Before setting timings, run through the entire slide show two or three times. Make sure that your audience will have time to read the title, read each point, and see how a graphic illustrates the points. It helps to read the contents of each slide out loud, slowly, while rehearsing and setting the timings.

When you are ready to record timings, click the Rehearse Timings button on the Slide Sorter toolbar. The first slide appears, and the Rehearsal dialog box opens.

In the dialog box are two timers. The timer on the right shows the total time for the presentation. The left timer shows the elapsed time for the current slide. The Rehearsal dialog box also contains three buttons: Next, Pause, and Repeat. Click the Next button to move to the next slide or animation. If you are interrupted in the middle of rehearsal, click the Pause button; then click Pause again to resume. If you make a mistake while rehearsing a slide, click Repeat to set new timings for the current slide. If you don't catch a mistake before a slide has been advanced, you can either finish and then edit the slide time manually, or close the dialog box and begin again.

When you complete the entire rehearsal for a presentation, you are prompted to save the timings. Choosing Yes assigns the timings to the slide transitions and animations. In Slide Sorter view, the timing appears below the slide. To edit an individual transition time, select the slide, then click the

Slide Transition button on the Slide Sorter toolbar. The rehearsed time, which you can edit, is displayed in the dialog box.

Rehearsing Slide Timings

1. In Slide Sorter view, click the Rehearse Timings button.
2. Click the Next button in the Rehearse Timings dialog box to advance each transition or animation. Click the Pause button to Pause rehearsal. Click the Repeat button to try new timings for the current slide.
3. At the end of the rehearsal, choose Yes to record the timings or No to discard them.

Incorporating Feedback

Before showing the presentation, it's a good idea to get some feedback from others. PowerPoint lets reviewers add comments to slides that you display or hide, allowing you to keep the comments with the presentation. Comments do not appear in Slide Show view.

To add a comment, in Slide view, choose Insert ➣ Comment from the menu bar. The Review toolbar appears. Begin typing, and the comment, including your name, appears on the slide. Use the comment's handles to move or re-size the comment. Press Delete to delete the selected comment.

To insert a new comment, click the Insert Comment button on the Reviewing toolbar.

The Show/Hide Comments button displays or hides all comments in the presentation.

Inserting a Comment

1. In Slide view, navigate to the slide on which you want to comment then choose Insert ➣ Comment from the menu bar.
2. Begin typing the comment. Click away from it when you're done.
3. Select a comment and use the handles to move or re-size it.
4. Click the Insert Comment button on the Reviewing toolbar to insert another comment.

Objective PP2000E.9.3

Another way to get feedback about your presentation is to use the Online Collaboration feature. To use this feature, you must be connected to a local area network or an intranet, and all participants must have NetMeeting installed and running on their computers. Using NetMeeting, you can share PowerPoint with others who can then edit your presentation.

Collaborating Online

1. Choose Tools ➢ Online Collaboration ➢ Schedule Meeting to open Microsoft Outlook's Appointment form. Complete the form and send it to those you want to invite to the meeting. (See Chapter 10 for information on how to do this.)
2. When the time for the online meeting arrives, choose Tools ➢ Online Collaboration ➢ Meet Now to open the Place a Call dialog box.
3. Enter a name or select it from a list. If necessary, click the Advanced button and type the computer name or network address of the person with whom you want to meet.
4. Click the Call button to place the call.

Customizing Shows for Different Audiences

Objective PP2000E.2.10

Sometimes you need to create multiple versions of the same slide show to present to different audiences. For instance, you might have an East Coast and a West Coast version of the same sales presentation. Both versions use identical slides one through 12, but slides 13–25 are different depending on where the client is located. The versions may differ only slightly, but until now you had to save each as a separate file. In Office 2000 you can create a presentation within a presentation using PowerPoint's new Custom Shows feature. Essentially, you group slides together under a certain name and then display or skip them depending on which version of the show you need for the current audience.

To begin customizing, choose Slide Show ➢ Custom Shows from the menu. The Custom Shows dialog box opens.

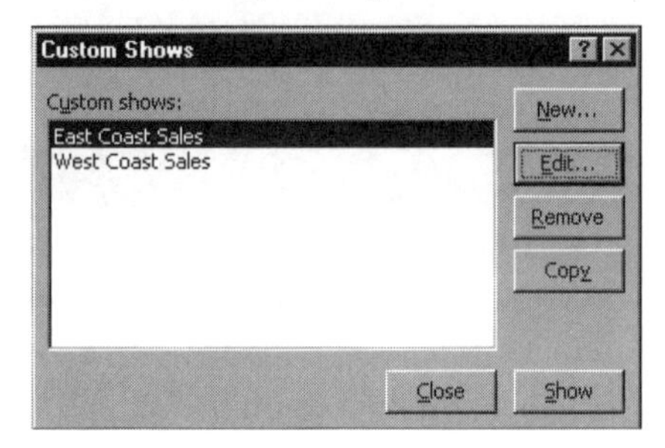

Click New to open the Define Custom Show dialog box.

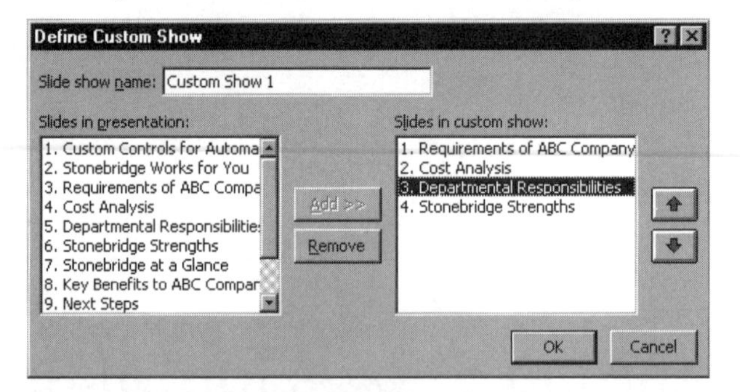

Name your show, overwriting the default of Custom Show 1. Select the slides you wish to include in this version of the show and click Add to move them to the list on the right. If you change your mind and want to remove a slide from the included list, simply select it and click the Remove button.

Use the arrows to change the order of the selected slide. Click OK to finish defining your custom show and return to the Custom Shows dialog box. Your newly defined show is displayed there. Define another custom show using the New button, or edit the selected show by clicking Edit. If you no longer wish to keep a custom show, you can remove it here as well.

During the presentation, you can right-click, choose Go ➢ Custom Show on the shortcut menu, and then click the show you want. However, the shortcut menu is rather intrusive. You may prefer to set up the presentation so it displays the custom version when you start the slide show. (See the next section, *Setting Up the Slide Show*.)

Using Action Buttons

Objective PP2000E.2.11

Action buttons are often used in circumstances where the audience views the show autonomously, such as at a trade show kiosk or on a company intranet. The buttons are of various shapes, such as right and left arrows. They represent commonly understood symbols for going to next, previous, first, and last slides so the person viewing the show can proceed at their own pace.

Once you know how to add a hyperlink, adding action buttons is a snap! Often, you want the same action button on every slide (a Next button, for example.) In this case, put the button on the Slide Master. If you only need the button on a particular slide, then navigate to that slide and click Slide Show ➢ Action Button to see a palette of button choices.

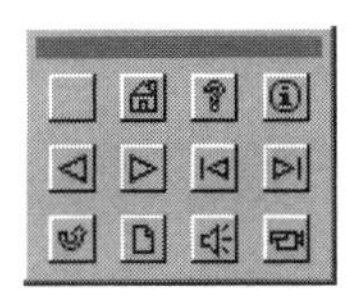

Select the button you want — Forward or Next, Back or Previous, Beginning, End, Document, etc. – by clicking it. Then click the slide to insert the button or drag the button if you want a size other than the default you get when you click the slide. Regardless of whether you click or drag, the Action Settings dialog box appears when you release the mouse. Create the hyperlink following the procedures you learned in the *Adding Links to Other Slides* section of this chapter.

Setting Up the Slide Show

You've designed a good presentation, and the reviewers are raving. Before you present the slide show, choose Slide Show ➢ Set Up Show or hold Shift and click the Slide Show button to open the Set Up Show dialog box, shown in Figure 8.43. In the Show Type area, select a presentation method. In the Advance Slides area, choose Manually or Using timing, if present. To show the presentation continuously, choose Using Timings and click the Loop

Continuously Until 'Esc' check box. In the Slides area, you can choose to show the entire presentation or part of the slides.

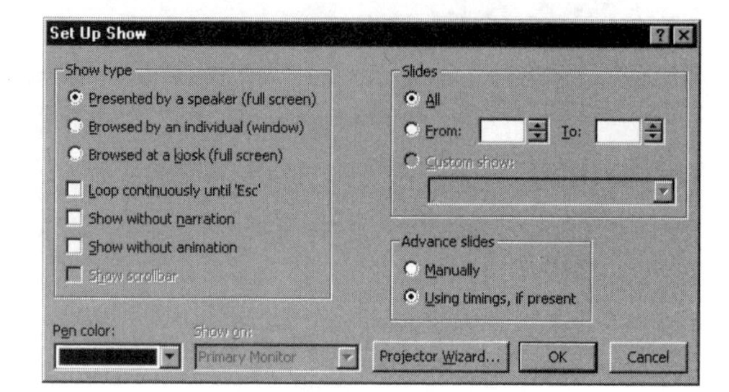

FIGURE 8.43 Set Up Show dialog box

During the presentation, you can use the mouse pointer to draw on the slides to emphasize a point (see *Drawing on Slides* below). You have a choice of colors for the pen. Choose a color that contrasts with both the background and text colors used in the slides.

Setting Up a Slide Show

1. Hold Shift and click the Slide Show button to open the Set Up Show dialog box.
2. Select a presentation method.
3. Select an Advance method and Pen Color.
4. If you want the slide show to run continuously, turn on the Loop Continuously check box.
5. Click OK to save the settings.

The slide show settings are saved with the presentation. Clicking the Slide Show View button runs the slide show with the settings in the Set Up Show dialog box.

When you click on the final slide in a Slide Show, you return to the PowerPoint window. To end on a blank slide, choose Tools ➢ Options to open the Options dialog box. Click the View tab, and then click on End with Black Slide.

It's Showtime!

Objective PP2000.7.2

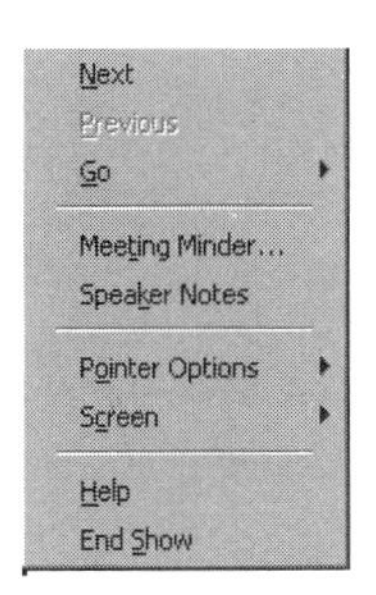

To start the slide show, select the slide you want to begin on and click the Slide Show view button. When the show begins, a shortcut menu button appears in the lower left or lower right corner of the slide. Clicking the button opens a shortcut menu.

You can choose Previous or Next (or use Page Up and Page Down on the keyboard) to move to the previous or next slide. To move to a specific slide, choose Go ➢ Slide Navigator to open the Slide Navigator dialog box. Select a slide to move to, and click Go To. To jump to the first slide quickly, without using the Slide Navigator, hold both mouse buttons down for 2 seconds.

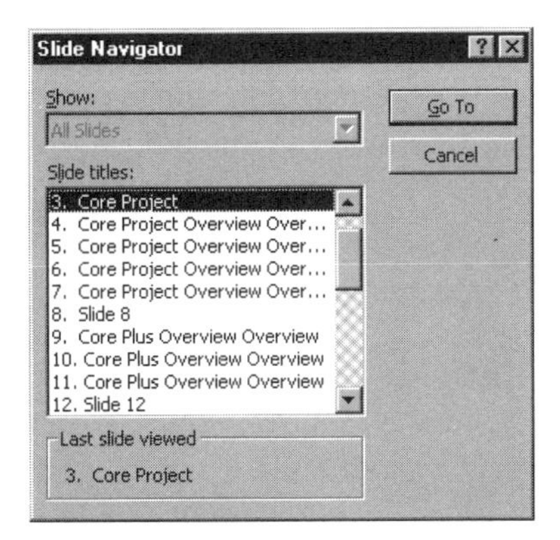

The pop-up menu and Slide Navigator are rather intrusive when giving a presentation. You may prefer to advance slides with a single mouse click anywhere on the slide in Slide Show view.

While you're presenting, you may wish to draw attention away from the screen for a moment. Press either the B or W keys to switch to a black or white screen. Pressing the letter again returns you to the slides.

Generating Meeting Notes

Objectives PP2000E.6.2 and PP2000E.5.2

During the presentation, you can enter minutes or action items in the Meeting Minder. Right-click a slide, and choose Meeting Minder from the shortcut menu to open the Meeting Minder dialog box.

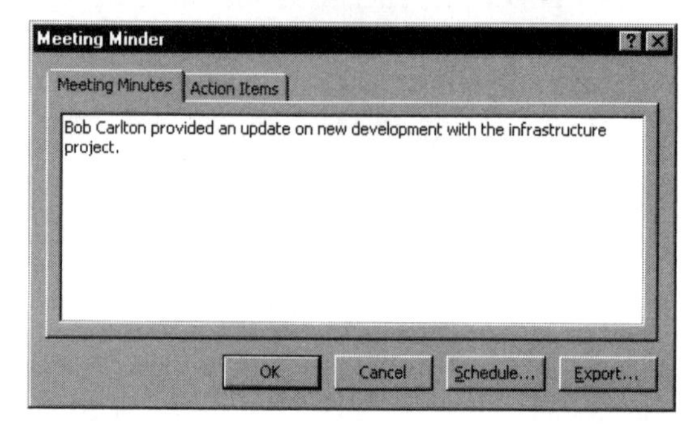

In the Action Items page, enter the "to do" list generated during the meeting, including due dates and the person responsible for the item. If the date or responsible person changes, or if the item is eliminated in later discussion, select the item from the list and edit or delete it.

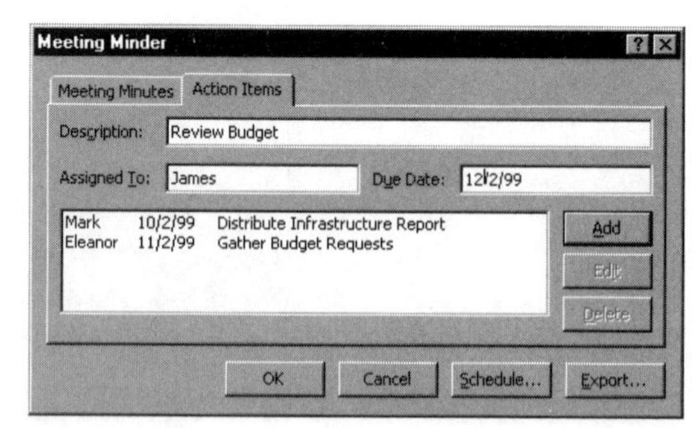

When the presentation is finished, click the Export button to export the minutes to Word, and the action items to Word and/or Outlook.

Drawing on Slides

Objective PP2000.7.4

During the Slide Show, you can use the Pen tool to draw on a slide, underlining or circling an object or text to make a point. Hold Ctrl and press P, or choose Pen from the shortcut menu, and the mouse pointer becomes a pen. Drag to draw on the current slide. Right-click, choose Pointer Options, and choose Arrow, or hold Ctrl and press A on the keyboard to turn the pen off. The drawing isn't saved, so there isn't any damage done to the slide.

Saving a Presentation for Use on Another Computer

Objective PP2000E.6.1

Office 2000 includes a PowerPoint Viewer that you can copy so you can display a presentation on a computer that doesn't include PowerPoint. To bundle your presentation and the viewer in one easy, compressed package, choose File ➢ Pack and Go to launch the Pack and Go Wizard. As you proceed through the Wizard, you are asked to select a presentation, a destination drive, linking and embedding options, and whether the file should include the PowerPoint Viewer.

Objective PP2000E.7.1

If your presentation includes linked objects or fonts that may not appear on the computer used to display the presentation, choose to include linked files and embed fonts.

Saving a Presentation for Use on Another Computer

1. Choose File ➢ Pack and Go from the menu bar. Click Next to advance to the second step.
2. Select the active presentation or another presentation you want to pack, and then click Next.
3. Choose a destination drive and/or folder. Click Next.
4. Turn the object-linking and file-embedding options on or off. Click Next.
5. If the destination computer does not have PowerPoint 2000 installed, include the PowerPoint Viewer. Click Next.
6. Click Finish to create the Pack and Go file and copy it to the selected destination drive. If the file does not fit on one disk, you are prompted to insert additional disks.

Unpacking a Presentation

1. Insert the disk created by Pack and Go.
2. In Windows Explorer, select the drive where the disk is located, and double-click the `pngsetup.exe` file.
3. Enter the destination you want to copy the unpacked presentation and viewer to.
4. To start the Slide Show, double-click the PowerPoint Viewer (`ppview32.exe`), and then click the presentation.

Hands On: Objectives PP2000.7.2, 7.4 and PP2000E2.10, 5.2, 6.1, 6.2, 7.1

1. Using an existing presentation:
   a) Rehearse and record slide timings.
   b) Create a custom show within the presentation. Create an action button to skip to the custom show.
   c) Set up the slide show.
   d) Show the presentation with the timings.
   e) Have a colleague review the timed presentation and add comments.
   f) Using Pack and Go, save the presentation for use on another computer. Embed the presentation's fonts and include linked files.
2. With an existing, rehearsed presentation, give a presentation to a couple of friends or colleagues. During the presentation:
   a) Use the Meeting Minder to record minutes and at least one action item.
   b) Draw on a slide to underline a point.
   c) Use the Slide Navigator to return to a previous slide.
   d) After the presentation, export the minutes and action items to Word.

CHAPTER 9

Tracking Data with Access

In this chapter, you'll learn about creating and using Access databases. We assume that you're a knowledgeable Windows user and have experience with sorting and filtering in Excel or another database. If you haven't worked with sorting and filtering, see Chapter 6. If you are new to Office 2000, you may want to review Chapter 1 then return here to work in Access 2000.

Designing and Creating a Database

A *database* is a collection of information about groups of items or individuals. Database structure is provided by *fields*—categories of information. For example, a telephone directory is a printout from a database. Fields in a telephone directory include last name, first name, middle initial, address, and telephone number. Each entry in the database for one individual (a last name, first name, middle initial, address, and telephone number) is called a *record*.

Simple database programs only allow you to work with one list of information at a time: one set of fields and records. More capable programs like Access let you group multiple lists together and relate lists to each other, creating a type of database called a *relational database*. In a relational database, each list is stored in a separate *table*; for example, a training course database might have a table listing classes offered, another table of information about trainees, and a third table that lists instructor information.

Designing Your Database

Before you begin constructing the database, you need to spend some time designing the database. A bad design virtually ensures that you'll spend time needlessly reworking the database. Database developers often spend as much time designing a database as they do constructing it. To design a database, you should follow these steps:

1. Determine the need or purpose of the database.
2. Decide what kinds of things (tables) the database should include to produce the desired output.
3. Specify the fields that comprise the tables and determine which fields in each table contain unique values.
4. Construct and relate the tables and populate the database with sample data.
5. Create forms, reports, queries, and Data Access Pages to use with the data.

Determining Need or Purpose

Every database begins with a problem that can be solved or a need that can be met by creating a data-tracking system. You might, for example, need to keep track of certain data about customers. Focus on the outcome you want to achieve: what will the database allow you to do better than you do now? Send mailings to existing customers? Track orders? Study current customers to identify characteristics to help identify potential customers? You could create a database for any of these needs, and each would be different.

Objective AC2000.1.2

Every piece of data that comes out of the database on a report or form needs to be included in the database. Talk with other potential users to determine what the output of the database needs to be. If you're replacing part or all of a manual system, look at the output you already create, for example: merged letters, labels, reports, and other documents. Determine any additional information that needs to be provided from the system.

Organize the information about data output requirements in an Access table, an Excel worksheet, or even a Word table. You'll add columns to this table later, so we generally do this work in Excel where we can easily insert rows and columns and sort the information in the table. For each field, list a name for the field, description, output (the name or description of a report, for example), and a contact for further information. Table 9.1 shows several rows of a sample table.

TABLE 9.1: Sample Data Output Requirements

Field Contents	Description	Output	Contact
first name	customer's first name	1. customer reports 2. mailing labels 3. promotions	1, 2. A. Marquis, 5/27/99 3. K. Browning, 5/27/99
last name	customer's last name	1. customer reports 2. mailing labels 3. promotions	1, 2. A. Marquis, 5/27/99 3. K. Browning, 5/27/99
street address	customer's address	1. mailing labels 2. promotions	1, 2. A. Marquis, 5/27/99 3. K. Browning, 5/27/99
postal code	customer's postal code	1. customer reports 2. mailing labels 3. promotions 4. order demographics	1, 2. A. Marquis, 5/27/99 3. K. Browning, 5/27/99 4. S. Roberts, 6/3/99

Objective AC2000.1.1

Every field on your list of data outputs must have a corresponding data input. Table 9.1, for example, includes fields for a customer's first and last names, so there is (or needs to be) a means of collecting this data about a customer: an input source. Input source and input method are intertwined; the source (for example, an order form) is where the data comes from, the method (for example, typing) is how it is added to your database.

Manually keying data from a paper form should be the input method of last resort – it's error prone as well as tedious. Only genuinely new data should be typed into your database. Here are some alternatives:

- If data that changes infrequently already exists in a usable form, you can *import* it from another data source. For example, you don't need to type in the list of U.S. zip codes, cities, and states: it's widely available in several formats that Access can import.

- You can *link* to data (like current prices) that changes frequently that is updated elsewhere in your organization. There's information about linking and importing later in this chapter.
- Investigate *source data capture* hardware: wands and guns for bar codes, scanners and OCR software for forms, and specialized software like Corex CardScan for business cards.
- Some output fields might be *calculated* from other fields in your database. For example, if you know an item's unit cost, you can calculate the total cost for the items in a customer order by multiplying the quantity ordered by the unit cost. Unit cost and quantity are the data inputs for the total cost field.

Deciding What Should Be Included

A customer database generally includes fields such as customers, items that can be ordered, shipping options, sales representatives, payment options, and actual order data. Each of these units is an *entity*. Each entity you include becomes a table in the database: a table for customers, another table for sales representatives, a third table for orders. The information about one individual or item appears in only one table. It would be redundant to keep the first name, last name, and address of the customer in each of their orders. Customer data belongs in a customers table, and order information belongs in an orders table. When the customer moves, you only have to change their address once in the customers table, not in every order they've placed.

Objective AC2000.1.3

Determining Table Fields

After you've identified the database entities, review your field list and determine what fields should be included in each entity's table. Review all the fields to make sure that they are *atomic*, that is, that you will be storing data in its smallest logical components. Store street address, city, state, and zip code separately, rather than in one big field, so that you can find all the customers in one state or zip code later on. It is a database convention that field names do not include spaces (even though Access allows it) and that the initial letter of each word is capitalized. Field names should be descriptive, for example, OrderDate, and should not be ambiguous: CustomerFirstName and SalesRepFirstName rather than FirstName for both of these fields.

Each field has a data type: the kind of information that can be stored in the field. Table 9.2 lists the Access 2000 data types. Text is the least restrictive type; you can enter a date in a text field, but Access won't allow you to enter non-date text in a Date/Time field.

TABLE 9.2: Access 2000 Data Types

Data Type	Description
Text (default)	Words or non-value numbers (such as phone numbers and social security numbers)
Memo	Open field used for comments; cannot be sorted or filtered
Number	Numbers, or integers, that are negative or positive values
Date/Time	Dates, times, and combinations of the two
Currency	Numbers in the Windows currency type (dollars in U.S.)
AutoNumber	Numeric field automatically entered by Access, used as a primary key when none of the fields in a table is unique
Yes/No	Boolean (logical) field that can have only one of two values
OLE Object	An object such as a picture or document created in another application
Hyperlink	URL or UNC address

If you're documenting your design in Excel, insert or append columns to your worksheet to record the name and data type for each field. When you're finished entering names and data types, copy the fields for each table to a separate worksheet in your workbook in preparation for creating your tables.

Identifying Primary Keys and Relationships

In a relational database, tables are connected to each other by unique fields: a field or combination of fields with values that occur only once in a table. A social security number, for example, uniquely identifies one living person. A field or combination of fields that uniquely identifies a specific record in a table is called a *primary key*. Other common primary key fields are the item number in a catalog, an employee ID, and a UPC for retail products. In a relational database, every table must have a primary key. If you can't identify one from the fields in the table, you can add a field that Access automatically enters unique values into.

After you've planned the tables and before you begin constructing tables and typing names and social security numbers, re-examine the tables and fields in your database. When you're convinced that the design is well conceived, you're ready to create tables in Access 2000.

Creating the Database

Objective AC2000.2.1

The first time the Access 2000 application window opens, you immediately see the Office Assistant and the Access dialog box. The Assistant offers help while you work in Access. If you want Clippit or the character you've chosen to disappear, right-click and choose Hide. (See Chapter 1 for more information on working with the Office Assistant.) In the Access dialog box, you can create a new blank database, create a database with help from a wizard, or open an existing database.

Objective AC2000.2.5

The Access 2000 Database Wizard lets you quickly create a database by customizing one of the predesigned databases that come with Access. If a database you want to create is already in the list, you can use the Wizard: choose the Access Wizards, Pages, and Projects option then click OK. The New dialog box opens so you can select the template for the database you want to start with. If you're creating a database from scratch, as we will in our example, choose Blank Database and click OK.

Enter a filename and location for the database in the File New Database dialog box. Databases must be saved before you begin creating tables. Access 2000 databases get very large very quickly; save your database on a hard drive or a large removable disk, not a floppy disk. Once you've saved the database, the Database window, shown in Figure 9.1, opens. The Database window has an icon on the Objects bar for each type of object that can be included in an Access database. Access 2000 databases include seven types of objects: tables, forms, reports, queries, macros, Visual Basic modules, and data access pages.

When you name objects, we suggest that you follow the *Leszynski/Reddick* (L/R) naming convention so that your databases are easily understood by other designers. In the L/R convention, an object name begins with a tag that identifies the kind of object it is: `tbl (table)`, `frm (form)`, `rpt (report)`, `qry (query)`, `mcr (macro)`. There are no spaces or punctuation in object names, and the first letter of each word other than the tag is capitalized. For example, a table of customer orders might be named `tblOrders`; a query showing order details might be called `qryOrderDetails`.

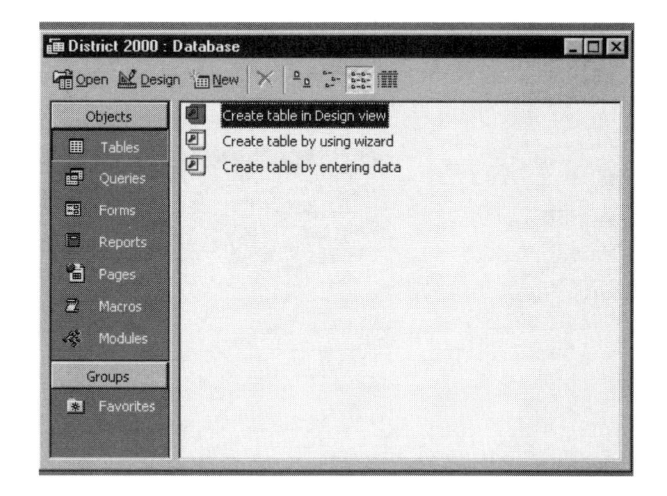

FIGURE 9.1 The Access 2000 database window

Creating a Table Using the Table Wizard

Objective AC2000.2.2

Click the Tables button on the Database Window's Objects bar to open the Tables page of the Database window. Then click the New button in the Database window to open the New Table dialog box, which lists five ways to create a table:

- In Datasheet view, by entering field names at the top of each column.
- In Design view, where you list field names and properties for each field.
- With the help of the Table Wizard, which includes suggested field lists for over 100 tables.
- By importing a table created from another database or spreadsheet.
- By linking (connecting to) a table that exists in another database.

We'll create our first table using the Table Wizard. There are two advantages to using the wizard. You start from sample tables, so you will have an opportunity to add fields to your design. More importantly, some of the fields will have additional properties set. For example, when you choose a telephone number field, the field automatically includes the parentheses and hyphen used to format a phone number. The first step of the Table Wizard is shown in Figure 9.2.

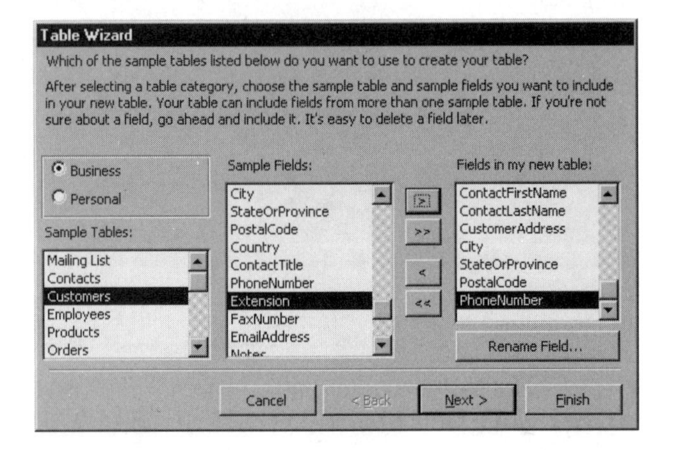

FIGURE 9.2 Use the Table Wizard to select a table and fields.

Objectives AC2000.3.1 and AC2000.3.2

Creating a Table Using the Table Wizard

1. Select Create Table by Using Wizard and click either Open or Design, or double-click Create Table by Using Wizard to open the New Table Wizard.
2. Choose either Business or Personal to display tables you're likely to include in your database.
3. Select a table that closely resembles the table you want to create from the list of Sample Tables.
4. Use the pick buttons to move fields from the Sample Fields list to the Fields In My New Table List. Select the primary key field(s) first, and the remaining fields in the order you want them to appear in the new table. You may select Sample Fields from more than one Sample Table.

Creating a Table Using the Table Wizard *(continued)*

5. To rename a field, select the field in the Fields In My New Table List then click the Rename button. Enter a unique name for the field in the Rename Field dialog box, then click OK.
6. When all fields are selected and renamed, click Next.
7. In the next step of the wizard, enter a name for the table. Click Next.
8. If there are existing tables, you'll be prompted to define a relationship between the new table and existing tables. Confirm the suggested relationships or click the Relationships button to open the Relationships window and identify relationships for this table. Click Next.
9. Choose the No, I'll Set the Primary Key option. Click Next.
10. Select your primary key field. Choose the option that describes the type of data that will be entered in the field. Click Next.
11. Choose an option to have Access open the table for modification, open the table for data entry, or create a form for data entry after the table is created.
12. Click Finish.

OR

9. If you cannot identify a primary key field and want Access to create an additional field, choose Yes, Set a Primary Key for Me. Click Next.
10. Choose an option to have Access open the table for modification, open the table for data entry, or create a form for data entry after the table is created. (You can discard the form later if you wish.)
11. Click Finish.

Access creates the table and, optionally, a form, then opens the table or form as you've specified in the last step of the Wizard. To close the table or form, choose File ➢ Close or click the Close button on the form or table. When you close the form, you are prompted to name and save it, or discard it.

Creating and Modifying a Table in Design View

Objectives AC2000.3.4 and 3.5

When you create a table in Design View, you start with a blank slate. In the Design View window, shown in Figure 9.3, begin by entering a name for the first field in your table. The Data Type indicates the kind of data that can be entered in the field (see Table 9.2 earlier in this chapter). Click the Data Type drop-down list to select a type. (We'll look at the last item on this list, Lookup Wizard, later in this section.) Select a data type for the field, and enter a Description for the field if the name isn't descriptive enough. Press Enter to drop to the next blank row and enter the information for the next field. Continue until all fields are entered.

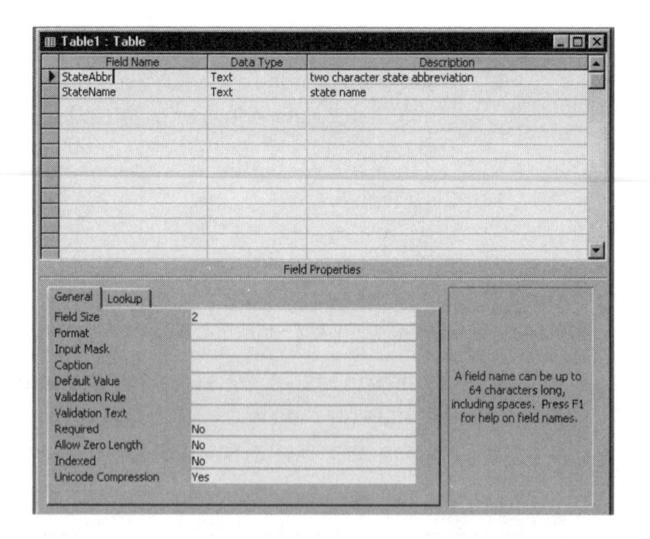

FIGURE 9.3
In Design View, enter field names, types, and descriptions for table fields.

Setting Primary Keys

Objective AC2000.3.2

To set the key, select the row selector(s) to the left of the Field Name column for the field or fields that will serve as the primary key. Right-click and choose Primary Key from the shortcut menu, or click the Primary Key button on the toolbar.

If a single field can't serve as a primary key, look at a combination of two fields that are, in combination, unique. For example, in a student registration table, neither the class number nor the student ID could be a primary key, since either could occur several times in the registration table. However, if a student could only sign up once for a class, you could use both the student ID and class number fields as the table's primary key. If no combination of fields are suitable, then add an AutoNumber field for a primary key. AutoNumber fields are, by definition, always unique.

Setting Field Properties

Objective AC2000.3.3

Every field has properties that control how the field's contents are displayed, stored, controlled, or validated. Some properties are common to all fields, and some properties are only relevant to particular data types. In Table Design view, the field's properties are shown at the bottom of the window. The field properties for the PhoneNumber field in `tblCustomers` (which we created using the Table Wizard) are shown in Figure 9.4.

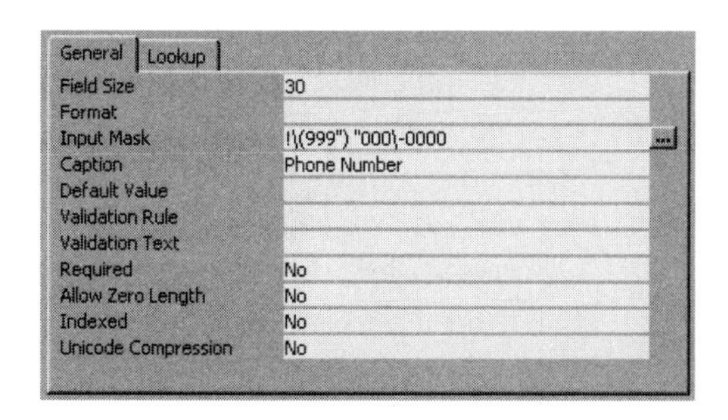

FIGURE 9.4 Properties set by the Table Wizard for the PhoneNumber field

All field types except AutoNumber and OLE Object have the following general properties:

Format How the field's contents will be displayed.

Caption The default label attached to the field on a form or report.

Default Value The value for new entries.

Validation Rule A range of acceptable entries.

Validation Text Message displayed when invalid data is entered.

Required Indicates whether the field must have an entry.

The following general properties apply primarily to text fields:

Field Size The maximum number of characters allowed in the field.

Input Mask Formats data entered in the field.

Allow Zero Length Yes/No setting that determines whether a text string with no length ("") is a valid entry.

Indexed Creates an index to speed sorting, searching, and filtering the field's contents. The primary key for a table is always indexed. You should index fields that will be frequently sorted for reports or forms.

Unicode Compression Unicode is an encoding scheme capable of encoding every known character; every character is represented by two bytes instead of one. When this property is set to Yes, Access compresses any character whose first byte is 0 when it is stored and uncompresses it when it is retrieved to optimize database performance.

Number and Currency fields have one additional general property: Decimal Places, which specifies the number of digits that will be displayed and stored after the decimal. To change a property, click in the property's textbox and enter a value or select from a list. The Caption property, for example, is easy to change and will save you lots of time later, because every form and report that you create will use the caption from the table to label the field. If you don't specify a caption, then Access uses the field name.

Access includes builders to help with more complex properties, like input masks. *Input masks* are formats for data entry like the parentheses and hyphen in a telephone number.

Setting Input Masks

Objectives AC2000.3.7 and AC2000E.1.3

To set an input mask, click the Input Mask property box, then click the Build button that appears at the right end of the property box (see Figure 9.4) to open the Input Mask Wizard. (You are required to save the table first.) In the first step of the Wizard, select the type of input mask you want to add to the field, then click Next.

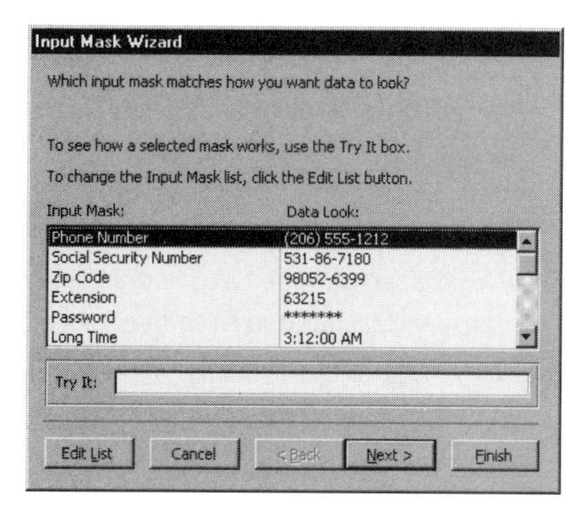

If you wish, you can modify the input mask by typing or deleting characters in the Input Mask text box. (See Access 2000 Help for a list of valid input mask characters.) Select the placeholder that will appear where the user should enter text, and click Next.

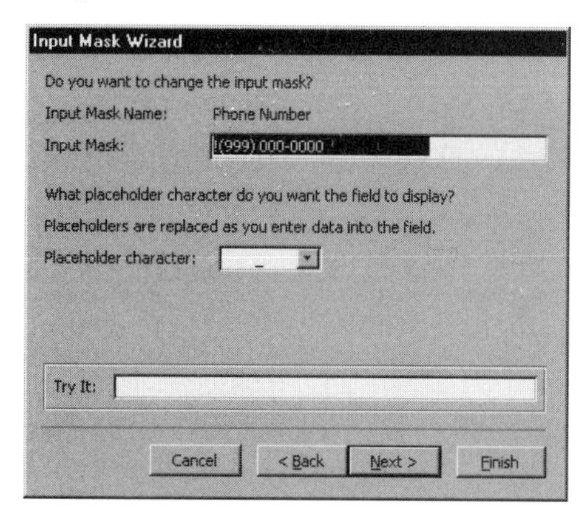

Choose whether you want the data stored with or without the input mask. Storing the data with the input mask makes the database file larger but preserves the format for reports. Click Finish to close the Input Mask Wizard and add the input mask to the field's Properties. See the Phone Number input mask in Figure 9.4.

If you have a custom format that you use multiple times in a database, click Edit List in the first step of the Input Mask Wizard and add the format to the list of Input Masks.

When you've entered all the fields and set the primary key and field properties, click the Datasheet View button or choose View ➢ Datasheet View to switch to the table's Datasheet view. You are prompted to save the table. Choose Yes. Enter a name for the table in the Table Name dialog box. If you forgot to assign a primary key, a warning appears. Click Cancel, assign a primary key, then save.

Databases include two distinct types of tables: those that include primary data and those that hold lists of values used in other tables. These supporting tables are called *lookup tables* and are named using a tlkp tag. We'll save the table we created in Figure 9.3 as tlkpStates and use it as a lookup table later in this chapter.

Creating a Table in Design View

1. Select Tables in the Object bar and click the New button in the Database window

   OR

1. Choose Insert ➢ Table from the menu.
2. In the New Table dialog box, choose Design view and click OK.
3. In Design view, enter the field name and data type for each field.
4. Select a field or fields to designate as a primary key, and click the Primary Key button on the toolbar or right-click and choose Primary Key from the shortcut menu.
5. Save the table. Enter a unique table name when prompted.

We'll return to tables and table properties later in this chapter. First, we'll enter data in the tables we have already created.

Entering Data in a Table

Objectives AC2000.5.2 and 5.3

To switch between views in Access 2000, use the View button and its drop down menu, or open the View menu and select from the list of views. When you change to a different view, the toolbars change to correspond to the view you are in, so don't be surprised if a toolbar looks different when you switch from Design to Datasheet view. Datasheet view (see Figure 9.4) looks much like a spreadsheet, and skills that you've learned with Excel 2000 will serve you well here.

Entering Records in Datasheet View

1. Open the table you want to use. If you are not in Datasheet view, click the Datasheet View button or choose View ➢ Datasheet.
2. Begin typing data in the first field. Press Tab to move to the next field. Continue entering field information and pressing Tab until you reach the end of the record. Press Tab again to start another record.

The table columns are all the same default width, so some of the field data, like addresses, don't fit in the column. Maximizing the window displays more of the data, and you can adjust the widths of individual columns. Move the mouse pointer between the column headings. When the pointer changes to a column adjustment tool, drag or double-click. When you close the table, you are asked if you want to save the layout changes made when you adjusted the columns.

Objective AC2000.2.4

Move around in the datasheet using the arrow keys on the keyboard and pan the width of the table with the horizontal scroll bar at the bottom of the screen. The vertical scroll bar at the right screen edge moves up and down through the datasheet. (Scroll bars only appear when there is data that cannot be viewed within the current window.) The navigation buttons at the bottom of the screen are used to move to the first, previous, next, last, or a new record, and appear in forms as well as in Datasheet View.

Adding Objects to Records

An Access database isn't limited to typed entries. The OLE Object data type allows you to store different types of objects in a database. OLE stands for Object Linking and Embedding, and you can store a variety of objects in an OLE field: for example, you could include graphics, pictures, sounds, or

Word documents. A customers table could include pictures of customers or their company's logo.

You can't just type an OLE object; you have to insert it. During data entry or editing, right-click in the OLE field in the record, and choose Insert Object to open the Insert Object dialog box. You can create an object to place in the field by choosing Create New. If the object already exists on a local or network hard drive, choose Create from File. Click the Browse button, and locate the OLE object file. If you want the object in the database to be updated if the disk file changes, choose Link. If, instead, you want a copy of the object in the database, don't choose Link, and the object will be embedded in the database. Click OK to insert the file in the OLE object database field. The object, the object's type (Word document, WAV file), or an icon representing the object appears in the field. If the type or icon is displayed, double-click on it to open the object in its native format. For example, a Word document will open in Word; a sound or video file will open the Windows Sound or Media Player and begin to play.

Modifying and Deleting Data in a Table

To edit data, move the pointer over the field you want to edit; the pointer changes to an I-beam, and when you click in the field, an insertion point appears. Double-click the I-beam to select a single word then type over a word. To select and overtype the entire field, move the pointer to the left edge of the field then click.

Objective AC2000.5.5

To delete a record, click the Record Selector to the left of the record's first field to select the entire record, then press the Delete key on the keyboard or click the Delete Record button on the toolbar. (Drag on the Record Selectors or hold Shift and click to select consecutive records to delete.) Or, right-click on the Record Selector and choose Delete Record from the shortcut menu. You are prompted to confirm the deletion. When you are finished entering or modifying table data, close the table. If you have changed table layout, you are prompted to save the changes. You aren't prompted to save the data you entered; each record was saved as you entered it.

Printing in Access 2000

Objective AC2000.2.3

Preview and print data (records) anywhere you can see it—in a table, in a query, form, or report—as it is presented. If you're in the Datasheet view of a table with 1000 records and you click the Print button or choose File ➢ Print, Access starts chugging out the table and won't stop until all 1000 records, about 20 pages, have been printed. If you only want to print the first 100 records, select the records, then choose File ➢ Print and select the Selected Records option. If you print from a form, the records appear in the form, complete with the form's background and labels. You can print an object's data from the Database window, too. Select the table, query, report, or form you want to print, then choose Print Preview or Print from the toolbar, File menu, or shortcut menu.

You can't print the Design view of a database object this way. When you're in Design view, the Print and Print Preview buttons and commands are disabled. To print information about a table or other object including fields and properties, you use an analysis tool called the Database Documenter: Tools ➢ Analyze ➢ Documenter.

Hands On: Objectives AC2000.1.3, 2.2, 2.3, 2.4, 2.5, 3.1, 3.2, 3.4, 3.5, 3.7, 5.2, and 5.5

1. Create a database using the Database Wizard.

   a) Using the Object bar in the Database window, open and close each of the tables in Datasheet view.

   b) Open one of the tables in Design view. Examine the properties of each field then switch to Datasheet view.

   c) Switch back to Design view and add a phone, fax, or social security number field to the table. Create an input mask for the field.

   d) Switch to Datasheet view and enter a new record to test the input mask.

   e) Return to Design view and delete the field you added.

2. Identify a database that would be useful in your work or personal life.
   a) Identify tables and fields, field types, and a primary key for each table.
   b) Create the table you feel is most central to your database. Make sure the table has a primary key. Close and save the table.
   c) Open the table from the Database window. Enter two or three sample records in the table.
   d) Print the table.
   e) Delete the second sample record.
3. Your company's Human Resources Department needs a database to track employee data and the results of employees' annual evaluations. Design the database and create tblEmployees using the Table Wizard.

Setting Table Relationships

Objective AC2000.1.4

Relationships tie the database tables together using primary keys. In a relational database, tables are related in one of three ways that reflect the relationships between the tables' entities in the real world. The three types of relationships are called one to one, one to many, and many to many, and you'll use primary keys to model the relationship in your database.

In a *one-to-one relationship*, one record in table A is related to no more than one record in table B, and one record in table B is related to no more than one record in table A. Generally, this means that you could have had one large table, but chose to separate it into two tables because there's a clear division in the types of data you'll store in the table. For example, you have an employees table with fields relevant to a person's employment. However, some of your employees are interns or co-op students, and you need to store additional, school-specific information about those employees. You might choose to create both tblEmployees and tblCoOpEmployees. If two tables have a one-to-one relationship, give them the same primary key.

In the more common *one-to-many relationship*, one record in table A can be related to many records in table B, but one record in table B will refer to only one record in table A. For example, one customer can place many orders, but an order is placed by only one customer. If two tables have a one-to-many relationship, the primary key from the one table (table A) is included in the many table (table B) to tie the two tables together. In our example, the primary key from tblCustomers will be included in tblOrders.

A *many-to-many relationship* means that a record in table A can be related to many records in table B, and a record in table B can be simultaneously related to many records in table A. For example, a student can enroll in multiple classes and a class can have many students. Access doesn't allow you to create many-to-many relationships directly. But these relationships abound in real data. If two tables have a many-to-many relationship, create a linking table whose primary key is the primary keys from the two tables. In the example above, a linking table (probably named tblRegistrations) will include the primary keys from tblStudents and tblClasses.

When you include a primary key from one table in another, it's called a *foreign key*. The foreign key field in the related table must have the same data type as the primary key in the primary table—with one exception. If the primary key uses an AutoNumber data type, then the foreign key field must use the Number type.

There are three ways to create relationships in Access 2000: by placing a lookup field in a table, by assigning a relationship in the Table Wizard, or by creating the relationship directly in the Relationships window.

Creating a Lookup Field

Objective AC2000.3.6

Lookup fields help the user and the designer by providing a list of choices that restrict and standardize data entry. For example, when users enter a state, you may want to restrict their choices to the two-letter state abbreviations. If you provide the list, then users don't have to look up (or worse, make up) the abbreviations. And there's one more benefit: when you create a lookup field that uses values from another table like the tlkpStates table we created earlier in this chapter, Access also creates the one-to-many relationship between the two tables.

With a lookup field, the user clicks a drop-down arrow and chooses a value from a list rather than typing the state abbreviation. The list can come from a table or from a list you enter when you create the field. If the list of possible entries for a field is short and doesn't change much, you might prefer to create a lookup based on a typed-in list of values rather than a table. For example, if one of the fields in a table is Gender, you might just type in a list of values. It's a short list that's not likely to change a lot.

Creating a Lookup Field with a Typed-in List

1. Open the table that you want to create the lookup field in.
2. Enter the field name.
3. Choose Lookup Wizard as the data type.
4. In the first step of the Lookup Wizard, indicate that you will type in the values.
5. In the second step, choose the number of columns that should be included, then enter data in each column.

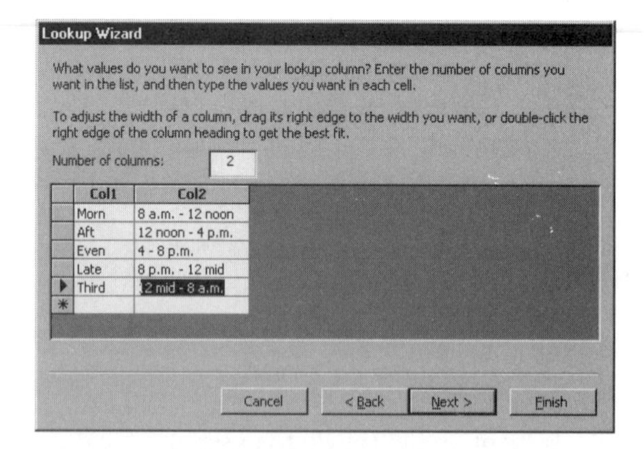

6. Adjust the column width(s). Click Next.
7. If you have more than one column, choose the column that contains the data you want to store in the table. Click Next.
8. Enter a label for your lookup field, and click Finish.

Longer lists, lists used in more than one table, and lists that change should be based on a table where you can more easily change the values. You must create the lookup table before you can use the table to create a lookup field in another table.

Creating a Lookup Field Using a Table

1. Open the table that you want to create the lookup field in.
2. Enter the field name.
3. Choose Lookup Wizard as the data type.
4. In the first step of the Lookup Wizard, indicate that you will use values from a table or query. Click Next.
5. In the second step, choose the table or query that will supply the values. Click Next.
6. In the third step, use the pick buttons to select, in order, the field(s) to include in the lookup. One of the fields should be the primary key for the table you selected in the second step. Click Next.
7. In the fourth step, choose to hide or display the key column. Adjust the column widths, then click Next.
8. Enter a label for your lookup field, and click Finish.
9. Save the table.

When you click Finish, the field changes to the appropriate data type and Access creates the relationship between the two tables.

Working with Relationships

Objective AC2000.6.1

To look at the relationship Access created, choose Tools ➢ Relationships to open the Relationships window, shown in Figure 9.5. (There may be a number of relationships already defined depending on how many lookups you've created.) Primary keys are bolded in each table. Click the Show All Relationships button to make sure all the relationships are displayed.

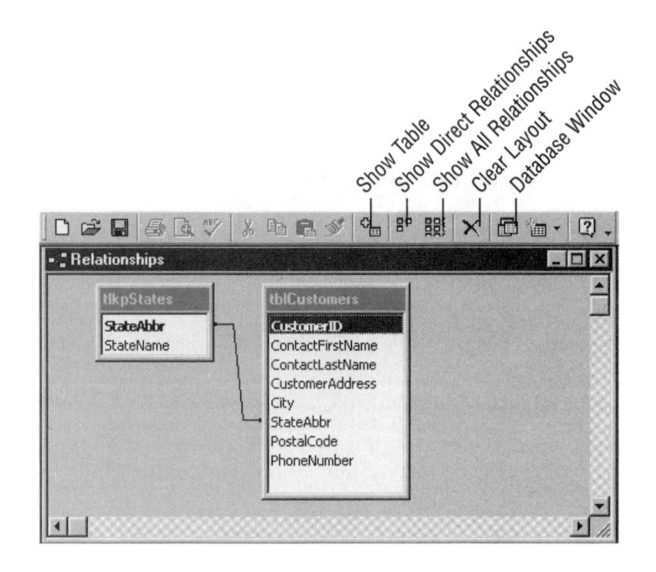

FIGURE 9.5
The Relationships window shows tables and relationships.

To create a new relationship, first click the Show Tables button or right-click in an empty area of the window and choose Show Tables to open the Show Tables dialog box. Select a table you want to add to the window then click Add. When you're finished adding tables, click Close to close the Show Table dialog box.

Creating a One-to-Many Relationship

If you haven't added the foreign key field in the many table, right-click on the table and choose Table Design to open the table in Design view. Add the field, then close and save the table to return to the Relationships window. To create a new one-to-many relationship, drag the primary key from the one table (the table where it is the primary key) and drop it on its corresponding foreign key field in the many table.

After you drop the field, the Edit Relationships dialog box opens. You can open the dialog box for an existing relationship by double-clicking the relationship's line. The primary table and primary key are shown in the left column, and the related table and foreign key are displayed in the second column. The relationship between tblCustomers, which includes a lookup field, and the tlkpStates table used in the lookup is shown in Figure 9.6

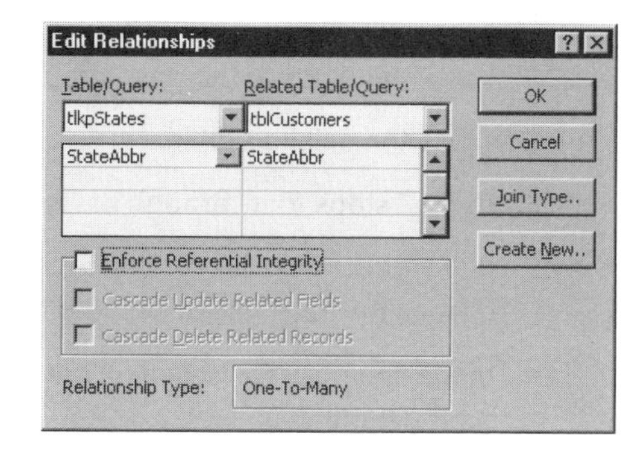

FIGURE 9.6 The Edit Relationships dialog box provides detail about the relationship.

Creating a One-to-One Relationship

Objective AC2000E.5.1

To create a new one-to-one relationship, drag the primary key from the primary table and drop it on the primary key of the related table.

Creating a Many-to-Many Relationship

Objective AC2000E.5.2

When you need to relate two tables in a many-to-many relationship, you have to create a third table called a linking table. If you're comfortable using the clipboard, this is easy to do from the Relationships window. Using copy and paste, you can ensure that the fields in the linking table have the same properties as the fields in the primary tables.

Creating a Many-to-Many Relationship

1. Open the Relationships window.
2. Click the New button to open the New Table dialog box.
3. Choose Design view. Click OK to open a Design View window for the linking table.
4. In the Relationships window, right-click on one of the tables you need to relate and choose Table Design.
5. Select and copy the primary key field(s) from the table.

Creating a Many-to-Many Relationship *(continued)*

6. Paste the fields in the new table.
7. Close the existing table.
8. Repeat steps four through seven for the other table you need to relate.
9. If any of the fields in the linking table have an AutoNumber data type, change the data type to Number and the Format property to Long Integer.
10. In the linking table, select all the fields and click the Primary Key button on the toolbar.
11. Add other fields to the linking table if you wish.
12. Close the linking table. Use the `tbl` tag and the names of the two primary tables for the linking table name: tblCustomersOrders.

Objective AC2000.9.1

A hard copy of the Relationships window helps you explain design to other members of your team or users helping you design the database.

Printing Relationships

1. Open the Relationships window.
2. Arrange the tables as you'd like them to appear in the printed report.
3. Choose File ➢ Print Relationships to create and preview the report.
4. Click the Print button in the Preview window.
5. Close the Preview. Save or discard the report; the report will not change if you change relationships in the database.

Setting Referential Integrity

Referential integrity (refer to Figure 9.6) ensures that records in a related table have related values in the primary table and prevents users from accidentally deleting or changing records in a primary table when records in a related table depend on them. This ensures there are no *orphaned records* in the related table: orders without customers, class registrations without students, or pay rates without employees.

When referential integrity is enforced in the relationship between the tlkpStates and tbtCustomers tables, three restrictions are applied. First, Access won't allow you to use a state abbreviation in tblCustomers that doesn't already exist in tlkpStates. Second, foreign key values (state abbreviations) that have been used in the Customers table protect their matching records in the primary table, so a user can't delete a state that's already been used in tblCustomers. Finally, the actual data in the primary table is protected. A user can't change MC, erroneously entered as the abbreviation for Michigan, to MI in tlkpStates because MC is used in tblCustomers. When you try to enter, delete, or change data that violates the referential integrity rules, Access displays a warning dialog box and ignores the change. You can apply referential integrity to all three types of relationships. When a relationship has referential integrity enforced, the relationship line displays symbols that indicate the one and many ends of the relationship.

Cascading Updates and Deletes

Objective AC2000E.5.3

You can override the second and third integrity restrictions and still maintain referential integrity by enabling Cascade Update Related Fields and Cascade Delete Related Records. When *Cascade Update Related Fields* is enabled, changing the value of a primary key in the primary table automatically updates that value in the foreign key of the related table's matching records. With cascade update enabled, you *can* change MC to MI; the change is automatically reflected in any customer record that included MC. When *Cascade Delete Related Records* is enabled, deleting a record in the primary table deletes any related records in the related table. Deleting MC from tlkpStates deletes the record for any customer with MC as their state. In this case, cascading updates may be fine, but cascading deletes is clearly a bad idea—a good example that illustrates the importance of deciding about cascades on a relationship-by-relationship basis, beginning with the question: do I really want to limit entries in the related table to values that I've already entered in the primary table? If you don't, you can skip referential integrity for that relationship.

You can't set referential integrity if existing table data already violates the rules. For example, if you have entered customer addresses that include abbreviations that aren't in tlkpStates, you'll get an error. Add the states to tlkpStates and try again.

Setting Referential Integrity

1. Double-click on the existing relationship lines and set referential integrity, cascade deletes, and cascade updates.
2. Click OK to close the Edit Relationship dialog box.
3. Click Save to save the layout of the Relationships window.

Displaying Related Data in a Subdatasheet

Objective AC2000.5.10

Drilling down into your tables refers to the process of tracing relationships between specific records in different tables to get an extended view of your data. For example, looking up all customers for a given state from tlkpStates is drilling down. Access 2000 uses *subdatasheets,* datasheets-within-datasheets, to support drill downs. The best part about subdatasheets is that most of the work is automatically done when you create relationships. Any table that is related through its primary key to one or more other tables contains subdatasheets when viewed in Datasheet view. When you open a table with subdatasheets, the subdatasheets are collapsed. To drill down, click one of the expand buttons (the plus signs at the left edge of the table) to open the subdatasheet, as shown in Figure 9.7.

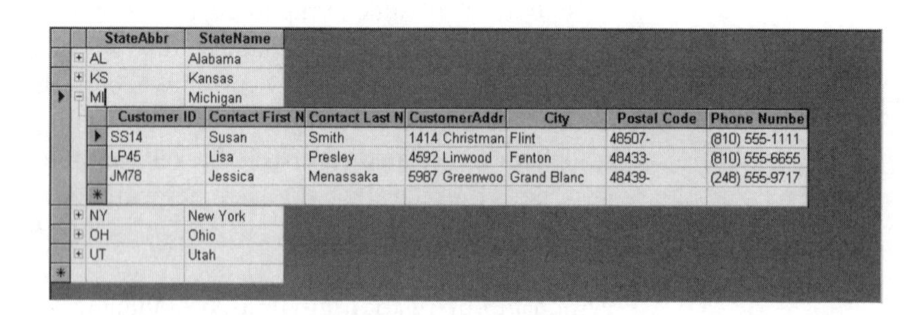

FIGURE 9.7
Subdatasheets display information about related tables.

When you click on a plus sign, the immediate result depends upon exactly how many other tables are related to this one. If there is only one related table, then the row expands to reveal all the rows in the other table that are related to the one you selected. You can now fully view, add, modify, and delete related rows in the other table directly from this datasheet! Click the collapse button (the minus sign) to hide the subdatasheet.

On the other hand, if more than one related table is in your database, clicking on an expand button opens the Insert Subdatasheet dialog box. Access can only display subdatasheets for one related table at a time, so the dialog box asks you to choose the table or query for which you would like the related rows to be shown. The problem with this dialog box is that it displays every table and query in the database; if you're not sure which tables are related to the active table, open the Relationships window, select the active table, and click the Show Direct Relationships button.

Displaying Related Data in a Subdatasheet

1. Open a table related via its primary key in Datasheet view.
2. Click on any of the plus signs to access the rows related to the row in the current table.
3. If more than one table contains rows related to this one, choose a table from the Insert Subdatasheet dialog box.

Hands On: *Objectives AC2000.1.4, 3.6, 6.1, 6.2, 9.1, and AC2000E.5.1, 5.2, 5.3, and 5.10*

1. In an existing database, create, populate, and save a lookup table that can be used to supply data for a field in a related table. Create a lookup field in the related table using the Lookup Wizard. Test the lookup field.
2. In the database you've been creating, add lookup tables you feel would be helpful for data entry and validation. Create any other relationships that are required to maintain data integrity and relate tables. Print the Relationships window.
3. Examine the relationships in an existing database, and if necessary, enforce referential integrity with or without cascading updates and deletes.
4. View, add, modify, and delete rows in related tables using subdatasheets.

5. Create a new database with three tables, created using the Table Wizard or in Design view. Primary key fields are bolded: tblEmployees (fields: **EmplNum**, EmplFName, EmplLName), tblEmployeeCoOp (fields: **EmplNum**, EmplGradYear, EmplCoOpYr), and tblSchools (fields: **SchoolID**, SchoolName). Make SchoolID an AutoNumber field. Create the following relationships:

   a) One-to-one relationship between tblEmployees and tblEmployee-CoOp that prohibits users from entering CoOp information unless there's a related record in tblEmployees and that automatically updates tblEmployeeCoOp if the primary key changes in tblEmployees.

   b) Many-to-many relationship between tblEmployeeCoOp and tblSchools. Analyze this relationship and determine whether or not cascading updates and deletes should be enabled.

   c) Print the relationships you created.

Building and Modifying Forms

Forms provide a way for users to enter data without having to know how a table is designed. One form can include data from multiple tables, providing one-stop data entry. You can create a customized layout so that a form looks just like its source document—the membership application, customer data form, or other document used to collect data—to minimize data-entry errors.

As soon as you begin creating forms, you create a dependency. Forms depend on tables. If you need to rename a table, the form may no longer work – unless you've enabled Name AutoCorrect. AutoCorrect helps repair any damage done to links between database objects during renaming procedures. By default, this feature should be turned on for every new database that you create in Access 2000. To verify this, simply select Tools ➢ Options and click the General tab to examine the status of the check boxes in the Name AutoCorrect control. You must select the Track Name AutoCorrect Info option *before* renaming your tables for Access to automatically repair your forms. This option tells Access to note whenever you rename a database object. To have Access repair damaged forms when table names change, select the Perform Name AutoCorrect option.

Access provides three form-creation methods: AutoForms, the Form Wizard, and Form Design view. This section focuses the most used of the three methods: the Form Wizard.

Forms *inherit* some of a field's properties from the table. For example, if you specify a field's input mask in the table, the field has an input mask when placed in a form. Before you use a table in a form, review and set each field's Field Size, Caption, Format, and Input Mask properties.

A form can have one of three different layouts: datasheet, tabular, or columnar. Simple forms of each type for table tlkpStates are shown in Figure 9.8. The datasheet layout looks a lot like the table's Datasheet view, right down to the navigation buttons. You can move the columns and rows around, just like in the table. Like the Datasheet form, the tabular form presents multiple records, as though you were looking at the table. However, the form itself looks a bit classier. The columnar form displays one record at a time. If the primary purpose of a form is data entry or editing one record at a time, a columnar form is best. If you're designing a form to allow users to view multiple records, a datasheet or tabular form is a better choice. In any of the forms, use the navigation buttons to move between records or to enter a new record.

Objective AC2000.4.1

The Form Wizard lets you create forms that display data from related tables. The related part is important: if you haven't already created a relationship between two tables, you can't relate them in a form. In the first step of the Form Wizard, you can access all the tables in the database from the drop-down list in the tables/queries section. When you have selected a table, its fields are displayed in the Available Fields list box, so you can move from table to table to pick fields.

If you choose fields from unrelated tables, the Form Wizard stops and displays an error message that tells you to cancel the Wizard, set the relationships, and then start the Form Wizard again. If the tables have a one-to-many relationship, you are asked how you want to view your data—whether you want the form's primary focus to be the primary or related table. With our

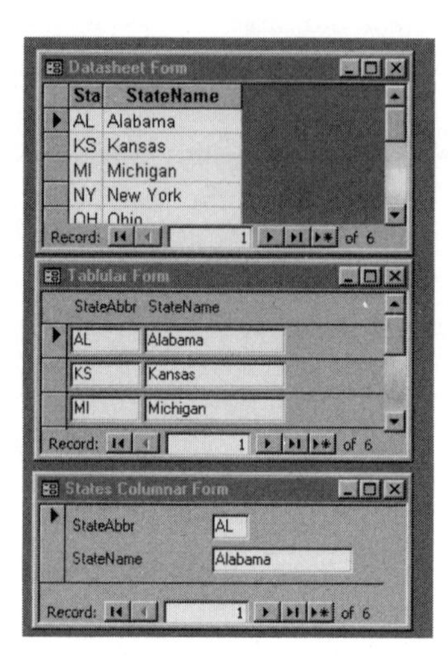

FIGURE 9.8
Datasheet, tabular, and columnar form layouts

Creating a Form with the Form Wizard

1. Choose Insert ➢ Form from the menu, choose Form in the Object bar and click the New button, or open the New button drop-down list and select Form to open the New Form dialog box.
2. Choose Form Wizard and click OK.

   OR

1. Choose Form in the Object bar and double-click Create Form by Using Wizard.
2. Select a table or query, then use the pick buttons to select fields for the form. Click Next.

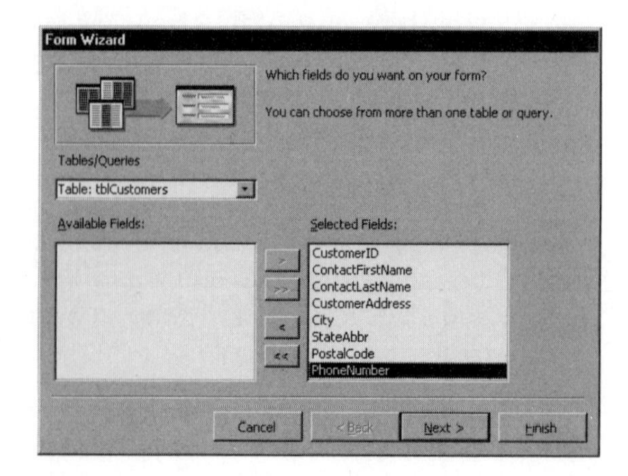

Creating a Form with the Form Wizard *(continued)*

3. Choose a layout for your form. Click Next.
4. Select a form style. Click Next.
5. Enter a name for the form. Choose to open the form in Design view or to enter data. Click Finish.

sample Customers database, switching between By tblCustomers and By tlkpStates changes the sample in the right pane.

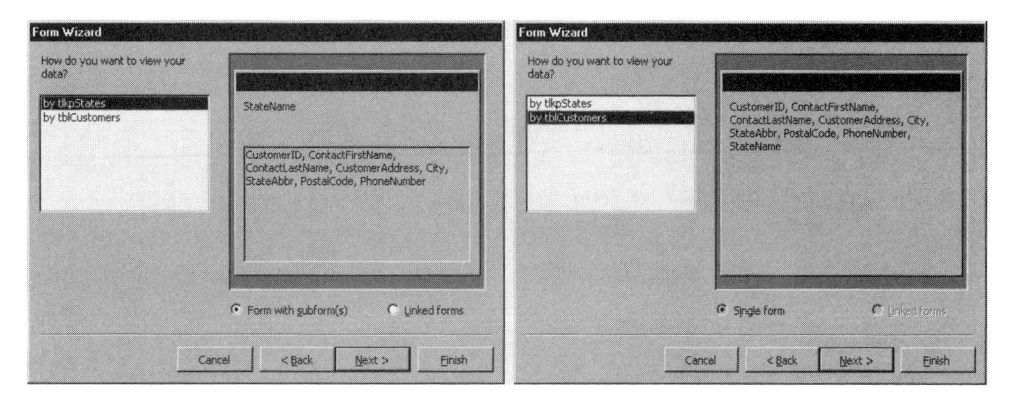

When the form is arranged by states, the customer data appears in a sunken area of the preview: a subform. A *subform* allows you to show related records from different tables when there is more than one record to display. The subform is embedded in the *main form*, and is a visual representation of the one-to-many relationship between states and customers. If the main form is already fairly complex, you can choose to display the subform as a linked form by choosing linked form option in the Form Wizard. The Form Wizard creates a main form with a button that opens the linked subform.

When the primary focus of the form is the table on the many side of the relationship, there is only one related record to display, so the data from the related table is displayed on the main form. The By tblCustomers layout doesn't include a subform.

Creating Forms for Multiple Tables

1. Select Form Wizard from the New Form dialog box. Click OK.
2. Select the fields you would like to include on your form.
3. Choose how you'd like to view the form data.
4. Select the type of layout you would like for each form.
5. Choose the style you would like for the form. Click Next.
6. Name the form(s) and click Finish.

Modifying Form Design

Access 2000 includes many tools to help you modify forms. Open a form in Design view. The Design window includes horizontal and vertical rulers and Form Design and Formatting toolbars, as shown in Figure 9.9.

FIGURE 9.9 frmStatesAnd-Customers form in Design view

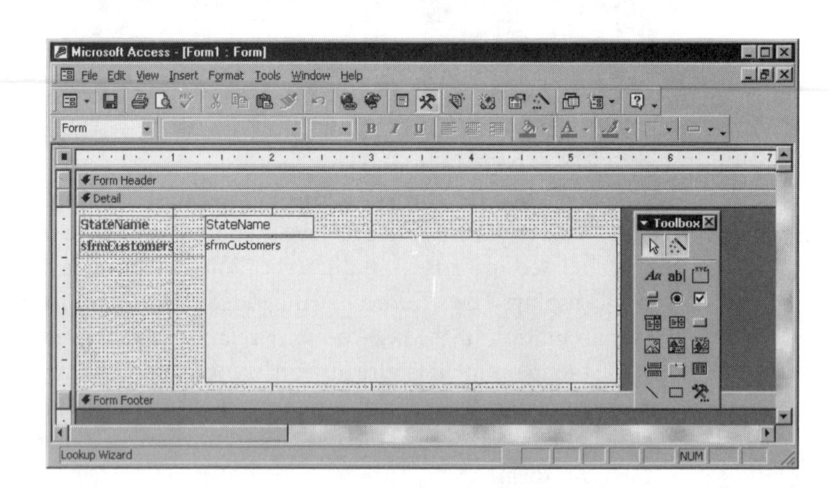

Forms can be displayed in three views: Design view, Datasheet view, and Form view. To switch between views, open the View menu or click the down-arrow on the View button.

Objective AC2000.4.4

Forms include five possible sections and a number of different controls. The sections are:

- A form header at the beginning of the form, usually used for titles.
- A form footer at the end of the form, used for user tips or other miscellaneous information.
- A page header at the top of each page of a form – on the first page, the page header follows the form header. A page header only appears on printed forms.
- A page footer at the bottom of each page of a form – on the last page of the form the page footer appears directly above the form footer. A page footer also only appears on printed forms.
- A detail section, a scrollable section generally used to display one or more records.

Any section can include various graphic objects like horizontal lines. The detail section includes individual text box controls for data elements and a label control for each text box. In tabular and datasheet forms, labels appear in the form header, and text boxes appear below the labels in the detail section.

When a form is displayed in datasheet view, only the detail section is displayed. If the form header and form footer sections aren't visible in other views, choose View ➢ Form Header/Footer from the menu bar to turn them on. Unlike the detail section, the header and footer sections do not scroll in Form view.

If you want to rearrange a form, it's easiest to begin by enlarging the form's area. Move the mouse pointer to the bottom of the detail section, just above the form footer. The pointer changes to an adjustment tool. Drag the footer bar down to increase the height of the detail area. To increase the header section, move between the header bar and the detail bar, and then drag the detail bar down to open the header area.

Like tables and fields, forms have properties that determine their appearance and behavior. For example, you can display a form as a single form, a continuous scrolling form, or a datasheet by setting the form's default View property. Set the Views Allowed property to prevent users from switching between Form and Datasheet views.

Working with Objects

To select an object, click it so that handles appear. If you select a text box, the corresponding label also appears to be selected. Actually, it is only partially selected; it *moves* with the text box, but if you change the *format* of the text box, the label format does not change.

To select multiple objects, move the pointer to either ruler bar. The pointer changes to a bold arrow pointing toward the form. Press the mouse button, and a line drops directly through the form. When you release the button, all the objects the line passed through are selected. You can also hold the mouse button down and drag the arrow to select a range of objects. If the objects you want to select aren't all in a line, you can select one object, and then hold the Shift key while selecting additional objects. Delete selected objects by pressing the Delete key on the keyboard.

Moving and Sizing Objects To move an object, first select it, and then move the pointer to an edge of the selected object being sure not to point directly at any of the resizing handles; the pointer changes shape to a small hand. Hold the mouse button and drag the object to its new location. If you move an object beyond the form's current area, the form area increases.

If you point directly at the handle in the upper-left corner of a text box or label, the hand changes to a finger pointing at the handle. If you drag using the pointing finger, only the object you are pointing at moves. If you point to the text box and drag it, the label remains in place. If you drag the label, the text box doesn't move.

Adjust the size of controls as you would any graphic object: by dragging the resizing handles at the corners and sides of the object. For extra precision, select controls and use Shift+arrow keys to resize and Ctrl+arrow keys to move. Note, however, that changing the size of a text box control does not change the size of the field. To change field size, you must go to the table's Design view and change the field size property.

Working with Text

Click once on a selected label, and you can edit the text in the label. *Don't* change the field name in a text box control. If you do, data from the table won't appear in that field.

Adding a Title

Objective AC2000.4.2

Click the Toolbox button on the Form Design toolbar or choose View ➢ Toolbox to open the Toolbox, shown in Figure 9.10.

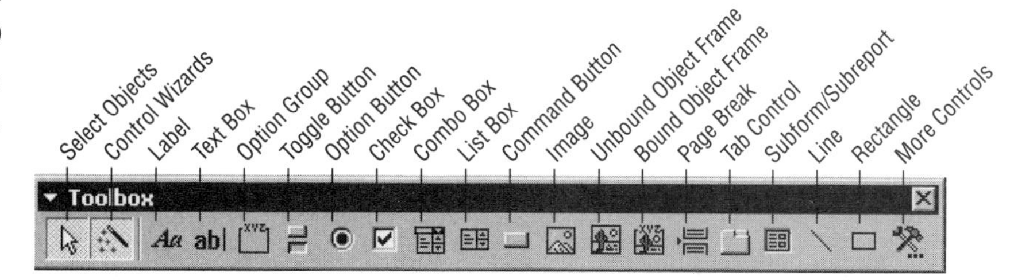

FIGURE 9.10 Use the Toolbox to add controls to a form.

The detail section is usually used for information from table(s). The header section is used for a form title. Use the Toolbox Label tool to create a title or other text to label the form. Click the Label tool; when you move the pointer back into the design area, it changes to a large letter *A* with crosshairs. Move the pointer into the header area, and click where you want to begin entering text. When you are done entering text, click elsewhere in the form to close the label control.

Formatting Text

Objective AC2000.4.3

Much of the formatting for controls is the same as text formatting in other Office 2000 applications (see Chapter 1). Select one or more controls, and then choose options from the Formatting toolbar (shown in Figure 9.11), or right-click and select options from the shortcut menu. If you're formatting a number of controls, first format one, then use the Format Painter on the Standard toolbar.

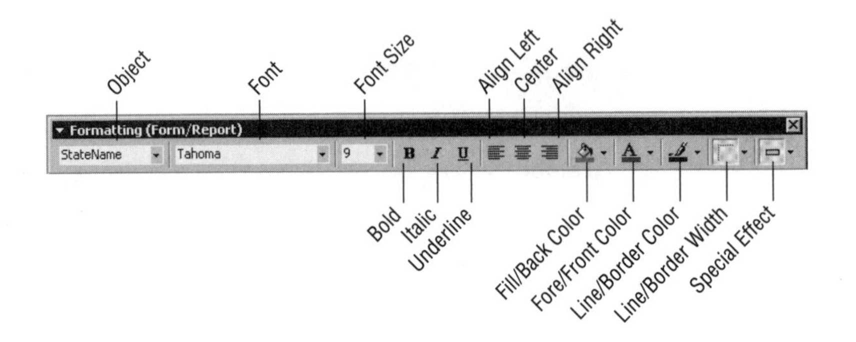

FIGURE 9.11 Change a control's style, border, font, and other attributes with the Formatting tools.

Sometimes you will want a field to appear differently depending upon certain conditions that vary from one record to the next. For example, if you're thinking about opening a new office in Kansas, you might want to bold or color the customers' names from Kansas. To use conditional formatting, select the fields that contain the text you want to format and choose Format ➢ Conditional Formatting to open the Conditional Formatting dialog box. Choose formatting styles in the Default Formatting control area just as you format other fields. Access will apply this formatting whenever one of the conditions specified in the Condition control area is met by the value in the field.

Changing Borders

Every Access control has a border around it. Borders have three properties: color, line width, and special effect. Although you can't delete the border, you can disable all three properties by choosing Transparent as the border color. A transparent border has no visible width, color, or effect.

You can change border width using the Border Width button on the Formatting toolbar, selecting widths from a hairline thickness to a six-point width. Typically, a one- or two-point border is appropriate. Special effects also help differentiate control type. There are six special effects, each of which has standard uses:

Flat controls that are not designed for data entry

Sunken text boxes where users can edit or enter data

Shadowed titles

Raised is a useful choice for data entry, titles, or to draw attention to a part of the screen

Etched text boxes with contents that cannot be changed by the user

Chiseled titles

When you apply Sunken, Raised, Etched, or Chiseled special effects, you turn off any other choices for border color and line width. Only Flat and Shadowed are affected by the border-color and line-width formatting options.

Relative Sizing and Alignment

Forms have one-inch horizontal and vertical guidelines and grid points which make up a grid. (If the grid points aren't visible, choose View ➢ Grid). When you move a control, it automatically lines up with the grid both horizontally and vertically. This is called *Snap to Grid*. Sometimes you might want to place two or more controls so they aren't on a grid point—closer together than the grid allows or not as far apart as two grid points require. To do this, you must first turn off Snap to Grid (choose Format ➢ Snap to Grid). The Snap-to-Grid feature is not one you will need to turn off very often, but working without Snap to Grid is essential for small refinements in your Access forms.

Adjusting Control Alignment, Size, and Spacing Access 2000 automates size and positioning features so you can manipulate multiple controls at one time. Begin by selecting two or more controls, then choose Format ➢ Align or choose Align from the shortcut menu to see the list of options. Choosing Align ➢ Left aligns all selected controls with the control closest to the left edge of the form. Use Align ➢ Top or Align ➢ Bottom to adjust controls on the same horizontal line. Access has trouble differentiating between controls that are overlapped. Separate overlapping controls before attempting to align them to ensure that you only select the controls you want to align.

Sizing Controls Choosing Format ➢ Size ➢ To Fit or double-clicking any sizing handle instantly resizes labels based on length of their content. You can select two or more controls and use the other sizing options. Tallest and Shortest refer to vertical height and Widest and Narrowest refer to horizontal width.

Spacing Controls Spacing allows you to increase or decrease the relative position of selected controls by one grid point either horizontally or vertically. This is valuable if you need to spread out the controls or move them closer together. You can also use Spacing to make sure controls are evenly spaced. Select controls, then choose Format ➢ Vertical Spacing (or Horizontal Spacing) ➢ Make Equal (or Increase or Decrease).

Customizing Form Sections

Objective AC2000E.2.4

The form's header, details, and footer sections each have their own set of properties. To view a section's properties, right-click on the section background and choose Properties from the shortcut menu. One exceptionally useful property is the Display When property. You can display a section only on screen or only when the form is printed, so you can add a footer or explanatory information in the Form Footer section, then set the Display When property to Print Only to suppress the explanatory text on screen. Use the Force New Page properties of one or more sections to print an entire form or part of a form on a new page.

Adding Controls to Forms

Objectives AC2000.4.2, 4.5 and AC2000E.2.2 and 2.3

If you add a field to a table, existing forms won't include the field. To add a field to a form, click the Field List button on the Standard toolbar (or choose View ➢ Field List), then drag the field from the list and drop it in the form. You can create *calculated controls* that perform a mathematical or logical operation and display the results. For example, a library database might subtract the date a book was checked out from today's date, and display the number of days until the book is due back in the library so that a user would know when to return. Calculated controls use functions similar to the functions used in Excel 2000 and a special builder called the *Expression Builder*, shown in Figure 9.12.

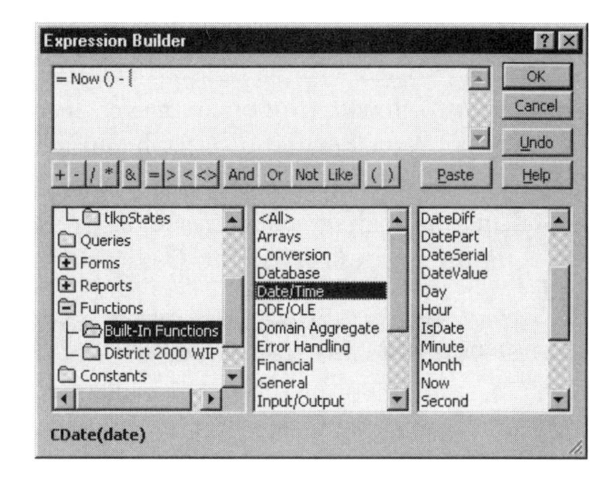

FIGURE 9.12 Use the Expression Builder to create calculated form controls.

In the Expression Builder, select a category of objects or expressions in the left column, then more specific items in the middle and right columns. For example, we're using the function NOW, which returns the current date/time in the calculated control we're building. We expanded the Functions folder to choose Built-in Functions in the first column, then chose Date/Time functions in the middle column and double-clicked on Now in the right column to add it to the formula pane at the top of the Builder. To select the CheckOutDate field from frmLoans, we'll expand Forms to see Loaded Forms and select frmLoans, choose Field List in the middle pane, then double-click the CheckOutDate field in the right column. As you're creating your calculation, you can enter symbols from the keyboard or click on the buttons below the formula pane.

Creating a Calculated Control

1. In Design View, drag a new text box control from the Toolbox into the form.
2. Right-click on the control and choose Properties.
3. In the control's Properties, select the Control Source property then click the builder button to open the Expression Builder.
4. Use the fields and functions in the builder to create a formula for the calculated control.
5. Click OK to close the Expression Builder and place the formula in the control.

To insert a graphic (for example a company logo) in a form, choose Insert ➢ Picture to open the Insert Picture dialog box. Locate the picture file then click OK.

A form with a lot of controls is cluttered and hard to use. Access provides two ways to create a form with multiple pages: page breaks and tab controls. Page breaks are cumbersome to use, whereas tab controls provide a simple and nicely designed interface for users. To create a form with tab controls, begin with a new form in Design view.

Creating a MultiPage Form with Tabs

1. Select the Tab Control from the Toolbox and place it on the form. Resize the control by dragging the handles on its border.
2. To add additional tabs, right-click on the tab control and choose Insert Page.
3. To change the name of the tab, right-click and choose Properties. Enter a name in the Caption box.
4. To add controls to a page, click the page tab and add fields from the Field List or copy controls from another form or add them from the Toolbox.
5. To remove a page, right-click on the page, and choose Delete Page.
6. To change the order of the pages, right-click on a page and choose Page Order.

Adding a Subform Control

Objective AC2000E.2.6

When a form contains information from two or more tables with one-to-many relationships, creating a form and subforms allows you to present information from the primary table in the main form, and records from the related table in the subform. The form created earlier in this chapter with the Form Wizard (see Figure 9.9) is a main form with a subform. The form and subform are synchronized by two properties of the subform control (as opposed to the subform itself) in the main form —Link Master Fields and Link Child Fields—which are the primary key of the main form's table and the related foreign key of the subform's table.

You aren't restricted to a single subform, but that's where the Form Wizard tops out. For example, you might have a database that coordinates information about corporate customers. A company can have employees, orders, shipping preferences, and a number of other attributes, so your database could have a number of tables related to tblCompanies. You could create a Company form and place various subforms on the form. One common design would place each subform on a different tab of a tab control.

Adding a Subform to a Form

1. Open the main form in Design View.
2. Click the Subform/Subreport button on the Toolbox.
3. Click in the form to place the subform control and open the Subform Wizard.
4. In the first step of the wizard, select an existing form to use as a subform. Click Next.

   OR

4. Choose to use an existing table or query to create a subform. Click Next. Select the table/query and fields to use in the subform. Click Next.
5. Choose the statement that best describes the relationship between the two tables, or choose Define and select the primary key/foreign key fields that relate the records in the two forms. Click Next.
6. Enter or confirm the name for the subform and click Finish.

Changing Properties of Forms and Controls

Objective AC2000E.2.5

Every Access object has properties. Form properties include the size of the form, how the form can be viewed, and its record source: the table or query the records come from. To view the properties for a control, double-click on the control in Design view to open the properties sheet. To open the form's properties sheet, double-click on the Form Select button to the left of the horizontal ruler bar. A form has four categories of properties, some of which are set for you when you use the Form Wizard:

Format properties determine the form's appearance.

Data is where the data comes from: the record or control source and whether or not the data can be edited.

Events are form behaviors that can trigger macros or visual basic code.

Other are any other properties that relate to the object or control including, for example, a field's tab order.

The properties sheet title bar includes the name of the selected object. If you want to look at properties for one of the form's other controls, just click the control.

A number of properties are enabled by default on every form, including scroll bars, record selectors, and navigation buttons. All these elements can be turned off, if desired, in the form's property sheet. The scroll bars are only needed if parts of the form don't fit on the screen. Record selectors are useful in tables and in some subforms but are not necessary in columnar forms. You have to decide whether it's necessary to have navigation buttons on both a main form and the subform. Turn off features you don't need by opening the form's properties sheet and changing the undesired item's property setting to No on the Format page. These changes, relatively easy to make, make the form much easier to use.

Rearranging the Tab Order

The sequence of controls a user moves through when pressing Tab is assigned when the form is created. After you rearrange controls on a form, the tab order may be out of sequence.

Adjusting Tab Order

1. Choose View ➢ Tab Order or right-click the Form Selector and choose Tab Order.
2. Click Auto Order to order the fields automatically.
3. To arrange tab order manually, select the field(s) you want to move by clicking/dragging the button at the left end of the field. Drag the fields up or down in the list.
4. Click OK to save the tab order and close the Tab Order dialog box.

Design view gives you the most control over your form's appearance and functionality. Plenty of Access developers create all their forms from scratch in Design view. You already know how to modify form controls; the only thing that's different is how you begin creating your form.

Objective AC2000E.2.1

Creating a Form in Design View

1. Choose Forms in the Object bar, then click New and choose Design View, or choose Insert ➢ Form and choose Design View in the New Form dialog box, or choose Forms in the Object bar and double-click Create a Form in Design View.
2. When the blank form opens, choose View ➢ Properties or double-click the Form Selector to open the Form Properties.
3. Click in the Record Source property, then select a table or query that serves as a record source for the form. Click the builder button if you want to create a new query.
4. Click the Field List button on the Standard toolbar or choose View ➢ Field List to display the field list.
5. Drag fields into the form.

Hands On: Objectives AC2000.2.3, 4.1, 4.2, 4.3, 4.4, 4.5 and AC2000E.2.1, 2.3, 2.4, and 2.6

1. In an existing database, use the Form Wizard to create:
   a) A datasheet form.
   b) Two different forms that include data from two related tables: a form with a subform and a form with a single main form.
2. Format the forms created in step one. Size and align all controls appropriately. Change the borders for text box controls. Edit and format labels as needed. Add and format a form title in the form header area. Add your name and the creation date in the form footer. Turn off form features that aren't required.
3. Print a single record in each of the forms created in step one above.
4. Create a new form in Design View for one of the tables in your database. Add the Tab control to the form. Place fields from the table on more than one page of the Tab control. Add a calculated control to the form. Save the form.

5. In an existing database, check the tab order for all forms.
6. Create and place a subform in a main form using the Subform Wizard.
   a) Open the main form in Design view.
   b) View the Link Child Fields and Link Master Fields properties for the subform control.
7. Modify a form so that the printed version of the form includes title and footer text, which are not displayed on screen. Change the footer section's properties so that each form prints on a new page.

Entering and Editing in Forms

Objective AC2000.5.4

In the datasheet form, enter and edit information exactly as you would in the table's Datasheet view; select and edit a field by moving to the left edge of the field and clicking. In tabular and columnar forms, drag to select all the text in a field before entering the correct data. To move to the next record on a columnar or datasheet form, tab out of the last text box control. In all forms, you can use the navigation buttons to move between existing records and the Delete Record button to delete the selected record.

Sorting Records

Objective AC2000.5.7

Records can be sorted in ascending order (A-Z) or descending order (Z-A) using the buttons on the Standard toolbar. Although you can sort records in Form view, it is easiest to see the results if you work directly in a table or in a form's Datasheet view. If you are sorting a table, Access asks whether you want to save the changes to the table's design when you attempt to close the table. Choosing Yes saves the sort order so that when you open the table again, the records will still be sorted. While a table is sorted, added records are automatically sorted.

Sorting Records

1. Switch to Datasheet view of the table or form.
2. Click anywhere in the column you want to sort by.
3. Click the Ascending or Descending Sort button.
4. To return records to their original order, choose Records ➢ Remove Filter/Sort.

A *multi-level sort* sorts the records on the first field you specify, then sorts records with the same value using another specified field. In a telephone book, for example, all the Smiths are alphabetized by first name.

Sorting by Multiple Fields

1. Open the desired form or table in Datasheet view.
2. Move the columns you want to sort so they are adjacent and in the order you'll use them in the sort. To move a column, select the column and then drag it to the desired position.
3. Click the Ascending or Descending Sort button on the toolbar.

Sorting in Columnar or Tabular Form view is similar to sorting in Datasheet view, except you cannot apply multi-level sorts. Select the field you want to sort by and click the sort button on the toolbar. To see the results of the work, move through the records.

Searching for Records

Objective AC2000.5.6

Access provides an easy way to find individual records by entering part or all of the contents of a field. To use Access's Find feature, click the Find button on the toolbar to open the Find dialog box, shown in Figure 9.13.

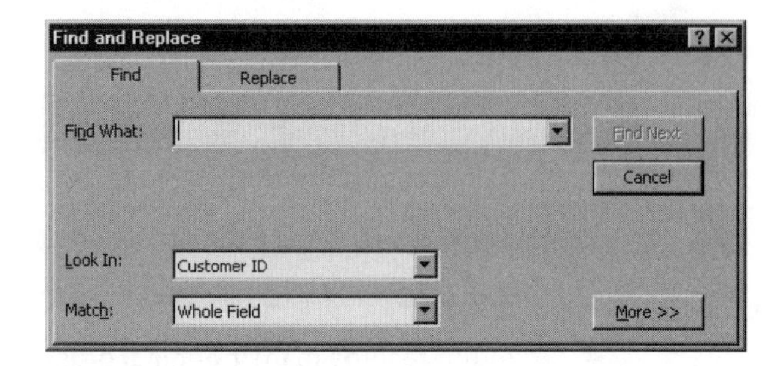

FIGURE 9.13

Use the Find dialog box to search for a record.

Searching for Records

1. Click the Find button on the toolbar or choose Edit ➢ Find from the menu to open the Find and Replace dialog box.
2. Select the field you want to search from the drop-down list.
3. Enter the search string you are looking for.
4. Choose a search method from the Match drop-down list.
5. Click the More button if you wish to specify a search direction or case sensitivity.
6. Click Find Next to move to the first record that meets your search criteria.

Access searches the field you selected and finds the first occurrence of the text you entered. If the search string occurs more than once, you can click the Find Next button again to see the next occurrence. When you have moved to the last record that contains the search string, clicking Find Next again results in a Search Item Was Not Found message.

Using Wildcards

You can construct search criteria using *wildcards*, symbols that represent one or more characters. Table 9.3 lists wildcard characters you can use in Find.

TABLE 9.3: Wildcard Symbols

Wildcard	Usage	Example
*	Can be used at the beginning or the end of a string to match any number of characters	`Par*` finds Parker and Parson. `*son` finds Parson and Williamson.
?	Matches any single alphabetic character	`w?ll` finds wall, well, and will.
#	Matches any single numeric character	`4#5` finds 405, 415, 425, etc.
[ ]	Matches any single character specified in the brackets	`w[ai]ll` finds wall and will, but not well.
-	Identifies any one of a range of characters in ascending order	`[c-h]ill` finds dill, fill, gill, and hill, but not kill, mill, etc.
!	Used within brackets to specify any character not in the brackets	`w[!a]ll` finds well and will, but not wall.

Filtering Records

Applying a *filter* to an Access form or table temporarily hides records that don't meet your criteria. You can filter in a Table, Query, or Form. There are three ways to create filters in Access:

Filter by Selection *and* **Filter Excluding Selection** are filter-based on a text string or value you have selected.

Filter by Form creates a blank form or datasheet where you can type in the values you want to see.

Advanced Filter/Sort opens a query form so you can enter more complex filtering and sorting criteria.

Filter by Selection/Filter Excluding Selection The easiest way to apply a filter in Access is with Filter by Selection. To find all the records from Indiana, for example, click in the State field or text box control for an Indiana record, right-click, and select Filter by Selection from the shortcut menu. Only the records for Indiana will be visible, and the navigation buttons show the number of filtered records. You can apply a filter to filtered data to narrow the search even further. Right-click and choose Remove Filter/Sort to remove the filter.

You can also use the Filter by Selection, Filter By Form, Apply Filter, and Remove Filter buttons on the toolbar.

If you would like to see all the data except for a certain value—for example, all the companies that aren't in Indiana—locate a record with the value you want to exclude and right-click to open the shortcut menu. Choose Filter Excluding Selection. If you have created a filter that you will re-use, use the filter just before closing the form. Access asks if you want to save changes to the design of the table. If you choose Yes the last filter you created is automatically saved. When you open the form again, all the records will be visible, but you can simply click the Apply Filter button to re-apply the filter.

Filter by Form The Filter by Form feature works the same way as the Filter by Selection method, except that you set up your criteria on a blank form or datasheet. Click the Filter by Form button to open a blank form in Form view or a single row datasheet in Datasheet view. When you click in a field, a drop-down list containing all the values in the field appears. Select the value to use as a filter, then click the Apply Filter button. Using this method, you can apply multiple filters to display records that meet all the criteria you select.

If you would like to see records that meet one or more of the specified criteria but not necessarily all of them (an OR filter), click the Or tab at the bottom of the Filter By Form window before selecting the additional criteria. Selecting part of a field works just as well in Filter by Form as in Filter by Selection.

Hands On: Objectives AC2000.5.4, 5.6, 5.7, and 5.8

1. Open an existing database. Open a table in Datasheet view and sort the records on one column and on two or more columns. Filter the records by Selection and by Form.
2. In a table that contains names, sort the records by last name. Filter the records by two or more criteria.
3. Enter data using a form.

Creating Queries

A *query* selects records from one or more tables based on user-specified criteria. If you use the Form Wizard to create a form that draws data from more than one table, Access automatically creates a query to retrieve the data. You can also use queries to append, modify, and delete data from your tables. You can create five different types of Access queries: select queries, parameter queries, crosstab queries, action queries, and SQL (Structured Query Language) queries.

Queries, like other database objects, can be created a variety of ways. You can enter SQL code manually, use Design view, or use one of the query wizards. If you're creating a query simply to enter or report data from multiple tables, it is easiest to use the Form or Report Wizard to retrieve the data you want because the wizard creates the query. If, however, you need to work with a data set independent of a form or report, use the Simple Query Wizard to create a select query. When one or more of the query fields are numeric, you can create a Totals query by choosing a summarization method.

Creating a Simple Select Query

1. Choose Query in the Object bar and click New, or click the New Object button and choose New Query. Choose Simple Query Wizard in the New Query dialog box and click OK.
2. From the Tables/Queries drop-down list, choose the table/query that contains the fields you want to include in this query.
3. Use the pick buttons to move fields into the Selected Fields column.
4. Select any additional tables/queries from the Tables/Queries drop-down list and repeat Step 3. Click Next when all fields have been selected.
5. If the fields you selected include a number field, you are asked to select a summary or detail query. To see each record, choose Detail. To see totals, averages, or other summaries, choose Summary and set the summation options. Click Next.
6. Enter a name for the query. Click Finish to run the query.

Move through a query using the Tab key. The results of some queries can't be edited, either because a primary key wasn't included in the results set or the relationships between the tables prevent editing. If the results can't be edited, a message appears in the status bar to let you know that it is a *non-updateable recordset*. If the results of a query can be edited, edit as you would in a table.

You can sort and filter the query results, which look like the Datasheet view of a table using the Sort and Filter buttons on the Database toolbar or the filter and sort options from the shortcut menu. When you sort, then close a query, you are asked whether you wish to save the changes to the query layout. If you save the changes, you're saving the sorting criteria, and the query will still be sorted the next time it is opened. If you choose not to save the changes, the query returns to its original order.

Objective AC2000.5.12

Clicking the Design View button opens the query for modification. The query window is separated into two panes, as shown in Figure 9.14. The lower pane, called the QBE grid (Query by Example), uses one column for each field included in the query. This indicates the field name, the table the field comes from, whether the query is sorted based on the field, whether the field is shown in the query results, and criteria that have been applied to the field to limit the query results.

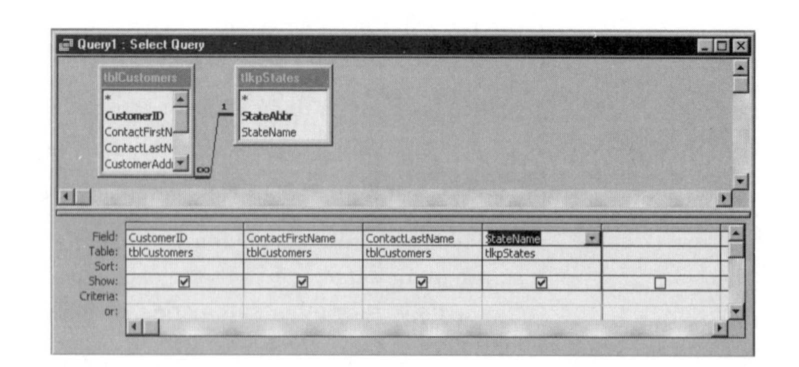

FIGURE 9.14 Open the query in Design view to modify the query.

Objective AC2000E.3.8

The upper pane shows the tables included in the query and the relationship between the tables. If you create a new query from related tables, the relationships appear as the tables are placed in the upper pane. If you haven't defined the relationships between the tables, you can create relationships in the upper pane the same way you do in the Relationships window. However, these relationships are only created for the query—they aren't automatically placed in the Relationships window. Relationships have a specification called a *join*. There are two types of joins: inner joins and outer joins. Outer joins are further divided into right outer joins and left outer joins. Don't worry too much about the names; instead, focus on how each join defines the data that the query will return. Double-clicking the join line opens the Join Properties dialog box, shown in Figure 9.15.

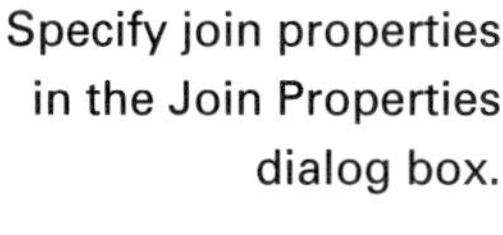

FIGURE 9.15

Specify join properties in the Join Properties dialog box.

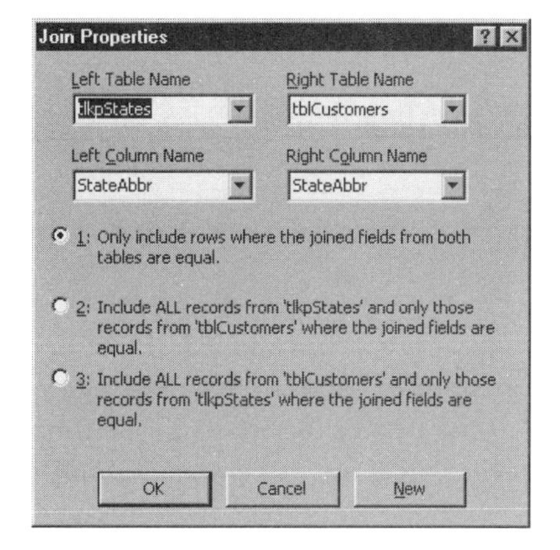

The first join type listed is an inner join, which is the default join in queries. In an *inner join*, the only records displayed in the query are those with identical values in the joined fields. If there are no customers in one of the states, the state won't be listed. The second join type is a *left outer join*. With a left outer join, all the records in the primary table in the relationship (tlkpStates) are displayed, even if they don't have matching entries in the related table.

A *right outer join* includes all the records from the related table, even if no matching records exist in the primary tlkpStates table. The join symbol points from the table that will have all records listed to the table that will only have matching records displayed. All three joins use the same tables and relationships, but each returns a different query results set. To remove a join, select the join and press the Delete key on the keyboard.

Sorting a Query

To sort a query, choose Ascending or Descending in the Sort row of the column you want to sort by. You can sort on multiple fields. Although the fields to sort on don't have to be next to each other, they do need to be in order from left to right. If necessary, re-arrange the query so that the primary sort field is to the left of the secondary sort field, and so on.

Printing a Query

When you print a query results set, the results appear in Datasheet view. To improve the appearance of the printed results, create a tabular form or report based on the query.

Setting Criteria

Objective AC2000.5.9

Field:	StateName
Table:	tlkpStates
Sort:	
Show:	☑
Criteria:	"Michigan"
or:	

In a select query, you can enter criteria that operate as a filter. For example, if you only want to see the customers in Michigan, enter Michigan in the Criteria row of the StateName field.

You can use operators such as <>, >=, <=, >, and <. If you want to show records where a field is blank, enter `Is Null` as the criteria. For all the fields that aren't blank use <> `Null` or `Is Not Null`.

Objective AC2000E.3.4

You can specify criteria in more than one column to display all the records that meet more than one criteria (AND), or that meet at least one of multiple criteria (OR). To show records that meet multiple conditions, enter all the criteria in the same row in the grid. To display records that meet one criteria or another, enter the criteria on different rows of the grid. If you need to use a field more than once for an AND condition, just add the field to the grid again. (Click in the field's Show check box to hide the second occurrence of the field in the query's results set. Figure 9.16 shows a portion of a query that returns all the customers in Kansas and Indiana, as well as customers in Michigan with zip codes that begin with 484.

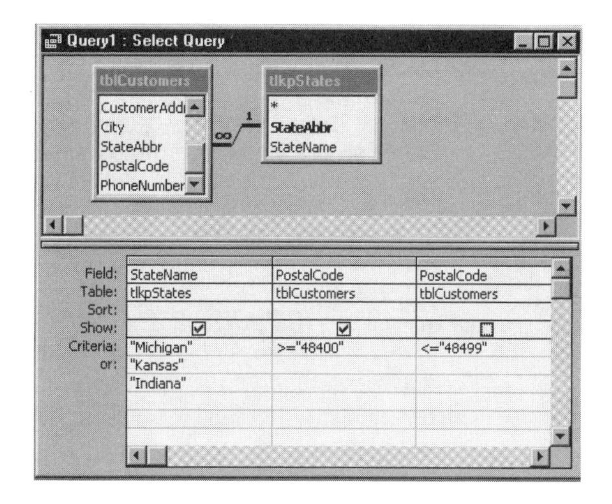

FIGURE 9.16 Combine criteria for a complex query.

Creating a Parameter Query

Objective AC2000E.3.3

A *parameter query* is a select query that displays a dialog box prompting the user for parameters. Use parameter queries when users frequently need to access a subset of a table or tables. Rather than creating 50 state queries, for example, you can create one parameter query and let the user enter the state abbreviation. You can easily create a parameter query from an existing select query. Enter a prompt, enclosed in brackets [ ] on the Criteria line of the field you want to use as a parameter: `[Enter a two letter state abbreviation]`.When the user runs the query, the prompt appears in an Enter Parameter Value dialog box to tell the user what information should be entered. You can see how the dialog box looks by clicking the Datasheet View button and running the query.

Creating a Parameter Query

1. Open an existing select query in Design view.
2. Enter the parameter statement in brackets in the Criteria row of the desired field.

Creating a Parameter Query *(continued)*

3. Run the query to make sure it works correctly. When the Enter Parameter Value dialog box opens, enter an appropriate value and click OK.
4. Choose Save As to save the parameter query with a new name.

Creating a Totals Query

Objective AC2000E.3.2

A *totals query* or *summary query* is a select query that returns summaries or totals rather than detailed records. If the fields you select in the Simple Query Wizard include numeric fields, you're given the choice to create a detail or summary query. But you can turn any select query into a summary query. Table 9.4 lists the functions, results, and field types used in queries.

TABLE 9.4: Functions, Results, and Field Types

Function	Results	Used with Field Types
Avg	Average of the values in the field	AutoNumber, Currency, Date/Time, Number
Count	Number of records that hold data in this field. Count includes zeros, but not blanks.	All
First	The contents of the field in the first record in the result set.	All
Last	The contents of the field in the last record in the result set.	All
Min	Lowest value in the field.	AutoNumber, Currency, Date/Time, Number, Text
Max	Highest value in the field.	AutoNumber, Currency, Date/Time, Number, Text
StDev	Standard deviation of the values in the field.	AutoNumber, Currency, Date/Time, Number

TABLE 9.4: Functions, Results, and Field Types *(continued)*

Function	Results	Used with Field Types
Sum	Total of the values in the field.	AutoNumber, Currency, Date/Time, Number
Var	Variance of the values in the field.	AutoNumber, Currency, Date/Time, Number

In Figure 9.17, the data in the query will be sorted by StateName, grouped by StateName, and the results will show the number of customers in each state.

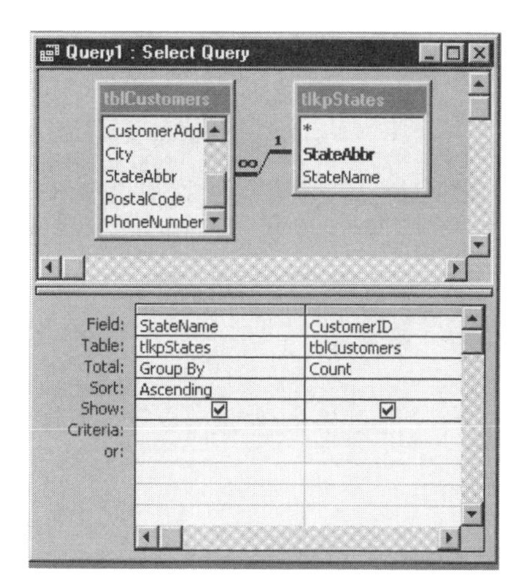

FIGURE 9.17
Totals queries summarize data in one or more fields.

Creating a Totals Query

1. In Design view, open a select query that includes the field you want to base the summary on and the fields you want to summarize.
2. Click the Totals button to open the Totals row of the query grid.
3. Set the Totals row for the field you want to base the summary on to Group By.
4. For every other field, choose an aggregate summarization method from the Totals drop-down list.

Adding Calculations to Queries

Objective AC2000.5.11

The table in our library database, tblLoans, includes the date each book was checked out. We'd like to print a list that shows each book on loan, the date it was loaned, the date it was to have been returned, and whether or not it is overdue. To do this, we'll add two calculated fields to a select query using the Expression Builder we used earlier in this chapter. The query design's calculated fields are shown in Figure 9.18.

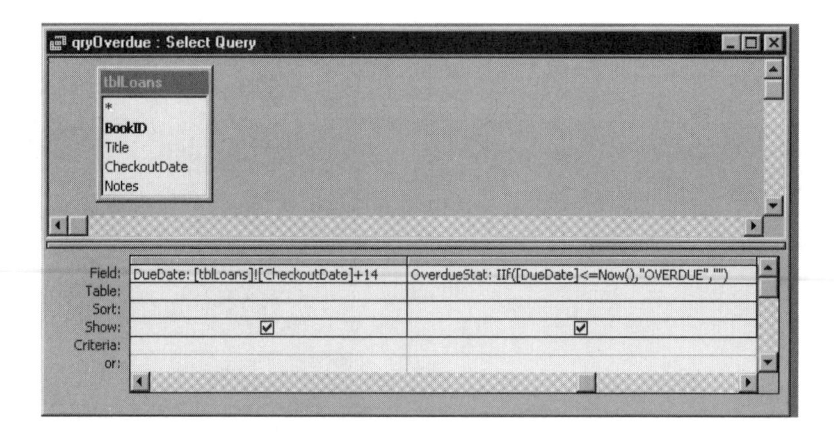

FIGURE 9.18 Use the Expression Builder to add calculated fields to a query.

To calculate the return date, we added 14 days to the loan date. In a second calculated field, we used the Access version of the IF function (IIF) to display OVERDUE if the return date was prior to today's date.

When you create a calculated query field, Access names the column `Expr1`. Select the name in query Design view and enter a new name. You can base a form or report on a query, so calculated query fields provide the tool you need to calculate many types of values for reporting on screen or on paper.

Adding a Calculation to a Query

1. Open the query in Design view.
2. In the Field row of an empty column, enter the calculation expression.

Adding a Calculation to a Query *(continued)*

OR

2. Click the Build button to open the Expression Builder. Using the Built-in Functions and list of field names from the active query, create the calculation, and then click OK.

3. If you wish, change the name of the calculated query field from Expr1 to a more descriptive name.

Modifying Query Properties

Objective AC2000E.3.5

Both query fields and the query have properties that you'll want to know about. Right-click on a query field in Design view and choose Properties to change the field's Format, enter a caption that will appear when you use the query as the source for a report or form, add a description, or create an input mask. Right-click in the top pane and choose Properties to open the query's Properties, shown in Figure 9.19. Two of the properties are beyond nifty. Change the Unique Records property to Yes to have Access filter the query results set and only display unique records. In the Top Values property, choose a number or percentage of records to display.

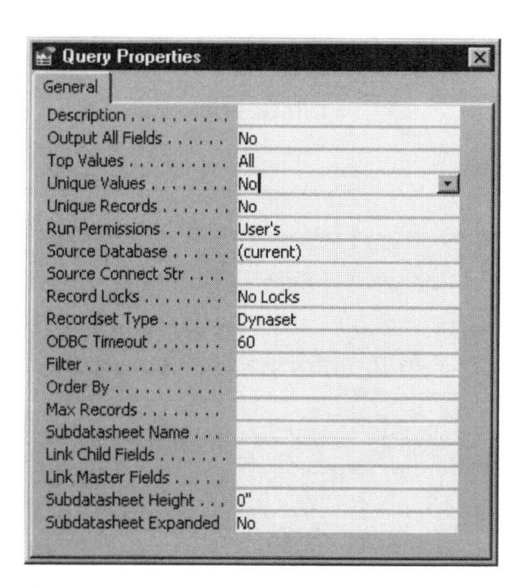

FIGURE 9.19 Change query properties such as Unique Records to alter the recordset returned by the query.

Creating Action Queries

Objective AC2000E.3.6

With Access 2000, you can create four different types of *action queries* to delete, update, append, or make a table from records that meet the criteria you specify.

Creating an Action Query

1. In Design view, create a select query that includes the fields you want to delete, update, append, or create a table with.
2. Enter criteria to select the records you want to include.
3. In datasheet view, ensure the correct records are selected.
4. Return to Design view and choose Query from the menu or open the menu on the Query toolbar button and select a type of action query.
   a. For an update query, enter an update value in the field's Update row.
   b. For an append query or Make Table query, enter a table name when prompted.
   c. For a delete query, verify that the table(s) used in the grid are the table(s) you want to delete records from.
5. Save the query.
6. Click the Run button in Design view, or close and open the action query to run the query.

Access *Crosstab queries* summarize information about two or more columns in a table or query, just like an Excel pivot table. See Access 2000 Help for information about creating crosstab queries.

Hands On: Objectives AC2000.5.9, 5.11, 5.12 and AC2000E.3.1, 3.2, 3.3, 3.4, 3.5, 3.6, 3.8

1. In an existing database:

   a) Create a select query to show information from a single table sorted in a different order than the table.

   b) Apply filters (by form and by selection) to the query's results set.

   c) Remove the filter. Add multiple criteria using both AND and OR. Run the query and examine the results.

   d) Modify query properties to format a query field.

   e) Modify query properties to return Unique Records, Top Values, or both.

   f) Modify the query to return all records in the results set.

   g) Add a parameter to the query so a user can look for records based on the value in a particular field.

2. Create a new query that includes information from more than one table. Save and run the query. Change the inner join to each type of outer join and note any differences in the query results sets.

3. In an existing database:

   a) Create a select query that includes a calculated field.

   b) Turn the select query into a summary query to total the calculated field and count at least one other field.

Optimizing Field Properties

You can tweak specific field properties to make your database easier to use and improve the quality of data entry and overall performance. In this section, we'll look at three specific issues: validating data entry, optimizing data storage, and modifying lookup fields.

Validating Data Entry

Objective AC2000E.3.7

The lowest level of validation mandates that a field must have an entry by changing its Required property. When a field's Required property is set to Yes, a user must enter data before saving the record. The Indexed property has three possible values: No, Yes (No Duplicates), and Yes (Duplicates OK). Choosing Yes speeds up searching, sorting, and filtering by creating an index for the field. Yes (No Duplicates) means that the value entered in the field must be unique. There is a speed tradeoff when you create an index: queries that search, sort, and filter are faster, but editing and adding records slows down as Access indexes each added or modified record.

For a single-field primary key, Access sets the Required property to Yes and Indexed to Yes (No Duplicates). With a multiple-field primary key, all fields are required, but duplicates are allowed within a field. You can set either property to constrain and/or require entries in a field.

Validating Entries

Entering a value in a field's Default property is a passive way to validate data. For more active validation, create a Validation Rule that screens the data, and Validation Text that lets the user know what constitutes a valid entry. In Access 2000, you can validate fields and records in tables, and controls in forms.

- *Field validation* is set in a field's Validation Rule property. When you tab or click out of the field, Access checks to make sure the data you entered matches the rule. If not, the Validation Text is displayed.
- *Record validation* is set in the properties sheet for the table. When you move to a new record, Access checks to make sure the entire record is valid. Record validation is used to compare one field to another to check, for example, that an employee's HireDate occurred before the TerminationDate.

Many field properties set in a table are inheritable. That means that the Validation Rule set in a table passes through to any form control based on the field. So normally you won't use control validation, which is set in a form control's property sheet. It's better to validate once in the table than four times in four forms. However, there are times that you can only validate in a form. For example, linked tables from Excel or other Access databases aren't included in your database, so you can't validate at the table level, only in a form control.

Objectives AC2000E.1.1 and 1.2

To enter a validation rule for a field, select the field in the upper pane in Table Design view, and click in the Validation Rule property box in the lower pane. If the rule is simple (minimum pay rate is $10), enter it using logical operators: >=10. In the Validation Text property box, enter the error message that should appear on the status bar when invalid data is entered, as shown in Figure 9.20. If you would like a larger space in which to type validation text, right-click in the property box and choose Zoom to open the Zoom box. When you are done entering text, click OK to close the Zoom box. To validate records, right-click in the table and choose Properties to open the table's properties sheet.

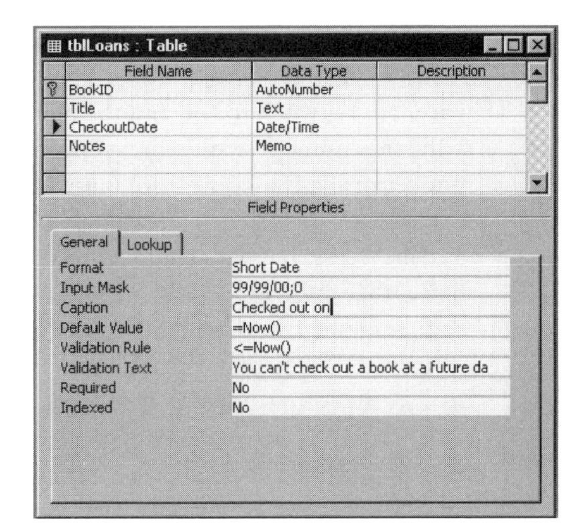

FIGURE 9.20 Enter validation rules and text in the Table Properties sheet.

Validating Data Entry

1. Open the table in Design view.
2. Select the field you want to add validation to.

   OR

2. To add record validation, right-click and select Properties.

Validating Data Entry *(continued)*

3. Enter a rule in the field or table's Validation Rule property box, or click the Build button and create the rule using the Expression Builder.
4. Type the message that you want displayed when invalid data is entered in the Validation Message property box.
5. Save the table. If you created validation rules for fields that contain data, you'll be asked whether you want Access to apply the rules to the existing data when you save the table.

Optimizing Data Type Usage

Objective AC2000E.1.5

In the good old days (shudder) when a small hard drive cost twice as much as a television, developers worked tenaciously to store data in the smallest possible space on a costly drive. These are the days of relatively cheap hardware, but network traffic and the memory required to process huge tables with large numeric requirements provide ample reason to minimize the number of bytes used to store information in a database.

For text fields, specify a reasonable field length. It won't make much difference in Access, but data entered in Access could end up in another database system that reserves string space and will believe that a two-letter state abbreviation requires the default 50 characters. For numeric fields, choose the most compact data type that will accommodate the numbers entered by users. Table 9.5 lists the Access numeric data types and their storage requirements. You'll notice that the Currency data type isn't on the list. Currency is a separate data type, but its fixed decimal point format is better than either Single or Double data types as long as you only need to store numbers with up to four decimal points. To change the data type used in a field, open the field's table in Design View, select the field, then change the Format property.

TABLE 9.5: Numeric Data Types

Name	Stores	Size
Byte	Whole numbers from 0 to 255	1 byte
Decimal	Numbers from $-10^{28}-1$ to $10^{28}-1$	12 bytes

TABLE 9.5: Numeric Data Types *(continued)*

Name	Stores	Size
Double	Negative numbers from –1.79769313486231E308 to –4.94065645841247E–324 and positive numbers from 1.79769313486231E308 to 4.94065645841247E–324 for positive values	8 bytes
Integer	Whole numbers from –32,768 to 32,767	2 bytes
Long Integer	Whole numbers from –2,147,483,648 to 2,147,483,647	4 bytes
Single	Negative numbers from –3.402823E38 to 1.401298E–45 and positive numbers from 1.401298E–45 to 3.402823E38	4 bytes

Modifying Lookup Fields

Objective AC2000E.1.4

When you add a lookup to another table using the Lookup Wizard , Access creates a select query to populate the drop-down list. By adding criteria to the query, you can have Access populate the list with records of a specific ListType (for example, STATE or WNBA). To access the query behind the lookup, open the table that contains the lookup field in Design view. Select the lookup field then click the Lookup tab in the lower pane.

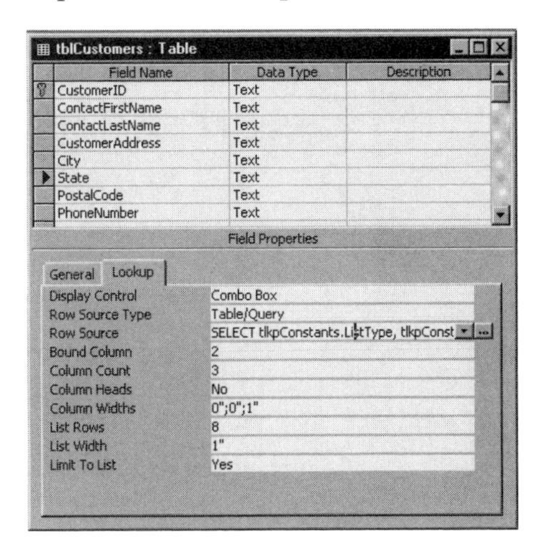

Enable the Row Source property then click the Build button to open the query. In the ListType column, enter the name of the list type in the Criteria row. While you're in there, make sure the query includes an appropriate sort order, then close the query and save the changes when prompted.

Hands On: Objectives AC2000E.1.1, 1.2, 1.4, 1.5, and 3.7

1. In an existing table:
   a) Review and set FieldLength properties for text fields where data length is known.
   b) Set Required properties where appropriate.
   c) Set the Index property to Yes for the fields that you will sort or filter on most frequently.
2. In an existing table:
   a) Establish a ValidationRule and enter a ValidationMessage for at least one field. Test the rule and message by attempting to enter invalid data.
   b) Set and test a DefaultValue property for at least one field.
3. In an existing database, review the field sizes for text fields and data types for all numeric fields.
4. In an existing database, examine and modify the properties for one or more lookup fields.

Working with External Data

With Access 2000, you can add copies of tables from other applications to your database or work with tables that exist in a separate database or spreadsheet. Access 2000 can *import* (copy) or *link* (connect to) data from prior versions of Access, other databases like FoxPro and Paradox, spreadsheets like Excel and Lotus 1-2-3, and HTML tables from the Internet or an intranet. The ability to work with data from a variety of sources makes Access a powerful tool in today's workplace, where data can originate in a variety of applications. Before you re-key data that already exists, it's worth your time to see if you can import it directly into Access or transfer it to a program like Excel that Access can import

Importing vs. Linking

Objective AC2000.8.1

Importing data creates a copy of the data in your database. The original data isn't affected, and changes in the original data are not reflected in Access. With *linked* data, you are working with original data; when the source file changes, the changes are reflected in Access, and changes in Access are reflected in the source file. If you know that the data doesn't need to be updated in another program, you should import it. If you need "live" data, you need to link.

Importing from a Spreadsheet or Database

1. Choose File ➢ Get External Data ➢ Import.
2. Choose a File Type from the drop-down list. Select the file you want to import and click Import.
3. Using the Import Wizard, select the data you want to import. When prompted, provide specifications about the data, including the columns/fields you wish to import, primary key, and location for the data. Proceed through the Wizard to create the table or add the data to an existing table.

If you import from another Access database, you aren't limited to data. You can import forms, reports, macros, queries, pages, modules, and even relationships. When you choose an Access database in the Import dialog box, the Import Objects dialog box opens.

Importing Objects from an Access Database

1. Choose File ➢ Get External Data ➢ Import.
2. Select the Access database you wish to import from and click Import.
3. Select the object(s) you wish to import. To set import options, click the Options button.
4. Click Import.

Linking to a Spreadsheet or Database

Objective AC2000.8.4

Linking to a table or worksheet is even less complex than importing. You can't change the structure of the linked table or worksheet, so you don't get an opportunity to skip columns.

Linking to an External Data Source

1. Choose File ➢ Get External Data ➢ Link Tables.
2. Select the type of data source you want to link to in the Files of Type drop-down list.
3. Select the file you want to link to and click Link to open the Link Wizard.
4. Select the worksheet, named range, or table you wish to link to. Click Link.
5. In a spreadsheet, indicate whether the first row contains data or column labels. Click Next.
6. Enter the name you will use to refer to the external table or worksheet, and click Finish.

If you decide later that you don't want to be linked to the data, select and delete the link in the Table page of the Database window. The link is deleted, not the original table.

Cut, Copy, and Paste with Excel 2000

Objectives AC2000.5.1 and AC2000E.8.1

If the data you want is currently stored in an Excel spreadsheet, the Windows Clipboard provides an excellent way to transfer your data back and forth from Access.

Importing from Excel

To import data from Excel into Access, select the portion of your spreadsheet that contains the information that you want to import. Then cut or copy it to the Clipboard, depending upon whether you want a copy of the data to remain in your spreadsheet. Note that you cannot select non-contiguous data.

Return to Access and select Paste. A dialog box opens asking if the first row of your selection contains column headings. If you answer No, Access generates the field names: "F1," "F2," "F3," etc. Access creates a table named after the Excel worksheet. If that name is already taken, Access appends it with a number to ensure uniqueness.

Importing from Excel

1. Select the region on your spreadsheet that you want to move to Access.
2. Cut or copy your data to the Clipboard.
3. Return to Access and select Paste, either using the first row of your data for column names or allowing Access to assign them for you.

Exporting to Excel

If importing from Excel is easy, then exporting to it is even easier! To transfer an entire table or query from Access, simply select it in the Database window and cut or copy it to the Clipboard. To transfer a certain number of rows from within the table or query, open it in Datasheet view, select the rows in question, and then cut or copy them to the Clipboard. Finally, go to Excel, place the cursor your spreadsheet where you want to import your data, and select Edit ➢ Paste from the menu bar.

Exporting to Excel

1. Select an entire table to export from the Database window, or just the rows that you want from the Datasheet view.
2. Cut or copy your data to the Clipboard.
3. Click in the Excel worksheet and paste.

Objective AC2000E.8.2

If you're really feeling adventurous, you can use drag and drop to move or copy records and rows between the two applications. For example, open the table you want to paste into in Access. Select data in Excel, then drag the selection to the Access button on the Windows taskbar, and wait for Windows to switch focus to the Access window. Drop the selection in the table.

To create a new table from an Excel worksheet, drop the selection in the Access Database window. Select an Access table or query in the Database window and drop it in an Excel worksheet to copy all the records from the table or query into the worksheet.

Hands On: *Objectives AC2000.8.1, AC2000E.8.1, 8.2*

1. In a new or existing database, import data from a spreadsheet or a database other than Access. (If you need a worksheet to import, choose one of the Excel worksheets from the Sybex Web site.) View and, if necessary, change the design of the imported table.
2. In a new or existing database, import at least one table and one form from another Access database.
3. In a new or existing database, link to a table in a worksheet or database.
   a) Change one or more values in the link source.
   b) Switch to Access and view the changes in the linked table.
   c) Delete the link.
4. Use drag and drop to create a table from an Excel worksheet selection.
5. Use drag and drop to copy an entire Access query results set to Excel.
6. Copy the first four records from an Access table to an Excel worksheet.

Producing Reports

A *report* is the output of the data in a database. Reports can be based on a table or a query. The flexibility to customize reports and to organize data in useful ways—in other words, to make it accessible—is really what gives Access its name. When a report is saved, only the structure of the report is saved. Data shown in a report is always live, as current as the information in your database. A simple report based on our Customers table is shown in Figure 9.21.

FIGURE 9.21

A report displays output from your database.

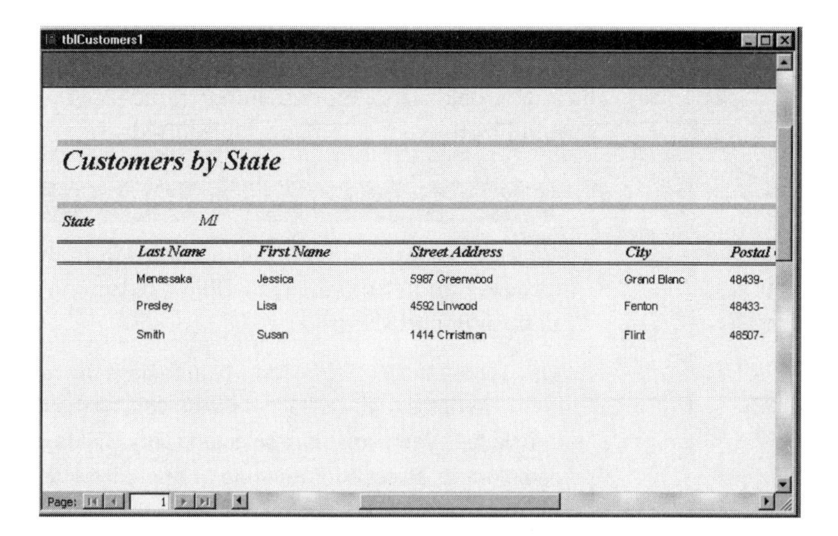

Most reports are either columnar or tabular reports. A *columnar report* shows each field on a separate line in a single column down the page. The columnar report is the printed version of a columnar form. A *tabular report* is like a tabular form.

You can develop reports in five ways:

- In Design view
- Using the Report Wizard
- By choosing one of two AutoReports, which automatically include all of the fields in the table or query
- In the Chart Wizard, which walks you through the steps to create a chart
- With the Label Wizard, which creates mailing and other labels

Creating a report in Access is as simple as creating a data form. AutoReports are very limited, so we'll move directly to the Report Wizard.

Using the Report Wizard

Objective AC2000.7.1

The Report Wizard lets you choose the fields you want in the report—including fields from more than one table—and designate how the data should be grouped, sorted, and formatted.

Creating a Report Using the Report Wizard

1. Choose Create Report by Using Wizard from the database window, or choose Report from the New Object button on the toolbar and then choose Report Wizard.
2. Choose the table or query on which to base the report. Click the pick arrow to move fields to the Selected Fields box, or the double arrow to move all the fields. When you have selected all the fields you want from the first table/query, select another table or query from the list, if desired.
3. Click Next when you have finished selecting fields.
4. Choose the levels you want to group by, if any. Use the up or down Priority buttons to reverse the order of the grouping levels. Click Next.
5. Choose the fields you would like to sort by, and indicate whether you'd like the records in ascending or descending order. Click Next.
6. Select the layout you'd like for the report, portrait or landscape orientation, and whether you'd like the fields truncated so they fit on one page. Click Next.
7. Select the style you'd like for the report and click Next.
8. Enter a title for the report and choose whether you'd like to open the report in Print Preview or Design view. Click Finish to create the report.

Printing and Previewing Reports

Objective AC2000.7.2

To preview a report, select the report in the Database window, then click the Preview button in the Database window or choose File ➢ Print Preview from the menu. Click the Print button in the Preview window to print the report.

To print a report from the Database window, select the report then click the Print button on the toolbar or choose File ➢ Print to open the Print dialog box and specify print settings.

Modifying a Report

Objective AC2000E.4.3

Most of what you know about Access form design can be applied to report design. After you open the report in Design view, maximize the report so you have more room to work. Figure 9.22 shows the rptCustomers report in Design view.

FIGURE 9.22 Modifying a report in Design view

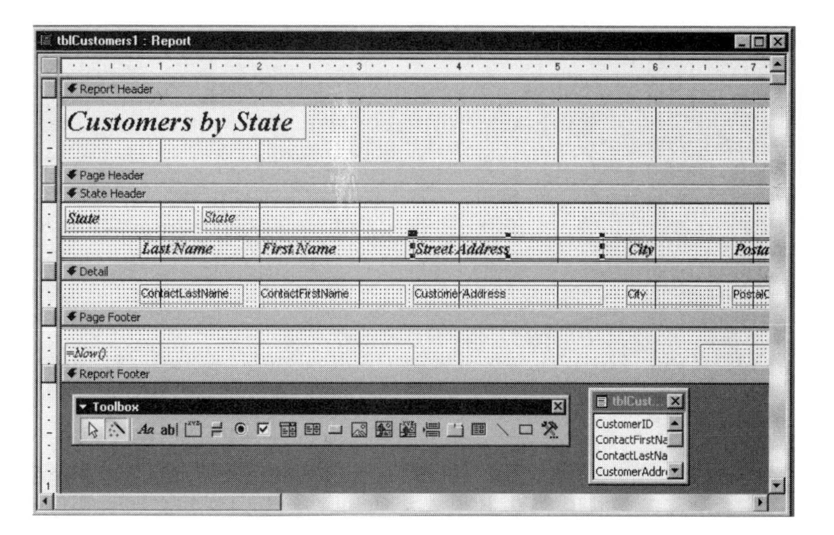

Objectives AC2000.7.6 and AC2000E.4.5

A report has seven possible sections:

Report Header is displayed at the top of the report (page one) and includes the title and other report information.

Page Header is at the top of every printed page of the report.

Group Header is at the top of an identified group; there is a separate group header for each grouping level.

Detail is where the data from the tables/queries will appear.

Group Footer is at the bottom of an identified group; there is a separate group footer for each grouping level.

Page Footer is at the bottom of every page.

Report Footer is on the last page of the report.

You can choose to incorporate any or all of these sections into your report. Use the adjustment tool to increase or decrease the size of the sections. Right-click in a section's background and choose Properties from the shortcut menu to set section properties.

Objective AC2000.4.2

The section properties can be overridden by changing the report's properties. For example, you can change the form's Page Header property so a page header doesn't appear on a page that also has a report header. To access the report properties, double-click the Report Selector button or right-click on the Report Selector and choose Properties. To modify a property, enter a new value or select a value from the property's drop-down list.

Objective AC2000.7.4

The Snap-to-Grid, alignment, and size features all work the same as they do in Access forms. All the colors, lines, borders, special effects, fonts, and other formatting features are available in reports. You can edit any of the report's labels without worrying about affecting the contents of the report. However, be careful not to edit the text boxes that contain data fields. If you do, the control will no longer be bound to a field, so it won't display data. Most text boxes are in the detail section. However, at least one text box appears in each group header. To be certain that you're editing a label rather than a text box, look at the control's properties.

In Report Design view, there are two preview choices on the View menu: Print Preview and Layout Preview. Print Preview produces the entire report just as it will look when printed. However, if you have a database with thousands or even hundreds or records, it takes time to produce a preview of all the pages. By using sample data, Layout Preview quickly generates a preview so that you can check design features.

Modifying Page Number Control Properties

Objective AC2000E.4.4

Each of the objects in a report has properties. For example, the Page Footer section contains a date field that shows today's date and a page number field that shows the current page number out of the total number of pages. The control is a calculated field that includes text strings and fields.

As with form controls, these controls can be customized if you would like to change their appearance. The date field, which displays today's date, includes the function `=Now()`. You can choose different date formats by opening the control's properties sheet. Click the Format drop-down list on the Format page and then scroll the list to select an option: general date, long date, medium date, or short date.

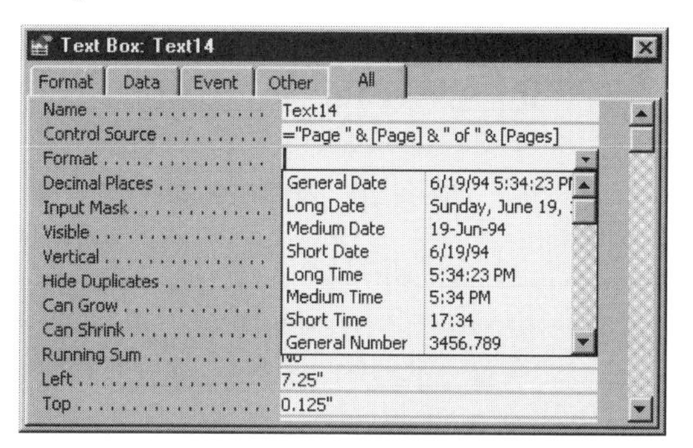

If you want to add a date to a different part of the report or to a report that doesn't already have a date, choose Insert ➢ Date and Time from the menu bar to open the Date and Time dialog box. Set your preferences and choose OK, and a text box control with the appropriate code is inserted at the top of the active report section. Drag the control to its location in the report. If your report is only one page, you might want to delete the page number field control altogether; select the field and press the Delete key on the keyboard.

Adding and Deleting Report Controls

Objective AC2000.7.3 and 7.5

Add and delete report controls just as you add or delete form controls. To add a field to a report, click the Field List button on the Report Design toolbar to open the Field List. Drag a field from the list into the appropriate section of the report. You might have to format and re-size the label and the text box controls once you drop the field into place. To delete a field's text box control from the report, select the text box and press the Delete key on the keyboard.

Inserting Graphics

Objective AC2000E.4.1

To add a graphic (for example, a company logo) to a report, click in the section (like the Report Header or Page Header) where you want to place the image then choose Insert ➢ Picture from the menu to open the Insert Picture dialog box. Browse to locate the picture, then click OK to insert the image.

Adding Calculated Controls

Objective AC2000.7.7

One of the rules of relational database design is that you don't store calculated values; you perform the calculation when you need it. You'll frequently need to add calculated fields to reports. There are two ways to do this:

- Add a calculated field to a query underlying the report, then place the field in the report.

OR

- Add a control to the report and perform the calculation in the control.

In either case, you can type an expression or use the Expression Builder to create the formula. For instructions on adding a field to a query, see *Adding Calculations to Queries* earlier in this chapter.

Adding a Calculated Control to a Report

1. Click the Text Box control in the Toolbox.
2. Click in the report to place the control.
3. Right-click on the text box control and choose Properties.
4. Select the Control Source property.
5. Enter a formula or click the Build button to open the Expression Builder then use the Builder to create the calculation.

Use the Subreport Control

Objective AC2000E.4.6

A subreport serves the same function in a report as a subform in a form; displaying records from a related table in an object that displays information from the primary table. However, you can use a report *or a form* for the subreport. A subreport prints within the detail section of the report. As with a subform and form, the subreport and report are synchronized by the Link Child Fields and Link Master Fields in the subreport control.

Using the Subreport Control

1. Open the report in Design View.
2. Click the Subform/Subreport button on the Toolbox.
3. Click in the report to place the subreport control and open the Subreport Wizard.
4. In the first step of the wizard, select an existing report or form to use as a subreport. Click Next.

   OR

4. Choose to use an existing table or query to create a subreport. Click Next. Select the table/query and fields to use in the subreport. Click Next.
5. Choose the statement that best describes the relationship between the two tables, or choose Define and select the primary key/foreign key fields that relate the records in the two reports. Click Next.
6. Enter or confirm the name for the subreport and click Finish.

Hands On: Objectives AC2000.7.1, 7.2, 7.4, 7.5, 7.6, 7.7, and AC2000E.4.2, 4.3, 4.4, and 4.6

1. In an existing database, create a report based on two or more tables using the Report Wizard. Modify the font and alignment of the report title. Add a subtitle to the report in the same font style with a smaller font size.
2. Preview and print a report.
3. Create a report with:
    a) The page number in the page header, with no number on the first page.
    b) Your name in the footer of each page.
    c) A report header and a page header.
4. Change the report's properties to suppress the page header on pages with a form header. Preview the report.
5. Create a report with a subreport. Preview the report.
6. Add a calculated control to your report.

Using Access 2000 Tools and Utilities

In the final section of this chapter, we'll focus on tools and utilities designed to help you maintain and improve your Access 2000 database. Like any well-used toolbox, the top drawer contains a variety of different tools, each designed for a particular task.

Converting, Backing Up, and Compacting Databases

Objective AC2000.E.7.8

Microsoft Access 2000 allows you to convert a database so it can be opened in Access 97. Once it is saved in the earlier format, you can no longer use any of the new Access 2000 features, but you can create databases that Access 97 users in your office can open. To convert an Access 2000 database to Access 97, open the Access 2000 database that you would like to convert. Choose Tools ➢ Database Utilities ➢ Convert Database ➢ To Prior Access Database Version, then enter a filename for the converted version of your database and click Save.

Backing up a Database

Objective AC2000.9.2

Databases quickly become mission critical applications in almost every company. When you design a database, you need to plan and implement a backup scheme. The backup frequency depends on how important the data is, whether it can be reconstructed from manual records, and how often it changes. No matter how often you plan to backup, backups need to become part of the work routine. For example, if you decide that you need to backup about every 10 days, then plan weekly backups: for example, Wednesdays at the end of the business day. Everyone knows when it's Wednesday, but it's hard to keep track of "10 days since the last backup."

To backup an Access database, copy the database file (with the mdb extension) to a floppy disk, zip disk, backup tape, or a drive on another network workstation or server. For truly important data, backup to a removable media and take the backup off premises. If your database is secured with user level security, you also need to backup the workgroup information file every time you add or remove a user or group.

Compacting Your Data

Objective AC2000.9.3

Access 2000 can automatically compact a database every time you close it, reclaiming unused space that can make a database file run slower and take up more disk space.

Configuring Access to Compact on Close

1. Choose Tools ➢ Options ➢ General from the menu bar.
2. Verify that the check box labeled Compact on Close is checked.
3. Click OK.

Manually Compacting Your Database

1. Choose Tools ➢ Database Utilities ➢ Compact and Repair Database.

Using the Access 2000 Add-Ins

Objective AC2000E.7.3

Beginning with Access 97, Access has included tools to make it easier to develop and distribute databases. The Analyzer examines a table or database and makes recommendations to improve performance. The Database Splitter Wizard converts a database to a *file server database*, by separating the tables from the forms and reports that users interact with. After you've split a database (or if your database includes linked tables from other databases or applications) you can use the Linked Table Manager to refresh links when the data source is moved or renamed.

Using the Analyzer

Open the database you wish to analyze and choose Tools ➢ Analyze ➢ Performance to open the Performance Analyzer dialog box.

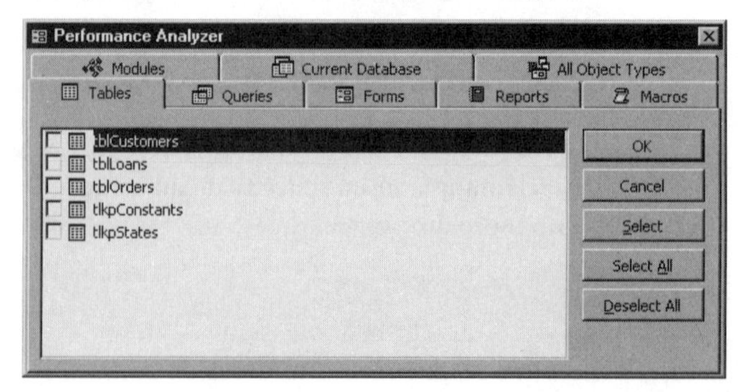

On each tab, select the object(s) to be included in the analysis then click OK to start the analyzer. The results of an analysis for a complex and poorly designed database (that we obviously didn't design!) are shown in Figure 9.23. Analysis results in order of the severity of the problem are couched as Recommendations, Suggestions, and Ideas. To implement a recommendation or suggestion, select the result and click the Optimize button. Access makes the change and marks the suggestion or recommendation as Fixed. Note the Analyzer's Ideas (or capture the screen and print or save it) for correction after you've closed the Analyzer.

FIGURE 9.23 The Analyzer highlights potential areas for improvement.

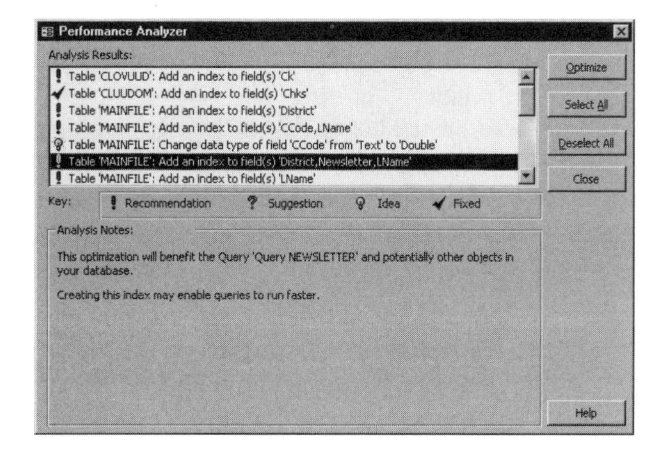

The Table Analyzer Wizard analyzes the records in a populated table to determine if the table really represents two or more entities. It makes this determination by looking for lots of duplicate values in a field, then helps you separate the table into two or more tables. You'd think that the Table Analyzer is only useful if you did a poor job of designing your database, but it has a real use for good designers by separating tables imported from other sources. To run the Table Analyzer, choose Tools ➢ Analyze ➢ Table from the menu.

Both the Table and Performance Analyzers can make suggestions that are incorrect—that's why both tools leave it up to you to accept or reject their suggestions.

Splitting Your Database

If you have multiple users for your database, you can often improve performance by splitting the database and saving the back end (tables) on a server and placing the front end (forms, reports, and queries) on each users' workstation. To split a database, first open the database. Choose Tools ➢ Database Utilities ➢ Database Splitter to launch the Splitter Wizard.

Click the Split Database button and the Create Back-end Database dialog box (similar to the Save As dialog box) opens so you can enter a name and select a location for the back-end database. Access assumes that you may already have people using the database, so the front-end database that users open is saved using the current database's name and location. Click the Split button to begin splitting the database. You are prompted when Access has completed the operation. Examine the Tables tab in the Database window, and you'll notice that each table name is preceded by the linked table icon.

Updating Table Links

With any type of linking, it's possible (even easy) to unlink objects. If you change the name or location of the back-end, the front-end won't be able to find the linked tables. When users forget to log in and open the front-end when Access 2000 can't access the shared network folder that holds the back-end, the tables may unlink. Or, you may decide that you want to move the back-end to another folder or a server with more free space. Access includes a Linked Table Manager that you'll use to re-connect the front-end and back-end databases. Choose Tools ➢ Database Utilities ➢ Linked Table Manager to open the Linked Table Manager.

Select the table link or links you wish to refresh, then click OK. Access checks the listed location for each selected table. If it cannot find a table in the listed location, a Select New Location of *tablename* dialog box opens so you can locate the table. Access checks the table's listed location first. But what if you've copied and changed the back-end and want to link to the tables in the changed database? Enable the Always Prompt for New Location check box in the Linked Table Manager dialog box to have Access ask you for the location for each selected table.

Using Security and Startup Options

Objective AC2000E.7.1

There are two types of security you can apply in Access 2000: user level security and a database password. User level security is robust, like network level security. You can create groups, grant permissions, and assign users to groups, and grant users different levels of access to individual database objects. For more information on user level security, see Access Help.

A database password prevents unauthorized users from opening your database. Once a user is "in", he or she can do anything with the database that you can do. Passwords are case-sensitive. If you lose your password, you can't open the database at all, ever again. We encourage you to create a non-protected copy of the database for archival purposes before setting a password.

Setting a Database Password

1. Make sure other users are not using the database.
2. Close the database.
3. Choose File ➢ Open from the menu.
4. Click the arrow attached to the Open button and choose Open Exclusive from the menu.
5. In the open database, choose Tools ➢ Security ➢ Set Database Password from the menu.
6. Type your password in the Password and Verify text boxes.
7. Click OK.

Encrypting and Decrypting a Database

Objective AC2000E.7.4

Encrypting a database compacts and protects the data so it can't be read in a text editor or word processing program. You decrypt a database to remove encrypting. Before encrypting a database, we recommend that you create a backup on removable media.

Encrypting/Decrypting a Database

1. Make sure other users are not using the database.
2. Close the database.
3. Choose Tools > Security > Encrypt/Decrypt Database.
4. Select the database you want to encrypt or decrypt.
5. Choose a location and name for the encrypted/decrypted database. Choose the current database name and location to replace the current database with the encrypted/decrypted version.

Creating a Switchboard and Setting Startup Options

You set startup options to control the environment that a user enters when the database opens. If, for example, the first thing a user sees is the Database window, they'll be tempted to play with the database objects. You probably don't want your users to delete tables just to see what happens. Before you hide the Database window, though, use the Switchboard Manager Add-in to create a switchboard that you can display when a user opens your database. Include all the activities your users will want to access on the switchboard to make your database easy to use. To see a switchboard in action, create an Access database using the Database Wizard. The wizard automatically adds switchboards to the databases it creates.

Objective AC2000E.2.7

Creating a Switchboard

1. Open the database.
2. Choose Tools > Database Utilities > Switchboard Manager.
3. Click Yes when prompted to open the Switchboard Manager dialog box.
4. Click the Edit button to open the Edit Switchboard Page dialog box.
5. Edit the Switchboard name from the default Main Switchboard if you wish.
6. Click the New button to add another page to the switchboard.

Creating a Switchboard *(continued)*

7. Select a page you want to add items to and click the Edit button to open the Edit Switchboard Page dialog box.
8. Click New to open the Edit Switchboard Item dialog box.

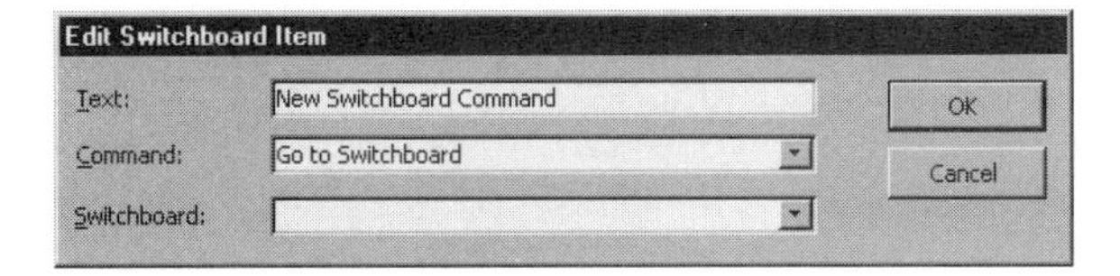

9. Enter the text your user will see for this choice in the text box.
10. Choose a command from the Command list.
11. If you choose a command that requires an argument (for example, a form or report name), another control will open below the Command control. Make a selection.
12. Click OK to return to the Edit Switchboard Page dialog box.
13. Repeat Steps 8–12 to add all the items to this switchboard page.
14. Use the Move Up and Move Down buttons to rearrange the switchboard items. On the main switchboard page, the last item should run the Exit Application command to close the database and Access 2000. On other pages, the last item should open the main switchboard page.
15. Click Close to close the Edit Switchboard Page dialog box and return to the Switchboard Manager.
16. Close the Switchboard Manager.

Choose Forms in the Object bar and double-click Switchboard to test the switchboard. Run the Switchboard Manager again when you need to modify the switchboard.

Objective AC2000E.7.2

To open your switchboard automatically when the database opens, choose Tools ➢ Startup to open the Startup dialog box. Click the Advanced button to display all the options, as shown in Figure 9.24.

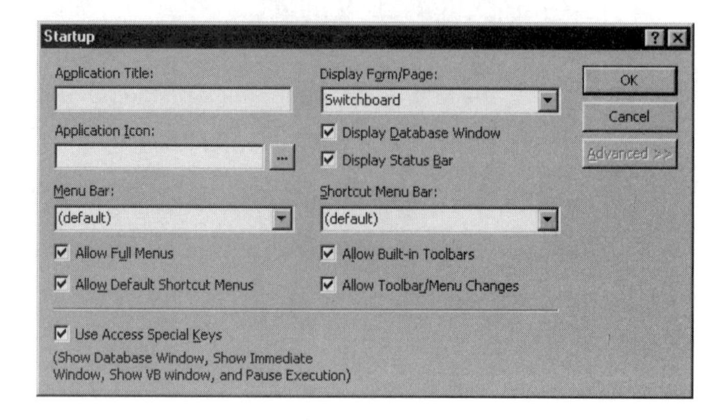

FIGURE 9.24 Set the database's properties when opened in the Startup dialog box.

Select Switchboard in the Display Form/Page drop down. Change a few other settings while you're here:

- Disable Display Database Window to keep users away from the objects in your database.
- Enter an Application Title that will appear in the Access title bar.
- Disable Allow Toolbar/Menu changes to prevent users from customizing toolbars.

For information on other startup options, click the Help button then click on the control. Click OK to close the Startup dialog box.

To test the startup settings, close the database then choose File ➢ Open and select the database. To bypass the startup options, simply hold down the Shift key while you open the database.

Creating a Briefcase Replica

Objective AC2000E.7.5

Replicas are synchronizable copies of a database. If you have users who need to take a copy of a database for work outside the office, you can create a simple replica using the Windows Briefcase. The Briefcase must be installed before you create the replica; if it is not installed, choose Add/Remove Programs in the Windows Control Panel. Find your Windows CD-ROM, then in the Add/Remove Programs dialog box, click the Windows Setup tab, double-click Accessories, and add the Briefcase feature.

Creating a Briefcase Replica

1. If the database has a database password, remove the password.
2. Open the Windows Explorer.
3. Select the folder that the database file is stored in.
4. Drag the database file and drop it on the My Briefcase icon on the desktop.
5. Move the Briefcase to the user's mobile computer.

When your mobile user returns to the office, you need to synchronize the databases to swap updated records.

Synchronizing a Briefcase Replica

1. Move the user's Briefcase folder back to the desktop.
2. In the Windows desktop, open the Briefcase, then select the database file.
3. Choose Update Selection from the Briefcase menu.

CHAPTER 10

Getting Organized with Outlook

Do you ever find a few of those myriad corporate details falling through the cracks? Does your follow up "system" consist of hundreds of sticky notes posted all over your office? Are you carrying an organizer that weighs more than your briefcase? Outlook 2000 can help you streamline your desktop organization. With six application modules available from a single window, you can manage appointments, contacts, meetings, e-mail messages, tasks, projects, files, and notes in one place. Set reminders for yourself so you don't drop the ball. Create categories for viewing data in ways that make sense to you. Print portions of your data to take on the road or synchronize your PC with a hand-held unit.

Outlook is a desktop information manager (DIM) rather than the more common personal information manager (PIM), because it is more than "personal." You can manage all your business activities with Outlook 2000 and stay on top of those details that make the difference between doing business and doing business well.

Understanding Outlook Basics

Because Outlook 2000 does so many different things, it takes a little while to find your way around. Outlook includes six major modules and several minor ones. The major modules are:

Outlook Today: Provides a quick overview of the day's calendar and tasks, along with current e-mail.

Inbox: Sends and receives e-mail and faxes.

Calendar: Used to schedule appointments, track recurring meetings, plan meetings with others, and receive reminders of important events.

Contacts: Stores names, addresses, and other contact data.

Tasks: Keeps your To Do list, assigns tasks to others, and tracks progress on projects.

Notes: Computerized sticky notes that can be stored in Outlook or posted on the Windows desktop.

You interact with each of the modules using *forms*. Each form window has its own toolbars and menu bar and operates independently. Even closing the Outlook application window doesn't close all the open forms. If a form window is open, you must choose File ➢ Exit & Log Off to exit Outlook completely. Otherwise, the Outlook application window will close, but form windows will remain open.

Outlooks supports three different mail configurations: Internet Only, Corporate/Workgroup, and No E-Mail. Each configuration provides different options. To check or to change your configuration, choose Tools ➢ Mail Delivery ➢ Reconfigure Mail Support. This chapter focuses mainly on the Internet Only configuration with a few topics addressing a Corporate/Workgroup configuration. If you need more information about the workgroup tools and options included only in the Corporate/Workgroup configuration, see *Mastering Outlook 2000*, also from Sybex.

Navigating Outlook

Objective OL2000.4.3

Before you can begin exploring Outlook, you must establish a user profile so Outlook knows who you are, what your e-mail address is, which information service(s) you use, and where you want your data stored. If your profile wasn't established when you installed Office 2000, you will be prompted to establish a profile using the Outlook Setup Wizard.

If you use a networked computer, your network administrator should be able to help you set up your profile (or they may have already done it for you).

When Outlook opens, you may see the Inbox (shown in Figure 10.1) or Outlook Today, a window that provides an overview of current information from several modules. The vertical Outlook Bar on the left of the window activates other modules: click an icon on the Outlook Bar to open the module. Use the navigation button at the bottom of the Outlook Bar to scroll the list of choices; as you scroll down the list, another scroll button appears at the top of the bar. The Outlook Bar's icons are grouped; the Outlook Shortcuts group includes the six main applications. The My Shortcuts and Other Shortcuts groups open additional lists of shortcuts you can customize and personalize (see *Creating Shortcuts*, later in this chapter). Click any group button to open the group and display its icons.

FIGURE 10.1

The Outlook Window

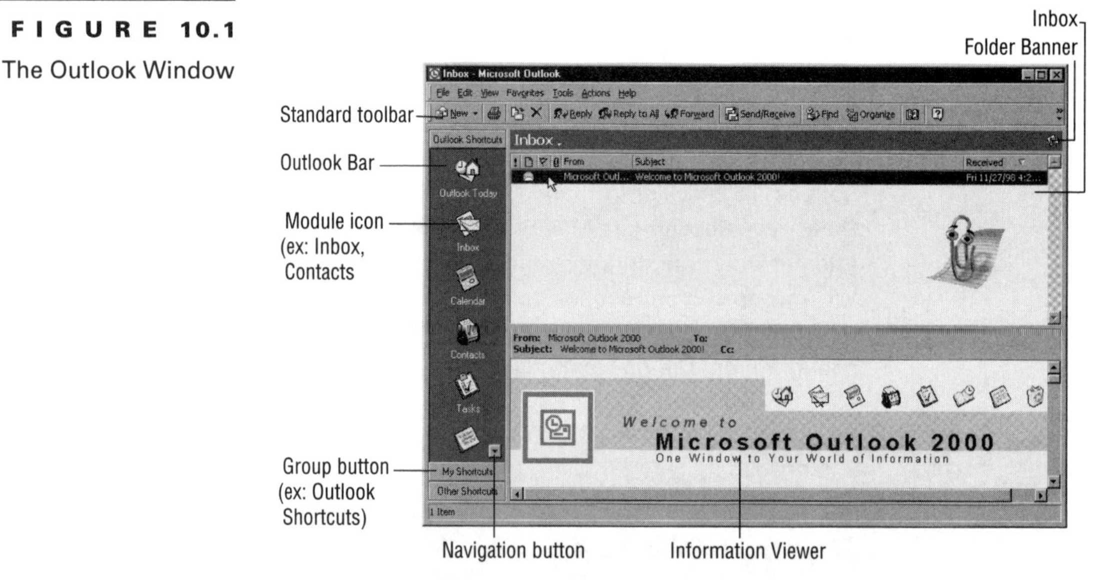

Opening an Outlook Module

1. Click the Outlook Shortcuts button to display Outlook modules.
2. Click the module's icon in the Outlook Bar.

Entering Data

You'll generally enter or edit data in an Outlook form. Clicking the New button on the Standard toolbar opens the default form for the selected module. In the Inbox, for example, the default form is a blank e-mail form. Open the drop-down list attached to the New button to access forms for all the modules.

Each module also provides easy ways to open a new form. For example, the Tasks module has an area at the top of the Information Viewer where you can click to add a new task.

You can click once then type information in this area, or double-click to open a new Task form.

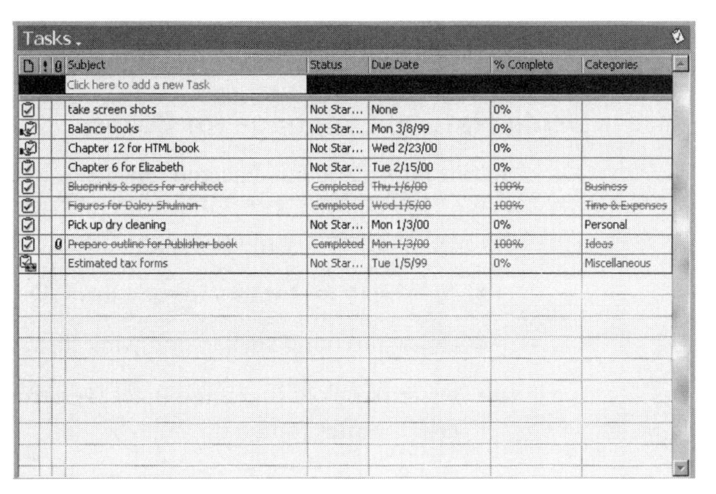

Entering text in an Outlook form is simple. Just type the information you want in the appropriate field. Press Tab to move between fields, and use Backspace or Delete to make corrections. Select text for editing by dragging over it; right-click to choose Cut, Copy, or Paste. The Edit menu has an Undo option, but you can only use it to reverse the last action you took, so use Undo promptly or you'll have to edit to fix mistakes.

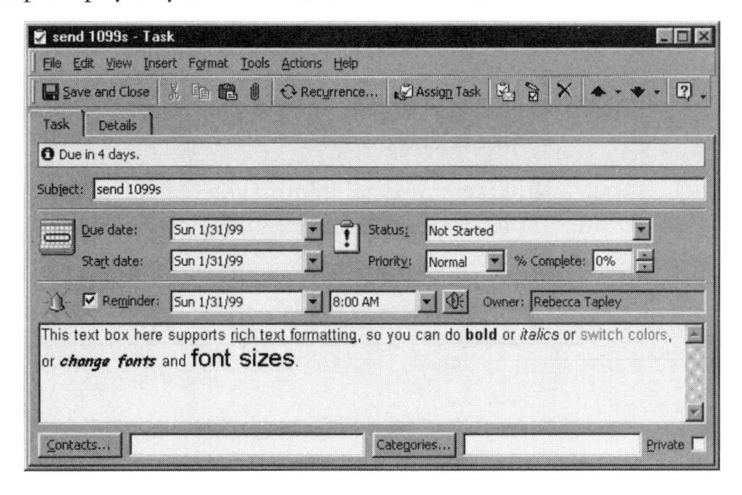

Outlook supports *rich text formats* in text boxes designed for entering paragraphs of text like the details or comments about a task. If the Formatting toolbar is not visible in the form window, choose View ➢ Toolbars ➢ Formatting. Toolbar buttons are only enabled in areas that support rich text. You won't find as many formatting choices as you do in Word, but the toolbar buttons include font, font size, color, text enhancement, paragraph alignment, bullets, and indenting.

Using Natural Language for Dates

Entering information in date and time fields is about as free as it can get. You can type 5/2/00 if you wish, but you can also enter 'three days before Cinco de Mayo.' Go ahead—try it! Outlook's natural language feature recognizes:

- Abbreviations for months and days (Oct, Mon).
- Dates and times spelled out (May fifth, third of Sept, noon).
- Descriptions of times and dates (yesterday, from today through next Fri, day after tomorrow).
- Holidays that fall on the same date every year (Christmas, Boxing Day, Cinco de Mayo).

Entering Text in Forms

1. Click the Tasks icon in the Outlook Bar to open the task list.
2. Double-click Click Here to Enter a New Task to open a new task form, or click the drop down arrow beside the New button and choose Task. Enter a Subject. Tab to a date field.
3. Enter a description of a date, such as 'tomorrow' or 'next Fri,' and press Enter.
4. Enter any other information about the task. Use the drop-down arrows to set options for fields like Priority and Status.
5. When you are finished entering information, choose Save and Close to add the task to the task list and close the form.

Organizing Your Data

Each Outlook record (information about one task, one contact, etc.) is called an *item*. Just as you use forms to create items and view details about one item, you use views to display multiple existing items. Every module offers a variety of ways to organize and to view the items it contains.

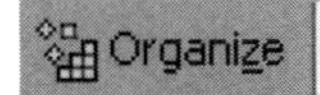

Click the Organize button on the main toolbar to view your organization choices in each Outlook module. Available options appear at the top of the module window, listed on the left side as links; click the organization method you want, then fill in the details.

Objectives OL2000.6.3, 4.5, and 5.3

To categorize your tasks, for example, activate the Tasks module and click the Organize button. Choose the Using Categories link, then select a task (hold Ctrl and click to select multiple tasks) from the list. Click the drop-down list next to Add Selected Tasks Below To and choose a category. Click the Add button to categorize the task(s).

You can quickly categorize items in any module this way.

Changing Your View

Objective OL2000.6.6

The easiest way to alter your view of data is to re-arrange the fields. In Tasks, for example, you can point to one of the column headers (the field names at the top of the columns) and drag the header horizontally to a new position. Red arrows will appear above and below the row of column headers, showing where the column will be placed.

To adjust the column width, drag the right edge of the column header as you would in Excel. To delete a field from the display, drag its header vertically off the header row and drop it when a large, black X appears. To move a column, drag its header left or right and release the mouse button when the red arrows line up where you want the column to go.

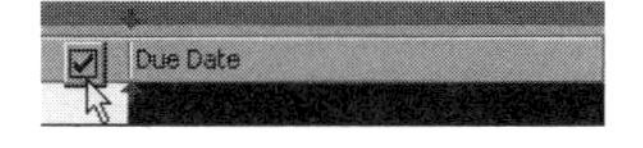

Sorting Items in a View To sort items in a view, click a column header. An upward triangle appears in the column header to show ascending order. Click the header again to reverse the sort order; the triangle will point down.

Grouping Items Together

Objective OL2000.5.3

You can easily group information in an Outlook module using the View menu. To group contacts, for example, switch to the Contacts module by clicking the Contacts shortcut on the Outlook Bar. Choose View ➢ Current View and select a view that includes the word By in the name, like By Category. The items on your task list will be re-arranged according to the information you provided in the Category box when you first created the task.

This graphic shows all contact groups expanded to show detail. Click the expand button (with the plus) to display subheadings or subgroups within the grouped view. Click the collapse button (with the minus symbol) to contract the headings and hide detail.

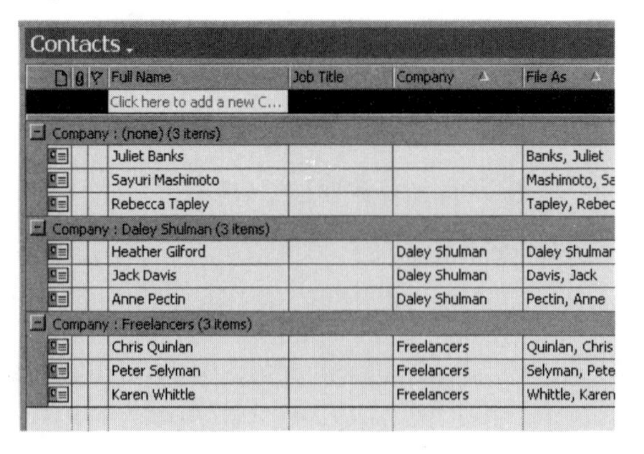

If you were an Outlook 97 user, you may be wondering what happened to the Current View drop-down menu and other familiar toolbars buttons. They have been placed on the Advanced toolbar, which you can turn on by choosing View ➢ Toolbars ➢ Advanced.

Now that you know how to work in Outlook 2000, we'll move on to the individual modules.

Hands On: Objectives OL2000.4.3, 4.5, 6.3, and 6.6

1. Switch between each of the Outlook modules using the Outlook Bar. Explore the menu and toolbar options for each module.
2. Switch to Tasks and then follow these steps:
   a) Add at least three tasks to the list; two or more tasks should have the same subject and category.
   b) Re-arrange the order of the Tasks columns. Adjust the column widths if necessary.
   c) Change the view of Tasks three times using different predefined views on the View menu.
   d) Sort Tasks by Subject.
   e) Use the Organize feature to assign tasks to another category.

Tracking Contacts with Outlook 2000

Of all of the modules that make up Outlook 2000, none is more central than Contacts. Developing a better system for tracking communications is, after all, what most people are looking for in a tool like Outlook.

Adding Contacts

Objectives OL2000.5.1 and OL2000E.5.4

Adding business and personal contacts is one of the first things you'll want to do when you start working in Outlook. It's a way to personalize Outlook and make it immediately useful.

If you have contacts in another application—Excel, Access, Schedule+, or another database file—you can import the data into Outlook. After you've learned how Contacts works, choose File ➢ Import and Export to launch a Wizard and import your data. See *Importing/Exporting,* later in this chapter.

To enter data, click the Contacts icon in the Outlook Bar to activate the Contacts module, then click the New Contact button on the Standard toolbar. (If you want to remain in another module, use the drop down list on the New button to open a New Contact form.) The Contact form opens with the General page displayed, ready to receive your data.

The Full Name and Address fields have buttons that open a secondary form to separate the data into the proper fields. You may enter data here, or use the form to verify that the data was entered correctly.

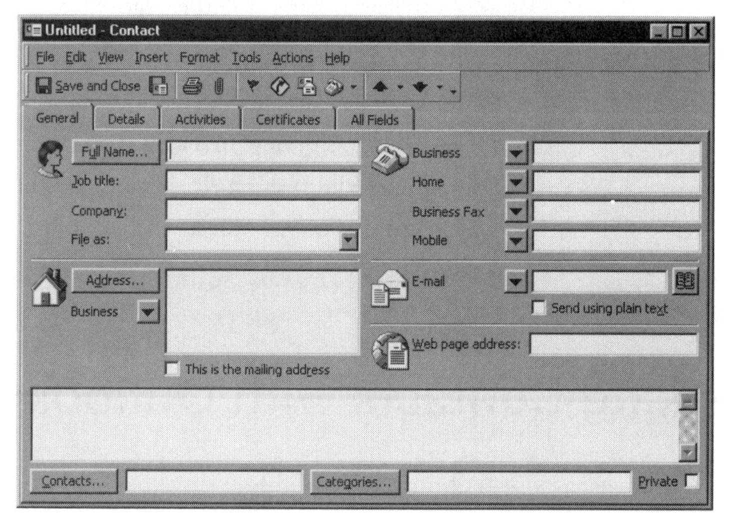

When you enter the Full Name, the name is automatically displayed as last name, first name in the File As field. If you'd rather file names by first name, nicknames, or some other system, choose a different format from the File As drop-down list.

Because many of your contacts may have separate home and business addresses and multiple phone numbers, click the drop-down arrows for Address, Phone Number, and E-mail fields to identify the kind of information (home, business, fax, etc.) that you are entering in the field. Outlook 2000 even has a place for the URL for a contact's Web page.

Entering a Web URL for a Contact

If one of your contacts or their company has a site on the World Wide Web, you may want to visit the site occasionally. If you enter the Web address (URL) on the Contacts form, you can access the site directly from the form (provided, of course, that you can connect to the Internet). Enter the entire

URL, exactly as it appears in your browser, in the Web Page Address text box. Outlook will underline the URL and highlight it to show that it's a hyperlink.

To visit the Web page, click the link in the Web Page Address text box to launch your browser and go directly to the contact's Web page.

Assigning Contacts and Categories

In this version of Outlook, you can assign other contacts to a contact. This is an excellent way to track referrals and other less obvious connections between your contacts. Once you assign a contact, the reverse assignment is created automatically. To make the assignment, click the Contact button at the bottom of the Contact Form and select a contact from the list.

Objective OL2000.4.4 and OL2000.4.5

Each Outlook item can also be assigned to one or more *categories*. Click the Categories button (in the New Contact form, for example) then select the appropriate categories for this contact. If you would like to create your own category, click the Master Category List button, type a name for the category in the New Category text box, and then click Add.

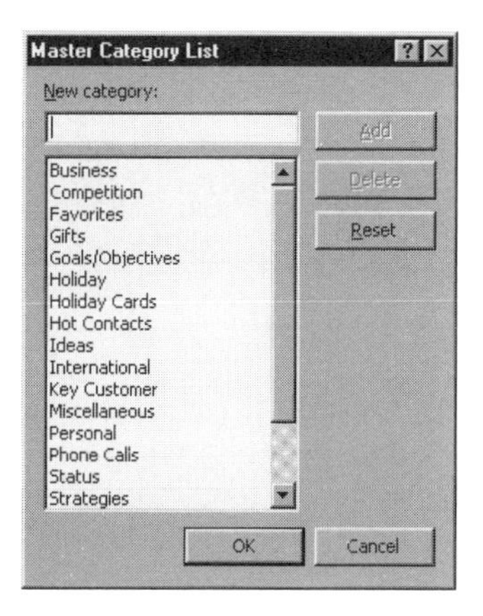

You can select existing categories and click Delete to remove them from the list. If you change your mind about adding or deleting categories and would like the original list back, click Reset and the original category list will be restored. Note, however, that you'll lose your additions as well as restore the deletions.

Categories can be applied to all Outlook items. If the Categories button isn't readily available, select the item (hold Ctrl to select multiple items in the Information Viewer) and choose Edit ➢ Categories to make the assignment.

Entering Additional Data

On the Details page of the Contacts form, you'll find fields for supporting data. Click the drop-down arrows in the Birthday and Anniversary fields to select dates using a calendar control.

Use the Certificates page to store certificates (also called digital ID's) that you can use to send encrypted mail to a contact. When you use a digital ID to send a message, only the intended recipient can decrypt the message. To use a digital ID you must first ask the recipient to send you an e-mail message that includes their digital signature. Right-click the name in the From field of the message, and then click Add to Contacts on the shortcut menu. This will copy the e-mail address and the certificates to the person's Contact form.

You can obtain a digital ID for your own use from a certifying authority such as Verisign, Inc. (`http://www.verisign.com`).

The Activities page replaces the Outlook 97/98 Contact form's Journal page. When you open a contact's Activities page, Outlook searches all internal data and displays those journal entries, e-mail messages, tasks, and other items that are related to this contact.

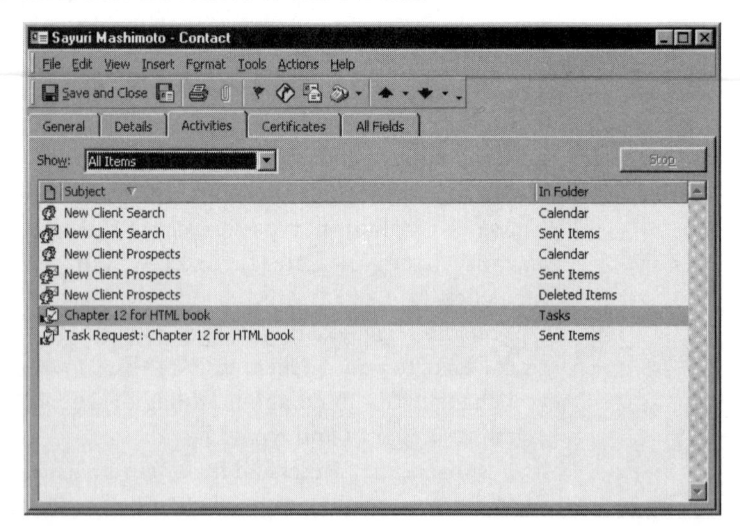

The All Fields page provides access to all the Contact form fields, including fields that are automatically entered by Outlook such as the item's creation date and time. Open the drop down list in the Select From text box to see the lists of fields you can display.

If you imported data from another database, you may find data here that did not fit into the standard fields on the Contact form. You can also enter data here, but there are no Calendar controls or drop-down lists to assist you.

Adding a Contact

1. Click the Contacts icon in the Outlook Bar and click the New Contact button on the Standard toolbar.
2. Enter data on the form, tabbing between fields.
3. Enter a new File As name if you would like to use something other than the suggested options.
4. Click the Full Name and Address buttons to enter data into individual fields.
5. Use the drop-down lists in the Address and Phone Number fields to identify the kind of data you are entering.
6. Assign the contact to other contacts or to categories, if desired.
7. Click the Details tab to enter more data about the contact, the Activities tab to view items related to this contact, and the All Fields tab to enter data in fields other than those represented on the form.
8. To return to the Contacts list, click the Save and Close button.

Deleting a Contact

Delete a contact by selecting it in the Informationer or other table view and pressing the Delete key on the keyboard. You'll also notice that when you open an existing contact there is a delete button (the X) on the Standard toolbar within the Contact form. The same Delete button exists in Outlook's Standard toolbar and it works the same way: select the item you want to delete and click the Delete button.

Adding Another Contact from the Same Company

Outlook makes it easy to add another contact from the same company without reentering all the standard company information. With the original contact form open, choose Actions ➢ New Contact from Same Company. Outlook will open a new contact form with the company name, address, and Business Phone already completed.

Viewing Contacts

Seven default Contacts views are available from the View menu: Address Cards, Detailed Address Cards, Phone List, By Category, By Company, By

Location, and By Follow-up Flag. Switch between views by choosing a different view from the menu. (See *Creating Custom Views,* later in this chapter to learn how to create a view.)

Objective OL2000.5.6

If you choose a table view such as Phone List, you can easily re-arrange fields and sort by column headings as described previously in the *Changing Your View* section of this chapter.

Locating a Contact

The easiest way to search through a long list of contacts is to enter a first or last name in the Find a Contact text box on the Standard toolbar–it's the empty text box next to the Address Book. If Outlook only finds one name that matches your entry, it will open the Contact form for that person. If it finds more than one possible match, Outlook will display a list of possibilities that you can choose from.

When you can't remember the contact's first or last name, you can search for other information about the Contact by clicking the Find button on the Standard toolbar to open the Find pane. Enter the data you would like Outlook to search for, make sure Search all text in the contact is enabled, and click the Find Now button. Even if you just remember part of the last name, Outlook will find every occurrence of those letters. In Figure 10.2, a search for '`Schulman`,' part of a company name, returned all employees of the same company, Daley Shulman:

Double-click a name in the list to open the form for that individual.

Viewing and Locating Contacts

1. Click View ➢ Current View to select from among the available views.
2. In table views, drag column headers to rearrange columns. Click a column header to sort that column.
3. Locate a contact by entering their first or last name in the Find a Contact text box.
4. To locate a contact based on other information, click the Find button. Enter the word or words you want to search for and click Find Now.

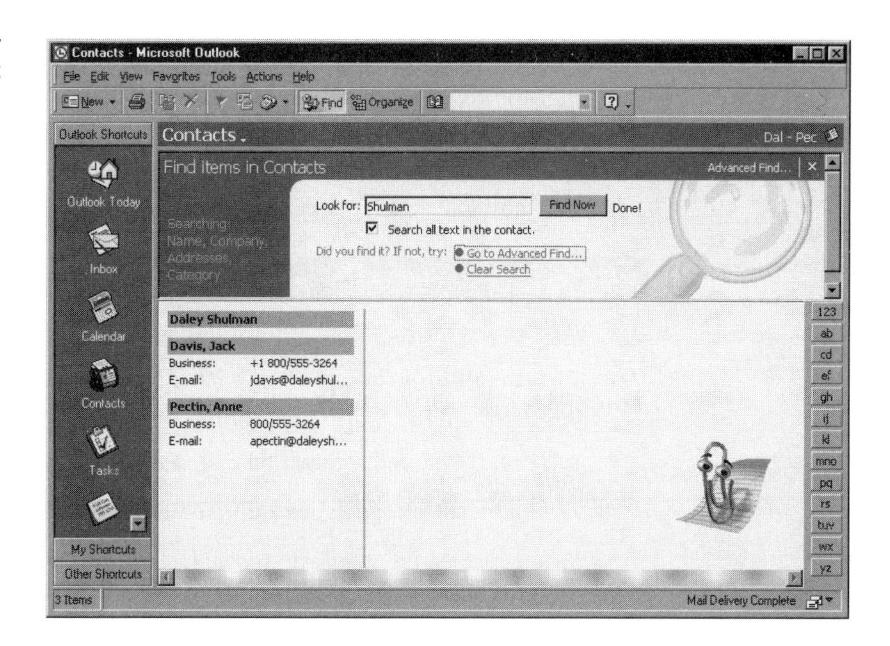

FIGURE 10.2 Results of a search on 'Schulman'

For even more Find options, click the Find button and then click Advanced Find to open the Advanced Find dialog box.

Communicating with Your Contacts

Now that you have a well-developed contact list, it's time to start putting it to good use. Outlook has a number of things you can do with contact information:

- Dial a phone number
- Write a letter in Word
- Hold online conferences with NetMeeting
- Send an e-mail message
- Schedule an appointment
- Assign a task
- Create a journal entry to document communication

Dialing a Contact

If you have a telephone connected to your PC's modem, you can place telephone calls from Outlook. Double-click the contact you want to call to open the Contact form, and click the AutoDialer button. Choose a phone number from the AutoDialer drop-down list. When the call connects, pick up the receiver and click the Talk button.

Using AutoDialer to Call a Contact

1. Double-click the contact you want to call.
2. Click the AutoDialer button, or click the down arrow, to select the number to call.
3. Click Start Call in the New Call dialog box.
4. When the call connects, pick up the handset and click Talk.
5. When you are finished with the call, click End Call to disconnect.

To record a Journal entry about a call (see *"Using the Journal and Notes,"* later in this chapter), enable the Create New Journal Entry When Starting New Call checkbox. When you click Start call, a new Journal form opens and the timer starts.

Creating a Letter to a Contact

Objectives OL2000.7.1 and OL2000E.6.4

Integration is one of the best features of Office 2000. With Outlook, you can generate regular "snail mail" letters directly from the Contacts list using the Letter Wizard.

Creating a Letter to a Contact

1. Double-click a contact to open the Contact form.
2. Choose Actions ➢ New Letter to Contact. This launches Word 2000 and starts the Letter Wizard.
3. Choose the Letter Format you would like to use, including Page Design and Letter Style. Click Next.

Creating a Letter to a Contact *(continued)*

4. The Recipient Info should include the contact you have open in Outlook. If it doesn't, or you want to change whom the letter is addressed to, click the Address Book button and select the recipient. Enter a salutation in the Salutation field. Click Next.
5. Other Elements includes more information about the address and mailing instructions. Choose options from the drop-down lists or enter your own text. Use the Address Book button to select additional addresses for courtesy copies. Click Next.
6. Enter Sender Info and Closing options. You can select the Sender Info from one of your address books (you may want to enter yourself as a contact so you can select yourself). Click Finish.
7. The Letter Wizard creates the structure of your letter. Choose if you would like to Make an Envelope, Make a Mailing Label, Rerun Letter Wizard, or Cancel the Office Assistant. Enter the body of the letter and send it to the printer.

Other Forms of Communication

Although Outlook 2000 handles the more traditional forms of communication like letters and phone calls, it was really designed to support newer modes of business communication. Effective use of e-mail, group appointment scheduling and meeting planning, and team management are all hallmarks of the new networked workplace.

Objective OL2000.1.16

Select a contact, open the Contact form, and click the New Message to Contact button on the Standard toolbar to open an e-mail form pre-addressed with the contact's e-mail address. If you want to assign a task to the contact, choose Actions ➢ New Task for Contact, enter the task information, and click the Assign Task button.

To invite the contact to attend a meeting, choose Actions ➢ New Meeting Request to Contact to open a new appointment form. The default form is an e-mail form, but if you enable the This Is an Online Meeting check box, the appointment form will display other options. Use the Online Meeting Planner page to invite meeting participants, send real-time reminders, and choose your online meeting software. You'll learn more about this feature later in the chapter.

Printing Options

Outlook 2000 features several pre-defined print styles that make it easy to print Outlook information. To print Contacts, first switch to the Contacts view you want to print. Address card views print directories, whereas tables, such as Phone List view, print lists of data. Once you've chosen the view you want, click File ➢ Page Setup and choose the style you want. Click the Print Preview button to preview the print style, and click Print if you are satisfied.

If you'd like to make some changes to the document before you print it, you can customize the print style, adjust the paper size and fonts, and change other settings in the Page Setup dialog box. You can also adjust the settings to print page sizes used in several popular types of day planners.

Printing Contact Lists

1. Choose File ➢ Page Setup to select a report style. Choose the style you want to use.
2. To customize the style, adjust the various paper, size, and other settings, or choose the type of day planner you carry, make changes on the various tabs of the Page Setup dialog box before printing.
3. Click Print Preview to see a preview of the report.
4. Choose Print to open the Print dialog box. Change the Print Style, if desired. Choose which pages you want to print and how many copies you want. Click Collate to have each copy print completely before the next copy begins. Click OK to send the report to the printer.

Objective OL20003.4

You'll go through the same process to print in any Outlook module. Select a view that supports the output you desire, then preview the output in Print Preview. Change views, if necessary, and tweak the Page Setup options to further define the preview before sending it to the printer.

Importing/Exporting Contact Information

Objective OL2000E.8.1

Contact information can be kept in dozens of different file formats, many of which can be imported directly into Outlook 2000. A colleague may have started out keeping his names and addresses in a simple Excel spreadsheet. Now you need to share this contact information. Don't retype it in Outlook–Import it.

Click File ➢ Import and Export to start the Import and Export Wizard. In the first step, you'll choose an action to perform. Using the example above, you would select Import From Another Program or File and click Next. Select the type of file to import (in this example, Microsoft Excel) and click Next. Browse to select the file and choose an option for dealing with potential duplicates. Click Next, then select the folder you want to import to, in our example Contacts.

If you're importing from Excel, Outlook looks for a named range. See Chapter 6 for information about naming an Excel range.

The Wizard will tell you which actions it will perform when you click the Finish button. If you know that the fields in the data you're importing are different than the fields that exist in Outlook, you'll want to use the Map Custom Fields feature to match up incoming data with Outlook fields. Click Finish to begin the import.

When you export data from Outlook, you'll follow the same basic steps. You'll choose which Outlook folder(s) to export and you'll choose a destination for the data.

Exporting to an Outlook .pst file is a great way to back up your Outlook data.

Hands On: *Objectives OL20001.4, 3.4, 4.3, 4.4, 4.5, 5.1, 5.3, 5.6, 7.1 and OL2000E.6.4 and E8.1*

1. Open Contacts and then complete the following steps:
   a) Add at least five contacts.
   b) Add two contacts from the same company.
   c) Create a "dummy" contact and delete it.
   d) If you have Internet access, locate the URL of one of your contacts and enter the URL in the Web Page field. Click the link in the field to test the URL.

2. Switch your contacts to the Phone List view.
   a) Rearrange the column order and sort by city.
   b) Group the items by company.
   c) Use Find to locate a contact.
   d) Create a new category on the Master Category list and assign the category to a group of records.
   e) Change the view so you're seeing your contacts By Category. Expand and collapse the category headings to show/hide contacts in each category.
3. If you have a modem and a telephone line connected to it, call one of your contacts using the AutoDialer.
4. Create a letter to send to a contact using the New Letter to Contact feature.
5. Print a directory of your contacts customized to the type of planner you carry.
6. Switch to the Calendar module and change to a list view. Print that view.
7. Export your Contacts folder to a .pst file. If you have contact data in Excel or another windows based program, import it.

Using Outlook Today

If you've ever wanted a place to keep track of the day's appointments, things to do, and other important, immediate information, you'll love Outlook Today. Outlook Today displays everything you need to know about your day: where you have to be, when you have to be there, what you have to get done, and who has sent e-mail you may need to respond to.

Viewing the Day's Information

Objective OL2000E.5.1

Outlook Today filters information from your Calendar, Tasks, Inbox, and Outbox to display your day at a glance. Click the Outlook Today shortcut, on the Outlook Bar, to display the Outlook Today window, shown in Figure 10.3.

FIGURE 10.3
The Outlook Today window

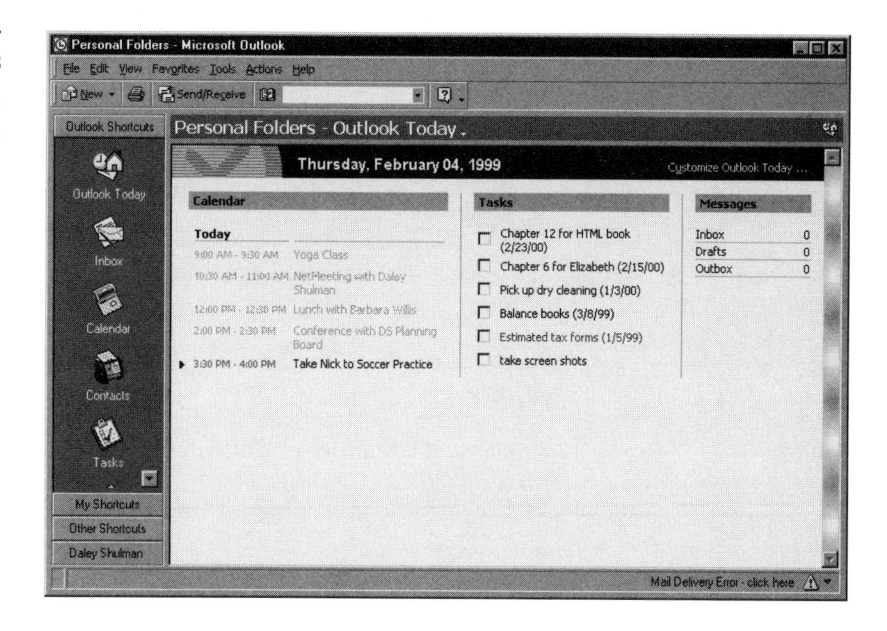

To view the details of any calendar item, task, or e-mail message, click the link that appears when you point the mouse at the item. You can also click the gray column headers to open the Calendar, Tasks, and/or Inbox modules. As you tend to the day's events, Outlook will dim completed tasks or meetings to gray, allowing you to concentrate on unfinished business.

Customizing the Outlook Today View

If you want to customize your view of the Outlook Today contents, click the Outlook Today icon and then click the Customize Outlook Today button in the Outlook Today window. You can:

- Make Outlook Today your default module when Outlook starts up.
- Decide how many days the Calendar portion should display
- Determine how your Tasks should be sorted
- Select which e-mail folders should be listed.

The Styles options give you more sophisticated choices. Table 10.1 lists your choices and how they affect the Outlook Today window.

TABLE 10.1: Outlook Today Style Customization Options

Style	What You Get
Standard	Calendar, tasks, and messages listed in three individual columns
Standard (two column)	Calendar items listed in the left column, tasks and messages listed in the right
Standard (one column)	Calendar, tasks, and messages information displayed in three horizontal rows
Summer	Similar to the Standard 2-Column view, only displayed in greens and yellows
Winter	Similar to the Standard 2-Column view, only displayed in blues and white.

Make your choices in the Customize Outlook Today window and click Save Changes to apply the changes. Outlook will reorganize your information and apply the changes. For more details on how to use Outlook's Calendar, Tasks, and E-Mail modules, see this chapter's specific sections for each module.

Hands On: Objective OL2000E.5.1

1. Open Outlook Today and view the day's events.
2. Customize the Outlook Today environment by changing to another style.

Using Outlook as a Mail Client

Although electronic mail has been around since the 1960s, it wasn't until the late '80s that it really took hold in the business world. Today, some businesses have grown so dependent on e-mail that their entire operations grind to a halt when their e-mail systems go down. Outlook 2000 has turned e-mail into an even more valuable tool by adding message-handling options, voting, and a score of other useful features.

Creating Mail

All your e-mail work can be handled using the My Shortcuts group on the Outlook Bar. This group contains shortcuts to email folders and add-ons associated with e-mail. If you're using synchronization software to transfer Outlook data into a handheld device, the software shortcuts will appear here. At the very least, My Shortcuts contains shortcuts to your mail folders as shown in Figure 10.4.

FIGURE 10.4
My Shortcuts group

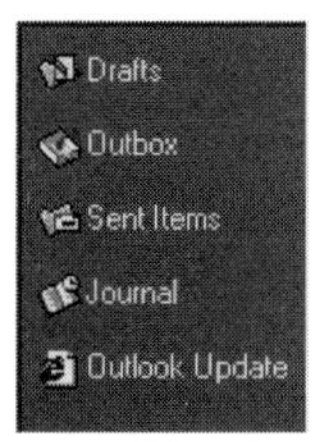

Inbox: E-mail and fax messages you've received.

Drafts: Unfinished messages.

Outbox: Temporarily stores outgoing messages.

Sent Items: Copies of messages you've already sent.

Deleted Items: The Recycle Bin for Outlook items.

Journal: Notes and records of meetings, phone calls, and other events.

Outlook Today: Tasks, calendar events, and other information applying to the current day.

As you start sending and receiving messages, you can add folders to keep your mail organized. (We discuss how to add folders and put shortcuts to folders on the Outlook Bar later in the chapter.)

Creating and Addressing E-Mail

Objectives OL2000.1.3, OL2000.1.5, and OL2000.1.7

To create an e-mail message, open the Inbox and click the New button on the Standard toolbar. A blank Message form opens.

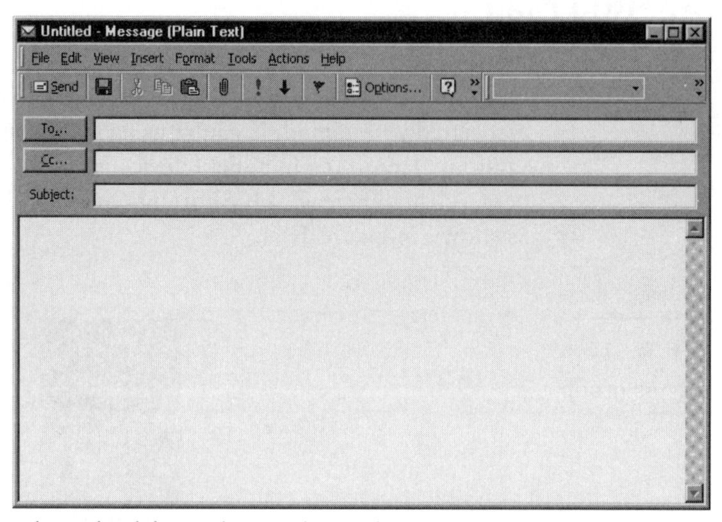

In order to be delivered, e-mail must be correctly addressed. To access the address book, click the To button on the Message form to open the Select Names dialog box to display the names of people in your Outlook Address book that have e-mail addresses and/or fax numbers.

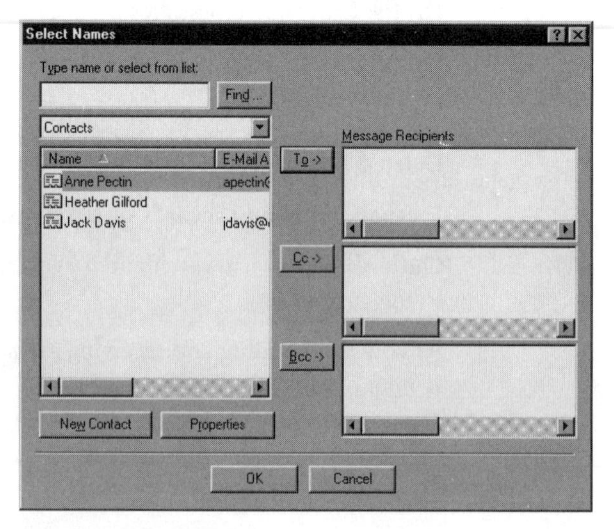

Select a name from the list by clicking it, then click the To, CC, or Bcc buttons to place the recipient's name in the appropriate field for addressing. Clicking To addresses the message to the recipient(s). Choosing Cc sends a copy of the message (and attachments) to recipients. Choosing Bcc sends a copy of the message and attachments to other recipient(s) but the names in the Bcc field do not appear in the header of the email message received by the To and Cc recipients. (The B in Bcc stands for "blind" because it's hidden from other recipients.) Click OK when you're finished choosing message recipients.

If you're connected to a network, you may have a global address book listing other users on your network as well as your regular Outlook Address Book. If you have more than one address book, choose the Address Book you want to use in the Show Names From list in the Select Names dialog box.

If the person you want to send e-mail to is not on the list in the Select Names dialog box, you can click the New button (if you're using the Contacts folder as your primary address book, the button will say New Contact) and type the information, including e-mail address, for that person. Once you finish the form and click OK, you'll see the name on your address list.

You don't have to use the Select Names dialog box to address mail. Sometimes it's easier to just type e-mail addresses in the To and Cc fields of the blank message form. However, e-mail addresses can be rather long and typing them leaves the door wide open for error. A misplaced period or forward slash will cause the mail to be returned undelivered.

After your message is addressed, type a subject for your message in the subject field. Press Tab or Enter to move the insertion point to the main window and compose your message.

Objectives OL20001.14 and OL2000E.2.1

Format selected text using the buttons on the Standard toolbar. (For more information on formatting text see Chapters 2 and 3.) Choose Tools ➢ Spelling to check spelling before sending your message. Insert pictures (a company logo, for example) by placing your insertion point in the message window and clicking Insert ➢ Object. Choose the Create from File option. Browse to find the picture file, select it, and click OK. Click OK in the Insert Object dialog box to place the picture in your e-mail message.

If you choose to use pictures in your e-mail messages, make sure the file size for the picture is very small (or the pictures are worth waiting for!). You'll quickly frustrate your message recipients if they have to wait for your message to download because of its large size.

If your default message type is plain text, formatting options will be disabled. See *Changing Mail Formats* below.

Creating and Addressing E-Mail

1. Open the Inbox or Outbox and click the New button on the Standard toolbar.
2. Enter e-mail addresses in the To and Cc fields or Click the To button to open the Select Names dialog box and choose your message recipients from a list.
3. Select the first person's name and click the To button. Select any additional names, and place them in the appropriate field by clicking the To, Cc, or Bcc button.
4. To check the properties of a name, select the name and click Properties.
5. To add a name that is not on the list, click New, choose the Entry type, select where you'd like to store the address, and click OK. Enter the data about the new address in the Mail Properties dialog box. Click OK to add the name.
6. Click OK to close the Select Names dialog box.
7. Type a subject for your message in the subject field.
8. Enter the body of the message in the main window and format the text as desired.

Adding a Custom Signature

Objective OL2000.1.13

A *custom signature* is text you add to the end of a message to identify the sender, pitch products or services, advertise a Web site, or note that your message should not be forwarded without your consent. Custom signatures have become fairly common and Outlook allows you to create multiple custom signatures and choose the one you want for each message you compose.

To create a custom signature click Tools ➢ Options then click the Mail Format tab. Click the Signature Picker button to open the dialog box shown in Figure 10.5. Existing signatures are displayed in the list.

FIGURE 10.5
Signature Picker

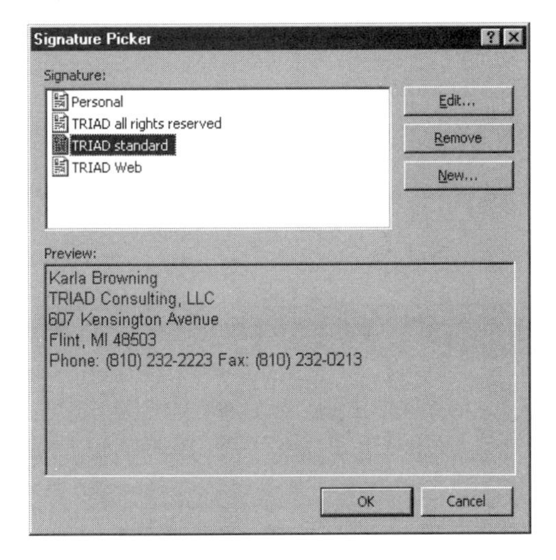

Click New to open the Create New Signature dialog box. Type a short but descriptive name for your signature then choose how you want to create your signature. You can start with a blank window, or base your signature on a template. If you choose the template option, browse, and select the template you want to use.

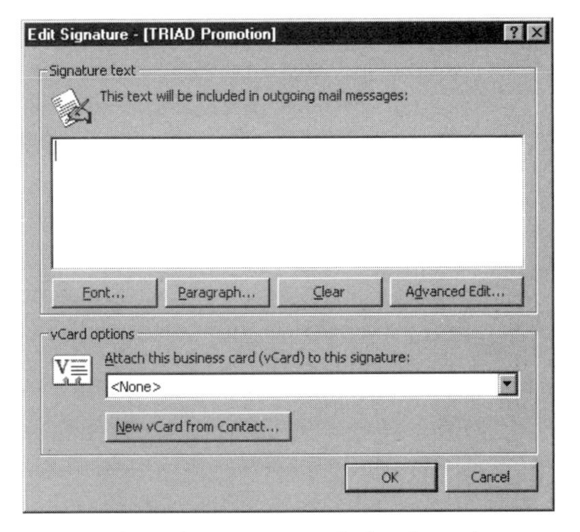

Click Next to open the Edit Signature dialog box then enter the text you want to use for the signature. Format the text using the Paragraph and Font buttons. (If you're using plain text as your default message format, the Paragraph and Font buttons are not available.) Click Clear to erase all message text and start over.

Objective OL2000E.1.2

You may wish to type minimal text then attach a vCard (virtual business card) to your custom signature. A vCard takes contact data and attaches it to the e-mail message. The recipient can transfer the vCard to their contact data in Outlook or other contact management software. Because vCard is an Internet Standard, chances are that recipients of your vCard will be able to open it, even if they're not running Outlook.

To attach a vCard, choose a contact from the list in the Edit Signature dialog box. If there are no contacts listed, click the New vCard from Contact button and select a contact from the list. Again, it's a good idea to keep your own data in Contacts so you can select yourself.

You can send a vCard directly from the Contacts module by selecting the contact then clicking Actions ➢ Forward as vCard to open an e-mail message with the vCard attached. Address and send the mail as you normally would.

When you're finished creating and formatting your signature in the Edit Signature dialog box, click the Finish button to return to the Signature Picker. If you want to create another signature, click the New button again to open the Edit Signature dialog box. You can edit a signature in the Signature Picker by selecting it and clicking the Edit button. Remove the selected signature with the Remove button. Click OK to close the Signature Picker and return to the Options dialog box. Before you click OK to close the Options dialog box, choose the signature you want to set as the default.

When you start a new e-mail message, the default signature will appear in the message. If you wish to use another signature, select the entire signature in the message window, then click Insert ➢ Signature and choose the signature you want to use.

Changing Mail Formats Outlook 2000 lets you create e-mail messages in three different message formats: plain text, Rich Text, and HTML. Rich text supports fonts, styles, weights, and other formatting. HTML supports HTML text formats and background graphics. To set the default format for messages choose Tools ➢ Options, then click the Mail Format tab. Choose a format from the drop down list.

When you create a message, you can choose between the default format and plain text on the message's Format menu.

Objective OL2000E.2.1

Customizing the Look of Mail If you're using Rich Text or HTML for your mail format, you can really jazz up your messages with fonts, colors, pictures, and stationery. Format text in a message just as you would in Word: select it and use the tools on the Formatting toolbar within the message window. Insert a picture, your company logo for example, by clicking Insert ➢ Object and choosing the Create From File option. Browse select the file and click OK to insert it.

Outlook offers another tool for customizing mail messages, but only if you choose HTML as your message format. When you choose HTML on the Mail Format tab of the Options dialog box, the stationery and fonts features are enabled. You can use stationery that includes fonts, background color, and images to create eye-catching e-mail.

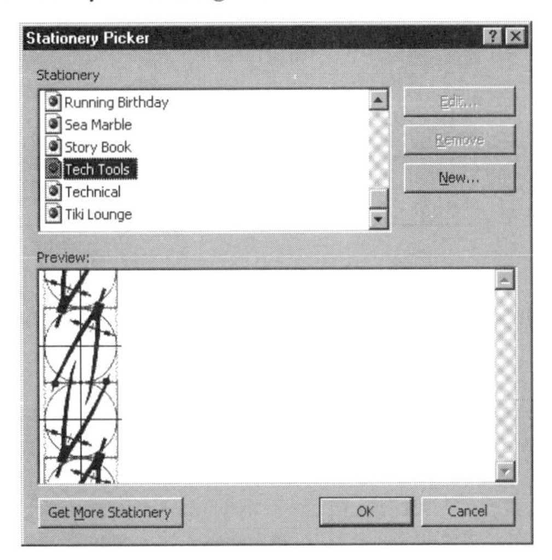

From the Mail Format tab of the Options dialog box, click Stationery Picker. Select from the list of available stationery and click OK. Clicking the Get More Stationery takes you to the Web where you can download more stationery choices. When you choose stationery, Outlook makes it the default stationary for e-mail, so when you start a new mail message, you'll see the stationery you selected. Change the default stationery, or create your own, by returning to the Stationery Picker.

When you create your own stationery, you can choose to start from scratch, or use an existing stationery or document as a starting point. Click New in the Stationery Picker and type a name for your stationery. Then choose how you want to start. Click Next to begin customizing. Change the font by clicking the Font button. Choose a picture for a background or eliminate the background altogether. When you're through, click OK three times to close all three of the dialog boxes.

Sending the Message

Objective OL2000.1.2

After you have addressed the message, entered the message body, and signed the message, it is ready to send. Click the Send button and it's on its way. If you're not online when you click the Send button, the message will be moved to your Outbox for sending later (see *Receiving Mail* below for more about how to send messages from your Outbox). When the message is sent, a copy is saved automatically in the Sent Items folder.

It's likely that most of the e-mail you send will be a quick message requiring an address, subject, and a paragraph or two of body text. There are, however, additional options you might want to consider when sending mail.

Setting Message-Handling Options There are several features that determine how your message will be handled. In the message form, click the Options button to access the message-handling options shown in Table 10.2.

TABLE 10.2: Message Handling Options

Option	Description
Importance	Puts a flag on the message to alert the recipient to its importance. Click to select Normal, Low, or High.
Sensitivity	Puts a flag on the message to alert the recipient to its sensitivity. Click to select Normal, Personal, Private, or Confidential.
Voting options	Used to poll recipients; only available in Corporate/Workgroup Configuration.
Have replies sent to	Allows you to designate an individual to collect replies to your message.

TABLE 10.2: Message Handling Options *(continued)*

Option	Description
Save sent message to	Indicates which folder you want the sent message stored in.
Do not deliver before	Keeps the message from being delivered before the date you specify.
Expires after	Marks the message as unavailable after the date you specify.
Tracking options	Notifies you when messages are delivered and/or read.

Flagging E-Mail Messages for Follow Up

Objectives OL2000.1.8 and OL2000E.6.1

Certain messages may require action on the part of the recipient; other messages only require a quick scan on their way to the Deleted Items folder. You can flag messages sent to other Outlook users so it's obvious when and what action is expected, or flag incoming messages as a reminder to yourself.

To flag a message, open the message and click the Flag for Follow Up button on the message toolbar. The Flag for Follow Up dialog box has two settings: Flag To and Due By. Choose a Flag To action from the list—Call, Do Not Forward, Follow Up, For Your Information, Forward, No Response Necessary, Read, Reply, Reply to All, Review—or type other text if you wish. In the Due By control, select a date for the action. The details of the flag appear in the message header. When you complete the flagged action, right-click on the message in the Information Viewer and choose Flag Complete from the shortcut menu, or open the message, open the Flag Message dialog box, and click the Completed check box. To delete a flag, right-click the message and choose Clear Flag. The flag information disappears from the open Message window.

You can flag any Outlook item for follow up by right-clicking it in the Information Viewer and choosing Flag for Follow Up from the shortcut menu.

Tracking E-Mail Messages

Objective OL2000E.2.4

If it's important to know whether someone receives and reads your message, you can turn on tracking options and it that will let you know when they have opened your message. You probably don't want these options set all the time or you'll double or triple the amount of mail you get, but for that important document, tracking options can't be beat.

Receipts are sent by the recipient's mail server. Many mail servers do not support read receipts, but most support delivery receipts.

To use Outlook's tracking features, click the message's Options button. The Message Options dialog box, shown in Figure 10.6, offers several choices for delivery and notification.

FIGURE 10.6 Message Options window

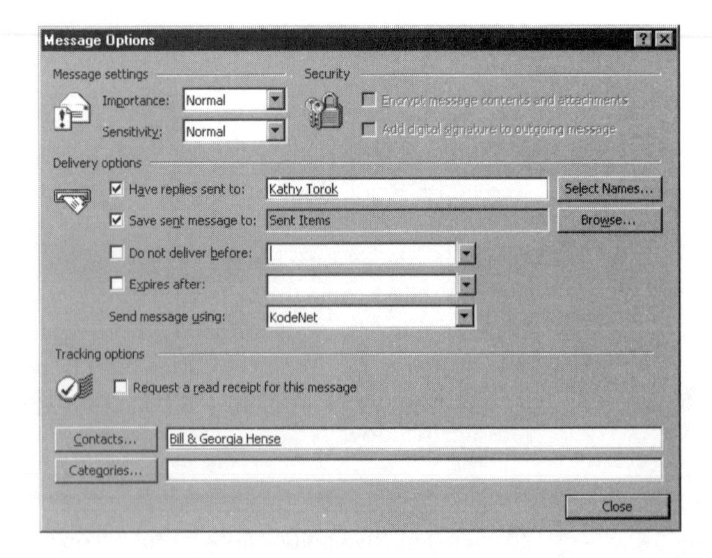

Choose to automatically store a copy of the e-mail in a separate folder or to send a copy to a third party, select an expiration date if the e-mail is time-sensitive, and set notification options by enabling the check box in the lower part of the window to request notification. Link a contact to the message by clicking the Contacts button; assign a category using the Category button. Click OK to close the Message Options dialog box, then send the message as usual. A notification e-mail will be automatically sent to your Inbox when the recipient has opened the e-mail.

Outlook allows you to choose whether to send a read receipt when one is requested by someone sending you e-mail through the Internet (Tools ➢ Options ➢ E-Mail Options ➢ Tracking Options). That means your mail recipients who use Outlook may decline your requests for read receipts as well.

Setting Tracking Options

1. Create an e-mail message and click the Options button. The Message Options dialog box opens.
2. Choose a recipient, an expiration date, and other options from this window. Check the box near the bottom requesting notification that the message has been received.
3. Send the message. You will receive notification in your Inbox when the recipient opens the e-mail.

Forwarding Outlook Items

Objectives OL2000.5.2 and OL2000.1.16

If you want to send a copy of an Outlook item—a contact, a task, an appointment, or even a note to a colleague who uses Outlook—you can right-click the item in the Information Viewer and choose Forward. A mail message opens with the item attached to it. Address your mail message and send it as usual. The item is sent along with the message, and the recipient just has to double-click the item to open it in Outlook.

Personal Distribution Lists

Objective OL2000E.2.5

Personal distribution lists help you manage contacts and information by sending e-mail to a group of people. You'll find distribution lists useful if you e-mail many people several times a week, or route messages within your organization.

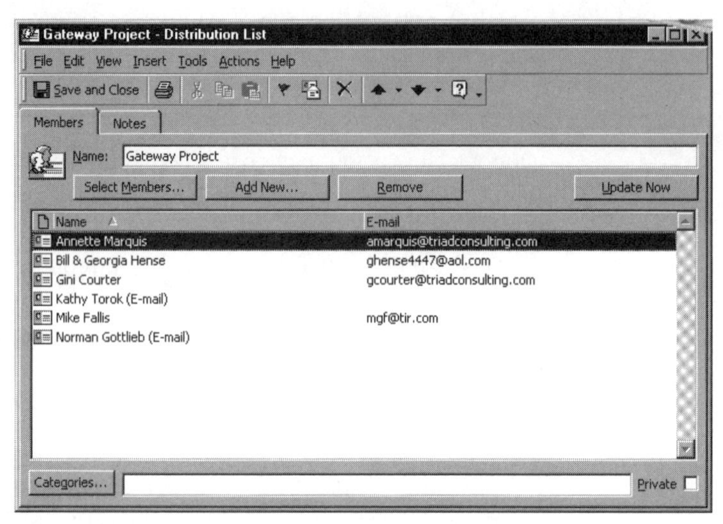

To create a personal distribution list, choose File ➢ New ➢ Distribution List to open the New Distribution List dialog box. Enter a name for the list in the Name field on the Members tab, then select members for the list by clicking the Select Members button. You'll recognize the familiar Select Names dialog box, where you can choose who you want to include in the distribution list. When you're finished adding names, click OK in the Select Names dialog box. If you want to add notes about the list, such as its purpose or when it was last updated, click the Notes tab. When you're through, click Save and Close in the New Distribution List window. The list name will appear in your Address Book. When you send a message to the list, the message is sent to each list member.

Creating a Distribution List

1. Choose File ➢ New ➢ Distribution List.
2. On the Members tab, enter a list Name in the Name text box.
3. Click Select Members to choose list members from Contacts or another address book.
4. Click the Notes tab to add any personal notes.
5. Click Save and Close to create the list.

Creating Re-usable Templates for Standard Messages

Objective OL2000.1.15 and OL2000E.1.3

If you're responsible for sending out a standard message each month (for example, a list of events or reminders), there's no point in recreating the message every time you want to send it. You can create and format it once, then enter the parts that vary each month. The first step in creating a re-usable message is to write the message the way you want it to look as a template. Enter and format the standard text: the portion that remains constant. (If all the recipients are on the same e-mail system and you know they can receive graphics and color, you can spice it up so it looks great.) When you have the standard message all set, choose File ➢ Save As to open the Save As dialog box. Select Outlook Template from the Save as Type drop-down list to open the Outlook templates folder.

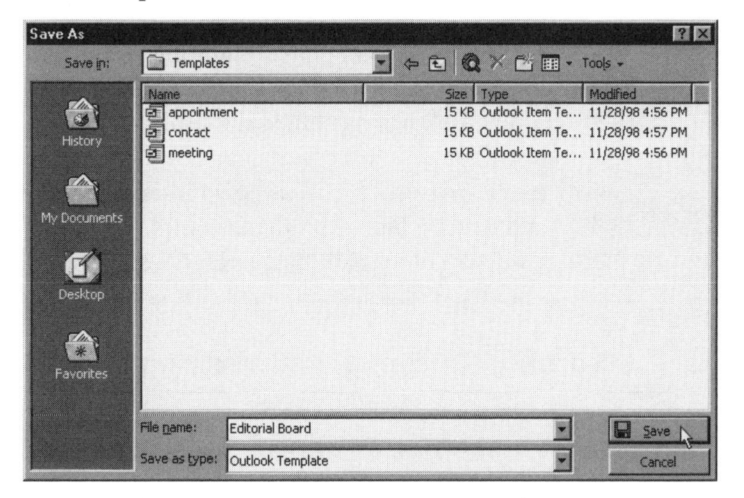

Enter a name for the template in the File Name field and click Save. To open and use the template, click File ➢ New (or click the drop-down arrow beside the New button) ➢ Choose Forms. In the Choose Forms dialog box, change the Look In field to User Templates in File System. Select the template you want from the list (or browse to find it) then click Open.

Creating a Reusable Template

1. Create and format a standard message.
2. Choose File ➢ Save As.
3. Select Outlook Template (`*.oft`) from the Save as Type drop-down field.
4. Enter a name for the template in the File Name field. Click Save.
5. To use the template, click File ➢ New ➢ Choose Form. Change the Look In field to User Templates in File System. Select your template and click Open.
6. Edit (if necessary) then send the message.

Receiving Mail

If you're connected to a network mail server or have a full time connection to your Internet Service Provider, you receive mail continuously in your Inbox. If you do not have a full-time connection, you need to connect to the Internet to receive or send Internet mail.

Outlook has combined the sending and receiving mail functions in one operation on the Tools menu, called Send/Receive. You can also initiate sending/receiving mail using your default mail service by clicking the Send and Receive button on the Standard toolbar. When you choose this option, Outlook connects to the mail service you select, sends the mail in your Outbox, and places any mail that is waiting for you in your Inbox.

Sorting, Grouping, and Viewing Mail

Objectives OL2000.1.1, OL2000.1.9, and OL2000.2.2

Mail in the Inbox is displayed in the Information Viewer. Mail messages are presented in a table view at the top of the viewer; an optional Preview Pane appears at the bottom. (Display or hide the Preview Pane by choosing View ➢ Preview Pane or click the Preview Pane button on the Advanced toolbar.)

To read a message with the Preview Pane turned on, simply select the message in the Information Viewer and you'll see its contents in the Preview Pane. If you choose to hide the Preview Pane, double-click any e-mail message to open the message in a separate window and view its contents. Close the window when you're through.

Sort your Inbox as you would any table view. Click a column header for an ascending sort by that field. Click the header again to sort in reverse order.

Finding Messages

Objective OL2000.1.10

You can also use the Find feature to locate a particular e-mail message. Click the Find button to open the Find pane, type a keyword in the Find What field, then click Find Now. For more information on using Find, see *Locating a Contact*, earlier in this chapter.

If you want to focus your search, or if you want to search for a message by other criteria, click the Advanced Find button to open the Advanced Find dialog box. In this dialog box, you can search for items from a particular person by entering the Sender's name in the From field. The More Choices tab offers additional search options, including searching by category.

Replying to Mail

Objective OL2000.1.6

One of the primary reasons e-mail has become so popular is that it's easy—easy to send, easy to view, and easy to respond to. When was the last time you responded to a written letter within minutes of receiving it? With e-mail, you can receive mail from across the globe, click the Reply button, write your response, click Send, and return a response within minutes. If the message you received was originally sent to more than one person, you can respond to all recipients by opening the message and clicking the Reply to All button on the Standard toolbar. To send a copy of a message to a colleague or friend, click the message's Forward button, enter the address, and click Send.

Sending, Receiving, and Replying to Messages

1. To send all messages in your Outbox and receive waiting mail, choose Tools ➢ Send/Receive, and then choose your mail account.
2. Sort the messages by clicking the column headers.
3. Choose View ➢ Current View to select how to group messages.
4. Double-click a message to open it.
5. Click Reply to reply to a message or Reply to All the send the responses to all the names on the To, Cc, and Bcc lists.
6. Click Forward to forward the original message to someone else. Enter the address in the To field. Enter a message of your own above the original message if desired. Click Send to forward the message.

Attaching a File to a Message

Objective OL2000.1.12

There's a frequent need in most offices to send drafts of documents to co-workers. It's easy to send files along with an e-mail. Just click the Insert File button on the Standard toolbar to open the Insert File dialog box, then locate and select the file(s). At the right side of the Insert File dialog box are three options for inserting the file. Only choose Text Only if the file contains unformatted text like a `.txt` or `.bat` file; if you insert, for example, a Word file as Text Only, the result is garbage. Choosing Shortcut inserts an icon representing a link to the file. This is a helpful option if you're on a company network. Attaching a shortcut makes it possible for you and your co-workers to edit the same file, eliminating the problem of multiple drafts. The default, Attachment, attaches a copy of the file to the task. Double-click the Shortcut or Attachment icon to open the document in the appropriate application.

You can insert an Outlook item by choosing Insert ➢ Item from the menu.

Recalling a Message

Objective OL2000.1.6

It doesn't take very much time working with e-mail before you click the Send button and immediately wish you hadn't. (How many times have you sent an e-mail that begins "Attached is...." only to forget the attachment?) If you're using the corporate/workgroup configuration, you have the ability to recall messages that haven't been opened by the recipients on your network.

Open the Sent Items folder (by clicking its shortcut on the Outlook Bar or by choosing that folder from the Folder List). Open the message you want to recall and choose Tools ➢ Recall This Message. You have the option of deleting unread copies of the message or deleting unread copies and replacing it with a new message. You can also ask Outlook to report back with a message that tells you if the recall was successful. If you choose the replace option, the original e-mail message opens in Edit mode so you can make changes to it and re-send it. If you click the report option, you'll receive an e-mail message notifying you of the results of each recall attempt.

Keeping Track of Your Mail

It doesn't take long before you need to develop some system to organize your messages. Outlook 2000 offers you two ways to get the junk mail out of your Inbox. You can delete it from your Inbox or you can route it directly to Deleted Items without even seeing it!

Deleting mail is as simple as dragging it to the Deleted Items folder. You can also select a message (hold Ctrl to select multiple items) and press Delete on your keyboard. Deleted Items is a recycle bin for Outlook items. In order to permanently delete items, you have to open and empty the Deleted Items folder.

Deleting Mail

1. Select the message you want to delete. Click to select the first message; hold down Ctrl and click to select additional messages.
2. Point to the selected messages and drag them to Deleted Items on the Outlook Bar.
3. Open Deleted Items.
4. Select messages you want to delete for good. Point to the selected messages, right-click, and choose Delete, or click the Delete button on the Standard toolbar, to remove them completely. (You can also use the Delete key on the keyboard.)
5. Click Yes to confirm you want to permanently delete the selected items.

Messages deleted from the Deleted Items folder cannot be recovered using Undelete tools.

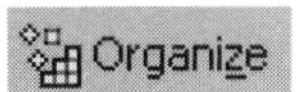

Outlook 2000's Junk E-Mail feature on the Actions menu gives you options when you see a piece of unsolicited e-mail in your Inbox. First, click the Organize button on the Standard toolbar, and then click the Junk E-Mail option in the Organize window.

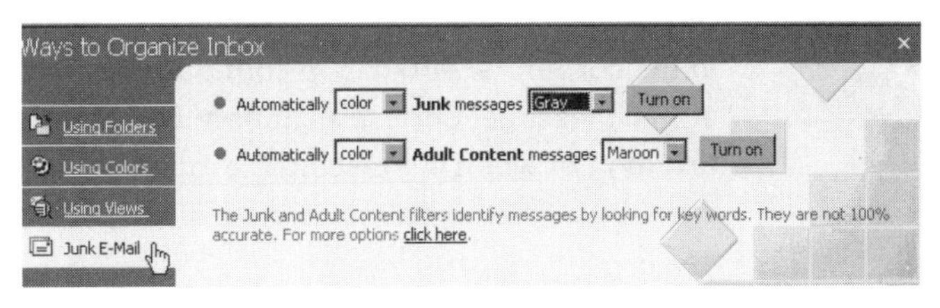

By default, Outlook will filter incoming e-mail for certain keywords to determine if the messages contain junk or adult content. The default options are simple: you can route junk e-mail directly to the Deleted Items folder or to a Junk E-Mail folder, and/or you can automatically color or move adult items depending upon your preference. Set your preferences and click the Turn On button to activate the feature. For more options, click the Click Here link and add a sender's name directly to the Junk E-Mail or Adult Content lists.

Using the Inbox to Send a Fax to a Contact

Objectives OL2000E.9.2 and OL2000E.9.3

Outlook comes with the all the things you need to send a fax to an Outlook contact. The first time you create a fax, Outlook prompts you to install Symantec Fax Starter Edition. (In the corporate/workgroup configuration, you'll use Microsoft Fax.) After you walk through the Fax Wizard, you can create a fax message to a contact just like any other type of message. With the Internet Only installation you have to send faxes from the Inbox. Choose Actions ➢ New Fax Message to open a message form. Click the To button and select the contact you want from the list. (Make sure you select a contact that has a fax number in their Contacts form.) Attach the document you want to fax then click the drop down arrow beside the Send button. Choose Symantec Fax Starter Edition to send the fax.

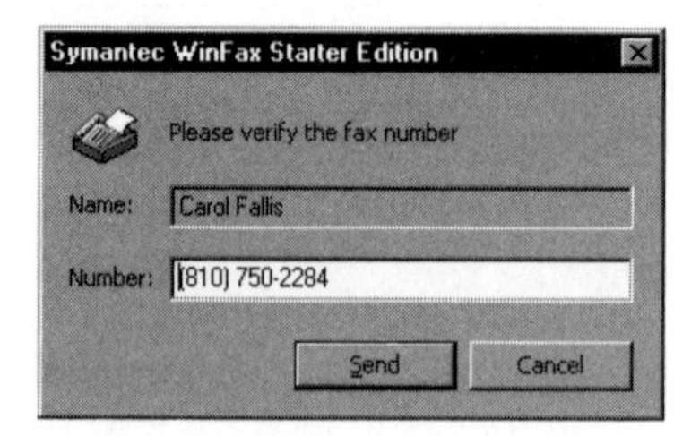

You will be prompted to confirm the contact's fax number. Choose Tools ➢ Send and Receive messages to send the fax.

In the corporate/workgroup configuration, create a fax as you would an e-mail message. Choose Actions ➢ New Message to Contact, then select a fax number when addressing the mail message. Click Send to send the fax.

Objective OL2000E.9.1

Receiving a Fax When a fax is sent to your computer's modem number, you'll receive it in your Inbox just like a regular message.

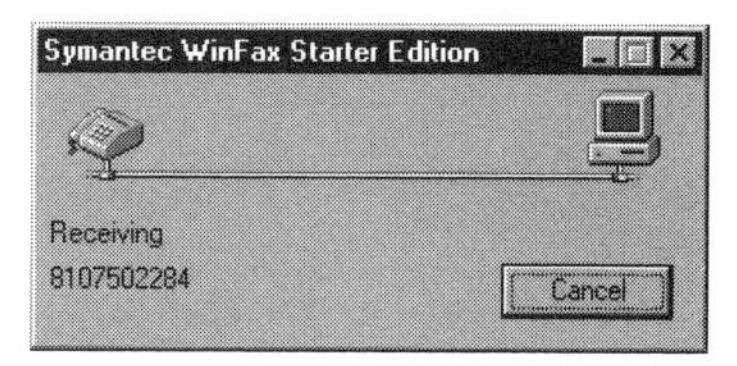

The From field will display the number from which the fax was sent. If you happen to be working on your computer when a fax arrives, you'll see a Receiving message.

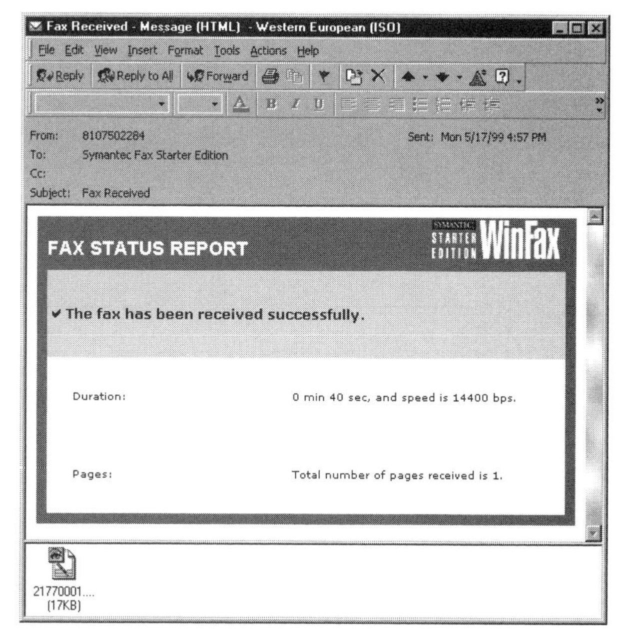

Double-click the message header to open the fax message. Then double-click the attachment icon at the bottom of the message and either Open it or Save it to Disk. If you choose to open it, you'll see the fax in a Quick Fax Viewer window.

Creating Bulk Mailings

Sometimes you want to mail, fax, or e-mail the same information to a large group of people. In Outlook 2000, this is called a *bulk mailing*, and you use the Mail Merge feature. You'll actually initiate this process from the Contacts folder, so switch modules then select the contacts to whom you want to send bulk mail. Choose Tools ➢ Mail Merge to open the Mail Merge Contacts dialog box shown in Figure 10.7.

FIGURE 10.7

Mail Merge window

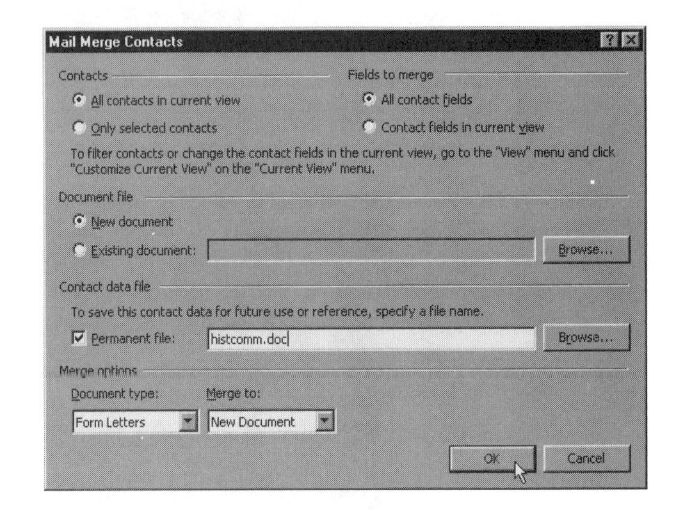

To select recipients, choose either All Contacts in Current View or Only Selected Contacts. Select the main document by browsing for an existing document or choosing New Document if you haven't created the document yet. To save the mail merge list click Permanent File and save the file under a new name. Merge Options include form letters, mailing labels, envelopes, and catalogs, and you can Merge To or export this information as a new document, to the printer as an existing document, to a fax machine, or to e-mail.

Outlook then launches Word 2000 so you can create your main document with merge fields and continue the process there (see Chapter 4 for more about Word documents and Mail Merge).

Storing Mail in Folders

Objective OL2000.2.1

After you delete or re-route all the messages you don't want, you can organize the remaining messages into a system of logical folders. To create a new folder in the Inbox, choose File ➢ Folder ➢ New Folder, or choose Folder from the New button drop-down menu on the Standard toolbar. This opens the Create New Folder dialog box.

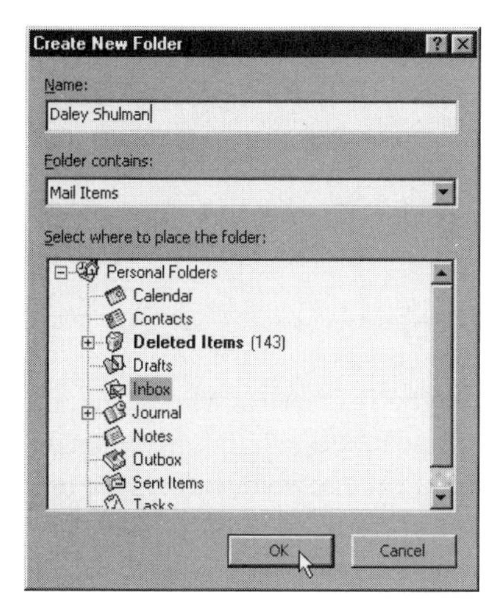

Enter a name for the new folder and make sure the Folder Contains control is set to Mail Items. In the Select Where to Place the Folder control, click the folder you want to house your new subfolder. Click OK to create the new folder. To view all Outlook folders, including your new folder, open the Folder List, either by choosing View ➢ Folder List or by clicking the Folder List button on the Advanced toolbar. To temporarily display the Folder List, click the button that displays the name of the current folder (for example, Inbox or Contacts) in the folder banner at the top of the Information Viewer.

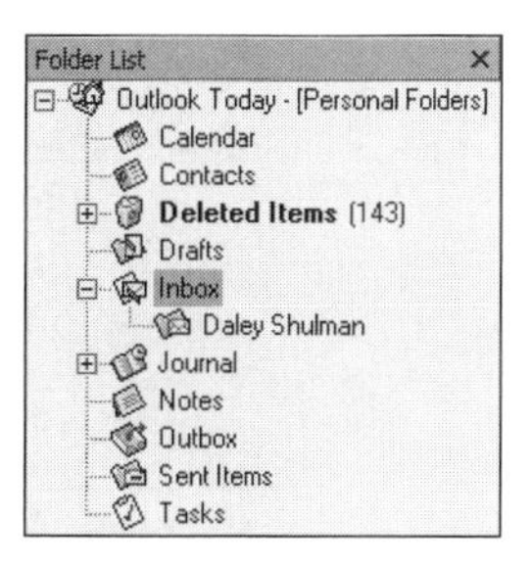

Click the Expand buttons (with plus symbols) in front of folders to display subfolders; the Collapse buttons (with minus symbols) hide lower level folders.

Objective OL2000.4.2

To move items to other folders, select the items and right-click. Choose Move to Folder and select the folder you want in the Move Items dialog box. Outlook also supports drag and drop moving of items and folders, so it's often easiest just to drag an item to the folder you want it in.

Using the Rules Wizard to Manage Mail

Objectives OL2000E.2.8 and OL2000E.5.4

If you're a person who receives a large volume of e-mail, you'll want to automate message handling whenever possible. With Outlook's Rules Wizard you can move messages to a particular folder based on who sent them, flag messages from a particular person, assign categories to mail based on the contents of the message, and automate dozens of other processes in your Inbox or other folders. You create the rules and Outlook does the rest!

Click Tools ➢ Rules Wizard to create and edit rules. Click New to begin creating a new rule. Your goal in working through the Rules Wizard is to set up a condition, then tell the Wizard how to treat items when they meet the condition. Let's say you wanted to have Outlook play a specific sound and display a specific message when mail from your boss arrives. Proceed as follows:

In the first step of the Rules Wizard, choose Check Messages When They Arrive, then click Next to move to the Conditions step shown here.

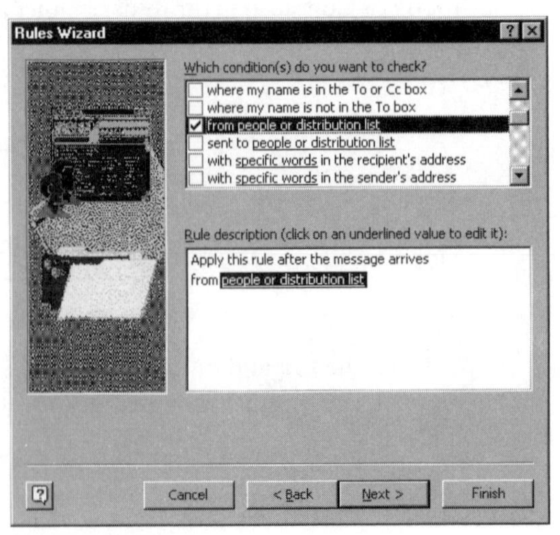

Enable the From People or Distribution List checkbox in the scroll list, then click the link to People or Distribution List in the bottom part of the Wizard window. Clicking this link opens the Rules Address dialog box where you can choose your boss's name from the list. Click OK, then click Next. Now choose what you want Outlook to do when it receives a message that meets the condition you just set. Continuing with the example above, you would want to enable both Notify Me Using a Specific Message and Play a Sound. Then be sure to click each link to specify your specific message and select a sound file.

Click Next and the Wizard allows you to choose exceptions to your rule. Set exceptions the same way you set conditions and handling options, then click Next again. In this last step of the Wizard, specify a name for your rule. You can choose to run your rule on existing messages if you wish; you might do this if you create a rule that moves or deletes messages. If you just want to set up the rule, but not activate it yet, disable the Turn On This Rule check box. Click Finish when you're through and then click OK to close the Rules Wizard.

You can import rules from other mail applications, or export Outlook rules to other mail applications, by opening the Rules Wizard and clicking the Options button. Choose whether you want to Export or Import, and select the drive and folder you need. Click Save (or Open, if you're importing) then click OK twice to close the dialog boxes.

Printing Mail

Objectives OL2000.1.4 and 1.11

You can quickly print a mail message by selecting it in the Information Viewer and clicking the Print button on the Standard toolbar. If the message is open, you can click the Print button on the Standard toolbar within the mail message.

If you click File ➢ Print to open the Print dialog box, you can choose to print Table Style, which prints the message fields as shown in the Information Viewer. Or you can print Memo Style, which prints the selected message as it appears when it is open. If you click the Define Styles button in the Print Dialog box, then click the Edit button, you can modify the selected style by changing default fonts, page size, header/footer, etc.

Hands On: Objectives OL20001.1, 1.2, 1.3, 1.4, 1.5, 1.6, 1.7, 1.8, 1.9, 1.10, 1.11, 1.12, 1.13, 1.15, 2.1, 2.2, 4.2, 5.2 and OL2000E.1.2, E1.3, E2.4, E2.8, E2.5, E5.4, E6.1, E9.1, E9.2, E9.3

1. Create an e-mail message to a colleague on your office network or to a colleague who has Internet e-mail.
   - a) Create and attach a custom signature to the e-mail message.
   - b) Request a Read Receipt for this message.
   - c) Flag the message for follow-up.
   - d) Send the message.
   - e) If you're using the corporate/workgroup configuration, recall, then resend the message.
2. Create an e-mail message to yourself by typing your own e-mail address in the To field.
   - a) Type some "dummy" text for the subject and message body.
   - b) Attach a file, then send the message.
   - c) When you receive the message in your Inbox, view it using the Preview Pane.
   - d) Turn the Preview Pane off and view the message by double-clicking it. View the attachment by double-clicking it. Close the attachment then print the message memo style. Close the message when you're through.
3. Reply to an e-mail message that you received. Flag the message for follow-up. Forward another message you've received to a colleague.
4. Send a contact to a colleague as a vCard.
5. Sort your Inbox using the column headers at the top of the information viewer.
6. Search for a message using the Advanced Find options. Provide as much information in the search text boxes as you can.

7. Create a Personal Distribution List of colleagues to whom you regularly send group e-mail.
   - a) Create and save a template for an e-mail message you use frequently.
   - b) Use the template to generate an e-mail to the list of recipients you created.
8. Create two new folders to store your e-mail messages:
   - a) Move existing mail from your Inbox to the new folders.
   - b) Use Find to locate a message sent by a certain individual.
   - c) Delete one or more messages.
9. Print the message fields in the Information Viewer, but change the table style so that it has a header with your name, your company name, and the current date and time.
10. Use the Rules Wizard to complete the following:
    - a) Automatically flag messages from your boss, or use another handling option that suits your work style.
    - b) Move messages from a certain sender into one of the subfolders you just created.
    - c) Export a rule for use in another mail application.
11. Send a fax to a colleague. Have your colleague fax you back. Open and view the fax.

Accessing Newsgroups with the Newsreader

Objectives OL2000E.10.1 and 10.2

Many companies host News Servers where individuals and groups can post messages to be viewed by others with access to the server. The collection of messages posted to the news server is called a *newsgroup*. Newsgroups tend to be topical; you can find a newsgroup for any interest area from the rainforest to software related issues. If your organization doesn't have a news server, don't despair; there are thousands of newsgroups on the Internet.

In order to read and reply to newsgroup messages, you need a *newsreader*. If you're not currently using a newsreader, Outlook automatically sets up the Outlook Express Newsreader. To start the default newsreader, click the View ➢ Go To ➢News. The first time you use the newsreader, you'll need to configure it. The Internet Connection Wizard will open and you'll be prompted to enter your name, e-mail account, and the name of the News Server you'll use to access news. (Contact your Internet Service Provider if you don't know the name of their news server.)

After you finish the Internet Connection Wizard, you'll need to download the list of Usenet groups available through your server. You only need to do this once but it takes a few minutes, because there are thousands of available newsgroups. In Outlook Express, click Subscribe to Newsgroups to begin the process of downloading. Once you have a list of available newsgroups in your newsreader, you'll want to search for the name of one that posts the types of messages you're interested in. This can be tricky, as not all group names have their topics included, so you may have to experiment a bit. If you find a newsgroup you want to revisit frequently, click the Subscribe button to keep it on the Subscribed tab of the Newsgroup Subscriptions dialog box, and save it as a quick link back to the newsgroup. Newsgroups that you visit but don't subscribe to are not saved when you exit the newsreader. You have to search for them again from that long list!

Select a newsgroup and click Go To. Click a message header to read its contents. Click the New Post button to post your own message.

For the complete low-down on newsgroups, see *Mastering Outlook 2000*, also from Sybex.

Managing Tasks in Outlook

Outlook takes the To Do list to a new dimension by adding the ability to track progress, assign the task to another person (our personal favorite), set reminders for the task, and insert the task into your calendar to make sure it gets completed.

The Tasks feature is available from the Outlook Bar, the New button, the Folder List, and the Calendar. From the Outlook Bar, click the Tasks icon to open the task list. The default view shows the task and the due date. The icons in the first column indicate whether the task is your responsibility or has been assigned to someone else, and whether it is a recurring task. The second column indicates whether the task is completed. As in any Outlook module, choose other views from the Current View menu drop-down list. Figure 10.8 shows a Detailed List view.

FIGURE 10.8

The Detailed List view of the Tasks window

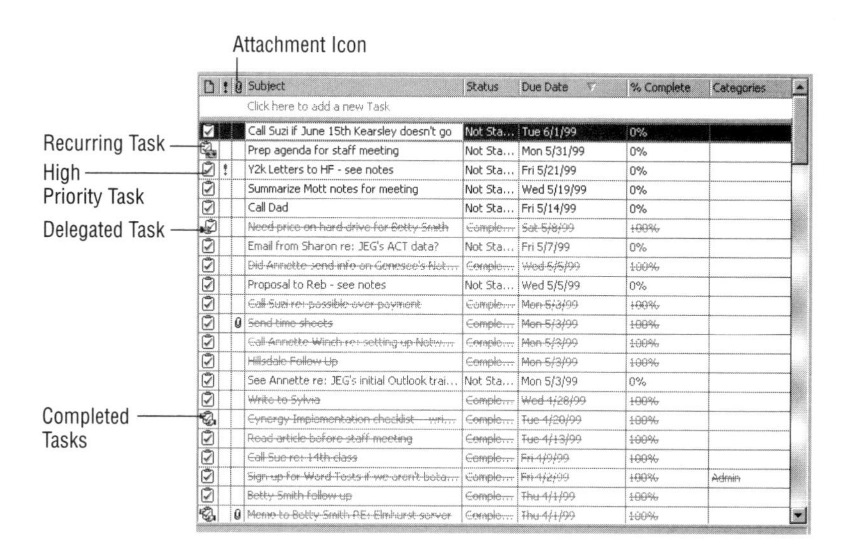

Creating a Task

Objective OL2000.6.1

To create a task, click in the Subject column where it says Click Here to Add a New Task. For a simple entry, enter the subject, date, and task. To enter more detail, double-click the entry to open the Task form. In the Task form, you can edit the task subject and due date information in addition to establishing a start date, assigning a status, setting a priority, and indicating how much of the task has been completed.

Subject: Provides a description of the task, which will be displayed on the Task list.

Due Date: Indicates when the task should be completed.

Start Date: Indicates when the task begins.

Status: Refers to whether the task is Not Started, In Progress, Completed, Waiting on Someone Else, or Deferred.

Priority: Can be set at High, Medium, or Low.

Percent Complete: Used to track progress.

Reminder: Sets a date and time at which you'll be reminded to work on the task.

Owner: Person responsible for task completion.

Categories: Allows you to assign the task to category.

Contacts: Links the task to a Contact.

Assign Task: Lets you delegate this task to someone else.

Private: Hides the item from other users who have permission to view your Outlook folders.

In the Subject text field, enter details about the task, for example, "Follow up with client to see if they received the proposal." You can also insert a file into the task if, for example, the task requires a Word or Excel document.

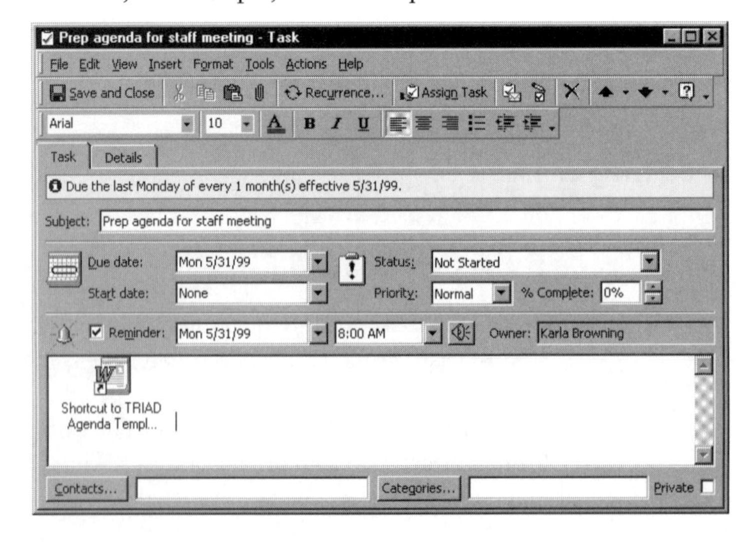

If you're creating a task with an attachment for your own use, consider attaching the file as a shortcut. This will save space on your hard drive, as Outlook duplicates a regular attachment and keeps a full copy of the file on hand. Shortcuts will not do, however, if you are delegating the task to someone who doesn't have access to the drive where the file is stored.

Objective OL2000E.6.3

Link a task to a particular contact by clicking the Contacts button at the bottom of the task form. To view all tasks associated with a contact, open the Contact in the Contacts module then click the Activities page. Choose Upcoming Tasks/Appointments from the Show list.

Creating a Recurring Task

Objective OL2000E.7.1

Many of the tasks you're responsible for are never really completed. It probably seems you just finish the task and it's time to do it all over again for a different week, a different month, or a different year. Outlook lets you designate recurring tasks and then reminds you when it's time to gear up for the next round.

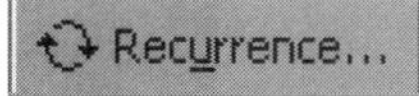

To make a task recurring, click the Recurrence button on the Standard toolbar in the Task form window. The Task Recurrence dialog box asks you for the recurrence period—daily, weekly, monthly, or yearly. Each choice opens a different list of settings to help you describe the pattern you want to establish. Set the recurrence options you want and click OK, then Save and Close to set the recurring task in motion. The task will continue to re-appear on your task list with the frequency you designate until you open the Task Recurrence dialog box again and click Remove Recurrence or until the End Date you indicate is reached.

Creating a Task

1. Click the Task icon on the Outlook Bar to open the task list.
2. Click in a blank row of any list view and Enter the Subject and Date or double-click a blank row to open the Task form.

Creating a Task *(continued)*

3. From the Task form, enter the Start Date, Status, Priority, and Percent Complete.
4. Set the date and time you would like to be reminded of the task in the Reminder fields.
5. Enter details about the task in the open text field.
6. Insert a file into the task by clicking the Insert File button on the Standard toolbar (the paper clip) and locate the file on your drive.
7. Set a recurrence pattern for the task by clicking the Recurrence button.
8. Click Save and Close to close the Task form and view the task list.

Tracking Tasks

One of the more useful Task views is the Task Timeline. This shows each task on the date it needs to be completed, so you can plan your time accordingly.

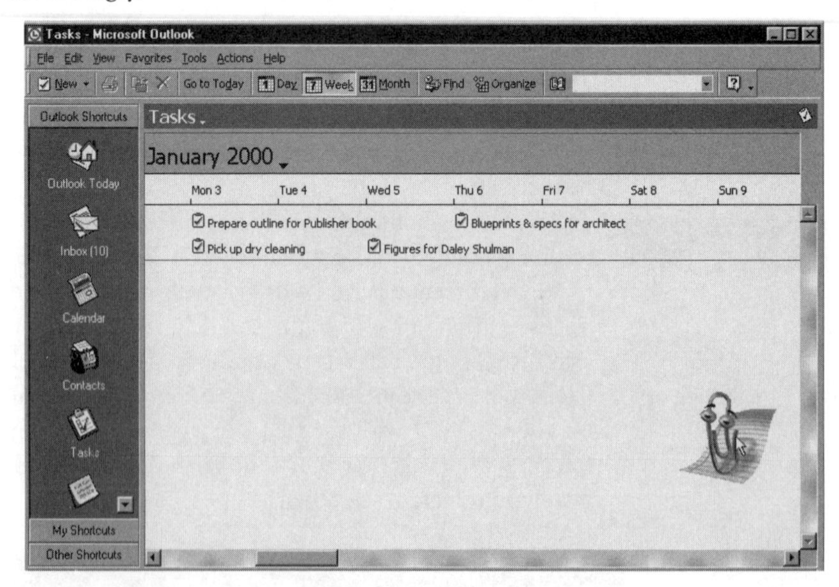

To display your tasks using the Task Timeline, choose View ➢ Current View ➢ Task Timeline. Use the horizontal scrollbar at the bottom of the Tasks window to browse future tasks—the Tasks module opens your view at the current day by default.

Delegating a Task

Objectives OL2000.6.4 and OL2000.1.16

It's always nice when you can generate a list of tasks to be completed—by someone else. Outlook makes delegation a snap, as long as you can reach the person you want to delegate to by e-mail.

Delegating a Task

1. Double-click the task you want to delegate to open it.
2. Click the Assign Task button on the Standard toolbar.
3. Click the To button and choose the address book that contains the person you want. Select a name from the Select Task Recipient list, or add a new person by clicking the New button.
4. Click the Cancel Assignment button on the Standard toolbar if you change your mind.
5. Click the Send button to send the task.

Tasks that have been delegated have an icon showing a hand holding the clipboard in the Task list. (See Figure 10.8) If you switch to the By Person Responsible view, you'll see the tasks listed by owner. When you double-click to open a task that has been assigned to someone else, the Task page of the Task form displays the e-mail message that was used to delegate the task, rather than the default Task page. The Details page stays the same, except that the Create Unassigned Copy button is activated. If you click it, Outlook will create a copy of the task and assign the copy back to you. However, you'll lose the ability to receive updates about the task, and the task will no longer show up under the other person's name in the By Person Responsible view.

Updating the Status of a Task

Objective OL2000.6.1

To update the status of a completed task or a task in progress, double-click to open the task and click the Details page. The Details page is the place to record how things are going or, if the task is completed, how things went.

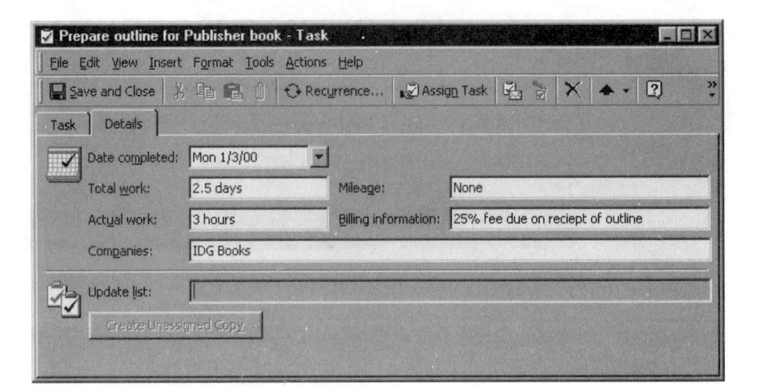

Only the owner of a task can update the task's status. If you've delegated a task, you have to wait for the assigned person to respond.

Tracking an Assigned Task

Objective OL2000.6.2

If you're the recipient of a delegated task, you can choose to accept or decline the invitation to take over the task (theoretically, at least). Figure 10.9 shows an assigned task from the recipient's end.

Click the Accept button to accept the task, or the Decline button if you're unable (or unwilling) to complete the task.

You can choose to edit your response before you send it. This is always a good idea if you're turning down a task assignment from your boss! When you Accept or Decline a task, the sender receives notification of your decision, with your comments if you added them.

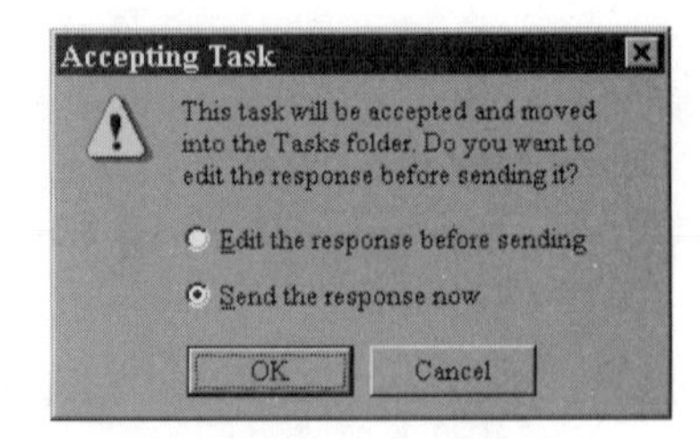

FIGURE 10.9
Delegated task, recipient's view

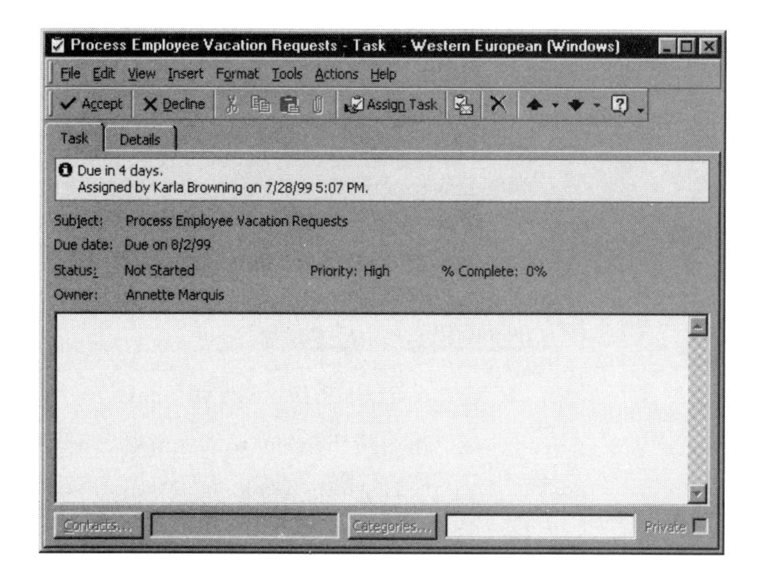

Once you accept a task, you can update the task's status in the Task form and send status updates by clicking the Send Status Report button on the Standard toolbar. The updates can be sent to the person who delegated the task or to anyone else in your address book.

Completing a Task

It's always great to check something off a long To Do list. Outlook provides several shortcuts to that warm feeling of accomplishment. In the Simple List view, you can literally check an item off a list. In other views, you have to mark the task as completed in some other way. If there is a Percent Completed column, change the percentage to 100%. In any view, you can right-click and choose Mark Complete from the shortcut menu.

If you prefer to open the task, changing the status to Completed or choosing Mark Complete from the Task menu will mark the task. But the biggest advantage of opening the task is that you can enter a Date Completed and other final task information on the Details page. If you need a thorough record of the task's completion, this is clearly the best choice.

Updating the Status of a Task

1. Double-click to open the task you want to update.
2. Click the Details tab and enter status information in the fields provided.

Updating the Status of a Task *(continued)*

3. Click the Send Status Report button to send information about the task's status to people in your address book.
4. Complete a task by checking it off in Simple List view or by double-clicking the task to open it, clicking the Details tab, and entering a Date Completed.

Hands On: Objectives OL2000.6.1, 6.2, 6.4 and OL2000E.7.1, E6.3

1. Create a list of 10 tasks you have to accomplish in the next month.
   a) Change the view to Detailed List.
   b) Enter details about three of the tasks on the Task form.
   c) Set at least one task as a recurring task.
   d) Establish a task as high priority.
   e) Link a task to a contact.
   f) Complete the Details form and mark two tasks complete.
2. Identify a task that you can delegate to another person in your address book (preferably someone using Outlook), and ask the person to provide you with a status report.
3. Send or forward a status report to someone else.
4. Have someone send you a task request. Accept or decline the request and add your comments to it.
5. Update the status of one of your recurring tasks and one of your regular tasks.

Keeping Your Calendar

Of all the Outlook modules, the hardest for many people to make a transition to is the electronic Calendar. The Calendar requires a shift in how you handle one of the most important aspects of your work—planning and organizing your time. However, the benefits and flexibility that Outlook affords, particularly in a networked environment, make the transition worth the effort.

Viewing and Navigating the Calendar

Objective OL2000.3.1

The Calendar default view, shown in Figure 10.10, is the Day/Week/Month view that includes an hour-by-hour daily calendar, a monthly calendar (Date Navigator), and a Task Pad.

FIGURE 10.10

Day/Week/Month view

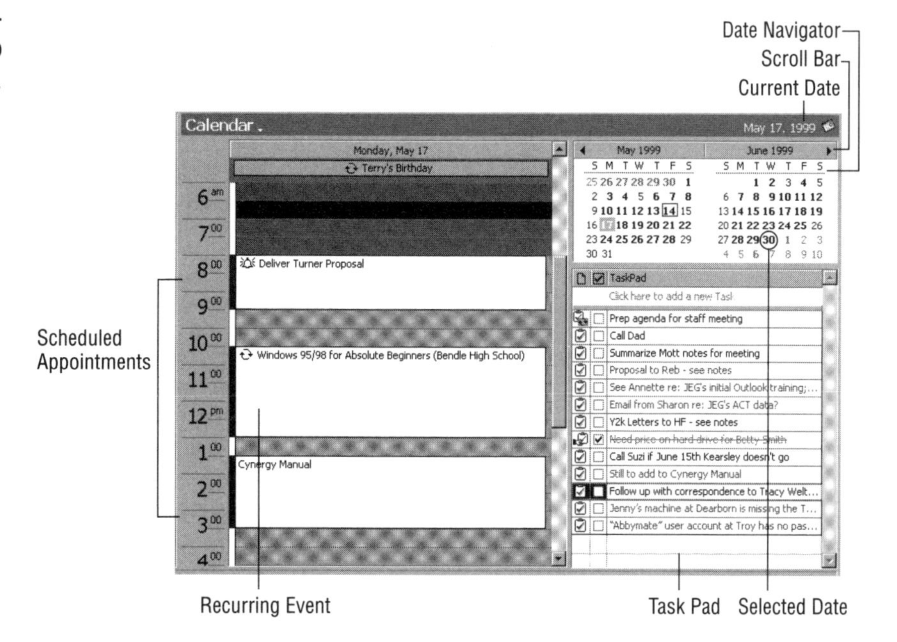

You may be wondering, though, where the weekly view that's part of Day/Week/Month is. Four additional buttons on the toolbar are actually the prime movers in this view. These buttons, located on the Standard toolbar, control whether you're viewing today, any day, a week, or a month:

The easiest way to move to another date is to click the date in the Date Navigator. Use the left and right arrow navigation buttons to move forward and backward a month. Click Month headers on the Date Navigator scroll bar to open a list of the three months preceding and three months following the current month.

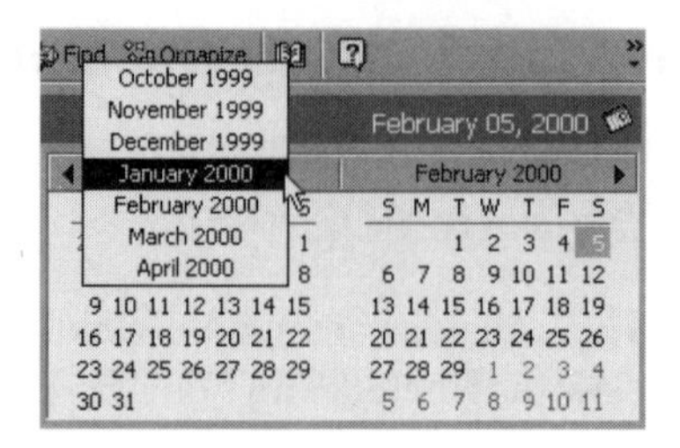

Scheduling Appointments

To schedule an appointment, switch to Day/Week/Month view and click the Date Navigator to bring you to the day you want to schedule. Click in the time slot that corresponds to the start time of the appointment you want to enter. Type the name of the appointment, and then drag the appointment block down to its end time.

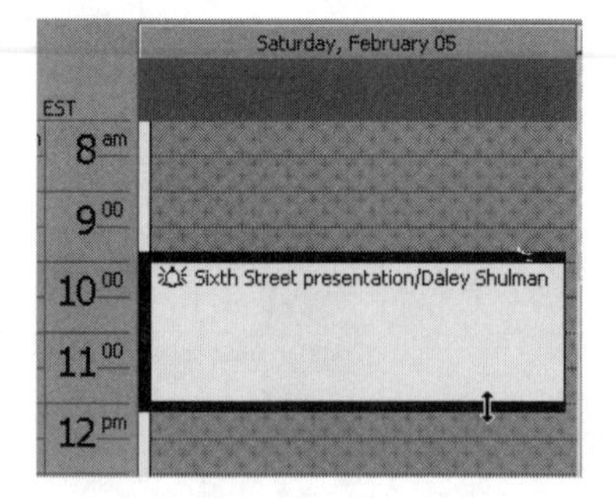

The blue line next to the appointment marks that time as busy, and the alarm clock represents a reminder that you'll receive 15 minutes before the appointment.

Setting a Reminder

Objective OL2000.3.3 and OL2000.3.2

Outlook's default reminder time is 15 minutes. That's great if you just have to walk down the hall, but what if you have a drive an hour to get to the appointment? You can change the reminder time and other reminder options by double-clicking the appointment to open the Appointment form.

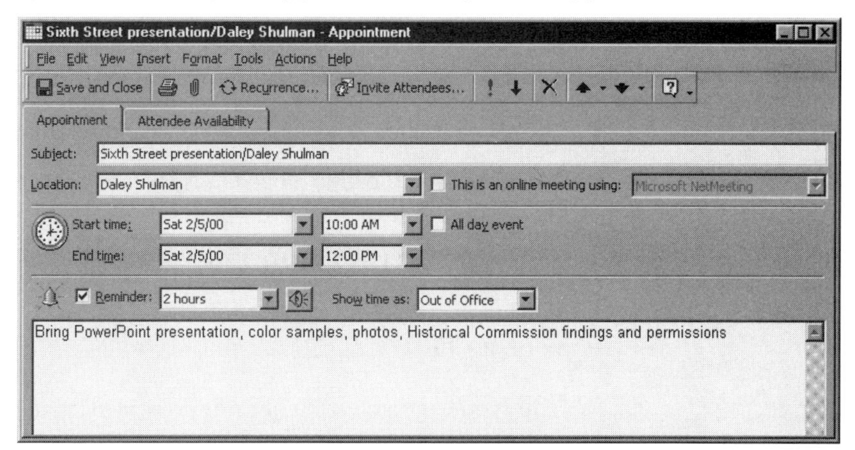

If you want to change the default reminder time, choose Tools ➢ Options and change the reminder time on the Preferences tab. Change the Reminder default to a different duration.

To change the reminder for this appointment, select a duration from the Reminder drop-down list, or type a duration in the text box.

To change the sound the reminder makes when it activates, click the Sound button and enter the path to a .wav file on your hard drive. When it's time for a reminder, the sound will play and a message will open on your screen with the appointment information. You can choose to Dismiss the reminder with no additional reminder, Postpone the reminder to a new time (like an alarm clock's snooze feature), or Open the item.

Use the Appointment form to enter other information about the meeting as well. Indicate the location of an appointment by typing it in the Location field. The Location information will show up in parentheses next to the Subject information in Day/Week/Month view. If the appointment you're scheduling is an all day event, enable that check box, then click Save and Close.

Setting a Reminder

1. Double-click the appointment on the calendar to open it.
2. Open the list of options in the Reminder field and choose a different duration.

Setting a Reminder *(continued)*

3. Click the Reminder Sound icon to select a sound file to play when the reminder pops up on your screen. Locate and select the file you want to use.
4. Clear the reminder check box to remove the reminder.
5. Click Save and Close to close the Appointment form.

Setting Up a Recurring Appointment

Objective OL2000.3.8

Any time you have a meeting or an appointment that occurs more than once, you only have to enter it once and then let Calendar know when and how often it will recur. Calendar will enter it on the subsequent dates for you. Any changes you make to a recurring appointment can be made to the specific individual appointment or to the series of recurring appointments.

Open the appointment by double-clicking it. Click the Recurrence button on the Standard toolbar to set the recurrence pattern. The Recurrence options are the same here as for recurring tasks. See *Creating a Recurring Task* for more information about recurring items.

Scheduling a Multi-Day Event

Objective OL2000.3.5

If you have an event that lasts all day, or for several days, you can set it up as an all-day event. All-day events appear at the top of your calendar for that day and show your time as Free on the Appointment form. You can make events recurring, just like appointments. Birthdays, anniversaries, and other important dates can be set up as recurring events like the one shown in Figure 10.10. If you plan to be unavailable for other appointments during an all-day event, click the Show Time As field and change your status to Busy or Out of the Office.

Scheduling a Multi-Day Event

1. Open the Appointment form for the all-day or multi-day appointment.
2. Click the All Day Event check box. The time fields disappear.
3. Enter the dates for the Start Time and the End Time of the event.
4. Enter a recurrence pattern, if needed.
5. If you're unavailable for the day or days in question, change the Show Times As field to Busy or Out of the Office.

Planning a Meeting with Others

Objectives OL2000.3.11 and OL2000.3.10

You can use the Outlook Calendar to plan and invite others to meetings. If you and all potential attendees are connected with Microsoft Exchange, Outlook 2000 will find the first available time for everyone, send out notices to invitees, tabulate their responses, and confirm the meeting.

Choose Actions ➢ Plan a Meeting or click the Plan a Meeting button on the Advanced toolbar in the Calendar to open the Plan a Meeting form shown in Figure 10.11.

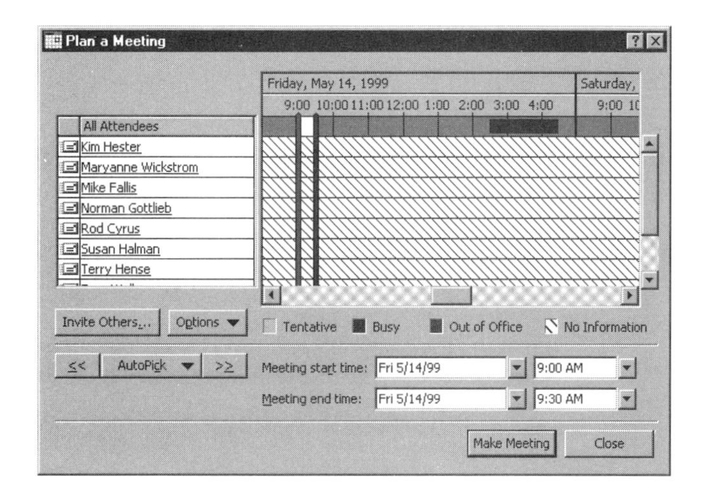

FIGURE 10.11 Plan a Meeting form

Click the Invite Others button and enter the people who are required to attend the meeting and those whose attendance is optional. Click OK. If attendees' schedules are available on your network, they show as blocked-off time on the timeline. If you want to remove someone from the list of attendees, right-click their name and choose Clear from the shortcut menu. You can also choose not to send an electronic invitation to a meeting attendee by clicking the icon that precedes her name in the Attendees list and choosing Don't Send Meeting to This Attendee.

If you have access to your invitees' Outlook calendars and would like Outlook to select the first available time for the meeting, set the desired start time of the meeting and the first possible date in the Meeting Start time field. Enter the desired end time in the Meeting End Time field. The most critical element here is to show the duration of the meeting. (You can adjust the actual time later if need be.) Click the AutoPick button, and the meeting selection bars will move to the first available time for all attendees.

You can drag the Meeting Selection bars to set a meeting's duration. The white area represents the meeting length, the green bar the start time, and the maroon bar the end time.

When you have found an acceptable time, click the Make Meeting button. Enter the details about the meeting: Subject, Location, Reminder, Description, and Categories. When all the details have been entered, click the Send button. All attendees will receive an e-mail message requesting them to choose among Accept, Reject, or Tentative. They can then choose to write a message and return it to you.

To review the status of a meeting, open the meeting in the Calendar and click the Attendee Availability tab. This shows you who was invited and the status of their responses. If you decide to invite others at this point, you can do so by clicking the Invite Others button. You can return to the default page by clicking the Appointment tab.

Planning a Meeting with Others

1. Switch to Calendar and click the Plan Meeting button on the Advanced toolbar.
2. Click Invite Others and select the people you would like to have attend, either as Required, Optional, or Resources. Click OK. If Outlook has access to your invitees' calendars, it will search the network and get their schedules to display in the Meeting Planner.

Planning a Meeting with Others *(continued)*

3. Enter a preferred Start and End Time for the meeting and click AutoPick to find the first available time for all invitees.
4. When you have decided on a time, click Make Meeting.
5. Enter the details about the meeting: Subject, Location, Reminders, and Categories. Enter additional information in the open text box.
6. Click Send to send messages to all invitees.
7. When messages are returned with responses, open the appointment to view the status of the responses by clicking the Attendee Availability tab.

Schedule Online Meetings Using NetMeeting

Objective OL2000E.3.3

You can't always be in the same room as those with whom you're meeting. Office 2000 supports online collaboration so that you don't have to be! Start a New Meeting Request as you normally would (File ➢ New ➢ Meeting Request) and enable the This Is an Online Meeting check box. Choose Microsoft NetMeeting from the list to the right of the check box then select the names for your meeting by clicking the To button and using the Select Names dialog box as you normally would. Enter subject, date and time, and reminder options like you would in any meeting request. To have NetMeeting start automatically, enable that feature.

You have to enter the path to a directory server to host your NetMeeting. If you're on an office network, your administrator can give you an address. If not, you'll need to locate and choose a directory server. (You can see which accounts already exist by clicking Tools ➢ Accounts and choosing the Directory Service tab.)

Browse to select an Office document for collaboration and set additional fields as you would in any form, then click Send to send the NetMeeting request.

Join a NetMeeting

Meeting participants will receive a meeting request in their Inbox. When it's time for the meeting, they will open the meeting request and click Join Meeting. Alternatively, meeting participants could right-click the appointment in their calendar and choose Join from the shortcut menu.

If the meeting organizer set up the meeting to start automatically with a reminder, the reminder will have a Join button for participants to click. (The meeting organizer's button will say Start.)

Showing Two Time Zones

Objective OL2000E.5.2

If you travel from Pacific to Eastern Standard, or plan telephone conferences with people in another time zone, it's handy to know the time in both locations. Calendar lets you view two time zones simultaneously.

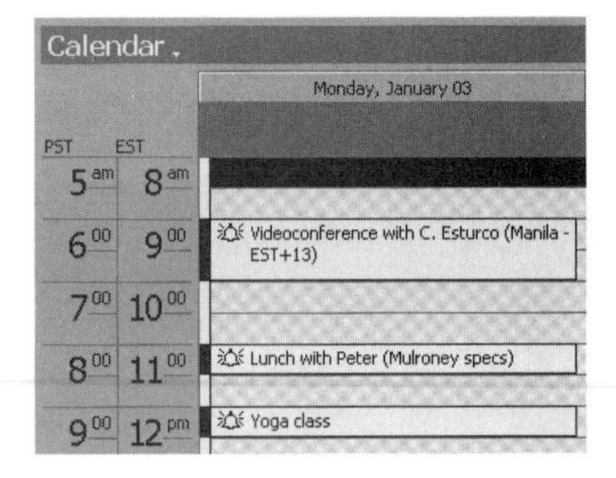

Viewing Two Time Zones

1. Choose Tools ➢ Options.
2. Click the Calendar Options button on the Preferences page.
3. Click the Time Zones button in the Calendar Options section.
4. Check the Show an Additional Time Zone options. Enter the other relevant information, and choose a time zone from the drop-down list.
5. To switch time zones, click Swap Time Zones. (Your calendar is always based on the time zone in the top pane.)
6. Click OK to close the dialog box. Click OK again to close the Calendar Options, and click OK once more to close Options.

Scheduling Resources

Have you ever scheduled a presentation only to find out someone else was using the LCD projector that day? Have you spent valuable time attempting to find out if the conference room was available for your sales meeting with a client? Most offices have a limited amount of meeting space and meeting equipment. With Outlook, however, your organization can keep a calendar for resources just like individuals keep their own calendars.

The way you schedule resources depends largely on how you're using Outlook. If you're in a small office using the Internet Only configuration with just a few resources to schedule, using folders will work for you.

Turn on your Folder List and create a subfolder in the Calendar folder. Name the subfolder to match the resource you're setting up: Small Conference Room or LCD Projector, for example. Select the subfolder and schedule "appointments" as you would in your own calendar. Create additional subfolders for each resource you have to schedule.

If your company does not have a network, resource schedules should be kept on one computer, usually that of the administrative assistant who reserves rooms and equipment. In networked environments, a shared public calendar folder for resources can be set up so that anyone with access to the network can view and/or reserve resources. See the section on *Shared Folders*, later in this chapter.

Objective OL2000.3.13

Scheduling Rooms and Equipment Using an Exchange Server Configuration If your office is running Microsoft Exchange Server, the administrator needs to set up separate mailboxes for all resources, that is, for each of the rooms and each of the pieces of equipment. The resource mail addresses can be kept in a separate global address book available to all users on the network. The people or person responsible for maintaining the schedule of resources needs to have permission to use each of these mailboxes. (For more information about setting up mailboxes and setting folder permissions, see *Mastering Outlook 2000*, also from Sybex, Inc.)

When you schedule a meeting you can select the meeting room and other resources from the address list in the Select Attendees and Resources dialog box (the Exchange Server version of the Select Names dialog box). When you check attendee availability, the availability of room and other required resources can also be considered.

Publishing a Calendar as a Web Page

Objective OL2000.3.12

If you embark on a business trip with three or four colleagues, it would be very useful for you all to have the same calendar listing. Outlook 2000 lets you publish a calendar as a Web page so that your colleagues, clients, and other important people can keep track of what's going on.

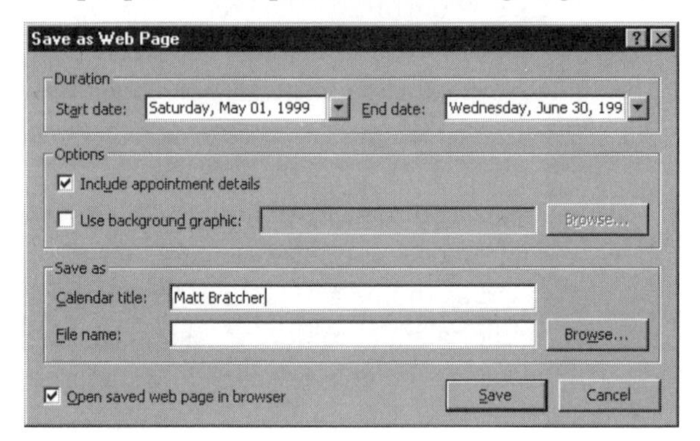

To save your calendar as a Web page, choose File ➢ Save as Web Page. In the Save as Web Page window, choose the span of days you wish published by choosing a Start Date and an End Date in their respective drop-down menus. You can opt to include your appointment details and whether or not to provide a background graphic, and you should enter both a Calendar Title and a File Name. Finally, if you want to preview the calendar page in your browser, check Open Saved Web Page in Browser before clicking Save. For more about publishing to the Web, see Chapter 13, "*Internet Publishing with Office 2000.*"

Publishing a Calendar as a Web Page

1. Choose File ➢ Save as Web Page.
2. Choose a Start Date and an End Date using the calendar controls.
3. Include appointment details and/or a background graphic.
4. Give the calendar a title and filename.
5. Preview the calendar as a Web page, if desired, by checking the available option.
6. Click Save.

Configuring the Calendar

Objectives OL2000E.3.1 and 3.2

In the One Day option of Day/Week/Month view, Outlook shows "work time" and "off time" with different color backgrounds. The default workday is from 8:00AM until 5:00PM excluding Saturdays and Sundays. This isn't very helpful if you're a third shift programmer!

Reconfigure the calendar to fit your life by clicking Tools ➢ Options ➢ Calendar Options. Choose your workdays and work hours. Choose a background color and enable the Week Numbers feature if you wish.

There are an abundance of Web sites that will publish your calendar so anyone with an Internet connection can view your availability. Click the Free/Busy Options button and choose the number of months' worth of data to publish. Set an update interval then enter the URL of the hosting site.

To make your calendar available on the Web for others to see, check out `www.when.com`, `www.visto.com`, or other similar sites where you can upload your calendar. Others can use the login name and password you supply to access your calendar to see what's happening.

Objective OL2000.3.6

You can choose to print a day's worth of calendar appointments, a week's worth, or several months at a time. You can also print the details of a single calendar appointment.

Click File ➢ Print and choose the Print Style you want from the scroll list in the Print dialog box. As with any module, you can click the Page Setup button to change how your calendar will look. The formatting options will vary slightly depending on which style you select. Some highlights are:

- Format the calendar to print on blank planner pages in a number of popular planner formats like Franklin or Day Runner. Click the Paper Tab of the Page Setup dialog box and choose from the Page Size scroll list.
- Choose to print the task pad and/or a notes area along with your calendar on the Format Tab of the Page Setup dialog box.

- Choose whether to print weekends in the Monthly Style on the Format Tab of Page Setup.
- TriFold Style lets you choose what to print on each 1/3 of the page. You could, for example, print your daily calendar on the left, task pad in the middle, and a lined notes section on the right.
- Calendar Details style lets you print attachments along with the details of each calendar appointment.

Hands On: *Objectives OL2000.3.1, 3.2, 3.3, 3.4, 3.5, 3.6, 3.8, 3.10, 3.11, 3.12, 3.13 and OL2000E.3.1, E3.2, E3.3, E5.2*

1. In the Calendar:
   - **a)** Configure calendar options to fit your workweek.
   - **b)** Enter at least five appointments.
   - **c)** Enter at least one meeting that recurs monthly.
   - **d)** View the Calendar in three different views and use the Day, Week, and Month buttons to examine your calendar.
   - **e)** Enter a one-week vacation using the all-day event option and indicate that you will be out of the office.
2. Plan an online meeting using NetMeeting:
   - **a)** Invite at least one other person to your meeting.
   - **b)** Set the meeting to start automatically with a reminder.
3. Print your calendar tri-fold style, with the selected date's appointments on the left, the week's appointments in the middle, and your task pad on the right.
4. Publish two days in your calendar as a Web page and preview it in Internet Explorer.
5. Find a site to host your calendar on the Internet. Type the URL in the Free/Busy options dialog box (you get there through Calendar Options under Tools ➢ Options).

Creating Shortcuts

By default, the Outlook Bar contains three different groups, each with different shortcuts. The Outlook Shortcuts group contains shortcuts to the Outlook modules. The My Shortcuts Bar has shortcuts to different e-mail folders, the Journal, and Outlook Today; and the Other Shortcuts Bar contains default shortcuts to My Computer, your My Documents folder, and your Favorites folder. All of this is customizable, however, so you'll want to set up groups and shortcuts that fit your own work style.

Creating Shortcuts to Files or Folders

Objective OL2000E.5.6

Outlook lets you add shortcuts to any Outlook module, or to any file, folder, or Web page to the Outlook Bar. To create a link to a file or folder, open the Outlook module, click the New button, and choose Outlook Bar Shortcut. You can also right-click the Outlook Bar and choose Outlook Bar Shortcut. The Add to Outlook Bar window opens:

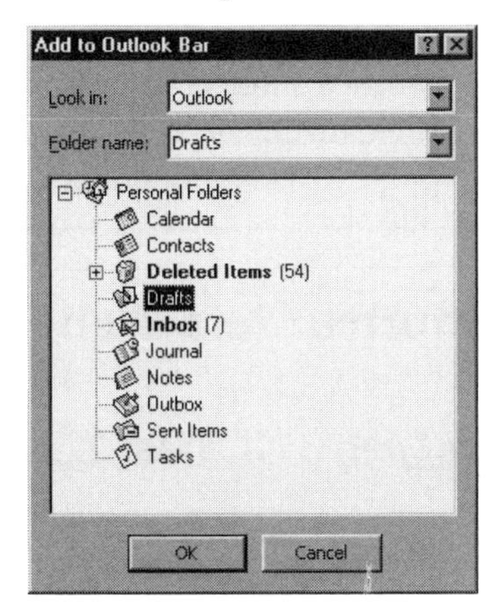

To create a shortcut for an existing item, such as the Tasks folder, click it once to select it and then click OK. An icon for the new item will appear in the Outlook Bar.

To add a shortcut to a folder from your hard drive, open the Add to Outlook Bar window and choose File System from the Look In drop-down menu. Outlook lets you browse the desktop and other areas of your computer. Choose the folder and double-click it to select it. An icon for the new item will appear on the Outlook Bar. Click the icon for the folder to view its files in the Information Viewer.

Once you've created a shortcut to a folder, you can make a shortcut to any file in that folder by dragging it to the Outlook Bar.

Remove unwanted shortcuts by right-clicking and choosing Remove from Outlook Bar.

Creating a Shortcut to a File or a Folder

1. Open the Outlook module of your choice, and then click the New button and choose New Outlook Shortcut, or right-click the Outlook Bar, and choose Outlook Bar Shortcut.
2. Set the Look In control in the Add to Outlook Bar dialog box to Outlook or File System.
3. Select the folder you want the shortcut to point to.
4. Click OK, and the new Shortcut will appear on the active bar.
5. Create a shortcut to a file from your hard drive by first creating a shortcut to the folder it's in, then viewing the contents of the folder and dragging the file to the Outlook Bar.

Creating a Shortcut to a Web Page

Objective OL2000E.5.3

Once you're familiar with navigation in Outlook, it's relatively simple to view internal items (like tasks, calendar appointments, etc.) and external items (like folders and files on your hard drive.) It should come as no surprise, then, that you can also view Web pages in Outlook.

Make sure you're connected to the Internet then activate Outlook's Web toolbar (View ➢ Toolbars ➢ Web). Type the address of the Web site you want to visit and press Enter to display it in the Information Viewer.

To create a shortcut to the displayed Web page, click File ➢ New ➢ Outlook Bar Shortcut to Web Page. Outlook places the shortcut in the My Shortcuts group.

You can add Web URLs to your Favorites folder by choosing Favorites ➢ Add to Favorites from the menu bar. Select a folder for the Web address in the Add to Favorites dialog box, then click Add. To open one of your Favorites Web sites, open the Favorites folder from the Other Shortcuts group on the Outlook Bar. The Favorites folder is accessible from Internet Explorer, so placing URLs in Favorites makes them available in Outlook and your browser.

Creating New Shortcut Groups

As mentioned, the Outlook Bar includes three default shortcut groups: Outlook Shortcuts, My Shortcuts, and Other Shortcuts. If you want to add a new, custom shortcut group, simply right-click on an empty part of the Outlook Shortcut Bar and choose Add New Group.

A blank text box appears at the bottom of the Outlook Bar where you can type in the name of the new shortcut group. Press Enter when you're finished, and the new shortcut group will appear with the others. Add shortcuts to your newly created group like you would with the regular Outlook Bar.

You can re-name or delete a shortcut group with the same right-click menu. Point the mouse to the group name in the Outlook Bar, right-click it, and choose Rename Group or Delete Group.

You can change the size of Outlook shortcuts by choosing Large Icons or Small Icons in the right-click menu. Outlook displays the Outlook Shortcuts as large and the rest of your shortcuts as small by default.

Creating a New Shortcut Group

1. Right-click on the empty part of any Outlook Shortcut Bar and choose Add New Group. A blank text box appears at the bottom of the Outlook Shortcuts pane.
2. Type the name of the new shortcut group and press Enter. The new shortcut group appears at the bottom of the Outlook Bar.
3. Right-click the shortcut name and choose the appropriate command from the menu if you want to delete or re-name the group.

Hands On: *Objectives OL2000.2.1, OL2000.E5.3, and E5.6*

1. Create a subfolder in your Inbox or Tasks folder, and drag several items into it. Create a shortcut to the new folder on the Outlook Bar.
2. Create a shortcut to a folder in Outlook and add it to the My Shortcuts group.
3. Create a shortcut to a folder elsewhere on your hard drive and add it to the Other Shortcuts group. Then create a shortcut to a file within that folder. Delete the shortcut to the folder, but leave the shortcut to the file.
4. Create a shortcut to a Web page and add it to the My Shortcuts Bar. Rename the shortcut.
5. Create a new group and add a shortcut to it.

Using the Journal and Notes

The Journal serves as your automated, online diary. It will automatically record work you are doing or let you add entries manually. You can track time spent on projects, phone calls, documents, e-mail messages—whatever you want to monitor. The Journal is located on the Outlook Bar. To open the Journal, click the Journal icon.

Automatically Recording Journal Events

Objectives OL2000E.7.3 and OL2000.5.5

One of the useful features of the Journal is that you can have it working in the background, silently recording the work you do. You have to configure the Journal to work automatically.

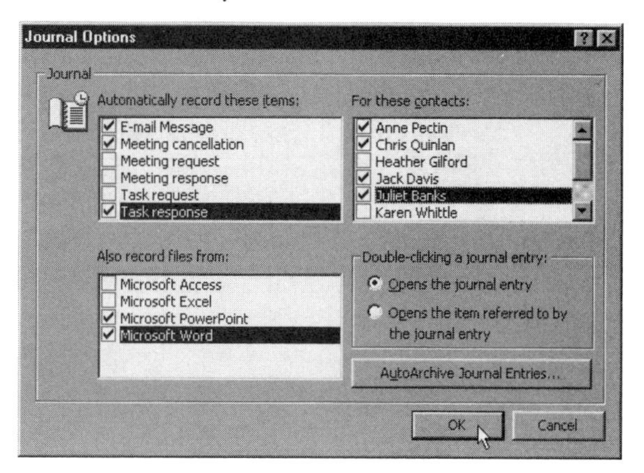

Choose Tools ➢ Options and click the Preferences tab. Click the Journal Options button in the Contacts section. Choose the contacts for who you wish to automatically record certain actions, then choose those actions. You can also choose to automatically record when and for how long you work on a file in other Office applications. Click OK twice to close both dialog boxes.

If you choose to automatically record your work in the Office applications, your Outlook file size becomes very large very fast. Unless you have the need to strictly track your time, it's better to manually record journal entries when you need them.

Automatically Recording Journal Entries

1. Choose Tools ➢ Options and click the Preferences tab. Click the Journal Options button.
2. Mark the items you want to record automatically.
3. Click OK.

Manually Recording an Event

Objective OL2000.5.4

Although automatically recording events is helpful, the real power of Journal is its ability to let you enter information manually to track phone calls, conversations, meetings, and any other kind of communication. To make a new journal entry, choose File ➢ New ➢ Journal Entry or choose Journal Entry from the list on the New Item button. If you're going to be creating a number of entries, it's fastest to choose Journal in the Outlook Bar then click the New Journal Entry button on the toolbar.

On the Journal Entry form, shown in Figure 10.12, you can enter a Subject, Entry Type (from a list of 20 choices), Contact Name and Company, Start Time, Duration, and Notes. If you want to clock the time you spend on the phone or working on a document, click Start Timer and let it run while you work on the entry. Outlook will automatically record the time in the Duration field.

FIGURE 10.12 Enter information about an activity in the Journal Entry form

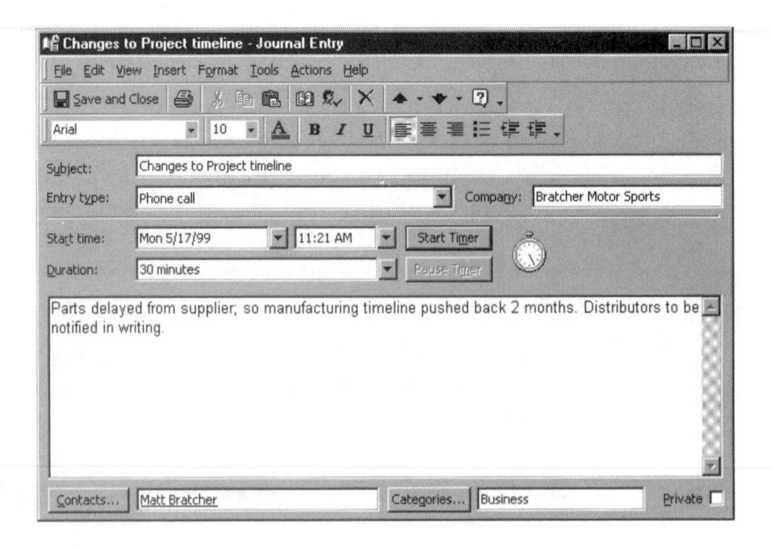

Objective OL2000E.6.3

You can insert files into journal entries, as you can with all Outlook items. Choose Insert ➢ Object and select the type of object you want to link to your

Journal entry. You can't insert Outlook items in Journal entries, but you can link the entry to a contact by clicking the Contacts button in the Journal Entry form. Select the contact(s) you want to link this entry to. To see all the journal entries linked to a contact, open the Contact form, activate the Activities page, and choose Journal from the Show drop-down list.

Creating a Manual Journal Entry

1. Choose File ➢ New ➢ Journal Entry to open a Journal Entry form.
2. Enter the Subject and Entry Type.
3. Enter a Start Time or click the Start Timer button. Either enter the Duration manually or click Pause Timer when you're finished to have Outlook enter the duration for you.
4. Enter details about the entry in the text box.
5. To link the entry to a Contact, click the Contacts button and choose a contact from the Select Names dialog box.
6. Choose a category for the journal entry, if you wish.
7. Click Save and Close to close the entry.

Locating Events in the Journal

The Journal is organized as a timeline and can be displayed in timeline or table form. The first three views available from the Current View list—By Type, By Contact, and By Category—are timeline views. The other three views in table format are Entry List, Last Seven Days, and Phone Calls. To locate an entry in a timeline view, click the Day button, Week button, or Month button on the Standard toolbar.

Click the plus symbol to expand the entries in the view; use the Collapse button (with the minus symbol) to hide entries. Double-click an item to open the Journal page for that item. Use the Find Items button to find entries based on criteria: for example, all the items that pertain to a particular company or subject.

Locating an Entry in the Journal

1. Select a view from the Current View menu.
2. If you've chosen a timeline view, click the Go to Today, Day, Week, and Month buttons to choose a particular date. Use the horizontal and vertical scroll bars to scroll through the dates.
3. Use the Expand and Collapse buttons to hide and display entries in a timeline view.
4. Click the Find Items button on the Standard toolbar to search for an item by words, entry type, contact, categories, or other criteria. Click Find Now to initiate the search.

Creating Notes

Objectives OL2000.8.1, OL2000.8.2, and OL2000.8.3

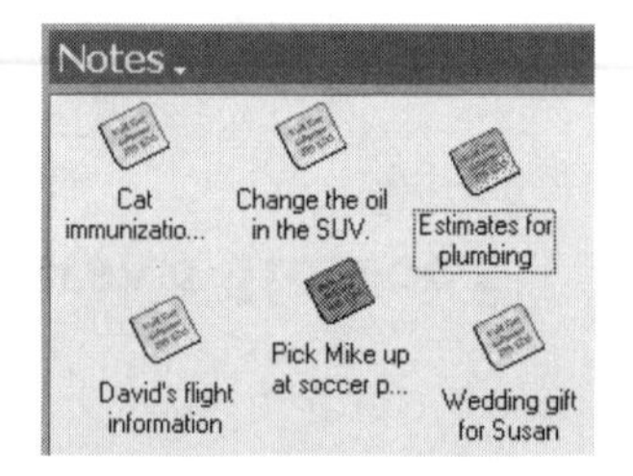

Even in the age of the computer, most people still use a paper memo pad or sticky note to write short notes to themselves. Outlook includes an easy way to computerize notes. Choose Note from the New button on the Standard toolbar or hold Ctrl and Shift and press N to open a Note window. Each note is automatically time and date-stamped. Closing the Note window automatically saves the note. To view a note, click the Notes icon on the Outlook Bar to go to the Notes module.

Double-click a note to open it. Edit the content of the Note by moving the insertion point and deleting old text and/or typing new text. Click the Note icon in the upper left corner of the Note to access options for deleting, saving, and printing notes. Click the Close button on the note to place it back in the Notes window as an icon.

You can move individual notes to the Windows desktop by dragging them onto the desktop.

Creating a Note

1. Choose Note from the New button on the Standard toolbar, right-click in the Note window, and choose New Note, or press **Control+Shift+N**.
2. Type the note and click the Close button.
3. Click the Notes icon on the Outlook Bar to open the Notes window. Click once to open a note.
4. Click the Note icon in the top-left corner of a note to access Save As, Print, and other options.

Customize the appearance of your electronic notes by clicking Tools ➢ Options ➢ Note Options. Choose a color, size, and font for your notes. Previously, created notes will still be formatted as they were, but newly created notes will have the new formatting.

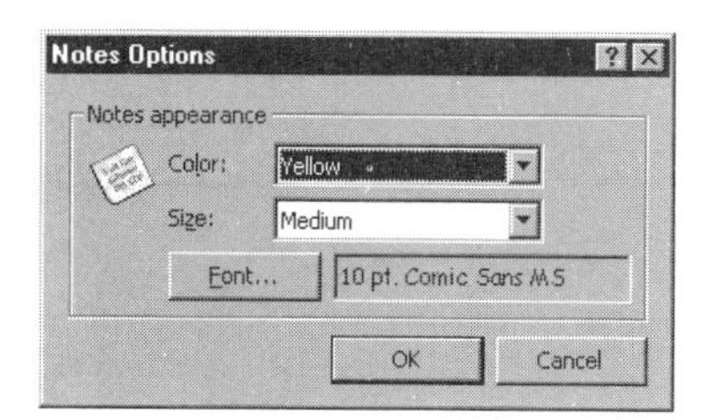

Hands On: *Objectives OL20005.4, 5.5, 8.1, 8.2, 8.3, OL2000.E6.3, and E7.3*

1. Set Journal options to automatically record your work on Word files and e-mail messages.
2. Make a Journal entry for a phone call to a contact in your Contacts folder. Use the timer to time the call.
3. Locate a Journal event using Find Items. Locate a Journal event using the Go to Month button and the scroll bars.
4. Create three notes and then complete the following:
   a) Delete one of the notes.
   b) Change the message content on one of the notes.
   c) Drag one of the notes to the Windows desktop. Double-click the Notes icon to open the note. Close it again.
   d) Change the Notes options to customize the appearance of your notes.

Integrating the Outlook Modules

The Outlook modules are designed to work together, to help you organize and manage your time and data most effectively. In this section, you will learn how to keep track of data and other files in Outlook and how to further customize the Outlook environment.

Managing Data and Files in Outlook

You may be surprised to discover that Outlook can be used for all your file management needs—moving, copying, opening, finding, re-naming, and deleting files; creating new folders; and even printing documents. The Outlook Bar can be customized to include shortcuts to other folders, making it possible to access any document or module on your system from within Outlook. To open a list of options for customizing the Outlook Bar, right-click it.

Click the Other group button on the Outlook Bar to see drives and folders on your computer. Click any folder shortcut to see the contents of that folder in the Information Viewer. Double-click icons for folders in the Information View to see their contents.

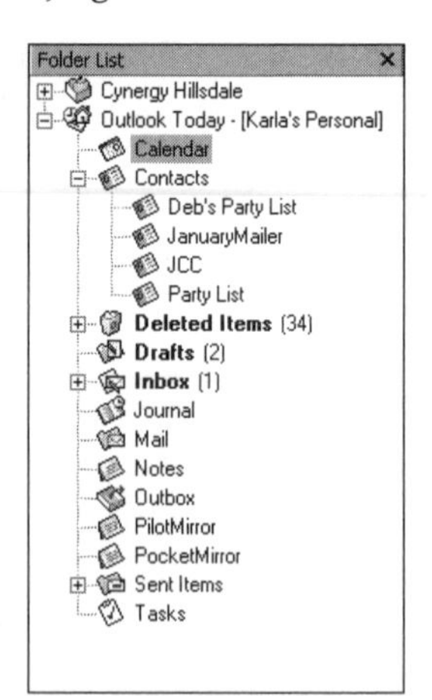

If you want to keep a Windows Explorer-type list of folders visible, open the Folder List by clicking View ➢ Folder List or clicking the Folder List button on the Advanced toolbar. If your screen is getting a little crowded, you could buy a bigger monitor. Or you could close the Outlook Bar (choose View ➢ Outlook Bar). It's up to you.

Objectives OL2000.6.5 and OL2000.3.14

Automatically Creating a New Outlook Item from an Existing One

With Outlook's AutoCreate feature, you can use an item to quickly create an item of another type. For example, to create a task from a mail message item, select the message, then drag and drop it on the Task icon or folder in the

Outlook Bar. Outlook will copy information from the mail message to the appropriate fields in the task form. If you drag a task request to the Calendar or to Tasks, Outlook automatically notifies the sender that you accepted the task. This also works with meeting requests.

Drag a calendar appointment to the Inbox and you've got a message with dates, times, and location already typed for you. Use this as an alternative to meeting requests for notifying colleagues of important events.

AutoCreate has another unique use. If you drag an Outlook item onto the desktop, you create a copy of the item that you can open from the desktop—a convenient way to remember to follow up on a task.

Archiving Items

Objective OL2000.2.4

If you use Outlook to its full potential, you'll be creating a mountain of data. Eventually, you'll want to clean out your folders to eliminate out-of-date items. Outlook gives you two ways to handle spring-cleaning: *AutoArchive* and *Archive*. Before you use either archiving method, you should review and set the Archive properties for individual folders.

Setting Folder Archive Options

1. Right-click the first folder for which you want to set Archive options, and choose Properties.
2. Click the AutoArchive tab.
3. Enable the Clean Out Items Older Than check box, and set a length of time.
4. Choose whether old items should be moved or deleted.
5. Click OK.
6. Repeat steps one through five for each folder.

AutoArchiving is the easiest option; simply tell Outlook how frequently it should check the folders.

Setting AutoArchive Options

1. Choose Tools ➢ Options from the menu.
2. On the Other page, click the AutoArchive button to open the AutoArchive dialog box.
3. In the AutoArchive dialog box, set the length of time between AutoArchive operations.
4. Enable or disable prompting and the deletion of expired mail items.
5. Click OK.

You don't have to use AutoArchiving. Instead you can archive folders and their subfolders individually as you need to. Or, you can use the Archive options you set for each folder, but start the archiving operation manually when you have time.

Manually Archiving Folders

1. Choose File ➢ Archive to open the Archive dialog box.
2. Select Archive All Folders According to Their Archive Settings and click OK to begin archiving all folders.

   OR

2. Choose Archive This Folder and All Subfolders.
3. Select the folder you want to archive.
4. Select a date in the Archive Files Older Than drop-down list.
5. Click OK.

Customizing the Outlook Environment

Outlook 2000 gives you two ways to customize its environment most effectively, by views and by forms. By designing your own Outlook environment and Outlook documents, you can tailor Outlook to your own specific needs without losing the ease and functionality of Office 2000.

Creating Custom Views

Objectives OL2000.2.3, .2.5, and 3.7

You can create a custom view in two ways. If you already have a view open, you can alter it, select a different view, and Outlook saves the changes. Or you can choose View ➢ Current View ➢ Define Views, and select a view to base the custom view on.

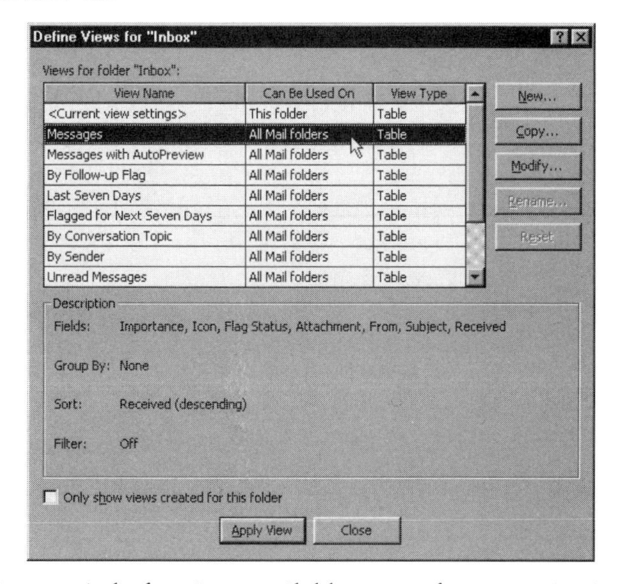

There is a myriad of options available to you for customization. Essentially, click an existing view and then click Modify, or Copy to customize an existing view, or create a copy to work from. Select fields to display, options for groups, filters, and formatting. Click OK to save the new view and return to the Define Views dialog box.

Objectives OL2000.6.3 and OL2000.4.6

When you're customizing, it helps to know which feature to change to get the result you're hoping for. You can choose from one of these features:

Fields: Adds or removes fields from the current view. (You already know how to remove fields from a view without using the dialog box. Just drag a column header into the folder banner above it.)

Group By: Displays all related items under a header. For instance, you could display all the tasks assigned to each of the categories you're using by clicking the Group By button and choosing Categories from the first Group Items By drop-down list. Expand and contract category headers to show/hide tasks under each category.

Sort: Changes the order in which your items appear in the Information Viewer. If you're customizing a list view that shows the categories field, you could sort by categories to show like items together, without the header you get when you use grouping.

Filter: Allows you to show or hide certain items based on criteria you set. For instance, you might want to hide your personal calendar appointments before you print it to post for your staff. Or you may want to filter contacts so that you only see those contacts from a certain company. Then you could select them and send a bulk e-mail, for instance. In this second example, you would open the View Summary dialog box from the Contacts module.

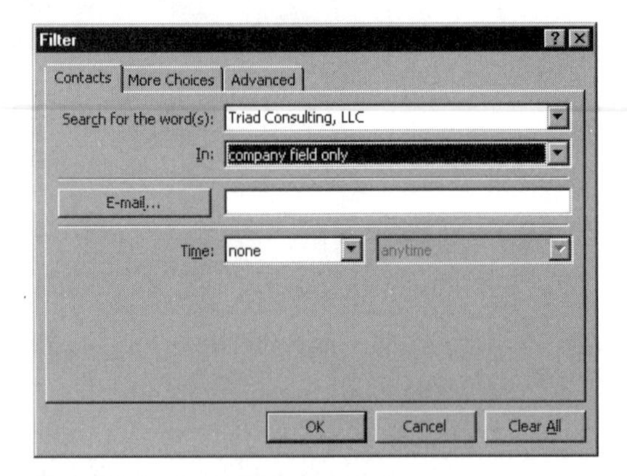

Click the Filter button to open the Filter dialog box, then set your filter criteria. Using the example in the Filter dialog box, you should type the company name in the Search for the Word(s) field, then set the In control to the appropriate field—in this case Company. Click OK twice to close both dialog boxes and see your filtered view.

Other Settings: Changes fonts and other display settings for table views. You can, for instance, choose not to display gridlines.

Automatic Formatting: Applies formatting to items that meet certain criteria you set. In mail folders, you might decide to display unread mail using a different font color.

Modifying an Existing View

1. Choose View ➢ Current View ➢ Define View.
2. Select a view that's similar to the one you want. Choose Copy to work with a complete duplicate, or Modify to customize an existing view without saving an original. Click Apply Settings (if you created a copy) to continue.

   OR

2. Click New to create a view from scratch. In the Create a New View dialog box, name the view, choose its contents, and indicate whether or not you wish to share the view with others. Click Apply Settings to continue.
3. Set options in the View Settings for Fields, Group By, Sort, Filter, and Format controls.
4. Click OK to return to the Define Views dialog box.
5. Click Apply View or Close to save the view.

Creating an Outlook Form

Objective OL2000E.5.5

As you know, every Outlook item is based on information entered into a form. High-end Outlook users quickly discover there is data they might want to track, and there are no existing Outlook forms that contain those data fields. When this is the case, it may make sense to modify an existing Outlook form to include the data field you need. To do this, you have to open the Design Form dialog box.

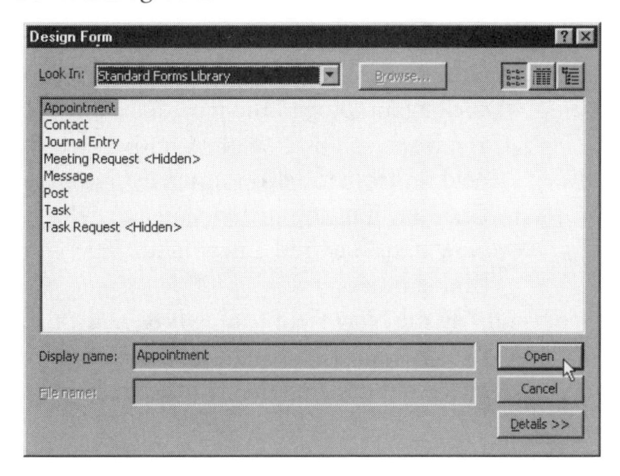

Click Tools ➢ Form ➢ Design a Form. Choose the type of form you wish to modify and click Open. The new form opens in Design view.

In Design view, extra tabbed pages appear beside the main page (see Figure 10.13). Mail items can have up to six visible pages; other items are limited to five pages. The (Properties) and (Actions) pages are permanently hidden. You can't modify the predesigned pages in the default form, but you can add information to other pages, and display or hide the default pages.

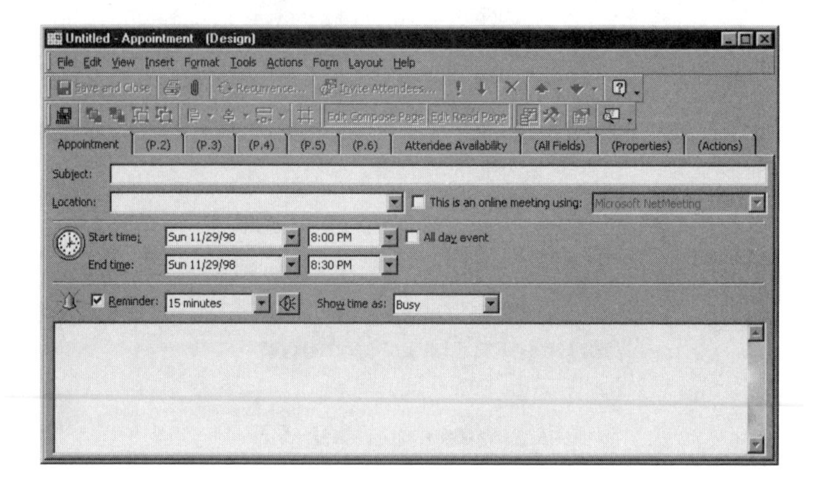

FIGURE 10.13 The Appointment window in Outlook Design view

Adding Controls to Form Pages To add a control to a form page, you must be in Design view. Click the form page you want to customize, and the Field Chooser opens automatically.

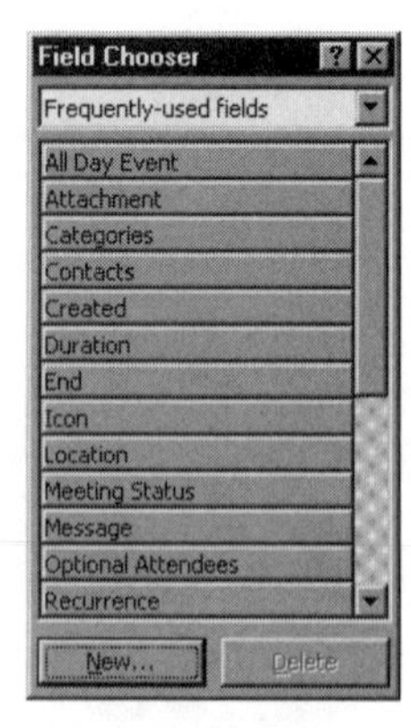

Drag a field from the Field Chooser onto the page to create a text box control and an accompanying label control. To change the label, click once, then click again to open the label for editing. If the field you want isn't listed in the Chooser, select a different field set from the drop-down list in the top of the Chooser. If it isn't included in any field set, click the New button to add a new field. The New Field Dialog box opens.

In the New Field Dialog box, name the new field and select the field type; the different ways to format these new fields will depend on the field type, so make that decision first. Click OK to insert the new field into the form. After you place the field in the form, right-click the text box control, and use the shortcut menu options to format the field. If you need to remove a control, right-click the control and choose Delete from the shortcut menu. Right-click the control and select Properties from the shortcut menu to set the control's properties. The Properties dialog box opens.

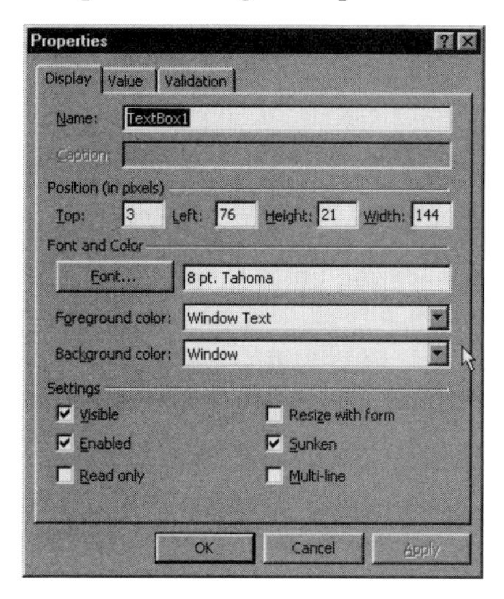

For more information about the settings in any of the Properties sheets, click the dialog box Help button (the question mark), and then click the setting you want to know more about.

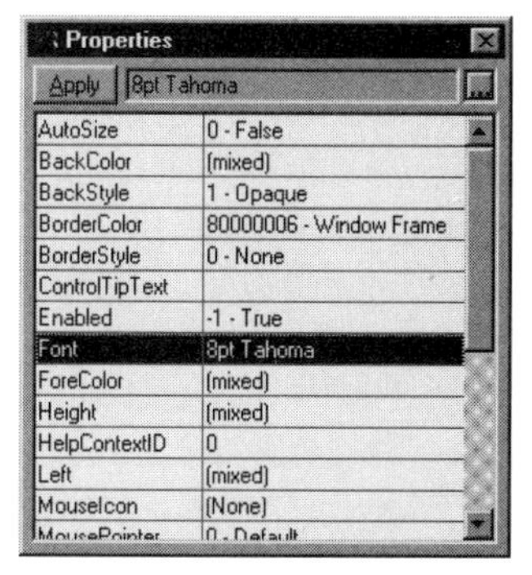

Click the Display tab to set font and formatting properties and to verify or enter a name for the control. Click the Value and Validation tabs also to establish other form field properties such as field and format field specifications. Click OK, and then right-click the new field again. This time, choose Advanced Properties from the right-click menu, and the Advanced Properties dialog box opens.

The Advanced Properties dialog box reveals more fundamental ways to customize your form controls. Double-click an item in the list (such as Font) to view and edit your options. A Font Customization dialog box will open in this example, showing you all the various type faces, sizes, and more. Make your choices and click Apply to put them into effect. See Chapter 9 for more information about adding controls to forms.

Naming, Hiding, and Displaying Pages To change the name on a page tab, activate the page and choose Form ➢ Rename Page to open the Rename Page dialog box. Enter a name and click OK. If you add fields, or other controls to a hidden page, the page will be displayed automatically. To hide or display other pages, activate the page, then choose Form ➢ Display This Page to turn the check mark on or off. If you want one of your newly designed pages to appear as the default page in the form, hide the first page (which you can't modify), and create your default page on (P.2).

Setting Form Properties Forms also have properties, which you can view by clicking the Properties tab while the form is open in Design mode. On this Properties page, you can establish a category and subcategory for the form, create a password to protect the form's contents, and provide description information, a form number, and other relevant information.

Saving Your Form To save your form, *don't* choose Save and Close—this saves only the item. Choose Tools ➢ Forms ➢ Publish Form from the menu bar to open the Publish Form As dialog box. Enter a name for the new form. (If you have permission to save shared forms, click the Publish In button to select a library.) Click the Publish button to save the form. The form can only be used with records created or imported *after* the form was created.

Creating a New Form

1. Choose Tools ➢ Forms ➢ Design a Form and select the form you want to modify. Click Open to open the form in Design view. The Field Chooser automatically opens.
2. Re-size the form using the mouse to click and drag the corners.
3. Drag a field from the field chooser to the form. To create a completely new field, click the New button on the Field Chooser. The New Field Dialog box opens.
4. Choose the field type first, and then name it. Click OK to insert the new field into the form.
5. Right-click the new form and choose Properties; the Properties dialog box opens. Use the Properties dialog box pages to establish font and formatting properties and to verify or enter a name for the control. Click OK.

Creating a New Form *(continued)*

6. Right-click the new form again and choose Advanced Properties. Customize the new form at a more basic level here, including fonts, colors, and so forth. Click Apply.
7. Change the properties of the entire form by clicking the Properties tab in the Design window. Choose a category, a subcategory, a password, and/or a form number, plus other special customizations. Click OK.
8. To save and publish the form, choose Tools ➢ Forms ➢ Publish Form. In the Publish Form As dialog box, give the form a new name and click Publish.

To open the form, click the New button on the Standard toolbar and choose Choose Form.

More on Customization in Outlook 2000

There are other ways to customize and use Outlook. Some of Outlook's features are only accessible in the Corporate/Workgroup configuration in combination with Microsoft Exchange Server. Others features are designed for use by programmers or developers. In addition to the forms customization features mentioned above, you can use Visual Basic for Applications and VBScript in Outlook 2000 to automate Outlook and create customized applications that involve other Office 2000 applications. For more information on this topic, we recommend *Mastering Outlook 2000* (Sybex 1999).

Hands On: *Objectives OL20002.3, 2.4, 2.5, 4.6, 6.5, and OL2000E.5.5*

1. Customize the view for your e-mail messages so that you're seeing the fields you want to see. Set automatic formatting so that e-mail received last month turns a different font color. (View ➢ Current View ➢ Customize Current View ➢ Automatic Formatting, click Add, type a title, choose the new font color, then set the condition by clicking the Condition button and using the Advanced tab of the Filter dialog box.) Click the Field button, choose Date/Time fields, and click Received. Set the Condition to Last Month then click the Add To List. Click OK, OK, and OK. Whew!

2. Review and set the Archive properties for each of your Outlook folders. Set AutoArchive options. Manually archive all folders according to their settings.
3. Customize a list view in any module to include the Categories field. Sort the items by Categories in descending order.
4. Drag a calendar appointment to the Tasks icon. Set a reminder for one hour before the appointment so you can prepare for the meeting.
5. Create a new Outlook form based on an existing one. Add and format two of your own fields.

Sharing Outlook Information over Your Network

Objective OL2000E.4.1

You can create shared Outlook mail, calendar, and task items on any network using Net Folders or Public Folders. Net folders can be used by anyone running Outlook—public folders are limited to users of Exchange Server.

Creating Shared Outlook Items

Shared folders are used to share schedules, contact information, and other kinds of Outlook items. The easiest way to create shared items is to copy an existing folder to a public folder in Exchange Server configurations. For example, you can copy your Contacts folder as a public Contacts folder, then delete the contacts that don't need to be shared. Or you can simply create a new folder in All Public Folders.

You can share a folder on non-Exchange Server networks by clicking File ➢ Share and choosing one of the options. (If the folder you want to share is not tasks, contacts, or calendar, you have to select it first then choose File ➢ Share ➢ This Folder.) The Net Folder Wizard opens to the introductory screen. Click Next to proceed.

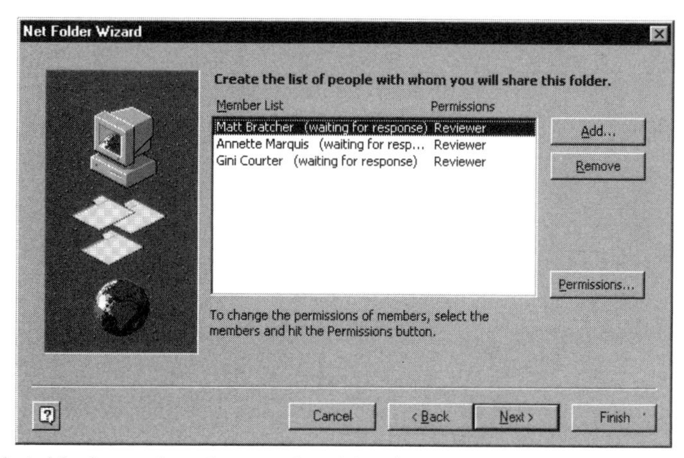

Click Add, then select the people with whom you want to share the folder. Members are given Reviewer permissions by default. (See *Setting Permissions for Others* below.) Select a member and click the Permissions button to change the level of access you wish to grant. Click Next to proceed. Type a description of the folder for your subscribers, if you wish, then click Finish. Outlook generates a subscription message and sends it to each of the members you selected. When they receive the message, they'll have to click the Accept button in order to subscribe.

Objectives OL2000E.4.2, OL2000E.4.3, and OL2000E.7.4

Setting Permissions for Others

Outlook's default Calendar settings allow other users to find out when you are busy or available, but not to see details about appointments. You might want to allow other people—for example, an assistant—to see more details or add new appointments to your calendar. Before they can do so, you need to change the default permissions for the folder.

Roles are bundled groups of folder permissions; to change a user's permissions for your folder, you assign that user to a role for the folder. The roles for folders, from the least privileges to the most, are:

None: No access to the contents of a folder.

Contributor: Allowed to create new items.

Reviewer: Allowed to read existing items.

Author: Allowed to create new items, edit or delete their creations, and read existing items.

Publishing Author: Same as Author, but includes access to subfolders.

Editor: Same as Author, but can edit or delete all items.

Publishing Editor: Same as Editor, but includes access to subfolders.

Owner: All permissions, including the right to change folder permissions.

You change permissions for other users in the folder's Properties dialog box.

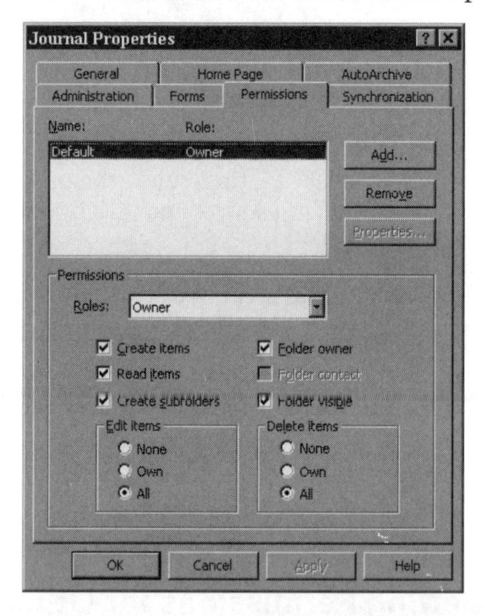

Changing Permissions for a Folder in Exchange Server

1. Open the folder.
2. Choose File ➢ Folder ➢ Properties for [Folder Name].
3. Click the Permissions tab.
4. Click the Add button to open the Add Users dialog box.
5. Select the person you want to allow access to your folder, and click OK.
6. Select the person's Name in the upper pane.
7. Choose the appropriate role in the Roles drop-down list.
8. Click OK.

Sharing a Folder on the Internet

Net folders automatically share information from your Outlook folders using the Internet. You can share Calendars or Contacts with other Outlook users. You can't share your Inbox or Outbox. And if you work on an NT/ Exchange network, you can't share Exchange public folders—only your personal folders are shareable. When you share a folder, you select other users as *subscribers* to the folder; a copy of the folder is placed in each subscriber's folder list. When you add an item to the folder, it is copied to their folder (unless you've marked the item Private). You set permissions for each subscriber as you would with any shared folder. There are four permission levels for net folders: Reviewer, Contributor, Author, and Editor.

Sharing a Folder as a Net Folder

1. Select the folder you want to share.
2. Choose File ➢ Share ➢ This Folder to launch the Net Folder Wizard. Click Next.
3. In the second step of the Wizard, choose subscribers.
4. Select each subscriber and click the Permissions button to set subscriber permissions. Click Next.
5. Type a description for the folder. Click Next.
6. Click Finish to send an invitation to each subscriber.
7. Each subscriber can choose to subscribe, or decline the subscription.

Working away from the Office

To complete the tasks shown in the rest of this section, you must have your home or laptop computer configured to use Dial-Up Networking. To use Offline Folders, you must have Dial-Up access to a Microsoft Exchange Server. See your system administrator for Dial-Up permissions and information on configuring Dial-Up Networking.

Outlook has two separate methods for handling work while you're out of the office: Remote Mail and Offline Folders. With *Remote Mail*, you can download and read the messages that have been delivered in your absence, but you can't send messages. *Offline Folders*, a second set of folders kept on your remote computer, allow you to send *and* receive mail, tasks, and other items.

Managing Remote Mail

Objective OL2000E.1.1

Remote Mail allows you to download selected messages from a computer at your office while you're using your laptop at home. Before you can use Remote Mail, you must:

- Install Outlook on your remote computer.
- Establish a personal folder file (`.pst`) on your work computer so messages can be delivered to your computer rather than the server. Choose Tools ➢ Services to see if Personal Folders is listed. If not, click Add.
- Establish a Dial-Up connection from your remote computer and choose Tools ➢ Synchronize ➢ Download Address Book to copy the Address Book.
- Set options for your Personal Folder in the Services dialog box.
- Have Outlook send new mail to your Personal Folders (choose Tools ➢ Services ➢ Delivery).

To connect to Remote Mail, click the Inbox and choose Tools ➢ Remote Mail ➢ Connect from the menu bar. After the connection is established, you can download messages or just the message headers. If you download the headers, you'll be automatically disconnected after the download is complete.

Browse through the headers and mark headers for messages you'd like to see by clicking the Mark to Retrieve or Mark to Retrieve a Copy buttons on the Remote Mail toolbar. You can click the Delete button to delete messages; however, when you delete messages remotely, they're actually deleted, not just moved to the Deleted Items folder, so use this feature cautiously. After you've marked all messages, re-connect to download or delete marked messages.

It's a good idea to make sure you've set up Remote Mail correctly and practice using it before you grab your laptop and leave for the Bahamas.

Working Offline

Offline folders allow you to use a folder remotely, work with all the items in the folder, then synchronize (update) both the offline folder and the folder on your work computer so the two are identical. Before you can work offline, you must:

- Install and configure Dial-Up Networking.
- Establish an Offline Folder File on your remote computer. If you indicated that you travel with the computer during Outlook Setup, it already exists. To check, open the Inbox and choose Tools ➢ Services. If Offline File Folder isn't listed, add it.
- Download the Address Book (see the previous section, *Managing Remote Mail*).
- Add any public folders you want to use offline to Public Folders Favorites.
- Choose the folders you want to make available offline. Select the folder in the Folder List, choose File ➢ Folder ➢ Properties For ➢ Synchronization, and enable the When Offline or Online check box. Click OK.
- Synchronize the offline folders (see the next section).
- Set Outlook to work offline.

You might also choose to create offline folders on your work computer so that you can work when you're not connected to your network server. On a network computer, you don't need to set up Dial-Up Networking.

Setting Outlook to Work Offline You can tell Outlook to always work offline, or to prompt you each time you start Outlook. If, for example, you have a laptop and use a docking station at work, you should choose to be prompted. However, if you only use your laptop for offline work, then set Outlook to always start offline.

Setting Outlook to Work Offline

1. Select the Inbox and choose Tools ➢ Services.
2. Choose Microsoft Exchange Server from the list, and click Properties.

Setting Outlook to Work Offline *(continued)*

3. On the General page, enable either Automatically Detect Connection State or Manually Control Connection State. If you choose manually, click the Choose the Connection Type When Starting check box to have Outlook ask you whether to connect or work offline. Use the Default Connection State options: Connect with the Network or Work Offline and Use Dial-Up Networking to set your typical connection state.
4. Click OK twice.
5. Choose File ➢ Exit and Log Off and restart Outlook.

Objectives OL2000E2.6 and E2.7

Synchronizing Folders Offline *Synchronizing* your folders compares the contents of the offline and regular folders and adjusts items in both so that they are identical. For example, synchronization moves messages you've received at work to an offline folder and sends messages from your offline folder Outbox. If you delete a Contact item in your Offline folder, synchronizing will delete the item in your regular folder.

To set synchronization options, choose Tools ➢ Synchronize ➢ Offline Folder Settings. Here you can identify the folders you want to synchronize and set various download options.

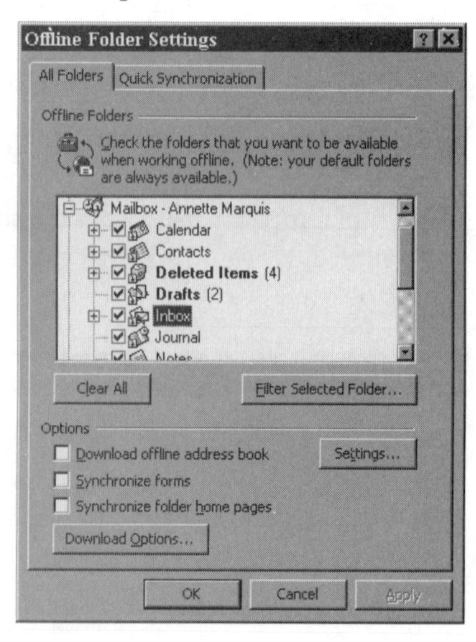

If you are concerned about connect time, you can set a rule that tells Outlook not to download a file if it's larger than a certain size. Instead it will move these files to a folder you specify on the server. To access message size limit, click the Download Options button. Enter the maximum size you want to download in kilobytes. If you want to set exceptions to this maximum size, like a message from your company's president, set the From, Marked as High Priority, or Flagged To options. Click OK to save the settings or Restore Default Rule to discard your changes.

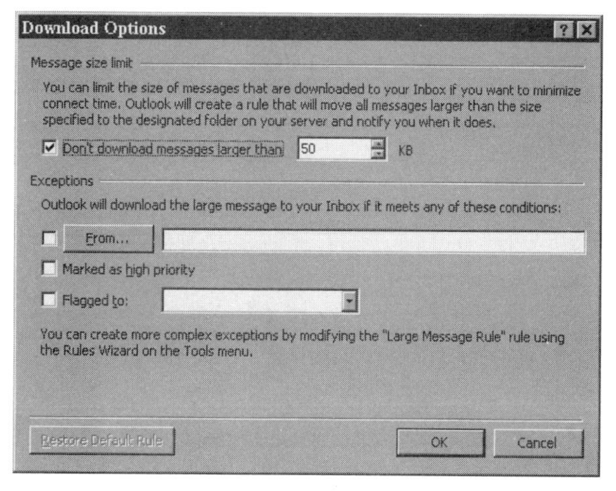

If you want to dial in and get essential information without bothering to wait for a full synchronization, you can create Quick Synchronization groups to synchronize only specific folders. Click the Quick Synchronization tab of the Offline Folder Settings dialog box and click the New button.

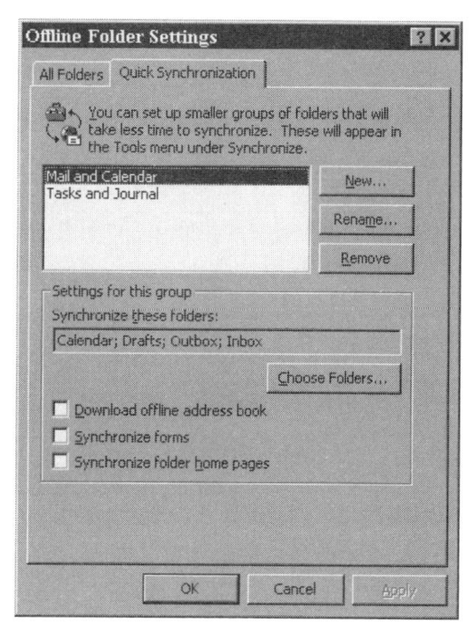

Enter a friendly name for the group that adequately describes the folders it contains. Click OK and then click the Choose Folders button. Select the folders you want to include in the Quick Synchronization group and click OK. When you choose Tools ➢ Synchronize you can select the group you want to synchronize.

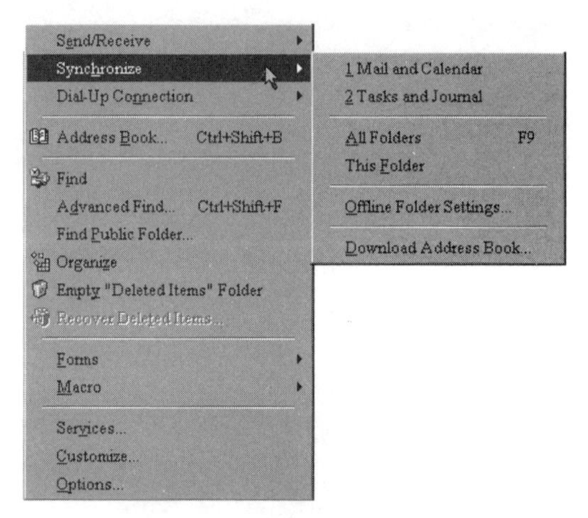

Synchronizing Folders

1. Choose Tools ➢ Synchronize.
2. To synchronize the current folder, select This Folder.
3. Choose All Folders to synchronize all offline folders and their corresponding folders on your workstation or server.

Hands On: *Objectives OL2000E.1.1, E2.6, R2.7, E4.1, E4.2, E4.3, E7.4*

1. Share your Contacts folder with a colleague, granting them Author permissions.
2. Grant another user permission to view existing appointments and add new appointments to your Calendar. Have the user add a new appointment. Remove the permissions. Verify that the user can add appointments.

3. Work with your network administrator to set up Remote Mail for yourself or another user. Use Remote Mail to download message headers, mark messages, and download messages.
4. Set up your workstation, or remote computer, so you can work offline. While working offline, create at least one new appointment and one e-mail message. Synchronize all folders.
5. Set the message size limit to 60KB, unless it's a message from your supervisor.
6. Set up a Quick Synchronization group for Journal and Tasks. Synchronize just those folders.

CHAPTER 11

Working with Objects and Graphics

Too often a well-written document, presentation, or spreadsheet is overlooked because it simply isn't eye-catching enough to cause the audience to take a second glance. You can avoid this potential downfall with object and graphic tools. Spice up text-heavy documents with a quote displayed in a nicely formatted text box. Give your statistics brand new life by creating charts to illustrate them. Insert your company logo onto a slide and clip art and pictures into less formal documents to grab the attention of your audience and make your message a memorable one!

Converting, Linking, and Embedding

An *object* is data that can be embedded or linked in another application. Object Linking and Embedding, or *OLE*, is a protocol that allows applications to communicate with each other to create or update objects. Word documents, Excel worksheets and charts, and PowerPoint slides are all examples of objects you can convert, embed, or link in other Office 2000 documents. As you'll see below, you can also embed or link graphics, sounds, video, and virtually anything else you can select and copy to the Clipboard.

Converting, Embedding, and Linking in Word

Objectives W2000E.3.1, W2000E.3.3, and XL2000E.1.4

The easiest way to convert, embed, or link data in an Office 2000 application uses a modification of copy-and-paste operations. Open the *source application* (also called the *native application*) that contains the text, picture, or other object you want embed or link in the *destination application*. Select and copy the object to the Clipboard. You can close the source application if you wish; in some programs, you'll be asked if you want to retain the contents of the Clipboard. Choose Yes. Then open the destination document and place the insertion point where you want to paste the selection. Choose Edit ➢ Paste Special to open the Paste Special dialog box, shown in Figure 11.1, where a range from an Excel worksheet is being pasted into a Word document.

FIGURE 11.1
Paste Special dialog box

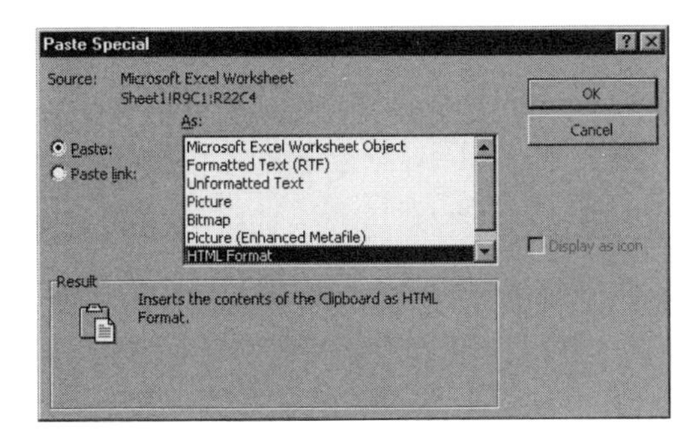

You choose to convert, embed, or link the selection in the destination application, depending on how you want to use the selection after it arrives. *Converting* the selection changes it from its native format to a format used in the destination document. For example, an Excel range pasted in Word can be converted to a graphic or text. From the time of conversion, you'll use Word's tools to work with the converted selection. If you *embed* a chart object, a *copy* of the object that retains its native format is saved within the destination Word document. If you double-click the object to edit it, the Excel toolbars will open.

With a *link*, each time you open the destination document, Word will reload the chart object from its native application file. If you double-click to edit the linked object, the source document opens; you can't change the linked object, only its source. Linking has two advantages: it saves disk space, but, more importantly, it is *dynamic*. If the object's source changes, the change is reflected in all linked documents. There is a downside: If the link's source file is moved or renamed, opening the destination document results in an error message and the destination document will load without the linked object. This means you can only open the destination document on a computer that contains both the native application and a path to the source document.

When you choose Paste Special from the Edit menu the source for the object is displayed at the top of the dialog box (see Figure 11.1). The As list allows you to select how the information should be pasted:

- Microsoft Excel Worksheet Object creates an embedded Excel object in the Word document that you can edit using regular Excel tools.
- Formatted Text (RTF), the default, converts the worksheet to a table.
- Unformatted Text converts the selection to Word tabular columns.
- Picture and Bitmap both convert the worksheet into a graphic that you can work with in Word using all the Word graphic tools.
- Picture (Enhanced Metafile) converts the selection into a Windows Metafile graphic.
- HTML inserts the contents of the Clipboard as HTML-formatted text.
- Unformatted Unicode Text inserts the worksheet without any formatting.

If you chose the Microsoft Excel Worksheet Object option, you can click the Display As Icon checkbox to insert an icon rather than text. To change the icon that's displayed in the destination, click the Change Icon button in the Paste Special window. You can choose from Excel's icon library or click the Browse button and choose from another icon library. You can customize the icon's caption as well.

To link—rather than embed—the selection, choose the Paste Link option. You can link any of the converted file types listed except for Enhanced Metafile. The Enhanced Metafile option is replaced with Word Hyperlink. Choosing Word Hyperlink creates a hyperlink in the Word document; clicking the hyperlink takes the user to the source Excel worksheet. You can access the Paste as Hyperlink option directly from the Edit menu.

Converting, Embedding, and Linking (Excel to Word)

1. Open the source document that contains the data to be converted, embedded, or linked.
2. Select the data and copy the selection to the Clipboard.
3. Open the destination document.
4. Place the insertion point where you want to paste the selection.
5. Choose Edit ➢ Paste Special.

Converting, Embedding, and Linking (Excel to Word) *(continued)*

6. Select a type in the As control. Choose the Paste or Paste Link option.
7. Select the Display As Icon option if you want to display an icon rather than the object.
8. Click OK to paste the selection in the destination document.

From the computer's point of view, OLE is a complex operation. Give the destination document a moment to accept and place the new object.

Objective W2000E.3.4

Click once on the pasted object to select it. Use the object's handles to size it, or press Delete to delete the object. The real magic of OLE occurs when you double-click the object. After you click, wait a moment. If the object was embedded, the toolbars from the object's native application will open in the destination application. The embedded object is a copy. Changing the object doesn't change the original worksheet, and changes in the source worksheet have no effect on the object. With a linked object, double-click and you'll be transported to the source document to edit the object. Change a number or formula, insert rows or columns, or make any other editing changes you need. Click away from the object to return to Word tools, and have your changes reflected in both documents.

OLE in Excel, PowerPoint, Access, and Outlook

Convert, embed, or link data in Excel as you do in Word. Copy the data in the source document, then switch to Excel and click on the destination location. Choose Edit ➢ Paste Special to adjust the settings in the dialog box. PowerPoint creates slide and presentation objects, which can be embedded in Word and Excel documents. PowerPoint also accepts embedded objects from Word and Excel.

OLE requires a source application that can create an OLE object (an *OLE server*) and a destination application that can accept OLE objects (an *OLE client*). Access and Outlook are OLE clients, but not OLE servers, so they cannot create OLE objects. You can paste Access tables, fields, or records and Outlook items in Excel or Word, but the result will be an Excel worksheet or a Word table, not an object. Selections pasted from Access and Outlook can't be linked. As OLE clients, Access and Outlook accept objects from other applications. You can embed part of a document from Word or a worksheet from Excel in an Access form or report or Outlook item. You can also choose Insert ➢ Object (or, in Access, use the Unbound or Bound Object Frame buttons in the Toolbox) to embed a new or existing object in an Access form or Outlook form.

You can use an Excel worksheet to create an Access table, but you don't use copy and paste. Access uses importing to create a new table from an Excel worksheet or to create a link to a worksheet. Activate the database that will contain the new table. Choose File ➢ Get External Data ➢ Import (or Link Tables). Select Microsoft Excel (*.xls) from the Files of Type control. Select the Excel workbook from the file list, and then follow the steps of the Import Wizard to create a table from the file. From Excel, you can choose Data ➢ Convert to Access to convert a worksheet to a table if you have installed the AccessLinks add-in for Excel. Use Outlook's Import and Export Wizard (choose File ➢ Import and Export) to swap data with Excel and Access.

Automatic and Manual Updating

When you create a link with Paste Special, *automatic link updating* is enabled. The object is updated each time the destination document is opened; if the source changes while the destination document is open, the link will reflect the change. You can choose to update links manually rather than automatically, giving you control over when a file is updated. To change to *manual link updating*, select the linked object and then choose Edit ➢ OLE/DDE Links to open the Links dialog box. In the Update method option, at the bottom of the dialog box, choose Manual. When you are ready to update links in the destination document, open the Links dialog box again and click the Update Now button. If you use manual linking, you should adopt a consistent method for updating so you don't pass off last month's information as the latest data.

OLE with Files

If you want to embed or link an entire file instead of a selection, it is often easier to insert the object. Choose Insert ➢ Object ➢ Create from File to open the Create from File page of the Object dialog box, shown in Figure 11.2.

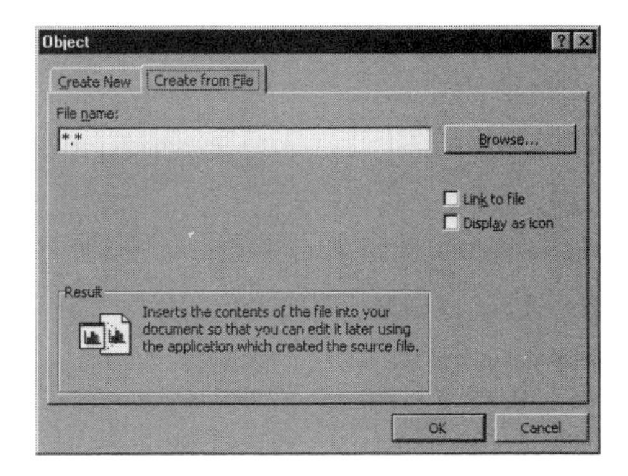

FIGURE 11.2
Create from File page of the Object dialog box

Select and open the file you want to embed or link and set the other options as you did in the Paste Special dialog box. Click OK to insert the object in the destination document. Some files are inserted as icons, whether or not you choose Display As Icon. Sound files, for example, place an icon in the destination document. Double-clicking the icon plays the sound file.

Embedding or Linking a File

1. Open the destination document and place the insertion point where the object is to be inserted.
2. Choose Insert ➢ Object from the menu bar. Click the Create from File tab.
3. Select the file you want to embed or link.
4. Click OK to embed the file, or choose Link to File, and then click OK to link the file.

Creating New Objects

You can use the Object dialog box to create a new object. For example, you might want to have an Excel worksheet in a Word document. You don't have to open Excel and create the worksheet; you can create an Excel worksheet object in Word. Because new objects don't exist as separate source files, they cannot be linked, only embedded.

Office 2000 includes other programs (such as Microsoft Graph) that are OLE servers. You probably have other non-Office applications on your computer that also create objects. Choosing Insert ➢ Object from the menu bar opens the Object dialog box. The scroll list in the Create New page displays the objects that can be created using applications installed on your computer, as shown in Figure 11.3.

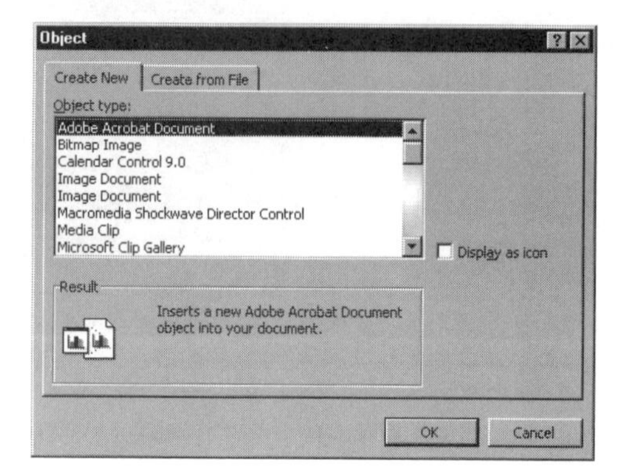

FIGURE 11.3
Creating a new object

Select an Object Type and then click OK. The appropriate OLE server will open within the current document. Create the object, then click in the destination document (outside the object) to close the OLE server.

Creating a New Object

1. Position the insertion point in the document and choose Insert ➢ Object from the menu bar.
2. Click the Create New tab. Select an Object Type from the scroll list.
3. Click the OK button to insert the newly created object.

The Object Type list is amended as new applications are installed. Applications may remain on the list, even if they have been removed from the computer. If you select an application that has been moved or removed, the destination application displays an error message.

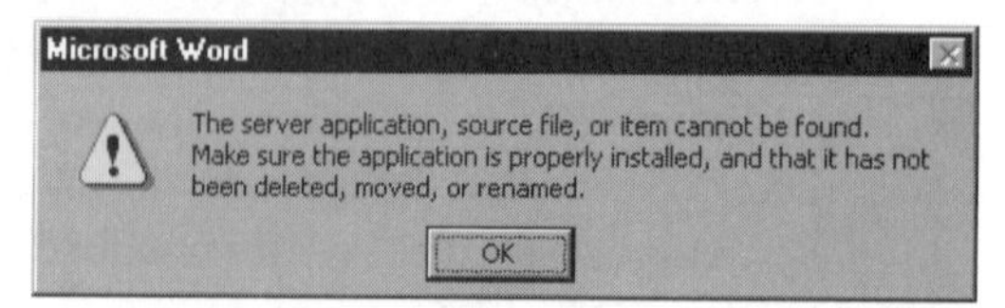

Importing a Text File into Excel

Objective XL2000E.1.1

There are two ways to import a text file. If you simply want to import the data into Excel and you don't care whether the data changes in the source file, just open the text into a blank workbook. Click File ➢ Open and browse to the drive and folder that contains the text file. You'll have to change the Files of Type control in the Open dialog box to see text files. Select the file you want and click Open. Proceed through the steps of the Text Import Wizard as described below.

However, if you want linked data (and the ability to refresh the data in Excel when the original data changes) you'll want to follow a slightly different procedure. Click the cell where you want to place the imported data. If you don't want to overwrite existing data, make sure the worksheet has no data below or to the right of the selected cell. Choose Data ➢ Get External Data ➢ Import Text File. Locate and select the text file you want to import, and click Open to activate step one of the Text Import Wizard shown in Figure 11.4.

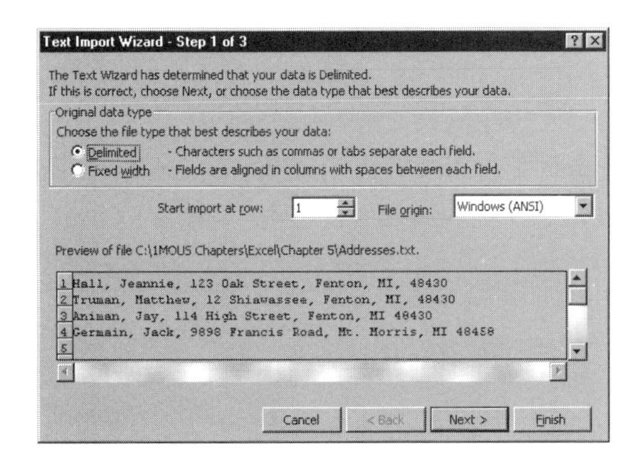

FIGURE 11.4 Text Import Wizard, Step 1

The Text Import Wizard attempts to determine whether your data is delimited (separated by tabs or commas or some other character) or of a fixed width (like columns in a Word table.) If Excel guesses wrong, change the file type option to match your data. Use the spin box to set the Start

Import at Row control. You can look at the data preview below to see the row numbers Excel has assigned. Set the spin control to 1 if you want all the data. Choose a file origin if your data comes from a location other than the one Excel has selected. Click Next to move to Step two of the Wizard.

Step two looks different depending on whether your text file is delimited or fixed width. Figure 11.5 shows options for delimited files. Your goal at step two is to specify how Excel divides the text into columns. So choose a delimiter or, in the case of fixed width files, create the column breaks as specified in the dialog box for Step two. Now, click Next to proceed to Step three and choose the format for your data.

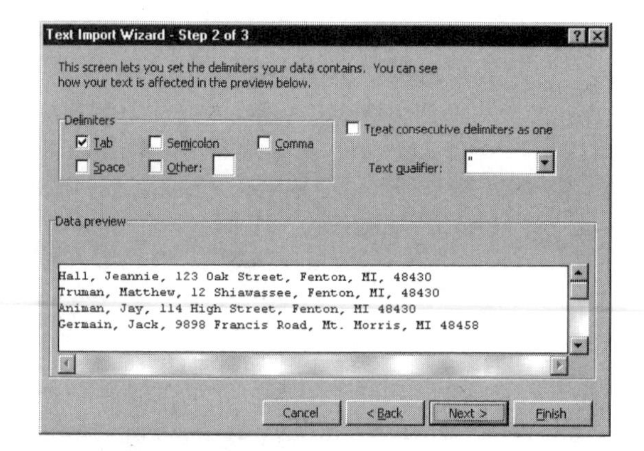

FIGURE 11.5

Step 2 of Wizard, delimited files

Click Finish and the Import Data dialog box opens. The default is to place the data in the selected cell, but you can collapse the dialog box and select another cell, or choose to insert the data in a new worksheet. Clicking Properties allows you to set additional formatting and layout options. Click OK to close the dialog box, import the data into Excel, and open the External Data toolbar.

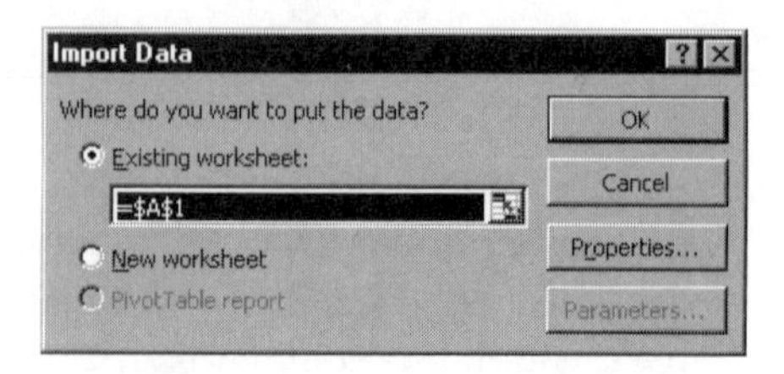

Dragging and Dropping Between Applications

Just as you might drag and drop text between Word documents, you can drag and drop to import data from text files to other applications. To do this, open a Word document and another application such as Excel. Resize the applications so you can see them both on the screen. Select text from the Word document and drag it across to the open Excel worksheet.

Importing a Text File

1. Click Data ➢ Get External Data ➢Import Text File.
2. Locate, select, and open the text file you want to import.
3. Choose a file type and enter a number to specify which row of data you want to use as a starting point for the data import. Choose a data origin from the list and click Next.
4. Specify how you want to divide the text into columns. You'll choose a delimiter if you're importing a delimited file. You'll set column divisions if you're importing a fixed width file.
5. Set data format options in the third step of the Wizard, then click Finish.
6. Choose a location for the imported data in the Import Data dialog box.
7. Click Properties in the Import Data dialog box to set additional formatting and layout options.
8. The External Data toolbar opens when the data import is complete. (Click View ➢ Toolbars ➢ External Data if it doesn't.)

Hands On: Objectives W2000E.3.1, E.3.3, E.3.4, XL2000E.1.4, E.1.1, and E.1.2

1. Create or open an Excel worksheet. Select and copy a range of cells and place them in a Word document:
   a) As a converted table using Paste.
   b) As a picture using Paste Special.

   c) As an embedded Excel object using Paste Special.
   d) As a linked Excel worksheet object.
   e) As a linked picture.
2. Double-click either of the linked objects, and make changes to the Excel worksheet. Return to the Word document and notice the differences between the converted, embedded, and linked objects.
3. In Access, follow these steps:
   a) Use Get External Data to import an Excel worksheet as a table.
   b) Use Get External Data to link to an Excel worksheet.
   c) Select records in a table and copy them to Word or Excel.
4. Create a new Excel chart object in Word or PowerPoint.
5. Paste a slide from a PowerPoint presentation as a linked graphic in a Word document. Update the slide in PowerPoint, and note the changes in the Word document.
6. Place a sound or video file in PowerPoint, Word, or Excel using Insert ➢ Object ➢ Create from File. Play the media file.
7. Create a small text file in Word using names and addresses of people you know.
   a) Separate the data fields using a tab or comma as a delimiter then save the data as a text file.
   b) Open a blank Excel workbook and import the text file.
8. Open a Word document and drag a portion of it into an Excel worksheet.

Inserting Clips and Graphics

You can insert graphics, sound, and video in every Office application, but each application includes menu or toolbar access to the types of media objects you'd likely place in the application. For example, PowerPoint and Publisher include Movies and Sounds on the Insert menu, while Excel does not. In any Office 2000 program, begin by choosing Insert from the menu bar. If the type of media you want to insert is listed on the Insert menu, select it. If not, choose Object and select the media type from the list in the Insert Object dialog box.

Adding Clips to a Document or Spreadsheet

Objectives W2000.6.2 and XL2000.7.4

The Microsoft Clip Gallery, included with Office 2000, has a broad selection of media clips. When you add other media files to your system, you can add them to the gallery for easy selection. You can access the Clip Gallery from Word, Excel, and PowerPoint. Choose Insert ➢ Picture ➢ ClipArt to open the Insert ClipArt dialog box shown in Figure 11.6.

The first time you use clip art with Office 2000, you may be prompted to index your existing ClipArt files. It can take ten minutes or more to index the files. You can postpone indexing clip art, but you won't be able to use all your clips and you will prompted to index every time you attempt to insert clip art.

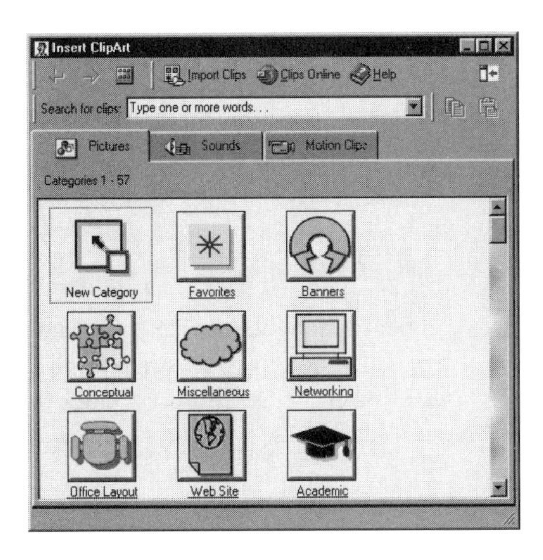

FIGURE 11.6
Microsoft Clip Gallery

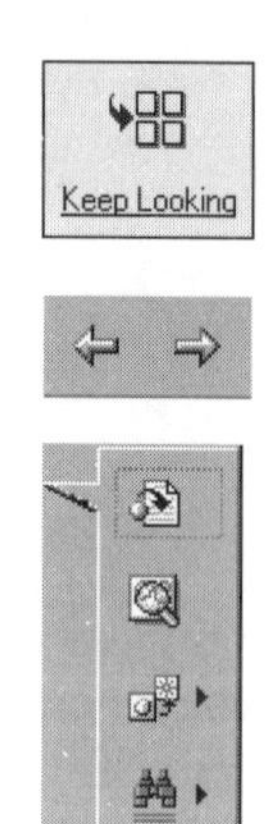

The Clip Gallery is arranged in categories. Click one of the icons displayed in the gallery to choose a category and load thumbnail versions of the first 60 clips in the category. If you wish to see the next 60 clips, scroll to the bottom of the clips and click Keep Looking or press Shift + Backspace; choose Keep Looking or Shift + Backspace again to display additional clips. Use the Back and Forward buttons at the top of the dialog box to navigate between current and previous screens in the Clip Gallery.

Click once on the object you want to select it and open a shortcut toolbar with Insert Clip, Preview Clip, Add Clip to a Category or Find for Similar Clips buttons. Choose the Preview option to enlarge the thumbnail so you can see more detail. Close the preview and choose Insert Clip if you decide you like it. You may decide to include this clip in another category. Choosing the third option on the shortcut toolbar allows you to reference the clip in an additional category you select from a list.

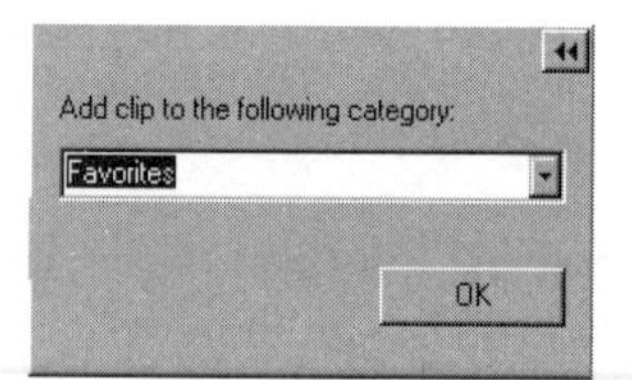

The Find option allows you to search for similar clips. You have the option of searching for clips with the same artistic style (for example, drawings with a thick black border), or clips with the same color and shape, or categorized using one of the keywords associated with the selected clip. Click Artistic Style, Color & Shape, or one of the keywords to move to a page of similar clips.

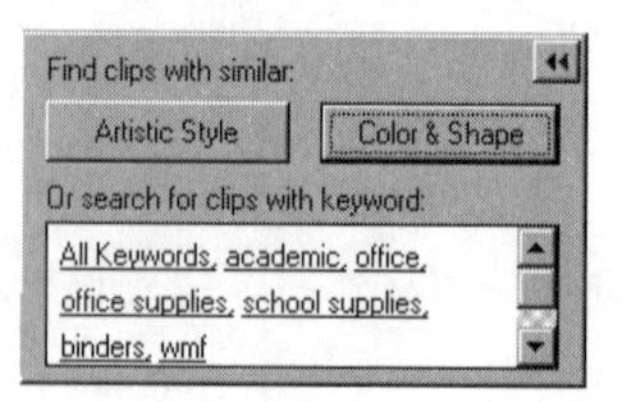

Your search history is kept on a drop-down list at the top of the Clip Gallery dialog box. If you wish to duplicate a past search, simply choose the keyword from the list and press enter to perform that search again.

When you choose Add To Category, or Search For Similar Clips, the pane that opens stays in view until you click the Hide Pane button at the top-right corner of the dialog box to close the Insert ClipArt dialog box.

Even though the Insert menu command is *Clip Art*, you can insert any of the files in the Gallery: pictures, sound, and motion files. Just click the corresponding tab for the type of media file you want. In Word and Excel, it's faster to choose Insert ➢ Clip Art and then choose a sound or video clip than to insert a sound or video object in the Insert Object dialog box. Once you've inserted a clip, you can edit it using tools from the Drawing toolbar. See *Grouping and Ungrouping Objects* later in this chapter for information on editing Clip Art graphics.

Inserting Clips from the Clip Gallery

1. Position the insertion point where you want to insert the clip.
2. Choose Insert ➢ Picture ➢ Clip Art to open the Clip Gallery.
3. Click the file-type tab. Choose a category and select a clip.
4. Preview or insert the clip, or add it to another category if you wish. You can also search for similar clips by clicking the Find option.
5. Use the Back and Forward buttons to navigate if you are several layers deep in the Clip Gallery.
6. Close the Gallery when you find and insert the clip(s) you need.

Importing Clips

If your company has a logo or other clip art you want to import into documents created in Word, Excel, PowerPoint, and other Office applications, you can use the Import Clips feature in the Clip Gallery to store your graphic files in an easily accessible place.

Click the Import Clips button in the Insert ClipArt dialog box to open the Add Clip to Clip Gallery dialog box shown in Figure 11.7. Change the Look In location and locate the file. You can import a copy of the new clip art by checking Copy into Clip Gallery or move the original by checking Move into Clip Gallery. To create a shortcut to the file, choose the last option in the Clip Import Option control.

You can import new clips from the Web by clicking the Clips Online button to launch your browser and connect to Microsoft's online Clip Art Gallery. Search the Web site for additional clip art to be imported to the Clip Gallery.

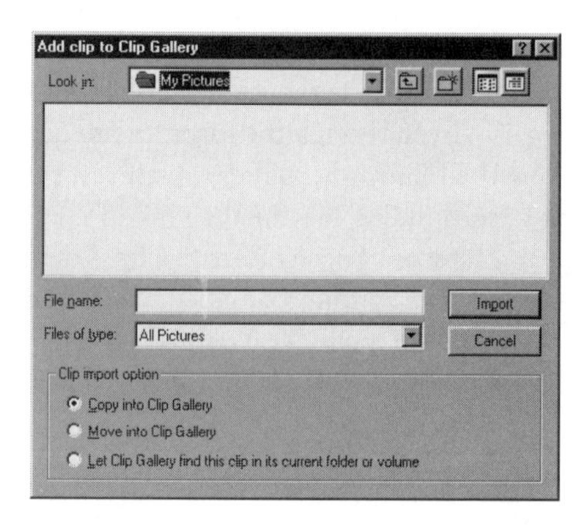

FIGURE 11.7 Add Clip to Clip Gallery

Categorizing Clips

Objectives PD2000E.6.1 and PD2000E.6.2

You can create a new category by clicking the New Category button. You'll be prompted to enter a name for the category. Click OK to add the new category to the Clip Gallery.

After you've created a category, you'll want to recategorize some clips, or add keywords to a clip's description. Right-click the clip you want to recategorize and choose Clip Properties from the shortcut menu. The Clip Properties dialog box opens to the Description tab. Enter a new description if you wish, then click the Categories tab.

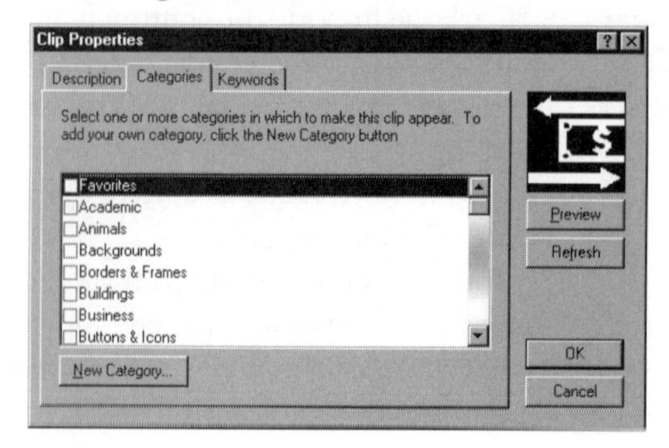

Click the categories to which you want the clip assigned. Disable the categories from which you want the clip removed. Click the New Category button to add a new category.

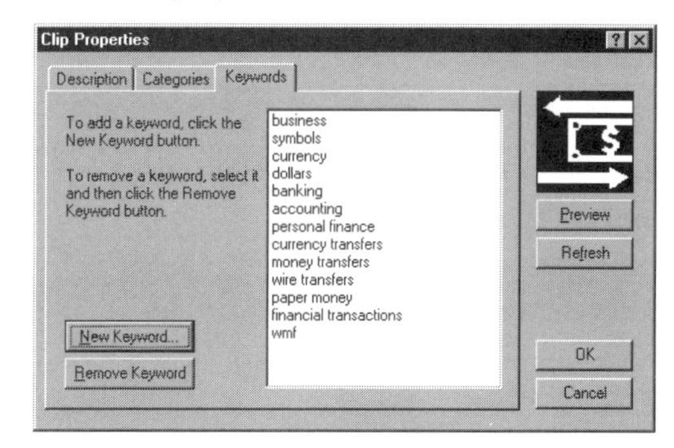

Choose the Keywords page to see a list of the keywords currently associated with the clip. Click the New Keyword button, type another keyword, and click OK to add it to the list. Select and click Remove to do away with unnecessary keywords. When you're done editing clip properties, click OK to close the dialog box.

Moving and Resizing Clips

Objectives W2000E.4.2 and XL2000.7.4

Use the mouse to drag a selected clip to move it. Drag the clip's handle to resize the clip. You can resize a video clip as you can any other object by dragging a sizing handle. However, badly resized video is blurry, difficult to see, and sometimes skips during playback. PowerPoint includes a resizing feature designed for video that sizes it at its best size for viewing. If you need to resize a video clip for an on-screen document in Word or Excel, consider placing the clip in PowerPoint and resizing it. You can use the clipboard to move the resized clip to Excel or Word.

Inserting Other Pictures

Objectives W2000.6.2 and W2000E.4.1

If the picture you want to insert isn't in the Clip Gallery, choose Insert ➢ Picture ➢ From File from the menu bar to open the Insert Picture dialog box (see Figure 11.8). Locate and select the file to insert it in your document. If you're looking for a particular type of file, such as a JPEG, bitmap, TIF, or other picture format, change the Files of Type control to filter for that file type. Select and insert the picture file.

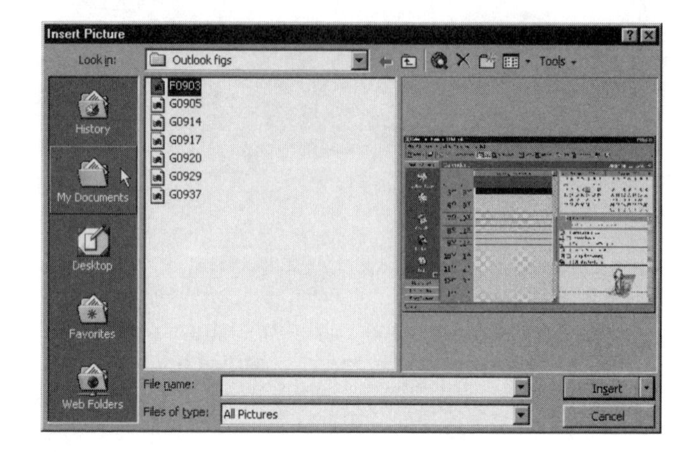

FIGURE 11.8 Insert Picture dialog box

Modifying Pictures

After you've placed a picture from a file or the Clip Gallery, you can adjust the picture using the Picture toolbar. Right-click the picture and choose Show Picture Toolbar from the shortcut menu. Table 11.1 describes the buttons on the Picture toolbar.

TABLE 11.1: Picture Toolbar Buttons

Button	Name	Use
	Insert Picture from File	Insert another picture
	Image Control	Choose from Automatic, Grayscale, Black & White, or Watermark
	More Contrast	Increase color intensity
	Less Contrast	Decrease color intensity

TABLE 11.1: Picture Toolbar Buttons *(continued)*

Button	Name	Use
	More Brightness	Add white to lighten the colors
	Less Brightness	Add black to darken the colors
	Crop	Trim rectangular areas from the image
	Line Style	Format the border that surrounds the picture
	Recolor Picture	Swap one color for another (PowerPoint only)
	Format Picture	One-stop shopping for picture properties
	Set Transparent Color	Used like an eyedropper to make areas of the picture transparent; used extensively for Web graphics
	Reset Picture	Return the picture to its original format

The Crop, Recolor Picture, and Set Transparent buttons are used with areas of the picture. All other buttons affect the entire picture.

The Recolor Picture button is only available on the Drawing toolbar in PowerPoint, but you can place an image in PowerPoint, recolor it, then move it to another Office application. See Chapter 8 for more information on recoloring pictures.

Inserting Scanned Graphics

If your computer is hooked to a scanner, you can scan images into Excel, Word, and PowerPoint through the Microsoft Photo Editor. Choose Insert ➢ Picture ➢ From Scanner or Camera, and the Photo Editor will launch.

You'll be required to set some scanner options; the actual options vary for different scanner models.

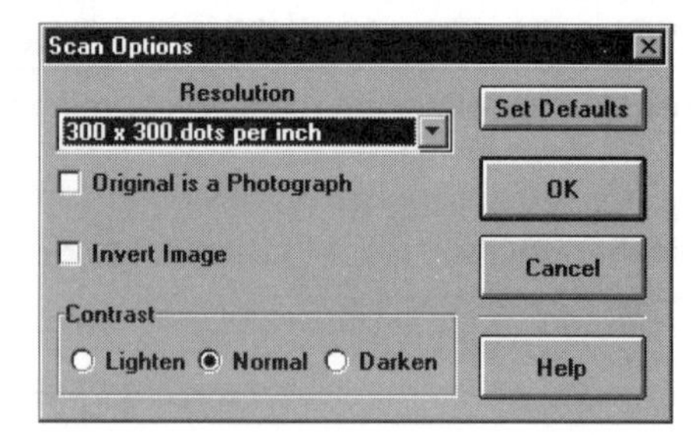

Make sure the document you want to scan is in the scanner, and then click OK. After the image scans, you can alter it in the Photo Editor. (See the Photo Editor's Online Help for more information.) When you close the Photo Editor, the image will be placed in your Office document.

Inserting a Scanned Image

1. In Excel, Word, or PowerPoint, choose Insert ➢ Picture ➢ From Scanner.
2. In the scanner's dialog box, set the scanning options, then click OK.
3. When the scanned image is placed in the Photo Editor, make any changes you desire.
4. Choose File ➢ Exit and Return To in the Photo Editor to close the Photo Editor and place the image in your Office document.

Deleting an Object

Objectives W2000E.4.2 and XL2000.7.4

Select any object in your document. Press Delete on the keyboard to remove the object. You can also right-click an object and choose Cut from the shortcut menu. This removes the object from your document and places it on the Windows clipboard.

Hands On: Objectives W2000.6.2, W2000E.4.2 and XL20007.4, W2000E.4.1, PD2000E.6.1 and PD2000E.6.2

1. Complete these tasks in Word, PowerPoint, *and* Excel:
   a) Insert Clip Art from the Clip Gallery.
   b) Size and position the clip.
   c) Insert a video or sound clip.
   d) Play the clip.
   e) Delete one of the clips.
2. In Word, PowerPoint, *or* Excel complete these tasks:
   a) Download a picture from the Microsoft online Clip Gallery.
   b) Insert the downloaded picture into a document.
   c) Use the tools on the Picture toolbar to retouch the picture.
3. In Word complete the following:
   a) Insert a bitmap picture.
   b) Size and position the picture.
   c) Add the clip to the Clip Gallery and assign it to a newly created category (you choose the name for the category). Add keywords to the description of the clip.

Doing It Yourself with Draw

Objective W20006.1

Microsoft Draw is an Office application that lets you create line art and other objects, such as Word Art. To design your own graphics, choose Insert ➢ Picture ➢ New Drawing or Insert ➢ Object and choose Microsoft Draw object in the dialog box. The new object is placed in a separate layer in front of the document. While working with the object, you'll have access to all the available drawing tools, including the Drawing toolbar. When you complete your drawing, simply click outside the object to return to the document layer.

To access the Drawing toolbar without creating a new object, right-click on any toolbar and select Drawing; choose View ➢ Toolbars and select Drawing; or in Word and Excel click the Drawing button on the Standard toolbar.

There is no Drawing toolbar in Access; appropriate drawing tools are found in the Toolbox. However, you can create drawings in other applications and copy/paste them into Access.

The Drawing toolbar includes two broad categories of menus and buttons. The first set, beginning with AutoShapes and ending with WordArt, is used to create drawing objects. The buttons on the second half of the toolbar are used to format existing objects.

Inserting AutoShapes

Clicking the AutoShapes drop-down opens a list of AutoShape categories.

Choose a category, and a menu of AutoShapes opens. Select an AutoShape, and then click or drag to insert the shape in the document. If you intend to add a lot of AutoShapes (for example, when creating a flow chart), you can drag the bar at the top of the menu to place the menu in the document as a free-standing palette.

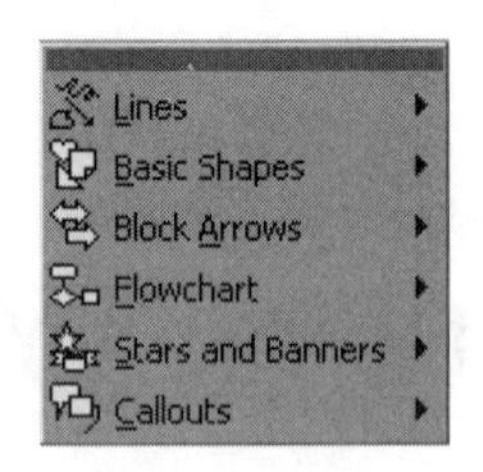

Objectives PP2000.3.7 and PP2000.E2.2

Callout AutoShapes are used for annotating other objects or elements, so when you place a callout, the insertion point will automatically appear. To place text in any other AutoShape, right-click on the AutoShape and choose Add Text.

Inserting Line Art Objects

Objective XL2000.7.5

To draw a line or arrow, click the Line button or the Arrow button. Move the crosshair pointer to one end of the line you want to draw. Hold the mouse button and drag to draw the line. Release the button to create the line and turn the Line or Arrow tool off. (With the Arrow tool, the arrowhead appears at the end of the line where you release the mouse button.) If you want a line that is absolutely horizontal or vertical in relation to the page, hold the Shift key while dragging the line. The Line button and other object buttons work like the Format Painter button: When you have more than one object to draw, begin by double-clicking the object button. The button will stay depressed, allowing you to draw more objects, until you click any button.

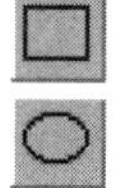

With the Rectangle and Oval buttons, drag from one corner of the object to the opposite corner, and then release the mouse button. Hold the Shift key while dragging to create circular ovals or square rectangles.

If you need a series of identical objects, create one object and then use copy and paste.

Objectives PP2000.3.6 and PP2000.4.4

Use the Text Box tool to create text that floats on a layer above standard document text. Draw the text box as you would a rectangle. When you release the mouse button, an insertion point appears in the text box. Select and format the text using the Formatting toolbar. As you already know, you can right-click and choose Text to insert text inside any AutoShape. If you wish to place text on or "inside" an object that *isn't* an AutoShape, you can use the Text Box tool to create and position the text.

Adding Drawing Objects

1. If the Drawing toolbar is not open, right-click on any toolbar and select Drawing from the list, or click the Drawing button on the Standard toolbar.
2. Choose an AutoShape category and shape from the AutoShapes menu, or click on any of the drawing tools in the first cluster of buttons to change the pointer to crosshairs for drawing lines and shapes. Double-click the tool to draw more than one object.

Adding Drawing Objects *(continued)*

3. Drag the crosshairs from a starting point to the point where you want the line or shape to end. Hold the Shift key while dragging to create straight lines, round ovals, or square rectangles.
4. Release the mouse button to end the line or shape and turn off the Drawing tool.

Adding WordArt

Objectives W2000.6.2 and PP2000.4.2

WordArt is used to create a graphic object from text. You'll use WordArt to create logos, emphasize titles, and design exciting text-based graphics for a document.

To create WordArt, place the insertion point where you want the graphic, and click the WordArt button on the Drawing toolbar to open the WordArt Gallery, shown in Figure 11.9.

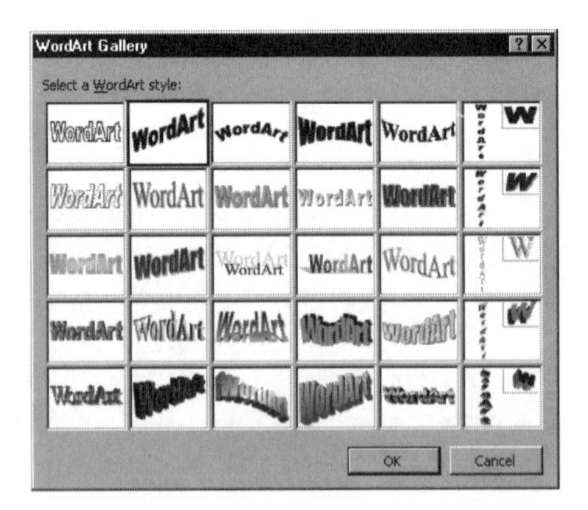

FIGURE 11.9
WordArt Gallery

In the Gallery, select a WordArt style and click OK. (You can apply a different style to the graphic at any time.) When the Edit WordArt Text dialog box opens, enter the text you wish to create WordArt from. Use the Font and Size drop-downs and Bold and Italics buttons to format the text. Click OK to place the WordArt object in your document and open the WordArt toolbar. The toolbar buttons are described in Table 11.2.

TABLE 11.2: WordArt Toolbar Buttons

Button	Name	Use
	WordArt	Creates a new WordArt object.
 Edit Text...	Edit Text	Opens the Edit WordArt Text dialog box to edit text.
	WordArt Gallery	Opens the WordArt Gallery.
	Format WordArt	Opens the Format WordArt dialog box so you can format colors, position, and wrap properties.
	WordArt Shape	Opens a Shape menu so you can select the basic shape the text should be poured into.
	Free Rotate	Changes the object handles to rotation handles so you can rotate the text. Click again to turn off.
	Same Letter Heights	Makes all letters the same height, irrespective of case.
	Vertical Text	Changes the WordArt orientation from horizontal to vertical. Click again to reverse.
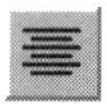	Alignment	Opens an alignment menu with standard options and unique WordArt options.
	Character Spacing	Opens an adjustment menu so you can change space between characters.

Use the WordArt toolbar buttons or the Drawing toolbar buttons (see "*Formatting Objects*" later in this section) to enhance the Word object.

Creating WordArt

1. Place the insertion point where you want the WordArt to appear.
2. Click the WordArt button on the Drawing toolbar.
3. Select a style from the WordArt Gallery and click OK.
4. Type the text that you want to convert to WordArt in the Edit WordArt Text dialog box. Change fonts, font sizes, and styles as desired, then click OK.
5. Use the WordArt toolbar buttons to format the WordArt object.

Formatting Objects

Objective PP2000.4.3

Use the Drawing toolbar's formatting buttons to format selected objects, including WordArt. To select a single object, just click on it.

To select multiple objects, either hold Shift while clicking on each object, or use the Select Objects tool and drag a rectangle around the objects you want to select.

Objective PP2000.4.7

Clicking the Fill Color button opens a menu of colors. If you just want an object without any "filling," choose No Fill. No fill is *not* the same as the colorless sample on the bottom row of the palette—that's the color white.

If you want to rotate an object, select it and click the Free Rotate tool. The object handles will change to green circular rotation handles. Place the Rotate tool over any of the green object handles and drag to rotate.

Objective XL2000.7.5

Change the line color of the selected object by clicking the down arrow next to the Line Color button to open a color menu. Click the color you want to apply.

The Font Color button changes the text color in a selected object like a text box or callout. With all three color buttons, if there is no object selected, the color you choose is the new default color and will be applied to objects you create in the future.

The Line Style button opens a line style menu. Selecting More Lines from the menu opens a Format AutoShape dialog box, where you can select other line widths and object attributes.

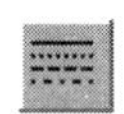

The Dash Style menu includes solid lines, dotted lines, dashed lines, and other combinations thereof.

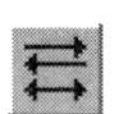

In the Arrow Style menu, select the style that should appear at the ends of the selected line from arrowheads and terminators of various types. If the combination of line endings you desire isn't in the menu, choose More Arrows to open the Format dialog box and set a beginning and ending style for the line.

Special Shadow and 3-D Effects

Shadow and 3-D effects add bulk to the selected drawing object. You must choose one or the other; if you apply a 3-D effect to a shadowed object, the shadow is removed, and vice versa.

From the Shadow menu, choose a shadow style for the selected object. To format the shadow, choose Shadow Settings from the Shadow menu to open the Shadow Settings toolbar. The toolbar includes buttons to nudge the shadow up, down, left, or right, and a Shadow Color menu.

You can add a 3-D effect to any object. With the options on the 3-D Settings toolbar, you can change the extrusion (depth) of the object as well as rotation, perspective angle, lighting direction, surface texture, and color. When you change the color of a 3-D effect, the change affects only the 3-D effect, not the object itself.

Arranging Objects

The Draw menu on the Drawing toolbar includes other options for manipulating objects. Drawing objects are placed in separate *layers* on top of the text in a document. To move objects from layer to layer, choose Draw ➢ Order to open the Order menu.

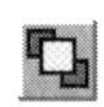

Bring to Front and Send to Back move the selected object(s) in relation to text and other graphic objects. If you draw an oval and place a rectangle over the right half of it, the rectangle covers part of the oval. If you want the entire oval to show, covering part of the rectangle, either send the rectangle to the back or bring the oval to the front.

 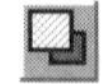

If you're working with more than two layers, use the Bring Forward and Send Backward buttons to move the selected objects one layer at a time.

Objective W2000E.2.5

In Word, you can send objects behind or in front of the text layer. Use Send Behind Text to create a single page watermark. (Place the watermark in a header or footer to have it appear on every page of a document.)

Ordering Objects

1. Select the object that you want to bring forward or move back.
2. Choose Bring to Front, Send to Back, Bring Forward, or Send Backward to switch the position of one graphic relative to another.
3. In Word, choose Draw ➢ Order from the Drawing toolbar, then click Bring in Front of Text or Send behind Text button on the Drawing toolbar if you want to position text in relation to a graphic.

You can adjust individual objects in a drawing using the Nudge, Align and Distribute, and Rotate or Flip options on the Draw menu. If you're doing detailed work, consider turning on a grid (choose Draw ➢ Grid) to help you properly align various objects in the drawing.

Grouping and Ungrouping Objects

Objective PP2000.4.2

When your drawing is complete, you can *group* all the drawing objects so that they are treated as a single object.

Select all the objects, then choose Draw ➢ Group from the Drawing toolbar. The handles on the multiple selected objects will be replaced with one set of handles that can be used to size or move the entire object.

If an object contains more than one element, you can *ungroup* it into separate objects, each of which can be individually moved, sized, formatted, or deleted. This is the easiest way to format Clip Art images. Ungroup the image, then change fills and line colors, or delete portions of the image. When you have finished editing, select all the objects and group them again so you can move or size the entire image.

Creating Charts

Objectives W2000E.4.3 and W2000E.4.4

In Office, there are two programs that create charts: Excel and Microsoft Graph. If you already have a chart in Excel, you can easily copy it and embed or link it to your Word document or PowerPoint slide. To embed an Excel chart object, open the Excel file that contains the chart. Select the chart object and click the copy button on the Standard toolbar or right-click and choose Copy from the shortcut menu. Switch to PowerPoint and navigate to the slide where you want to place the chart. Click the Paste button on the Standard toolbar.

If you don't have access to Excel, however, Microsoft Graph will let you create charts quickly and easily in PowerPoint, Word, and Access. See Chapter 8 for more information on working with Microsoft Graph.

Hands On: Objectives W2000.6.1, W2000.6.2, XL2000.7.5, PP2000.3.6, PP2000.4.2, PP2000.4.4 and PP2000.4.3, PP2000.3.7, PP2000.4.7 and PP2000E.2.2

1. In Word, PowerPoint, or Excel follow these steps:
   - a) Use the Drawing tools to draw a simple picture that includes AutoShapes and lines.
   - b) Use the formatting tools on the Drawing toolbar to format individual objects in the drawing.
   - c) Add a text box that floats over one of the objects.
   - d) Select and group all the drawing objects.
   - e) Create and format WordArt.
2. In PowerPoint follow these steps:
   - a) Place an AutoShape.
   - b) Fill the AutoShape with color.
   - c) Rotate the AutoShape.
   - d) Apply 3-D effects to the AutoShape.
   - e) Use the 3-D Settings toolbar to format the 3-D effects.
   - f) Add text to the AutoShape.

CHAPTER 12

Using PhotoDraw

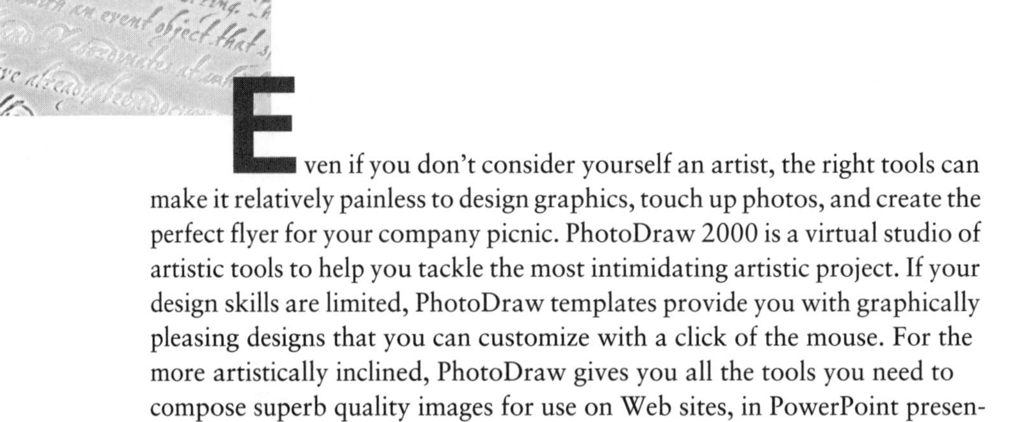

Even if you don't consider yourself an artist, the right tools can make it relatively painless to design graphics, touch up photos, and create the perfect flyer for your company picnic. PhotoDraw 2000 is a virtual studio of artistic tools to help you tackle the most intimidating artistic project. If your design skills are limited, PhotoDraw templates provide you with graphically pleasing designs that you can customize with a click of the mouse. For the more artistically inclined, PhotoDraw gives you all the tools you need to compose superb quality images for use on Web sites, in PowerPoint presentations, in Word and Excel documents, on Access forms, and in printed publications.

Finding Your Way around PhotoDraw

PhotoDraw works a lot like any other Office program so you'll find many familiar features in the PhotoDraw interface. Some tools, such as AutoShapes, you can find in a number of the Office programs. At times, you may find it difficult to decide which application to use to create a certain graphic object. However, PhotoDraw's strengths lie in its ability to create pictures consisting of different pieces of clip art, photos, or art you create yourself. Once you learn its special features, you're sure to find it a valuable companion to the other graphics tools in the Office 2000 Suite.

PhotoDraw is another incarnation of a product included with FrontPage 97 and FrontPage 98 called Image Composer. If you used Image Composer, you'll notice some of the same tools and options. However, PhotoDraw uses more of the standard Office interface and is a broader and friendlier program.

Exploring the PhotoDraw Application Window

The PhotoDraw application window, shown in Figure 12.1, contains a menu bar, a visual toolbar, a standard toolbar, a picture list, a workspace, a status bar, and scrollbars.

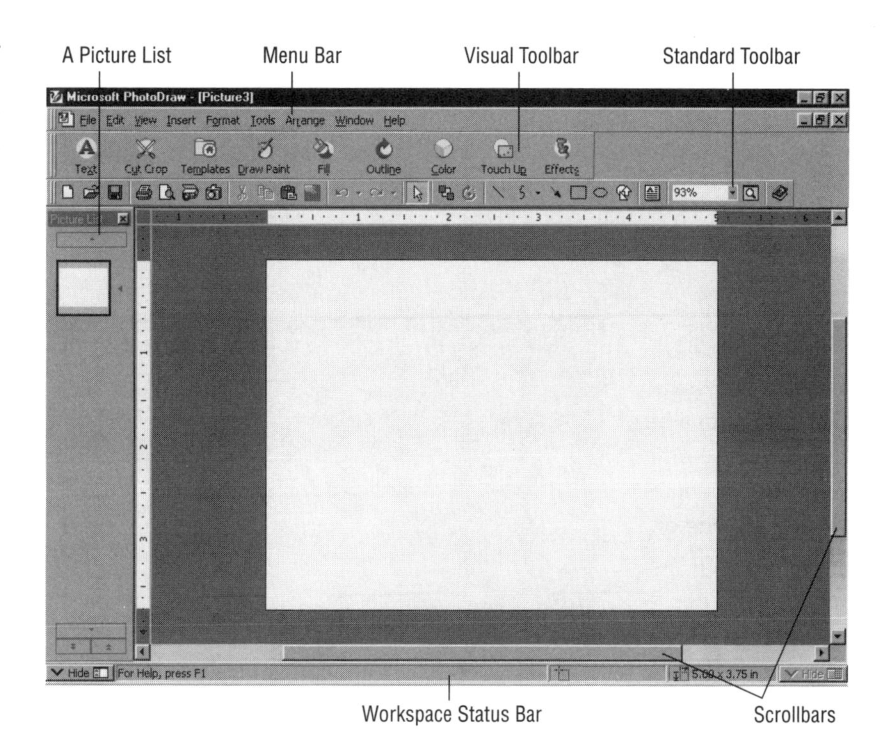

FIGURE 12.1
The PhotoDraw application window

Using PhotoDraw Menus and Toolbars

The Visual toolbar contains many of PhotoDraw's graphic tools, including text, drawing, painting, and color tools, among others. The Visual toolbar opens like a menu but contains illustrations of each tool's effect. For example, the Fill tool, shown in Figure 12.2, shows the five Fill effects you have to choose from.

The tools available on the Visual toolbar generally have multiple settings and options. When you select one of the tools on the Visual toolbar, a separate workpane, like the one shown in Figure 12.3, opens up on the right side of the workspace with the available choices for that effect.

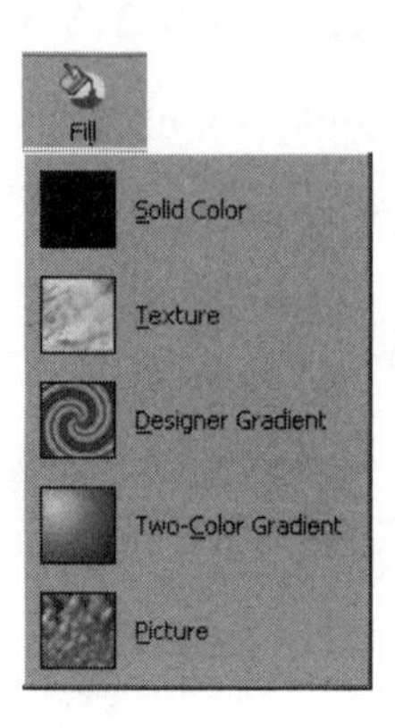

FIGURE 12.2
The Fill menu, an option on the Visual toolbar, shows you an illustration of each effect

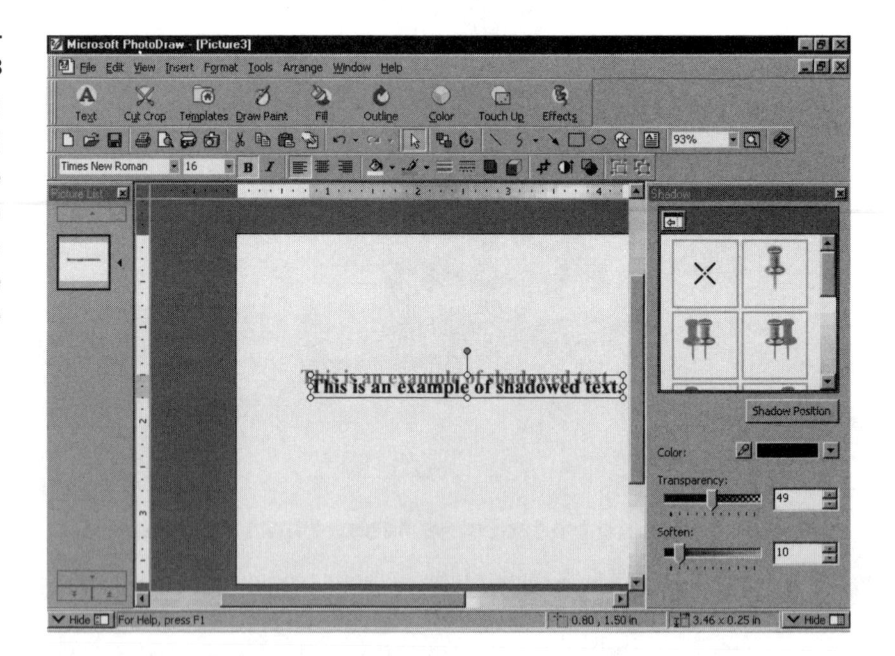

FIGURE 12.3
The tools on the Visual toolbar contain several options that are made available to you in a separate workpane on the right side of the workspace

To close a workpane, click the Close button at the top of the window. To temporarily hide a workpane to see more of the workspace area, click the Hide button at the bottom of the workpane in the Status bar. Click the Show button to make it visible again.

The Standard toolbar in PhotoDraw is a combination of the tools you would expect to find in the Standard toolbar of other Office applications such as New, Open, and Print, and tools from the Drawing toolbar such as Line, Rectangle, and AutoShapes.

A Formatting toolbar is available but is not turned on by default. The Formatting toolbar contains traditional formatting tools such as text and alignment tools and also contains additional drawing tools such as 3D and Shadow. Many of the tools available on the Formatting toolbar are also accessible from the Visual toolbar so there is generally no reason to display them both.

Making Use of the Workspace

The *workspace*, shown in Figure 12.4, is the area made up of a picture area and scratch area. The picture area is the primary work area. Objects in the picture area are considered to be part of the final composition. Objects in the scratch area are considered temporary and are not saved when the picture is saved in any format besides the default PhotoDraw format (.mix).

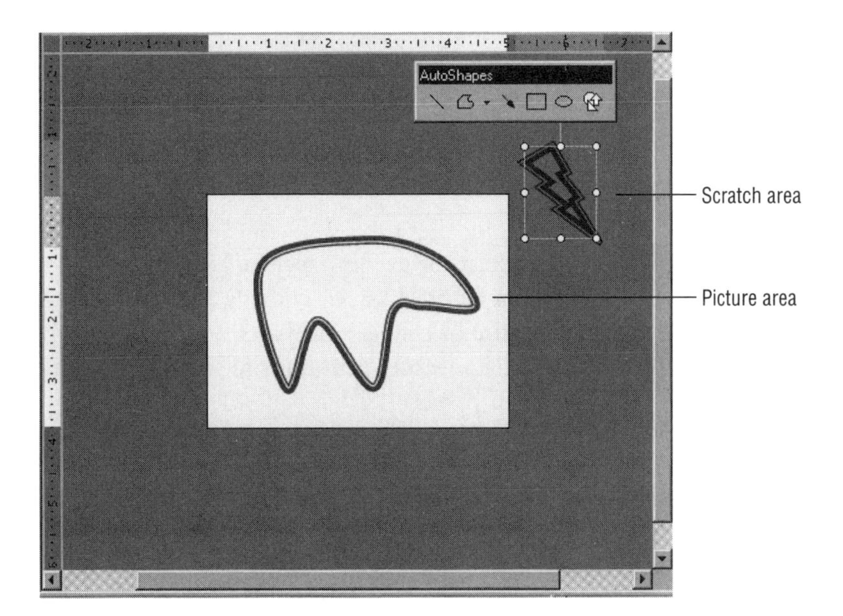

FIGURE 12.4
The workspace is made up of the picture area and the scratch area

You can drag any objects into the scratch area for holding until you are ready to work with them.

Defining the Picture Area

Objective PD2000.8.5

The *default picture area*, the area you get when you choose File ➢ New ➢ Default Picture, is 5 inches by 3.75 inches. You can choose another picture area from the New dialog box, shown in Figure 12.5, or you can adjust the picture area to your needs.

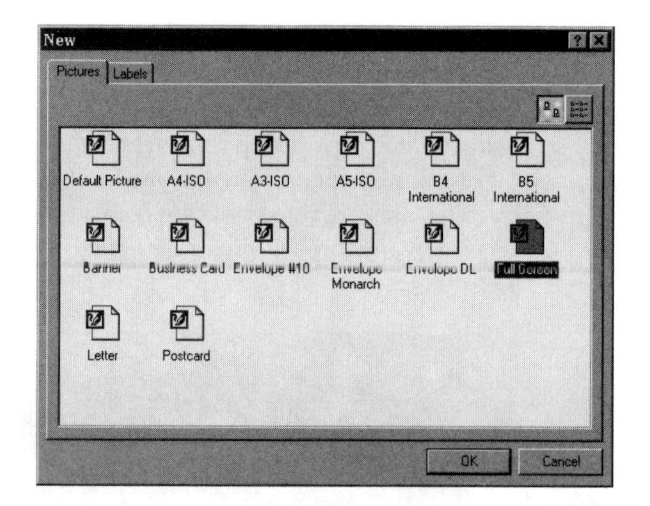

FIGURE 12.5 Choose from a number of picture areas in the New dialog box

To adjust the existing picture area, open the Picture Setup dialog box, shown in Figure 12.6, by clicking File ➢ Picture Setup. Choose a different picture size or change the Width and Height of the picture. You can also change the measurement units to centimeters (cms), inches, millimeters (mms), or pixels.

Change the picture orientation from Landscape to Portrait to reverse the Height and Width measurements.

If you want to change the default picture area, click the New Picture Default tab of the Picture setup dialog box. Any changes you make here are reflected in all future default pictures you create. To restore original picture defaults, choose Default Picture on the New Picture Default tab.

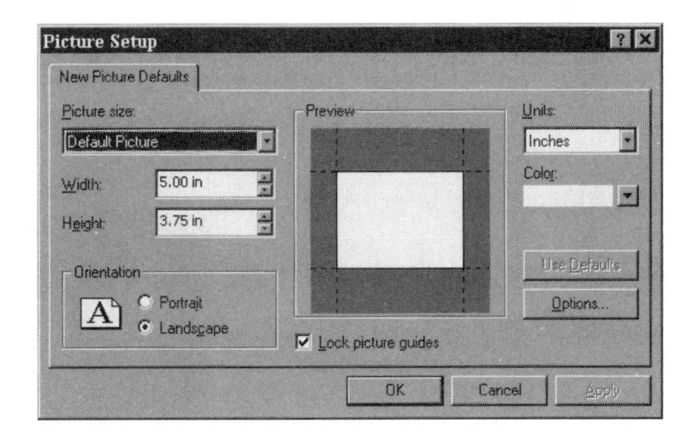

FIGURE 12.6
Change the size of the picture area in the Picture Setup dialog box

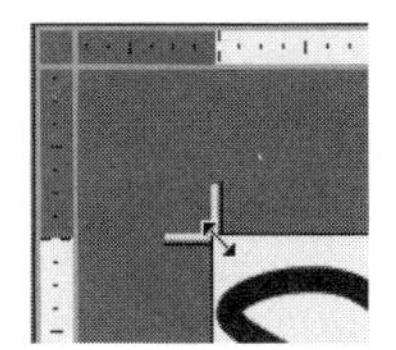

You can also change the picture area manually by unlocking and dragging the picture guides. Clear the Lock Picture Guides checkbox in the Picture setup dialog box or choose View ➢ Lock Picture Guides. Drag the picture guides to the desired size.

The final option for changing the size of the picture area allows you to re-size the picture area to fit the selected objects.

1. Choose Edit ➢ Select All in Picture Area, or hold down the Shift key, and click on the objects in the picture area you want to include.
2. Select Fit Picture Area to Selection from the View menu.

Determining Size and Location

The Status bar at the bottom of the workspace contains valuable information about the size of the picture area and the size and location of specific objects within the picture area. When no objects are selected the Status bar displays the size of the picture area. When you click an object to select it, the left display shows the location of the object in the picture area and the right display shows the actual dimensions of the selected object.

Using Pan and Zoom

The Zoom control on the Standard toolbar can be used to zoom in by 600% or zoom out by 10%. You can also find options here to zoom to Selection, zoom to Fit All, and zoom to Picture area.

The Pan and Zoom button opens a miniature Pan and Zoom window, shown in Figure 12.7. Use the Zoom In and Zoom Out buttons or drag the Zoom Slider to control the magnification. Inside the picture area, drag the viewfinder to focus on a part of the picture.

FIGURE 12.7

Use the Pan and Zoom Window to zero in on a particular part of a composition

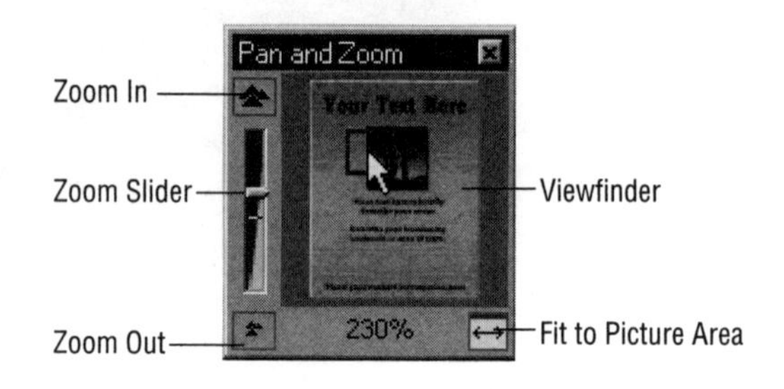

Using the Picture List

Objective PD2000.6.8

PhotoDraw is an image composition tool, which means that you can create new pictures by combining several images into one. An individual PhotoDraw picture may consist of photos, clip art, text objects and drawings all rolled into one. To help in the composition process, PhotoDraw keeps each image separately in the picture list and allows you to work with each one independently of the other. In Figure 12.8, the picture list shows the composite picture and each of the photos that make up the composite.

To insert a picture into the picture list, click New on the Standard toolbar to create a new picture or Open to open an existing file.

If you would like an object contained within a picture to become a separate picture, drag the object from the workspace into the picture list.

Click any of the objects in the picture list to move that object into the picture area. To add an object to a picture, drag the object from the picture list into the workspace.

FIGURE 12.8
The picture list keeps track of each of the objects that make up a picture

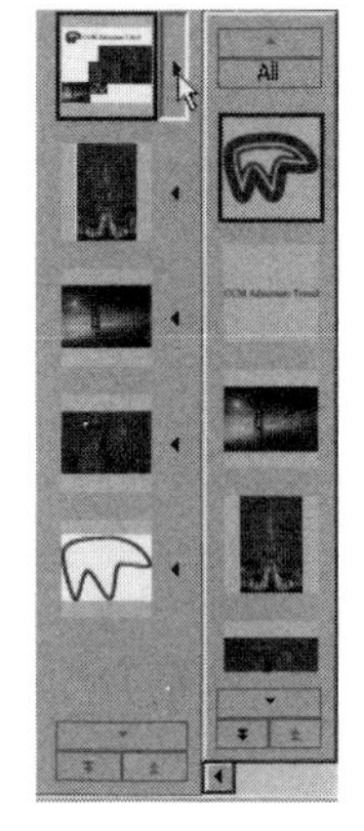

PhotoDraw also separates out each object contained in a picture, making it easy to concentrate on a specific object. Click the Open/Close Object List arrow on the right side of an object in the picture list to see each of the individual objects that compose a picture.

Click on any object to select that object in the picture area. Click the Open/Close Object List area again to close the object list.

Importing Artwork from Other Sources

Objective PD2000.4.3

With today's digital cameras, scanners, and endless CD-ROMs filled with photos and clip art, it's pretty easy to capture just the right images for your PhotoDraw creation. It may take a little legwork but if it's out there, there is a way to turn it into a digital image. PhotoDraw has built-in tools to accept images directly from scanners and digital cameras. The Office 2000 Clip Gallery is at your disposal and, in addition, PhotoDraw comes with its own gallery of images for use in PhotoDraw compositions.

To import images from a digital camera, scanner, or other TWAIN device, you must first install the device in PhotoDraw. Make sure the device is connected to your computer and the software for the device is installed through Windows. Then, follow these steps:

1. In PhotoDraw, choose Tools ➢ Options and click the Scanner/ Camera tab.
2. Select the device you want to install and click Modify.
3. Select the type of device.
4. Under Performance, select Enhanced.

If the device you want to install is not listed here, check the documentation for the device and make sure it is installed and working correctly outside of PhotoDraw.

Once the device is installed, open the File menu and choose Scan Picture, Digital Camera, or Other TWAIN Device to transfer the image, or choose Select All to transfer all the images.

Using Visual Insert to Preview Graphics

Objective PD2000.4.1

PhotoDraw's Visual Insert feature is a fabulous way to locate graphic files you have scattered around your hard drive. Visual Insert instantly renders a thumbnail of any graphic file it encounters. To use Visual Insert, choose Insert ➢ Visual Insert. Select the drive you want to look in and double-click the particular folder the files are in. Visual Insert displays all the graphic files it can find in the selected folder, as shown in Figure 12.9

If you want to focus on a particular graphic file type, click the Files of Type down arrow and choose the file type from the list. If you have a large number of images in a folder and know the file name you want, enter the name in the File Name text box, and press Enter.

When you locate the image you want to insert, select the image and click Insert. To insert more than one file at a time, hold down the Ctrl key when you are selecting them.

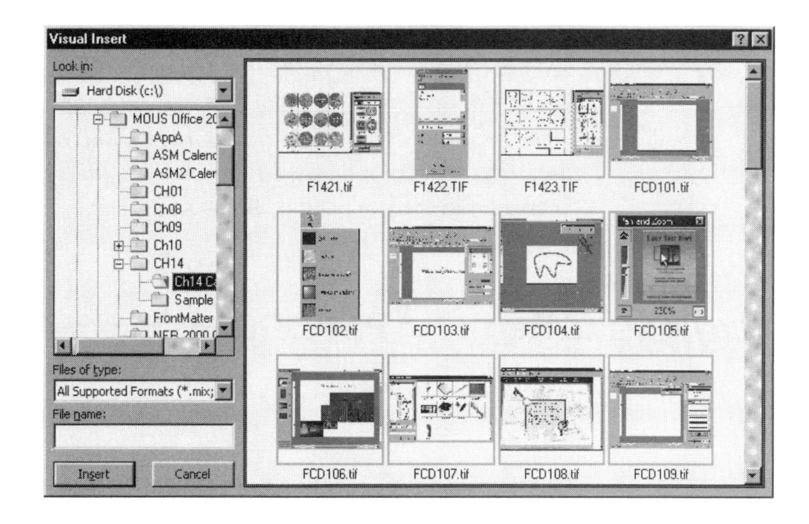

FIGURE 12.9
Visual Insert lets you preview pictures before you insert them

Inserting PhotoDraw Content, Clip Art, and Other Images

Objective PD2000E.6.3 and PD2000.4.2

PhotoDraw CD 2 is filled with photos, clip art, and other images for use in PhotoDraw. To access these images, shown in Figure 12.10, choose Insert ➢ PhotoDraw Content.

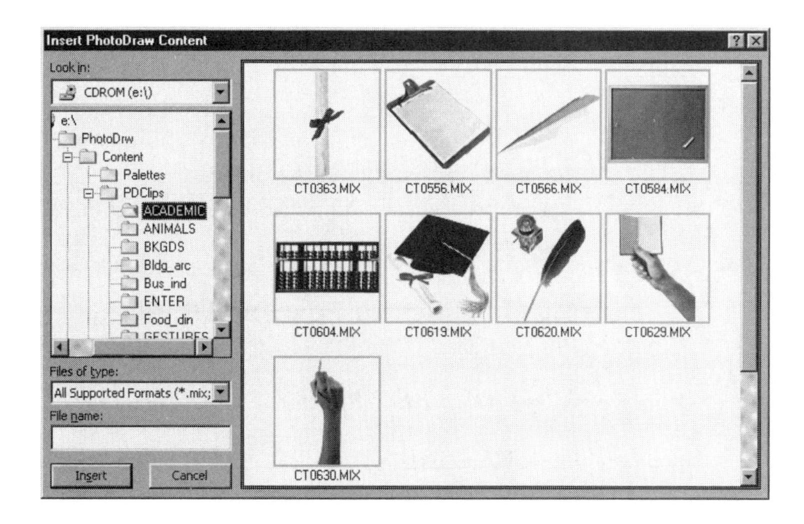

FIGURE 12.10
PhotoDraw comes with its own extensive collection of images

Choose a category from the available folders displayed in the left pane. When you find the clip you want, select it and click Insert to insert the image into the open picture.

The Microsoft Clip Gallery that you are already familiar with from Word, Excel and PowerPoint is also available to you in PhotoDraw. Choose File ➢ Insert Clip Art to open the Insert Clip Art dialog box. Choose from among the available categories and click Insert. (For more about using the Clip Gallery, see Chapter 11.)

Moving and Re-sizing PhotoDraw Objects

Objective PD2000.5.1 and E.4.10

A selected object has handles around it. When an object is selected, you can move it and re-size it. Move it by pointing to the border of the object and dragging with the four-header Move arrow. Re-size using the handles themselves. To maintain the proportion of the object, drag the handles in the corners of the object. Hold Shift to re-size the object vertically and horizontally without maintaining proportions.

You may be used to holding down the Shift key to drag the corner handles of an object when you want to maintain proportions. In PhotoDraw, you do just the opposite. Hold down Shift when you want to change proportions. Dragging the corners without holding down Shift maintains proportions. Go figure!

To skew an object in PhotoDraw, hold down Ctrl and Alt while dragging the midpoint handle on the object.

For more precise dimensions and positioning, use the Arrange workpane discussed in the next section.

Setting Gridlines to Position Objects

Objective PD2000E.7.1

PhotoDraw uses an invisible grid to position objects in the picture area. By default, this grid is .10 inches by .10 inches and objects "snap" to this grid when you move them around the picture area. You can temporarily disable the grid by opening the View menu and clicking Snap to Grid or hold down Alt while you are dragging an object. To change the size of the gridlines, choose File ➢ Picture Setup. To change the gridlines for only the picture you are working on, click Options on the Active Picture tab. To change gridlines for all future pictures, click Options on the New Picture Defaults tab. In the Options dialog box, enter new values in the Horizontal Spacing and Vertical Spacing boxes.

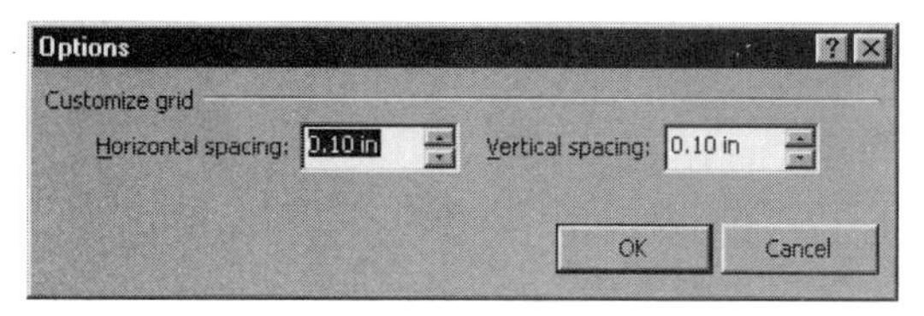

Arranging Objects

Objective PD2000.5.1 and 6.2

When you are working with several objects in one picture, it's important to be able to change their relationship to each other. PhotoDraw provides you with several tools on the Arrange menu to arrange objects on a page. To open the Arrange workpane, shown in Figure 12.11, choose Arrange from the Arrange menu. Here you can change size and position of an object, and rotate and flip an object.

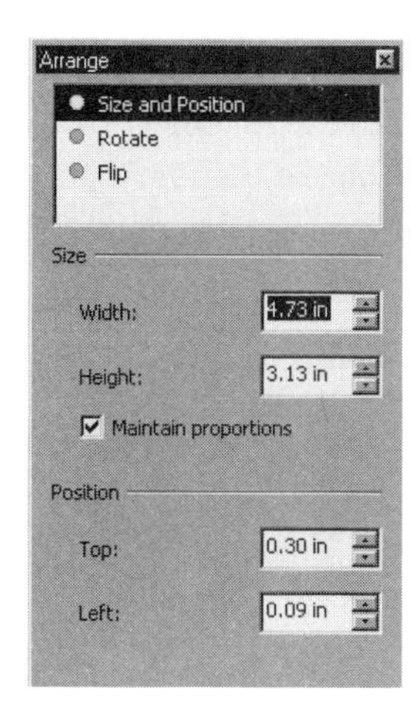

FIGURE 12.11 Use the Arrange workpane to change the size and position of an object and flip objects

To enter the actual dimensions of an object, choose Size and Position from the Arrange workpane. Enter the desired Width or Height and as long as Maintain Proportions is checked, the opposite value is entered automatically. Clear the Maintain Proportions checkbox if you want to change the proportions.

When you are creating a composite of several images, you may want to enter the exact location of an object within the picture area. Enter Top and Left values in the Position section of the Size and Position workpane.

Rotating and Flipping Objects

Objective PD2000.5.4

To rotate an object, click Rotate on the Arrange workpane and choose one of the four options or enter a custom value from 0 to 360 in the Custom Degrees text box.

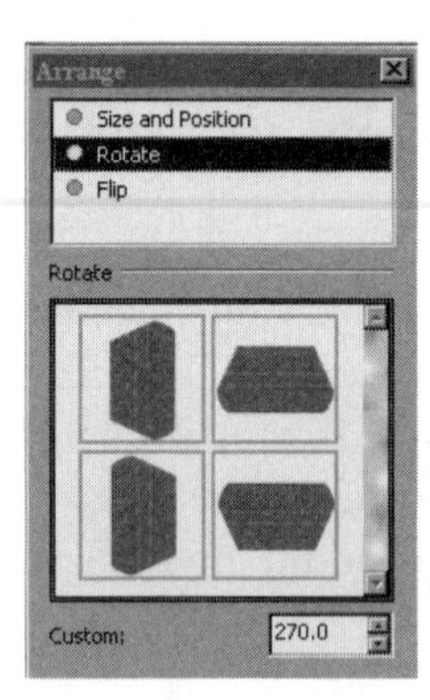

To flip an object, click Flip on the Arrange workpane. There are only four ways to flip an object so you won't find any choice for custom values here. Click one of the four options to flip the object in the direction you want it.

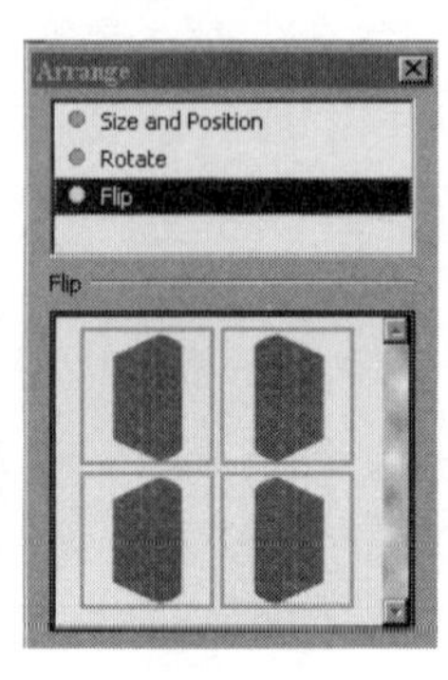

Objective PD2000.5.2 and 5.3

On the Arrange menu, you will find additional options for Group, Ungroup, Order, and Align. Grouping objects make them one object. Once objects are grouped, they can be re-sized, repositioned, and modified as a single object. In order to change an individual object within the group, they must be ungrouped.

Order allows you to position objects in front of or behind other objects. PhotoDraw is not limited to a single layer. In fact, you can position several objects on top of each other and use the Order options of Bring to Front, Send to Back, Bring Forward, and Send Backwards to order them correctly.

Align repositions multiple objects so they line up. Select two or more objects and choose Align Left to align the left edges of the objects, Align Right to align the right edges and Align Center to align the centers of the objects. Align Top, Middle and Bottom work the same way when you want vertical alignment.

Hands On: Objective PD2000.4.1, 4.2, 4.3, 5.1-5.4, 6.8, 8.5 and PD2000E.6.3

1. Use Visual Insert to insert an image into a blank picture.
   a) Re-size the image so that it fits in the picture area.
   b) Reposition the image by dragging it to the desired position in the picture area.
2. Insert a clip art image from the Clip Gallery or from another file location.
   a) Flip the clip art horizontally.
   b) Re-size and reposition the clip art.
   c) Fit the picture area to the object.
3. Select the objects from the previous two exercises and align them horizontally or vertically.
   a) Group the two objects and move them to the opposite side of the picture area.
   b) Rotate the new grouped object 45 degrees.
   c) Ungroup the objects.

4. Insert a background from the collection of PhotoDraw content.
   a) Use Order to send the background to the back of the picture.
   b) Reposition one of the foreground objects so it is precisely positioned .5 inches from the top and left of the picture area.
5. To complete the picture, insert a digital image from a digital camera or scanner.

Saving PhotoDraw Creations

Objective PD2000.8.3

PhotoDraw's default file format is MIX but it accepts pictures in almost any graphic format. You can also save pictures in a wide variety of graphic formats such as GIF (.gif), TIFF (.tif), JPEG (.jpg), and PNG (.png). Choose File ➢ Save As and change the format in the Save As Type box.

When you save a picture in a format other than MIX (.mix), PhotoDraw flattens the image and combines it into a single image. You can no longer edit individual parts of the picture.

If you save a picture in another format, save it first as a MIX file and then save it again in a different format. You can always open the MIX file for editing and re-save it in another format for use in other applications.

Saving Artwork for Use in Other Programs

Objective PD2000.8.2 and E.8.2

When you've planned how to use an image, PhotoDraw can help you choose the best format and set other display options. Choose File ➢ Save For Use In and then choose On the Web, On the Web as a Thumbnail, In a Microsoft

Office Document, In an On-screen Presentation, or In a Publication. Follow the steps of the wizard to complete the save.

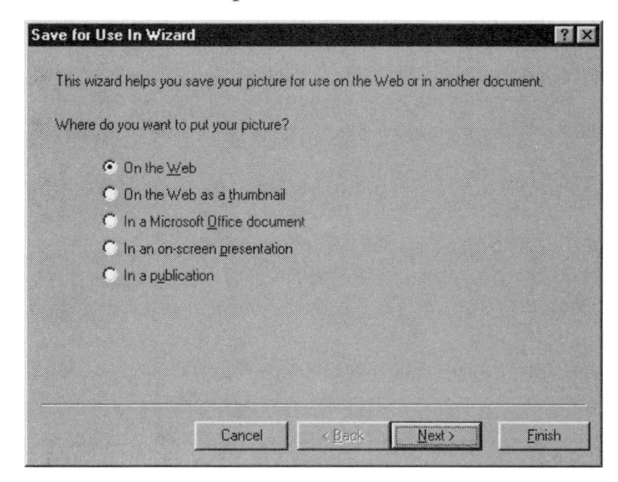

If you want a JPEG image and want to identify the specific size of the exported (saved) file, choose File ➢ Save As, change the Save As Type box to JPEG File Interchange Format (.jpg) and click the Options button.

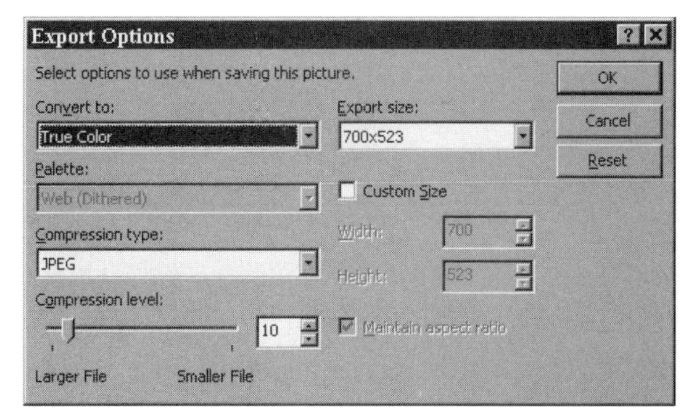

Click the Export Size down arrow to choose another export size or enter a custom size by clicking the Custom Size checkbox. You can also change the level of compression to adjust for file size vs. quality (A higher degree of compression gives you a smaller file but reduced quality). When you are finished with the Options, click OK, and complete the save.

You can also adjust the export size of GIF, JPEG and PNG files by clicking the Options buttons on the Save As dialog box.

Storing Pictures in the Clip Gallery

Objective PD2000E.8.3 and E.8.1

In Chapter 11, you learned how to effectively use the Microsoft Office Clip Gallery to locate and organize clip art. To make the Clip Gallery really useful, add your PhotoDraw creations to it so you can find them anytime you need them. To add PhotoDraw pictures to the Clip Gallery, open the Clip Gallery just as you would to insert a picture. Click Import Clips on the Clip Gallery toolbar to open the Add Clip to Clip Gallery dialog box shown in Figure 12.12.

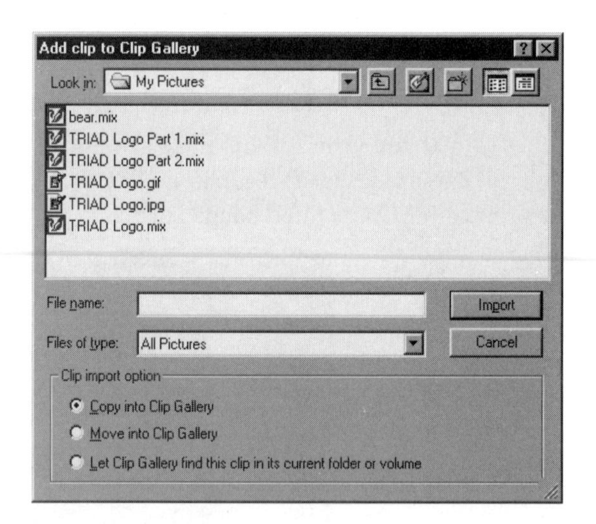

FIGURE 12.12 Add PhotoDraw pictures to the Clip Gallery

Locate the picture you want to add and select it (or select multiple pictures if you want to add more than one). Choose if you want to move the picture to the Clip Gallery, copy it there, or link to it in its current location. Click Import to import the picture(s).

The Clip Properties dialog box opens automatically and lets you enter a description of the picture, assign it to categories, and list keywords so you can use Search to locate it. Enter a description on the first tab of the dialog box. On the Categories tab, you can select one or more pre-existing categories, or click New Category, to create a new category of your own.

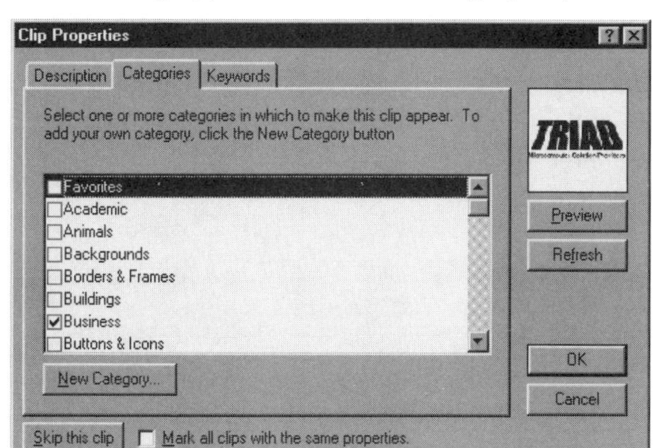

To enter Keywords, click the Keywords tab and click the New Keyword button. When you are finished setting the properties, click OK to finish importing the picture.

Printing

Objective PD2000.8.1, 8.4, and E.8.1

To print a PhotoDraw picture, choose File ➢ Print so you can review any of the print settings before sending the picture to the printer. The Print dialog box, shown in Figure 12.13, has standard print settings, such as Orientation and Number of Copies, and also has a number of options unique to PhotoDraw.

If you want the picture to print at the highest possible resolution, change Print Quality from the default of 150dpi (dots per inch) to 300dpi. Depending on the features of your printer, you may also have the option to Match Screen Colors. If your printer supports it, this option is checked by default. You can also print crop marks that show the size of the picture area.

On the Size tab of the Print dialog box, shown in Figure 12.14, you can change the size of the printed output from Exact Size to Fit to Page, Photographic Size, or Custom Size. If you choose Photographic Size, you have your choice of 3 x 5 up to 8 x 10 in and several sizes in centimeters. Custom Size maintains proportions if you enter either a Width or Height and click the Maintain Proportions checkbox.

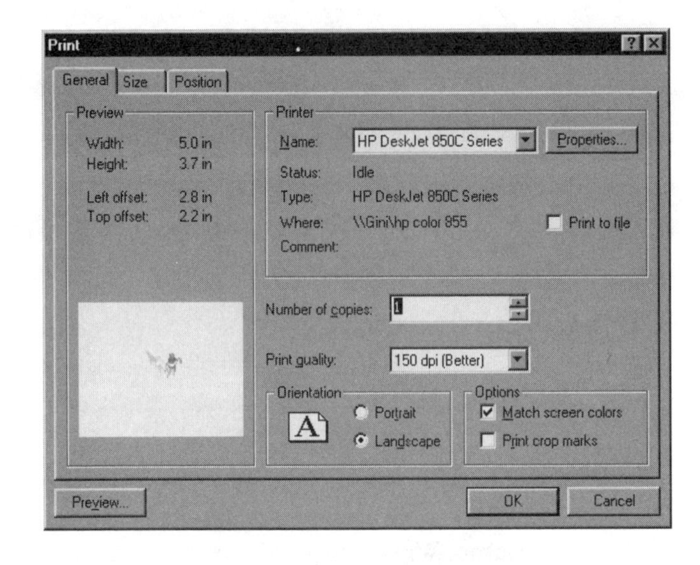

FIGURE 12.13 The Print dialog box has settings for Size and Position in addition to the General print settings.

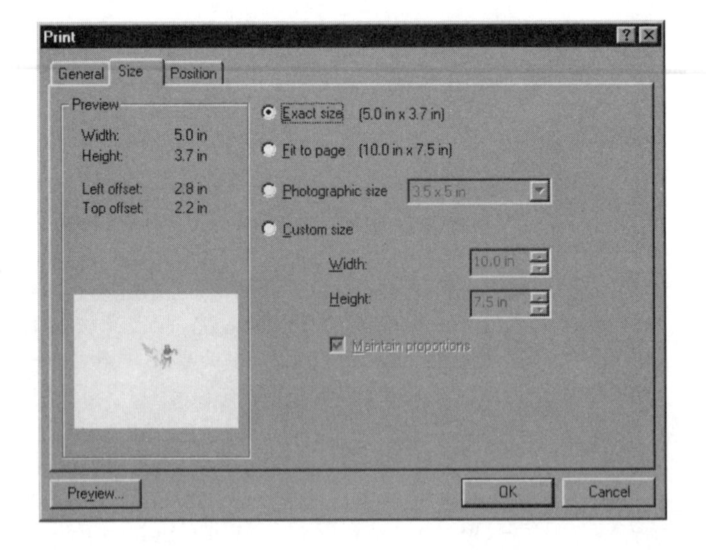

FIGURE 12.14 Choose the size of the printed output on the Size tab of the Print dialog box

If you would like to identify where you would like the picture to print on the page, click the Position tab of the Print dialog box, shown in Figure 12.15 (these options are not available if you choose Exact Size on the Size page). The default position is centered on the page both horizontally and vertically. If you would like to change this position, enter exact coordinates in the Left Top, Right, and Bottom Offset boxes.

FIGURE 12.15
Indicate the position of the picture on the printed page on the Position tab of the Print dialog box

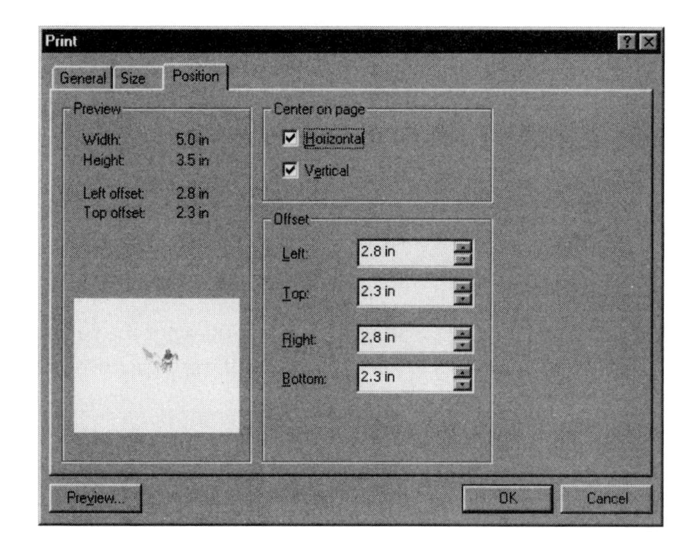

Previewing Before You Print

Objective PD2000.7.11

While you are working in the Print dialog box, PhotoDraw shows you a miniature of the picture. If you want to see what the entire page looks like before you print it, click the Preview button on the bottom of the print dialog box or choose File ➢ Print Preview. You can change the zoom level by clicking the Zoom down arrow. When you are ready to print, click Print or click Close to exit Print Preview.

Printing on Labels

Objective PD2000E.9.1

Have you ever wanted to created great looking labels but couldn't find a way to insert graphics onto Word labels? PhotoDraw lets you print your creations on hundreds of different labels styles.

Printing Labels

1. Open the picture(s) you want to print (you can print one picture on multiple labels or different pictures on each labels).
2. Choose File ➢ Print Reprints and walk through the wizard to create the labels.
   a. In Step 1, designate a printer.
   b. In Step 2, select a label template from twenty categories.
   c. In Step 3, choose if you want the same picture repeated on each label or choose to print different pictures on each label.
   d. In Step 4, drag the picture(s) into the template.
3. When you click Finish, PhotoDraw sends the labels to the printer and closes the wizard.
4. Save the picture of the Reprint Sheet if you ever want to print the labels again.

Hands On: Objective PD2000.8.1-8.5, PD2000E.8.1-E.8.3, E.9.1 and E.7.1

1. Add an object from PhotoDraw Content to a blank picture.
   a) Save the picture in the Photo Draw MIX format.
   b) Save the picture again as a GIF and adjust the export size to the smallest available size.
   c) Save the picture as a JPEG, specifying 192 x 132 as the export size.
   d) Save the picture in the PNG format.
   e) Close all open pictures.
2. Open a saved picture and resave the picture for use in a Microsoft Office document.
   a) Preview the picture in Print Preview.
   b) Print the picture, fitting it to the page.
3. Add a preview of the open picture to the Microsoft Clip Gallery.

4. Open a saved picture and print it on Avery 5161 labels (don't worry about adding text or other objects to the labels at this time).

Creating Art in PhotoDraw

Now that you know your way around, you are ready to begin creating your own artwork. You can start by drawing or painting, importing an image, or opening a saved picture file. Once you have a picture, PhotoDraw gives you many tools to manipulate the image to your heart's content.

Drawing and Painting on Your Own

Many of the drawing tools are available from the Standard toolbar, but to access all of the tools, click the Draw Paint button on the Visual toolbar and choose between Draw, Shapes, and Paint.

Using Drawing Tools

Objective PD2000.2.2, 2.3, 6.3

When you click either Draw or Shapes, the Outline workpane and the AutoShapes toolbar open, as shown in Figure 12.16. The only difference between Draw and Shapes is which tool is selected when you click it: the Curve tool is selected when you choose Draw and the Rectangle tool when you choose Shapes.

You may need to move the AutoShapes toolbar out of the way to see all of the available workpanes.

Choose the tool you want to start with and then choose between these options on the workpane window.

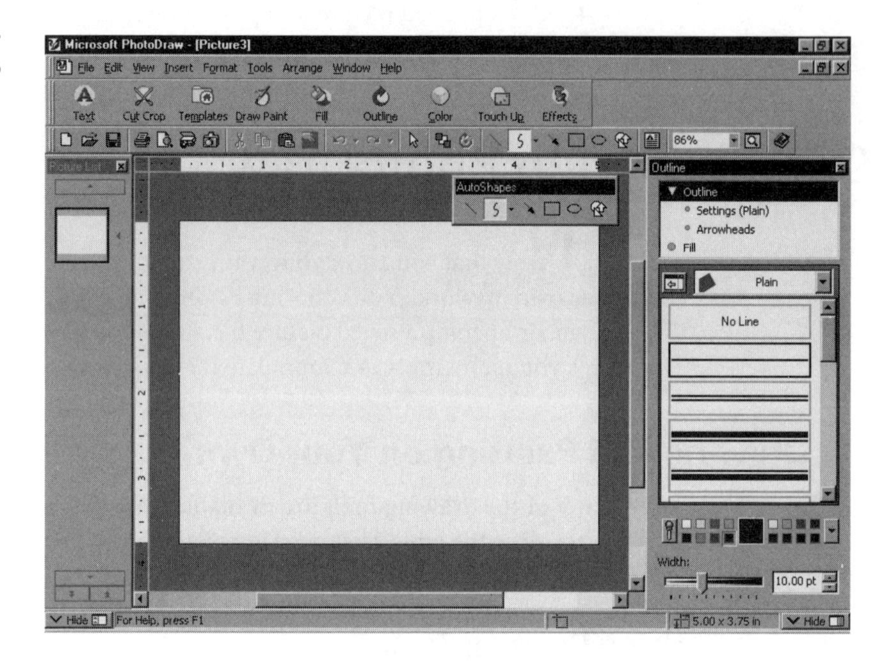

FIGURE 12.16
Draw and Shape tools let you create objects of any shape

Outline:

- Plain, Artistic, and Photo Brushes give you plenty of choices for how you want the outline to appear.
- Use line Color (Plain and Artistic brushes only) or use the Eyedropper to select a color to copy (see *Applying Color* and *Using the Eyedropper* later in this chapter).
- Line Width determines the width of the line in point size.

Settings:

- Line Style lets you change line style from the original brush selection.
- Line Color lets you change Line Color from the original selection.
- Transparency determines how light or dark the outline is.
- Line Width lets you change the width form the original selection.
- Placement indicates if the line is on top or beneath other objects.

Arrowheads (applied only to Lines and Arrows):

- Begin Style and Size is the style and size of an arrow placed at the beginning of a line.
- End Style and Size is the style and size of an arrow placed at the end of a line.

Fill:

- Fill List has options for Solid Colors, Textures, Designer Gradients, Two-Color Gradients, and Colors.
- Choose a fill from the options below the Fill List.
- Transparency affects how light or dark the fill is. Use a higher transparency percentage to make the image lighter.

When you are ready to actually draw the outline of the shape you selected, click in the picture area and drag to create the object. If you are using the Curve or the Freeform tool, click once to change directions and double-click to complete the object.

Objective PD2000.2.1

You can modify the line style, colors, or any of the other settings of existing objects in one of two ways. You can open the Draw/Paint workpane, select the objects you want to change, and change the settings. Or you can click Fill, Outline, or Color on the Visual toolbar and choose the tool you want to use.

To select an object when the Drawing tools are active, click the Select button on the Standard toolbar and click the object you want to select.

Working with Paint Brushes

Objective PD2000E.4.5

Paintbrushes come in a variety of shapes and styles and can be found throughout PhotoDraw. Three primary types of paintbrushes are available: Plain, Artistic, and Photo brushes. To use a paintbrush, you must have a workpane open that supports paint brushes, such as the Outline or Paint workpanes. Click the Expand Gallery arrow next to the brush style to see all of the available brushes. Select the brush you want to use from the Brush gallery and drag the pointer across the picture where you want to apply the brush.

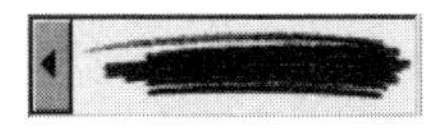

Paintbrushes are also available to use with other tools such as Distort, Clone, and Smudge (see *Applying Special Effects* later in this chapter). Select the brush you want to use from the Brush gallery and drag it over, or click an area of the picture, to apply the effect.

Point to any of the brushes or outline styles in the Brush gallery to see the name of that style. Make a note of any styles you use so you can reuse them without guessing which one it was.

To modify a brush, click Settings on the open workpane. Change the brush style, transparency, width, and placement.

Applying Color

Objective PD2000E.4.11, E.4.12 and E.7.4

PhotoDraw comes with a number of predefined color palettes and lets you create your own to fit your particular needs. To apply color, choose a color from the Color list that's available in most workpanes. If the color you want does not show up on the list, choose one of the other options available when you click the Color list arrow button. These options include:

Active Palette—Lets you select a color form the active palette. The default active palette is Web Dithered.

True Color—Gives you more colors to choose from by clicking a color in the color display.

More Colors—Opens the More Colors dialog box shown in Figure 12.17.

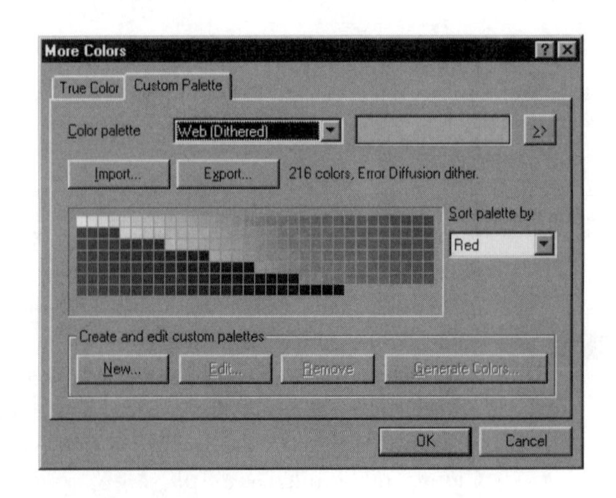

FIGURE 12.17

The More Colors dialog box gives you options for importing and exporting custom palettes and selecting colors by the RGB and HSV values.

To use a different color palette, select one from the Color Palette list, or if the palette you want is on the list, click Import. PhotoDraw comes with over 50 custom palettes to choose from. Click any of the Custom Palettes to import it into PhotoDraw.

If you would like to create your own custom palette that includes standard colors for your company's publications or other uses, click New on the Custom Palette tab. This opens a dialog box for you to specify a palette name, a size, and the type of dithering you would like to use (dithering is used to mix colors in order to approximate colors that are not available on the display).

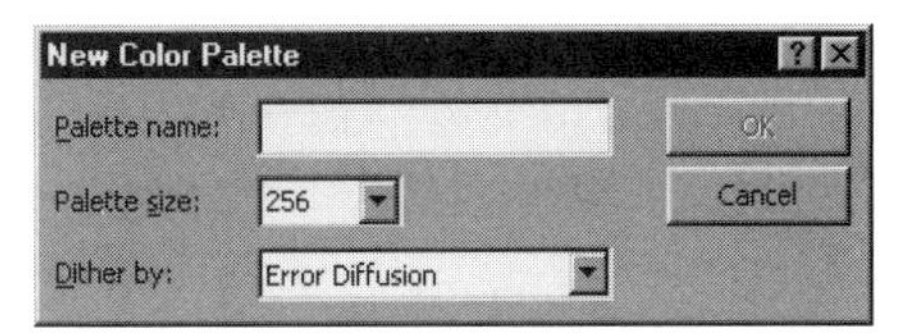

Once you have created the palette, choose Generate Colors to add colors to the palette.

If you want to export palette for use in other graphics programs, click Export and open the folder where you want to store the palette.

Using the Eyedropper

Objective PD2000E.7.4

To match color in a PhotoDraw picture, the Eyedropper is a handy tool to use. The Eyedropper is similar to the Format Painter in Word, Excel, and PowerPoint. The eyedropper lets you copy colors from one place to another on the screen (and the color doesn't even have to be in a PhotoDraw picture). To use the eyedropper, click the Eyedropper button. The pointer changes to an eyedropper, which you can use to click on any color you want to capture. The color you've chosen appears in the Color list. You can then apply the color using whatever line style or brush you want to use.

See *Correcting Brightness and Contrast* later in this chapter for information about matching brightness and contrast.

Using AutoShapes Using AutoShapes is a quick way to insert shapes into a picture. Click the AutoShapes button on the AutoShapes toolbar or directly on the Standard toolbar. This gives you a choice of Lines, Basic Shapes, Block Arrows, Flowchart, Stars and Banners, and Callouts. Choose the type of shape you want and then select the specific shape that most closely resembles the shape you are looking for (you can edit it later to make it perfect!), as shown in Figure 12.18. Drag the shape in the workspace to create the shape.

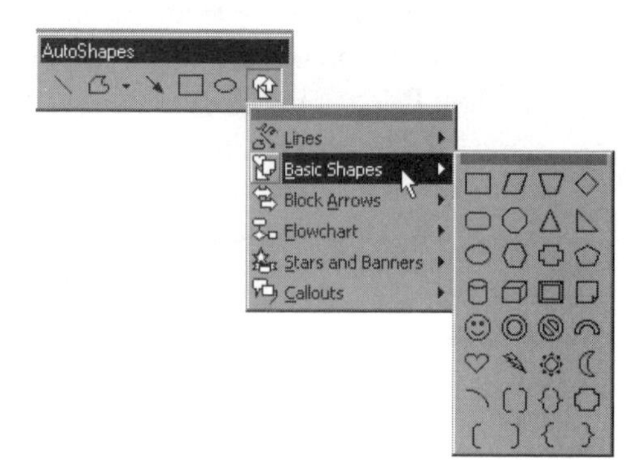

FIGURE 12.18
Select an AutoShape from one of the six categories

Once you have an AutoShape, you can apply any of the Custom Draw options to it the same way you would with an original shape.

Editing Points

Objective PD2000E.2.1

As soon as you create an object, an Edit Points workpane becomes available in the workpane window. Edit Points lets you stretch and reshape an object any way you want. Select Edit Points to switch to Edit Points mode, as shown in Figure 12.19

Drag any of the points to reshape the object or drag the outline to create new points. To add several new points to the object to make it more malleable, click the Add Point button in the Point Properties section of the workpane.

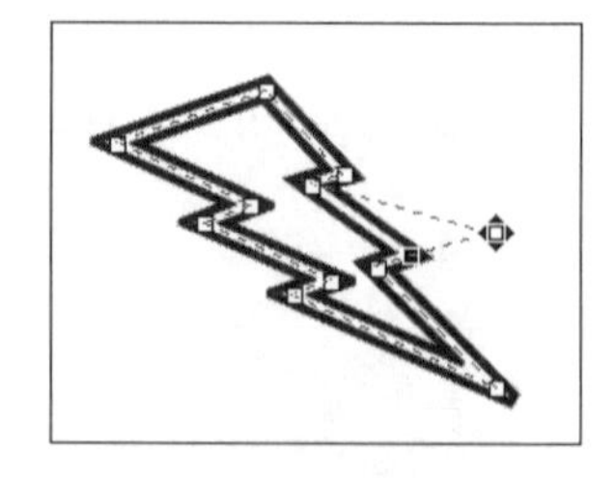

Delete a point by selecting it and clicking the Delete Point button on the workpane. If you want to open a curve in the drawing, click the Open Curve button. To turn a straight line into a curved line that you can then bend, click on the line and click the Curved Line button. Change it back to a straight line by clicking the Straight Line button.

When you are finished editing points, click the Exit Edit Points button or any other tool.

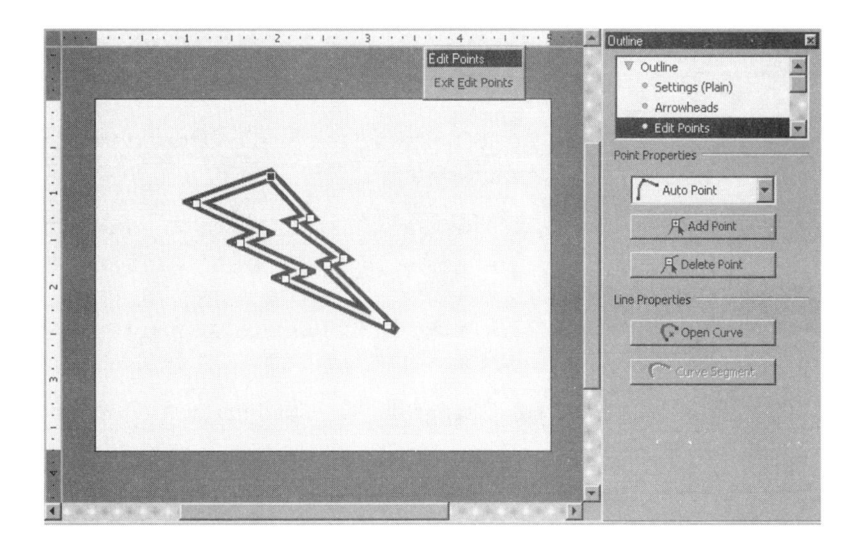

FIGURE 12.19 Switch to Edit Points mode to reshape an object

Painting

Objective PD2000.2.3

Painting is similar to drawing except you can't edit or reshape the line once you've drawn it. When you paint, the brushstrokes are combined into a single object so you have a complete picture when you click the Finish button on the Creative Paint toolbar. You have a choice of Artistic brushes, Plain brushes, and Photo brushes *and* you can change the Color, Transparency, Width, and Placement by clicking to open the Settings workpane.

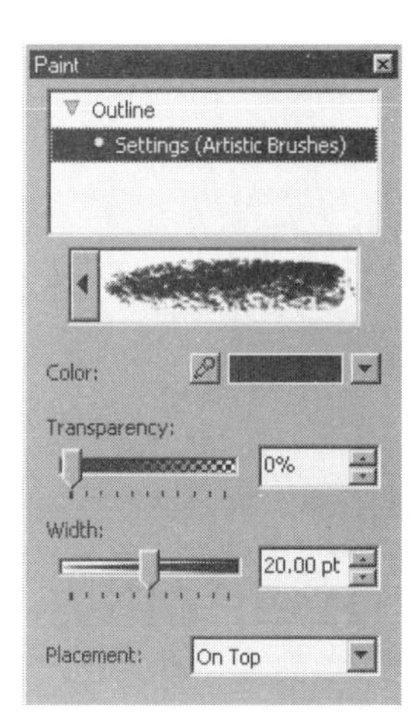

To add to the painting, click the Paint button on the Creative Paint toolbar. This actually creates a new painting within the same picture. When you click Finish on the Creative Paint toolbar, you can select any individual painting by clicking on it within the picture.

Hands On: Objective PD2000.2.1, 2.2, 2.3, 6.3, and PD2000E.2.1, E.4.11, E.4.12 and E.7.4

1. Create a new default picture. Draw a freeform object using the Plain outline style.
   a) Move the object to the center of the picture area.
   b) Re-size the object.
   c) Change the Outline style to Artistic Brushes, then choose a brush from the gallery.
   d) Change the Transparency and Width of the brush.
2. Create a rectangle and two additional objects using Shapes.
   a) Choose a Photo brush for the outline style.
   b) Add a point to each side of the rectangle.
   c) Drag the four new points to give it eight sides.
   d) Delete two points to make it only six-sided.
   e) Change the line style on one of the objects to Thick-Thin Line, the color to blue and the width to 12 points.
   f) Import a custom color palette and apply colors to the objects.
   g) Use the Eyedropper to match the color of one object to another.
3. Use an artistic paintbrush to paint a picture.
   a) Add to the painting using photo brushes.
   b) Use a Sisal Braid artistic brush to paint a line across the top.

Enhancing Artwork

PhotoDraw not only helps you create artwork, it includes tools to modify and enhance existing artwork. You can enhance artwork in three primary ways: cutting and cropping, touching up, and applying special effects.

Cutting, Cropping, and Erasing

Objective PD2000.6.1, 7.10, and PD2000E.4.1

If you have a favorite photo that looks great except for an unwanted object in the background, use PhotoDraw to crop the picture and throw the rest away. There are several ways to eliminate parts of a picture using the cutting, cropping, and erasing tools.

Cutting makes a copy of part of a picture and leaves the original intact. Cropping preserves part of an image and throws the rest away. Erasing is similar to cutting but allows you to adjust the transparency of the erased portion of the image.

Because the three tools, Cut Out, Crop, and Erase, are essentially variations of the same, once you've learned one, you can experiment and decide which tool you want to use with a particular image.

To start, click the Cut Crop button on the Visual toolbar and choose Cut Out, Crop, or Erase.

When you choose Crop from the Cut Crop menu, the workpane displays about 50 shapes that can be used to select an area of a picture. Pick a shape that most closely resembles the area you want to preserve. Use the handles to re-size the area or click Stretch to Fit to maximize the selected shape around the image. When you are ready, click Lock Crop—or if you think you will ever want to crop the original image using a different shape—click Finish on the Crop toolbar instead. You still get a cropped image, but a portion of the picture is just hidden. The entire picture can be re-cropped at a later time.

Erasing By Shape

With the Erase tool, you select an area of the picture you want to preserve and discard the rest. You have four options for using Erase: By Shape, By Drawing, Edge Finder, and By Color. To begin, select the picture you want to cut.

Choose the shape you want to use to see a representation of what the finished product will look like, as shown in Figure 12.20. Drag the handles around the object to adjust the size of the area to be erased. Decide if you want to erase the shape or the opposite area. You can also adjust the hardness or softness of the cut by dragging the slider right or left. When you are ready, click Finish to erase.

FIGURE 12.20
All of the area outside the heart will be discarded when the Erase By Shape is applied

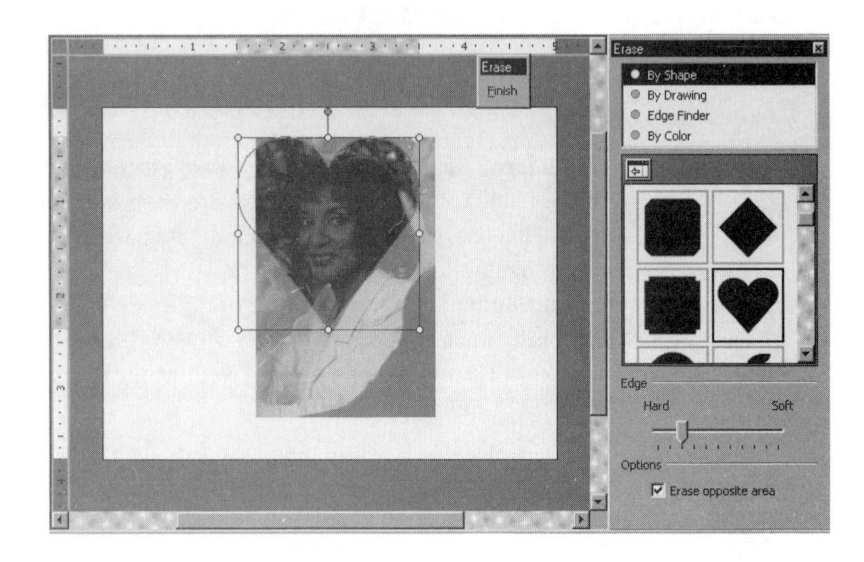

Erasing By Drawing

Use the By Drawing option to draw a line around the area of a picture you want to erase, as shown in Figure 12.21. Altering the hardness or softness of the path gives you cleaner lines in some pieces. Drag the Path Smoothness slider to make an adjustment. Click Erase Opposite Area if you want to preserve the area inside the lines. Click Finish when you are ready to make your cut.

FIGURE 12.21
Draw a line around an area you want to erase using the By Drawing option

Using the Edge Finder

Objective PD2000E.7.3

The Edge Finder option is the trickiest to use but allows you to trace around a portion of an object and remove it from the image. This option works best when you have objects with high contrast between them. To use the Edge Finder, click on an outside edge of the image you want to erase. From the yellow diamond, drag the rectangle to the first turn and click. The Edge Finder will draw a line as precisely as it can around the edge. Drag another rectangle around the next section of edge and click again.

Proceed all the way around the image and rejoin the yellow diamond to close the image, as shown in Figure 12.22. If the Edge Finder missed an edge, drag the line at the section it missed and let it recapture the edge.

FIGURE 12.22 The Edge Finder finds the precise edge of an image

When you use Cut Out instead of Erase you can choose to create the resulting picture in a new picture or keep it in the picture it is in. The default is Put in New Picture. If you keep it in the same picture, the original picture stays intact and after you create the cut out, you can pull out a copy of the picture in the new shape by moving the rectangle surrounding it.

Erasing by Matching Colors

The By Color option is an interesting way to take a part of the image that is not clearly definable by edges or shapes. The By Color option lets you erase all the parts of an image by their color. For example, in Figure 12.23 the colors in this piece of clip art were removed, leaving only an outline of the original image.

FIGURE 12.23 By Color lets you erase parts of a picture distinguished by their colors

To use the By Color option, select the object you want to use and select By Color from the Erase workpane. Click a section of the image that you want to capture. The section changes color to indicate it is selected. If there is more than one section you want, click the next section. Repeat this process until all areas of the image you want are selected. You do not have to choose sections of the same or even similar color. When you are finished selecting sections, click Finish on the Erase toolbar.

To erase every occurrence of a particular color, click the Global option on the By Color workpane.

Hands On: *Objective PD2000.6.1 and PD2000E.4.1, E.7.3*

1. Insert a photograph from PhotoDraw Content into a new picture. Crop a portion of the photo using one of the predefined shapes. Drag the handles to set the boundaries for the cropping. Click Finish rather than Lock Crop. Save the picture.
2. Using the graphic saved in Exercise One, crop it using another predefined shape. Choose Stretch to Fit and when you are ready, click Lock Crop. Save the new picture.
3. Open a previously saved picture or insert a graphic into a new picture.
   a) Erase a section of the picture using By Shape.
   b) Erase a section of the picture using By Drawing. Close the picture without saving changes.
   c) Open a new picture and erase a section of it using Edge Finder.
   d) Erase a section of the picture using By Color. Close the picture without saving changes.
4. Open a previously saved picture or insert a graphic into a new picture.
   a) Use Edge Finder to trace and cut out a portion of the picture and insert it into a new picture.
   b) Use Edge Finder to trace and cut out a portion of the picture and keep it in the existing picture.

Adjusting and Applying Color

PhotoDraw has a number of tools to help you adjust and work with color in clip art, photos, and other objects. Click Color on the Visual toolbar and choose Brightness and Contrast (or any of the Color choices) to open the Color workpane.

To discard all the changes you have made to a picture, you can choose Restore from the Effect list on the Color workpane. This restores the picture to its original state. Just to be on the safe side, save the picture before applying any Color adjustments so you can revert to an original if you are not pleased with the results. Use Save As to save a modified picture and preserve the original.

Correcting Brightness and Contrast

Objective PD2000.7.1 and PD2000E.5.1, E.7.4

Brightness refers to the lightness or darkness of an object and contrast refers to the difference between the lightest and darkest area of the picture. To adjust brightness and contrast automatically, click the Automatic button. To manually adjust the settings, drag the Brightness and Contrast sliders or enter values between -100 and 100.

For more precise correction, choose Correct by Painting in the Brightness and Contrast workpane. Move the slides to set the brightness and contrast levels and choose a brush from the Brush gallery. Click on the area of the picture you want to change. If you are satisfied with the results, click Finish on the Touchup Paint toolbar. Click Undo Last to undo the last brush stroke or Restore to restore the picture to its original brightness and contrast.

If Restore doesn't restore the picture to its original brightness and contrast, try clicking the Undo button on the Standard toolbar.

To match the brightness and contrast of one PhotoDraw object to another, hold Shift and click on both objects to select them. Drag the Brightness and Contrast sliders to the desired values.

Adjusting Tint

Objective PD2000.7.3 and 7.7

Tint works essentially the same way as Brightness and Contrast. Move the Hue slider to the desired tint and then adjust the amount of tint to be applied. If you'd like PhotoDraw to make those decisions for you, click the Automatic button and then click on an area of the picture that is supposed to be white or light gray. PhotoDraw will make the adjustments based on that color. You can also use Correct by Painting to change the tint in only one area of the picture.

Adjusting Hue and Saturation

Objective PD2000.7.8

Using Hue and Saturation on the Color menu, you can choose a color from the color wheel (values from –180 to 180) by moving the Hue slider and then determine how much of the color you want to apply and how dark you want it by adjusting the Saturation and Brightness sliders.

Colorizing an Object

Objective PD2000.6.6 and E.4.2

Colorizing applies variations of the same color to an object, giving it the appearance of having been dyed. Click Colorize on the Color menu and choose a color from the Color box. If you would like a different color, click the arrow button and choose from the available palettes. You can also use the Eyedropper to choose any color visible on the screen. Click the eyedropper and click the color you would like to apply. Use the Amount slider to adjust the amount of color that is applied.

Adjusting Color Balance

When you want to adjust the balance of a particular color in a picture, choose Color Balance from the Color workpane. Using Color Balance, you can adjust the specific colors without affecting others. For example, you can balance the amount of red and cyan without disturbing the amounts of magenta, green, yellow, and blue in a picture. Drag the sliders between –100 and 100 to make the desired adjustments.

Negative and Grayscale

Objective PD2000.2.4

The last two options on the Color menu, Negative and Grayscale, both have dramatic impact on a picture. Click the Negative button to turn a photo into a negative; click it again to restore the photo. Choosing Grayscale and clicking the Grayscale button removes all the color in a picture. It is not a toggle like Negative so clicking it again does not reapply the color. Use the Undo button on the Standard toolbar for an immediate reversal of the effect.

Hands On: Objective PD2000.2.4, 6.6, 7.1, 7.3, 7.7, 8.8, and PD2000E.5.1 and E.7.4

1. Insert a photo into a new picture. Adjust the brightness and contrast of the picture using the Automatic settings.
2. Insert a photo into another new picture. Adjust the brightness and contrast manually.
3. Re-size the photo in the second picture and drag the first photo into the second picture.
   a) Select both photos and match the brightness and contrast.
   b) Click on each picture to see the current brightness and contrast settings to verify that they are the same.
   c) Group the two photos together and adjust the tint automatically.
   d) Close this picture, saving it if you want to.
4. Activate the first picture.
   a) Correct the tint using Correct by Painting.
   b) Adjust the Hue and Saturation, making the colors darker and brighter.
5. Create a new picture by inserting a photo from clip art or your own digital camera or scanner.
   a) Colorize the picture using a color from a Custom palette.
   b) Apply a negative effect to the picture. Undo the negative affect.

Touching Up Photos

Objective PD2000.7.4, 7.5, and 7.6

Digital photos and other digital images occasionally need a little touch up to make them look their best. PhotoDraw has several tools to fix imperfections and improve their appearance.

Click the Touch Up button on the Visual toolbar to access the Touch Up tools. Here you'll find tools to fix red eye, remove dusts and spots, despeckle, and remove scratches. Click any of the first four choices on the menu to access the set of improvement tools, shown in Figure 12.24.

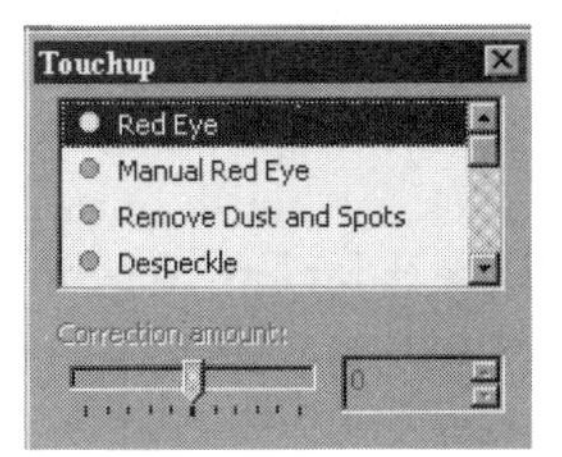

FIGURE 12.24 Digital images can be improved using PhotoDraw's Touchup tools

Fix Red Eye has two options, automatic and manual. Try the automatic tool first and, if PhotoDraw has a problem making the correction, you can try to fix it manually. Click the red portion of the eyes and click the Fix button on the Red Eye toolbar. After the Red Eye is fixed, use the Correction Amount slider to adjust the amount of the correction. If you have to fix Red Eye manually, zoom in so you have the eyes magnified. Click Manual Red Eye and drag around the eyes to select them. Click the Fix button.

Remove Dust and Spots cleans up a photo. Just click the spots on the object and click Finish.

Despeckle can help if the object is really dirty. Use the Despeckle slider to adjust the amount of despeckling you want to do. Be cautious because this option may reduce clarity in a photo or image.

Remove Scratch eliminates a scratch from a photo or image. Click at the beginning of a scratch and at the end of a scratch to remove it. Use the Scratch Width control to adjust the width of the scratch area.

Additional Touch Up Tools

Objective PD2000.7.9, and PD2000E.4.4, E.4.6, E.4.8, E.7.2

Three additional tools are available to touch up images. The first, Clone, helps when a portion of an image is unclear or when you want to cover up an area of a photo with another image. To use Clone, select it from the Touch Up menu. Select the density of the paint and choose a brush size. First, click the area you want to clone and then paint over the area you want cloned. Click Restore and drag back over the same area if you are not satisfied with the results.

Touchup tools are not limited to photos. Apply touch ups to clip art or any graphic image.

Smudge smears the colors in an image and can be used to blend edges in a picture. Choose Smudge from the Touch Up menu or from the Effects box on the Touchup workpane. Drag a brush over the area you want smudged and click the Finish button if you are happy with your work.

Erase Paint lets you choose the degree of transparency you want to apply when you erase part of an image. This creates some interesting effects if you want part of the image to recede to the background. To use Erase Paint, choose the degree of transparency you want to apply (the higher the number, the less visible the image is) and the brush you want use. Drag over the area you want to erase. To restore any part of the image, click the Restore button and drag over the image again. When you have erased as much as you want to, click Finish to close the tool.

Before applying any of the Touchup or Effects tools, save a copy of the picture – just in case the changes are not what you expect.

Hands On: Objective PD2000.7.4, 7.5, and 7.6, 7.9, E.4.4, E.4.6, E.4.8, 6.4, 6.7, E.7.2

1. Insert a photograph of a person or people into a new PhotoDraw picture from a digital camera or scanner.
   a) Fix the Red-eye in the photo (if you do not have a photo with red-eye, choose Help ➢ Tutorial and walk through the PhotoDraw tutorial on Enhancing Photos).
   b) Remove dusts and spots from the photo.
   c) Remove any scratches from the photo.
2. Insert a clip art object into a new picture.
   a) Use Clone to clone the object.
   b) Select a different brush and clone the object again. Compare the differences.

c) Using 25% transparency, apply Smudge to soften the edges of one of the cloned images.

d) Apply Erase Paint at 35% transparency to part of the original clip art.

Applying Special Effects

For those extra added touches, you'll find several special effects tools, shown in Figure 12.25, that change an image from something mundane into something out of the ordinary. Click Effects on the Visual toolbar to open the Effects menu. Each tool operates independently of the others so you have to select each tool from the Effects menu one at a time.

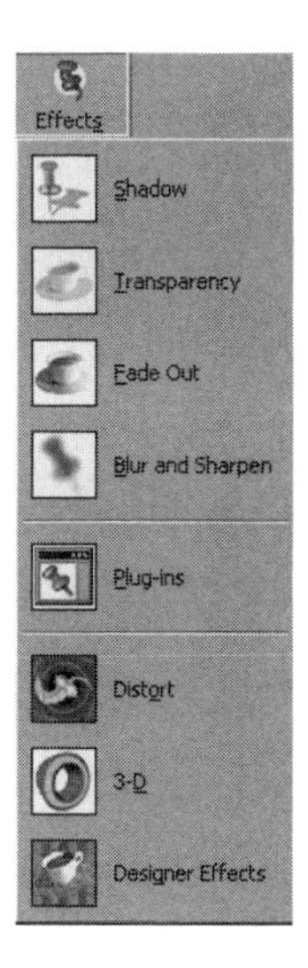

FIGURE 12.25 Effects tool change an ordinary photo into something special

The only way to get to know the Effects tools is to experiment with them until you find the right look. Select a tool from the Effects menu, adjust the settings in the workpane and watch the impact on the image. When you click a new option in the gallery, the effect is applied to the original image.

Applying Shadow, Transparency, and Fade Out Attributes

Objective PD2000.6.4

Shadow, shown in Figure 12.26, is the perfect tool for adding an attractive and interesting effect to an object. Click Shadow on the Effects toolbar to open the Shadow workpane. Click any one of the thirteen shadow choices.

FIGURE 12.26 Use shadow to add drama to an object.

If you want to change the position of the shadow, click the Shadow Position button to drag the shadow to a new location. You can also re-size the shadow if you would like to make it larger or smaller. Click Finish on the Shadow toolbar when you want to return to the Shadow workpane options.

To change the color of the shadow, click the down arrow next to the Color List or use the Eyedropper to capture a color from somewhere else. Use sliders to adjust the transparency of the shadow and to soften the shadow's lines.

Transparency and Fade Out are both features that lighten an image. Transparency lightens the entire image the same degree; fade out lightens the image gradually according to a defined shape. To access Transparency or Fade Out choose either option from the Effects menu—both options are available from the Transparency workpane.

To apply Transparency, move the slider or enter the desired percentage in the text box. To apply Fade Out, click Fade Out on the Transparency Workpane. Move the slider to adjust the Start and End settings as shown in Figure 12.27.

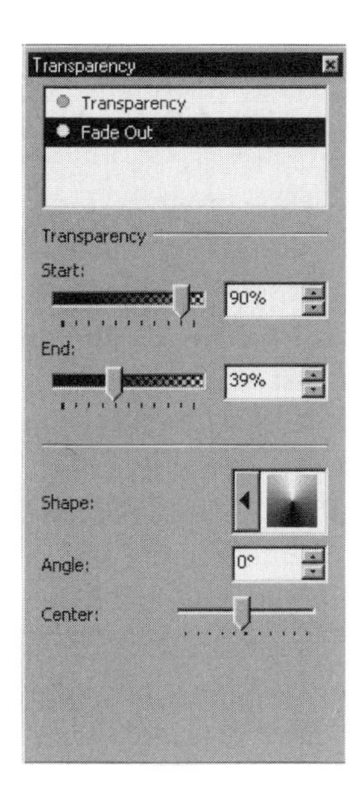

FIGURE 12.27 Move the sliders to adjust the Start and End settings of Fade Out

To change the shape of the Fade Out, click the Shape arrow and choose a shape from the gallery.

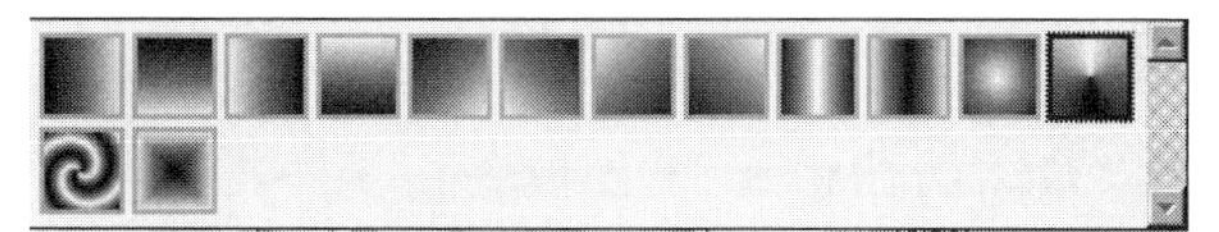

You can also adjust the angle of the Fade Out by entering a value between zero and 360 degrees in the Angle box. Drag the Center slider to change the center of the fade out.

Blurring and Sharpening Objects

Objective PD2000.6.7

Blur and Sharpen affects the focus of an object. Choose Blur and Sharpen from the Effects menu and adjust the slider from –100 (very blurry) to 100 (very sharp).

Applying a Plug-In Effect

Objective PD2000E.4.13

Plug-ins are programs from other manufacturers such as Adobe that enhance the functioning of PhotoDraw. They were designed to augment the functioning of programs such as PhotoDraw, adding different effects and tools to enhance photos and graphics. Before you can apply a plug-in effect, you must first have some on your system and direct PhotoDraw where to find them. Choose Tools ➢ Options and click the Plug-Ins tab of the Options dialog box. PhotoDraw knows to look in its default plug-in directory (...Microsoft Office\Office\PhotoDraw\PlugIns) but you can identify an additional directory for plug-ins you've stored.

To apply a plug-in effect, choose Effects ➢ Plug-Ins. Select the plug-in you want to use and click Launch. Because different plug-ins respond differently, follow the instructions that came with the plug-in to know how to apply each one effectively.

Plug-ins are available from many sources on the World Wide Web. One valuable source is `www.pluginsource.com`, or find out more about plug-ins at the Adobe Web site `www.adobe.com`.

Distorting an Object

Objective PD2000.6.9

The Distort tools include a number of interesting effects, as shown in Figure 12.28. Click an effect to apply it. If you want to adjust the amount and if applicable, frequency of an effect, click Settings on the Distort workpane.

Smearing, Bulging, or Shrinking a Portion of an Object

Objective PD2000E.4.5, E.4.7 and E.4.8

To distort only a portion of an object, choose Distort by Painting. You can smear paint or make a part of the picture bulge or shrink. Choose Smear, Bulge, or Shrink from the Distortion list and choose the brush you want to use from the Brush gallery. Click on the portion of the object you want to distort.

FIGURE 12.28
Use Distort to modify pictures in a number of interesting ways

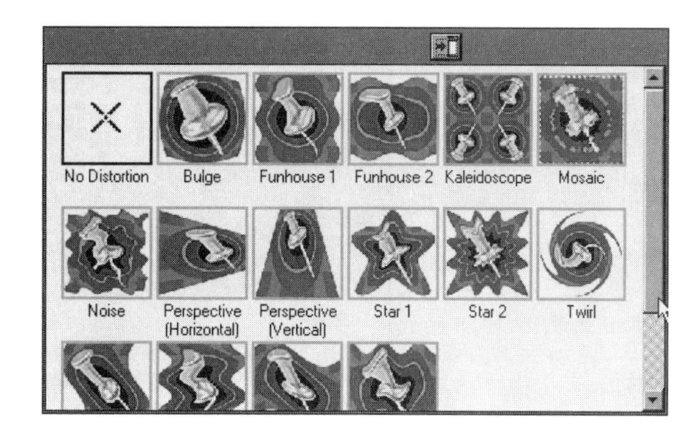

To apply a distortion effect by painting, click the mouse button repeatedly until you reach the desired degree of distortion.

If you want to reverse some, but not all, of the distortion you've applied, click the Restore button on the Distort by Painting toolbar and click on the portion of the object you originally distorted. To restore the object to its original condition, click Reset.

Applying Designer Effects

Objective PD2000.6.5, and PD2000E.4.3 and E.4.9

The Designer effects, shown in Figure 12.29, are categorized into 20 useful categories to help you narrow down the effect you want to apply. Click the Gallery Type arrow to select from the list of categories and then choose an effect from the list or click the Expand Gallery button to see all of the effects in a category.

Designer Effects let you lock an effect so you can layer one effect on top of another. Click Lock Effect and then apply an additional Designer Effect.

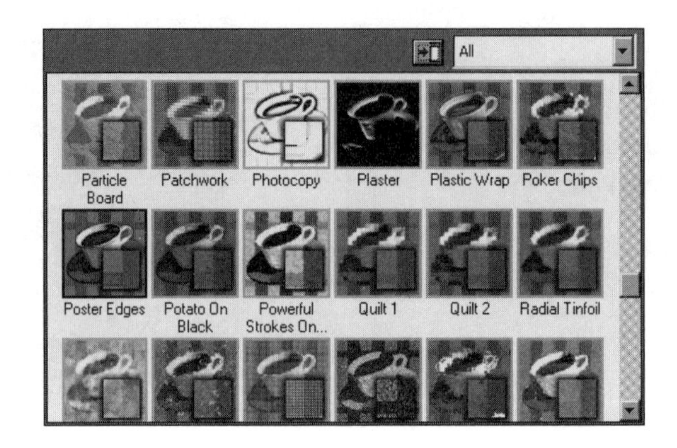

FIGURE 12.29 Click a preview to apply a Designer Effect from the gallery

To modify the settings of a particular effect, select the effect and choose Settings from the Designer Effects workpane. Here you can adjust Transparency, Edge Thickness, Edge Intensity, and Posterization.

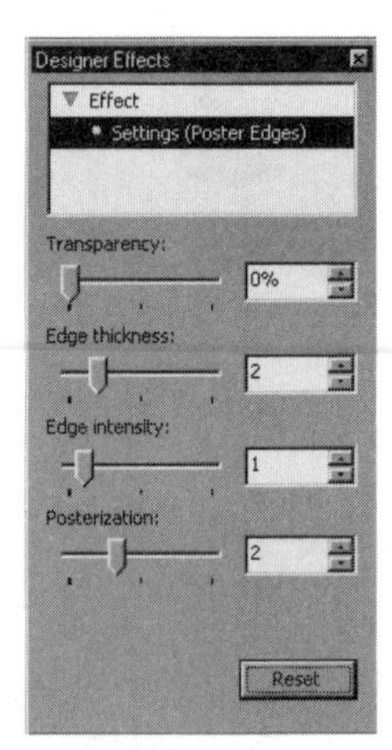

Hands On: Objectives PD2000.6.4, 6.5, 6.7, 6.9, PD2000.E.4.3, E.4.5, E.4.7, E.4.8, E.4.9, and E.4.13

1. Insert a piece of clip art into a new picture.
   a) Experiment with applying several different shadows to the object.
   b) Apply an 80% Start Transparency and a 25% End. Reverse the Fade Out and see if one looks better than the other.
   c) Change the Blur and Sharpen values to –49 and then to +49 to see the different effect.
   d) If you have access to a plug-in, apply the plug-in effect to the clip art. Insert a photo into a new picture and apply the plug-in effect to the photo.

2. Insert a photograph into a new picture.

   a) Experiment with several of the available Distortions until you find one you like.

   b) Smear a portion of the picture to accentuate it.

   c) Use Bulge and Shrink to the same portion of the picture to see the impact they have. (Remember to click multiple times to increase the bulging or shrinking.)

3. Create a new PhotoDraw picture using any tools you want.

   a) Save the picture before applying any effects.

   b) Experiment with several different Designer Effects, choosing a different one from at least five categories.

   c) When you find an effect you like, modify the settings to intensify and soften the effect.

   d) Save the picture again if you like the results or close it without saving.

Inserting and Designing Text Objects

Objective PD2000.3.1, 3.2, and 3.3

If you've worked with text boxes in PowerPoint or Publisher, you are already familiar with some of the text features of PhotoDraw. Click the Text Object button and choose Insert Text to open the Text workpane, shown in Figure 12.30.

Enter the text in the workpane window, not directly into the text object. Reposition the object by dragging it with the four-headed Move arrow. Select the text in the workpane to make any changes to it or to change text style or font.

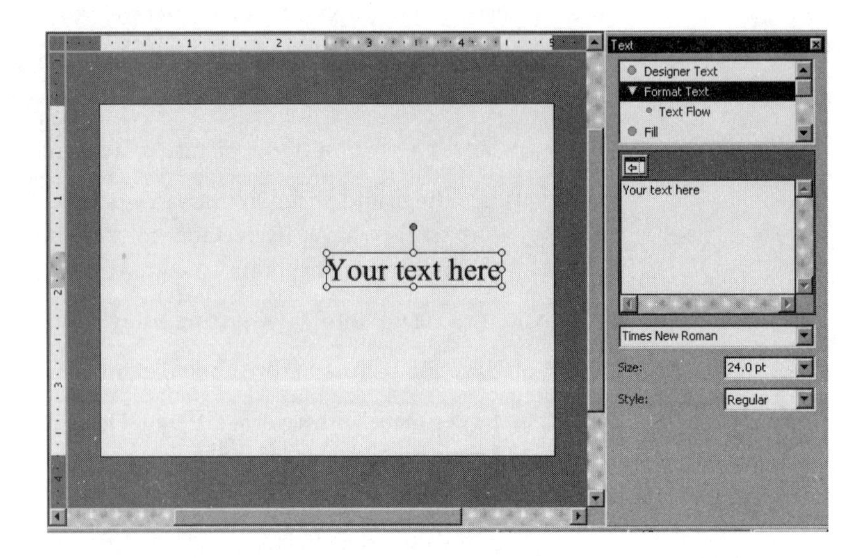

FIGURE 12.30 The Text workpane lets you customize text objects

Select from the following text object options:

Format Text—Change font, font size, and font style (Regular, Bold, Italic, or Bold Italic).

Text Flow—Change the alignment and orientation of the text.

Fill—Change the text color and transparency.

Bend Text—Choose from six different options for adding a curve to the text in the text box.

Outline—Apply different line styles or brushes to the text.

Stylizing Text

Objective PD2000.3.4

PhotoDraw is not limited to creating simple text objects. Using 3-D and Designer text, you can create fancy logos, mastheads, and other headings that make your text stand out from the crowd. To use 3-D and Designer text, you must first insert a text object. Format the text and make any changes to fill that you want to make.

Before applying any text effects, save the picture just in case you want to return to the original state.

To apply 3-D text, select the text and choose Text ➢ 3-D Text. Choose a 3-D style or click the Expand Gallery button to see all of the 3-D choices.

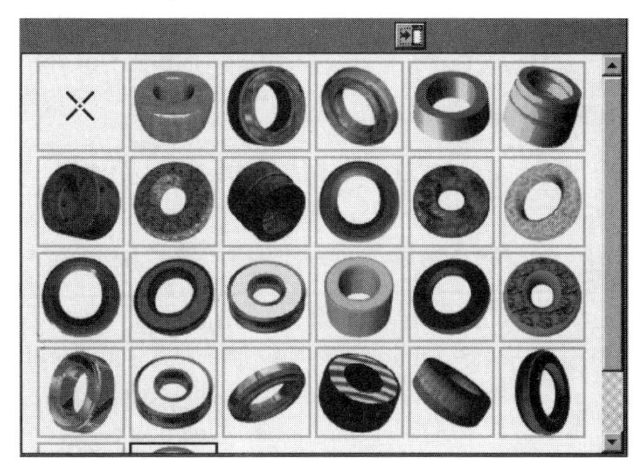

Choose the 3-D style you want and then wait a few seconds for PhotoDraw to apply the style.

Modifying 3-D Attributes of a 3-D Object

You can adjust the fill, rotation, tilt, beveling, extrusion, lighting, size, and position of the text object from the 3-D workpane.

Applying Fill

Objective PD2000E.3.1

Fill refers to the colors used in the object. Click Fill in the 3-D workpane to access the fill options.

Start by choosing the placement of the fill. 3-D objects have three possible placements: the face of the object, the bevel, and the sides. Click the placement you want the fill applied to. Fill can be applied to one or more placements at one time. Make sure the placements you do not want are not selected.

To select a fill, choose a fill from Solid Color, Texture, Designer Gradient, Two-Color Gradient, and Picture. If you choose a fill other than Solid Color, click the Expand Gallery button if you want to see the available fill options.

3-D effects can be applied to any object by selecting the object and choosing Effects ➢ 3-D.

If you aren't satisfied with any of the fill choices, you can use your own fill. Click the Browse button to locate a picture on a local or network drive.

Changing the Rotation and Tilt

Objective PD2000E.3.2 and E.3.3

Rotation and tilt are critical components of a 3-D style. By changing the rotation and tilt, you can create a completely customized 3-D object. Click Rotate and Tilt on the 3-D workpane to adjust these options.

Rotation changes the direction of the entire object, as shown in Figure 12.31. Enter a number between –360 and 360 to change the rotation of the object.

FIGURE 12.31

Rotate a text or other object from 0-360 degrees

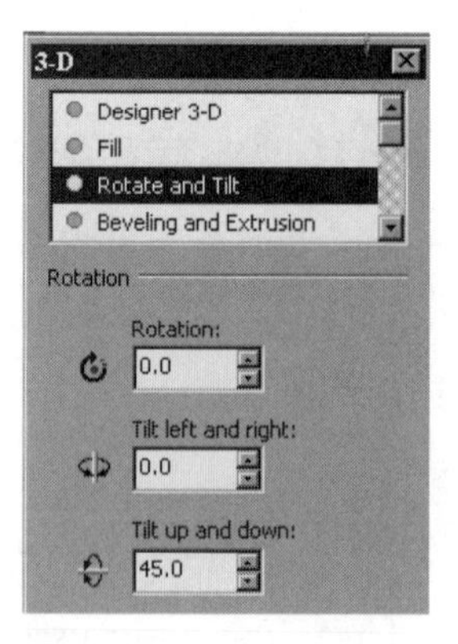

You can also rotate an object by dragging the yellow dot at the top of a selected object. The pointer changes to a 4-headed rotation arrow.

Tilt Left and Right and Tilt Up and Down change the actual shape of the object. Enter a number between –180 and 180 to change the tilt of an object.

Enter numbers rather than using the spin box controls on PhotoDraw text boxes to avoid re-drawing the object before you are ready.

Modifying the Beveling and Extrusion

Objective PD2000E.3.3 and E.3.5

Beveling and Extrusion refer to the depth of the sides of a 3-D object and how the sides connect to the face of the object. You can choose from a gallery of beveling styles by selecting Beveling and Extrusion from the 3-D workpane and clicking the Expand Gallery button under Bevel Style. After you select a style, you can change the Bevel Depth and Width and the Extrusion Depth by entering values between zero and 200.

Depending on the 3-D style and Bevel style you are using, the Bevel Depth and Width and the Extrusion Depth values may be more limited. If you enter an inappropriate value, a message appears giving you the available range.

Adjusting the Lighting of a 3-D Object

Objective PD2000E.3.6

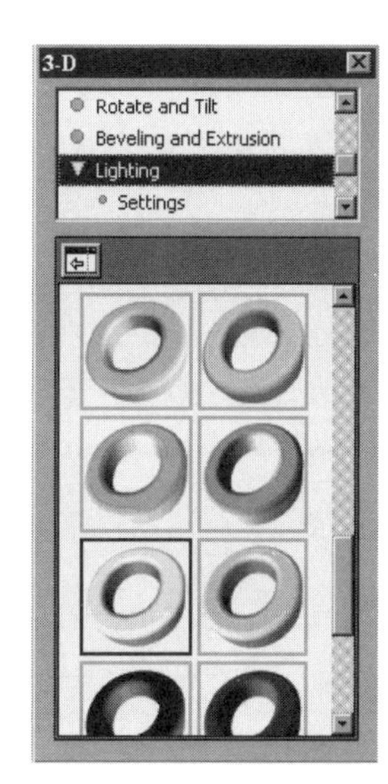

Lighting plays an important role with a 3-D object. It changes the focus of the object and makes it appear real. To change the lighting, select Lighting from the 3-D workpane and choose Settings to be able to access all of the lighting options.

Select the lighting style from the gallery and then change the direction of the light using the four pre-defined settings. If you want to change the color of the light, click a color or a color variation from the Active palette.

You can manually adjust lighting direction by entering new values between –180 and 180 in the Tilt Left and Right and Tilt Up and Down text boxes. To change the two-point perspective of the object, drag the slider left to bring the object closer and right to move it farther away.

Applying Designer Text Effects

If you are used to working with WordArt in the other Office applications, you'll find similarities with Designer Text. Designer Text gives you a choice of a number of predefined text effects that you can apply to your text objects. To use Designer Text, insert a text object into a picture. Choose Designer Text, either from the Text workpane or from the Text visual menu. Click the style you would like to apply.

Hands On: *Objective PD2000.3.1-3.4, and PD2000E.3.1-3.6*

1. Insert text into a picture.
   a) Reformat the text making it bold and italics.
   b) Pick a different font and change the font size.
   c) Apply a Bend effect to the text.
   d) Save the picture.
2. Insert text into another picture.
   a) Apply a 3-D style to the text object.
   b) Change the Fill color of the face of the object.
   c) Change the Fill color of the bevel.
   d) Choose a new bevel style.
   e) Increase the extrusion of the object.
   f) Save the picture.
3. Insert another text object into the picture you created in Exercise 1.
   a) Rotate the object –50 degrees.
   b) Tilt the object left and right by 15 degrees.
   c) Return the object to its original tilt settings.

Using Templates

Now that you know the basics of working in PhotoDraw, you might want to explore the many templates that come with the program. Choose File ➢ New Template to access the five categories of templates:

- Web Graphics
- Business Graphics
- Cards
- Designer Edges
- Designer Clip Art

Select the category from the drop-down list on the Templates workpane and then choose a style for that category. Figure 12.32 shows the styles available for the Business Graphics category.

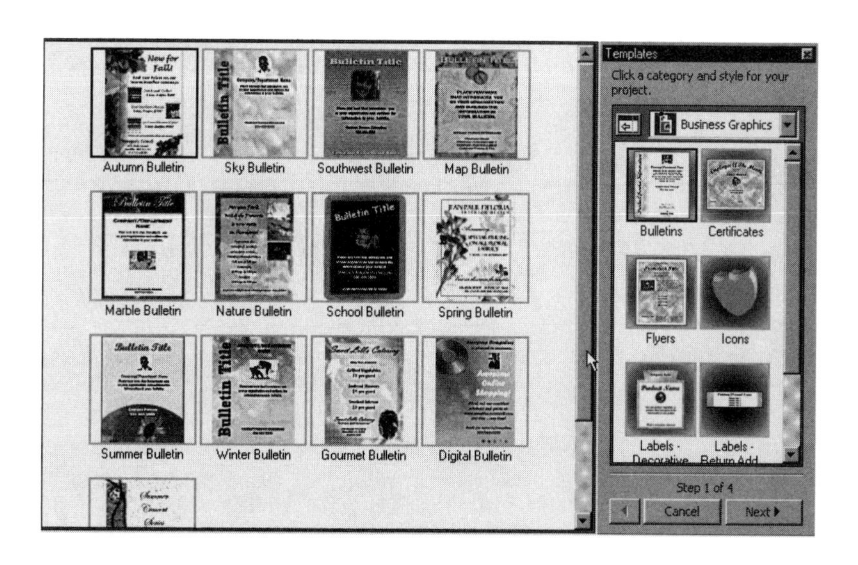

FIGURE 12.32 PhotoDraw comes with a number of templates in five different categories

Once you have chosen the style you want, follow the steps in the Templates workpane to customize the template. After you click the Finish button, you are free to customize the picture any way you want. You might want to save it first just to be on the safe side.

Many of the templates are available on PhotoDraw Disk 2. To access these templates, make sure PhotoDraw knows where to look for Disk 2. Choose Tools ➢ Options and click the File Locations tab. If you've copied Disk 2 to a drive, enter or browse for the path to the drive location. If you're using the CD-ROM directly, enter the path to the CD-ROM drive and click the Prompt to Insert PhotoDraw Disk 2 checkbox.

Creating Graphics for the Web

Objective PD2000.1.1

Creating custom navigation buttons and banners for a Web site has never been easier. PhotoDraw provides a variety of Web button and banner templates to get you started. Choose the Web Graphics category in the Templates workpane and select Banners, Circular Buttons, Connecting Buttons, Festive Buttons, or Rectangular Buttons to view the options shown in Figure 12.33. Scroll through the button options and when you find one you like, click to select it, and click the Next button at the bottom of the Templates workpane.

FIGURE 12.33 To create a button, select a button style from one of the four types of Web buttons

Objective PD2000.1.2

In the second step of the Wizard, shown in Figure 12.34, you can replace the graphic image of the banner or button with a graphic of your choosing. If the image you want to use is open, click the Replace button on the Templates workpane. Click the image you want to use and then click on the banner or button. The saved image replaces the existing template image. If the image you want to use is not open, click the Browse button, locate the image and click Open in the Browse window. This closes the Browse dialog box and replaces the image with the saved image.

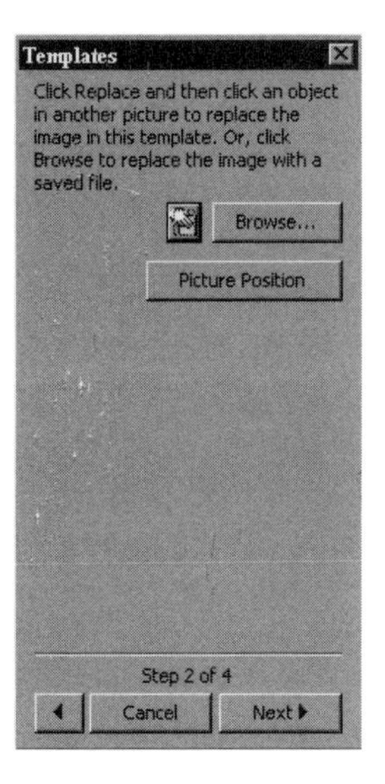

FIGURE 12.34 Replace the template graphic with one of your own choosing, by clicking Replace or Browse

If the image is larger than the banner or button, it is cropped to fit the picture area. To reposition the image to display a different part of it in the button, click Picture Position and drag the image to focus on the section you are interested in displaying. Click Finish to continue with the template steps. Click the Next button to move to Step 3.

Step 3 lets you edit the text and change the font and font style used on the button or banner. Enter the text you want in the text box on the Template workpane. Change the Font, Size, and Style for the text.

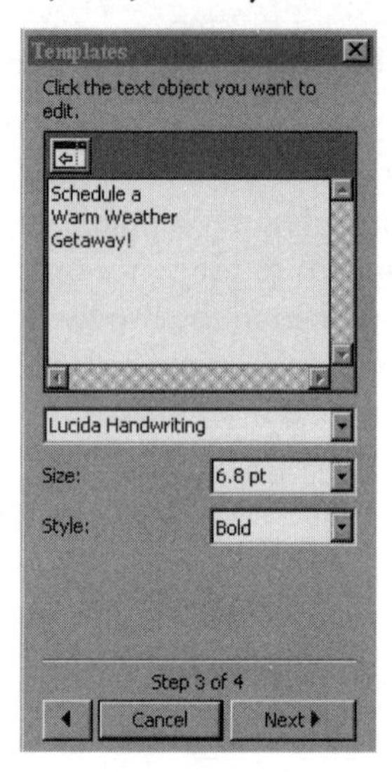

Click Next and Finish to complete the banner or button. You can still edit the image and text by selecting the image or double-clicking the text box.

Objective PD2000E.1.1

To apply a Designer Edge to a Web button template, click Effects ➢ Designer Effects, and choose Accented Edges. Click Settings in the Designer Effects workpane to adjust the Transparency, Edge Width, Edge Brightness, and Smoothness.

Create a Custom Clip Art Image

Objective PD2000E.1.2

If you've ever been frustrated because you couldn't find the perfect clip art image, PhotoDraw's Designer Clip Art feature is for you. You can select from a variety of basic shapes and then customize it and combine multiple shapes to meet your needs. To select a shape, choose File ➢ New Template. When the Templates workpane opens, choose Designer Clip Art from the list of available categories. Figure 12.35 shows you some of the 12 categories of Designer Clip Art you can choose from.

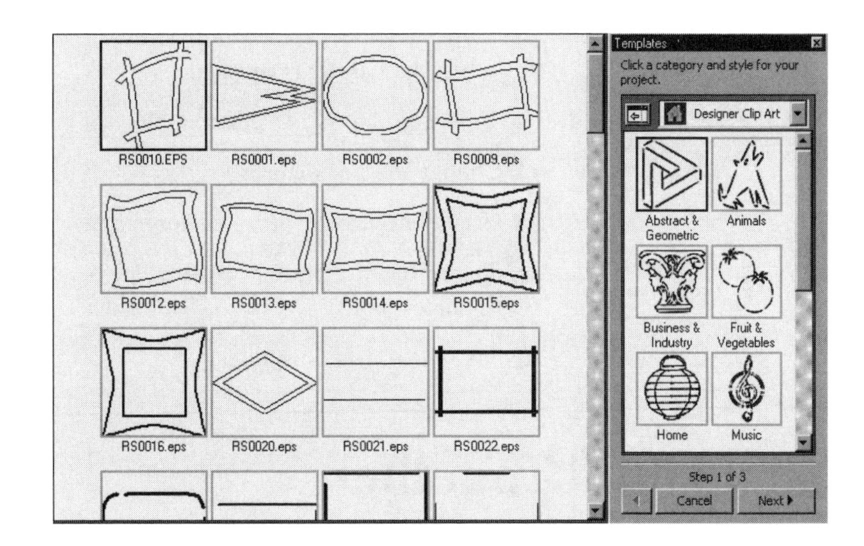

FIGURE 12.35 Choose from 12 categories of Designer Clip Art to start your project

Choose the shape you want to start with and click Next. In the second step, you can change the line or brush style, line width, and color used in the clip—you cannot add anything new to the clip at this point, only change the lines that already exist. Click next and Finish to finish the project.

Now that you have a design, you can add another piece of designer clip art by choosing File ➢New Template and repeating the process or you can customize the piece you just created. All of the PhotoDraw tools, such as Text, Cut, Crop, Draw, and Paint are at your disposal.

Hands On: *Objective PD2000.1.1, 1.2 and PD2000E.1.2*

1. Create a Home button to use on a Web site using a button template.
2. Create a series of four connecting buttons to identify the major sections of a Web site. These might include, for example, Home, What's New, Products, and About Us.
3. Use a banner template to create a Web banner.

a) Replace the existing graphic with a graphic you saved previously.

b) Use Picture Position to reposition the graphic you inserted.

c) Change the font and font size of the text.

d) When the banner is finished, save it.

4. Use Designer Clip Art to create a piece of custom clip art.

a) Change the line or brush style of the clip art.

b) Use PhotoDraw tools to customize the clip art.

c) Create another piece of custom clip art and then combine it with the first piece.

d) Save the finished product.

Pulling It All Together

PhotoDraw is an exciting new product with plenty of useful features and a wagon full of toys. With a little exploration and experimentation, you're sure to find the right combination to design the perfect picture. Remember to save your work in progress and you may even want to save different versions of it along the way in case you want to go back to a previous rendition.

If you find you need some addition help, Microsoft's sure to be posting PhotoDraw tips and troubleshooting help on its Web site. You may even find some additional graphics and templates free for the downloading. Click Help ➢ PhotoDraw on the Web to get there. Good luck and happy composing!

CHAPTER 13

Internet Publishing with Office 2000

Your supervisor has just asked you to create a series of Web pages for your corporate intranet. If you haven't created Web pages but have heard the lunchroom rumors about HTML, this new assignment can be pretty intimidating. Fear no more. Office 2000 is designed to put your anxiety to rest. All you need to do is add a few new skills to your bag of tricks, and you'll be producing dazzling pages in no time.

Creating Web Pages in Word

Word 2000 provides three ways to create Web pages:

- Using the Web Page Wizard
- Applying a Web template
- Converting an existing Word document

The Web Page Wizard not only creates Web pages but actually creates full Webs; collections of pages with links between them. If the project you are undertaking involves multiple documents, the Web Page Wizard is generally the best choice because it creates links for you and gives your pages a consistent look and feel. If you are providing content to your corporate intranet and you've been given a template to use, you may want to apply the template directly or convert an existing document without going through the Wizard. However, after you use the Wizard, you'll find it's a great tool whatever your goal.

Creating Web Pages Using the Web Page Wizard

The Web Page Wizard can create single pages or entire Webs. If you want to create more than one page, it's a good idea to draw up the layout of your

Web before you start the Wizard. You'll want to know the names of as many pages as possible so the Wizard can create the links between them. If you have existing documents you want to include in the Web, be sure to know their names and where to locate them. The Wizard isn't included in the Typical Office installation, but can be automatically installed on demand, so make sure you have access to the CD-ROM or network drive from which Office was installed.

When you are ready to create your Web pages, click File ➢ New. Click the Web Pages tab in the New dialog box and select Web Page Wizard. Click OK to start the Wizard and next to move on to the first step.

The Title and Location page, as shown in Figure 13.1, determines the official title of your Web. Although it can be changed later, it's important to give your Web a descriptive title because the various Web search engines use the site's title when they search for a site on the Internet. A good title could mean the difference between someone finding your site or not.

By default, the Wizard creates a new folder for your Web, so if you change the location be sure you change it to an empty folder. The Wizard creates additional subfolders for storing graphics and other supporting files, but the main pages are stored in the folder that you specify. If you don't designate a unique folder, your Web files will get mixed in with unrelated documents, making it difficult to manage the Web effectively. Enter the title and location and click Next.

FIGURE 13.1
Title and Location

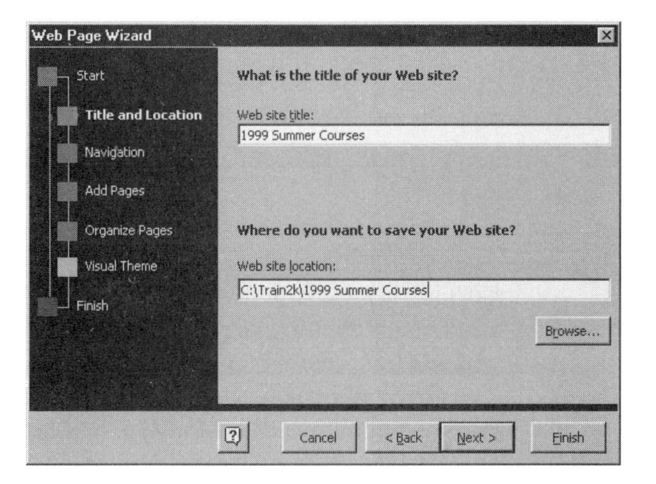

Using Frames for Navigation

The Web Page Wizard offers three choices (as shown in Figure 13.2) for the layout of your pages:

- A vertical frame runs down the left side of the page and contains links to the other pages in the Web.
- A horizontal frame is positioned across the top of the page and contains links to the other pages in the Web.
- The separate page option doesn't use frames; instead each page opens in a full window. Forward and Back buttons and appropriate links are added to the pages.

Choose the Navigation option you prefer and click Next.

FIGURE 13.2 Navigation types

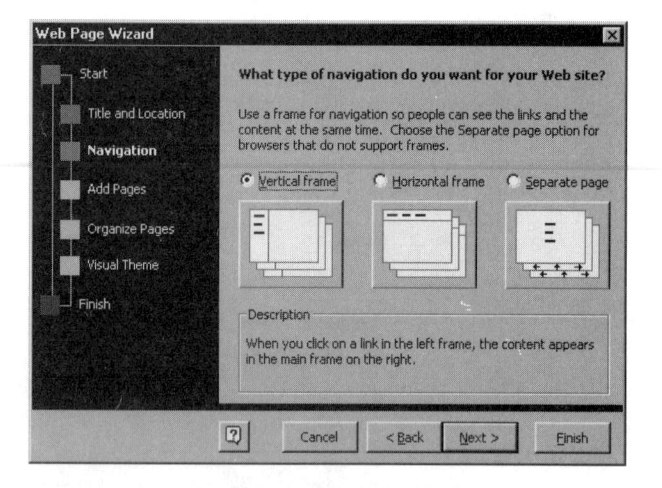

Not all browsers support frames, and text readers, used by people with vision impairments, can't read pages with frames. Many Web developers who use frames also offer visitors a no-frame alternative on the site's Welcome page, but if you can only choose one layout, choose the Separate Page option for the widest range of accessibility.

Differentiating Text Frames from Web Frames You may already be familiar with text frames for positioning text on a page. Text frames are used extensively in PowerPoint, in Publisher, and can be used in Word and Excel to position a block of text outside of the normal paragraphs or cells. Web frames also may contain text, but their primary purpose is to organize content on a Web page. Web frames typically appear on the top or left of a page and include navigational links that remain visible even when the visitor moves to a different page of your Web. See *Working with Frames,* later in this chapter for more information.

Adding Pages

A Web created by the Web Page Wizard comes with three pages: a Personal Web Page and two blank pages. The Personal Web Page is a template that includes sections for work information, favorite links, contact information, current projects, biographical information, and personal interests. If you are not creating a personal Web with you as the focus, you can delete this page by selecting it and clicking Remove Page. The first blank page moves into position as the new home page for your Web.

The home page is typically the first page a visitor sees when they visit a Web site, but it may be preceded by a Welcome page that gives visitors options such as no frames or no graphics.

If you want to add additional pages to your Web, now is the best time to do so. As shown in Figure 13.3, you can add a new blank page, add a page based on a template, or insert an existing document into the Web. To add a blank page, click the Add New Blank Page button, and the new page appears at the bottom of the list (you are given the option to re-name pages in the next step of the Wizard).

Using Templates Word includes seven Web page templates. Some of these templates give you specific page layouts, such as the Left-Aligned Column and Right-Aligned Column templates. Others provide a structure for Web content, such as the Frequently Asked Questions and Table of Contents templates. To review each template, click the Add Template Page button in the Add Pages step. This opens the dialog box and preview window (see Figure 13.4). Click any of the templates in the Web Page Template dialog box to see a full-page view of the template. When you have chosen the template you want to include in your Web, click OK. If you'd like to add another template page, click Add Template Page again and repeat the process.

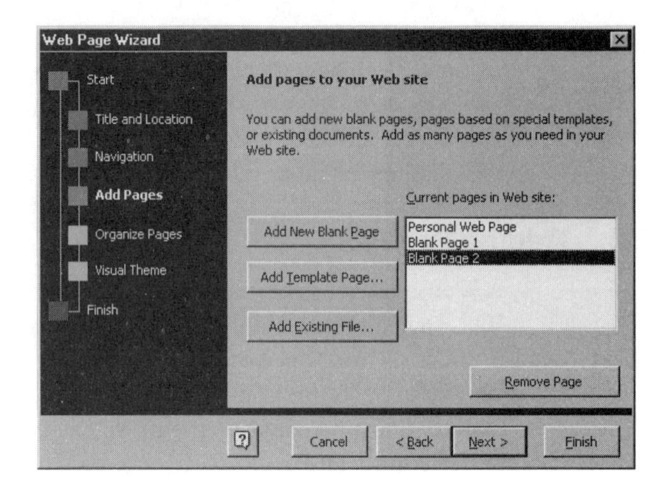

FIGURE 13.3
Add Pages step of the Web Page Wizard

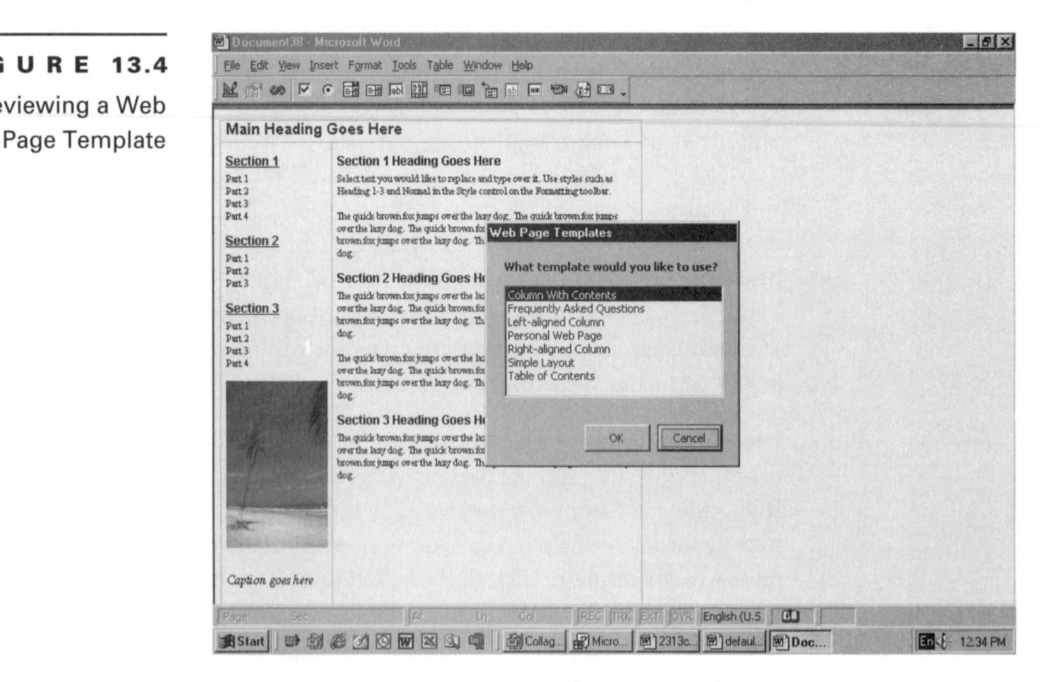

FIGURE 13.4
Previewing a Web Page Template

Adding Existing Documents If you would like to convert any existing documents and add them to your Web, click the Add Existing File button in the Add Pages step. Locate and double-click a file you would like to include.

The Wizard saves a copy of the file as HTML and includes it in the Web folder. Repeat the process to add additional documents.

If you try to add an HTML page created in FrontPage 2000, or a page created in Excel or Access that uses the Office Web Components, it opens in its native application instead of being added in the Wizard. When you have finished adding pages, click Next to move on to the Organize Pages step of the Wizard.

When you insert a file in the Wizard, it is added as a single page, even if it's a multi-page document. If you have a document that you want to include as several individual pages, use copy and paste to create and save a separate Word document for each page, before launching the Wizard, then insert each document.

Organizing the Links

Now that you have the pages in your Web, you can re-name each page and change their relative order as shown in Figure 13.5. This order determines the order of the links. Use the Move Up and Move Down buttons to rearrange the pages and the Rename button to change a page's name. Click Next to move on to the next step.

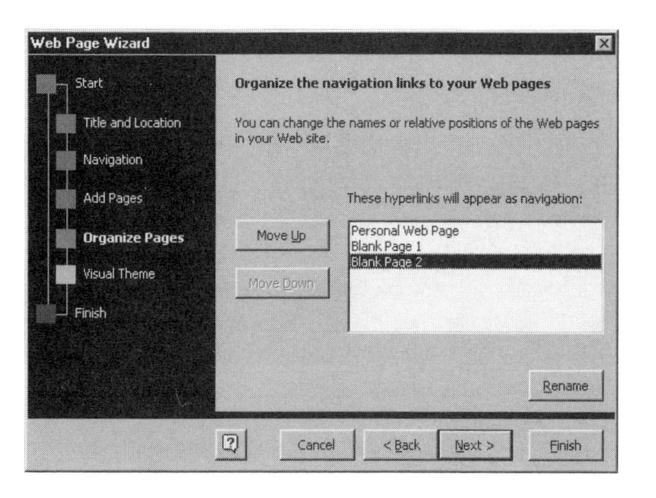

FIGURE 13.5 Putting the Web pages in order.

Applying Themes

A theme is a collection of colors, fonts, graphics, backgrounds, bullet characters, and styles that fit together. Office includes over 60 themes that can be applied to print publications, online documents, and Web pages. To select a theme, click the Browse Themes button in the Visual Theme step of the Web Page Wizard.

The Theme dialog box, shown in Figure 13.6, displays a preview of each theme listed on the left. Options for Active Graphics (typically appearing as animated bullets and horizontal lines) and Background Image are on by default. If you would also like to use Vivid Colors, click the check box. You can see the results of turning these options on or off in the preview window on the right, although you won't see active graphics actually move.

Once you decide on a theme (you can also choose No Theme from the top of the list), click OK. If you decide to use a theme, make sure Add a Visual Theme is selected on the Visual Theme step of the Wizard.

FIGURE 13.6
Web themes

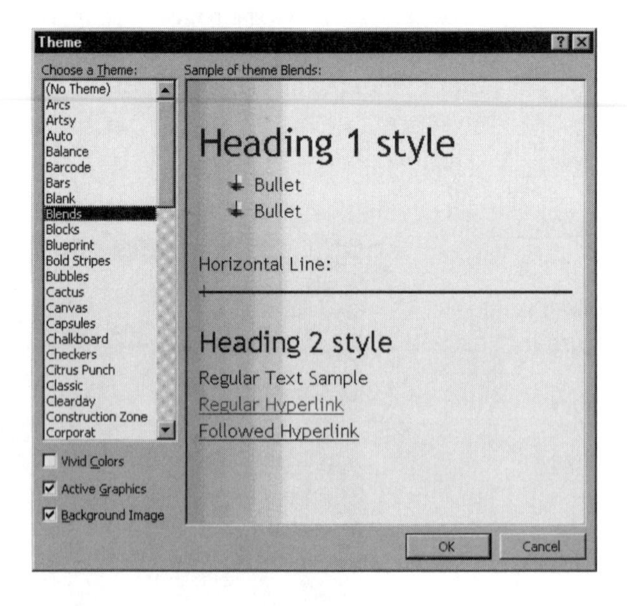

Click Next to move to the last step of the Wizard, and then click Finish. The Wizard creates your Web pages, adds the links you specified, and saves the pages to the folder you chose.

Creating a Web using the Wizard

1. Click File ➢ New and choose the Web Pages tab of the New dialog box.
2. Select Web Page Wizard and click OK to begin.
3. Click Next to move past the Start step of the Wizard to the Title and Location step. Enter a descriptive name and choose a file location for your Web.
4. At the Navigation step, choose a frame style.
5. Add blank pages, pages based on a template, or pages from existing files at the Add Pages step. Remove pages you don't want.
6. At the Organize Pages step, use the Move Up and Move Down buttons to put your pages in an order that makes sense. Re-name pages if you wish by clicking the Rename button and typing the new name. When you're finished with this step, click Next.
7. Browse to choose a visual theme for your page or choose the No Visual Theme option.
8. Use the back button to return to any step of the Wizard and make changes or Click Next and then Finish.

Exploring Web Files In addition to the Web pages, the Web Page Wizard creates additional folders and files for your Web. To view these, open the folder in My Computer or Windows Explorer, as shown below.

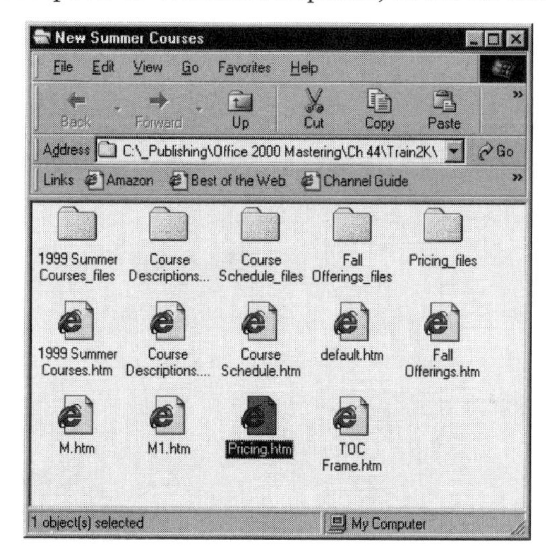

You may notice a number of subfolders and files that aren't familiar to you. `Default.htm` is the file name the Wizard automatically assigns to the first or home page of the Web (the home page of a Web that is published on a Web server is `index.htm`). The Wizard creates a subfolder for each page and uses it to house graphics and other objects related to the page. For example, when you insert a graphic on a page and save the page, Word automatically saves the graphic to the page's corresponding subfolder. Graphics and other objects are not saved as part of a Web page but rather are saved separately and linked to the page. This is standard Web design protocol and helps keep the myriad of individual files streamlined and organized.

Viewing Your Web

After the Web Page Wizard finishes its job, it opens the home page in Word. If you used frames in your Web site, the Frames toolbar opens (see more about frames in *Working with Frames* later in this chapter). The home page contains navigation links to other pages in the Web either in frames (as shown in Figure 13.7) or at the top the page if you choose the Separate Page option.

FIGURE 13.7

Home Page

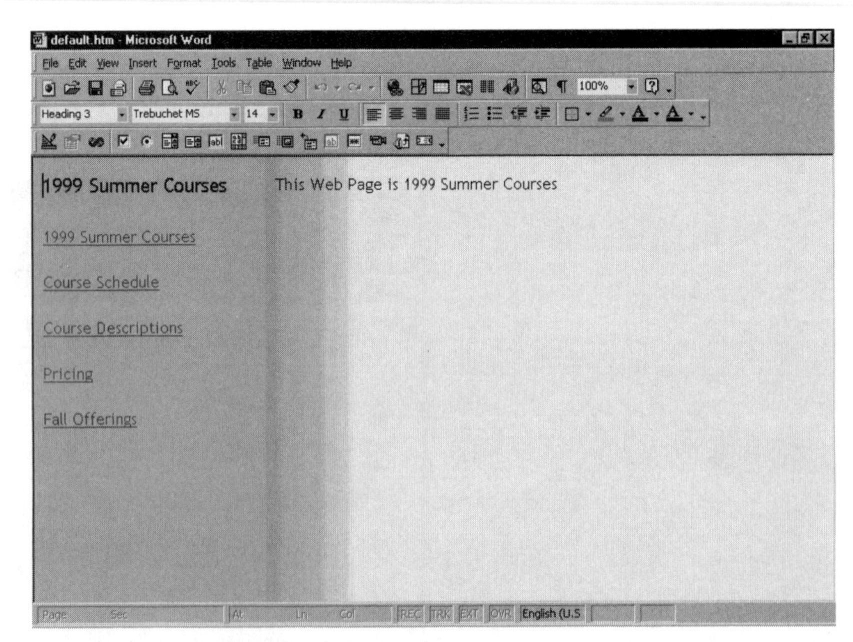

To view the other pages of the Web, point to any of the navigation links. The pointer changes to a hand and provides a screen tip about the file location of the hyperlink. Click the hyperlink to open the page. When the page opens, the Web toolbar, shown in Figure 13.8, also opens.

FIGURE 13.8
The Web toolbar

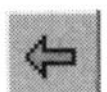

The Web toolbar is the standard Internet Explorer browser toolbar. Click the Back button to return to the home page.

Creating a Web with Page Wizard

1. Use the Web Page Wizard to create a Web.
   a. Give your Web a descriptive name. If you don't want to use the default, browse to select a location for your Web.
   b. Use a vertical frame.
   c. Remove the Personal Web Page and add three new pages: one blank, one with a template, and one from an existing file.
   d. Organize the pages in an order that makes sense. Re-name at least one page.
   e. Select a theme for your page.
2. When you finish the Wizard, browse the Web page by clicking the various links.

Creating a Web Page from Scratch

To begin a Word document for the Web from scratch, choose File ➢ New and select Web Page from the New dialog box.

You now have access to all of Word's editing and formatting features to help you create your Web page. In addition, you can add themes by choosing Format ➢ Theme, Hyperlinks by selecting text, and choosing Edit ➢ Hyperlink and Frames by choosing Format ➢Frames. Frames and hyperlinks are covered in-depth later in this chapter.

Adding Content to a Web Page

Editing Web pages in Word is not much different than editing other Word documents. You have access to all of Word's formatting and editing tools, including fonts, paragraph formatting, bullets, tables and borders, and shading. Although overall, you will find Word's HTML tools to be consistent with the typical Word features you are used to using, there are some minor HTML restrictions.

Web pages also include features that are not typically used in print documents: hyperlinks, frames, form controls, active graphics such as scrolling text boxes, and other special multimedia features. If you learn to use these tools effectively, you'll be able to design Web pages that are dynamic, attractive, and effective.

Saving and Reopening a Web

Objective W2000.4.6

If you create a Web using the Web Page Wizard, the Wizard automatically saves the Web pages and associated files. After you make changes to any of the pages, click the Save button or choose File ➢ Save to re-save the files just like you would any other document. When you start a Web page with a Web template, you can also save just as you would any other document.

Convert an existing document to a Web page by opening it and choosing File ➢ Save As Web Page. Select a location for your file, change its title if you wish, and click Save. If Word has to reformat existing objects, borders, shading, etc., you may be prompted to complete the conversion. After the document is saved as a Web page, you can reformat it, add a theme, and insert frames as desired.

When you re-open a Web, you can choose to open individual pages for editing or the entire Web. If you use frames, you can open each page displayed in the frames separately or open the page that contains all of the frame pages. To make changes to the structure of the frames page, open the file `TOC Frame.htm` (see more about working with frames later in this chapter). To open the home page, open the file called `default.htm`.

Saving a Web Page in Word

1. If you're converting a regular Word document to a Web page, Choose File ➢ Save As Web Page.
2. Open the folder (or create a new folder) where you want to save your Web page.
3. Enter a title for the Web page, if desired.
4. Enter a filename and click Save.
5. If you created your Web using a Wizard or Template, Word automatically saves the pages in HTML format. Simply re-save when you make changes by clicking the Save button on the Standard toolbar.

Round Tripping a Document from HTML

Objective W2000E.7.6

In Word 2000, you can create, save, and edit HTML documents without having to convert them to Word's native format. When you save a Word document as a Web page, you can open the document in your Web browser just like any other Web document. You can also open this HTML document directly in Word for editing and updating. This process of saving a Web page in Word and then re-opening it in Word for editing is called *round tripping*. Round tripping makes it easy to make changes to a Web page posted on a corporate Web server without requiring users to learn another Web page editing tool.

Creating Hyperlinks

Objective W2000.4.8

Hyperlinks are what make the Web what it is. When Tim Berners-Lee, CERN researcher, developed HTML, his primary interest was in being able to access related documents easily, without regard to computer platform or operating system, by connecting the documents through a series of links. Hyperlinks allow readers to pursue their areas of interest without having to wade through tons of materials searching for specific topics. And hyperlinks take readers down paths they might never have traveled without the ease of clicking a mouse. Adding hyperlinks to your documents moves information down off the shelf, dusts it off, and makes it a living, breathing instrument that people can really use.

Creating a hyperlink in an existing Web page is easy. First you'll enter or select some descriptive text anywhere in the page to define the link; for example, you could type, "Click here to view new courses" or select the existing text that says "New Courses." Then right-click the selected text, and choose Hyperlink to open the Insert Hyperlink dialog box, as shown in Figure 13.9. If you prefer, you can select the text and press **Ctrl+K** or Insert ➢ Hyperlink.

In the Insert Hyperlink dialog box, type a file or Web page name or click the File or Web Page buttons to Browse for the file. Click the Place in this Document button to create a link to another location in the same document, or click the e-mail Address button to create a link to an e-mail message form. If you want to change the hyperlink text, enter new text in the Text To Display box. Add a screen tip to the hyperlink by clicking the Screen Tip button and entering the text you want to appear in a screen tip. Click OK to create the link.

For more about creating hyperlinks and bookmarks in Word documents, refer to Chapter 4.

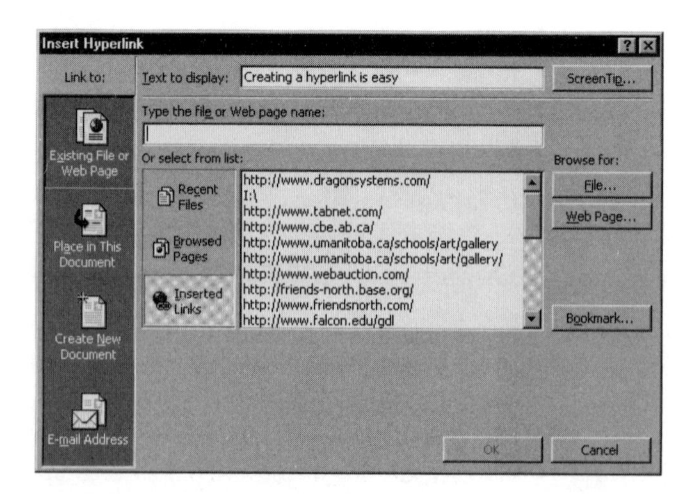

FIGURE 13.9 Insert Hyperlink dialog box.

Word automatically creates a hyperlink when you type an address it recognizes as an Internet or file path address. If, for example, you type `www.train2k.com`, Word creates a hyperlink to that address. To turn hyperlink automatic formatting on or off, choose Tools ➢ AutoCorrect. Click AutoFormat As You Type and check or clear the Internet and Network Paths with Hyperlinks check box. Check or clear the same check box on the AutoFormat tab.

Creating a Hyperlink to a Web Page or File

1. Enter and select text that will serve as the hyperlink.
2. Right-click the selected text or Choose Insert ➢ Hyperlink to open the Insert Hyperlink dialog box.
3. Choose a file, Web page, bookmark, or other existing document for the link by using the Insert Hyperlink dialog box options. After entering or selecting the filename and path, click OK to establish the link.

OR

3. To link to a page on the Web, enter the URL for the file. To locate the page, click the Browse for Web Page button, then click the Search the Web button to open the Link to File dialog box. Your default browser loads and opens a search engine at `http://www.microsoft.com`.
4. Use the search engine, Favorites list, bookmarks, or another search engine to go to the Web page you wish to link to.
5. Switch back to Word.
6. Click OK to create the link.

Troubleshooting Hyperlinks A hyperlink's effectiveness depends on its being able to locate the file or Internet address it is linked to. If the file has moved or been re-named, or the Web address no longer exists, clicking the hyperlink returns an error message. It's important to regularly verify hyperlinks you've included in your site. If a link does not work, check the following:

1. Do you currently have access to the Internet or an intranet site the link is calling? If not, check the link again when access has been restored.

2. Has the site or file moved? If so, right-click the link and choose Edit ➢ Hyperlink. Update the location of the linked file.
3. Does the file still exist? If not, right-click the link and choose Edit ➢ Hyperlink. Click Remove Link.

If the link still does not work after you have followed these steps, make sure the address is spelled correctly and there are no syntax errors in the address (for example, a comma instead of a dot).

If Edit Hyperlink does not appear on the shortcut menu when you right-click, it could be because the text contains a spelling or grammar error. Word displays the Spelling shortcut menu until the error is corrected.

Inserting Graphics Visitors to a Web site expect to see more than just text. Graphics add impact to your Web pages, as long as they are fast-loading. Fast-loading graphics add impact to your Web pages.

Inserting a graphic into a Web page is no different than placing one in a Word document. The Clip Gallery is available from the Insert menu; from the gallery, you can choose art or any other clipart or photos you want to use (for more about inserting graphics, see Chapter 5).

Not all graphics features available in Word are supported by Web browsers. To assure that your Web pages look as good being viewed by a browser as they do in Word, features that are unsupported have been disabled. For example, only some of the text wrapping styles available in Word documents are available for use in Web pages. As a result, you may find that once you've inserted a graphic, you have difficulty positioning it where you want it. To change how text wraps around the picture so you can more easily place the graphic where you want it, right-click the graphic and choose Format Picture or choose Format ➢ Picture from the menu. Click the Layout tab and change the Wrapping Style, as shown in Figure 13.10.

A number of other options are available in the Format Picture dialog box. Because not all browsers can display graphics, and some people don't want to wait for graphics to appear on Web pages, it's possible to insert alternative text that describes the graphic. When the Web page opens, the alternative text appears while the page is loading, allowing visitors to click when they find the text they want without waiting for the graphic. To specify alternative text, click the Web tab of the Format Picture dialog box.

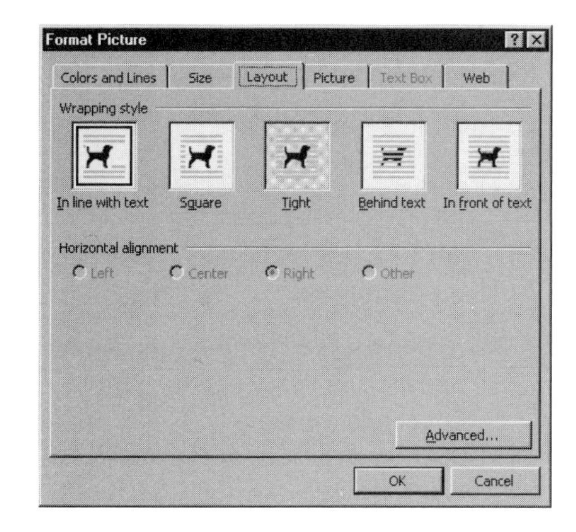

FIGURE 13.10 Changing wrapping style

Troubleshooting Graphics If you are having trouble positioning graphics on a Web page, you might want to try a Web designer's trick. Insert a table into the page. Three columns are usually sufficient, but add more columns if you want to line up a series of graphics. Then, position the graphic inside a cell of the table and change the table properties so the table expands to fill the screen:

1. Click inside the table and choose Table ➢ Table Properties.
2. Click the Table tab and change Preferred Width to 100% Measured in Percent. (Although this step is not necessary, it makes it easier if you aren't sure about precise placement and sizing.) Click OK.
3. Now place the graphic inside the cell of the table that corresponds to the position you would like for the graphic. Click the Center button on the Formatting toolbar to center the graphic in the cell.

Before publishing the Web page, you can change the table's borders to No Borders. To do this, select the table, choose Format ➢ Borders and Shading, click the Borders tab, and click None. Your table won't be visible on the page, but the graphics stay where you put them.

Web Tools Toolbar Word comes equipped with a Web Tools toolbar, shown in Figure 13.11, to help you add sounds and video, create forms, and add scrolling text. To turn on the Web Tools toolbar, choose View ➢ Toolbar and click Web Tools (not Web).

FIGURE 13.11
The Web Tools toolbar

Adding Background Sounds and Movies

Despite the fact that we don't seem to mind being constantly barraged by sounds from radio and television, we have not yet developed a fondness for sounds from the Web. Only occasionally will you happen upon a Web site that opens with background music drawing you in (or turning you away). However, if you'd like to add background sounds to your site, Word makes it easy for you to do.

Although you can add a sound or movie to a Web page in Web page view, it's helpful to be in Design mode so you know where the Sound or Movie icon is in case you want to remove it later. Open the Web Tools toolbar, and click the Design Mode button to go into Design mode. Before inserting the Sound or Movie button, move the insertion point to an obvious position at the top of the page. This is where the icon representing the sound or movie file will appear.

You can move into Design mode from any view, not just Web Layout view, but if you're working on a Web page, it's best to begin in Web Layout view so you know what your finished product will look like.

When you're all set, click the Sound button on the Web toolbar. Enter the name of a .wav file or click Browse and locate the file. Click the Loop down-arrow to choose the number of times you want the sound to play, either 1–5 or Infinite. Click OK. Click the Design Mode button to return to the view you were in when you clicked the Design Mode button. The sound file should begin playing immediately and plays every time you open the page (and as many times as you instruct it to play).

A user's browser (and add-ins like RealPlayer) determines the types of sound files they can play. MIDI and WAV files are common, but MP3 (MPEG audio) files are becoming the more popular. After you insert the file, test it in your browser.

To add a movie file, click the Movie button on the Web toolbar (remember to click the Design Mode button and position the insertion point first). Enter the settings in the Movie Clip dialog box, as shown in Figure 13.12. It's a good idea to include an alternative image that will display in browsers not supporting movie clips, or put the clip on a page so users can choose whether or not to download it. However, even if a browser does support movie clips, the image will be small and difficult to see on most systems. If possible, test out the display on several machines with different browsers to see how the movie file looks before making it a permanent part of your Web page.

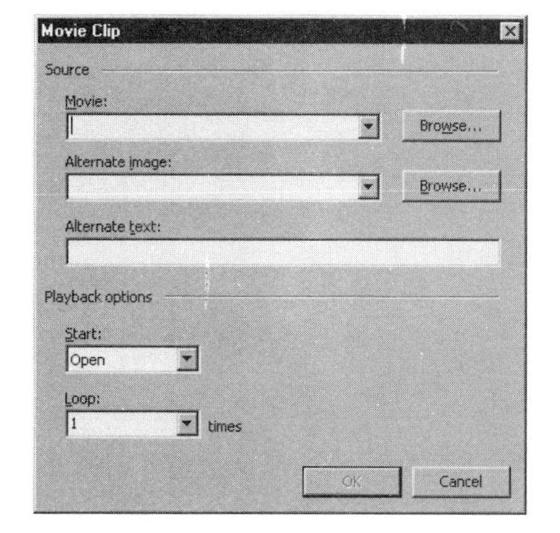

FIGURE 13.12 Movie clip settings

Removing Sound or a Movie from a Web Page

To remove a sound or movie clip, move into Design Mode. Locate the Sound or Movie icon, as shown here. Select the icon and choose Edit ➢ Clear.

Adding Scrolling Text

Scrolling text is a way to grab your visitors' attention with a special announcement or notice. If you've used Windows Scrolling Marquee screen saver, you're already familiar with the concept. To add scrolling text, click the Design Mode button on the Web Tools toolbar then position the insertion point where you want the scrolling text to appear.

Click the Scrolling Text button on the Web Tools toolbar and enter the text in the text box, as shown in Figure 13.13. Set the options for Behavior, Direction, Background Color, Loop, and Speed then click OK to insert the scrolling text box. If you want to view the scrolling text, click the Design Mode button to exit Design Mode. Note, however, that the text box doesn't scroll in Design mode.

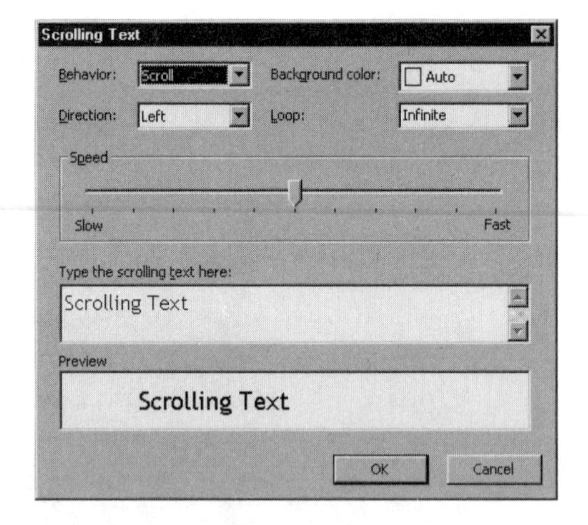

FIGURE 13.13
Entering scrolling text

You can re-size or move the scrolling text box in Design mode as you would any text box in Word. To delete a scrolling text box, switch to Design mode, click the box to select it, and press Delete.

Creating Web-based Forms

To make the Web truly interactive, information has to go in both directions. Web users need the ability to send information to the site owners and Web owners need to know about who their visitors are and what they are looking for. Web forms provide a way for visitors to respond to surveys, register with a site, voice their opinions about issues, search your site, or submit feedback.

You can add a form to any Web page. Word automatically adds Top of Form and Bottom of Form boundaries to the form, as shown in Figure 13.14, when you add a form control from the Web Tools toolbar.

FIGURE 13.14 Form control navigators

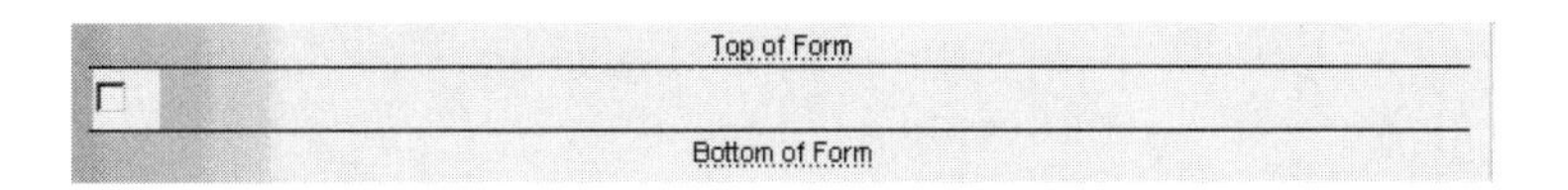

Word comes equipped with 11 built-in form controls for you to use on forms. These form controls are:

- Check box control
- Option control
- Drop-down box control
- List box control
- Text box control
- Text area control
- Submit control
- Submit with image control
- Reset control
- Hidden control
- Password control

Use check boxes when users are allowed to select more than one option within a group. For example, you could have your check box say something like, "Send me more information about" and then list various choices for the user to select from.

Option buttons indicate that a user can select only one item from a group of options, such as receiving information Daily, Weekly, or Monthly.

Drop-down boxes give users a list of specific options from which they can choose one. For example, from a drop-down list of cities you can pick yours to see its weather report.

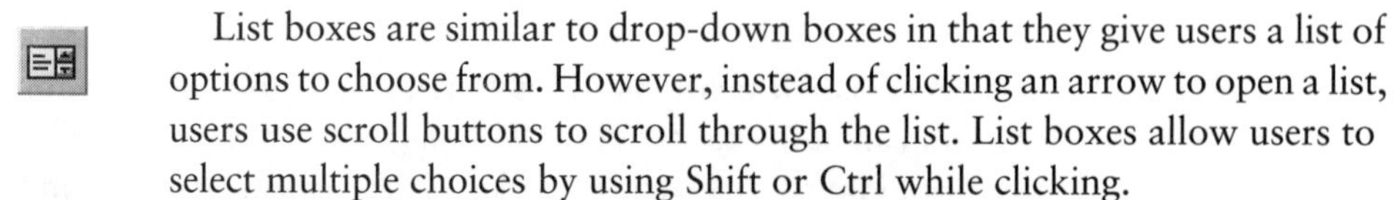

List boxes are similar to drop-down boxes in that they give users a list of options to choose from. However, instead of clicking an arrow to open a list, users use scroll buttons to scroll through the list. List boxes allow users to select multiple choices by using Shift or Ctrl while clicking.

Text boxes are fields where users can enter text, such as a name, address, or other specific information.

Text areas are open text boxes with scroll bars where users can write a paragraph or more to give feedback, describe a problem, or provide other information.

Submit buttons are essential elements on a form, because a user must click the Submit button so the data they entered is sent to the Web server for processing.

The Submit with Image control lets you substitute an image for the standard Submit button. Make sure users know they have to click this button to submit their data – and that clicking the button submits the data. For example, don't use the same image for a Next Page button and a Submit button.

Reset is a form control that clears the data in the current form so the user can start over.

Hidden is a form field, invisible to the user, which passes data to the Web Server. For example, a hidden control could pass information about the user's operating system or Web browser.

Password replaces typed text with asterisks so users can type passwords confidentially.

Laying Out a Form Tables are a big help in laying out a form so it looks organized. Create the table so it has twice the number of columns you would want to display in a single row. For example, in Figure 13.15, the third row contains three fields, so the table contains six columns. After you have inserted all the field names and form controls, save the page and open it in Internet Explorer or another browser to see how it looks. (See Previewing Web Pages below.)

Setting Form Field Properties All form controls have properties that determine how they behave. Some form controls require you to set the properties before the control can be used. For example, you must enter the values you want to appear in a drop-down box so the user has options to choose from. To set, or edit, a control's properties, double-click the control to open the Properties dialog box, as shown in Figure 13.16.

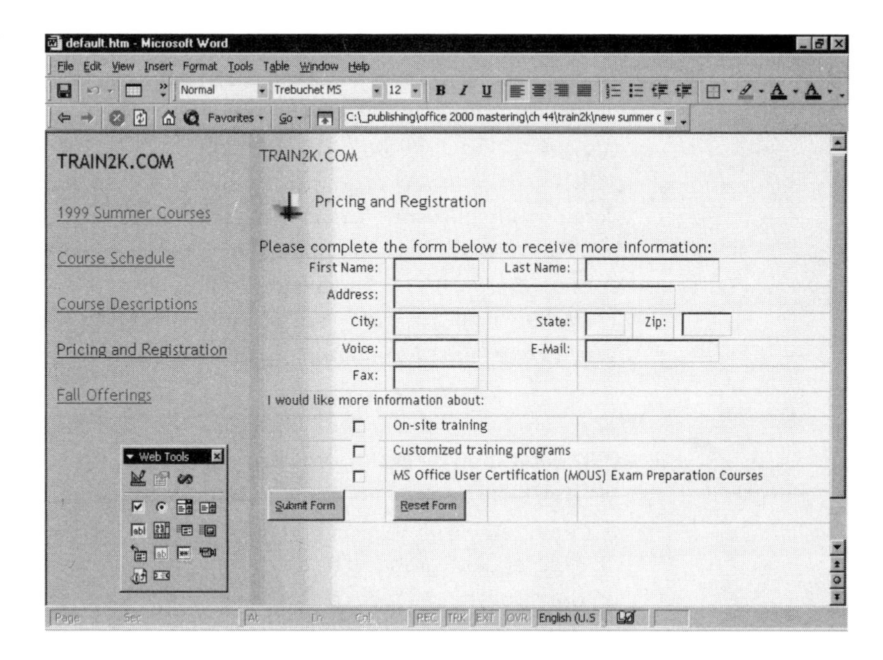

FIGURE 13.15
Using a table to lay out form fields

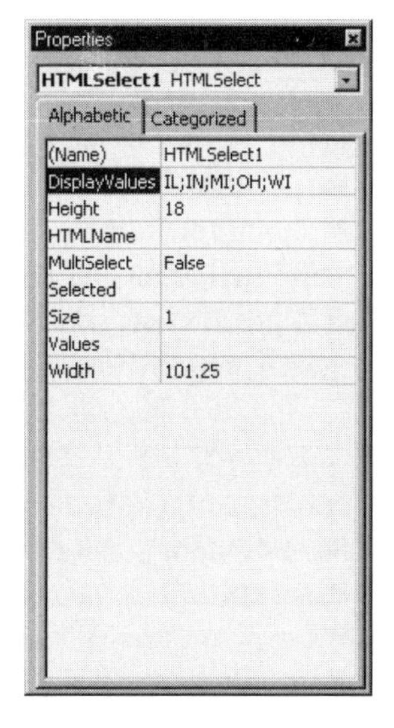

FIGURE 13.16
Properties dialog box.

To enter options for a drop-down list or a list box, type the first value in the DisplayValues property. Enter a semicolon and no space before entering the next value. The values you type each appear on a separate line in the drop-down list or list box. To test the drop-down box, exit Design mode and click the down arrow on the form control.

It's helpful to any other users who work on your Web site to change the default control name to a name that describes the field, for example, change `HTMLText1` to `FirstName`. Control names cannot contain spaces, but they can contain numbers and upper- and lowercase letters.

For more information about form control properties, refer to Microsoft's Word Help file: "*Form controls you can use on a Web page.*"

Data submitted by Web forms is processed by the Web server and stored in a database format either as a comma-delimited text file, an Access table, or other database format. For a form to work, the Web server has to be set up to accept and process the data. Talk with your Web server administrator before publishing a form on a Web site.

Previewing Web Pages

Objective W2000.3.3

The easiest and quickest way to see what your Web will look like in a browser window is to click File ➢ Web Page Preview. Your default browser launches, and the home page is displayed. Follow the links as you normally would and make notes if you see things you want to change. You can't edit in Web Page Preview, so when you're through previewing, close or minimize the browser window and return to Word to make necessary changes.

If you're already in a browser window and want to preview your Web, Click File ➢ Open. Locate the default.htm for the Web site you want to view. Click OK.

Using Web Page Preview

1. Click File ➢ Web Page Preview to open your default browser and view your Web.
2. Use navigation links to move from the home page of the Web site to the page you are working on.
3. After you have viewed the page, close or minimize the browser and return to Word.
4. Make any additional changes you want to and save the Word Web page again.
5. Maximize the browser and click the Refresh button on the browser toolbar to view your changes.

Because of the way different browsers display form fields, it is difficult to make every field line up perfectly with the fields above it unless you use tables.

Working with Frames

A frame is a structure that allows you to display and relate multiple Web pages in one page. The page that displays the frames is called a frames page. Although the Web Page Wizard is the easiest way to create a simple navigational frame, Word offers you the option of adding and deleting frames manually if you prefer.

Word has a Frames toolbar you can use to add, delete, and set the properties of frames. Right-click any toolbar and choose Frames to display the toolbar.

To add a frame, click Format ➢ Frames. If you only want to add a table of contents to the existing document, choose Table of Contents in Frame. This option creates a table of contents for the displayed document based on heading styles used in the document. Figure 13.17 shows an example of a Table of Contents Frame. A link is created for each heading formatted using a heading style (for more about using heading styles, see Chapter 3).

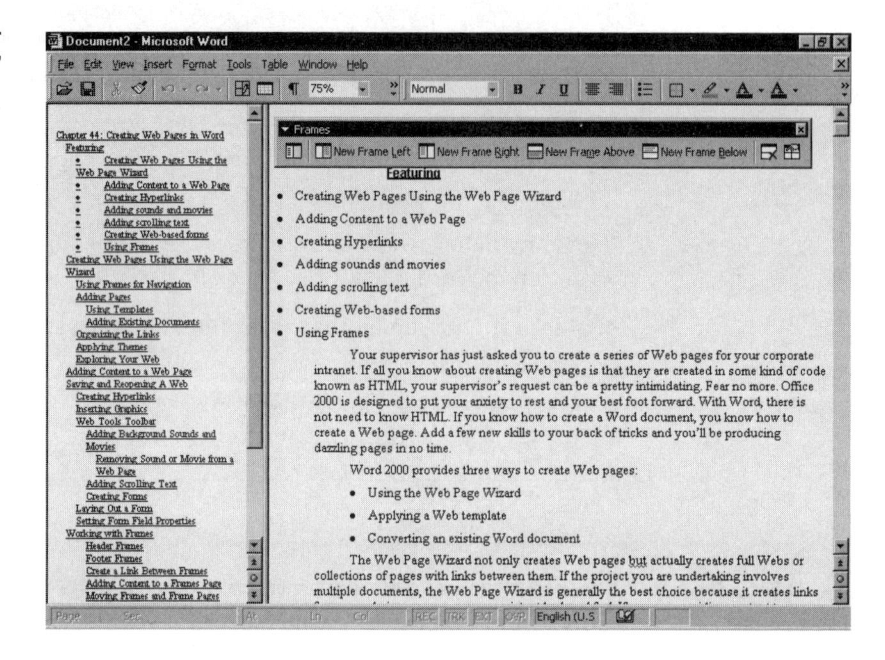

FIGURE 13.17

The Table of Contents in Frame option

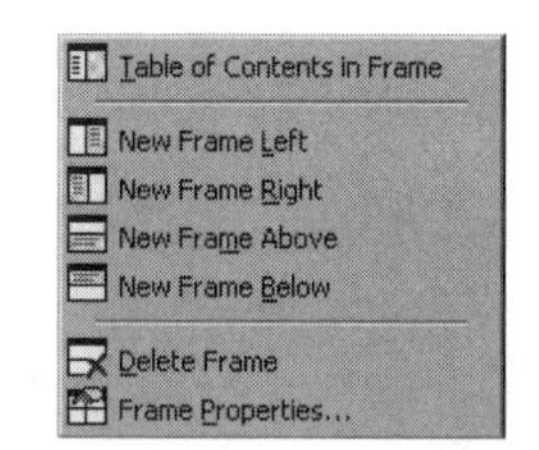

To create a frames page to which you can add frames, choose New Frames Page. Choose Format ➢ Frames again to choose the position of the frame you would like to add. You have several frame options, as shown below.

New Frame Above creates a header frame, and New Frame Below creates a footer frame. If you plan to add horizontal and vertical frames, add header and footer frames first so they extend the width of the page, as shown in Figure 13.18. Re-size frames by dragging the frame border in the direction you want.

Add content to each frame. When you save the frames page, each page is saved separately as M, M1, M2, and so on.

Before saving a frames page, create a folder to save it in. Word automatically saves the frames as individual pages in that folder. If you add graphics or other objects, Word creates subfolders to house them in. Give the frames page a name that reminds you it's a frames page. If it's the home page of the Web you are creating, save it as `default.htm`.

FIGURE 13.18
Add Header and Footer horizontal frames

Setting Frame Properties Right-click or select any frame and click the Frame Properties button on the Frames toolbar to open the Frame Properties dialog box, shown in Figure 13.19. The initial page should be set to the frame that is open. However, you can change the page that opens in a frames page by selecting a different initial page. Give the frame a name by selecting or entering one in the Name box. Adjust the size of the frame by adjusting the size controls. By default, frames are set to a relative size. You can change the relative size to a specific pixel size or a percentage of the screen display by changing the Measure In option.

On the Borders tab of the Frame Properties dialog, set whether you want to display frame borders and, if you do, what size and color you want them to be? You can determine if you want users to be able to adjust the frame size by clearing or checking the Frame is Resizable in Browser check box. Turn scrollbars on or off using the Show Scrollbars In Browsers setting.

If you move a frames page to a different folder or drive location, you must copy all of the related frames documents to the same location.

FIGURE 13.19
Changing Frame properties

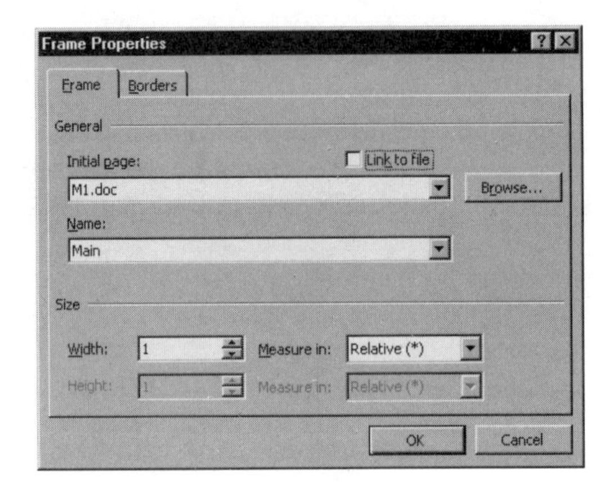

Removing a Frame from a Frames Page If you decide you want to remove a frame from a frames page, click in the frame and choose Format ➢ Frames ➢ Delete Frame or click the Delete Frame button on the Frames toolbar. You may want to save the frame under a different name before you delete it in case you decide you want to use it at a later time. To save the frame under a different name, right-click in the frame and choose Save Current Frame As.

View HTML Source of a Web Page Although Word 2000 provides some exciting Web page design options, creating a complex Web site requires some knowledge of HTML and other Web programming tools. While you are creating Web pages in Word, Word is writing the HTML code behind the scenes. You can view this code and even edit it directly by choosing View ➢ HTML Source. This opens the Microsoft Development Environment design window where you can edit HTML and active server page (`.asp`) files. If you are not a programmer, this is a good place to take a look at what it takes to produce the content you are creating and see HTML in actual application. If you are a programmer, you can edit the HTML file and add Microsoft Visual Basic, JScript, and VBScript to your files.

The default installation of Word does not include the HTML viewer, so you may be prompted to install it.

Hands On: Objectives W20003.3 and 4.6

1. In a new or existing Web Page:
   - **a)** Select some text and add a hyperlink to another Web page. Add a hyperlink to an e-mail address.
   - **b)** Test the hyperlinks.
   - **c)** Open the Web and Web Tools toolbars. Switch to Design view and insert a sound clip that plays once when the page is opened.
   - **d)** Create a simple Web form using two types of form controls. Edit the values using the Form Control Properties (right-click and choose Properties).
   - **e)** Add a frame and modify its properties so the border is displayed.
   - **f)** View the page in your browser using Web Page Preview.
   - **g)** Save the changes you've made.
2. Open a Word document and use the Save As A Web Page command to convert it to HTML.
   - **a)** Save the doc in the same folder as the Web you created (or modified) in Step 1.
   - **b)** Create a link to the new page from the Web you edited in Step 1.

Internet Publishing with Excel 2000

In previous chapters, you've learned how to create the entire spectrum of Excel spreadsheets, from simple one-sheet workbooks to complex analysis workbooks with databases, PivotTables, and charts. This section of the chapter focuses on using Excel with the Web, including saving and publishing Web pages.

We'll begin with saving and publishing simple Web pages, and then add advanced features that are more typically used on an intranet. In this section, we will use the Traverse Tree Sales workbook we've used in previous chapters.

Saving Worksheets and Workbooks for the Web

Web pages—documents that can be displayed on the World Wide Web—are pages of HTML code. *HTML*, or *Hypertext Markup Language*, is programming code that a browser program like Internet Explorer or Netscape Navigator can interpret and display.

When you publish Excel 2000 worksheets as Web pages, you can create *interactive* or *non-interactive* pages. Non-interactive, or static, pages let browser users view and print published pages. Interactive pages let users manipulate the page data using some of the same tools they would in Excel 2000. Interactive pages can take the place of printed reports, because they allow users to sort, filter, and print the spreadsheet data from their browser.

Objective XL2000.2.6

To create a Web page, begin by opening the spreadsheet you want to save for the Web. Then choose File ➢ Save As Web Page from the menu bar to open the Save As Web Page dialog box, shown in Figure 13.20.

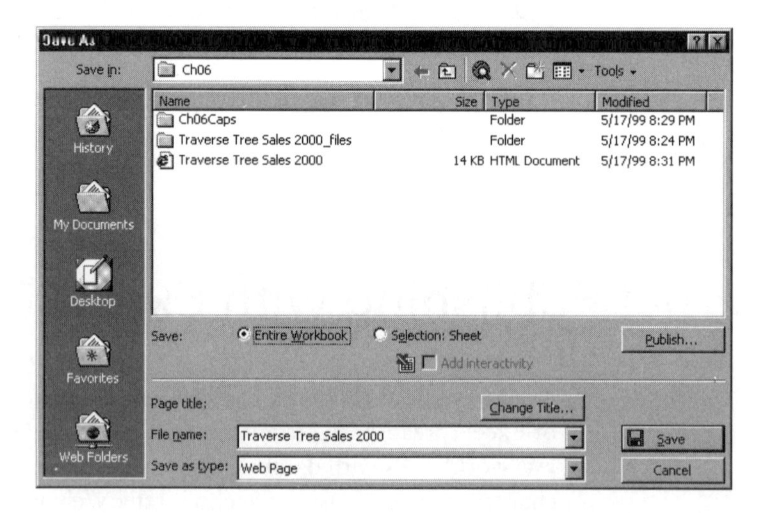

FIGURE 13.20 Use the Save As Web Page dialog box to create Web pages in Excel.

The default title displayed in a browser for your page is the workbook's filename. To create a new title, click the Change Title button in the Save As dialog box to open the Set Page Title dialog box, shown here.

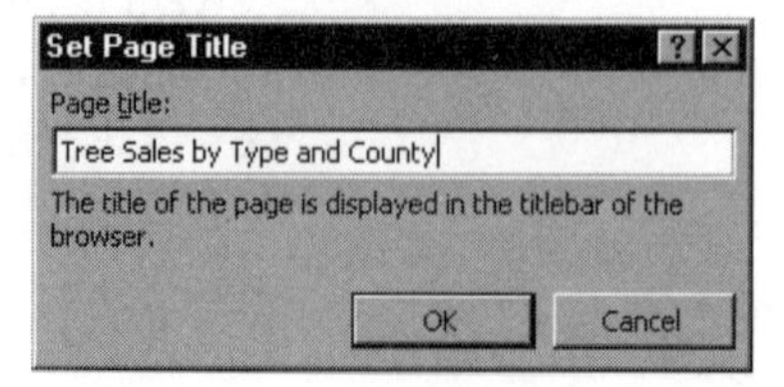

As shown in Figure 13.21, you can either save your entire workbook as a Web page, complete with sheet tabs, or you can save only the active sheet. To save an entire workbook as HTML, enter a location and a filename, then click the Save button to create the Web page and close the dialog box. Excel will create a master HTML page in the location you specify and place images and other files used in the page in a folder named *yourfilename_files* in the same directory. To open the page in your browser, use My Computer or Windows Explorer to locate the HTML file. Double-click the file to launch your browser and open the file.

To save only the active sheet as a Web page, choose the Selection: Sheet option in the Save As dialog box, and then click the Save button.

The easiest way to save a range of cells is to select the range before you choose Save As Web Page. In the Save As Web Page dialog box, the Selection option will list the selected range.

The HTML page is a copy of the data in your workbook or worksheet. If the data in your workbook changes, you have to save the workbook or worksheet as a Web page again to update the HTML page.

To Save a Range, Worksheet, or Workbook for the Web

1. Open the workbook that contains the items you want to save. Select a sheet or range to save part of the workbook.
2. Choose File ➢ Save As Web Page.
3. Choose a Save option: Workbook or Selection.
4. Click Change Title to open the Set Title dialog box. Enter a title that will appear in the browser window.
5. Click OK to return to the Save As Web Page dialog box.
6. Enter or browse to select a location and a filename.
7. Click Save to save the workbook or selection as a Web page.

Using Web Page Preview

Objective XL2000.4.2

You don't have to create a Web page to see what your workbook will look like in a browser. Excel's Web Page Preview lets you preview the HTML version of your workbook. Choose File ➢ Web Page Preview to launch your browser and open a preview of the active workbook. Use the tabs at the bottom of the browser window (see Figure 13.21) to move between pages.

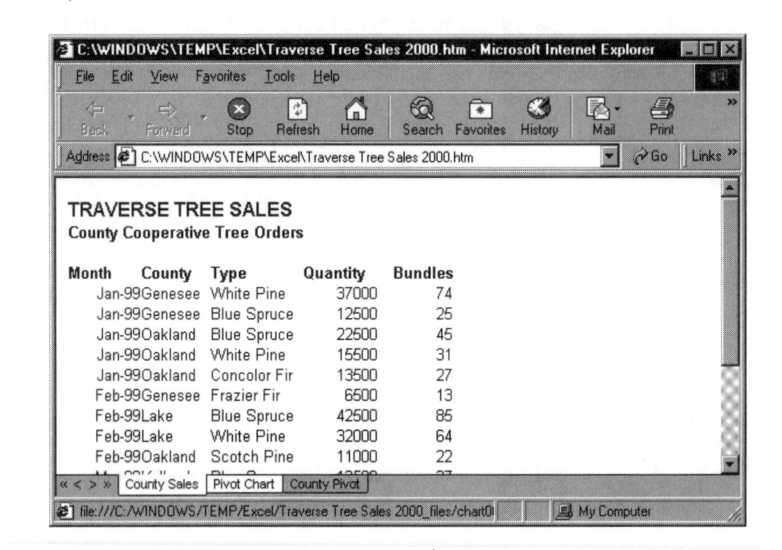

FIGURE 13.21 A Web Page Preview of the Traverse Tree Sales workbook

Publishing Interactive Web Pages

Interactive pages are a new feature in Excel 2000. You create interactive pages using one or more of the *Office Web Components*. There are three Web Components in Excel: the Spreadsheet Component, the Chart Component, and the PivotTable Component. You can use the same components in Access and FrontPage to present information from other data sources.

But don't run out and create a bunch of interactive pages yet. The Office Web Components require Office 2000. For a person to use the interactive features in a Web page, they have to have an Office 2000 license on their computer. And Web Components require Internet Explorer, and the newer version you have the better:

- You can't even see Office Web Components in browsers other than IE, and versions of IE prior to 4.
- With IE 4, you can see and use the page and component, but some features aren't available.

- With IE 4.01 and later, all features are available, but the page is reloaded each time you open it, even within a browser session.
- With IE 5, all component features are enabled. If you modify the component (for example, sorting or formatting cells), the changes will still be there if you return to the page in the same browser session.

If you can't predict or dictate the Desktop environment for your users, you can't rely on interactive pages as your primary means of communicating data. However, for companies or workgroups moving to Office 2000, interactive Web pages are seeing immediate application, because they're a fast and easy way to let end users create reports.

When you save an entire workbook as a Web page, the resulting page is always static. Web Page Preview previews your entire workbook, so the preview shows the static versions of your pages.

To create interactive pages, you have to publish rather than save the pages. Begin as you did when saving a page: Open the Save As Web Page dialog box. Change the page title if you wish. In the Save section, change the option from the default Entire Workbook to Selection. This enables the Add Interactivity check box. Click the check box before clicking the Publish button to open the Publish As Web Page dialog box, shown in Figure 13.22.

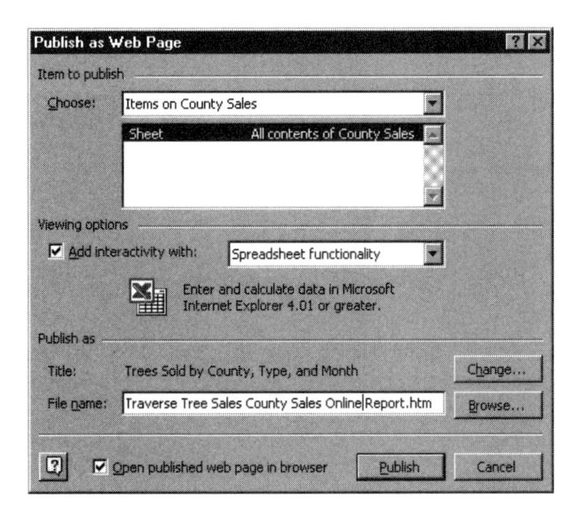

FIGURE 13.22 Specify a sheet or range to publish in the Publish As Web Page dialog box.

In the Items To Publish section, use the Choose drop-down list to indicate whether you're publishing a specific sheet, something that was previously published, or a range of cells in the workbook. (The range does not need to be named; use your mouse to select the cells you want to publish.)

If you enabled interactivity in the Save As dialog box, choose the component you wish to use from the drop-down list by selecting the kind of functionality you want browser users to have: Spreadsheet, PivotTable, or Chart. Click the Change Title button to supply a title that will appear above the component in the Web page. You can't preview an interactive page, but you can have it open in your browser as soon as it's created by enabling the Open Published Web Page In Browser check box at the bottom of the Publish As Web Page dialog box.

Click the Publish button and Excel creates the Web page including any interactivity you have specified. A Web page that includes the Spreadsheet Component is shown in Figure 13.23. The same sheet without interactivity is shown in the Web Page Preview in Figure 13.21.

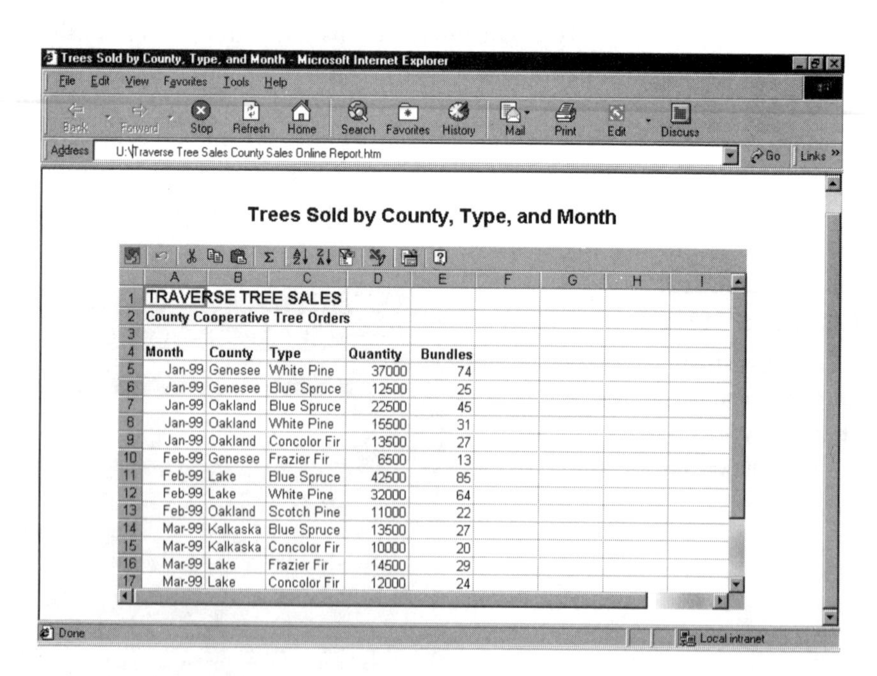

	A	B	C	D	E
1	TRAVERSE TREE SALES				
2	County Cooperative Tree Orders				
3					
4	Month	County	Type	Quantity	Bundles
5	Jan-99	Genesee	White Pine	37000	74
6	Jan-99	Genesee	Blue Spruce	12500	25
7	Jan-99	Oakland	Blue Spruce	22500	45
8	Jan-99	Oakland	White Pine	15500	31
9	Jan-99	Oakland	Concolor Fir	13500	27
10	Feb-99	Genesee	Frazier Fir	6500	13
11	Feb-99	Lake	Blue Spruce	42500	85
12	Feb-99	Lake	White Pine	32000	64
13	Feb-99	Oakland	Scotch Pine	11000	22
14	Mar-99	Kalkaska	Blue Spruce	13500	27
15	Mar-99	Kalkaska	Concolor Fir	10000	20
16	Mar-99	Lake	Frazier Fir	14500	29
17	Mar-99	Lake	Concolor Fir	12000	24

FIGURE 13.23
The interactive Excel worksheet displayed in IE 5

The second Office Web Component, the Chart Component, includes the chart and the data table the chart is based on. Users can change the data in the table to change the chart, just as you do in Excel. However, they can't choose a different chart type or do extensive chart formatting.

Objective XL2000E.11.7

In Figure 13.24, we've published the County Sales worksheet using the third component, the PivotTable Component, which creates a PivotTable List. We selected the PivotTable interactivity in the Publish dialog box. The component works like the Excel PivotTable Report with areas for row data, column data, and page data (filter data).

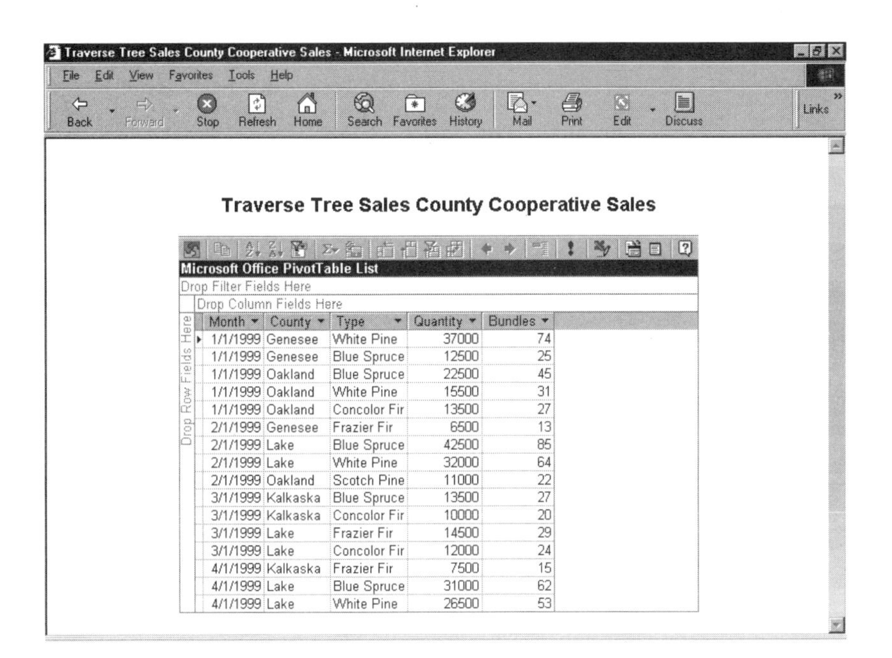

Month	County	Type	Quantity	Bundles
1/1/1999	Genesee	White Pine	37000	74
1/1/1999	Genesee	Blue Spruce	12500	25
1/1/1999	Oakland	Blue Spruce	22500	45
1/1/1999	Oakland	White Pine	15500	31
1/1/1999	Oakland	Concolor Fir	13500	27
2/1/1999	Genesee	Frazier Fir	6500	13
2/1/1999	Lake	Blue Spruce	42500	85
2/1/1999	Lake	White Pine	32000	64
2/1/1999	Oakland	Scotch Pine	11000	22
3/1/1999	Kalkaska	Blue Spruce	13500	27
3/1/1999	Kalkaska	Concolor Fir	10000	20
3/1/1999	Lake	Frazier Fir	14500	29
3/1/1999	Lake	Concolor Fir	12000	24
4/1/1999	Kalkaska	Frazier Fir	7500	15
4/1/1999	Lake	Blue Spruce	31000	62
4/1/1999	Lake	White Pine	26500	53

FIGURE 13.24

A PivotTable List lets users interactively analyze data.

See Chapter 4, "Taking Excel to the Max," for more information on working with Excel's PivotTable feature.

To Create an Interactive PivotTable, Spreadsheet, or Chart for the Web

1. Open the workbook and select the database, sheet, or chart you want to publish for the Web.

2. Choose File ➢ Save As Web Page to open the Save As Web Page dialog box.

To Create an Interactive PivotTable, Spreadsheet, or Chart for the Web *(continued)*

3. In the Save options, choose Selection: (the sheet or selected range will be listed here).
4. Enable the Add Interactivity check box.
5. Click the Publish button to open the Publish As Web Page dialog box.
6. Select the type of Item To Publish from the drop-down list.
7. Choose a type of functionality (PivotTable, Spreadsheet, or Chart) from the Add Interactivity Using drop-down list.
8. In the Publish As section of the dialog box, click the Change Title button to enter a title that will appear above the component and in the title bar of the browser window.
9. Select or enter a filename and location for the Web page.
10. To preview the completed page, leave the Open Published Web Page In Browser check box enabled.
11. Click Publish to create the interactive Web page.

Browsing an Interactive Page

Each of the Office Web Components supports specific kinds of interactivity. With the Spreadsheet Component, users can add formulas, sort and filter, and format the worksheet. The Charting Component is linked to a data table so users can change the chart display by changing the table data. The PivotTable List lets your users analyze database information using most of the sorting, filtering, grouping, and subtotaling features of Excel lists and PivotTable Reports. We'll examine the PivotTable List we created earlier in this chapter to see how the interactive page works in the Internet Explorer browser.

The interactive page opens with a toolbar above the list. Most of the buttons are familiar from Excel's Standard, Formatting, and PivotTable toolbars:

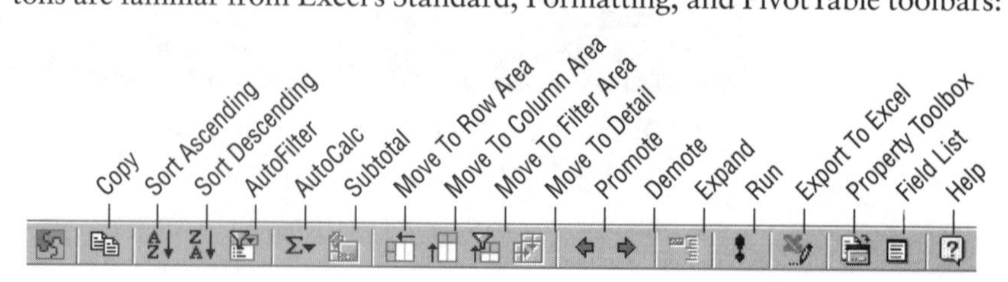

The Export To Excel button saves the worksheet data from the page in a user-specified location (like a user's hard drive). The Property Toolbox button displays tools that let your users format the data in the list (for example, prior to printing), as shown in Figure 13.25.

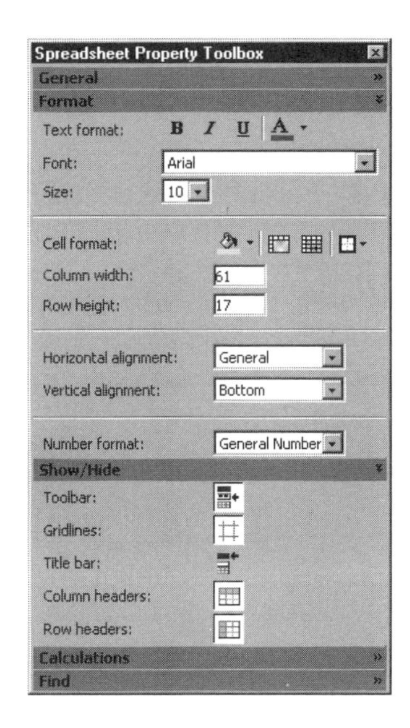

FIGURE 13.25
Users can change the properties of cells in an interactive page using the Properties toolbox.

Objective XL2000E.11.8

Users can sort and filter a PivotTable List using the toolbar buttons. The List has drop-down areas like an Excel PivotTable Report:

- Row
- Column
- Filter
- Detail

In Internet Explorer, drag buttons from one-drop area to another to re-arrange the List and create a PivotTable. To remove a field from the component, drag and drop its button out of the component onto the page background. Fields in the Column, Row, and Filter areas have drop-down arrows that open a list of the values in the column or row. Use the list to filter the values displayed in the table.

Select a field in a column or row area and click the AutoCalc button on the toolbar to choose a summarization method for the data area (choose from Count, Sum, Min, or Max for value fields; Count only for text or date fields). When you add totals, the details will still appear. Use the Expand and Collapse buttons on the Row and Column fields to display or hide the details. Select a Column or Row field and click the Subtotals button to add column or row "grand" totals to the PivotTable List.

To add fields that aren't currently used in the table, click the Field List button on the toolbar to open the Field List, shown in Figure 13.26. Fields in the Field List that are in bold are already displayed in the PivotTable list, and other fields can be added from the Field list. If there's an expand button in front of a field name, click the button to display additional fields.

FIGURE 13.26

Add fields or dimensions of a field from the Field List.

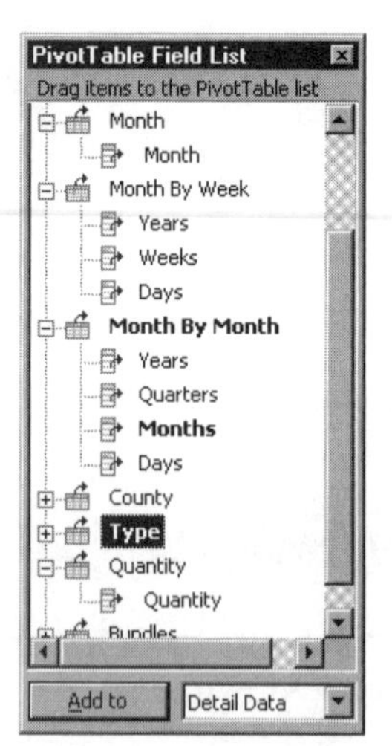

You can remove a field from the PivotTable List and the Fields List: Simply right-click the field and choose Delete.

Some of the fields in the Field List don't actually appear in the data source. For example, fields you've added to the table (like subtotals) are included in the Field List. For date fields, Excel includes different time dimensions. The Traverse Tree Sales worksheet includes a Month field. In Figure 13.26, the Month field appears three times—Month, Month By Week, and Month By Month. Expand the Month By Week field, and you see three different date divisions: Years, Weeks, and Days fields. Expand Month By Month, and you can choose Years, Quarters, Months, and Days fields.

Why are there three different lists? When Excel sees dates in a PivotTable List, it allows you to regard each unique date as an item, or group them into one or more logical divisions. There are 12 months in a year, and 52 weeks, but the weeks don't fall evenly into months or quarters. If you want to display more than one type of date unit, choose all the units from the same group.

To Add Fields to a PivotTable List

1. Open the PivotTable page in Internet Explorer.
2. Click the Field List button on the toolbar to open the Field List.
3. Select the field you want to place in the PivotTable List.
4. Drag and drop the field in the PivotTable List, or select the field in the Field List.
5. Choose the area where you want to place the field in the drop-down list.
6. Click the Add To button to place the field in the drop area.

Hands On: Objectives XL2000.2.6, 4.2, and XL2000E.11.7, E.11.8

1. Open an existing workbook.
   a) Use Web Page Preview to view the workbook in your browser.
   b) Save the workbook as a static Web page with an appropriate page title.
   c) Select a range of cells and save the range as a static Web page.
   d) Save a worksheet as a static Web page.

2. Open an existing workbook that contains a database.
   a) Use the PivotTable Component to create an interactive Web page.
   b) Preview the page in Internet Explorer.
   c) Use the toolbar command buttons to sort and filter the PivotTable List.
   d) Open the Properties Toolbox. Format the column and row headings.
   e) Remove all the fields from the PivotTable list.
   f) Open the Field List. Add fields to the Column, Row, and Detail areas.
   g) Use AutoCalc to summarize the results in the detail area.
   h) Hide and display details.
   i) Use the Field List to remove a field from the PivotTable List and Field List.

Creating Online Presentations with PowerPoint

With PowerPoint 2000, you can save or publish presentations for individuals to use online at their convenience, or deliver a real-time presentation on the Internet or an intranet for an audience of one or one thousand.

Preparing Presentations for the Web

There are two different methods you'll use to make PowerPoint 2000 presentations available for browsing on the Internet or your company's intranet: saving and publishing. When you save a presentation, other PowerPoint 2000 users can access the HTML document, which allows them to edit the presentation. A published presentation is like a published Web site; other users can view but cannot edit a published presentation.

Before saving or publishing your presentation, it's a good idea to use preview (File ➢ Web Page Preview) to see how the presentation will look in your default browser. Then, choose File ➢ Save As Web Page from the menu bar to open the Save As dialog box shown in Figure 13.27.

FIGURE 13.27

Use the Save As dialog box to save or publish presentations.

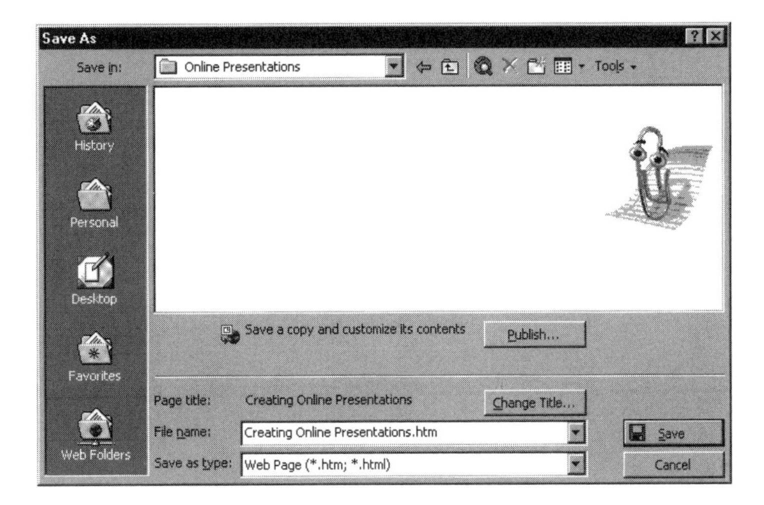

Saving a Presentation as a Web Page

The page title for the presentation is displayed near the bottom of the Save As dialog box. The title will appear in the title bar of the user's browser; the default title is the presentation's filename. To change the page title, click the Change Title button (see Figure 13.27), enter a new title in the Change Title dialog box, and then click OK to return to the Save As dialog box. Click the Save button to save the presentation and close the dialog box.

Publishing a Web Presentation

Objective PP2000.8.3

With PowerPoint 2000, you can publish an entire presentation, selected slides, or even a single PowerPoint slide. You can include Web scripts in PowerPoint presentations just as you would in Word Web documents; (see *Mastering PowerPoint 2000* by Sybex for more information about Web scripting in PowerPoint). The first page of a PowerPoint publication, displayed in Internet Explorer 5, is shown in Figure 13.28.

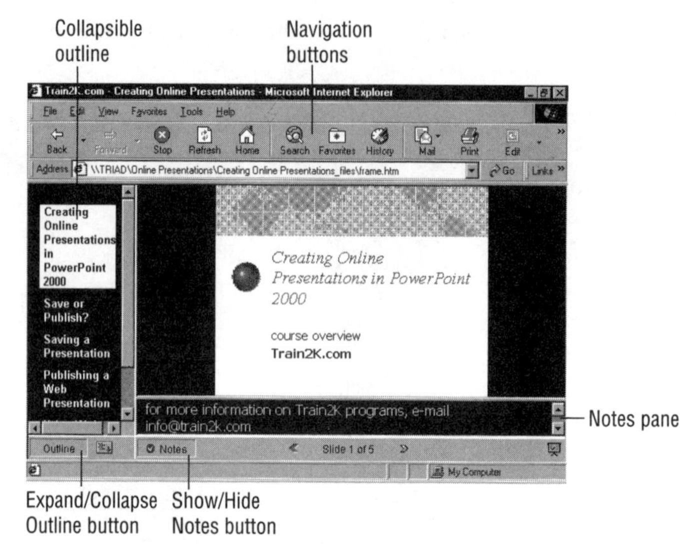

FIGURE 13.28 The published presentation includes navigation controls browser users expect to see.

To publish your presentation, first choose File ➢ Save As Web Page, then click the Publish button in the Save As dialog box (see Figure 13.27) to open the Publish As Web Page dialog box, shown in Figure 13.29.

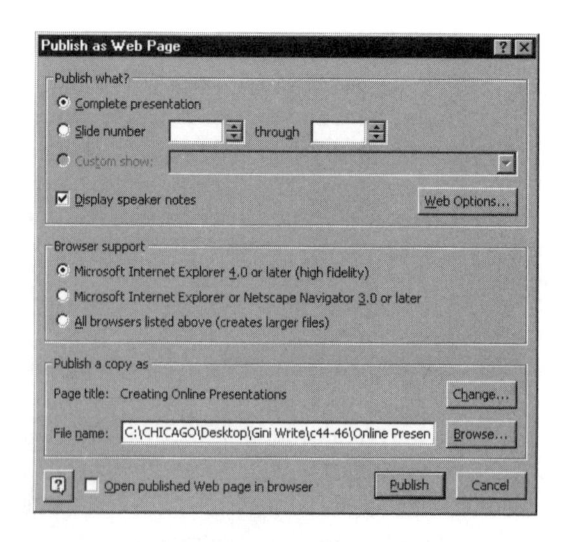

FIGURE 13.29 Set options for your Web presentation in the Publish dialog box.

In the Publish What section, choose to publish the entire presentation, a range of slides, or a custom show you created using the Slide Show ➢ Custom Shows command. Enable the Display Speakers Notes check box if your presentation includes speaker's notes that you want users to see in a separate notes pane.

Setting Web Publishing Options

Objective PP2000E.1.4

Click the Web Options button to open the Web Options dialog box. Use the four pages of this dialog box to set options for publishing the current presentation. When you've finished setting Web options, click OK to close the Web Options dialog box and return to the Publish As Web Page dialog box. The General options available only in PowerPoint are detailed below.

With the Slide Navigation Controls and Colors option is enabled, your presentation will include a collapsible outline (see Figure 13.28) in the color scheme you select and navigation buttons below the presentation. Turn this option off if you're publishing a single slide.

Show Slide Animation While Browsing displays animations within slides. If animations are manually advanced, the user will click the navigation buttons to switch slides, and click on the slides to move through the animations. There are no instructions to tell the user to do this, so we suggest you set automatic timings for all animation if you enable this check box.

Resize Graphics to Fit Browser Window is enabled by default. When you publish your presentation, this option automatically resizes graphics so they'll display best in the Screen Size setting specified in the Picture options.

Selecting Browsers to Support

Objective PP2000E.7.2

Choose the browsers you wish to support based on the intended distribution of your presentation. If you're publishing a presentation for your company's intranet you're fortunate; simply select your company's browser standard. For wider distribution (as with the Internet), there are issues to consider:

- Pages that link to your presentation serve as gatekeepers. If users need Internet Explorer 4 or better to effectively view your home page, you may as well choose IE 4 support for your presentation that's accessed via the home page.

- The newer the browser, the more bells and whistles it will support. For example, IE 4 supports multimedia including PowerPoint sound effects and movies. However, choosing the latest and most powerful browsers means that users may have to download a newer version of a browser to view your presentation. Even if you put a link to the browser's download page on your Web site, some users won't take the time to do this: they'll just browse elsewhere.
- The best browser format for WebTV is not the newest, but the IE/Netscape 3 standard. With the number of WebTV users increasing, you may wish to choose the less dramatic 3 standard to maintain a broader user base.
- Choosing to support all browsers is the least restrictive approach and guarantees the widest possible access to your publication. However, it results in larger files, which means that everyone who wants to view your presentation will need more time to download it.

In the Publish a Copy As section, change (or leave the default) page title. Click the Browse button to select a destination for the presentation. (To save to a Web folder, select Web Folders from the Places pane.) If you wish to display the presentation as soon as it is published, enable the check box at the bottom of the dialog box. Click Publish to publish a copy of active PowerPoint presentation. If you change the presentation, you'll need to publish it again if you want the published copy to reflect your changes.

Broadcasting Presentations

Objective PP2000E.9.4

You can broadcast a PowerPoint presentation over the Internet or over an intranet. Presentation Broadcasting is often used in place of a face-to-face meeting or conference call when you have participants at remote locations, lowering travel costs and travel time. Unlike a published presentation that users browse at their leisure, a broadcast is "real time", so you schedule the broadcast and invite participants in advance using Outlook (or another e-mail program). However, you can record the broadcast and save it so that participants who could not attend or wish to review the presentation can do so.

Broadcasts come in two sizes: 1 to 15 participants and 16 or more participants. This assumes that participants need their own Internet connections. If two people are sitting in front of the same monitor, feel free to count them as one participant! You can use Internet Explorer 4 or 5 to broadcast to up to 15 people. For 16 participants or more, you'll need access to a NetShow server, so talk to your Web administrator. A NetShow server is required if you include live video, regardless of audience size. There are three steps required to get ready for the actual broadcast: selecting the broadcast options; selecting a shared folder and server; and scheduling the broadcast.

Presentation Broadcasting uses Office automation to create appointments and invitations to the presentation in Outlook 2000. You can create and broadcast presentations regardless of your e-mail client, but if you intend to broadcast on a regular basis, you'll want to use Outlook and speak to your network or Web administrator about installing NetShow server.

Setting Up Your Broadcast

With the presentation you wish to broadcast open and active, choose Slide Show, Online Broadcast, Setup and Schedule to open the Broadcast Schedule dialog box, shown here.

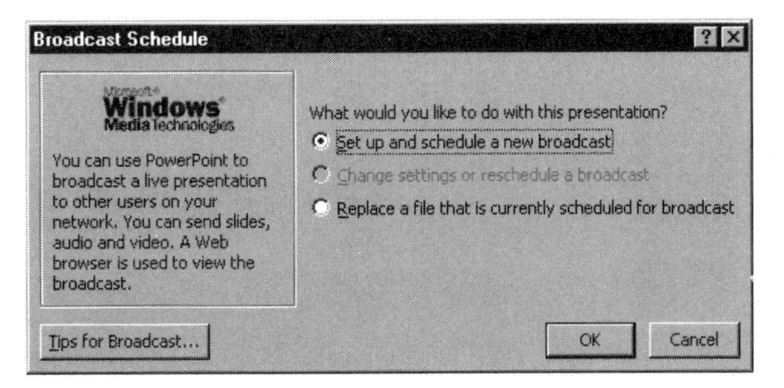

Select whether you want to set up a new broadcast or change an existing broadcast, then click OK to open the appropriate dialog box. A Description page used when scheduling a new broadcast is shown in Figure 13.30. Enter a title and (optional) description for the presentation. In the Contact text box enter (or click the Address Book button and select) the e-mail address that participants should use to send e-mail questions or responses to during the broadcast.

You can schedule and broadcast a presentation on different computers. It's easiest to schedule the broadcast on the computer of the person who's hosting the presentation so PowerPoint will pick up their default description information.

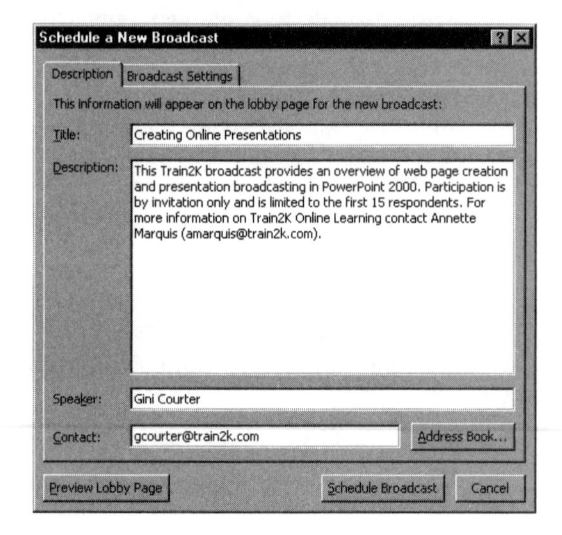

FIGURE 13.30 Information from the Description page is used to create a lobby page for the broadcast.

Set the options you want to use for the broadcast on the Broadcast Settings page, shown in Figure 13.31. Table 13.1 describes each of the options.

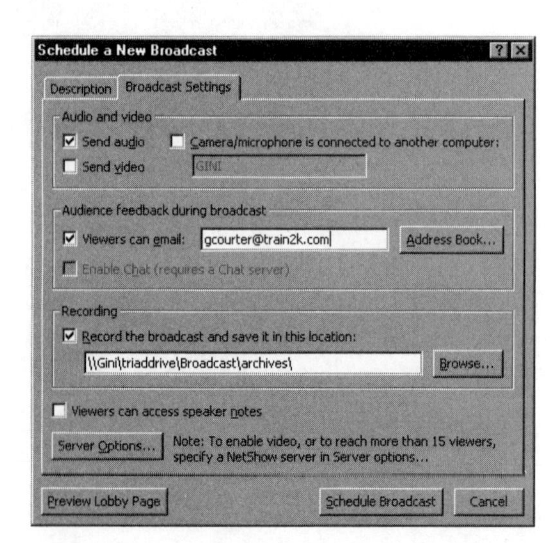

FIGURE 13.31 Specify broadcast options on the Broadcast Settings page.

TABLE 13.1: Presentation Broadcast Settings

Setting	Description
Send Audio	Broadcasts live audio during the presentation.
Send Video	Broadcasts live video; requires a NetShow server.
Camera/Microphone is Connected to Another Computer	If a different computer will be used for audio/video feed, specify its name here.
Viewers Can E-mail	Address for e-mail feedback during the broadcast.
Enable Chat	Enables Microsoft Chat; requires a Chat server.
Record the Broadcast and Save It	Records a copy of the broadcast for later viewing in the specified location.
Viewers Can Access Speaker Notes	Gives access to all speaker notes.

Selecting a Server Click the Server Options button to select a location from which your presentation will be broadcast: a shared folder and, optionally, a NetShow server, as shown in Figure 13.32. If a participant does not have permission to access the shared folder you specify, they will not be able to participate, so you may want to talk with your network administrator about creating a folder with very broad permissions for broadcasting presentations. After you specify a shared folder, you can select a NetShow server.

For the shared folder and the location where you save a recording of the broadcast, you must enter a server and folder with the file `URL:\\server\sharedfolder`, not a network path syntax such as `c:\My Documents\Broadcasts`. (See Figures 13.31 and 13.32.) Ideally, the shared folder's URL and the PowerPoint presentation's filename should not contain spaces; if they do, you'll have to edit the URL whenever it is referenced as the spaces will be represented by the characters `%20`. If the shared folder you want to use is on your computer or a mapped drive, click the Browse button and locate the folder through the Network Neighborhood to have the correct syntax automatically entered in the dialog box.

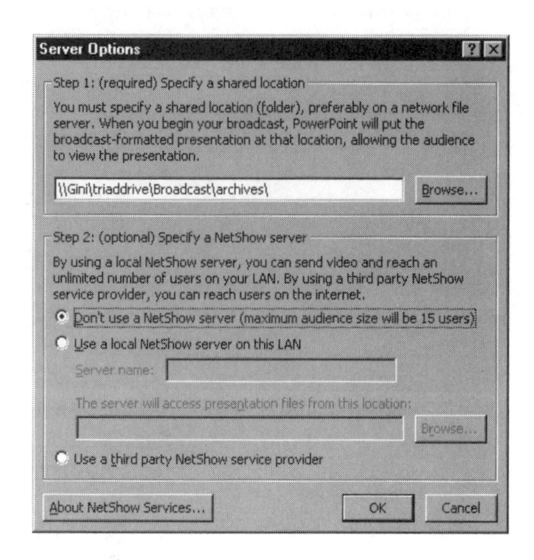

FIGURE 13.32
Select a shared folder for the broadcast.

Previewing the Lobby Page Click the Preview Lobby Page button to view the first page participants will see when they join the presentation. The *Lobby Page* created from the settings shown in Figures 13.30 and 13.31 is shown later in this chapter. A Lobby Page with typographical errors or other mistakes can set a poor tone for your broadcast, so examine the page carefully before continuing.

Scheduling the Broadcast

Objective PP2000E.9.3

After you set all your other options, click the Schedule Broadcast button to schedule the presentation broadcast. PowerPoint will validate your settings to make sure, for example, that the folder you selected exists. If you did not select a NetShow server, you'll be reminded that you are limited to 15 participants. Then, PowerPoint will open an Outlook appointment form so you can set a time and date for the meeting and invite participants, as shown in Figure 13.33. The Subject will appear as the subject of the e-mail invitations to potential participants, so feel free to change it. While you're entering information, check the Event Address text box—it's the location of your shared folder. If the address (which now includes the presentation filename) contains spaces, you'll need to edit the Event Address so it refers to the correct folder and file.

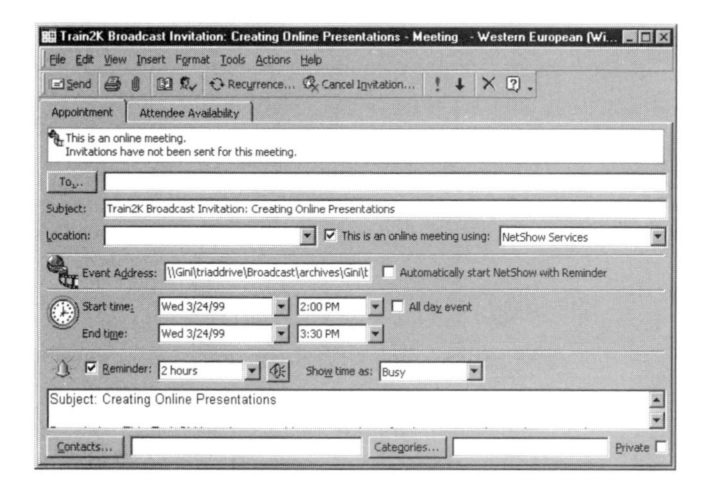

FIGURE 13.33

PowerPoint opens an Outlook appointment form so you can invite broadcast participants.

If you're the person presenting the broadcast, you might want to set a reminder at least 30 minutes in advance and have Outlook automatically launch NetShow when the reminder occurs.

After you send the appointment, PowerPoint will create and send e-mail invitations to the attendees. If you don't use Outlook as your e-mail client, you'll need to enter the broadcast date and time in the message; PowerPoint will automatically include a hyperlink to the broadcast location that the participants can click on to join the broadcast. PowerPoint then saves the broadcast version of the presentation. This can take several minutes for a lengthy presentation, but PowerPoint will let you know when the presentation is ready:

You'll receive e-mail responses from participants who use Outlook to let you know whether or not they will be attending the broadcast. After you read an e-mail response, the list of attendees on the second page of the Outlook appointment item will be automatically updated. The presentation appointment appears on your Outlook calendar. If you need to change broadcast times or cancel the broadcast, right-click on the appointment and use the shortcut menu in Outlook, or open the PowerPoint presentation and choose Slide Show ➢ Online Broadcast ➢ Setup and Schedule.

It's a good idea to rehearse your presentation between the time you send the invitations and the scheduled broadcast time.

Broadcasting the Presentation

You'll want to start preparing a few minutes before the advertised broadcast time. Open the presentation in PowerPoint, then choose Slide Show ➢ Online Broadcast ➢ Begin Broadcast to open the Broadcast Presentation dialog box, shown in Figure 13.34. PowerPoint launches the NetShow service or connects to the NetShow Server.

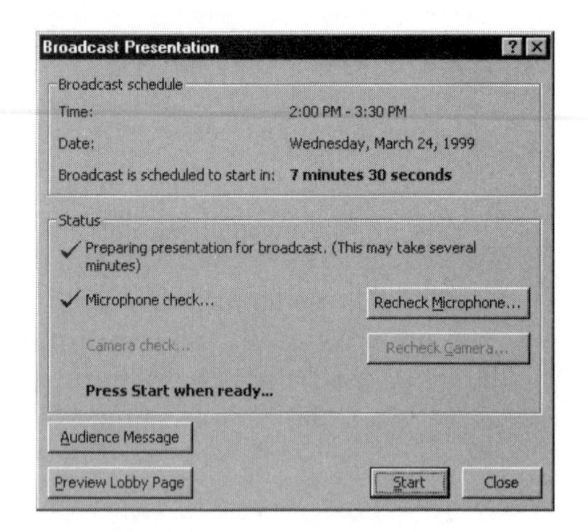

FIGURE 13.34 The Broadcast Presentation dialog box is used to set up the server, audio, and video.

You'll be prompted to check your microphone (and camera if you're using video) to make sure both are operational. If the check is not satisfactory, make adjustments then click the Recheck button to test again.

This is a good time to click the Preview Lobby Page button so you can see the participants' view, shown in Figure 13.35. As the time to broadcast approaches, your participants will begin to log in. They'll see their own version of the lobby page with the clock counting down to show time. The clocks are not synchronized: they simply subtract the system clock time from the scheduled broadcast time. Make sure your system clock isn't set ahead a few minutes, or you could begin the broadcast before all your participants have a chance to join the broadcast.

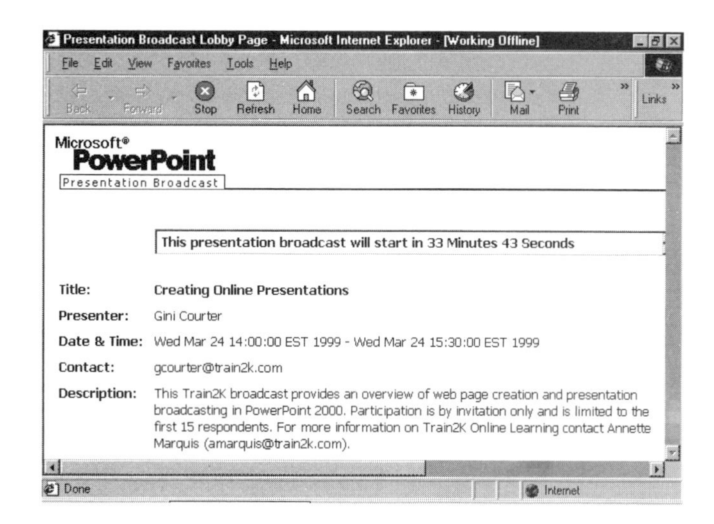

FIGURE 13.35
The Lobby Page greets participants prior to the broadcast.

If you have last minute information for participants, click the Audience Message button in the Broadcast Presentation dialog box to display a text box. Information you enter in the text box will be posted in place of the timer in the participants' browser.

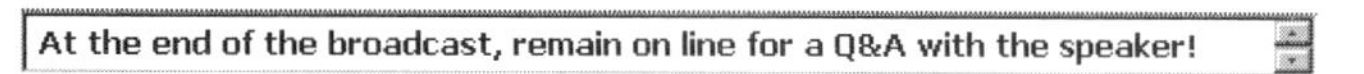

When you're ready to begin broadcasting, click the Start button in the Broadcast Presentation dialog box. The Lobby Page will be replaced with the first slide in your presentation. Advance slides and animate objects just as you would in a live electronic presentation. The presentation will end with a black slide. When you click the last slide, the broadcast ends, and participants are returned to the Lobby Page. If you recorded the presentation, participants can click the Replay Presentation button in their browser to view the presentation again.

Remember that a broadcast is not a NetMeeting. Participants can't easily remind you to slow down, or speak more clearly, so take your time as you move through the presentation.

Participating in a Broadcast

Objective PP2000E.9.3

You must have IE 4 or 5 to participate in a PowerPoint broadcast. To participate, you need an e-mail invitation. If you are using Outlook, you will see a reminder 15 minutes before the broadcast begins with a View NetShow button. Click the reminder's View NetShow button to launch IE and see the Lobby Page for the broadcast. When the broadcast begins, it will appear in the IE window. Adjust your audio volume so that the sound is clear. In many presentations, you'll be allowed to e-mail questions or responses from your browser during the presentation. Some presentations also let you use Microsoft Chat to have a dialog with other participants.

Hands On: Objectives PP2000.8.3 and PP2000E.1.4

1. Open or create a presentation.
   - a) Set browser support, animation, and other web publishing options.
   - b) Publish the presentation for the Web.
   - c) Preview the presentation in your browser.

Creating Web Pages in Access

You can create three very different kinds of Web pages with Access 2000: server generated HTML pages, static Web pages, and dynamic Data Access Pages. You use different tools to create the different types of pages. There are advantages and disadvantages to each type of page.

Server generated HTML pages let you present live data, but the data is not updateable. Microsoft Internet Information Server is required on the server side to generate the HTML pages, so these are not generic "publish anywhere" pages, but they work with a variety of browsers. Server generated HTML pages are useful in a heterogeneous environment like the Internet when you need to display current read-only data to a variety of client browsers.

You create static pages when you want users to view, but not change or manipulate data, and the data changes infrequently (or non-refreshed data is good enough). Static pages are wall to wall HTML, so you can even publish them on a Web server that isn't running Internet Information Server.

Data Access Pages, created with the Data Access Page Wizard, create DHTML (dynamic HTML) pages that support the Office Web Components. Data Access Pages are interactive. You can allow users to edit and enter database data from a browser, but they must have Office 2000 and Internet Explorer 5.0 or higher. Create Data Access Pages in a relatively closed environment like an intranet where users need to work interactively with up to the minute data and you know they have the required client-side software.

Creating Server Generated HTML Pages

Objective AC2000.8.2

Server generated HTML pages are the active pages you're used to seeing on the Web exported from forms, tables, or queries. They're not updateable in a browser, but they are live data. There are two flavors of server generated pages: ASP and IDC/HTX. ASP (Active Server Page) is a better format, but the pages contain ActiveX components so they require a Web server with Internet Information Server 3.0 or higher. The IDC/HTX format supported by earlier versions of Internet Information Server generates two files: a text file with instructions for connecting to the database and an HTML template for the Web page. With both formats you have to publish the page on a Web server, which creates the HTML page on demand. Ask your system administrator which version of Internet Information Server is installed on your Web server.

When you create a server generated page, you are asked to specify a data source: an ODBC connection to your database.

To create a server generated page, first select the form, table, or query you want to use for the page in the Database window. Then choose File ➢ Export from the menu. Choose either Microsoft IIS 1-2 to create IDC/HTX pages or Microsoft Active Server Pages from the Save As Type drop down list. Select a file location, enter a file name, and then click Save. A dialog box opens so you can enter additional information. The IDC/HTX Output Options dialog box is shown in Figure 13.36.

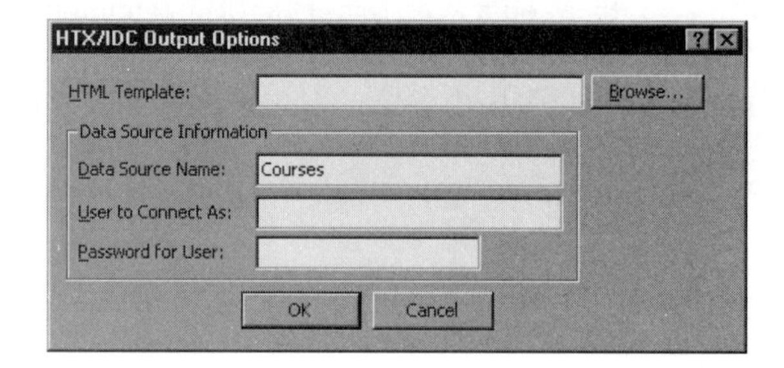

FIGURE 13.36
Enter connection information in the Output Options dialog box

Enter the information in the text boxes. An HTML Template is an HTML file that contains formatting and tags for Access. If you don't select a template, the server applies default formatting. The Data Source Name is the ODBC data source that connects to your database. Username and Password are for the data source. If you don't enter usernames and passwords, the defaults are used (Admin with no password for an Access database).

After you've created a server-generated page, you must publish the page before you can view it because the server generates the page. If you're not familiar with Web page publishing, read the Access 2000 Help topic entitled, "*Publish Server Generated HTML Files to a Web Server.*" Then have a chat with your system or Web administrator.

Creating Static HTML Pages

Static HTML pages are snapshots of the data at the time you create the page. There's nothing interactive, dynamic, or even linked here. However, don't overlook their usefulness for data that changes infrequently. Static pages load quickly and are exceptionally egalitarian. If your browser will let you view anything on the Web, it will let you view a static HTML page. To create a static page, choose the form, table, or query that you want to place on the page from the Database window. Choose File ➢ Export to open the Export...As dialog box. Choose HTML files as the Save As Type, select a file location, and click Export to create the page. A static HTML page created by exporting the Courses table is shown in Figure 13.37.

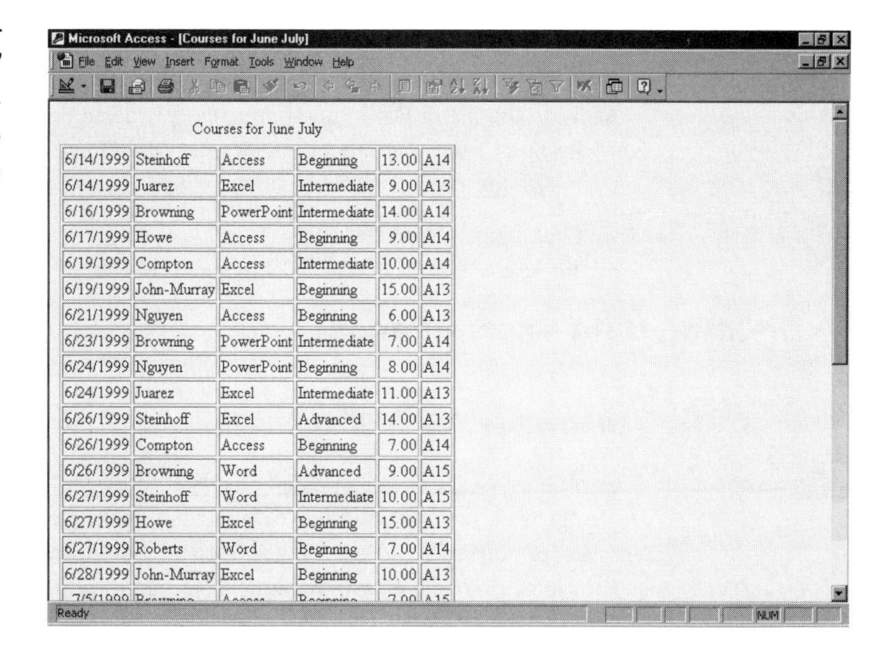

Courses for June July

6/14/1999	Steinhoff	Access	Beginning	13.00	A14
6/14/1999	Juarez	Excel	Intermediate	9.00	A13
6/16/1999	Browning	PowerPoint	Intermediate	14.00	A14
6/17/1999	Howe	Access	Beginning	9.00	A14
6/19/1999	Compton	Access	Intermediate	10.00	A14
6/19/1999	John-Murray	Excel	Beginning	15.00	A13
6/21/1999	Nguyen	Access	Beginning	6.00	A13
6/23/1999	Browning	PowerPoint	Intermediate	7.00	A14
6/24/1999	Nguyen	PowerPoint	Beginning	8.00	A14
6/24/1999	Juarez	Excel	Intermediate	11.00	A13
6/26/1999	Steinhoff	Excel	Advanced	14.00	A13
6/26/1999	Compton	Access	Beginning	7.00	A14
6/26/1999	Browning	Word	Advanced	9.00	A15
6/27/1999	Steinhoff	Word	Intermediate	10.00	A15
6/27/1999	Howe	Excel	Beginning	15.00	A13
6/27/1999	Roberts	Word	Beginning	7.00	A14
6/28/1999	John-Murray	Excel	Beginning	10.00	A13

FIGURE 13.37 Any browser can display static pages like this one

To apply a theme or add a title, scrolling marquee, or other elements, click Pages in the Database Window and choose Edit Web Page that Already Exists. Locate the page and add any additional components or formatting to the page that you desire. You can also add Office Web Components if your intended users have IE 5 and Office 2000.

Adding Hyperlinks to Web Pages

Objective AC2000.8.3 and AC2000E.6.1

When you open a Web page for editing, you can add hyperlinks to the page to send visitors to related pages.

Adding Hyperlinks to a Access Web Page

1. Open the Web page for editing and move the insertion point to the location where you want to enter the hyperlink.
2. Choose Insert ➢ Hyperlink from the menu.

Adding Hyperlinks to a Access Web Page *(continued)*

3. Enter the text you want to display for the hyperlink.
4. Type the file or Web Page name, click Browse For File, Web Page, or Bookmark to locate the page or select the file you want from the list in the dialog box.
5. Click OK to create the link.

Creating Data Access Pages

Objective AC2000E.6.3

Data Access Pages can be posted on a Web site or on your company intranet, or sent via e-mail to someone off your network. Data Access Pages aren't saved as objects in your database; rather, they're saved as separate files on your hard drive. They are dynamic Web pages bound directly to the data in your database. Data Access Pages are designed for Internet Explorer 5.0; earlier versions of Internet Explorer don't support Data Access Pages.

To create a Data Access Page from your data, click the Pages button in the left pane of the Access Database window. On the Pages page, click Create Data Access Page by Using Wizard. The Page Wizard starts, shown in Figure 13.38. It's very similar to the Report Wizard, and your Data Access Page will resemble an Access report. In the first Wizard dialog box, in the Tables/Queries drop-down, select a table to base your page on, then double-click fields in the table that you want to include in the page.

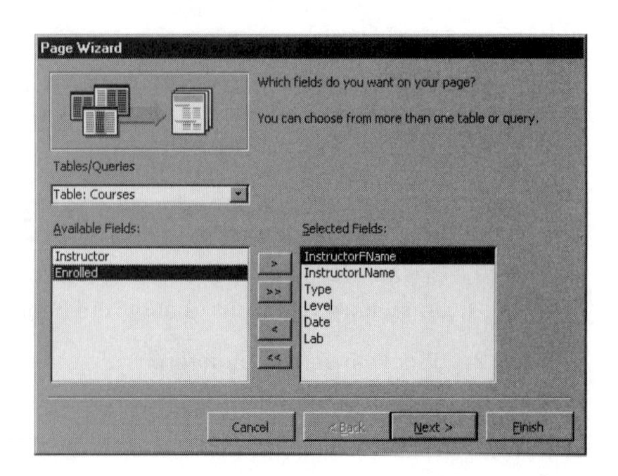

FIGURE 13.38 Select fields for your page in the Data Access Page Wizard.

If you want to create a page in which users can drill down for related records in another table, select the related table in the Tables/Queries drop-down, and double-click fields you want to add from that table. Then click Next. In the next step (if you've chosen related tables), you can group your data as you would in an Access report.

Adding grouping levels means that the data displays as read-only—it cannot be edited.

When you've set your grouping levels, click Next. The next dialog box lets you set sorting options for the data in the related records. In the last step of the wizard, name your page. To open the finished page, click the Open the Page option. To add text to the page such as a title, click the Modify the Page's Design option. Enable the Apply a Theme check box to select an Office 2000 theme for your Web page. When you've finished setting options, click Finish to create the Web page. Access creates a folder with the name of the page appended to "_ files" in the folder that houses the database. For example, if your page is named 'Courses,' the folder for the page will be called Courses_files. Data Access Pages are stored as HTML files and graphic files in the new folder. Figure 13.39 shows a Data Access Page displayed in Access 2000 form view. Choose File ➢ Web Page Preview to display a Data Access Page in your browser.

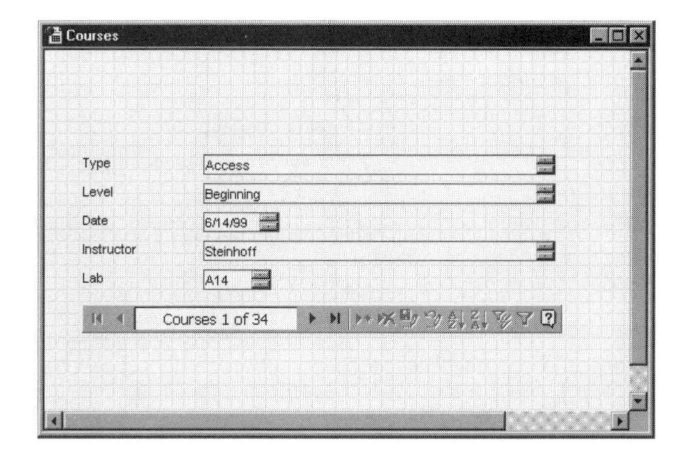

FIGURE 13.39

Data access pages are bound to your database

To delete the page, select the Pages group in the Database window, select the Data Access Page, and click the Delete button. When you delete a page, you'll be given the choice to delete just the link and keep the page (the unlinked page will be static: a snapshot of the data when the page was created), or delete all the page files.

Figure 13.40 shows a data access page created from the same data in Internet Explorer 5. In this case, we chose to group based on Instructor in the wizard. The result in the browser is a *Grouped Data Access Page*. This grouped list is read-only, but if you want a slick way to present large quantities of categorized data, grouping is the answer. Users can show or hide details by clicking expand indicators on the left side of the page. When a user prints the contents of the browser window, they only print the data that is displayed. Combine the power of grouping with the sorting and filtering toolbar buttons and you have the tools you need to create a fast and friendly reporting tool for end users.

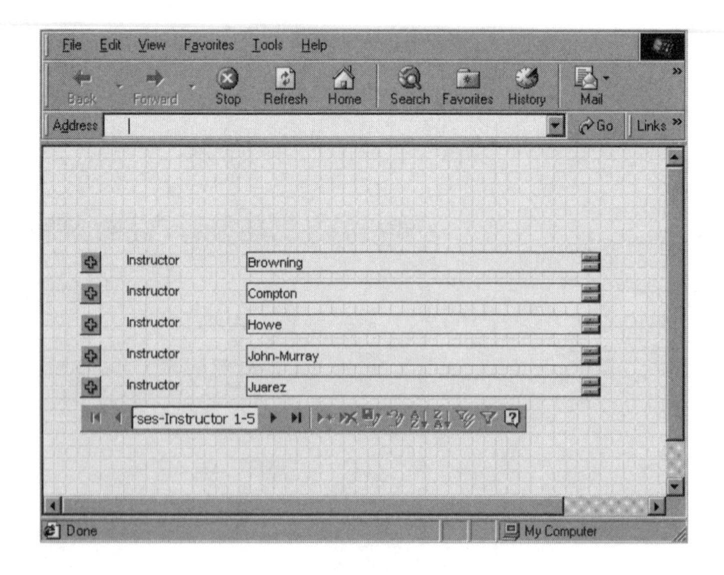

FIGURE 13.40

Selecting a group in the wizard creates a page with expandable groups

Using Data Access Pages

Objective AC2000E.6.2

After you've created a Data Access Page, users with a Microsoft Office 2000 license can open the page using the Internet Explorer browser (version 5 or higher). To test an interactive data access page in its intended environment, open it in IE. The page has a toolbar at the bottom that viewers can use to navigate, sort or filter the records (see Figure 13.40). Navigating, sorting, and filtering records works just like in Access database forms.

If the Data Access Page was created from an editable recordset, and you didn't group the data on the page, users can edit and enter records in the page as they would in a form. If a viewer makes changes to the data, they must save the changes by clicking the Save button on the page toolbar or undo changes by clicking the Undo button on the toolbar.

Any changes a user makes and saves are made directly to the data in your database so be careful who has access to your Data Access Pages.

Hands On: *Objectives AC2000E.6.1, 6.2, and 6.3*

1. Select a table that has a related form.
    - a) Save the table as a static Web page.
    - b) Preview the page in your browser.
    - c) Create a static Web page from the related form.
    - d) Preview the page in your browser.
    - e) In either page, add a hyperlink to another Web page.
    - f) In either page, add a hyperlink to an Excel spreadsheet or Word document.

2. Using the same table that you used above, create a data access page.

a) Preview the page in your browser.

b) Sort the data by the first field displayed in the page.

c) Sort the data based on values in another field.

d) Group and sort the displayed data.

e) Create a new page that opens with the data grouped and sorted as in step d above.

f) Preview the page in your browser.

CHAPTER 14

Creating Web Sites with FrontPage 2000

During the last five years, the world has witnessed an unprecedented explosion in an entirely new form of communication. The World Wide Web, the most exciting tool ever developed for sharing information, is providing a whole new outlet for creative and enterprising people to reach each other around the globe. Whether you want to provide information, entertain, sell a product, or collaborate on a project, FrontPage is the perfect tool to help you create a dynamic presence on the Web.

Working in FrontPage 2000

In simple terms, a Web site (or Web) is nothing more than a collection of documents—Web pages, images, multimedia files, databases—housed on a computer open to access by others. Some, or all, of the site may be open to the general public through the Internet; other parts may be restricted to employees of your company (an intranet) or to people, such as your company's suppliers, to whom you have given specific access privileges (an extranet). A Web site can provide product and services information, grant access to extensive databases of information, serve as a guide to other related sites, collect survey information, record product orders, host video conferences, answer questions, and allow you to perform just about every other communication function you can imagine.

Creating a Web is a lot like building a house: you can't build it one page or one room at a time and expect the overall design to have any continuity. When creating a Web site, you should lay out the entire design before you start building it. With the plans in hand, you're ready to create the basic structure and build the individual pages. You can always remodel it later, once the basic format is in place.

FrontPage 2000 offers all the tools you need to create and manage an outstanding Web site without your needing to know how to program HTML (hypertext markup language), the programming language of the Web. FrontPage creates all the HTML code you need behind the scenes, while you work with the elements you're already most familiar with—text and graphics. And to simplify Web maintenance, FrontPage provides a unified interface for Web page creation and Web site management.

Becoming Familiar with FrontPage

The FrontPage 2000 application window, shown in Figure 14.1, looks like a cross between Word and Outlook. It opens with a menu bar and single toolbar row at the top, a Views bar on the left side of the window, and a blank page on the right. When you create a Web page, you are working in the default view, which is Page view. Later in the chapter, we'll introduce you to the other FrontPage views.

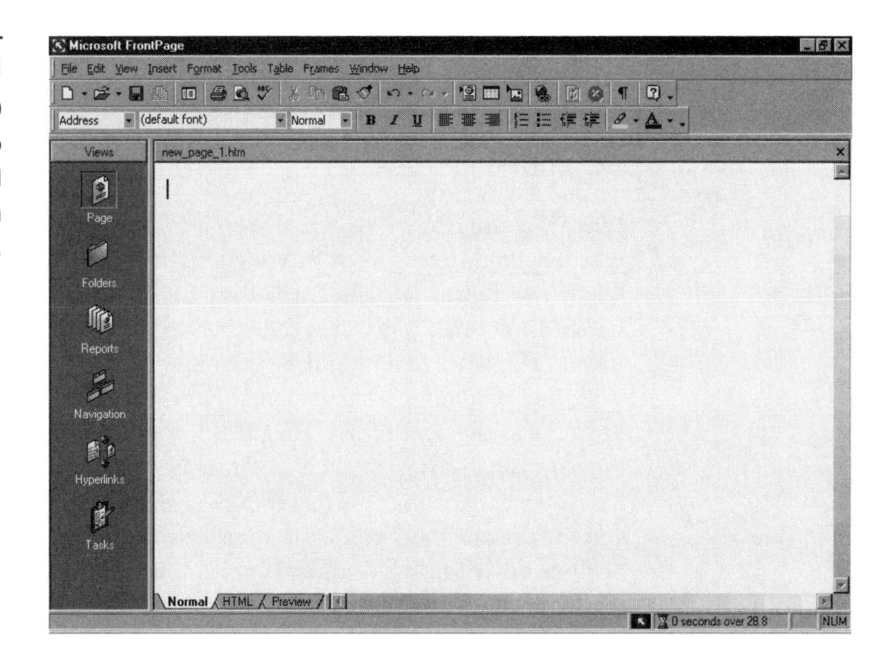

FIGURE 14.1
The FrontPage 2000 window displays Web page creation and management tools in a single interface.

When you launch FrontPage, a message box may indicate that FrontPage is not your default Web page editor and ask if you would like to make it your default editor. Unless you are using other Web editors, you will want to answer yes. If you are certain about your choice, clear the check box and you won't be asked again.

Building a Web Page from Scratch

Objective FP2000.4.2

When you launch FrontPage, you are immediately presented with a blank Web page. To add additional pages to your Web, click the New Page button on the Standard toolbar. If you have a clear idea what the major pages in your Web will be, you may want to create these pages first before entering the pages' content. This makes it easy to add links between pages and helps you organize the content more clearly. Refer to *Saving Pages to a Web* later in this chapter for information about how to save your new pages. To switch between pages, click the Window menu and choose the page you want to view.

Entering and Formatting Text

Objective FP2000.7.1

When you are ready to add text, you'll find that adding text to a Web page is not much different from entering text in Word. You will recognize all of the default buttons on the Formatting toolbar, including Style, Font, Bold, Italics, Underline, Alignment, Numbering, Bullets, Increase and Decrease Indent, Highlight Color, and Font Color.

Rather than displaying an actual Font, the Font text box displays `default` as the active font. The default font is typically a variable (proportional) width, serif font, such as Times New Roman. However, the actual font is dependent on the browser of the person viewing the Web page. While you can use any fonts you wish, some browsers only support Times and two or three other fonts. The more fonts you use, the greater the odds that visitors with various browsers will see strikingly different versions of your site.

There are six heading styles recognized by HTML and several additional styles shown on the default styles list. You can be assured that text formatted using one of the listed styles will look the same, no matter which browser your visitors are using. The majority of body text should be entered using the Normal style. Figure 14.2 shows the major styles.

FIGURE 14.2
FrontPage supports major HTML text styles.

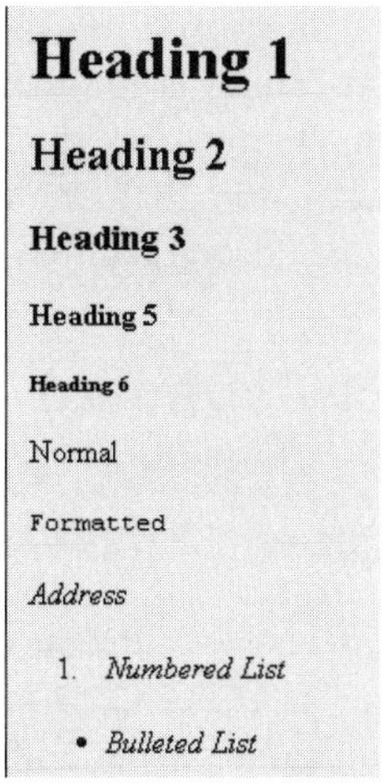

Heading 1
Heading 2
Heading 3
Heading 5
Heading 6
Normal
Formatted
Address
1. Numbered List
• Bulleted List

Text automatically wraps to the next line—just press Enter to start a new paragraph. When you press Enter, FrontPage inserts a special HTML code that inserts a blank line between paragraphs. If you want a new line without a blank line, choose Insert ➢ Break and select Normal Line Break to end a line.

To format existing text, start as you usually do, by selecting the text. The text-selection methods you use in Word also work here. Click any of the Formatting buttons on the toolbar, choose a new style, or change the font for selected text.

As you are entering text, don't forget the Undo and Redo buttons—you can Undo and Redo up to 30 actions. That should get you through most crisis situations. You also have full access to Cut, Copy, and Paste to move and copy text. If you've already prepared something you want to include on your page (even a Word table or an Excel worksheet), you can copy and paste it into FrontPage with no problem.

Using the Format Painter

Objective FP2000.7.5

The Format Painter, also available in the other Office 2000 applications, lets you copy formats from one paragraph to another. To use the Format Painter, select text with the format you want to copy, click the Format Painter button to copy the format, and drag over unformatted text to apply the format. The Format Painter is automatically turned off after you release the mouse button. Double-click the Format Painter button if you want to apply the format to more than one selection. Double-click again when you're finished using the Format Painter.

Using the Office Clipboard

Objective FP2000.7.6

In Chapter 1, we introduced you to the Office Clipboard in *Pasting Multiple Items*. The Office Clipboard is only partially available within FrontPage—although you can cut and copy items to the Office Clipboard, you cannot access those items in FrontPage. You can use the collect portion of collect and paste, but not the paste option. To turn on the Clipboard toolbar in Word, Excel, or PowerPoint, choose View ➢ Toolbars ➢ Office Clipboard. Then switch to FrontPage and cut or copy multiple items. When you switch back to the primary application, use the Office 2000 Clipboard toolbar to paste items from the Web page into the open document.

Checking Spelling on a Page

Objective FP2000.12.1

FrontPage 2000 checks spelling on the fly just like you are used to in Word. Right-click when you encounter a red wavy underline to choose a correct word from the shortcut menu. After you have entered all the text for a page, double-check the spelling by clicking the Check Spelling button on the Standard toolbar. The Spelling feature will run through your page and identify any words that it does not recognize.

To check spelling for all the pages in a Web, see "Checking Spelling Across a Web" later in this chapter.

Organizing with Lists

Objective FP2000.7.2

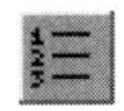
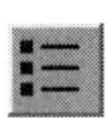

FrontPage supports bullets and numbering using the Bullets and Numbering buttons on the Formatting toolbar. Select the text to which you want to apply bullets or numbering and click the corresponding button before entering the text.

FrontPage 2000 also supports collapsible lists and multilevel lists, like the one shown in Figure 14.3.

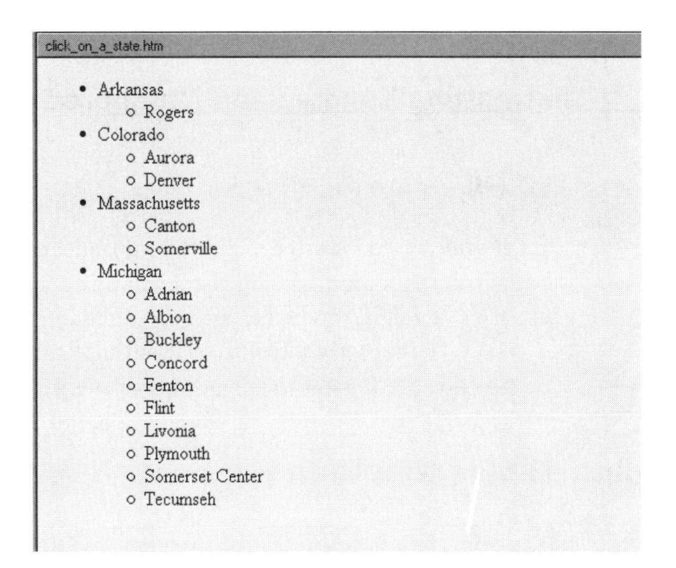

FIGURE 14.3
A multilevel list lets you present data in an organized way.

Creating a Multilevel list

1. In Page view (View ➢ Page), position the insertion point where you want to create a list.
2. Click Format ➢ Bullets and Numbering.
3. Click either the Plain Bullets tab or the Numbers tab and choose the style of bullets you want to use for the top level.

   OR

Creating a Multilevel list

3. To create a bullet from a graphic, click the Picture Bullet tab and choose Use Bullets from the Current Theme or click Browse to select a different graphic. Click OK.
4. Click OK again and begin typing the list, pressing Enter after each item.
5. To change the level of an item, click the Increase Indent button on the Formatting toolbar twice to demote the item.
6. To move items up to the previous level, select the items, and then click Decrease Indent one or more times as needed.
7. Press Enter twice to end the list.

Formatting Bulleted and Numbered Lists

Objective FP2000.7.3

If you would like to use a different bullet or number style for the sub items in the list, right-click on a list item and choose List Properties. Select the new style. It will be applied to all items on that level under the current main point. You'll have to reapply it to other similar sub-items or use the Format Painter to copy the format to the other sub-items.

Adding Tables to a Web Page

Objective FP2000.9.1

Despite the fact that Microsoft has done everything it can to make FrontPage look and act like Word, HTML has limitations that cannot be overlooked. One of the most significant problems Web page designers encounter is the inability to move and place text and graphics freely on a page. That's where tables come in. A table is a structure of columns and rows that allows you to enter and edit text and graphics within the cells of the table. By creating a table with the right number of cells, you can position things more precisely on your Web page. The recipe in Figure 14.4 is an example of a simple table used to place text in adjacent columns.

FIGURE 14.4
Use a table on a Web page to create columns.

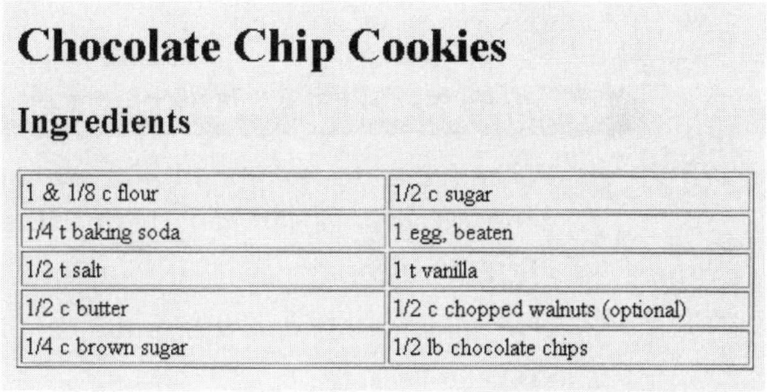

Chocolate Chip Cookies
Ingredients
1 & 1/8 c flour
1/2 c sugar
1/4 t baking soda
1 egg, beaten
1/2 t salt
1 t vanilla
1/2 c butter
1/2 c chopped walnuts (optional)
1/4 c brown sugar
1/2 lb chocolate chips

Figure 14.5 demonstrates a more complex use of tables to position both text and graphics precisely. The gridlines do not display in a browser.

FIGURE 14.5
Tables can be used to position text and graphics more precisely.

Adventures Unlimited, LLC
Your Source for Ecological Travel
About Us
Planning Your Adventure
Where Would You Like to Go?
South America
North America
Central America

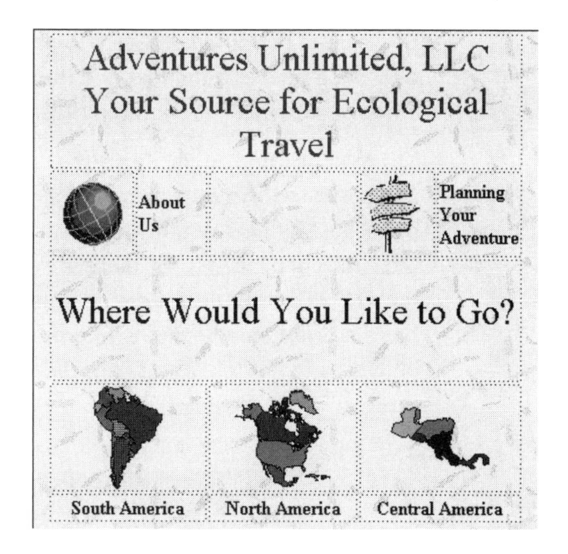

If you're familiar with tables in Word, you have a head start. Just as in Word, there are three ways to create a table in FrontPage:

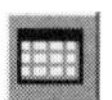

- Click the Insert Table button on the Standard toolbar and drag the numbers of columns and rows you want.
- Choose Table ➢ Draw Table to draw the cells that make up a table.
- Choose Table ➢ Insert ➢ Table to enter the table properties in a dialog box.

The last method is the most efficient, because you can set all the table options as you create your table.

Creating a Table Using the Insert Table Dialog Box

1. Position the insertion point where you want to create the table and choose Table ➢ Insert Table to open the Insert Table dialog box, shown in Figure 14.6.
2. Use the spin box controls to indicate how many rows and columns you want.
3. Choose how you would like the table aligned on the page: left, right, centered, or default (the position of the table when it was created).
4. If you want the table to look like a table, add a border—the higher the number, the thicker the border.
5. Set the Cell Padding and Cell Spacing in increments of 1. Cell Padding is the space between the text and the sides of the cell. Cell Spacing is the amount of space between the cells of the table.
6. To have the table adjust its size to the screen resolution your visitors are using, set the width in Percent: 100% will span the entire width of the page, 50% half the width, and so on. FrontPage will automatically adjust the width of each cell so cells are evenly spread across the width of the table. Pixels provide a more precise measurement than percentages, but are unreliable because different browsers interpret pixels differently. It's safest to avoid pixels when working with tables.

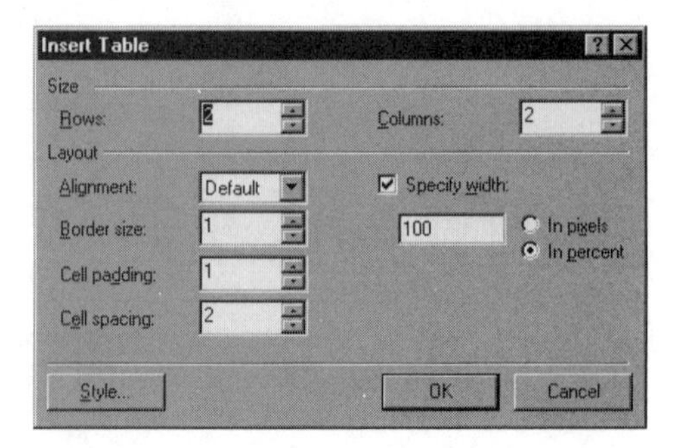

FIGURE 14.6
The Insert Table dialog box lets you set table properties before creating the table

If you are creating a complex page, you should divide the page into several separate tables rather than one large one. A large table takes longer to load. Smaller tables load one at a time and will begin appearing much more quickly.

Once you've created your table, entering text is a breeze. Use Tab to move between cells of the table or just click in the cell you want and start typing. When you reach the cell border, text will wrap around inside the cell, increasing the height of the cell.

Changing Cell and Table Properties

Objective FP2000E.8.1

Right-click on the table and choose Table Properties to make changes to the table's settings (see Figure 14.7). In addition to changing the properties you set when you created the table, you can add a background to the table and colors to the borders. Choose a solid color for the background from the color control. If you choose Use Background Image, click the Browse button and you will be given a choice between using an image in the current Web, another location on disk, or from FrontPage's Clip Art collection. After you choose the image, you must close the dialog boxes to view your selection. Make sure you can still read the text against the background. If you need to make a change, you have to go back into Table properties and do it all over again.

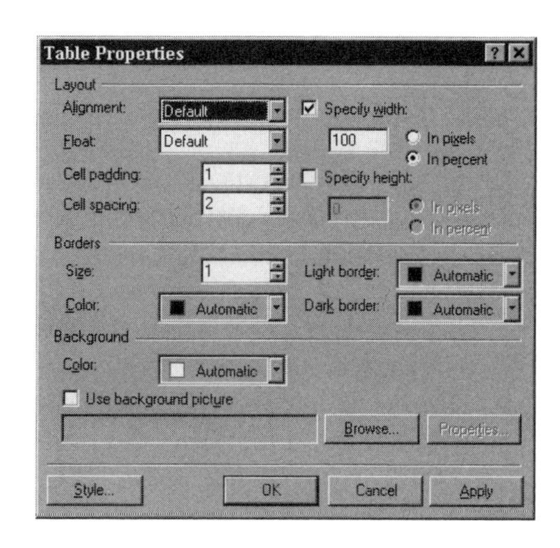

FIGURE 14.7 Change the layout, borders, and background of a table using the Table Properties dialog box.

If you like to keep things simple but still want your tables to stand out on the page, add borders to your tables. Border changes the color around the table and its cells. Light Border and Dark Border work together to create a dimensional effect like the one shown here.

There are many colors to choose from, or you can mix your own in the Color dialog box. To open the Color dialog box, choose Custom from the list of color choices.

Resizing Tables and Cells

Objective FP2000.9.4

FrontPage adjusts the width of a cell to the cell's contents unless you have specified a table width in the Table Properties or a cell width in the Cell Properties. Both are minimum widths, so if your content is larger than the minimums you set, the cells will still expand. As long as you use percentages rather than pixels, the cell widths are relative to the table widths. If your table width is set at 50% of the page, a cell set at 50% will actually be 50% of the table or 25% of the entire page width. Preview your page in a browser or two before you spend too much time fine-tuning it. Some pages look even better in the browsers than in FrontPage.

Changing Cell Properties

Objective FP2000E.8.1

If you select Cell Properties from the shortcut menu when you right-click a table, you find that the properties for individual cells are similar to the table properties. The horizontal and vertical alignment options, such as top, right, center, refer only to text or images within the cell, however, not to the entire table.

If you designate a cell or a group of cells as header cells, FrontPage will bold them automatically. You can also tell FrontPage not to wrap text within a cell by enabling the No Wrap check box. Use the cell background options to apply a background to selected cells. (There is no point in applying a background to a cell if you already have a table background, because the cell background will be ignored.)

Merging and Splitting Cells

Objective FP2000.9.5

To really get creative with tables, try merging and splitting cells. Use Table ➢ Merge Cells to join two or more cells together so they act as one. Use Table ➢ Split Cells to divide a cell into two or more cells. By merging and splitting cells, you can align text and graphics within a table using a variety of layouts, as you can see in Figure 14.5 earlier in this section.

You can also merge cells by using the Eraser on the Tables toolbar to erase cell borders. To access the Tables toolbar, choose Table ➢Draw Table. The Tables toolbar holds tools for formatting and designing tables.

Click the Eraser tool and drag it over the cell border you want to erase. When the cell border turns red, release the mouse button to erase the border.

Adding Rows and Columns

Objective FP2000.9.3

To add rows or columns to an existing table, click the Draw Table button on the Tables toolbar. Drag the pencil pointer horizontally or vertically across the table, as shown in Figure 14.8 to create rows or columns.

FIGURE 14.8 Draw rows and columns into a table using the Draw Table tool.

You can also add rows and columns to a table by choosing Table ➢ Insert ➢ Rows and Columns or right-clicking and choosing Insert Row or Insert Column. The Insert menu option opens an Insert Rows or Columns dialog box where you can indicate the number and placement of the rows or columns you want to add.

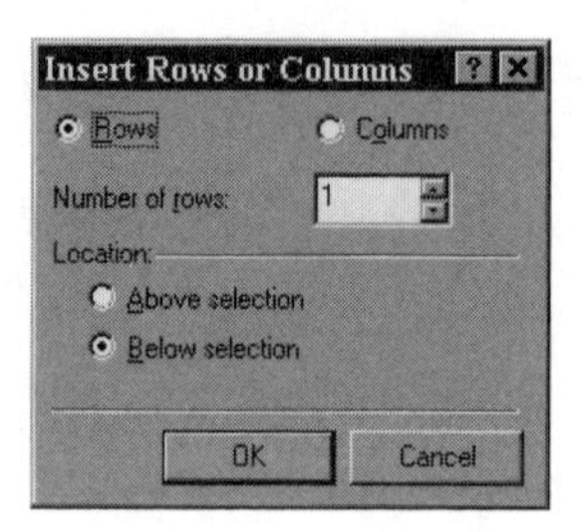

Deleting Rows and Columns

Objective FP2000.9.2

To delete a row or a column, select what you want to delete, right-click and choose Delete Cells. You can select columns by moving the insertion point above the column, so that the insertion point turns to a downward-pointing arrow, and clicking the mouse. Select rows or cells by dragging over them. To select only one row or column, click in a cell and choose Table ➢ Select Row or Select Column.

If you want to delete an entire table, choose Table ➢ Select Table and press the Delete key on the keyboard.

Adding Tables within a Table

Objective FP2000E.8.3

When you need even greater precision in the placement of text and images, you can insert a table inside a cell of another table. Each table maintains its own properties, so each table can have different borders. Table backgrounds can get a little complicated when you insert a table into another table, because changing the background of a parent table (the outside table) affects each of the cells, including the tables inside of the parent. Nevertheless, this table-in-table option makes it possible to lay out aesthetically pleasing and functional sites with minimal effort.

Hands On: Objectives FP2000.4.2, 7.1, 7.6, 9.1-9.5, 12.1, FP2000E.8.1-8.3

1. Launch FrontPage and explore the application window.
   a) Create a new page in Page view.
   b) Switch between open pages using the Window menu.
2. On *new_page_1*, enter heading text formatted as Heading 1, press enter, and enter additional text formatted as Heading 2.
   a) Change the font of the Heading 1 to Arial, 36 pt.
   b) Change the Font color to blue.
   c) Check the spelling on the page.
   d) Enter a bulleted list of at least four items.
   e) Enter additional heading text and then enter a numbered list of at least four items.
   f) Use the Office Clipboard and copy/paste in FrontPage and another Office application to rearrange the items in the bulleted list. Cut each one to the Office Clipboard in the order you want them to appear. Click Paste All to paste them all back in order.
3. Switch to *new_page_2*.
   a) Enter heading text formatted as Heading 1.
   b) Insert a table of at least three columns and three rows on the page.
   c) Draw an additional column.
   d) Insert an additional row using the table menu.
   e) Enter text in several of the cells.
   f) Select three adjacent cells that contain text and specify a cell width of 25% in the Cell Properties dialog box.
   g) Center the text horizontally in the cells.
   h) Open Table Properties and set a custom background for the table.
   i) Re-size the table so the width is 50%.
   j) Center the table horizontally.

k) Erase one of the columns in the table.

l) Delete a row using the shortcut menu.

4. Copy multiple items from the Web page into Word:

   a) Open the Clipboard toolbar in Word.

   b) Switch back to FrontPage and copy five items from various parts of the open page.

   c) Switch back to Word and paste those items into the Word document.

Creating a FrontPage Web

Objective FP2000.1.2 and 1.3

Until now, you've been working with individual Web pages; it's now time to bring those pages together into an actual Web. A Web is a collection of pages linked together for easy navigation. When a Web is published to a Web server, it becomes a live Web site that others can access.

FrontPage gives you the option of using a wizard or template or creating a Web from scratch. There are three wizards and four templates, shown in Figure 14.9, provided by FrontPage on which you can base a Web.

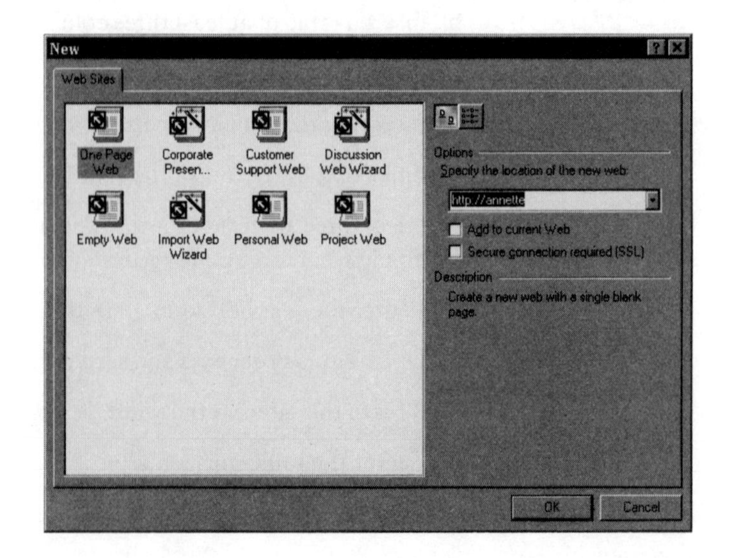

FIGURE 14.9 FrontPage provides templates and wizards to help you create a Web.

Templates provide you with a page or pages that relate to the type of Web you choose to create. For example, the Customer Support Web, shown in Figure 14.10, contains a number of sample pages that you can customize to meet your needs.

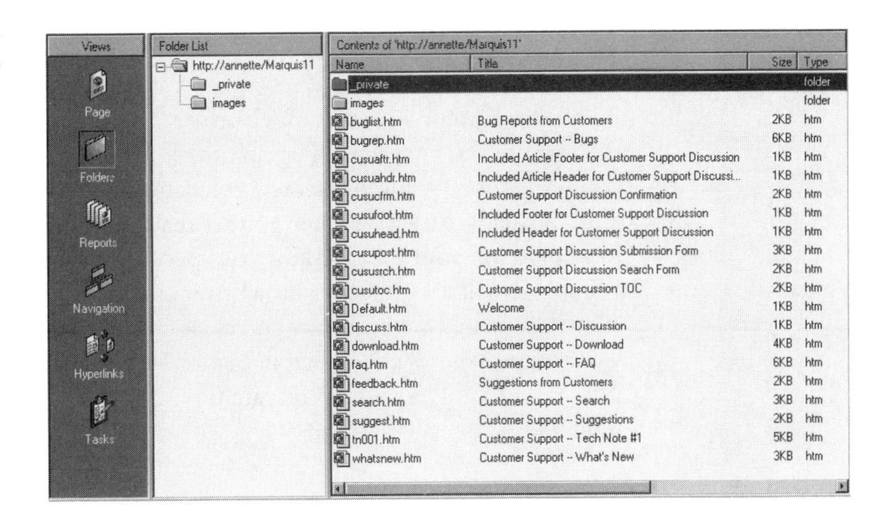

FIGURE 14.10 The Customer Support Web is an example of a Web created using a template.

Wizards actually take it one step further and walk you through the process of customizing some of the content of the Web. The Corporate Presence Web, for example, asks you questions about your company, as shown in Figure 14.11, before it creates the pages in the Web.

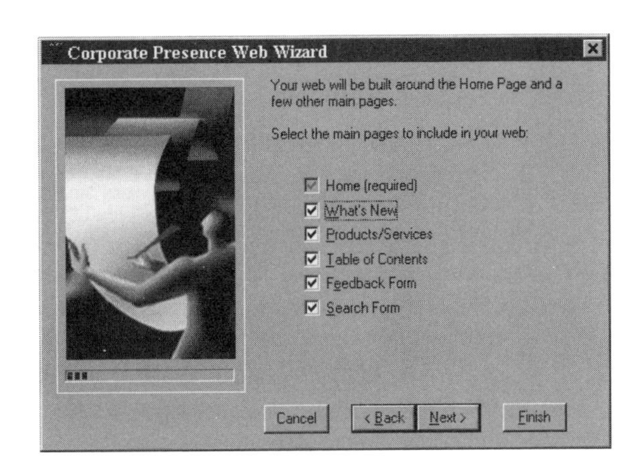

FIGURE 14.11 The Corporate Presence helps you design your Web before it creates the Web for you.

It's easier to understand what's going on with a complex Web created by a wizard or template after you've had a chance to work with all the features of FrontPage in your own Web. Because you already know how to create Web pages, you can create a blank web that you can add your pages to; choose File ➢ New ➢Web and choose Empty Web from the New dialog box.

Objective FP2000.1.1

If you have author access to a Web server (also called a host computer), enter the name of the server in the Specify the Location of the New Web text box. If you do not have author access, you can create a Web on your hard drive and transfer it to a server when you are ready to publish it. Enter the full path to a folder on your local disk; if you specify a folder that does not exist, FrontPage will create it for you when it creates the Web. The name of the Web itself is up to you. When you click OK, FrontPage creates the basic structure of your Web (shown in Figure 14.12), including a folder to store images and a folder to keep private files that you don't intend to make public.

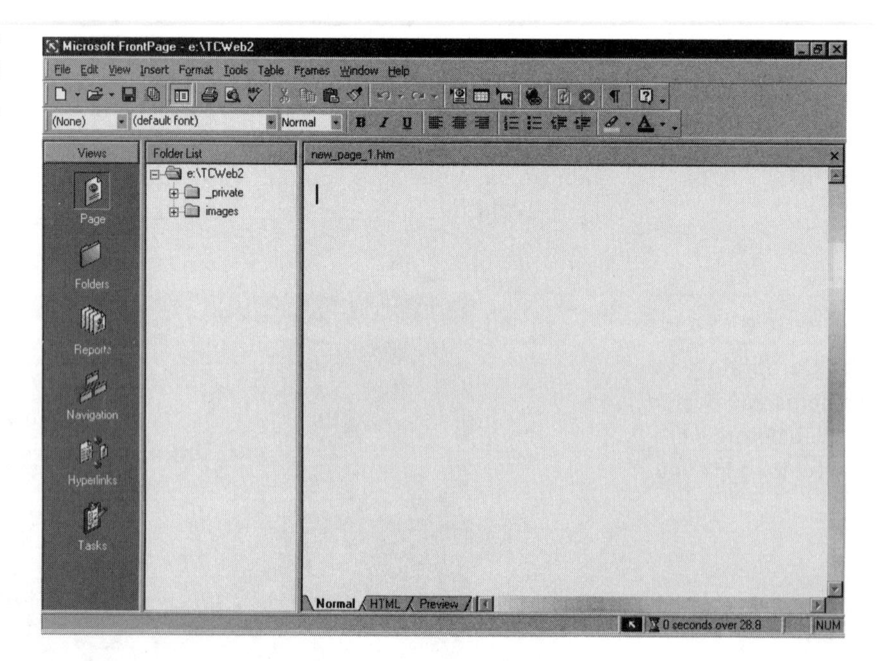

FIGURE 14.12 FrontPage creates the basic structure of an empty Web.

The Web server you are using (or going to use) may have restrictions on the characters, case sensitivity, and length of the name, so it's best to keep the name to eight characters or less if you haven't selected a server or if you are unsure of your server's naming conventions.

The default FrontPage Web window consists of two panes. The left pane shows the folders and files that make up the Web in a tree structure similar to the Windows Explorer. The right pane displays the active page.

If you don't see the folder list, click the Folder List button on the Standard toolbar.

Viewing a Web in Different Ways

Objectives FP2000.11.1, 11.2 and 11.3

FrontPage 2000 gives you six different ways to view and organize the work you are doing creating a Web. Each of these views has a special focus and gives you a new perspective on your Web.

The first view is the view you've been using to create Web pages up to this point. Page view combines the functionality of an editor with the tools you need to manage a Web.

Folders view, shown earlier in Figure 14.10, allows you to see all the pages, graphics, and files in your web. Double-click any page to open the page in Page view. Right-click on any folder and choose New Folder to add a folder to the folder. Use drag and drop to organize files into folders.

Reports view, shown in Figure 14.13, is your personal analysis tool. In Reports view, you can run reports to list slow pages, unlinked pages, recently added or changed files, broken hyperlinks, component errors, review status, assignments, categories, publish status, or checkout status.

Navigation view helps you define and create a navigational structure within a site, like the one shown in Figure 14.14. For more about using Navigation view to create internal links between pages in a Web, see *Creating the Navigational Structure for a Web* later in this chapter.

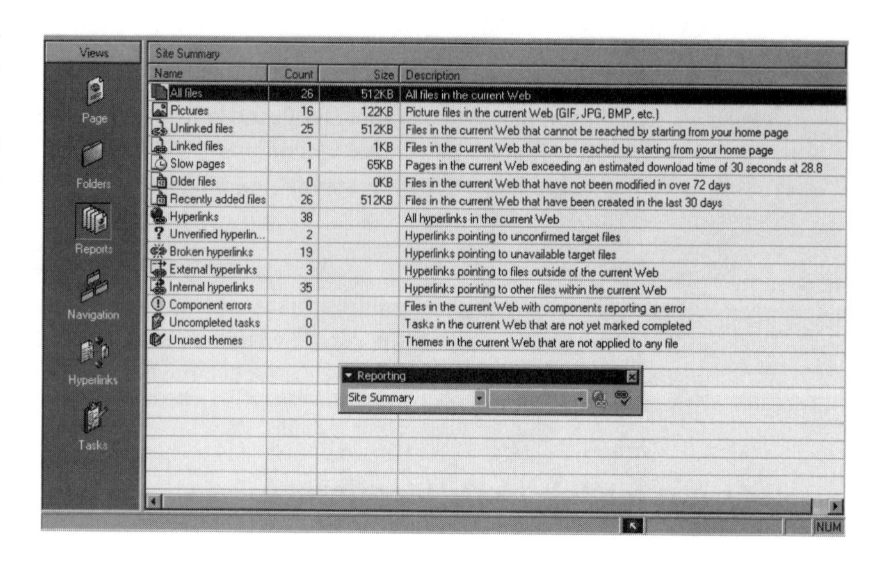

FIGURE 14.13 Reports view lets you analyze how a Web is functioning.

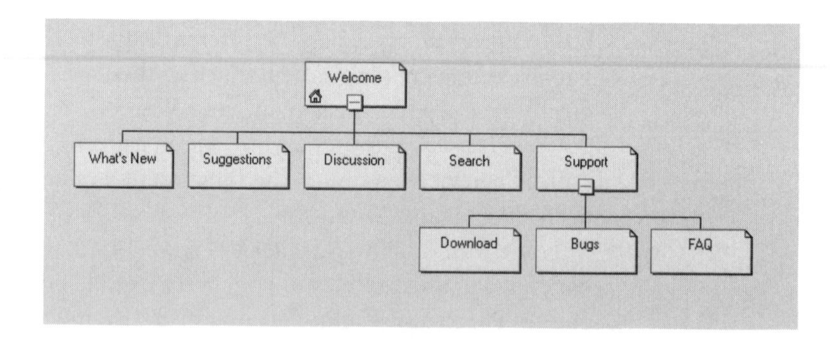

FIGURE 14.14 Navigation view helps you create the organizational structure and create links between the pages of the Web.

Hyperlinks view, shown in Figure 14.15, lets you see all of the items that link to or from a specific page or Microsoft Office document, and determine if any links are broken.

Tasks view helps the members of the Web design team track what needs to be done and to whom the tasks are assigned. As tasks are completed, they are marked off the list, as shown in Figure 14.16. For more about Tasks, see *Managing Tasks* later in this chapter.

Although you'll probably spend most of your time in Page view, these other views give you a dynamic way to manage all the pieces of your Web.

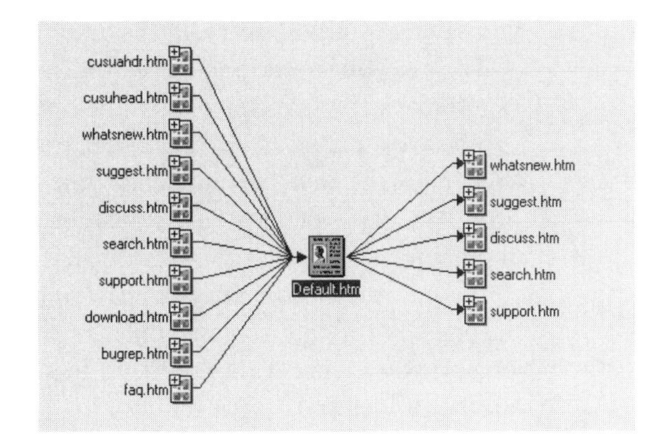

FIGURE 14.15
Hyperlinks view shows you a graphical representation of the links in a Web.

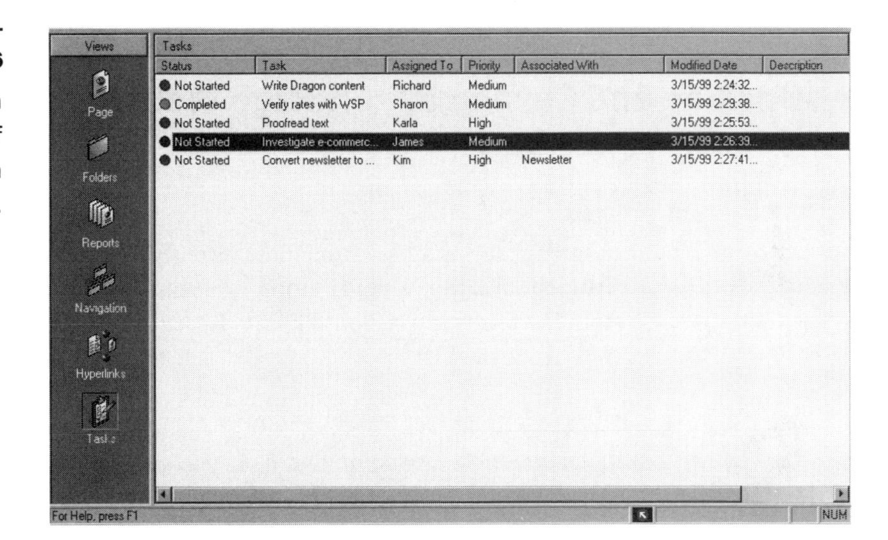

FIGURE 14.16
Tasks view helps a team keep track of what is left to do on a Web.

Saving Pages to a Web

Objective FP2000.2.1

Now that you have a Web, you can save pages directly to the Web, bringing your Web a step closer to publishing. To create a home page for your Web, switch to Navigation view and click the New button. This creates a home page (called `index.htm` if you are saving to a hard disk or `default.htm` if you saving to a Web server).

To save your home page, click the Save button on the toolbar. The page is automatically saved as part of the open Web.

To save a previously created page or to save a new page you add to the Web, click the Save button. When you save a page for the first time, FrontPage will open the Save As dialog box to ask you the page's location and name.

If you want to save a page as part of the open Web, just enter a name for the page. FrontPage suggests a filename based on the first line of text on the page. If you do not want the file to be saved with the open Web, switch to another folder and save it there.

The Page Title is the text that appears in the title bar of the browser window and is the friendly way to refer to the page. If you would like to change the suggested Page Title, click the Change button and enter a new name.

Opening and Closing a FrontPage Web

Objective FP2000.2.1

FrontPage keeps a list of the most recently opened Webs so if you're only working on a few Webs at a time, you can re-open a closed Web directly from the File menu. Choose File ➢ Recent Webs and choose the Web you want from the list.

If you are only working on one Web, you can have FrontPage open it for you when you launch the application. Choose Tools ➢ Options and check the Open Last Web Automatically When FrontPage Starts checkbox on the General page.

If the Web you want to open is filed away somewhere, choose File ➢ Open Web. The Open Web dialog box, shown in Figure 14.17, helps you locate the Web you want to open. If you have access to Web Folders, this folder is displayed by default. To locate a folder in another location, change the Look In setting to the correct folder and double-click the folder name that houses the Web you want.

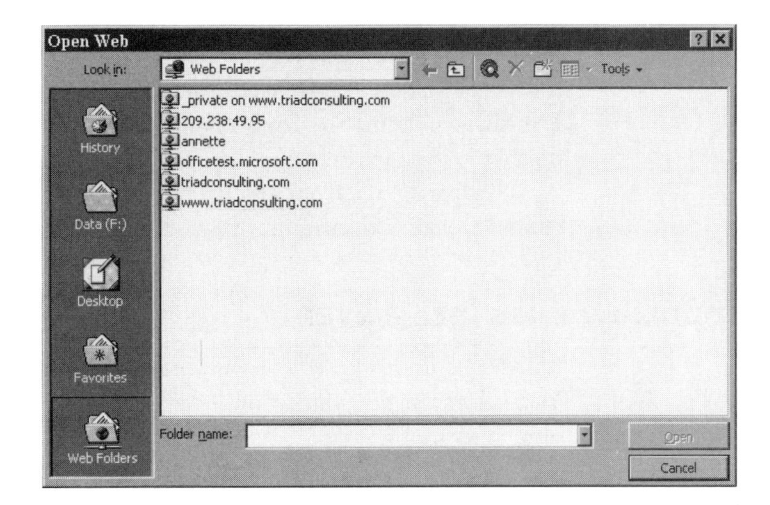

FIGURE 14.17 Use the Open Web dialog box to open a previously saved Web.

FrontPage opens each Web in its own application window. Use the Windows Taskbar to switch between open Webs.

To close a Web, choose File ➢ Close Web.

Renaming Web Pages and Webs

Objectives FP2000.5.3 and 12.2

Web pages have page URLs (Uniform Resource Locators or addresses) and page titles. To change the page title, open the page and choose File ➢ Properties or right-click on the file in Folder view and choose Properties from the shortcut menu. Enter a new title in the Title textbox. Click OK to save the change.

To rename the page URL, right-click on the page in Folder view and choose Rename. Enter a new name for the page.

Do not use Windows Explorer or My Computer to rename pages—renaming pages within FrontPage automatically updates its hyperlinks within the Web. The Windows file management tools don't do this.

Deleting a Web and Web Pages

If you want to delete a Web you have created, right-click on the Web in the folder list and choose Delete. FrontPage asks you if you want to remove FrontPage information from the folder but retain the folder contents or delete the Web entirely.

To delete a page from a Web, right-click on the page in Folder view and choose Delete. Confirm that you want to delete the page by clicking Yes.

Importing Files into a Web

FrontPage offers two ways to import existing content into a FrontPage Web. You can insert the content of documents into a Web page and you can import entire files.

Opening Text Files in FrontPage

Objective FP2000.6.2

You can convert many imported text files to HTML by simply opening them in FrontPage using these steps:

1. Import the file into an open Web (File ➢ Import).
2. Right-click on it in the Folder list and choose Open With.
3. Select FrontPage from the list of choices and click OK. If it can, FrontPage converts the file into HTML.

If FrontPage doesn't recognize the file format, it asks you if it is an HTML (probably not), RTF, or text file, or warns you that the file contains binary data (which means it probably can't be converted). Unless you know the file is a text file, choose RTF and see what happens. If FrontPage converts it, you're all set. If not, return to the Folder list and double-click on the document to open it in its native application, then see if you can use Save As to save the document as an HTML or RTF file.

Rich Text Format (RTF) is the standard format for exchanging Windows-based files. RTF files retain much of a document's original formatting, unlike text files.

Adding Elements from an Existing Web Site

Objective FP2000.6.3

Using your browser you can save images, text, and tables from a Web site and insert them into your Web pages. Right-click on any Web image and copy the image, then switch to FrontPage and paste it into an open page. You can also select text and tables and copy and paste them the same way.

Web content may be copyrighted. Be sure to read the copyright notices and legal disclaimers on a Web site before copying another site's content.

Importing Web Sites, Folders, and Files

FrontPage lets you import entire Web sites, folders, and files into a FrontPage Web so you can use the contents in your Web.

Using the Import Wizard

Importing Files into FrontPage

1. Choose File ➢ Import.
2. To add files, click the Add Files button and browse to locate the files you want to add. Hold the Ctrl key to select multiple files. When you have found the files you want, click Open.
3. To add folders, click the Add Folders button and locate the folder you want to add. Click OK to add the folder to the import list. Click Add Folder again to import another folder.
4. When you have added all the files and folders you want, click OK to import the files.

Objectives FP2000E.1.1 and E.1.2

To add content from a site on the Web or from a source directory of files on a local or network drive, click the From Web button in the Import dialog box. Follow the Import Web Wizard to select the site or location and what you want to import. When you finish the wizard, FrontPage imports the Web.

Creating Hyperlinks

Objective FP2000.7.4

The basic tenet behind the Web is that when you read something that interests you, you should be able to click on it and be whisked away to a document that contains more information about that topic. To create a Web site that is friendly to visitors, you want to establish useful and logical links from:

- One place on a page to another
- One page to another within your site
- Your site to other sites

Although you can clutter a page with too many links, incorporating valuable links makes your site worth coming back to—and isn't that, after all, the whole point?

Using Bookmarks to Move to a Specific Location on a Page

If you've used Word bookmarks or hyperlinks in any of the Office applications, you already know much of what you need to create internal page links. In FrontPage, a bookmark is a location on your page that you have named so that you can refer to it by name. Once you've created a bookmark on a page, you can create a link to the bookmark.

To create the bookmark, select the text or image you want to mark by dragging over it. Choose Edit ➢ Bookmark to open the Bookmark dialog box.

If you select text, the text will appear in the Bookmark Name box. (With an image, the text box will be blank.) Enter a name for the bookmark, then click OK. A broken blue line will appear to indicate marked text.

Creating a Link to a Bookmark

1. Select the text or image you want to act as your hyperlink and click the Hyperlink button on the Standard toolbar.
2. Select the bookmark from the Bookmark drop-down list, then click OK to establish the link.
3. Test your link by right-clicking on the link and choosing Follow Hyperlink. If the link is working, it takes you directly to the bookmark.

Linking to Another Page in Your Web

If you have more than one page in your Web, you'll want to create links between the pages so your visitors can easily navigate between them. Enter enough text to tell your visitors where the link will take them, then select the text. Click the Hyperlink button on the Standard toolbar to open the Create or Edit Hyperlink dialog box.

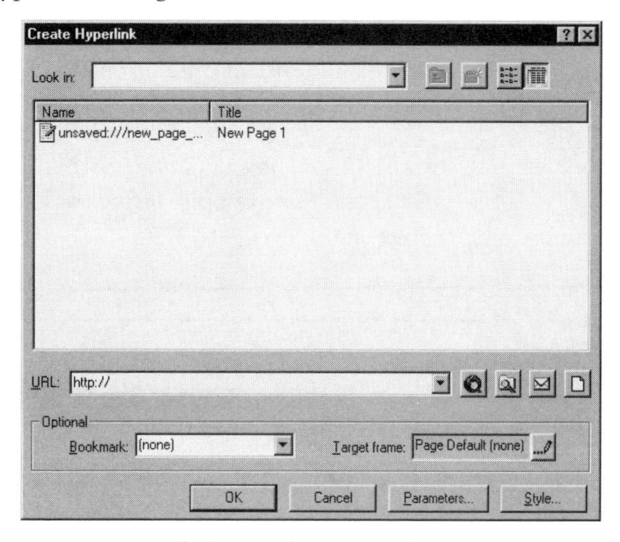

If the page you want to link is in the current Web, select the page from the list of pages.

When you click OK to close the dialog box, the selected text will be underlined and colored blue (unless you've chosen another color for hyperlinks in the Page Properties to indicate that it is a hyperlink. To test the hyperlink, right-click and choose Follow Hyperlink. The working link will take you to the page you designated. When you view the link in a browser, you'll just click on the link to be taken to the linked page.

Linking to the World Wide Web

The most effective Web sites strike a balance between providing information directly and linking visitors to other valuable resources located in the vast labyrinth of the World Wide Web. One of the reasons that people will return to your site is that they remember it as a valuable jumping-off point for other places of interest. If you pick your links with care and keep them up-to-date, your site will become a regular stop for repeat visitors.

Before you can create links to other Web sites, you must identify sites to which you want to link. Visit the sites and put them in your Favorites folder (if you're using Internet Explorer) or mark them as bookmarks (Netscape Navigator) so they are accessible.

Creating an External Hyperlink

1. On your Web page, select the text you want to use as a hyperlink, then click the Hyperlink button.
2. Enter the Hyperlink Type (if this is a WWW site, this will generally be *http*) and the URL of the site, as shown in Figure 14.18

   OR

3. In the URL text box, enter the full URL including the access method (generally *http*). For example, *http://www.sybex.com* is the URL for the Sybex site.
4. Click OK to create the link.

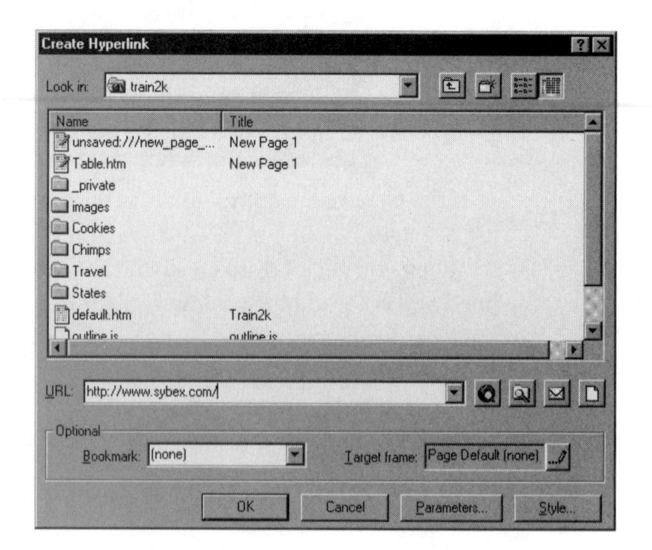

FIGURE 14.18 Creating a link to the World Wide Web.

Viewing a Web

Objective FP2000.5.1

When you are working on a Web page in Page view, you have three options for how you view the page. Typically, you are adding and editing content in

Normal view. This is the view in which you can use all of FrontPage's editing and formatting tools.

For a behind-the-scenes look at a Web, click the view tab at the bottom of the document window and choose HTML. This view shows all of the HTML code used to create the page.

To see what the page will look like when it's "live" on the Web, click the Preview tab. In this view, you can see how text, tables and graphics display on a page. Dynamic elements, like those you'll learn about later in this chapter, may not display correctly in Preview so you may see a warning at the top of the window: This page contain elements that may need to be saved or published to preview correctly.

Viewing HTML Tags

Objective FP2000E.1.3

This option, shown in Figure 14.19, clearly identifies how codes affect the various elements of the page. To view tags on a page, choose View ➢ Reveal Tags. You can modify the page and FrontPage displays tags to correspond to your modifications. For example, if you select text and click the Bold button, <b> and </b> tags appear around the text.

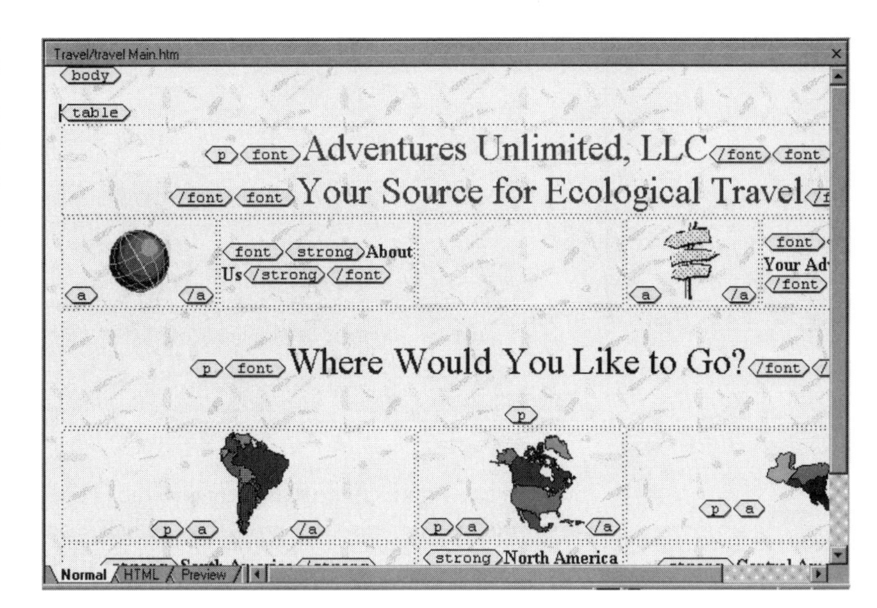

FIGURE 14.19 The new Reveal Tags option shows you exactly how the source code affects a page.

If you are new to HTML and would like to learn more about coding, see *HTML 4.0: No Experienced Required* or *Mastering HTML 4.0*, both published by Sybex.

Working Directly with Source Code

Objective FP2000E.1.4

If you would like to review or edit the source code directly, click the HTML tab at the bottom of Page view. This takes you behind the scenes into the real world of HTML, as you can see in Figure 14.20. The default view color codes the tags blue so you can easily distinguish them from the page content. To toggle color coding off, right-click on the page and choose Show Color Coding.

FIGURE 14.20 The HTML tab of Page view takes you directly to the HTML code that defines a page.

Travel/travel Main.htm

```
<html>

<head>
<meta http-equiv="Content-Type" content="text/html; charset=windows-1252">
<meta name="GENERATOR" content="Microsoft FrontPage 4.0">
<meta name="ProgId" content="FrontPage.Editor.Document">
<title>About Us</title>
</head>

<body background="Images/bd14712_.gif">

<table border="0" width="100%">
  <tr>
    <td width="100%" colspan="5">
      <p align="center"><font color="#008000" size="6">Adventures
        Unlimited, LLC</font><font size="6"><br>
        </font><font color="#008000" size="6">Your Source for
        Ecological Travel</font></td>
  </tr>
  <tr>
    <td width="17%"><a href="../images/about.htm"><img
        src="images/globe.gif" border="0" width="67" height="67"></a></td>
    <td width="16%"><font size="3"><strong>About Us</strong></font></td>
    <td width="33%"></td>
    <td width="17%"><a href="../images/planning.htm"><img
        src="images/directions.gif" border="0" width="51" height="67"></a></td>
    <td width="17%"><font size="3"><strong>Planning Your
```

Normal HTML Preview

You can enter text and tags directly into the HTML you see here. Now for the first time, you can also use FrontPage to help you set valid attributes and values for tags, saving you from learning them all yourself.

Setting Properties for a Tag

1. Click the HTML tab in Page view.
2. Position the insertion point inside the tag name (not inside an attribute or a value) of the tag you want to set properties for and right-click. Chose Tag Properties from the shortcut menu.
3. The tag's properties dialog box opens. Make the changes you want to make and click OK.

When you click OK to close the properties dialog box, FrontPage automatically rewrites the HTML for that tag.

FrontPage 2000 also allows you to use Formatting buttons such as Bold, Italics, and Underline while editing HTML code. Select the text you want to format and click the button. FrontPage inserts the tags for you.

Enhancing Design with Style Sheets

Objective FP2000E.9.3

A *cascading style sheet* consists of style definitions or style rules that apply to specific page elements or entire pages. The reason this is valuable is that it gives you more control over how a page appears irrespective of the browser. It still isn't possible to have complete control, but style sheets give Web developers many more tools than were possible before.

Let's look at a practical example. Without a style sheet, Heading 1 text appears in a large, bold version of the browser's default font. A style sheet lets you define parameters for the Heading 1 style, including font family, size, and other attributes. You can even define multiple font options to use rather than revert to the browser's default font if your first font choice isn't available on the viewer's browser.

There are three ways to apply style sheets to FrontPage web pages:

- By linking to an *external style sheet* (created in HTML and saved with a CSS extension). External style sheets are stored as individual pages. By creating an external style sheet, you can link all the pages in your Web to that one page. To make a style change to the web, you only have to change one page.

- By creating an *embedded style sheet* on a page in Page view. With an embedded style sheet, you can create styles that only apply to the active page in your web.
- By applying inline styles to individual elements on a page.

Style sheets are cascading because you can apply multiple styles to a page that are interpreted by a browser in a specific order. Styles that are applied to individual elements (inline styles) take precedence over styles embedded in the page (embedded styles), and those take precedence over styles included on external style sheets.

FrontPage Themes are based on cascading style sheets. For that reason, you should not apply cascading styles to a page or a web that is already using themes. You should also avoid editing a theme's CSS file, because it may destroy the theme (for more about themes, see *Applying Themes* later in this chapter).

You can specify styles for the following properties:

- Alignment: margins, padding, and text wrap
- Borders: style, color, width
- Colors: background, foreground, background image, attachment, repeat, vertical position, horizontal position
- Font: primary font, secondary font, font size
- Text: weight, style, variant, transform, decoration, indent, line height, letter spacing, alignment, vertical alignment

Creating and Linking External Style Sheets

FrontPage 2000 includes a number of pre-designed style sheets to get you started with CSS. To access these sheets, switch to Page view and choose File ➢ New ➢ Page from the menu. Click the Style Sheets tab. Although you can't preview the style sheets, click on each one to get a description of the sheet.

Once you select a style sheet and click OK, the HTML file will open in FrontPage.

```
new_page_1.css
a:link
{
    color: rgb(0,102,153);
}
a:visited
{
    color: rgb(0,153,102);
}
a:active
{
    color: rgb(0,102,102);
}
body
{
    font-family: Arial, Helvetica;
    background-color: rgb(204,204,153);
    color: rgb(0,51,51);
}
table
{
    table-border-color-light: rgb(102,204,204);
    table-border-color-dark: rgb(0,102,102);
}
h1, h2, h3, h4, h5, h6
{
    font-family: Times New Roman, Times;
}
```

Review the style sheet and make any changes that you want to make, then close and save the style sheet.

If you're creating a Web site as part of your company's intranet, check with your web administrator to find out if there is a company standard style sheet you should use. Most companies have a standard design they want Web authors within the company to follow.

To link an external style sheet to a page, follow these steps:

1. Open the page in Page view or select multiple pages in Folder view.
2. Choose Format ➢ Style Sheet Links.
3. Choose whether to link the style sheet to all pages or to selected pages.
4. Click Add to locate the style sheet you want to link to.
5. Click OK to link to the sheet.
6. Save the page and view it in your browser to see the impact of the style sheet changes.

Remember that if a page is linked to an external style sheet *and* has an embedded style sheet, the embedded styles are displayed. External styles are only displayed when there is no setting specified on the embedded style sheet.

Creating and Linking Embedded Style Sheets

Embedded style sheets only apply to the active page. Not to worry—if you want to apply a style sheet to other pages in your web, save the page as a template. You can then use the template that includes the embedded style sheet as the basis for other new pages in your web.

Follow these steps to create an embedded style sheet:

1. Create a new page or open the page in which you want to embed the style sheet in FrontPage.
2. Choose Format ➢ Style to open the Style dialog box.
3. Select the HTML tag you want to modify and click the Modify button or click New to create a new custom style.
4. Click the Format button and choose between Font, Paragraph, Border, Numbering, and Position.
5. Change the settings for each type of format you want to include. Click OK when you have designed the style.

Once you define the style sheet, save the page to embed the style sheet. To use the new styles, select the style from the Change Style drop-down arrow on the Format toolbar.

Remember that not all browsers support Cascading Style Sheets. If a user opens your web with an older browser, your pages may appear as if they have no styles at all. If you produce complex style sheets, you may want to add a notice to users about your use of style sheets. Better yet, include hyperlinks to Microsoft and Netscape to download their latest browsers.

Applying an Inline Style to Page Elements

You can apply *Inline styles* to specific page elements such as tables, graphics, or paragraphs. Inline styles supersede embedded and external style sheets so they allow even more precise formatting of individual elements.

To apply inline styles:

1. Select the element—table, image, or paragraph—to which you want to apply the style.
2. Right-click to open the shortcut menu and choose <element> Properties, where <element> is Table, Image, or Paragraph.
3. Click on the Style button to open the Style dialog box. If you can't apply inline styles to a specific element, there isn't a Style button.
4. Click the Format button and design the style you want to apply.
5. Click on OK when you've set all the desired properties.

Remember that inline styles only apply to the selected element, not to all the elements in that style. If you apply an inline style to a paragraph formatted as Heading 1, only the selected text changes.

Using Class

When you really want to be specific, you can define a subset of a style and save it in the external or embedded style sheet as a *class*. Think of a class as a new style that you create based on a pre-existing style. For example, you define the Heading 3 style as 14 point, bold, Arial, blue. You want to apply the Heading 3 style to text, but wish to differentiate the headings that contain tips for your users. You can define a Heading 3 Tip style that is 14 point, bold, Arial, green.

To define a class for the embedded style sheet, choose Format ➢ Style and follow the same steps you use to define any style. The only difference is that after you select the style you want to base the new style on, enter a dot and a name of the new class. For example, instead of using the selector H3 to define this particular style, use the selector `H3.Tip`.

The H3.Tip style has a different font size (24 rather than 18) and a different color (128, 128, 0 instead of 0, 128, 0) from H3. However, because H3.Tip is a class of H3, it inherits the font family and font weight attributes of H3, its parent class, rather than the default properties of the browser.

Hands On: Objectives FP2000.1.1-1.3, 2.1, 2.2, 5.1, 5.2, 6.2, 6.3, 11.1, 11.3, and FP2000E.9.3, E.1.3 and E.1.4

1. Create a new FrontPage Web using the One Page Web template.
   a) Save any previously created pages to this new Web.
   b) Switch to Folder view and add a new folder to the Web.
   c) Drag a couple of files into the new folder.
   d) Close the Web.
2. Create a new FrontPage Web using the Corporate Presence Wizard.
   a) Explore the contents of the Web in Folder view.
   b) Open at least three pages in Page view.
   c) View the HTML code for a page.
   d) Select some text in the HTML code and apply Bold.
   e) Press enter after the text and use Insert ➢ Table to insert table tags into the code.
   f) Preview the page to see how it will look in a browser.
   g) Switch to Hyperlinks view and Reports view to examine the Web more closely.
   h) Close the Web.
3. Open the One Page Web you created in Exercise 1.
   a) Add a new page to the Web and add content to the page.
   b) Save the new page to the Web.
   c) Turn on Reveal Tags.
   d) Select some text and change the heading style to make it bold. Verify that the tags appear correctly around the text.
4. Import a text file into the One Page Web.
   a) Locate the imported file in Folder view and open it.
   b) Close the file.

5. Create a blank Web and import a favorite Web site into it.
    a) Explore the files, folders, and pages of the Web.
    b) Delete the Web when you are finished with it.
6. Add a style sheet to the Web using one of the predesigned style sheets.
    a) Use the Style dialog box to modify the Heading 1 style in the sheet to be Centered.
    b) Modify the color of the Visited Hyperlinks.
    c) Modify the default font
    d) Save and close the style sheet.
    e) Link other pages in the Web to the style sheet.

Adding and Importing Images

The most successful Web sites communicate their message by finding the right combination of text, colors, images, and active content (objects that move). Having an eye for design helps, but even novices can create aesthetically appealing and interesting sites by using a few basic FrontPage tools to insert graphics and apply backgrounds.

Image Formats

FrontPage supports a number of different graphics file formats, including GIF (standard and animated), JPEG (standard and progressive), BMP (Windows and OS/2), TIFF, TGA, RAS, EPS, PCX, PNG, PCD (Kodak Photo CD), and WMF. The most common file formats for Web graphics are GIF (Graphics Interchange Format), JPEG (Joint Photographic Image Group) and PNG (Portable Network Graphics). Although some browsers can display images in other formats (like TIFF, PCX, and BMP), all graphics-capable browsers can display GIFs and JPEGs, and a growing number support PNG. There are advantages and disadvantages to each format:

- GIFs are the most common image format used on the Web. GIFs support 256 colors and are generally used for line art and simple graphics. They decompress quickly so they display faster than other formats.

One color of a GIF image can be made transparent so the image blends in with the background. GIFs also support animations by combining a series of images and displaying them consecutively.

- JPEGs, best used for photographs and artwork, use a lossy compression, which means certain parts of images are discarded so that the files take up less storage space. Higher levels of compression result in more degraded image quality. Most browsers support JPEG file compression by automatically decompressing the image. JPEG files support up to 16.7 million colors.
- PNG, the newest graphics format on the scene, was developed to replace the GIF format. PNG supports variable transparency, offering more options for how an image appears on a page. PNG also supports 14-bit true color and 16-bit grayscale and uses lossless compression so the image quality does not degrade in the compression process. Although you can convert a picture to the PNG file format in FrontPage 2000, you will not find any options for changing the properties of PNG images.

Whichever format your choose, it's better to keep it simple than to shoot for incredible graphic designs that clog up your loading time and discourage visitors.

Adding and Importing Images

A graphic on a Web page is called an inline image. To insert an inline image on an open Web page, position the insertion point where you want the image to appear and click the Insert Picture from File button on the FrontPage standard toolbar. The dialog box, shown in Figure 14.21, gives you several choices for finding an image:

- Use the Look In drop-down to locate an image in the current FrontPage Web.
- Enter a URL or click the Web Browser button to locate an image on the Web.
- Click the Select File button to locate an image on a local or network drive.
- Click the Clip Art button to access the clip art that comes with FrontPage and the Microsoft Clip Art Gallery.

- Click the Scan button to scan an image using a TWAIN-compatible scanner, camera, or other device.

Once you've found the image you want, click OK to insert the image.

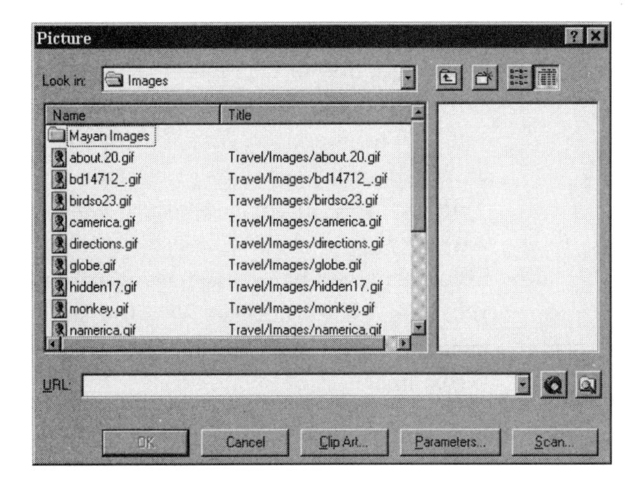

FIGURE 14.21 The Insert Picture dialog box gives you several options for locating image files.

Converting Images to GIF or JPEG

FrontPage easily converts GIF, JPEG, and PNG images from one format to the other. Open the Picture Properties sheet by right-clicking on the image and choosing Picture Properties (see the Picture Properties dialog box below), click the General tab, and choose the format you want in the Image Source section.

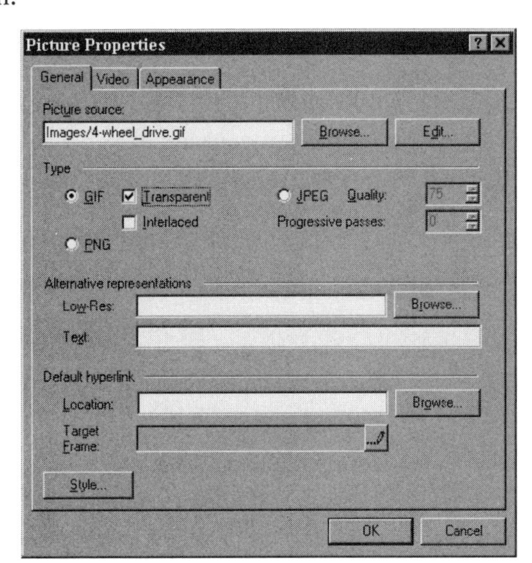

Some browsers support interlaced images, which means that the GIFs are displayed with increasing detail until the entire picture is represented. To mark a GIF as interlaced, select the Interlaced option. To make an image transparent or to make a transparent image opaque again, click the Transparent option (see later in the chapter for more about transparent images).

The default quality of a JPEG image is set at 75. You can increase it to 100 (higher quality) or decrease it to as low as 1. The higher the quality, the slower the image will load. JPEGs can be downloaded in progressive passes, similarly to interlaced GIFs. Indicate here how many passes you'd like to make before the entire picture appears.

If you insert an image that is not a GIF, JPEG, or PNG, you can convert it by opening up the Picture Properties and selecting one of the three formats. If you copy and paste an image into FrontPage that is not already a GIF, JPEG, or PNG, FrontPage will automatically convert it first to HTML, then make it a GIF. When you save the page, you'll be prompted to save the converted image.

Visitors to your site may not have graphics-capable browsers. To provide alternative text for the images, enter a *short* description of the image in the Alternative Representations Text box. The text will appear in place of the image so a visitor with a text-only browser knows what the graphic is. To provide faster response for visitors with graphics-capable browsers, you can have a small, low-resolution image appear while the main image is loading from the Web server. Enter the location of the temporary image in the Low-Res textbox.

Resampling an Image

Objective FP2000E.9.2

Resizing a picture affects how the picture displays on the Web page, but it does not change the actual size of the picture. Resampling changes the file size to match its current display size.

Resampling an Image

1. In Page View, resize an image by dragging its borders.
2. Activate the Picture toolbar if it is not currently visible (View ➢ Toolbars ➢ Pictures).
3. Click the Resample button.

Positioning Graphics on a Page

Objective FP2000E.4.1

If you're used to working with images in Word or PowerPoint and moving them anywhere you want them on the page, you're in for a bit of a disappointment here. Because of the restrictions of HTML, you have to employ a number of tools and a little ingenuity to position your images exactly where you want them. Click on the image to select it first, then try any of the following:

- Choose Format ➢ Paragraph and select left, center, or right alignment from the drop-down list, or click the alignment buttons on the toolbar
- Click the Increase Indent button as many times as you need (click Decrease Indent to move left)
- Insert the image into a cell of a table
- Right-click, choose Picture Properties, and choose the Appearance tab. Choose Left, Right, Top, Middle, Bottom, or Baseline from the list of alignment options. (Left and Right will cause the text to wrap around the image; Top, Middle, Bottom and Baseline will position the text alongside the image.)

Paragraph Alignment and Image Layout Alignment are not the same thing. If you try to apply both to the same image, conflicts may develop and your image may not appear where you want it. To resolve a conflict, delete the image and re-insert it onto the page.

Although hardly conventional, you can use hidden text to position images. Position the insertion point before the image and enter text until the graphic is in position (make sure the Layout Alignment is not set to Left or Right). Select the text and change the text color to match the color of the background.

Precise Positioning and Layering

Objectives FP2000E.4.1 and E.4.2

A new feature of FrontPage 2000 lets you position page elements, including text and graphics, much more precisely than previously allowed. This new feature, called Positioning, is supported by Web Browsers that support CSS 2.0 (cascading style sheets), such as Microsoft Internet Explorer 4.0 and later, and Netscape Navigator 4.0 and later. If you are developing for a corporate Intranet and know which Web browser and screen resolutions users are using to view your Web, Positioning takes much of the difficulty out of precise placement and layering of page elements.

To use Positioning, select the page element you want to position, and choose Format ➢ Position from the menu. The Position dialog box, shown in Figure 14.22, is divided into three sections: Wrapping Style, Positioning Style, and Location and Size.

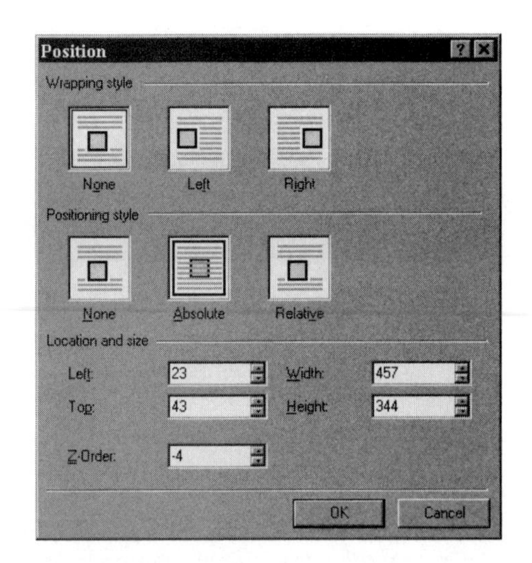

FIGURE 14.22 Use the Position dialog box to change the wrapping style, position style, and location and size of page elements.

Wrapping Style refers to how a picture affects the text around it. *None* means the text moves around the picture without wrapping. *Left* moves the picture to the left of the page and the text wraps around it to the right. *Right* moves the picture to the right of the page and the text wraps around it to the left.

Positioning Style has to do with how the picture is placed by the browser. *None* treats the picture as an ordinary page element and anchors it to the surrounding text. *Absolute* specifies the exact location of the picture, positioning it in front of or behind other elements (see about adjusting the z-order later in this section to adjust the picture's layering). *Relative* keeps the layout of page elements intact by placing pictures and other elements at a fixed point in the text flow. If the text moves, the picture moves with it.

The Location and Size section lets you input the exact location of the top left corner and height and width of the page element. To change the layering of a page element in relation to the main text-flow layer, change the z-order. A positive z-order positions the element in front of the text layer and a negative z-order positions the image behind the text layer.

It's also possible to adjust the position of a page element by using the Positioning toolbar, shown in Figure 14.23. To turn on the toolbar, choose View ➢ Toolbars and click Positioning. Most of the settings of the Position dialog box are available here, except Wrapping styles. In addition, there are Bring Forward and Send Backwards buttons to easily adjust z-order.

FIGURE 14.23

The Positioning toolbar.

Be careful not to apply absolute positioning to dynamic HTML effects (DHTML). The results are unpredictable.

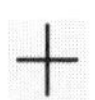

Moving Page Elements If you change the Position Style to Absolute in the Position dialog box, you can change the position of the page element by dragging it around the page. Point to the element, and when the pointer changes to a four-headed arrow, drag it to the new position.

Screen resolution can impact the position of a page element, even if you specify its absolute position. For best results, test your page at various screen resolutions before distributing it to others.

Using Picture Tools

Objective FP2000.8.1

Within FrontPage, the Picture toolbar, shown in Figure 14.24, provides you with a number of useful options for working with pictures.

FIGURE 14.24

The Picture toolbar

TABLE 14.1: Picture toolbar buttons

Button	Name	Description
	Insert Picture	Inserts a picture from the current Web, a local or network drive, or the World Wide Web.
	Text	Adds text to a GIF image.
	Auto Thumbnail	Creates a thumbnail that users can click on to view the full picture.
	Positioning buttons	Positions an element at an exact location and changes the z-order of a picture to layer page elements.
	Rotate and Flip buttons	Changes the direction of the picture.
	Contrast and Brightness buttons	Increases or decreases lightness and contrast.
	Crop	Allows you to display only part of a picture.
	Set Transparent Color	Sets the color that becomes transparent, blending into the background.
	Black and White	Changes the picture to black and white colors only.
	Wash Out	Bleaches out a picture for use in the background.
	Bevel	Places a bevel frame around the picture.
	Resample	Changes the actual file size of a resized picture.
	Hotspot buttons	Creates clickable hotspots on a picture.
	Restore	Restores the picture to its original appearance.

Adding Text over an Image

Objective FP2000.8.2

To add text over an image, you can add a text box that become part of the image.

Adding Text over an Image

1. Select the image to activate the Picture toolbar (it should appear at the bottom of the document window).
2. Click the Text button. If the picture is in JPEG format, you are prompted to save it in GIF format before proceeding. Click Yes.
3. Type the text inside the box that appears on the picture.
4. Resize and reposition the text box if you wish. Click outside of the picture to embed the text box.

Hyperlinking Images and Creating Hotspots

Objective FP2000.8.3

Earlier in this chapter, you learned how to create text-based hyperlinks to connect one Web page to another. You can also use graphics to help your visitors navigate around your site and follow links to other sites. An entire image can become a single hyperlink or it can contain multiple hyperlinks depending on where the user clicks.

Creating an Image Hyperlink

1. Right-click on an image and choose Hyperlink.
2. Locate the page you want to link to or enter the URL for the page. Click OK.
3. To test the image hyperlink, switch to Preview and click the image to take you to the linked page.

To remove a hyperlink from an image, right-click on the image and choose Edit Hyperlink. Delete the URL and click OK.

Creating Hotspots A hotspot is an area on an image designated as a hyperlink, not to be confused with a sunspot, which is the result of stellar hyperactivity. An image with several hotspots is referred to as an image map.

Creating an Image Map

1. Insert the picture you want to use for the image map.
2. Position and resize the picture the way you want it to appear.
3. Click the Rectangular Hotspot, Circular Hotspot or Polygonal Hotspot button on the Picture toolbar.

4. Drag the area you want to designate as a hotspot, as shown in Figure 14.25. When you release the mouse button, the Create Hyperlink dialog box opens. If you are using the Polygonal Hotspot tool, click to change directions and insert a handle. When you rejoin the first handle, the Create Hyperlink dialog box opens.
5. Identify the destination of the hyperlink and click OK.
6. You can re-size the hotspot by pointing to one of the handles and dragging it. If you used a Polygonal Hotspot, point to one of the handles and drag along one of the connecting lines to reshape the hotspot area.
7. Repeat steps three through six to designate additional hotspots on the image map.

To design an effective image map, see Chapter 12, "Using PhotoDraw," to learn how to combine several photos or clip art files into one picture.

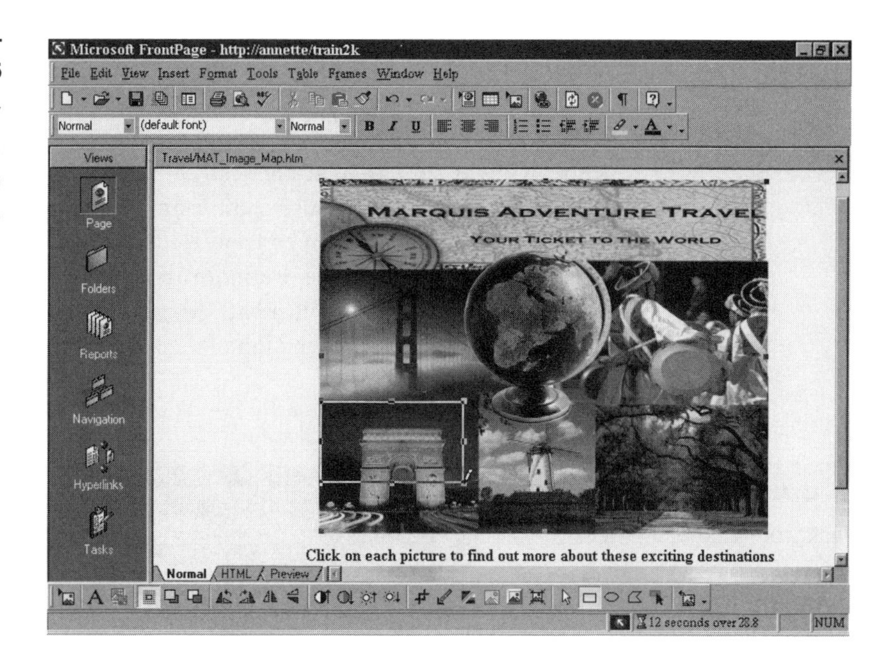

FIGURE 14.25
Designate a hotspot by dragging an area using one of the Hotspot buttons on the Picture toolbar.

Saving Images on a Page

Images are saved separately from the Web pages where they are displayed. When you save a Web page on which you have inserted images, you are prompted to save the images with the Save Embedded Files dialog box:

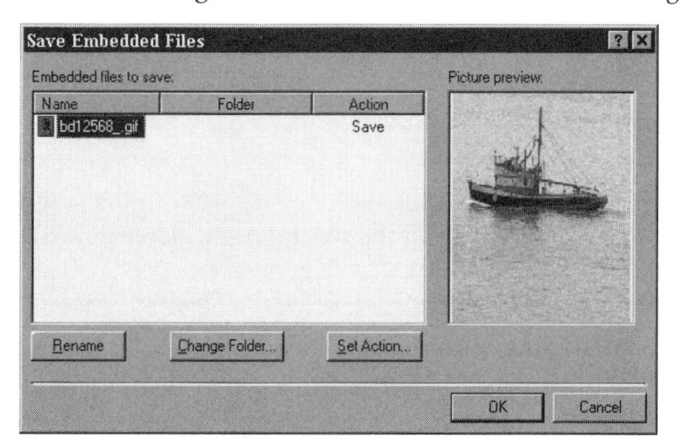

Here you can rename the image file and choose a folder in the open Web in which to store it. Click OK to save the image to the Web.

Setting Custom Backgrounds

Objective FP2000E.7.1

Although a Web site can be aesthetically appealing with a white background, many Web designers prefer using color or even images to get their message across. Background color can be applied to individual pages or applied to an entire Web as part of a theme (for more about themes, see *Applying Themes* later in this chapter). To apply a background color, choose Format ➢ Background to open the Background tab of the Page Properties dialog box shown in Figure 14.26.

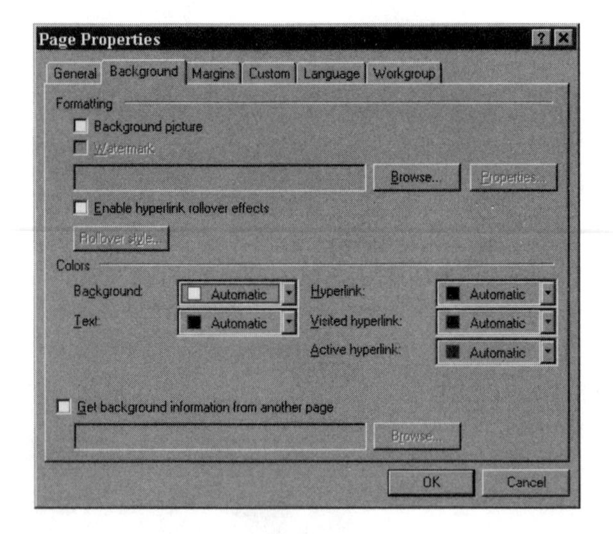

FIGURE 14.26 Set background colors and images on the Background tab of the Page Properties dialog box.

Click the down arrow next to the Color button to choose a background color from the palette of available colors.

Many Web designers create a separate Colors page that they link to every page in the Web. This allows them to make color changes to all the linked pages at one time. Create the Colors page first and then check the Get Background Information from Another Page checkbox on the Background tab of the Page Properties dialog box. Browse to select the Colors page. Repeat this process for each page in the Web.

Selecting a Background Image

Any picture can be used as a background by choosing the Background Picture option on the Background tab of the Page Properties sheet. Click the Browse button to locate the picture you want to use. You can choose to make this image a watermark by clicking the Watermark check box. A watermark image does not move when you scroll the page.

To remove a background image, open the Page Properties dialog box and delete the background image file name from the Background page.

Hands On: Objectives FP2000.6.1, 8.1, 8.2, 8.3, and FP2000E.4.1, E.4.2, E.7.1

1. Add an image from the Microsoft Clip Gallery or other source to a Web page.
   - a) Resize the image.
   - b) Use the Picture toolbar to rotate or flip the image.
   - c) Enter text on the image.
2. Add another image and create an image map on the image.
3. Insert a Word file on the page.
   - a) Wrap text around the image to the right and view the results.
   - b) Save and close the page.
4. Explore different background images and colors until you find one that you want to add to the page.

Creating the Navigational Structure for a Web

If you've ever been on the Web, you've already encountered navigation bars. A navigation bar is a strip of buttons or text that connects you to other pages in the same Web. You can find them at the top, bottom, or sides of a page. Figure 14.27 shows an example of a Web page with navigation bars at the top and left. Although it is possible to create individual Web pages and link them together by manually creating hyperlinks, you can save yourself a lot of trouble using FrontPage's built-in navigation tools. To automatically create navigation bars, you first need to create a navigation structure so that FrontPage knows how the pages in your Web are related. You can then add shared borders to the pages of the site and FrontPage will place the appropriate buttons on each page. If you change the structure, the links change automatically—you don't have to do a thing to keep your links up-to-date.

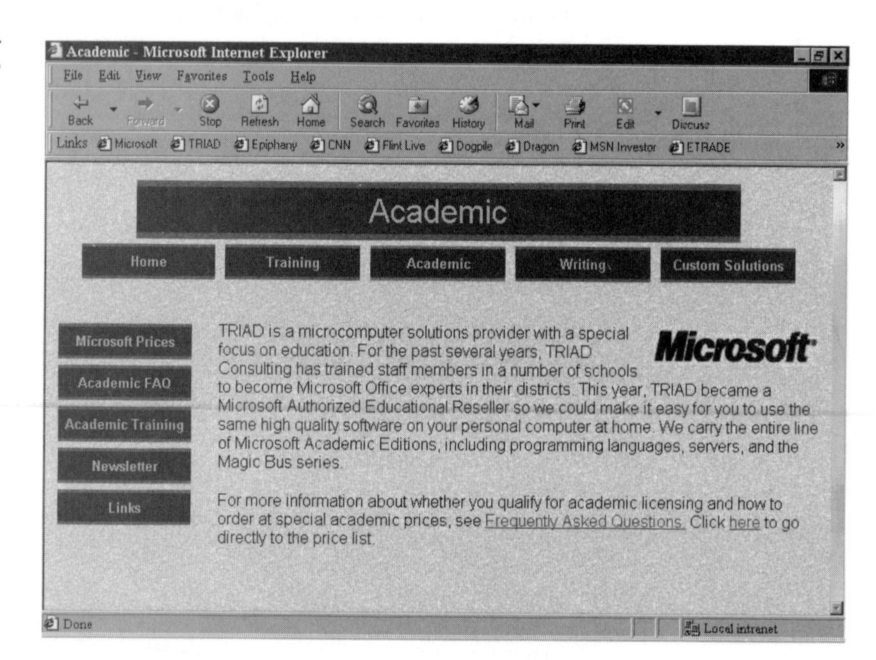

FIGURE 14.27 Navigation bars link pages within a Web site.

Using Navigation View to Create Linked Pages

Objective FP2000E.3.3-E.3.4

The first time you click on the Navigation button on the View bar, the Information viewer will probably be empty or may contain only the Home page. Unless you created the Web using a wizard or template, FrontPage has to rely on you to create the navigation structure of a Web. Once you've told FrontPage how you want the pages laid out, it will be happy to keep the links for you. Figure 14.28 shows the navigation view of a linked Web.

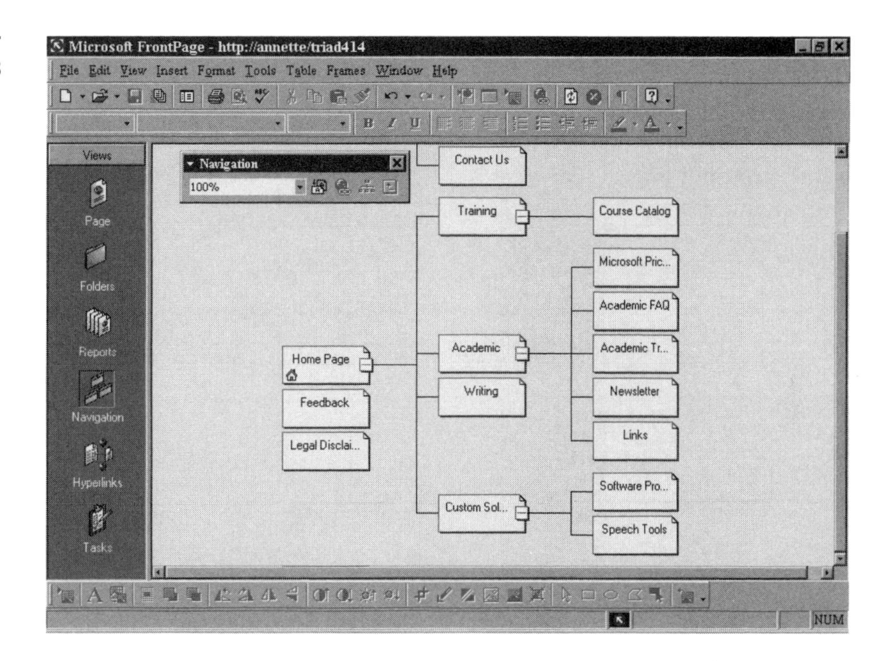

FIGURE 14.28

Once you've created a navigation structure in FrontPage, links between pages can be maintained automatically.

Creating a Navigational Structure for a Web

1. Switch to Navigation view.
2. Click the Folder List button on the Standard toolbar to open the Folder List.
3. Select a page and drag it into the Navigation view window and drop it when the connector line appears underneath the page you want it linked to, as shown in Figure 14.29.
4. Repeat Step 3 until you have linked all the pages in the Web.

Pages can be inserted into the Navigation structure at the same level as the Home Page, such as the Feedback and Legal Disclaimer page shown in Figure 14.30. FrontPage can still create links to these pages even though they are not child pages.

When you are working in Navigation view, the Navigation toolbar opens automatically (or you can access it by clicking View ➢ Toolbars ➢ Navigation). Use the Zoom button to change the Navigation display so you can see more of it at one time. Or, if you prefer a different perspective, switch the display from landscape to portrait. The other buttons on the Navigation toolbar relate to Navigation bars and you can learn more about them later in this chapter.

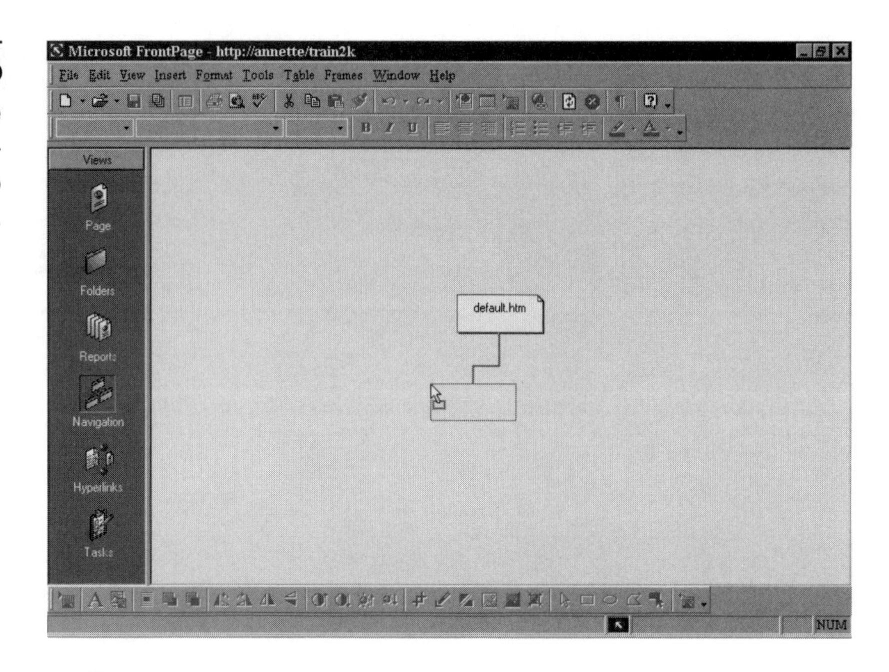

FIGURE 14.29 Drag a page into the Navigation view window and connect it to the home page.

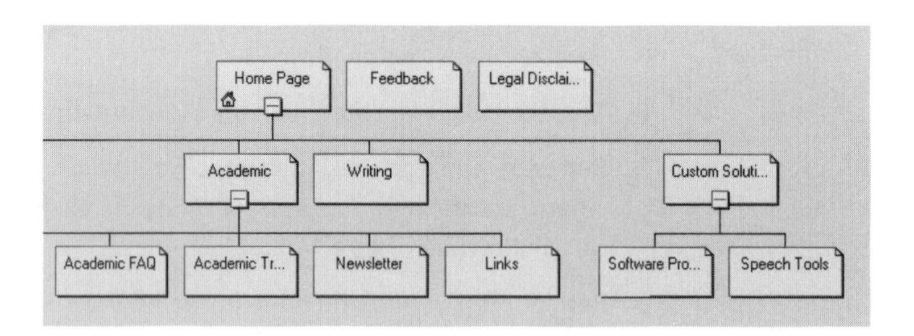

FIGURE 14.30 The Feedback and Legal Disclaimer pages in this example are included in the Navigation view at the same level as the Home Page.

Viewing and Printing the Navigational Structure

Objective FP2000.11.2

In the early stages of design, in particular, you may find it helpful to print the navigation structure of a Web to take to a meeting, report to your supervisor, or just see what's missing.

Viewing and Printing Your Web Site Structure

1. Switch to Navigation View.
2. Choose File ➢ Print Preview to view the navigation structure.
3. Click Print to send it to the printer.

If the navigation structure of the Web doesn't fit well on a printed page, try rotating it. Switch back to Navigation view, right-click on the Web, and choose Rotate.

Adding and Renaming Pages in Navigation View

Objective FP2000E.3.2

If you are starting a Web from scratch, switch to Navigation view and create new pages by clicking the New page button on the Standard toolbar. FrontPage automatically links all of the pages and allows you to move them around to your satisfaction.

FrontPage creates a new page underneath the page that is selected when you click the New Page button. If you want to add pages to a lower level (child) page, select that page before clicking the New Page button.

Objective FP2000E.3.1

To rename the title of a new page in Navigation view, right-click on the name and choose Rename. Enter a new name for the title.

To rename the new page's URL, right-click the name in the Folder List and choose Rename. This changes the name of the file and updates the hyperlinks.

Inserting Navigation Bars on Individual Pages

Objective FP2000E.6.1 and E.6.3

To become familiar with Navigation bars and how they work, it's helpful to open a page and insert Navigation bars directly into a simple Web.

Creating a Simple Web Structure for a New Web

1. Create a One Page Web (File ➢ New ➢ One Page Web) and switch to Navigation view.
2. Click the New button two times to add two new pages.
3. Click on New Page 1 and click the New button two times to create New Page 3 and New Page 4.
4. Click on New Page 2 and click the New button two times to create New Page 5 and New Page 6. Your Web structure should look like the one in Figure 14.31.

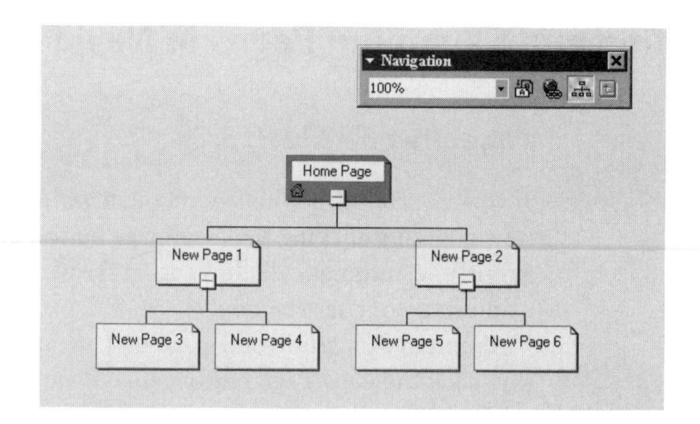

FIGURE 14.31
Creating this simple Web structure is a good way to experiment with Navigation bars.

Now you are ready to insert Navigation bars on the pages. Double-click the Home Page to open it in Page view. Choose Insert ➢ Navigation Bar to open the Navigation Bar Properties dialog box shown in Figure 14.32.

You can choose from six different navigation bar options:

Parent Level Builds links to pages above the current page.

Same Level Links pages on the same level as the current page.

Back and Next Inserts "Back" and "Next" links to pages on the same level as the current page.

Child Level Creates links to pages below the current page.

Top Level Creates links to all the pages at the Home Page level.

Child Pages under Home Links the pages immediately under the Home Page.

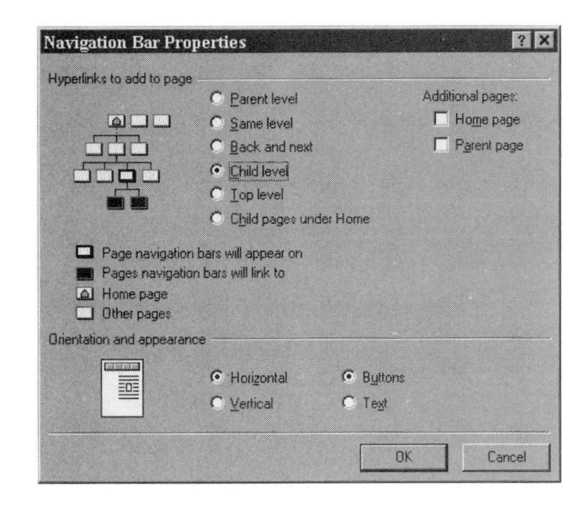

FIGURE 14.32 The Navigation Bar Properties box lets you choose how you would like navigation bars to appear on the page.

In addition, you can add links to the Home Page and to the Parent Page of the current page. As you click each option, the preview in the dialog box changes so you can see what pages each choice links. The final options relate to the appearance of the links on the page. You can choose if you want the links to appear horizontally on the left of the page or vertically at the top. If you have a theme applied (see *Applying Themes* later in this chapter), you can also choose to display the links as buttons or text. When you are satisfied with your choice, click OK to see the links on the page.

The preview in the Navigation Bar Properties dialog box is not directly related to the Web you are working on, so you may not have the pages it refers to.

To test the links, switch to Preview or press the Control key and click to follow a link in Normal Page view. Until you have links on all the pages, you have to choose File ➢ Close to close the linked page and return to the original page. Practice with different navigation bars to see which ones suit your needs.

To change the properties of an existing navigation bar, right-click on the bar and choose Navigation Bar properties from the shortcut menu. If you want to combine Navigation bars on a page, click where you want the second navigation bar to appear and choose Insert ➢ Navigation Bar again.

In this way, you could have a Parent Level navigation bar on the top and a Child Level navigation bar on the left, as shown here.

To center a navigation bar, click on it to select it and click the Center button on the Formatting toolbar. To remove a navigation bar from a page, click on it to select it and press the Delete key.

Adding Page Banners

Objective FP2000E.6.2

A page banner displays a page's title at the top of the page. To add a page banner, choose Insert ➢ Page Banner to open Page Banner dialog box. You have your choice in the Page Banner dialog box of displaying a picture or text. Editing the text in the box changes the title of the page, and even though you can select Picture here, you cannot choose an image to display. Page banner images can only be displayed when you are using themes (see *Applying Themes* later in this chapter).

Sharing Borders

Objectives FP2000E.5.1 and 5.4

Shared borders combine the concepts of headers/footers and Navigation bars into one easy-to-use feature. Like headers and footers you might apply in Word or Excel, shared borders appear on every page of a Web. You can add a copyright, contact information, a logo, or any other repetitive content to a shared border. Figure 14.33 shows Top, Left, and Bottom shared borders with Navigation buttons.

To create shared borders, switch to Navigation view and choose Format ➢ Shared Borders to open the Shared Border dialog box shown in Figure 14.34.

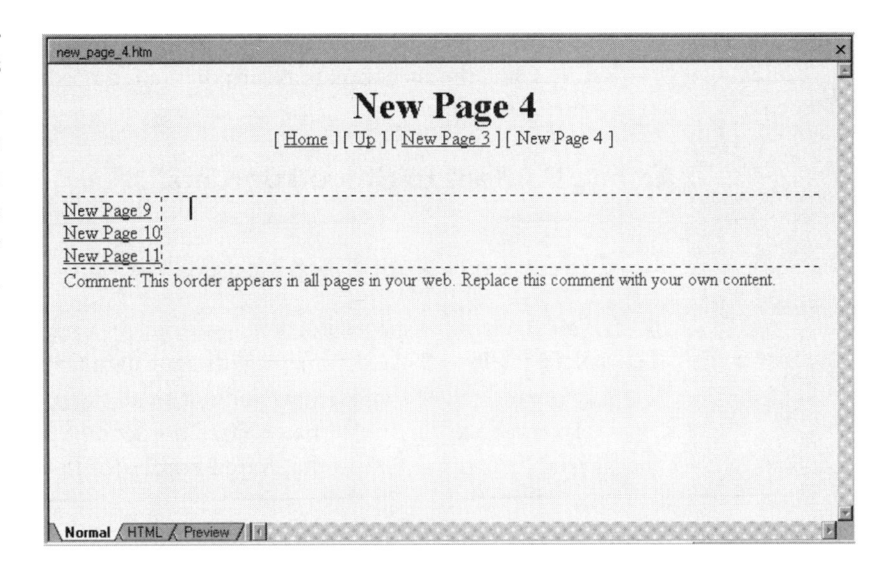

FIGURE 14.33 This page shows Top, Left, and Bottom shared borders with navigation buttons before adding any other content.

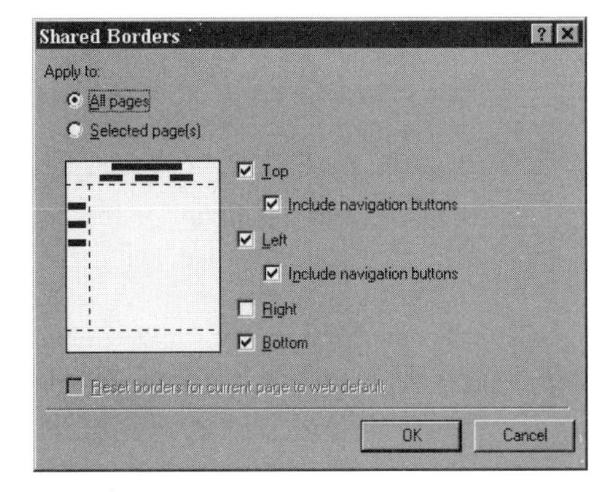

FIGURE 14.34 In the Shared Borders dialog box, choose where you would like Shared Borders and if you'd like them to contain Navigation bars.

Decide if you would like the Shared Border settings to apply to All Pages or only to Selected Pages. Select where you would like the shared borders to appear and if you'd like them to contain Navigation bars. Click OK to accept the shared border settings.

To edit the properties of the Navigation bars, double-click on them. If you would like to turn shared borders on or off on certain pages, select the page or pages in Folders view (hold Control to select multiple pages) and choose Format ➢ Shared Borders. Check the Selected Pages checkbox to only apply changes to the selected pages.

After you have made changes to selected pages, the Reset Borders for Current Page to Web Default checkbox in the Shared Borders dialog box is active. Click the checkbox to return the shared borders on the selected pages to the Web default.

Adding Content to Shared Borders

Objective FP2000E.5.2 and 5.3

To add content to shared borders for an entire Web site, open any page and replace the FrontPage comment with your own text and graphics. Save the page to add the shared borders content to all the pages in the Web.

To enter text for an alternate shared border on a particular page, open the page and enter the text in the shared border for that page.

Applying Themes

Objective FP2000.3.1 and E.2.2

Themes combine shared borders, navigation buttons, background colors and graphics, horizontal lines, font styles, and active graphics. FrontPage installs 15 themes as part of the standard installation. Over 50 more themes are available to install and many third-party developers have additional themes you can purchase.

To add a theme to a Web, choose Format ➢ Theme from any view to open the Themes dialog box shown in Figure 14.35. Click on each theme to see a preview of the theme's colors, buttons, and graphics. You can change the following attributes for a selected theme by checking or clearing the respective checkboxes:

Vivid Colors Adds brighter, more intense colors to the text.

Active Graphics Affects the buttons—they move or change color or shape when a user moves a pointer over them or clicks a link.

Background Graphics Adds or removes a graphic or color from the background.

Apply Using CSS Writes the theme elements to a cascading style sheet.

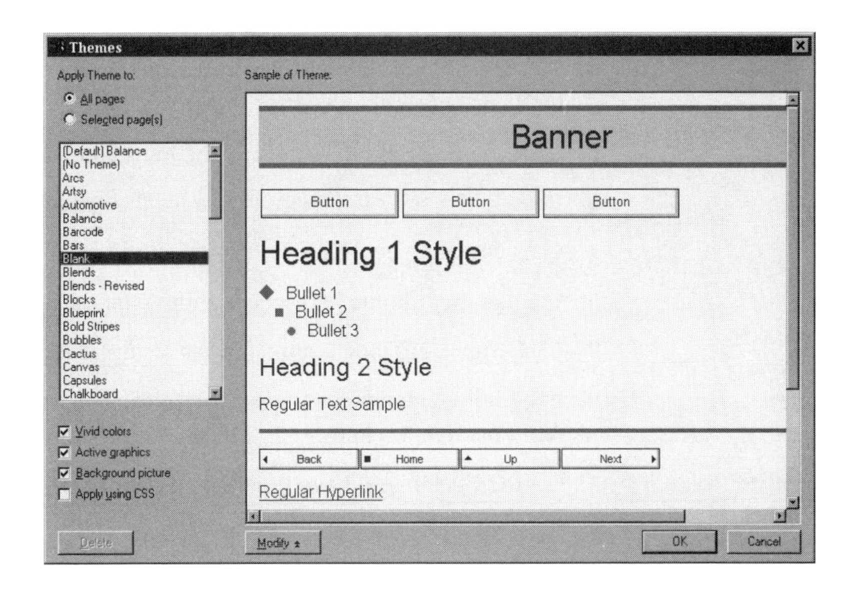

FIGURE 14.35 In the Themes dialog box, you can choose from a wide selection of themes to add graphic appeal to a Web.

Modifying an Existing Theme

Objective FP2000.3.2

For the first time, you can now modify an existing FrontPage theme and then save the theme under a new name. You can:

- Change the normal and vivid colors used for hyperlinks, body and heading text, banner text, navigation bar labels, table borders, and the background.
- Replace graphics (background picture, page banner, bullets, navigation buttons, and horizontal lines) with your own graphics. You can also change the font of graphical elements displayed with text, such as buttons.
- Change the body and heading styles of the text

Modifying an Existing Theme

1. Open the theme dialog box (Format ➢ Theme).
2. Select the theme you would like to modify.
3. Click the Modify button and then when the buttons become available, click Colors, Graphics, or Text.

Modifying an Existing Theme *(continued)*

4. Select a Color Scheme or customize colors by clicking the Colors buttons and then choose between Normal and Vivid colors.
5. Click the Custom tab to specify the item you want to change.
6. Choose the color you want to use for the specific item.
7. Click OK when you have finished customizing colors.
8. Choose the graphic item you want to change.
9. Click Browse to locate a picture file to replace the current file.
10. If the item contains text, click Font to replace the font style and alignment used in the item.
11. Click OK when you have finished customizing graphics.
12. Select the text item you want to change.
13. Enter the name of the font you want to use.
14. Click More Text Styles to modify a font style.
15. Click OK when you have finished customizing text.
16. To save the new theme, click Save As and enter a new theme title in the dialog box that opens.

Changing a theme is as simple as reopening the Themes dialog box and choosing a different theme or No Theme from the list.

Applying a Theme to an Individual Web Page

Objectives FP2000E.2.1 and E.2.3

You may also find that you want to turn off background graphics or in some other way modify the theme on a particular page. Open the page or select multiple pages in Folders view. Choose Format ➢ Theme and click the Selected Page(s) checkbox. Choose a new theme, change attributes, or customize the theme. Any changes you make will only apply to the selected pages.

Hands On: ***Objectives FP2000.3.1, 3.2, and FP2000E.2.1-2.3, E.3.1-E.3.4, E.5.1-5.4, and E.6.1-6.3***

1. Create a One Page Web.
   a) Switch to Navigation View and add at least five additional pages.
   b) Drag the pages around until you have a structure you like.
   c) Re-name the pages (title and page URL).
   d) Open a page and add a page banner to the top of a Web page.
   e) Add shared borders, including navigation buttons to the Web.
   f) Open the home page and edit the shared borders to include content you want to appear on every page.
   g) Switch to Preview and test the links between pages.
   h) Save and close the page.
2. Add a theme to the Web you created in Exercise 1.
   a) Turn on Vivid Colors and Active Graphics.
   b) Change the Color Scheme of the theme and save your change.
   c) Preview a page.
   d) Open a page in the Web and modify the theme for that page only.
   e) Change the top shared border for that page to include only the Home and Parent level.
   f) Add a graphic to the left shared border for the page.
   g) Preview the pages in the Web.
   h) Save the changes.

Using Templates to Design Web Pages

Objective FP2000.4.1

While the Web Wizard and templates create a structure for an entire Web, page templates help you create web pages or special elements within a

Web page. To access the page templates, switch to Page view and choose New ➢ Page from the File menu to open the New dialog box shown in Figure 14.36.

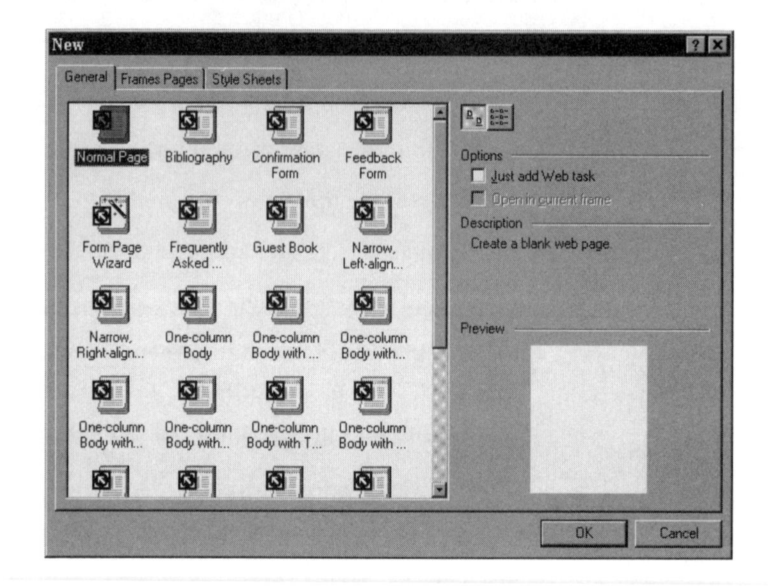

FIGURE 14.36 The New dialog box offers numerous options for creating pages or page elements.

The templates that come with FrontPage include a search page template (so guests can search for information in your site), a guest book, a frequently asked questions page, and a feedback form. As you create Web sites, you may find uses for all the templates at one time or another. You can combine elements from various templates to create the page you want. If you want to add a feedback form to an existing page, for example, you can create the feedback form, then cut and paste it into the existing page. Many of the pages created by the templates include components that automate certain portions of a form. To learn more about components and how to modify component properties, see *Animating a Web* later in this chapter.

Each template has comments with instructions or information at the top. Comments aren't visible in a browser, so you can leave them for later reference. Choose Insert ➢ Comment to insert your own comments.

As you're exploring FrontPage and deciding what to include in your Web site, it's not a bad idea to create and preview each of the templates and see what they include. If a template doesn't interest you, just close it without

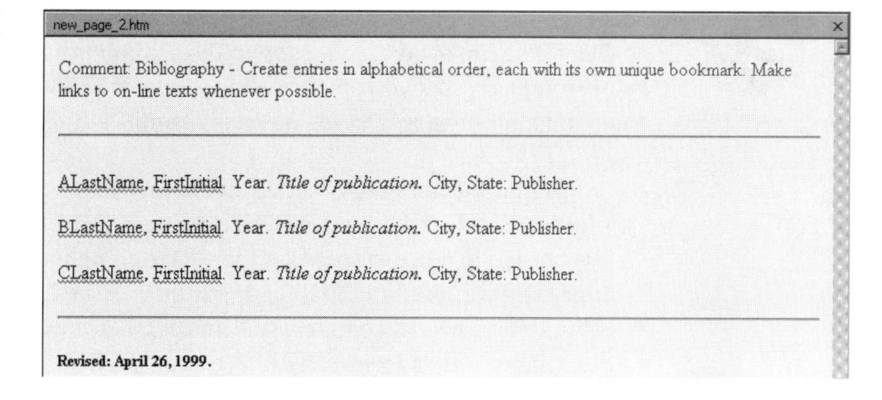
new_page_2.htm

Comment: Bibliography - Create entries in alphabetical order, each with its own unique bookmark. Make links to on-line texts whenever possible.

ALastName, FirstInitial. Year. *Title of publication.* City, State: Publisher.

BLastName, FirstInitial. Year. *Title of publication.* City, State: Publisher.

CLastName, FirstInitial. Year. *Title of publication.* City, State: Publisher.

Revised: April 26, 1999.

FIGURE 14.37 The Bibliography template includes instructive comments not visible when the page is displayed in a browser.

saving. If you like what you see, follow the instructions in the Comments section at the top. Select the existing content and enter yours in place of it, then add whatever additional content you would like. Or you can save the page as a template that you could use to create other, similar pages. Just change the Save As Type in the Save As dialog box to FrontPage template.

Hands On: Objective FP2000.4.1

1. Add four new Web pages to a One Page Web using different templates for each page.
   - a) Customize each page to contain your content.
   - b) Add a theme to unify the pages.
   - c) Preview the Web and save the changes.

Animating a Web with Pre-Built Components

Objective FP2000E.10.4

As Web browsers are becoming more sophisticated, the people browsing the Web are becoming more demanding. No longer content to scroll through static pages of text, today's Web users expect well-designed sites with lots of graphics and interactivity. FrontPage 2000 includes several tools to make your Web pages come alive.

Older Web browsers do not support the animation and interactive features of FrontPage, so if you are developing for a wide audience, test your Web on different browsers to see how they handle high-end features.

FrontPage components and Office Web components, shown in Figure 14.38, are built-in objects that execute either when the page is saved or when it is opened in a browser. Most FrontPage components automatically generate the appropriate HTML code for their defined tasks. Others work behind the scenes to complete specific tasks—for example, saving data that a user inputs into a form. Office Web components, such as the Office Spreadsheet, shown in Figure 14.39, insert Office toolbars and applications windows within FrontPage.

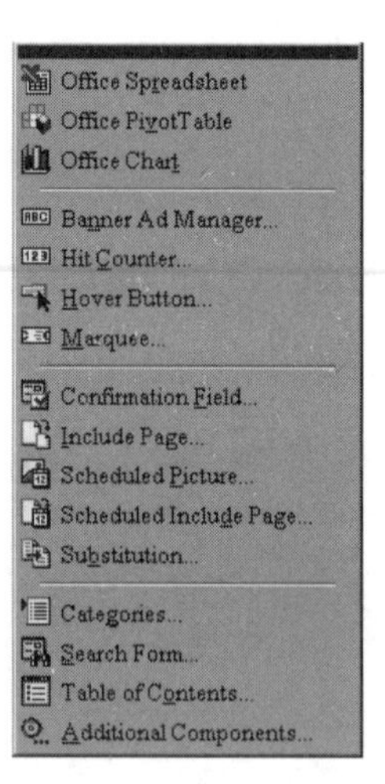

FIGURE 14.38
FrontPage components automatically generate the HTML code to add interactivity to a Web.

In early versions of FrontPage, FrontPage components were referred to as WebBots or Bots. WebBots are a subset of FrontPage components and are referenced in the HTML code when you insert a WebBot component. However, FrontPage 2000 consistently uses the broader and more generally accepted name of *component* to refer to these objects.

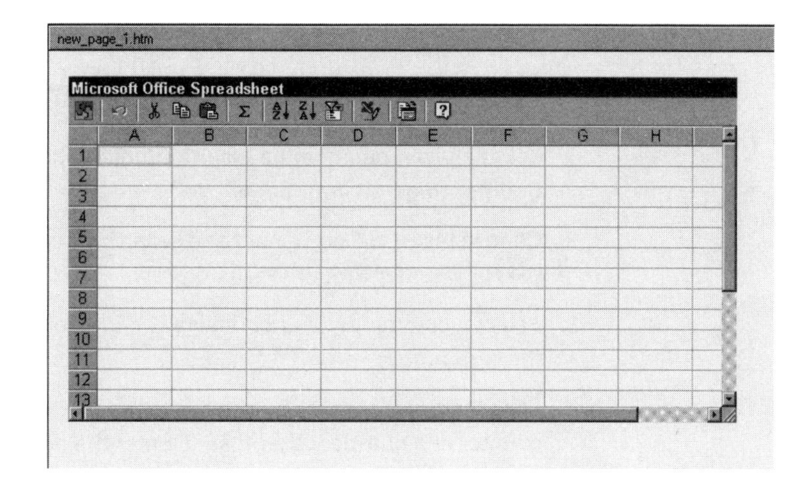

FIGURE 14.39 The Office Spreadsheet component incorporates the essential features of an Excel worksheet into a Web page.

You can incorporate FrontPage components into a page in several ways.

- In Page view, use the Insert ➢ Component command to insert a component.
- Create a new page from a template that uses a component, including Confirmation Form, Search Page, and Table of Contents.
- Create a new Web using a wizards or templates.
- Apply a theme to a Web.

The *Common Gateway Interface (CGI)* has been the traditional way to run automated tasks from Web pages. When you perform tasks with FrontPage components on a FrontPage-aware server, you avoid having to write CGI scripts and referencing their somewhat arcane parameters.

In this section, we'll introduce you to several of the most popular FrontPage components.

Counting Your Visitors

Objective FP2000.10.1

One of the nerve-racking parts of establishing a Web presence is waiting to see how many visitors find their way to your fabulous site. FrontPage takes care of counting for you with the Hit Counter component, so you can just sit back and watch the numbers grow.

Inserting a Hit Counter

1. In Page view, position the insertion point where you want the Hit Counter to go on your page.
2. Choose Insert ➢ Component and select Hit Counter from the list to open the Hit Counter Properties dialog box.
3. Select a counter style or choose a GIF image containing the digits zero through nine.
4. Click the Set the Reset Counter To checkbox if you want to start the counter at a number other than 0. Enter the number in the adjacent text box.
5. Select the Fixed Number of Digits checkbox if you want the counter to start over when it reaches a certain number. Enter the maximum number of digits you want to see in the adjacent text box.
6. Click OK to save the properties and insert the Hit Counter.

A Hit Counter actually counts how many times a page is opened, not how many unique visitors a site gets. Be cautious about using this number to calculate market reach or site visibility. You could be seeing the same five people over and over again.

To edit the Hit Counter, right-click on it and choose FrontPage Component Properties. Make any changes you want and click OK to save them.

Making Pages and Objects Move

Objective FP2000.10.2

If you like using transitions and animation in PowerPoint, you'll be happy to learn you can also apply them to Web pages and Web page objects in FrontPage. Any visitor using a browser that supports Dynamic HTML (DHTML) can watch objects fly in and pages checkerboard across your site.

Formatting Page Transitions

1. To access page transitions, choose Format ➢ Page Transitions. The dialog box, shown here, has only a few options you need to set.

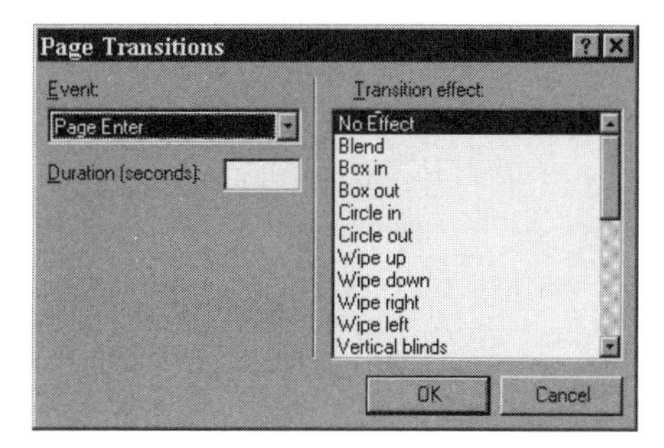

2. Choose the event you want to tie the transition to:

   - Page Enter–displays the transition when a user opens the page.
   - Page Exit–displays when a user leaves the page.
   - Site Enter–displays when a user initially enters the site.
   - Site Exit–displays when a user leaves the site.

3. Choose the transition. You have twenty-five transitions to choose from. You'll probably need to test a few of them out to see how they affect your pages.
4. Enter how long you would like the transition effect to last. More than a few seconds is typically too long—less than 2 or 3 is often too short.
5. Click OK and save the page.
6. Preview the page in a browser that supports Dynamic HTML. Because the transition is tied to entering or exiting, it's easiest to see the transition if you follow a hyperlink in or out of your page or site.

Animating Objects

Making objects change color and fly around the page are other examples of DHTML in action. To apply DHTML to an object or group of objects, select the object(s) and choose Format ➢ Dynamic HTML Effects. This opens the DHTML Effects toolbar.

Choose an event from the list of choices: Click, Double-Click, Mouse Over, and Page Load. This activates the Effect list and is dependent on which Event you choose. For example, if you choose a Mouse Over event, you only have an option of changing the formatting of the object. If, on the other hand, you choose a Click or Page Load event, you have animation choices such as Fly Out. Depending on the event and effect you choose, you may have to choose additional settings. If you choose a Mouse Over event, for example, and select the Formatting Effect, setting choices include Font or Border.

Many objects can be animated: text boxes, tables, buttons, or pictures. Some animations are more appropriate for some objects than others. For example, attaching a Fly Out effect to a Submit button when it is clicked may be disconcerting to a user giving feedback or placing an order.

Delivering a Message with a Marquee

Objective FP2000.10.3

Microsoft Internet Explorer first introduced the marquee, which is an HTML implementation of the scrolling message you might find on the marquee of a movie theater, where it displays the current schedule, or above a stock brokerage firm, where it displays a live ticker tape.

Figure 14.40 shows an example of a marquee in a page in the Page view. Here the marquee displays a newsy and timely message that you might change every few days.

FIGURE 14.40 A marquee can be an effective way to catch the viewer's attention and display an important message.

If a browser cannot display a scrolling marquee, it will simply display the text that would have instead scrolled across the screen.

Of course, the only problem with the marquee in Figure 14.39 is that you can't see its most important feature—the message scrolling across the marquee from right to left, again and again. To see a marquee in action, you need to open its page in a browser.

Creating a Marquee

1. In Page view, place the insertion point where you want the marquee to appear. As always, you can move the marquee later, if necessary.
2. Choose Insert ➢ Components ➢ Marquee, which displays the Marquee Properties dialog box (see Figure 14.41).
3. In the Text field, enter the text you want displayed in the marquee. In the example in Figure 14.40, that would be **TrainTrax is coming! Watch this site for an important announcement**.
4. To change the color of the marquee's background, select a color in the Background Color option.
5. Select the Specify Width check box. To size the marquee so it is half the width of the window in which this page is displayed, enter 50 for the width, and select Percent.
6. That's all you need in this dialog box, so click OK.

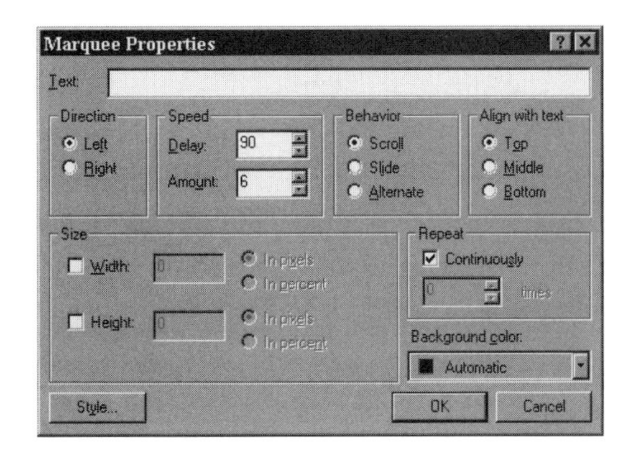

FIGURE 14.41 You can enter the text and define the size, shape, appearance, and behavior of a marquee in the Marquee Properties dialog box.

You can also change the size of a marquee. Select the marquee, then drag one of its selection handles to resize it.

The marquee is now half the width of the window and is aligned with the left edge of the window. Its text is in the default size and style.

Editing Marquee Text

1. Select the marquee not by clicking on it but by pointing to the left of it and clicking. This will highlight the marquee as though it were a line of text you had just selected.
2. Now click the Center button on the Format toolbar to center the marquee on the page.
3. Choose a Heading style from the Change Style list on the Format toolbar so the marquee's message appears in that heading style.
4. Save the page, and now you're ready to see the marquee in action.
5. Switch to Preview or click Preview in Browser. You'll see your message scroll across the marquee from right to left, endlessly repeating.

To modify the marquee, right-click and choose Marquee Properties. Experiment with the Behavior options, which affect the way the message moves across the marquee. Adjusting the Movement Speed options controls how fast or how slow the marquee runs. Make sure it's slow enough that your users can read it, but not so slow as to be boring.

Adding a Search Form to a Web Page

Objective FP2000.10.4 and E.11.3

One of the features users look for in a Web site is the ability to search for the topics they are interested in. By providing them with a search form, you make it easy for visitors to find what they are looking for without having to learn the navigational structure of your site. You can add a search form by using the FrontPage Search Page template or by inserting a FrontPage Component.

Inserting a Search Page Component

1. Choose Insert ➢ Component ➢ Search Form.
2. On the Search Form Properties tab, shown in Figure 14.42, enter the text you would like to appear for the search box label.
3. Enter the desired width of the search box.

Inserting a Search Page Component *(continued)*

4. Enter the desired text for the Start Search button and the Reset button.
5. Click the Search Results tab.
6. Enter the name of the Word List to Search. Enter All if you want users to have the ability to search the entire public portion of the Web; enter the name of a discussion group folder if you'd like the search limited to the items in a discussion group.
7. Set display options by checking the Display Options checkboxes:

   Display Score to display the closeness of the match to the search criteria.

   Display File Date to show when the file returned in the search results was created. If you use this option, set the Date Format and Time Format you want to use.

   Display File Size of the files returned in the search results.
8. Click OK to create the search form, as shown in Figure 14.43.

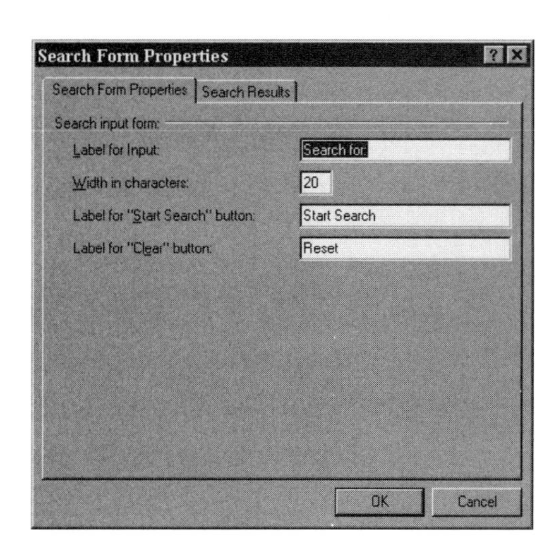

FIGURE 14.42
Use the Search Form Properties to create a search form for a Web.

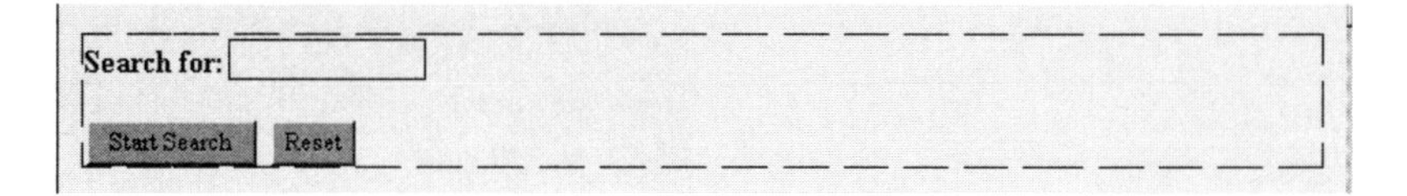

FIGURE 14.43
The Search Form component.

Changing FrontPage Component Properties

Objective FP2000E.10.3

When you point to a search form or any FrontPage Component, the pointer changes shape to indicate you are pointing to a component and you cannot edit it directly. Right-click on the component and choose FrontPage Component Properties or the specific component, in this case Search From Properties, from the shortcut menu to make changes to the component's settings.

Creating Hover Buttons

Objective FP2000E.10.1 and E.10.2

Hover buttons are buttons that change when you point to them. Hover buttons can change color, bevel in or out, change text, or even become a completely different button. You can use simple rectangles as the buttons and group them together as shown in Figure 14.44. Or you can use elaborate buttons you create using the Button Template in Microsoft PhotoDraw (for more about creating buttons in PhotoDraw, see Chapter 12). Whatever your choice, hover buttons add just a touch of sparkle.

FIGURE 14.44 Simple rectangular hover buttons.

Creating Hover Buttons

1. Position the insertion point where you want the first button to appear on your page.
2. Choose Insert ➢ Component ➢ Hover Button to open the Hover Button dialog box, shown on the next page

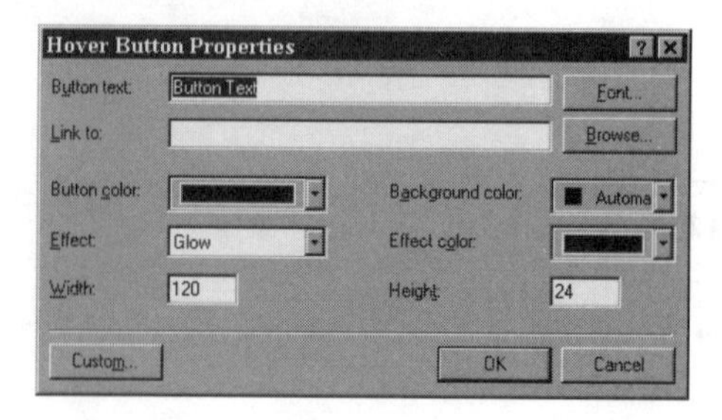

Creating Hover Buttons *(continued)*

3. Enter the text you want to appear on the button (unless your button GIF already includes text). Click the Font button to change the font, font style, size, and color, as shown here. Your choices are limited to four fonts.
4. Enter the URL you want to link the button to. Click the Browse button to choose a page from the active Web, the World Wide Web, or your computer.
5. Choose a color for the button. You can match the button color to the background color of the page so only the text appears on the page.
6. Choose a background color for the button.
7. Choose a transition effect for the hover button. Choose from Color Fill, Color Average, Glow, Reverse Glow, Light Glow, Bevel Out, and Bevel In.
8. Choose an effect color (the color the button will transition to).
9. Select a Width and Height for the button. If you plan to use a custom button, enter the size of the button here in pixels.
10. Click the Custom button to open the Custom dialog box, shown here, if you want to use a custom button on your page that plays a sound or changes to another button when you click or hover.
11. Click OK to close the Hover Button dialog box.
12. Repeat Steps 2-11 to create additional buttons.
13. Save the page and switch to Preview to see your buttons in action.

Now that you have the hang of it, if you want to edit your buttons, right-click on a button and choose Hover Button Properties to reopen the Hover Button dialog box.

Hands On: Objectives FP2000E.10.1 and E.11.3

1. Open an existing Web and create a search page using the Search Form component or the Search Page template. Edit the Search Form component properties:
   a) Change the width of the search box to 25.
   b) Change the label for the "Start Search" button to "Begin Searching."

c) Change the label for the "Reset" button to "Start Over."

d) Display the file date for files in the search results.

e) Save the changes.

f) If you are running a Web server, test your search form by previewing it in a browser.

2. Add a series of hover buttons to a page that link to the main pages in the Web.

   a) Change the Button Color, Button Effect, and Effect Color.

   b) Preview and test the buttons in Preview.

Building a Page for User Input

Objective FP2000E.11.5

You've already seen how the Web can be a great way to transmit information. It can also be a great way for you to collect information. Whether it is survey data or order information, interactive forms let you gather and process all kinds of data from your Web site visitors.

For a form to take data supplied by your visitors and convert it into a format you can use, each form is assigned a form handler. The form handler is a program, also called a CGI (Common Gateway Interface) script, that strips the data from the form and processes it as you have designated. You could have the form handler save the data to a file, save it to a Web page, import it to a database, or even calculate results, convert the results into HTML, and return them to the visitor. You don't have to write the CGI script yourself; FrontPage has several different types of form handlers included with the form templates and Form Page Wizard. These handlers are another example of components, because they handle tasks for you automatically.

Forms can be as simple as one question or as complex as multiple-page surveys. Regardless of how complex it is, every form contains the following components:

- One or more questions
- A field for the reader to answer each question

- A Submit button to transmit the data to the server
- A Clear button to clear or reset the form
- A form handler, called the Save Results bot, to process the data.

Although you can create your forms from scratch, FrontPage comes with a Form Wizard and all the templates you need to create fully functional forms.

Creating a Form with the Form Wizard

The Form Wizard comes fully packed with the tools to build all kinds of forms.

Creating a Form with the Form Wizard

1. Switch to Page view and choose File ➢ New ➢ Page, and select Form Page Wizard from the New dialog box. Read the first step, then click OK.
2. Click the Add button to add a question to the form. Choose the type of input you would like to collect from the list of categories presented.
3. Enter the question's text in the Enter the Prompt for This Question text box, then click Next.
4. Choose the data items you would like to collect in response to the question. This step differs with each input type. Enter a simple, one-word name for this group of responses in Enter the Base Name for This Group of Variables text box. Click Next.
5. Repeat Steps 3–5 until you have entered all the questions. (The questions can be modified after the form is created.)
6. To delete a question, select the question from the list and click Remove. To change a question, select the question and click Modify. To change the order of a question, select the question and click Move Up or Move Down. When all the questions are listed in the correct order, click Next.
7. Choose how you would like the questions to be presented on the Presentation Options page. Click Next.
8. Choose output options. You can save the responses to a Web page, create a text file, or use a custom CGI script to direct the output to a database. Enter a name for the results file to be stored with your Web. Click Next.
9. Click Finish to create your form.

After the Form Page wizard creates the form, you'll need to modify the form's purpose by editing the This Is An Explanation section. You may also want to modify or delete the copyright information at the bottom of the form and add other text and images to make your form complete. View the form in at least two browsers to ensure everything works the way it should.

Storing Form Results

Objective FP2000E.11.2 and E.11.4

When the FrontPage Form Page wizard creates a form, it attaches a form handler to the form to process the results and save them in the file you designated in the last step of the wizard. If you create a form from scratch, or if you want to change how the FrontPage Save Results component stores the data, you can modify the properties of the form by right-clicking on the form and choosing Form Properties, shown in figure 14.45.

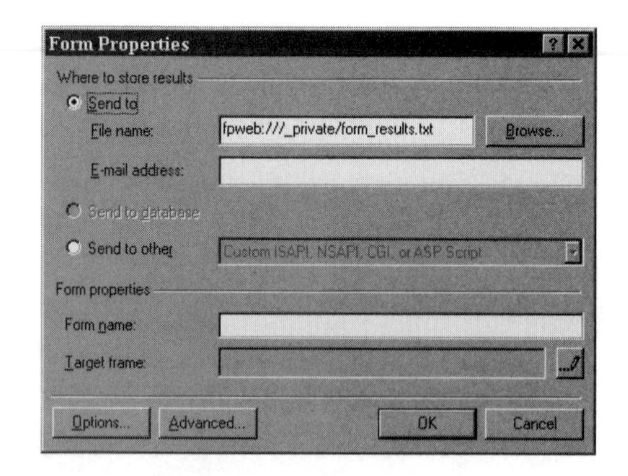

FIGURE 14.45
You can change where to store the results of a form in the Form Properties dialog box.

You can change the file that receives the results and you can change the format of the results. Choose where you'd like to store results, entering the full path if you would like the file located in a particular folder in or outside of the open Web.

If you choose to send the results by e-mail, enter the e-mail address you want the results sent to. Even if you are storing the results in a file, it helps to be notified by e-mail that someone actually completed a form.

Sending Form Results to a Database

Objective FP2000E.12.1

To send the results to a database, click the Options button to open the Options for Saving Results to Database dialog box, shown in Figure 14.46.

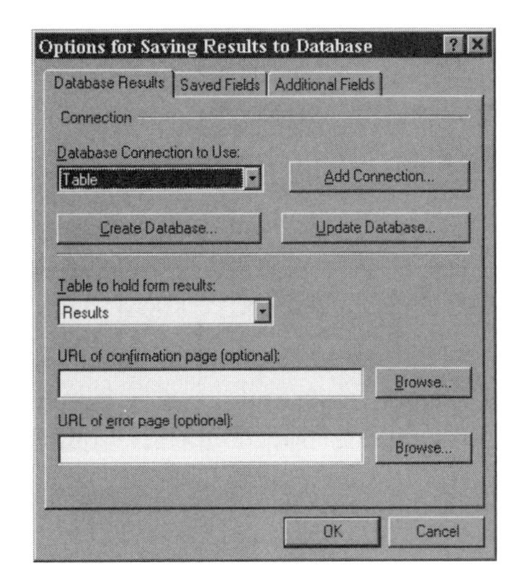

FIGURE 14.46 Use the Options for Saving Results to Database dialog box to set up the database, tables, and fields you want to use.

Using an Existing Database Connection

You can use an existing database connection, add a connection, or create a new database to house the data. To add a connection, click the Add Database button and choose from one of the available ODBC database connections or click Add to set up an entirely new connection.

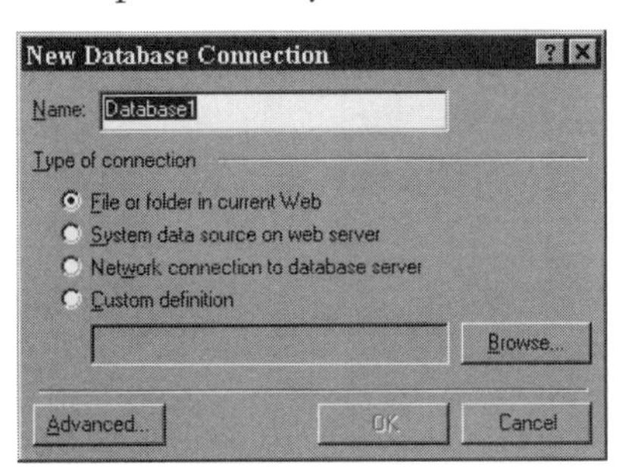

The connection can be a file or folder in the current Web, a system data source on a Web server, a network connection to a database server (such as a SQL server), or a custom definition. Click Advanced to set up a user name and password to access the database and to set timeouts for the connection and other parameters. After you create the database connection, click OK as many times as needed to return to the Options dialog box.

Click the Update Database button. FrontPage will add a column to the selected database for every form field added to the current form.

Creating a Database

If you don't have a database to store results in, FrontPage can create one for you. Click the Create Database button. FrontPage creates an Access database with one table called Results, and saves it in the open Web.

Other Form Results Settings

If you would like to specify a confirmation page, such as the one shown in Figure 14.47, and a page to be returned when an error occurs, such as when a user does not complete a required field, enter the URLs for those pages in the text boxes provided.

FIGURE 14.47 A Confirmation Form lets users review what they entered and print or save for their records.

Form Confirmation

Thank you for submitting the following information:

UserName: Janis Joplin
UserEmail: jjoplin@joplin.com
Subject: Products
SubjectOther: Mastering Outlook 2000

Comments

Me and Bobby just finished your latest Mastering book. It was great -- keeping them coming!

Return to the form.

Click the Saved Fields tab, shown in Figure 14.48, to select the fields you want to save and to verify the mapping of form fields to database fields.

The All Fields and Add buttons are not available if all form fields are already included on the form. If these buttons are available, you can use them to map fields that are not currently included in the form results.

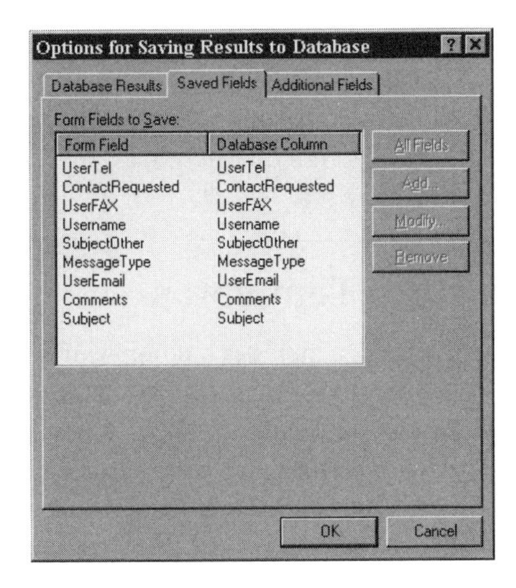

FIGURE 14.48 In the Saved Fields tab, you can select fields you want to save in the database and map form fields to database fields.

Click the Additional Fields tab to save additional data with each submission, such as TimeStamp, Remote Computer Name, User Name, and Browser Type.

The fact that you are collecting this data is not communicated to the user who completes the form, so you may only want to select these options if you're comfortable with electronic sleuthing.

After you've modified the settings for storing the results, click OK and enter a name for the form, and if desired, identify a target frame to display the results in a page such as a confirmation page. Click the button to the right of the Target Frame box to choose a target frame.

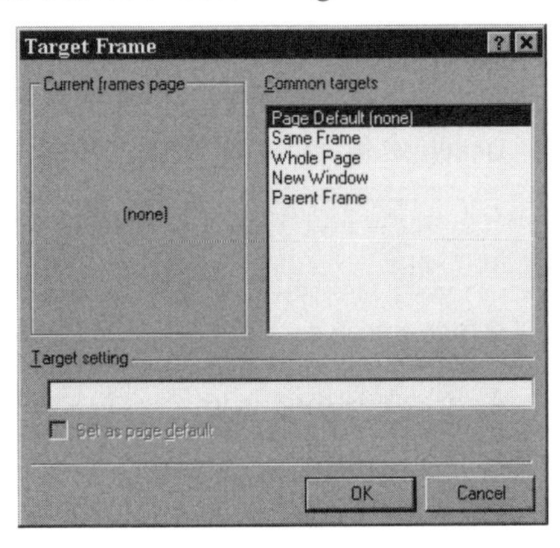

Click OK and then OK again to close the Form Properties dialog box. You're now all set to use your form on the Web.

After a user clicks the Submit button, the form handler automatically saves the results to the location you designate. You must have an active connection to the Internet to test the form handler by clicking the Submit button in a browser.

Using the Form Templates

FrontPage includes a number of templates that contain interactive elements so that your visitors can participate in your site. These include a Confirmation Form, Feedback Form, Guest Book, Search Page, and User Registration. Each of these templates requires some customization, but they provide you with the essential ingredients to design an exciting, interactive Web site. You can use each template as a separate page in your site or combine them to create pages that more closely meet your needs. To access the templates, switch to Page view, choose File ➢ New ➢ Page and choose from the list of available templates. Follow the instructions in the Comments section to customize your form.

Inserting Additional Form Fields

Objective FP2000E.11.1

The Form Page wizard and various form templates provide you with options for selecting the appropriate type of field, depending on the kind of response you are seeking. FrontPage also lets you create your own form fields whenever you need them. Each of the seven types of form fields is visible in Figure 14.49 and described in the table below.

TABLE 14.2: Form fields

Form Field	Description
One-Line Text Box	A box one line high and up to 999 characters long for (relatively) short text answers
Scrolling Text Box	A box with a scroll bar that can hold multiple lines of text
Check Box	A small box that users can click to indicate a positive response

TABLE 14.2: Form fields *(continued)*

Form Field	Description
Radio Button	Similar to a check box, except that users can only choose one option from a choice of more than one
Drop-Down Menu	A list of supplied choices that users can pick from
Push Button	A command button used to submit a form, clear (reset) a form, or complete another action designated by an attached script
Image	Same as a push button, except an image is used in place of the standard push button

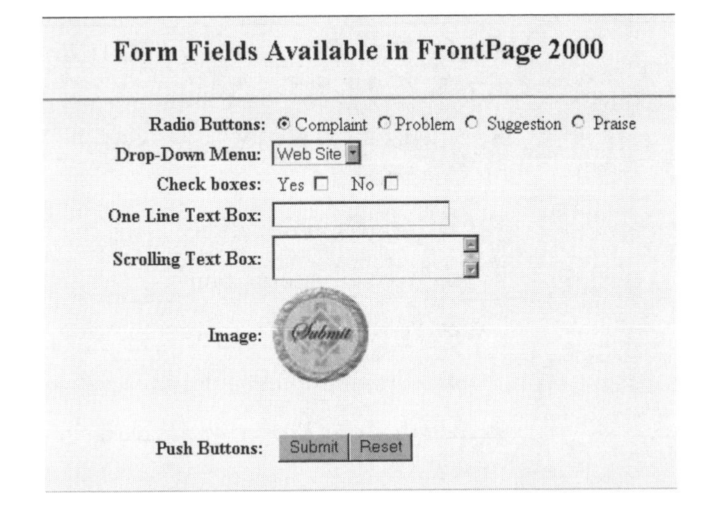

FIGURE 14.49
FrontPage form fields.

Inserting Individual Form Fields

1. Choose Insert ➢ Form and select the field you want to insert from the list of choices.
2. Right-click on a form field and select Form Field Properties to edit the property settings of the field. Modify field properties as desired.
3. Click the Validate button to create validation rules for the field, specifying the type of data you expect in the field. Click OK to save the validation rules.
4. Click OK to save the form field properties.
5. Click on a form field and drag it to move it to another position on the form.

When you add the first form field to a page, FrontPage creates a dashed border around the field, extending to the left and right margins, to designate the boundaries of the form.

Be sure to keep other fields within this boundary so that FrontPage will consider all the fields to be part of one form. You'll find it easiest to create the form if you place the field names (the questions you are asking) and their respective fields inside a table. You can then insert additional cells and change the cell sizes to position the fields appropriately. Once you've completed the form, make sure you test it multiple times in a couple of different browsers (and check the results file) before making it accessible to your Web site visitors.

Hands On: Objectives FP2000E.11.1, E.11.2, E.11.4, E.11.5, E.12.1

1. Use the Form Page Wizard to create a form with the following characteristics:
   a) Contact information
   b) Account information
   c) Personal information
   d) One question you designed.
2. Edit the Form Properties to save the results to text file and to an e-mail address.
3. Create a new page and use the Form menu (Insert ➢ Form) to create a form with at least one of each of the following:
   a) Text box
   b) Check box
   c) Radio buttons
   d) Drop-down pick lists
   e) Push buttons.
4. Save the results of the form page you created in Exercise 3 to a newly created Access database. If you are running a Web server, test the form by completing the form fields and submitting the form.

Adding Databases to a Web

Up until now, we've talked about collecting data from users. Equally important is the need to make data available to users of a Web site. If you want people to order your products, they need to know what the products are and be able to search for the ones they want. Whether it is product information, a directory of members, or a listing of available houses in a particular market, sophisticated Web users expect to be able to find data quickly and easily.

FrontPage offers several types of database connections:

- A file-based connection to a database, such as Microsoft Access, in your Web. When you import an Access database into your Web, FrontPage creates a database connection automatically.
- A System Data Source Name (System DSN) on a Web server. The data source can be a file-based database or a database management system.
- A network connection to a database server. A database server (for example, Microsoft SQL Server) is a computer dedicated solely to managing and maintaining large databases.

You can also create a custom connection using a file or string that defines all the necessary information.

The Database Results wizard lets you use an existing database connection or create a new one. You can also use a sample database, Northwind Traders, to help you understand database concepts and experiment without altering your own "live" database.

Incorporating Data Access Pages

Objective FP2000E.12.3

In Access 2000, you can create data access pages to display and work with live access data. Chapter 13 "Internet Publishing in Office 2000," explains how to create data access pages. Once you have a data access page, you can save it to a Web folder so it can be accessed as a page in a Web. You can also import the data access page into a FrontPage Web using the File ➢ Import command. Either way, the data access page, like the one shown in Figure 14.50, can be made available to users of a Web for viewing and data manipulation.

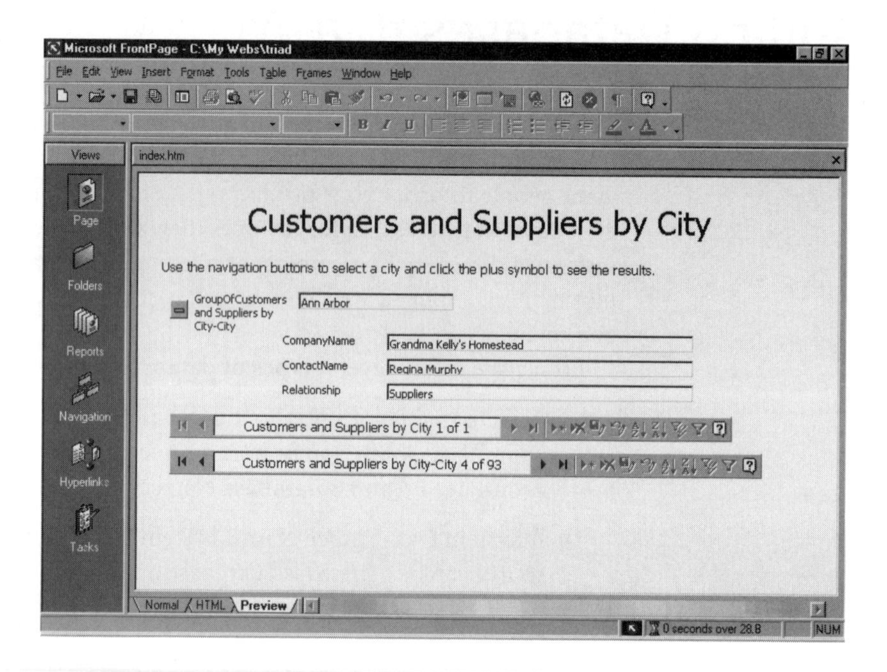

FIGURE 14.50 Publishing a data access page to a FrontPage Web is an effective way to make database data available to Web users.

Incorporating Queries Using the Database Results Wizard

Objective FP2000E.12.3

In addition to using Data Access Pages to integrate databases, FrontPage 2000 lets you attach a database to a Web page so users can view the data in a table or a query. If you plan to display a query, create the query first in Access and save it to the Access database.

Attaching a Database to a Web Page

1. Click Insert ➢ Database and choose Results to start the Database Results Wizard shown in Figure 14.51.
2. In Step 1 of the wizard, choose whether to use a sample database connection to experiment with databases, use an existing database connection, or create a new database connection.
3. In Step 2, select the table or query you want to display, or use SQL to create a custom query.

Attaching a Database to a Web Page *(continued)*

4. In Step 3, select specific fields from the table or query. Click the Edit button to remove fields or change the order in which they appear. Click the More Options button to establish criteria to filter, sort, or limit the number of records.

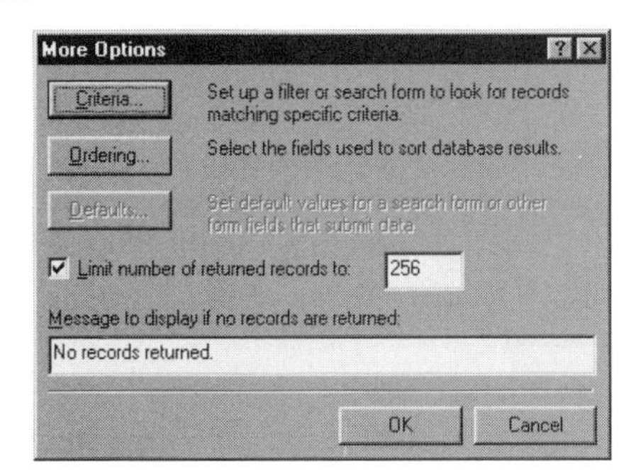

5. To set up a Search field that visitors can use to select the data they want to see, choose Criteria, click Add, and select the field you want visitors to be able to search. Choose the comparison you want to allow and verify that the field name appears as the Value. You can enter multiple search criteria indicating if you want each record to meet *both* criteria (And) or *either* criteria (Or). When you click OK, note that FrontPage puts the Value in brackets to indicate it is a variable.

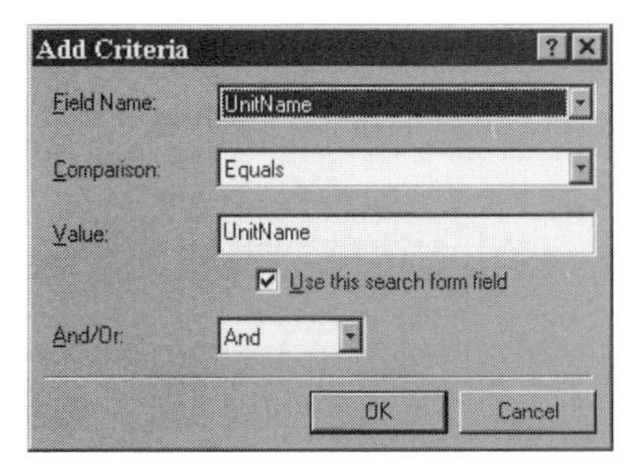

6. In Step 4, you can choose the format in which you want the records returned. Table displays one complete record on each row. List displays one field per line and Drop-down List creates a drop down of the values in one field.

Attaching a Database to a Web Page *(continued)*

7. In the final step of the wizard, Step 5, you can choose how you want to make the records available to the users. You can display the records all at one time or make them available in groups of a specified number of records. If you identified search criteria in Step 3 of the Wizard, you can also choose to add a Search form to the page (this option is not available if you did not specify search criteria in Step 3). Click Finish to create the database page.
8. You must save the page with an .asp (active server page) file extension for the page to work properly. To test the page, save it and then preview it in a browser.

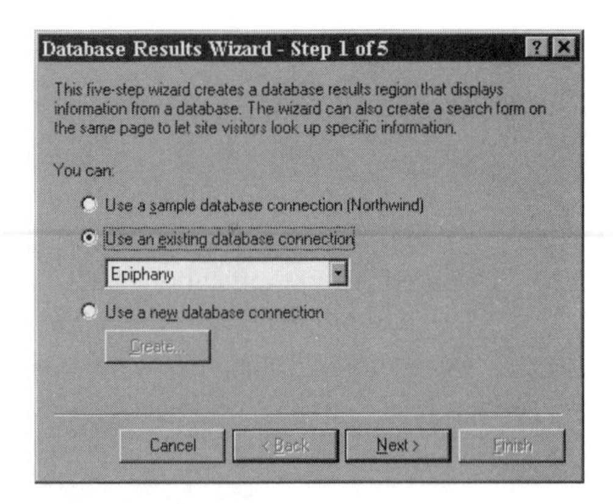

FIGURE 14.51
The Database Results wizard connects a Web page to a database to make the data available to visitors to the site.

To test an active server page, you must be running a Web server with the FrontPage server extensions installed. For more information about Web servers, see "Publishing the Web" later in this chapter.

If you'd like to improve the appearance of the list display, select the field placeholders on the page, right-click, and choose Paragraph. Change the Spacing Before and the Spacing After to 0.

Using Frames to Divide Your Pages

Objective FP2000E.14.4

Frames divide a page into two or more separate windows that operate independently or in a hierarchical structure. One frame, for example, can be a static display of a table of contents or site map, while another frame displays selected pages from the static frame. A frames page defines the groups of frames that make up a page. Frames aren't HTML objects like text, images, or tables; rather, they are a structure on which you hang other pages.

To develop a frames page, click the Frames Pages tab on the New dialog box. Figure 14.52 shows the frames page templates available in FrontPage.

FIGURE 14.52

Frames pages display multiple pages in one.

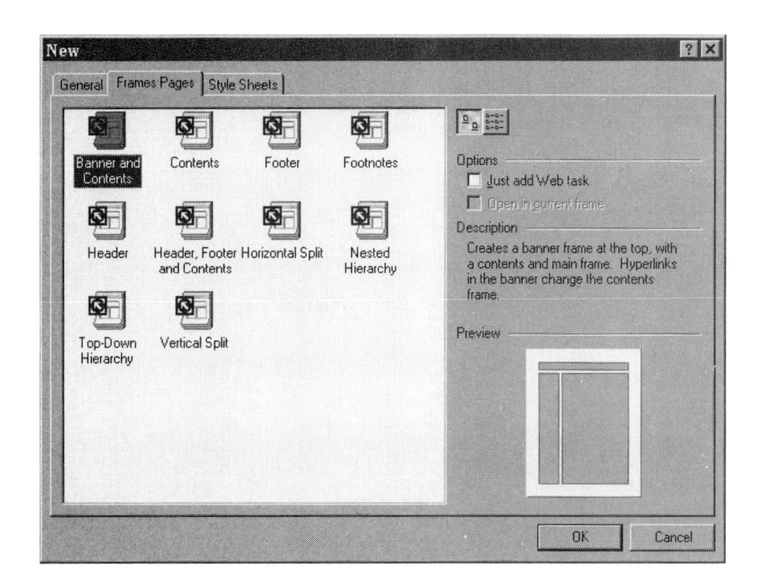

Click each template to see a description of the frames page. Select the frames page you would like to use and click OK. Figure 14.53 shows a newly created Banner and Contents frames page. You now have to tell it which pages to display in each of the frames. Display an existing page by clicking the Set Initial Page button in each frame or create a new page by clicking the New Page button.

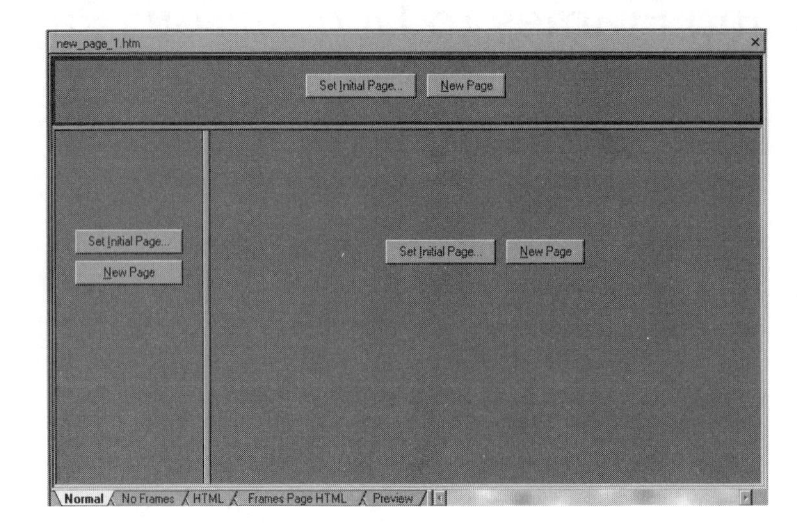

FIGURE 14.53 After you create a frames page, you must designate the pages you want to display.

When you close the frames page or click the Preview in Browser button, you are prompted to save the page and any new pages you created as part of the frames page.

Editing Frames

Objective FP2000E.14.1 and E.14.3

To edit the size of existing frames in a Frames page, drag the border lines of the frame until it is the size you want it. You can also create a new frame on a Frames page, by holding the Ctrl key when you drag a border. A new frame is created wherever you drop the border.

Objective FP2000E.14.2

To edit the content within a frame, click in the frame and edit it as you would any other full page.

Adding Target Content Within a Frame

Objective FP2000E.14.5

If you click the Set Initial Page button on a newly created frame, the Create Hyperlink dialog box opens and you can set the target page for the frame. If you decide you want to add a target page after you create the pages in a

Frames pages, right-click on the frame where you want the target content and choose Frame Properties, shown in Figure 14.54. Click the Browse button and locate the page you want to appear as the Initial Page. Select the page and click OK. Click OK again to close the Frame Properties dialog box.

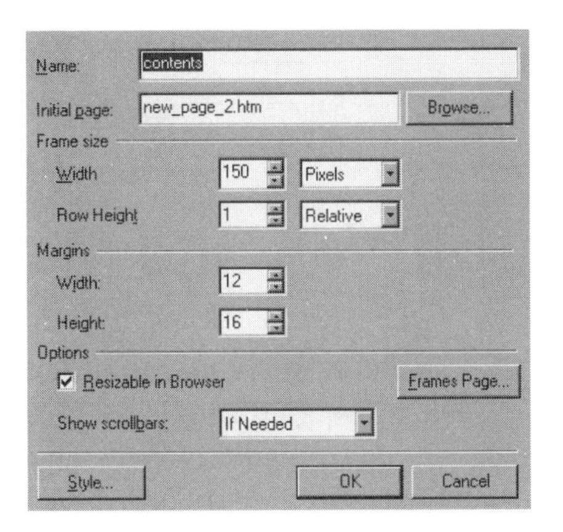

FIGURE 14.54
Click the Browse button to set target content for a frame.

Not all browsers are capable of displaying frames, and frames play havoc with text readers that visually impaired users require. You should always designate an alternate page for visitors who don't have frames-compatible browsers.

Hands On: Objectives FP2000E.14.1-E.14.5

1. Create a Frames page using a Frames template.
   a) Set one of the Initial pages to an existing page in the Web.
   b) Create new pages for the other frames.
   c) Edit the content of the new pages.
   d) Change the size of one of the frames using drag and drop.
   e) Replace one of the new pages with a targeted page.
   f) Save each of the pages in the Frame Page to the Web.

2. Create a second Frames Page using a different Frames template.
   a) Use drag and drop to create a new frame.
   b) Add content to the pages in the frame.
   c) Edit the left frame's properties to not display a scroll bar.
   d) Preview the Frames page.
   e) Save the changes to each page.

Overview of Web Site Management

Successful Web sites are sites that are well designed and well managed. It's staggering to know the number of companies that have paid big money to have a Web site designed and then left it to languish unattended and out of date. FrontPage 2000 can help you manage your Web site and make sure it stays current and functioning the way you had intended. Whether you are in the initial design stages or have a fully functioning Web site, FrontPage can help you keep track of incomplete tasks, verify and update hyperlinks, and assist with publishing Web sites.

Using Reports to See What's Going On

The quickest and easiest way to see what's happening in a Web is to click the Reports button on the Views bar. The default Site Summary report, shown in Figure 14.55, gives you an overview of critical information about the Web, including the number and size of files, the number and status of hyperlinks, the number of slow pages, and the number of incomplete tasks.

If the Reporting toolbar does not open automatically, choose View ➢ Toolbar and click Reporting to turn it on.

If you want to find out more about a particular item in the Site Summary, double-click it to drill down to a detail report. Figure 14.56 shows the detail report for Unlinked Files.

Use the Reporting toolbar to switch back to the Site Summary or choose another detail report from the drop-down list.

FIGURE 14.55

The Site Summary report gives you a quick snapshot of the status of a Web.

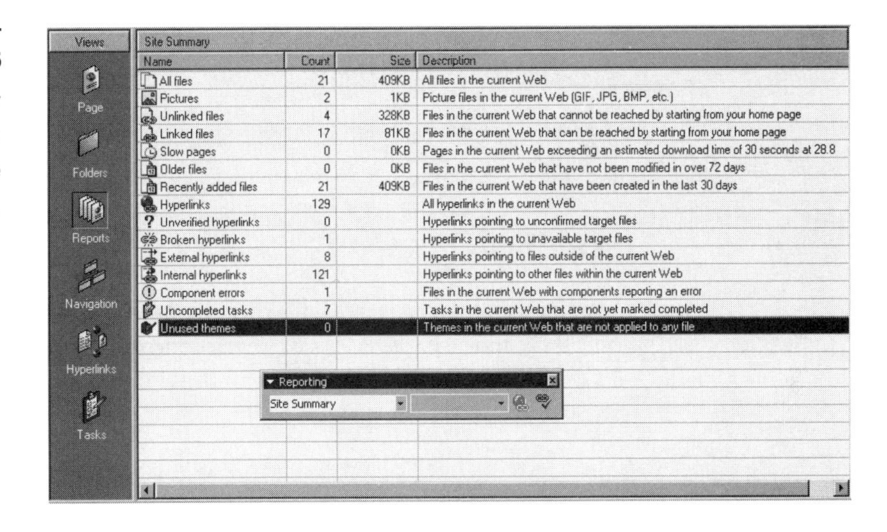

Site Summary

Name	Count	Size	Description
All files	21	409KB	All files in the current Web
Pictures	2	1KB	Picture files in the current Web (GIF, JPG, BMP, etc.)
Unlinked files	4	328KB	Files in the current Web that cannot be reached by starting from your home page
Linked files	17	81KB	Files in the current Web that can be reached by starting from your home page
Slow pages	0	0KB	Pages in the current Web exceeding an estimated download time of 30 seconds at 28.8
Older files	0	0KB	Files in the current Web that have not been modified in over 72 days
Recently added files	21	409KB	Files in the current Web that have been created in the last 30 days
Hyperlinks	129		All hyperlinks in the current Web
Unverified hyperlinks	0		Hyperlinks pointing to unconfirmed target files
Broken hyperlinks	1		Hyperlinks pointing to unavailable target files
External hyperlinks	8		Hyperlinks pointing to files outside of the current Web
Internal hyperlinks	121		Hyperlinks pointing to other files within the current Web
Component errors	1		Files in the current Web with components reporting an error
Uncompleted tasks	7		Tasks in the current Web that are not yet marked completed
Unused themes	0		Themes in the current Web that are not applied to any file

FIGURE 14.56

Double-click an item to see the underlying detail.

Unlinked Files

Name	Title	In Folder	Modified By	Type	Modified Date
fpnwind.mdb	fpdb/fpnwind.mdb	fpdb	amarquis	mdb	5/3/99 4:43 PM
global.asa	global.asa		amarquis	asa	5/3/99 4:43 PM
smallnew.gif	images/smallnew.gif	images	amarquis	gif	5/5/99 3:06 PM
undercon.gif	images/undercon.gif	images	amarquis	gif	5/5/99 3:06 PM

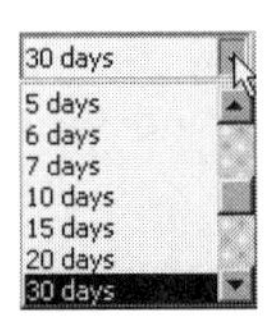

Reports that are date driven, such as Recently Added Files, let you customize the time period for the report. Choose the report from the Reporting toolbar and change the Report Settings using the drop-down list provided.

Not all available reports appear in the Site Summary. Use the Reporting toolbar or choose View ➢ Reports from the menu to access additional reports.

Viewing a Page's Estimated Time to Download

Objective FP2000E.9.1

An important quality of a successful Web site is that the pages load quickly so your users are not waiting around for your content. The Slow Pages report identifies those pages that download too slowly (pages that will take at least

20 seconds to download at a connection speed of 14.4 baud). Choose Reports ➢ Slow Pages to run the Slow Pages Report. Double-click to open any of the pages on this list so you can edit them to make them more efficient.

Managing Tasks

Objectives FP2000.13.1 and 13.2

Keeping track of the status of every file on a Web can be a daunting task, especially in the early stages of development. FrontPage offers a built-in Tasks list that helps you manage all those outstanding issues. Tasks can be created in several ways.

- Choose File ➢ New ➢Task. This works in any view, and if you use this option in Page view, the task is directly associated with the open file.
- Click the Tasks icon on the Views bar, right-click in the Information Viewer, and choose New Task.
- Right-click on a filename in Folder view and choose Add Task. Tasks created this way are also associated with the file you right-clicked.

- Click the down arrow on the New Page button and choose New Task.
- Creating a Web with a wizard automatically creates tasks related to pages in need of customization.

To enter a task, enter a Task Name in the New Task form, choose a Priority level, identify the Assigned To person or team, and enter a description, if desired.

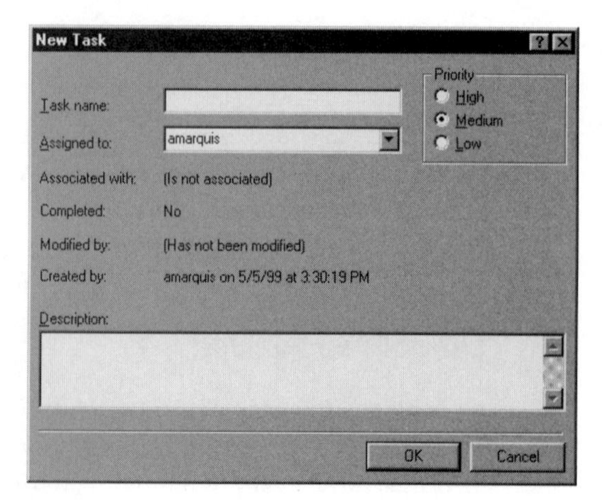

To add individuals or team names to the Assigned To list, either type their name into the Assigned To box in Tasks view or right-click any file in the Web and choose Properties. Click the Workgroup tab and click the Names button. For more information about adding names, see *Assigning Files to Teams and Team Members* later in this chapter.

Tasks are displayed in the Tasks window, shown in Figure 14.57, by clicking the Tasks icon on the Views bar.

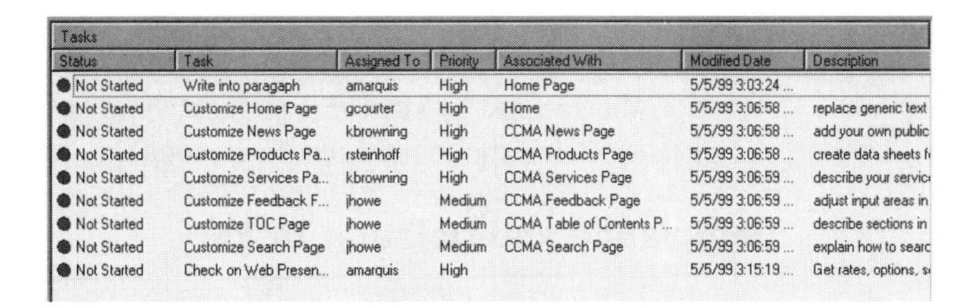

Tasks

Status	Task	Assigned To	Priority	Associated With	Modified Date	Description
Not Started	Write into paragaph	amarquis	High	Home Page	5/5/99 3:03:24 ...	
Not Started	Customize Home Page	gcourter	High	Home	5/5/99 3:06:58 ...	replace generic text
Not Started	Customize News Page	kbrowning	High	CCMA News Page	5/5/99 3:06:58 ...	add your own public
Not Started	Customize Products Pa...	rsteinhoff	High	CCMA Products Page	5/5/99 3:06:58 ...	create data sheets f
Not Started	Customize Services Pa...	kbrowning	High	CCMA Services Page	5/5/99 3:06:59 ...	describe your servic
Not Started	Customize Feedback F...	jhowe	Medium	CCMA Feedback Page	5/5/99 3:06:59 ...	adjust input areas in
Not Started	Customize TOC Page	jhowe	Medium	CCMA Table of Contents P...	5/5/99 3:06:59 ...	describe sections in
Not Started	Customize Search Page	jhowe	Medium	CCMA Search Page	5/5/99 3:06:59 ...	explain how to searc
Not Started	Check on Web Presen...	amarquis	High		5/5/99 3:15:19 ...	Get rates, options, s

FIGURE 14.57
Using Tasks helps you and your team keep track of incomplete pages and other outstanding issues.

Double-click a task in the Information viewer to open it. If the task is associated with a file, a Start Task button is added to the form. Click the Start Task button to open the page in Page view. When you save the page, this message appears.

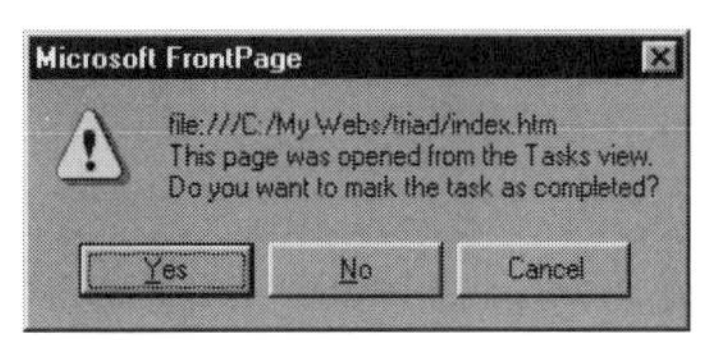

If you completed the task, click Yes. If you still have work to do, click No. In either case, the task stays on the Task list, but the Status of the task is automatically updated.

Status	Task	Assigned To	Priority	Associated With	Modified Date	Description
Completed	Check on Web Presen...	amarquis	High		5/5/99 3:37:06 ...	Get rates, options, s
In Progress	Write into paragaph	amarquis	High	Home	5/5/99 3:36:37 ...	
Not Started	Customize Home Page	gcourter	High	Home	5/5/99 3:06:58 ...	replace generic text
Not Started	Customize News Page	kbrowning	High	CCMA News Page	5/5/99 3:06:58 ...	add your own public
Not Started	Customize Products Pa...	rsteinhoff	High	CCMA Products Page	5/5/99 3:06:58 ...	create data sheets f
Not Started	Customize Services Pa...	kbrowning	High	CCMA Services Page	5/5/99 3:06:59 ...	describe your servic
Not Started	Customize Feedback F...	jhowe	Medium	CCMA Feedback Page	5/5/99 3:06:59 ...	adjust input areas in
Not Started	Customize TOC Page	jhowe	Medium	CCMA Table of Contents P...	5/5/99 3:06:59 ...	describe sections in
Not Started	Customize Search Page	jhowe	Medium	CCMA Search Page	5/5/99 3:06:59 ...	explain how to searc

In Task view, you can directly edit the Task, Assigned To, Priority, and Description columns. Select the task and click a second time in the column you want to edit.

Task information such as the date the task was created or modified, and the page, image, or file to which it is linked is not editable.

Viewing Task History

To view the history of tasks, right-click in the Tasks viewer and choose Show History.

Sorting the Task List

Sort the Task list by switching to Tasks view and clicking any of the column headers. Click the column header a second time to reverse the order of the sort.

Completing and Deleting Tasks

To mark a task complete, right-click it in the Task list and choose Mark as Completed. The red ball in front of the task changes to green, the Status changes to Completed, and the Modified Date changes to the current date. You can also delete an active task this way, but you cannot delete a completed task.

If you'd prefer that completed tasks no longer showed on the Task list, right-click in the Information viewer and clear Show Task History. You can always get them back by right-clicking and choosing Show Task History again.

Working with Webs

As a Web grows and develops, you may need to conduct some basic file management activities, such as renaming and deleting files. Because of the unique nature of Web files and folders, it is better to handle those tasks through FrontPage rather than through the Windows Explorer.

Renaming Pages and Webs

Every Web page has a title and a filename. The title is the friendly name that appears in the Title column in Folder view. The filename is the Windows name for the file and is the name used in links. When you rename a file, you can change either name or both names in Folder view or in Navigation view. However, if you are using Navigation view to manage internal links, you should change them there. Otherwise, the new filenames are not reflected in Navigation view or in Navigation bars.

To change the title of a page in Navigation view, right-click on it and choose Properties. Enter a new title in the Title box. To change the filename, right-click on the page in Navigation view and choose Rename. You are switched into Edit mode and you can enter a new name directly on the page icon.

Renaming a Web is just as easy. With the Web open in any view, choose Tools ➢ Web Settings. Enter the new name of the Web in the Web Name box on the General page, shown in Figure 14.58

FIGURE 14.58

Change the name of a Web in the General page of the Web Settings dialog box.

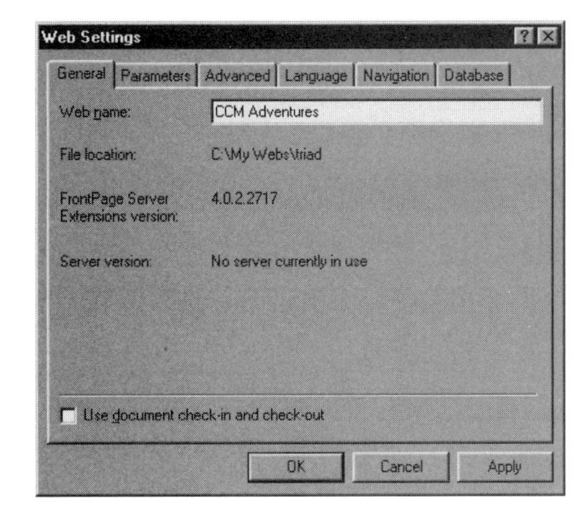

Moving and Copying Files

The techniques you already know for moving and copying files in the Windows Explorer work well in FrontPage's Folder view. Select the file or files you want to move or copy and right-drag them to the new folder. Choose Move Here or Copy Here from the shortcut menu that appears. FrontPage revises all the hyperlinks related to the file.

An unpublished Web saved to a folder on a local or network drive can be moved or copied safely in the Windows Explorer.

Deleting Pages and Webs

To delete an entire Web, right-click the main Web folder in Folder view and choose Delete. When the Confirm Delete dialog box appears, choose to convert the folder or delete the folder entirely.

Check Spelling for an Entire Web

Objective FP2000.12.1

Even if you can trust that every author created their pages with care and meticulously checked the spelling, it never hurts to do it again before you publish the Web for the world to see. Rather than open every page of the Web and run Spelling, you can use FrontPage's Spelling feature on an entire Web at once.

With the Web open that you want to review, choose Tools ➢ Spelling. You have two options: check the spelling of the entire Web or of selected pages. You can also have FrontPage create a task associated with the page for each misspelling. Click OK to start the checker. When it is finished, you receive a report like the one shown in Figure 14.59.

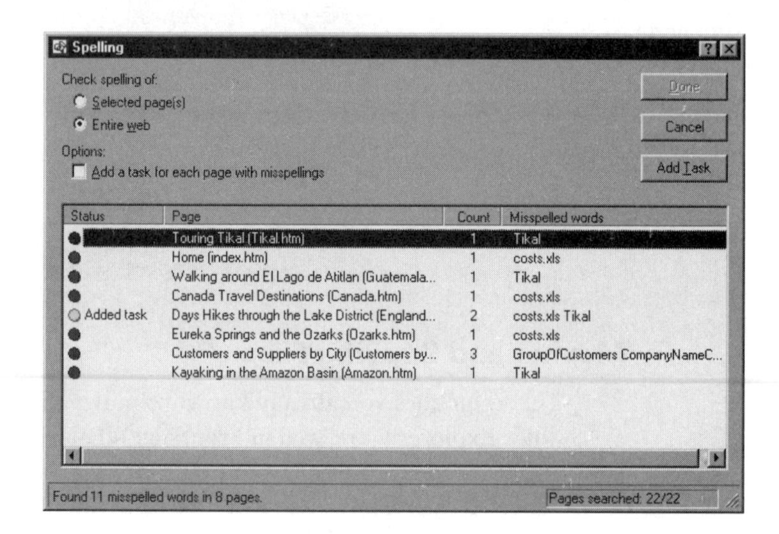

FIGURE 14.59 FrontPage reviews an entire Web for misspelled words and provides you with a summary of its findings.

If you didn't choose to create tasks, you have another opportunity to do so now. Check the Add a Task for Each Page with Misspellings or select an individual file and click the Add Task button.

Double-click each file to open any of the pages. A Spelling dialog box opens with the misspelled word. Make the appropriate correction and FrontPage prompts you to close the document and move on to another page.

After you have finished checking all the documents, the Spelling summary shows the status of each file as Edited.

Using Global Find and Replace across a Web

Objective FP2000.12.4

To change text that affects all or some of the pages in a Web, you can use Find and Replace to make global changes across the Web.

Using Global Find and Replace

1. Unless you want to replace text in all pages of the Web, switch to Folder view, and select the pages in which you want to replace text.
2. Chose Edit ➢ Replace.
3. Enter the text string you want to look for in the Find What box.
4. Enter the text string you want to replace it with in the Replace With box.
5. Click if you want to search All Pages or Select Pages.
6. Enter the direction you want to search through the files: Up or Down.
7. Check if you want to Match Case, Find Whole Words Only, or Find in HTML.
8. Click the Find in Web button.
9. When FrontPage finishes the Find operation, click Replace All to make the change in all the pages or Replace to replace the text one page at a time. Click Add Task if you want to mark the file and make the change at another time.

Working on a Team

Most Web sites, whether they are on corporate intranets or the World Wide Web, are the product of a team of people working together to design and provide content for the site. As Webs grow and develop, it makes sense to assign responsibility for specific parts of a Web to the people who have the most knowledge in that area. For example, a Human Resources Department, with a little training, is generally much more capable of maintaining the Human Resources pages on a Web than an IT Department. The IT Department is probably better-equipped to manage style sheets and database connections. By delegating tasks to particular individuals or teams, the Web becomes a vibrant reflection of the entire organization rather than a collection of stagnant documents.

As with any team project, however, it's not always easy to keep track of who is responsible for what and what the status of each task is. FrontPage has several tools to help teams manage Web development, such as source control to check files in and out and task delegation to assign jobs to specific people.

Source Control

Objective FP2000E.13.1

Up until FrontPage 2000, you've had to install special source control software to have a method of checking files out and in. FrontPage 2000 has a built-in source control feature that monitors if a file is checked out by another member of the team. The Web administrator can enable the source control feature and each team member can make use of it.

Enabling Source Control

1. Open the Web, but close any open files in the Web.
2. Choose Tools ➢ Web Settings.
3. Click the Use Document Check-in and Check-out on the General tab. Click OK to close the dialog box and save the changes.
4. Click Yes to the FrontPage message that recalculating the Web based on the changes in source control may take a few minutes and would you like to proceed.

With source control enabled, when authors try to open a file they are asked if they want to check out the file. They are informed if someone else has already checked out the file. If a file is already checked out, other authors can open a read-only copy. In the Folder view, as shown in Figure 14.60, files that are checked in have a green dot in front of them. Files checked out by the current author are designated by a red check mark, and files checked out by another author have a lock in front of them.

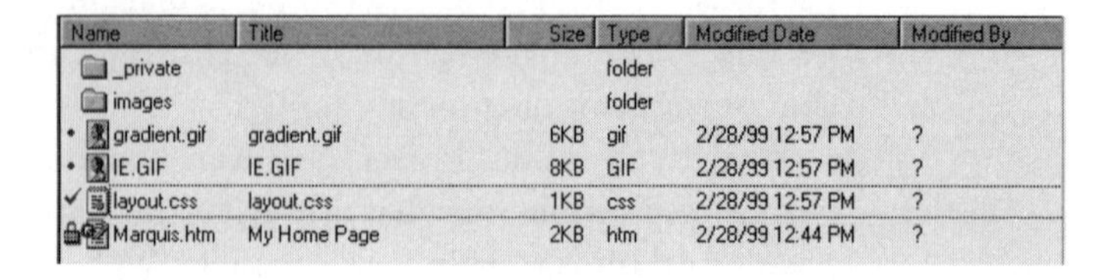

FIGURE 14.60 Source control protects files from being edited by more than one author at a time.

When an author has a file checked out, any changes they save are published, even if the file is not checked back in again. To restore a previous version of a file, right-click on the file in Folder view and choose Undo Check Out. This restores the file to the state it was in before the file was checked out.

To check a file back in, right-click on the file in Folder view and choose Check In.

Assigning Files to Teams or Team Members

To assign responsibility for a file to an individual or team member, you first want to set up the list of names. You've already worked with this list when you assigned tasks to specific individuals earlier in this chapter. To revisit the list and assign a file, right-click on the file you want to assign and click Choose Properties. Click the Workgroup tab, shown in Figure 14.61, and click the Names button. Type a name in the New Username box and click the Add button to add a name to the list. Select an existing name and click Delete to remove it. To discard your changes and return to the list of names that appeared when the dialog box first opened, click the Reset button.

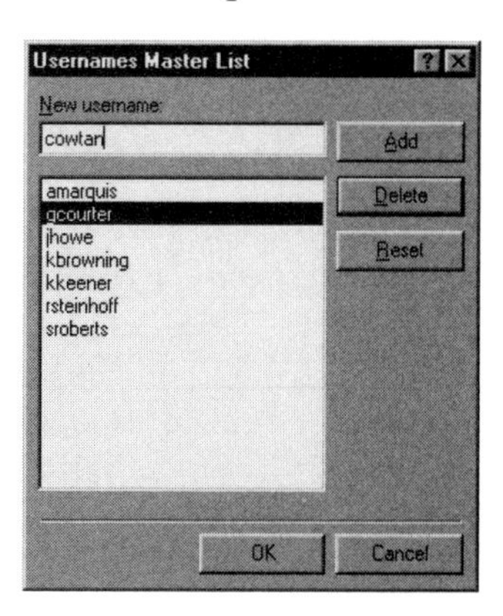

When you have finished creating the list, click OK to return to the Workgroup tab. Click the Assigned To down arrow to select a name from the list.

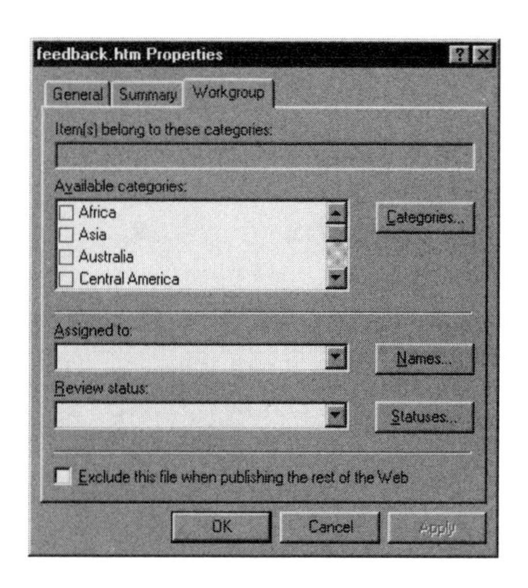

FIGURE 14.61

On the Workgroup tab, you can assign Web pages to specific users.

Setting Review Status Review status, also found on the Workgroup tab of the Properties dialog box, is set by an individual user responsible for a specific type of review. FrontPage identifies four types of review: code review, content review, legal review, and manager review. When a logged-in user conducts a review on a file, they can change the review status to reflect the type of review they conducted. FrontPage records the review status, the review date, and the name of the person conducting the review (based on the current login name). Choose View ➢ Reports ➢ Review Status to get a report of this information.

Review status is not directly associated with the Assigned To field. The person assigned to a file may be different from the person who reviews the file.

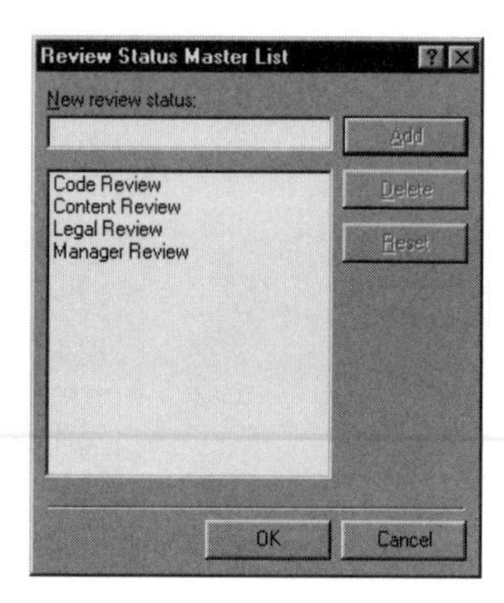

If you would like to add additional items to the Review Status list, right-click on a file and choose Properties. On the Workgroup tab click the Statuses button to open the Review Status Master List dialog box.

Add review statuses in the same way you added usernames. Click OK when you finish with the list.

A person responsible for reviewing files may find it easier to change the review status in the Review Status report directly rather than in the Properties dialog box. Click once on Review Status Field and then click a second time to switch into Edit mode. Choose a new status from the drop-down list.

Setting Permissions

Objective FP2000E.13.2

Depending on how the Web server you are using handles security, you may or may not be able to control security from within FrontPage. If you are running Internet Information Server under Windows NT, for example, users and groups cannot be created in FrontPage. Instead, FrontPage lets you choose who you want to give access to a Web from among the Windows NT accounts.

If you are uncertain if you can control security from within FrontPage, choose Tools ➢ Security. If Security is dimmed, you do not have access to security in FrontPage and it must be managed by your Web server and/or server operating system.

If Security is available on the Tools menu, you can add users and groups to a Web's user list and then specify the type of access each user has. You can choose from three types of permissions:

Browse A user can view the files in a Web but cannot modify them.

Author A user can add and edit files in the Web.

Administrator A user has the same permissions as Authors but can also add and remove users.

Permissions are set for the root Web, and all subwebs inherit the same permissions. However, you can set different permissions for subwebs. This option allows you to provide author permissions to people in a department on their department's subweb and browse permissions to the same people on another department's subweb.

For more about security with Internet Information Server, see *Mastering IIS 4,* also from Sybex.

Publishing a FrontPage Web

After hours, days, weeks, and maybe even months of work, you are finally ready to go live. Whether you have contracted for virtual hosting with a Web hosting service or are managing your own Web server, the process of publishing is relatively painless. But before you take that final step, there is one more precaution you may want to take and that is to check all the hyperlinks in the Web to make sure they are working correctly. Don't panic. FrontPage can do this for you in one easy step.

Updating and Verifying Hyperlinks

Objective FP2000.12.3

To see the hyperlinks in a Web, you can switch to Hyperlink view, shown in Figure 14.62, by clicking the Hyperlink icon on the Views bar.

To see the links related to a specific page, click the plus symbol to expand the links, as shown on the following page, or right-click and choose Move to Center to move the focus to that page.

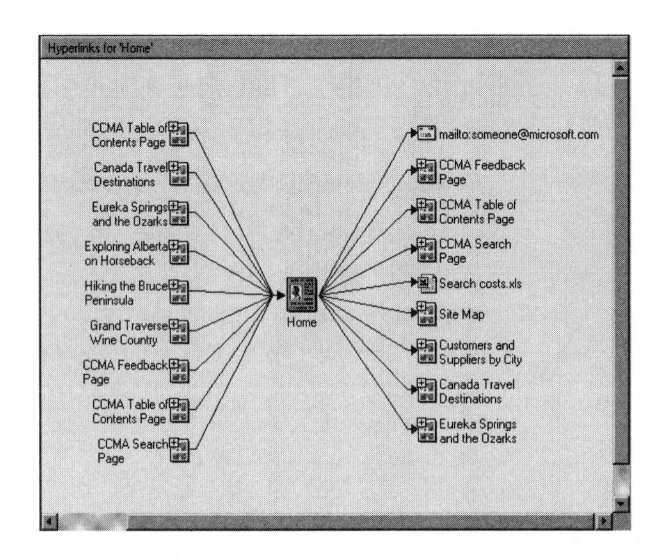

FIGURE 14.62 Hyperlinks view shows how pages are linked within a Web.

Double-click any icon to open the page it represents. If you'd like to view the page titles instead of the filenames, right-click on the viewer window and choose Show Page Titles from the shortcut menu. You can also choose to show Hyperlinks to Pictures, Repeated Hyperlinks, and Hyperlinks within Pages.

Show Page Titles
Hyperlinks to Pictures
Repeated Hyperlinks
Hyperlinks Inside Page
Web Settings...

Hyperlinks view is a good way to examine the connections in a Web and to see if any links are broken (represented by a broken line), but it does not help you verify external links. The Recalculate Hyperlinks command will check all the links, internal and external. To access this feature, click Tools ➢ Recalculate Hyperlinks. Recalculate Hyperlinks does more that just verify links. It repairs the links when it can; updates information for FrontPage components, including shared borders and navigation bars; and synchronizes Web data, database information, and categories. Definitely worth the effort!

View the reports named Broken Hyperlinks and Component Errors to review the results of the Recalculate Hyperlinks command.

Publishing the Web

In order to publish a Web, you must have access to a Web server. If you are publishing to a network server or Internet Service Provider, the Web server should be already set up and available to you. Just find out the Web server address from your network administrator or ISP and make sure they have given you permissions to publish to the Web.

Microsoft's Personal Web Server

Objective FP2000E.15.2

If you'd like to run your own Web server so you can fully test your Web's functioning before you publish it to a public server, you can install Microsoft Personal Web Server (PWS) that comes with Windows 98. You can find PWS on the Windows 98 CD-ROM under add-ons\pws. Double-click the setup.exe file to install PWS.

Once you've installed the PWS, you'll find it active in the Windows 98 system tray. Double-click the PWS icon to launch the Personal Web Manager, shown in Figure 14.63. To find out more about how to use the Microsoft Personal Web Server, click the Tour button on the PWS View bar. You can also choose Personal Web Server Topics or Readme/Troubleshooting from the Help menu.

FIGURE 14.63 Microsoft Personal Web Server, a fully functioning Web Server, comes with Windows 98.

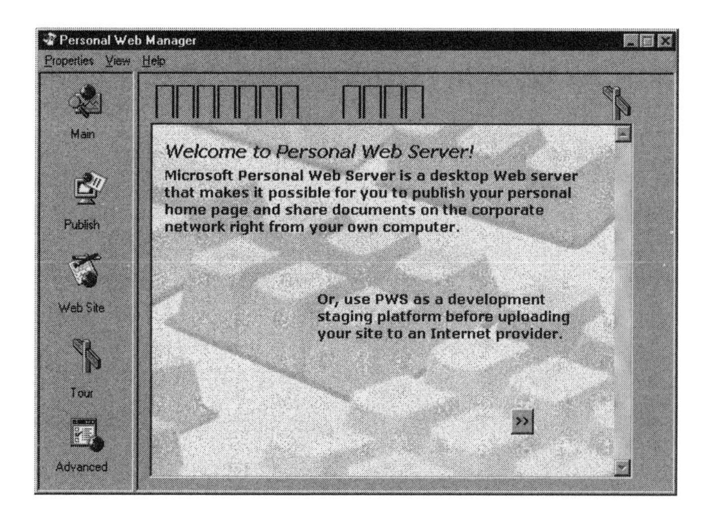

FrontPage 2000 Server Extensions

Objective FP2000E.15.3

The FrontPage 2000 Server Extensions are a set of programs installed on a Web server that support administering, authoring, and browsing a FrontPage-extended Web site. FrontPage 2000 Server extensions allow you to:

- Administer FrontPage-extended webs, including setting permissions for authors, administrators, and Web site visitors.

- Author FrontPage-extended Webs, including automatically maintaining hyperlinks, generating and maintaining navigation bars, and automatically formatting pages.
- Add functionality to your Web site through support of the FrontPage components such as hit counters, forms, and discussion groups.

To learn more about FrontPage Server Extensions and how to install them on your Web server, install the Server Extensions Resource Kit from the Office 2000 installation program.

Installing the Server Extensions Resource Kit

1. Click Start ➢ Settings ➢ Control Panel and double-click Add/Remove Programs.
2. Click Microsoft Office 2000 Premium (or FrontPage 2000 if you purchased FrontPage separately) and choose Add/Remove.
3. In the Update Features window, expand Microsoft FrontPage for Windows and set Server Extensions Resource Kit to Run from My Computer. If you are interested in remote administration of a FrontPage Web, you might also want to install Server Extensions Administrative Forms.
4. Click Update Now to install the add-ins.

The installation program adds a new folder to your Programs Menu, called My Administrative Tools. Choose FrontPage Server Extensions Resource Kit to find out how to install and administer FrontPage 2000 Server Extensions.

Publishing the Web

Objective FP2000E.15.1

When you are ready to publish the Web to a Web server, click File ➢ Publish Web. Click the Options button to see all the options shown in Figure 14.64. Enter the URL for the location you want to publish to. If you do not yet have Web Presence Provider to host your Web, Microsoft has a list of providers that support FrontPage Server extensions on their Web site. Click the WPPs button to explore a variety of companies.

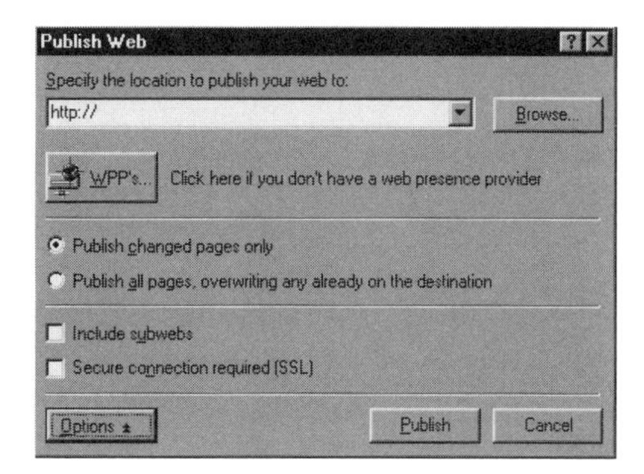

FIGURE 14.64 Identify where you want to publish the Web in the Publish Web dialog box.

If this is the first time you are publishing, you want to click the Publish All Pages option. If you are updating an already published Web, choose the Publish Changed Pages Only option. If your Web contains subwebs that you want to publish, click the Include Subwebs options. You also have an option to publish to a secure port on a Web server that supports Secure Socket Layers (SSLs). If you have a secure port available, click the Secure Connection Required checkbox.

When you have all the settings correct, click Publish. FrontPage copies all the files to the new location. If you are updating an already published Web and FrontPage encounters a conflict with the navigation structure because of changes you or another author made to the same structure, FrontPage lets you resolve the conflict in one of three ways:

- Do not replace the navigation structure.
- Replace the navigation structure.
- Let FrontPage merge the changes. In this case, FrontPage publishes the navigation structure but only replaces changes if yours are more recent.

Avoid conflicts by enabling source control discussed earlier in this chapter.

When your Web is successfully published, you have the option to view the published Web site. Click the Click Here to View Your Published Web Site link to be taken to the live site. Congratulations!

CHAPTER 15

Creating and Using Macros in Office 2000

A *macro* is a set of instructions that a program executes on command. The instructions can be simple keystrokes or complex menu selections. If you have tasks you regularly complete that include the same series of steps, creating a macro to automate the tasks save time and effort. If you're creating documents for others, adding a few macros can make the documents more user-friendly. In this chapter, you'll learn how to create and use macros in Word, PowerPoint, and Excel.

Recording a Simple Macro

Most macros complete repetitive tasks that involve several steps. You record (create) the series of steps you want to repeat. The next time you need to carry out the operation, you can run (play back) the macro to repeat the steps. Before recording a macro, you should practice the steps you want to record, because once you begin recording, all your actions are recorded, mistakes included. Then determine what conditions your macro will operate under and set them up. Will you always use the macro in a specific document? If so, open that document. Will the macro be used to change or format selected text or numbers? Then have the text or numbers selected before you begin recording the macro, just as you will when you play the macro back at a later time.

Objectives W2000E.6.2 and XL2000E.8.1b

When you have practiced the steps and set up the same conditions the macro will run under, select Tools ➢ Macro ➢ Record New Macro to open the

Record New Macro dialog box. The Excel Record Macro dialog box is shown in Figure 15.1.

FIGURE 15.1
Excel Macro dialog box

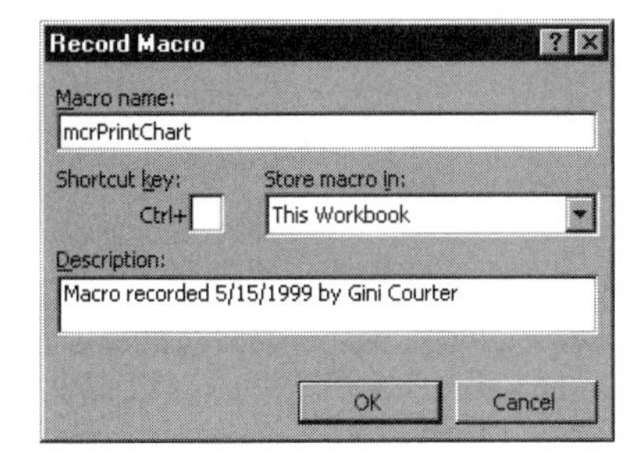

The suggested name is Macro1. (Microsoft didn't waste a lot of imagination here.) Enter a more descriptive name for the macro like the one shown in Figure 15.1. Macro names can be up to 255 characters long; they can contain numbers, letters, and underscores (but not spaces or other punctuation); and they must begin with a letter. Enter a new description. If other users will have access to the macro, include your name for reference. With the recent proliferation of macro viruses; anonymous macros are obviously suspect. The Record Macro dialog box from Word is shown in Figure 15.2.

FIGURE 15.2
Word Macro dialog box

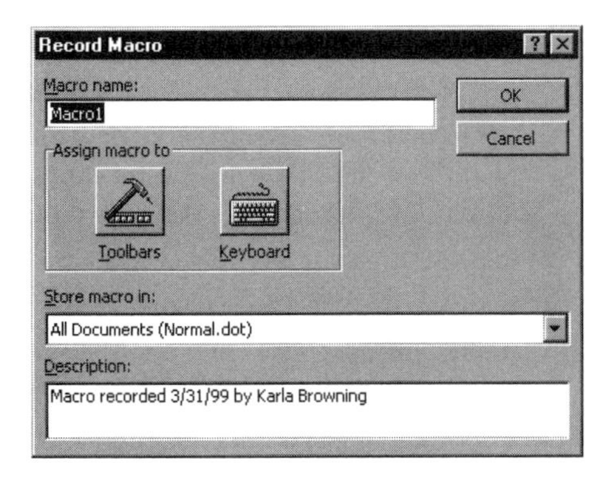

Storing a Macro

In the Store Macro In drop-down list, select which document you want the macro to be stored in. PowerPoint macros are stored with the presentation.

In Word and Excel, a macro's storage location determines how you'll be able to access it on playback.

- If you select the current document, then the macro will only be available in the current document. If you want the same macro somewhere else, you'll have to copy or recreate it. In Excel, you can also store the macro in a new workbook, then add other functionality to the workbook. Macros that are stored in a document are *local macros*.
- Storing a macro in `Normal.dot`, Word's default template, or the Personal Macro Workbook in Excel creates a *global macro*, available to all documents created in the program.

From the description, you'd think that you should save every macro as a global macro, but all the global macros are loaded each time you launch Excel or Word. They take up space in memory, and any macro names you use here can't be reused in individual documents. Unless a macro is going to receive wide usage, it's best to store it in the current document.

In Excel, you can assign a shortcut keystroke combination to macros, and Word lets you assign a shortcut or place the macro on the toolbar. While you can assign macros to shortcut keys, you should use extreme caution when making assignments. Most of the Ctrl+ combinations, and many of the Ctrl+Shift combinations, are already in use. It's safer to assign frequently used macros to a toolbar. You don't have to make this decision when you record the macro; you can always add a macro to a toolbar later (see *Customizing Toolbars*).

Once you've set the options in the dialog box, click the OK button to begin macro recording. The message "Recording" is displayed at the left end of the status bar to show that you are recording a macro.

The Stop Recording toolbar opens. The macro recorder records the actions you take, but not the delay between actions, so take your time. If you want the macro to enter text, enter the text now. Type carefully—if you make and correct a mistake, the mistake and correction will be included when you replay the macro until you edit the mistake (see *Editing Macros*). Make menu selections as you normally would to include them in the macro.

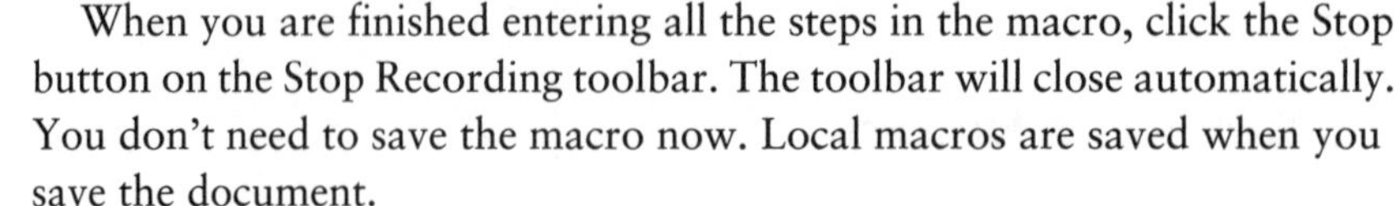

When you are finished entering all the steps in the macro, click the Stop button on the Stop Recording toolbar. The toolbar will close automatically. You don't need to save the macro now. Local macros are saved when you save the document.

Word prompts you to save changes to `Normal.dot` when you end your Word session if the Prompt to Save Normal Template option (choose Tools ➢ Options ➢ Save) is enabled, and Excel prompts you to save the Personal Macro Workbook. If the option is not enabled, global macros are saved automatically.

Formatting Options in Macros

If you want to format text while recording in a macro, choose the formatting options from a formatting dialog box rather than clicking toolbar buttons. If you use the buttons, the playback results will be unpredictable because the toolbar buttons are toggle buttons. If, for example, selected text is already italicized, clicking the Italics button will turn Italics off. If Excel titles are centered across a selection, clicking will revert to left alignment. Whenever possible, don't use format toggle buttons in macros unless you can guarantee that the text you select when you play back will be formatted exactly as the text was when you recorded the macro.

Excel Cell References in Macros

All macro cell references are absolute by default. If you click in a cell during macro recording, the macro will select that exact cell each time you play it back. This wouldn't be terribly useful. For example, you might want to format cells, and then move to the cell below the selection. When you record the macro, the cell below the selection is J22. But each time you play the macro, you don't want Excel to select J22; you want to select the cell below the cells you just formatted.

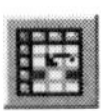

To instruct Excel to use relative cell references, click the Use Relative References button on the Macro toolbar. The macro will record references relative to the current cell until you click the button again to turn relative references off. Then you can record other actions using absolute references.

Creating a Macro

1. Create the same conditions that will be in effect when you play the macro.
2. Choose Tools ➢ Record Macro ➢ Record New Macro to open the Record Macro dialog box.
3. Enter a Macro Name and Description.

Creating a Macro *(continued)*

4. Choose a storage location from the drop-down list.
5. Click OK to begin recording the macro.
6. Perform the steps that you want included in the macro. If you want to include relative cell references in Excel, click the Use Relative References button on the Macro toolbar. Click again to turn relative references off if you need to include absolute references.
7. Click the Stop button on the Stop Recording toolbar when you have finished recording the steps of the macro.

Opening a File with Macros

A *macro virus* is a computer virus written as a macro. When you open a document that contains a virus, the virus copies itself into the default template. From that point forward, every document you save using the template will be infected, which means that every file you give to someone else on a disk or via the Internet will also contain the virus.

Office 2000 does not include virus detection software. You should install some unless you *never* receive files from another computer by disk, network, or Internet connection.

Office 2000 Macro Protection Word, Excel, Outlook, and PowerPoint will notify you if any macros exist in a document you are trying to open. (Outlook doesn't have a macro recorder, but you can type macros in the Visual Basic Editor for Outlook.) You can decide whether you want to open the document with macros enabled or to disable them. Disabling the macros gives you an opportunity to look at them in the Visual Basic Editor without endangering your computer. If you decide you want to enable the macros, just close and then re-open the file.

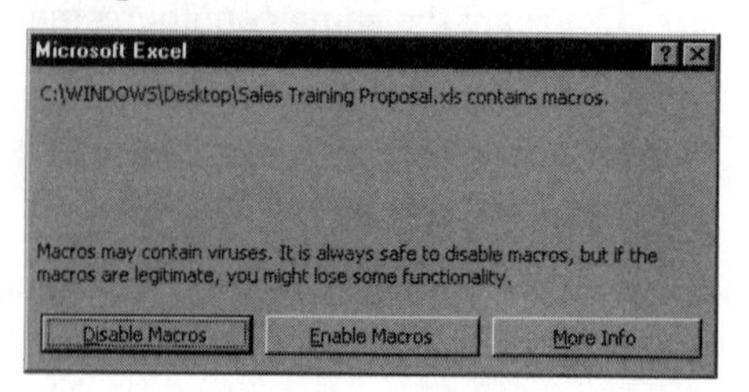

If you are opening a document that contains macros and you know that you or a co-worker created the macros, choose Enable. If, on the other hand, you received the workbook, unsolicited, as an e-mail attachment, consider disabling the macros or not opening the file.

Updating Macros from Previous Versions

Some earlier versions of Excel used a macro programming language called XLM (Excel Macro Language—"ELM" was already being used as a tree name). Visual Basic for Applications (VBA) replaced XLM as the programming language, beginning with Excel version 5.0. Excel 2000 supports both macro programming languages. If you have workbooks that contain XLM macros, Excel 2000 will let you play them. However, you cannot record XLM macros in Excel 2000. All Excel 2000 macros are recorded in VBA.

Word also had its own macro language in earlier versions called Word Basic. When you open a Word document from a prior version that contains macros, Word 2000 automatically converts the macros to Visual Basic.

Running Macros

Objectives W2000E.6.2 and XL2000E.8.2

It's always a good idea to save anything you have open before you run a new macro. If you make a mistake during recording, the playback results may not be what you expected. (If there was an error, you can record the macro again using the same name. You might also have to click Undo a few times to back out of any problems the macro created.) To run a macro, choose Tools ➢ Macro ➢ Macros to open the Macro dialog box, shown in Figure 15.3. Select the macro from the list of macro names in the Macro Name/Reference control, and then click the Run button. The macro will execute one step at a time. You can't enter text, or choose menu options, while the macro is executing. When the macro is done playing, the application will return control to you.

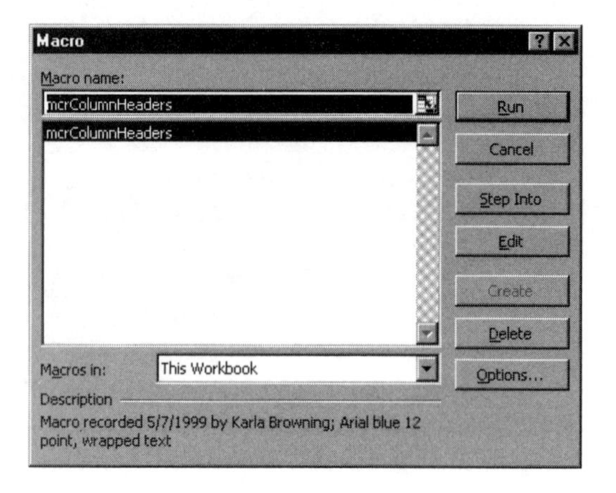

FIGURE 15.3
Macro dialog box

Running a Macro

1. Choose Tools ➢ Macro ➢ Macros.
2. Select the macro from list of available macros and click Run.

Examining and Editing Macros

Objectives W2000E.6.2 and XL2000E.8.3

Office 2000 macros are stored in Visual Basic *modules* and edited in the Visual Basic Editor. (Access 2000 is the exception; Access macros are stored as part of the database, but can be converted to VB and stored in a module.) To examine or edit a macro, choose Tools ➢ Macros ➢ Macros to open the Macros dialog box, select the macro you want to examine, then click the Edit button to open the Visual Basic Editor, shown in Figure 15.4.

The Visual Basic window may contain a number of windows. In Figure 15.4, a Properties window is open on the left and a Code window on the right. You can scroll through the Visual Basic Code window to see the information recorded in a macro. The macro name and description appear at the top of the macro. The macro code begins with the word Sub (for subroutine) and the macro name. The description appears on the following lines. If you know VBA, you can create macros and other procedures directly by typing VBA code into a module's code window. If you want to learn about Visual Basic, recording macros and studying the resulting code is a good way to begin. Even if you don't understand VB, you can do some simple editing here.

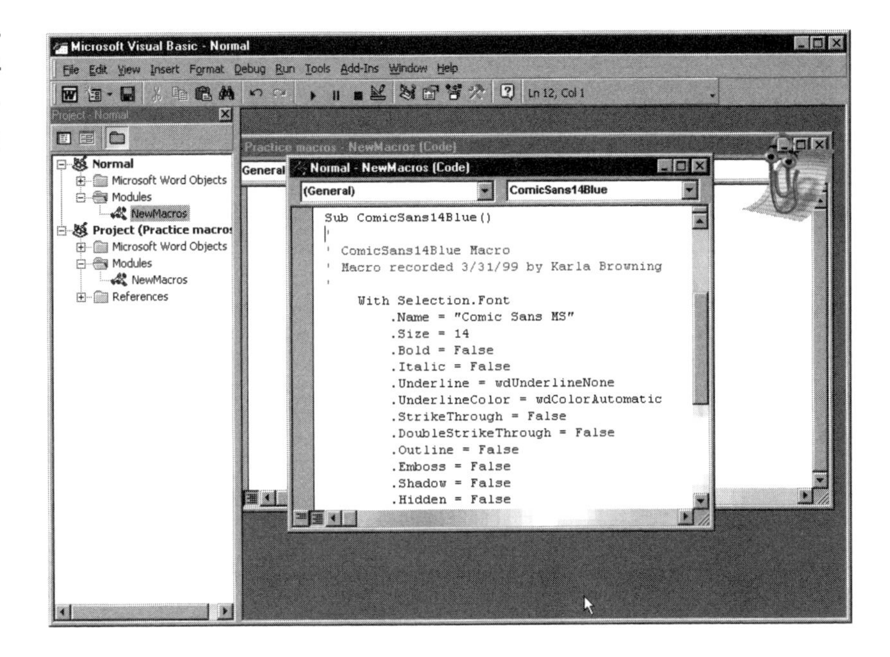

FIGURE 15.4 Visual Basic Editor in Word

You could edit the Word macro shown in Figure 15.4 by typing another font name or size. When you are finished editing a macro, save, and close the Visual Basic Window.

Editing a Macro

1. Choose Tools ➢ Macro ➢ Macros to open the Macros dialog box.
2. Select the macro and click the Edit button.
3. Make the changes you desire.
4. Save the macro and close the Visual Basic window.

Adding Macros to a Toolbar

Objective XL2000E.7.3

To add an existing macro to a toolbar, right-click any toolbar and choose Customize or choose View ➢ Toolbars ➢ Customize to open the Customize dialog box. Click the Commands tab to open the Commands page, shown in Figure 15.5.

FIGURE 15.5
Customize dialog box

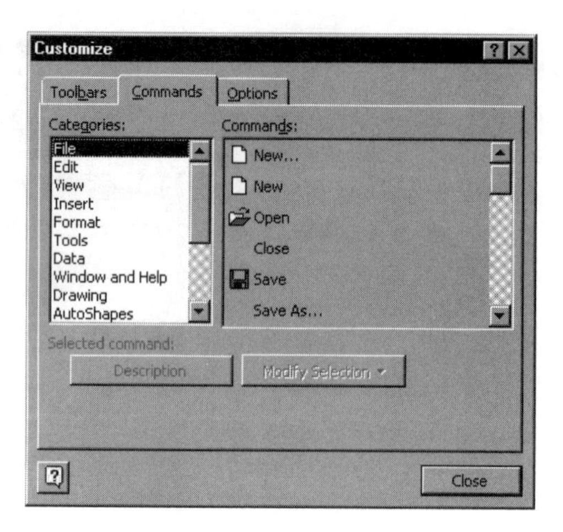

Select Macros from the Categories list. In Word and PowerPoint, the list of available macros appears in the right pane.

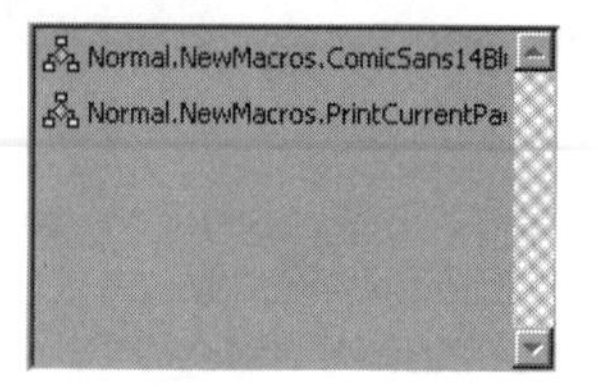

In Excel, two options will appear in the Commands List: Custom Menu Item and Custom Button. If you want to add the macro anywhere on the menu bar, choose Custom Menu Item. If you'd prefer a button (with a picture, text, or both), choose Custom Button.

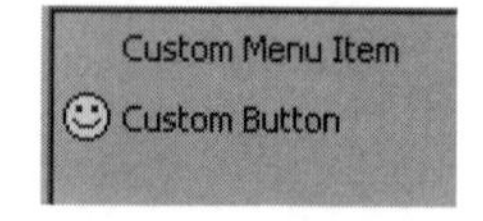

To add a menu item, drag the macro (Custom Menu Item in Excel) from the Command List to the menu bar. If you want to place the custom menu item on an existing drop-down menu, move to the menu, hover a moment, and the menu will open. Drop the menu item where you want it to appear on the menu.

To add a toolbar button, drag the macro (Custom Button in Excel) and drop it on the appropriate toolbar. If you drop it on an existing button, the other buttons will move over to make room for the new button. (Be careful here—buttons will move to the right, and can be forced off the right edge of the display.

Objectives W2000E.6.7, XL2000E.7.2, and PP2000E.8.1

While the Customize dialog box is open, you can modify all the command bars. Drag menu items or buttons to new locations to rearrange them, or drop them in the document window to delete them. To add something other than a macro, scroll the Categories and Commands lists until you find the command you want. Drag the command onto a menu or toolbar. If you mess things up completely, you can always select and reset the menu bar and the toolbars on the Toolbars page of the Customize dialog box. To create an entirely new toolbar, click the New button on the Toolbar page. Drag any buttons you wish onto the toolbar from the Commands list. To copy a button from an existing toolbar, hold Ctrl while dragging the button.

You can move and remove toolbar buttons without having the Customize dialog box open. Just hold Alt, drag the toolbar button to its new location and drop it. Or hold Alt and drag the button away from the toolbar until you see an X attached to your mouse pointer. Release the mouse to remove the toolbar button.

Changing Command Item Settings

After you've placed your button or menu item, right-click on the item to open the shortcut menu.

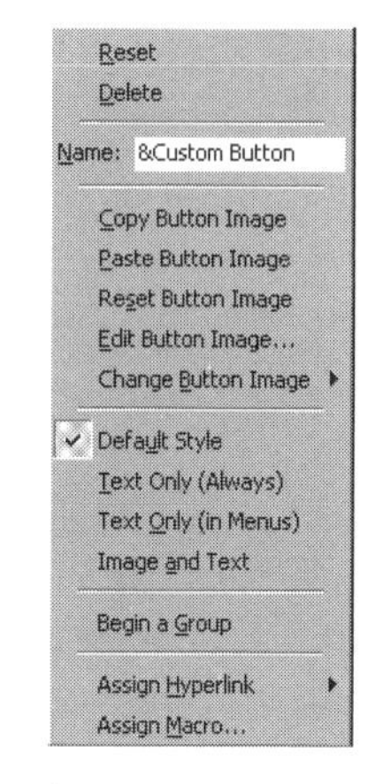

In Word and PowerPoint, the button or menu item is attached to the macro you dragged to the command bar. In Excel, you must assign the macro. Choose Assign Macro from the bottom of the menu, and the familiar Macro dialog box opens. Select the macro you want to assign from the list, and then click OK.

Changing Command Bar Item Options The default toolbar button picture is the yellow smiley face. With the Customize dialog box open, right-click on a button and choose Change Button Image to open a menu of icons you can assign to a command item. If you prefer, you can label the button or menu item by changing the contents of the Name box on the shortcut menu. The ampersand (&) is used on menu items and appears before the letter that a user can press to choose the menu item. The letter will be underlined on the menu bar like the F in File and E in Edit.

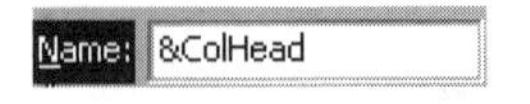

You can also create your own button images. While you are still in the Customize mode, select the button, right-click to open the shortcut menu, and then choose Edit Button Image to open the Button Editor to edit the button image.

When you are finished adding menu items, assigning macros, and sprucing up your button images, close the Customize dialog box. Now, you can play the macro by clicking a toolbar button or making a menu selection. To remove a button or menu item, open the Customize dialog box and drag the item off the menu or toolbar.

Adding a Macro to a Menu or Command Button

1. If the macro is not global, open the document that contains the macro.
2. Right-click on any toolbar and choose Customize. Click the Commands tab.
3. Choose Macros from the Categories list.
4. In Word or PowerPoint, drag the macro onto a toolbar or menu, then close the Customize dialog box.

   OR

4. In Excel, drag Custom Menu Item or Custom Button from the Commands List to the toolbar or menu and drop it in the desired location.
5. Right-click on the new item and select Assign Macro from the shortcut menu.
6. Choose the macro from the Macro dialog box.
7. Click OK to assign the macro to the button, then close the Customize dialog box.

Creating a New Toolbar

Objective PP2000E.8.2

Wouldn't it be great to have all your favorite command buttons in one place? Or maybe you'd like a separate toolbar to contain all your macro buttons. Create a brand new toolbar by opening the Customize dialog box, then click New.

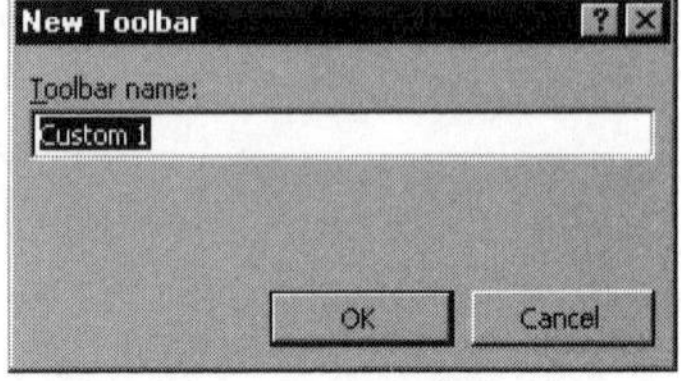

Type a descriptive name for your new toolbar, overwriting the default of Custom1. In Word, you'll also have to choose which template to store the toolbar in. Click OK to close the New Toolbar dialog box.

Look for a blank toolbar somewhere in your application window. It's little—so look closely! The Customize dialog box should still be open; your task now is to drag the commands you need to the new toolbar. Switch to the Commands tab, choose a category from the list on the left and drag the command (from the list on the right) to the new toolbar. It will stretch to accommodate more buttons as you drag and drop them.

Deleting Macros

Objective W2000E.6.3

You can delete a macro in two ways. If you have recorded a macro and are not pleased with the way it executes, you can record the macro again, using the same name. You will be asked if you want to overwrite (delete) the existing macro. You can also choose Tools ➢ Macro ➢ Macros, select the macro from the macro list, and click the Delete button to delete the macro from the template. If you delete a macro that has a command bar item, you also need to remove the macro's button from the toolbar.

You can copy macros from one document to another by copying and pasting from one module to another in the Visual Basic Editor. Rename an Excel macro by renaming the Visual Basic module. Rename a Word macro by clicking the Organizer button in the Macro dialog box. On the Macro Project Items tab, click the name of the entry you want to rename in the In box on the left. Click the Rename button and type a new name for the macro. Click OK then Close.

When you have mastered the information in this chapter, and want to learn more, activate the Office Assistant in an application and enter `macros` in the dialog box to find more information.

Hands On: Objectives W2000E.6.2, W2000E.6.7, XL2000E.7.2, XL2000E.7.3, XL2000E.8.1, XL2000E.8.2, PP2000E.8.1 PP2000E.8.2, W2000E.6.2, W2000E.6.3 and XL2000E.8.3

1. In Word or Excel, record a global macro that checks the spelling in the active document and then sends the document to the printer. Name the macro SpellPrint. Add it to the Standard toolbar and test it.
2. In Word or Excel, record a global macro that:
   a) Opens the Page Setup dialog box.
   b) Inserts a header with your name and the current date.
   c) Sets all four margins at 1 inch.
   d) Name the macro StandardPageSetup. Execute the macro to see that it works the way you designed it.
3. In PowerPoint, create a macro that prints the current outline. Add it to the Standard toolbar and test it.
4. In any Excel workbook, create individual macros to complete the tasks below. Create your own macro names. When all macros are recorded, create a new toolbar and add all the macros to the toolbar.
   a) Create a macro to format a range of cells for currency, no decimal places, Arial 12-point, dark blue.
   b) Record a macro that creates a header that includes "All rights reserved, *your company name* (or *your name*)," and the current date.
   c) Record a macro to change the paper orientation to landscape.
5. Open a macro you've created in Word.
   a) Use the Visual Basic Editor to edit the macro.
   b) Copy part of the macro to another module.
   c) Save the changes to both macros then rerun them to see that they work.
6. Rename one of your Word macros. Delete one of your Word macros.

APPENDIX

Preparing for the Microsoft Office 2000 User Specialist Exams

A *Microsoft Office User Specialist* (MOUS) is a person who has passed an exam administered through a Microsoft Authorized Testing Center on one of the Office 2000 products. Introduced in 1997 as the Microsoft Certified Office User Program, users today can receive designation as Microsoft Office User Specialists at the core level in Word, Excel, PowerPoint, Access, and Outlook (FrontPage and PhotoDraw core exams should be available soon). For those who really want to demonstrate their skills, exams are also available at Expert and Master levels.

Although the Office certification process is relatively new, Microsoft is experienced at certification. It currently offers several highly respected certification programs such as the Microsoft Certified System Engineer program and the Microsoft Certified Professional program. Up until now, all of these certifications focused on networking, systems, or programming skills. They were not intended for end users but rather, they were designed to establish recognizable standards for computer professionals—those people whose life work revolves around computer systems.

The MOUS Difference

The Microsoft Office User Specialist certification is fundamentally different from other certifications that Microsoft offers. Whether it is in a large corporation or in a small office, a MOUS is likely employed in a profession outside of the computer field, using applications such as Word and Excel to function effectively as an administrative assistant, a secretary, a manager, an account representative, or a myriad of other positions that require day-to-day problem-solving skills. The Microsoft Office family of products has helped this person accomplish the impossible by meeting a deadline, impressing their bosses, and performing their job more efficiently. The

MOUS is interested in improving their skills and increasing their opportunities. As more and more employers begin looking for verification of a person's software skills, there is no better way to stand out from the crowd than to show your credentials as a specialist in the software the job requires.

Although the MOUS program got off to a slow start, over 900 testing centers around the world have now delivered well over 30,000 exams.

Should I Become a Microsoft Office User Specialist?

If you were applying for an office job only a few short years ago, probably the only test you had to take was a typing test. This test would document your speed and accuracy at a typewriter. It didn't matter if you understood what you typed or if you could create a similar document from scratch, all you had to be able to do was re-create what someone handed to you and do it in an acceptable amount of time. With the infiltration of personal computers into large and small workplaces everywhere, the expectations placed on office workers have increased significantly.

Typing speed and accuracy may still be important, but even more valuable is knowledge about how to make the most efficient and effective use of new office technology. Microsoft Office 2000 is the fastest-growing office suite on the market today. Knowing how to apply this group of powerful applications to the demands of your work environment can clearly put you ahead of the pack. You immediately stand out from the typists and become recognized as a problem-solver and, in some cases, even a lifesaver to those who are in a position to help advance your career.

If you are in business for yourself, you may not care about whether you can prove your skills to someone else, but being able to influence potential clients with the quality of your written and verbal presentations may make the difference between your business's success and failure. With little validation available from co-workers, the small businessperson has to find other ways to feel confident using their skills and know they are effectively using state-of-the-art technology to impress their clients.

The Microsoft Office User Specialist Program provides a mechanism for all types of users, regardless of their motivation, to prove their competency in the family of Microsoft Office 2000 applications. Whether you are a student with little real world experience or a highly trained professional with a top-level staff position, you may find that it is beneficial to add the Microsoft Office User Specialist designation to your portfolio.

Getting Your Employer to Foot the Bill

Companies that place a high value on employee education and training may very well agree to pay for you to take one or more of the MOUS exams. As the credential is becoming more widely known, more and more employers are looking at the MOUS credential as a mark of excellence in their company. Certainly, there is no hard and fast rule about this—employers are by no means required to pay for the exams. However, it certainly doesn't hurt to ask your supervisor or your Human Resources Department. Some companies may agree to reimburse you only if you pass an exam—it doesn't pay for them to spend money for someone to fail it.

Unless your company has issued a company statement about paying for the exams, do your homework before approaching your employer. It helps if your company has already adopted or plans to adopt Office 2000 as the company standard. Visit the Microsoft Office User Certification Web site `www.mous.net` and other Office certifications sites, (such as the site offered by Quick Start Technologies,`www.officecert.com`) for more information (ammunition) to convince a company of the benefits of employing certified employees.

If you decide to give your employer the opportunity to demonstrate his or her commitment to quality improvement and staff development, here are a few tips for you to consider when you are preparing a proposal to give to your boss:

1. Plan to study for the exams on your own time. If you spend an hour after work or at lunch time three or four times a week working through this book, you'll be ready to take one or even two of the exams after just a few study sessions. By doing it on your own time, it shows that you can take initiative and that you are committed to personal improvement. Even if this doesn't impress your employer, you will have improved your skills to help you in other areas of your job (or to get a better job!).

2. Become familiar with Microsoft's requirements and the process for taking the exams so that you are prepared to answer any question your employer may ask about how the exams work.

3. List at least three specific benefits to the company of having certified employees. Be able to point out the financial savings resulting from fewer technical support calls and from less downtime figuring out how to do something.

4. Develop an argument that ties your getting certified into the company's overall quality initiative. Having certified employees in every field helps a company demonstrate to their customers and potential customers that they are committed to quality. It makes the company look good and that goes a long way in today's competitive market.

5. Offer to be a mentor to other employees—individually or as a group. If work time is too precious, organize a weekly bag-lunch of Office users and have someone present a different topic each week based on a project they just completed. However you approach it, show your employer that you are a leader and it may be easier to make a case for the value of the certifications to the company.

If all else fails, pay for the exams yourself. Being certified makes you a more valuable commodity and may make your employer think twice when he or she sees you using Word to update your resume!

What are the Microsoft Office 2000 User Specialist Designations?

Once you've decided to pursue certification, you have to determine if you want to take all of the exams or pick and choose among them. Unless you plan to train other users or you have a technical support type of job, you probably don't have a need to take all of the exams available. However, if you want a comprehensive knowledge base and you want the new Office Master designation that Microsoft is now offering, you may want to set up a plan of attack and go after them all.

It's possible to receive designation as a Specialist in each of the five applications that are a part of the Microsoft Office family. These include Word, Excel, PowerPoint, Access, and Outlook. Because Word and Excel are the most popular of the products and have the most widespread application, two levels of designation—Core and Expert—have been developed for these applications; that means that there is a separate test for each level. However, you do not have to pass the Core exam prior to taking the Expert Word or Excel exams.

Microsoft expects that a Microsoft Office User Specialist at the Core level is able to complete the everyday tasks that arise in a typical office setting. A Word Specialist should be able to format text and paragraphs, create tables and columns, manage files, and work with pictures and charts. An Excel Specialist should be able to format cells and worksheets, enter formulas and basic functions, work with multiple worksheets, create charts, and insert objects.

In order to become an Expert Specialist, you are expected to be able to create more complex documents. A Word Expert should be able to conduct mail merges to create personalized form letters with envelopes and mailing labels, work with master and subdocuments, add references, and use collaboration features. An Excel Expert should be able to use templates, work with multiple workbooks, create macros, use analysis tools, and also use collaboration features.

The eight Specialist designations currently available are:

- Microsoft Office User Specialist: Microsoft Word 2000
- Microsoft Office User Specialist: Microsoft Word 2000 Expert
- Microsoft Office User Specialist: Microsoft Excel 2000
- Microsoft Office User Specialist: Microsoft Excel 2000 Expert
- Microsoft Office User Specialist: Microsoft PowerPoint 2000
- Microsoft Office User Specialist: Microsoft Outlook 2000
- Microsoft Office User Specialist: Microsoft Access 2000
- Microsoft Office User Specialist: Microsoft Office 2000 Master

MOUS Exams To Be Developed

The MOUS program is still relatively new and administration of the program was only taken over by Nivo International in late 1998. As a result, not all of the anticipated exams have been developed as of the publication date of this book.

Exam objectives, however, have been released for the following anticipated designations:

- Microsoft Office User Specialist: Microsoft PowerPoint 2000 Expert
- Microsoft Office User Specialist: Microsoft Access 2000 Expert
- Microsoft Office User Specialist: Microsoft Outlook 2000 Expert
- Microsoft Office User Specialist: Microsoft FrontPage 2000
- Microsoft Office User Specialist: Microsoft FrontPage 2000 Expert
- Microsoft Office User Specialist: Microsoft PhotoDraw 2000
- Microsoft Office User Specialist: Microsoft PhotoDraw 2000 Expert

Check www.mous.net for updates on the availability of these additional exams.

What Are the Exams Like?

Taking an exam is a lot like completing the Hands On exercises in each chapter of this book. You will be expected to be able to apply your knowledge of an application to real-world tasks that you will complete within the application itself. Unlike other Microsoft certification exams, there are no multiple-choice questions. Instead, each user is expected to complete specific tasks, such as formatting a document in a certain way, creating a formula, sorting a list, etc. The exams must be completed within the designated timeframe, which is under an hour depending on the exam.

This is not a paper and pencil test. You will be working with a fully functional, live version of the product on which you are being tested. You can use all of the features of the product, including Help. However, if you access Help too often, you'll run out of time before completing all of the required tasks.

When you're ready to start, take a deep breath (be sure to exhale too!), and click the Start Test button. You complete each task on the sample documents provided to you so you don't have to spend time creating documents of your own. Each task has a set of instructions for you to follow. When you've completed one task, you click Next Task and move on to the next task.

Be aware: there is no going back to a previous task. Once you've moved past a particular task, it's gone forever.

Preparing to Take an Exam

Before you start studying, review the objectives for the test you are interested in taking. If you're an experienced user, you may even want to check off those activities in which you are already pretty comfortable. Spend some time reviewing those activities and making sure you are 100% confident in completing each of them. When you are ready to tackle new ground, either follow the topics of this book in order or use the certification map to jump to the activities on which you want to focus.

If you are a relatively new user, you will benefit most from following each of the topics in this book in order, completing the Hands On exercises and then moving on to the next topic. When you have completed the book, review the objectives again and make sure you can complete each activity comfortably. If you need to review a topic for a second time, refer to the certification map at the end of this chapter to find out where it is covered in the book.

If you'd like to get a taste of how the exams work, download the practice exams from www.mous.net. You'll find practice exams for Word, Excel, and PowerPoint. They help you get used to the format and the structure of the exams so you'll know what to expect when you sit down to take the real ones.

Registering to Take an Exam

You can receive information about a local Authorized Testing Center (ATC) by calling 800-933-4493 or visiting the Web site of the company that is managing the testing, Nivo International, at www.mous.net. Not every city has a testing center but the number of centers is growing rapidly—there probably is one within a couple hours' drive if not right in your city. Although some centers allow walk-in test-takers, it's best to call first to make sure.

Each test you take has a fee associated with it. You can usually pay by check or credit card—check out payment arrangements when you call to register. Be sure to bring a picture ID (driver's license, passport, credit card, etc.) to the testing center with you.

Taking More than One Exam

It's not unusual to take more than one exam in a day, especially if the testing center is long way away. Be careful not to overload yourself, however. Some people may be able to handle taking three or four in a day—others may faint after taking one. Evaluate how long you can realistically concentrate without affecting your ability to think clearly. There's no point in paying for an exam and then not allowing yourself optimal test-taking conditions.

If you plan to take more than one exam, talk with the testing center about spacing them out a bit throughout the day. Take one or two, then go to lunch before taking another one or two. You'll be fresher and have time enough to re-focus on the new topic (maybe even get in a little last-minute cramming).

Getting Help When You're Stuck

You can't bring notes, books, or a laptop computer into the testing center. However, you can use the application's Help files for a quick refresher during the test. If you are concerned that you might have to look something up during the exam, practice using Help extensively before going in. You may find yourself failing the exam because you wasted valuable seconds searching through Help files. Find the most efficient ways to locate the steps you need to accomplish a task. Use the Index to search for what you need.

If you know there are a couple of areas that you are weak on, look up the topics in the Index ahead of time so you'll know what you are looking for and when you have found it. Stay away from using the Office Assistant while you are taking an exam. Even though they may be cute, they take up precious time just appearing and disappearing. Save them for when you have the time to be entertained!

The Moment of Truth

The tests are scored electronically so you'll know your score immediately. You need to get about 80% correct to pass the tests. If you pass, you'll receive a certificate of completion in the mail in one to two weeks after taking the test. Take yourself out to dinner to celebrate or better yet have someone else take you out!

What Happens If I Don't Pass? If you need to take a test again, ask the test administrator for a printed score report which identifies where you need to focus your energy as you prepare for another round. Of course, you'll have to pay to take a test again but it was probably money well spent. You learned some things and although it would be nice to not be out the exam fee, being more experienced means you'll probably pass it next time.

If you thought you were prepared and still didn't pass, you may just have test anxiety that probably won't be as bad the second time around. You'll be in familiar surroundings and know very clearly what you are expected to do. You'll be told what areas you need to focus on. If you realize that you didn't know how to do certain tasks that were asked for, study up on those, and then be sure to review all the material before taking the test again.

The Certification Map

The tables on the following pages list the skill sets and activities required for the Microsoft Office User Specialist: Microsoft Word 2000 Core and Word 2000 Expert exams. Also listed are the page numbers in this book where you'll find information about each of the activities.

TABLE A.1: Word 2000 Core Activities

STANDARDIZED CODING NUMBER	ACTIVITIES	PAGE NUMBERS
W2000.1	**Working with text**	
W2000.1.1	Use the Undo, Redo, and Repeat command	27, 20
W2000.1.2	Apply font formats (Bold, Italic and Underline)	27
W2000.1.3	Use the SPELLING feature	21
W2000.1.4	Use the THESAURUS feature	40
W2000.1.5	Use the GRAMMAR feature	38
W2000.1.6	Insert page breaks	71
W2000.1.7	Highlight text in document	45
W2000.1.8	Insert and move text	21
W2000.1.9	Cut, Copy, Paste, and Paste Special using the Office Clipboard	25
W2000.1.10	Copy formats using the Format Painter	29, 34
W2000.1.11	Select and change font and font size	27
W2000.1.12	Find and replace text	67
W2000.1.13	Apply character effects (superscript, subscript, strikethrough, small caps and outline)	43
W2000.1.14	Insert date and time	53
W2000.1.15	Insert symbols	52
W2000.1.16	Create and apply frequently used text with AutoCorrect	65, 22
W2000.2	**Working with paragraphs**	
W2000.2.1	Align text in paragraphs (Center, Left, Right and Justified)	55
W2000.2.2	Add bullets and numbering	47
W2000.2.3	Set character, line, and paragraph spacing options	44, 59
W2000.2.4	Apply borders and shading to paragraphs	106
W2000.2.5	Use indentation options (Left, Right, First Line and Hanging Indent)	56
W2000.2.6	Use TABS command (Center, Decimal, Left and Right)	60
W2000.2.7	Create an outline style numbered list	118
W2000.2.8	Set tabs with leaders	62
W2000.3	**Working with documents**	
W2000.3.1	Print a document	75
W2000.3.2	Use print preview	69, 17
W2000.3.3	Use Web Page Preview	149
W2000.3.4	Navigate through a document	47
W2000.3.5	Insert page numbers	83

TABLE A.1: Word 2000 Core Activities *(continued)*

STANDARDIZED CODING NUMBER	ACTIVITIES	PAGE NUMBERS
W2000.3.6	Set page orientation	71
W2000.3.7	Set margins	73
W2000.3.8	Use GoTo to locate specific elements in a document	67
W2000.3.9	Create and modify page numbers	83
W2000.3.10	Create and modify headers and footers	85
W2000.3.11	Align text vertically	73
W2000.3.12	Create and use newspaper columns	90
W2000.3.13	Revise column structure	91
W2000.3.14	Prepare and print envelopes and labels	76
W2000.3.15	Apply styles	91, 110
W2000.3.16	Create sections with formatting that differs from other sections	82, 72
W2000.3.17	Use click & type	42
W2000.4	**Managing files**	
W2000.4.1	Use save	12
W2000.4.2	Locate and open an existing document	16
W2000.4.3	Use Save As (different name, location or format)	14
W2000.4.4	Create a folder	13
W2000.4.5	Create a new document using a Wizard	122
W2000.4.6	Save as Web Page	149
W2000.4.7	Use templates to create a new document	120, 12
W2000.4.8	Create Hyperlinks	163
W2000.4.9	Use the Office Assistant	8
W2000.4.10	Send a Word document via e-mail	15, 182
W2000.5	**Using tables**	
W2000.5.1	Create and format tables	94
W2000.5.2	Add borders and shading to tables	105
W2000.5.3	Revise tables (insert & delete rows and columns, change cell formats)	99
W2000.5.4	Modify table structure (merge cells, change height and width)	100, 102
W2000.5.5	Rotate text in a table	98
W2000.6	**Working with pictures and charts**	
W2000.6.1	Use the drawing toolbar	647
W2000.6.2	Insert graphics into a document (WordArt, ClipArt, Images)	639, 643, 649

TABLE A.2: Word 2000 Expert Activities

STANDARDIZED CODING NUMBER	ACTIVITY	PAGE NUMBERS
W2000E.1	**Working with paragraphs**	
W2000E.1.1	Apply paragraph and section shading	106
W2000E.1.2	Use text flow options (Widows/Orphans options and keeping lines together)	88
W2000E.1.3	Sort lists, paragraphs, tables	133
W2000E.2	**Working with documents**	
W2000E.2.1	Create and modify page borders	106
W2000E.2.2	Format first page differently than subsequent pages	84
W2000E.2.3	Use bookmarks	161
W2000E.2.4	Create and edit styles	111
W2000E.2.5	Create watermarks	67
W2000E.2.6	Use find and replace with formats, special characters and non-printing elements	67
W2000E.2.7	Balance column length (using column breaks appropriately)	90
W2000E.2.8	Create or revise footnotes and endnotes	158
W2000E.2.9	Work with master documents and subdocuments	170
W2000E.2.10	Create and modify a table of contents	167
W2000E.2.11	Create cross-reference	163
W2000E.2.12	Create and modify an index	165
W2000E.3	**Using tables**	
W2000E.3.1	Embed worksheets in a table	628
W2000E.3.2	Perform calculations in a table	107
W2000E.3.3	Link Excel data as a table	628
W2000E.3.4	Modify worksheets in a table	631
W2000E.4	**Working with pictures and charts**	
W2000E.4.1	Add bitmapped graphics	109
W2000E.4.2	Delete and position graphics	643
W2000E.4.3	Create and modify charts	655
W2000E.4.4	Import data into charts	655
W2000E.5	Using mail merge	126
W2000E.5.1	Create main document	136
W2000E.5.2	Create data source	127
W2000E.5.3	Sort records to be merged	133, 142
W2000E.5.4	Merge main document and data source	139

TABLE A.2: Word 2000 Expert Activities *(continued)*

STANDARDIZED CODING NUMBER	ACTIVITY	PAGE NUMBERS
W2000E.5.5	Generate labels	144
W2000E.5.6	Merge a document using alternate data sources	140
W2000E.6	**Using advanced features**	
W2000E.6.1	Insert a field	153
W2000E.6.2	Create, apply and edit macros	241
W2000E.6.3	Copy, rename, and delete macros	158
W2000E.6.4	Create and modify form	149
W2000E.6.5	Create and modify a form control (e.g., add an item to a drop-down list)	153
W2000E.6.6	Use advanced text alignment features with graphics	149
W2000E.6.7	Customize toolbars	891
W2000E.7	**Collaborating with workgroups**	
W2000E.7.1	Insert comments	179
W2000E.7.2	Protect documents	180
W2000E.7.3	Create multiple versions of a document	174
W2000E.7.4	Track changes to a document	176
W2000E.7.5	Set default file location for workgroup templates	122
W2000E.7.6	Round Trip documents from HTML	727

TABLE A.3: Excel 2000 Core Activities

STANDARDIZED CODING NUMBER	ACTIVITY	PAGE NUMBERS
XL2000.1	**Working with cells**	
XL2000.1.1	Use Undo and Redo	190
XL2000.1.2	Clear cell content	191
XL2000.1.3	Enter text, dates, and numbers	189, 201
XL2000.1.4	Edit cell content	191
XL2000.1.5	Go to a specific cell	188
XL2000.1.6	Insert and delete selected cells	206
XL2000.1.7	Cut, copy, paste, paste special and move selected cells, use the Office Clipboard	207
XL2000.1.8	Use Find and Replace	191
XL2000.1.9	Clear cell formats	219
XL2000.1.10	Work with series (AutoFill)	195
XL2000.1.11	Create hyperlinks	326

TABLE A.3: Excel 2000 Core Activities *(continued)*

STANDARDIZED CODING NUMBER	ACTIVITY	PAGE NUMBERS
XL2000.2	**Working with files**	
XL2000.2.1	Use Save	186
XL2000.2.2	Use Save As (different name, location, format)	186
XL2000.2.3	Locate and open an existing workbook	186
XL2000.2.4	Create a folder	186
XL2000.2.5	Use templates to create a new workbook	186
XL2000.2.6	Save a worksheet/workbook as a Web Page	744
XL2000.2.7	Send a workbook via email	182
XL2000.2.8	Use the Office Assistant	186
XL2000.3	**Formatting worksheets**	
XL2000.3.1	Apply font styles (typeface, size, color and styles)	271
XL2000.3.2	Apply number formats (currency, percent, dates, comma)	201
XL2000.3.3	Modify size of rows and columns	204
XL2000.3.4	Modify alignment of cell content	215
XL2000.3.5	Adjust the decimal place	199
XL2000.3.6	Use the Format Painter	218
XL2000.3.7	Apply autoformat	270
XL2000.3.8	Apply cell borders and shading	218
XL2000.3.9	Merging cells	217
XL2000.3.10	Rotate text and change indents	270
XL2000.3.11	Define, apply, and remove a style	271
XL2000.4	**Page setup and printing**	
XL2000.4.1	Preview and print worksheets & workbooks	220
XL2000.4.2	Use Web Page Preview	745
XL2000.4.3	Print a selection	223
XL2000.4.4	Change page orientation and scaling	224
XL2000.4.5	Set page margins and centering	224, 226
XL2000.4.6	Insert and remove a page break	232
XL2000.4.7	Set print, and clear a print area	230
XL2000.4.8	Set up headers and footers	227
XL2000.4.9	Set print titles and options (gridlines, print quality, row & column headings)	230
XL2000.5	**Working with worksheets & workbooks**	
XL2000.5.1	Insert and delete rows and columns	205
XL2000.5.2	Hide and unhide rows and columns	212

TABLE A.3: Excel 2000 Core Activities *(continued)*

STANDARDIZED CODING NUMBER	ACTIVITY	PAGE NUMBERS
XL2000.5.3	Freeze and unfreeze rows and columns	213
XL2000.5.4	Change the zoom setting	352
XL2000.5.5	Move between worksheets in a workbook	186
XL2000.5.6	Check spelling	312
XL2000.5.7	Rename a worksheet	209
XL2000.5.8	Insert and Delete worksheets	211
XL2000.5.9	Move and copy worksheets	211
XL2000.5.10	Link worksheets & consolidate data using 3D References	326
XL2000.6	**Working with formulas & functions**	
XL2000.6.1	Enter a range within a formula by dragging	197
XL2000.6.2	Enter formulas in a cell and using the formula bar	192
XL2000.6.3	Revise formulas	197
XL2000.6.4	Use references (absolute and relative)	236, 275
XL2000.6.5	Use AutoSum	196
XL2000.6.6	Use Paste Function to insert a function	245
XL2000.6.7	Use basic functions (AVERAGE, SUM, COUNT, MIN, MAX)	250
XL2000.6.8	Enter functions using the formula palette	243
XL2000.6.9	Use date functions (NOW and DATE)	251
XL2000.6.10	Use financial functions (FV and PMT)	248
XL2000.6.11	Use logical functions (IF)	252
XL2000.7	**Using charts and objects**	
XL2000.7.1	Preview and print charts	264
XL2000.7.2	Use chart wizard to create a chart	260
XL2000.7.3	Modify charts	265
XL2000.7.4	Insert, move, and delete an object (picture)	263
XL2000.7.5	Create and modify lines and objects	649, 652

TABLE A.4: Excel 2000 Expert Activities

STANDARDIZED CODING NUMBER	ACTIVITY	PAGE NUMBERS
XL2000E.1	**Importing and exporting data**	
XL2000E.1.1	Import data from text files (insert, drag and drop)	635
XL2000E.1.2	Import from other applications	332, 635

TABLE A.4: Excel 2000 Expert Activities *(continued)*

STANDARDIZED CODING NUMBER	ACTIVITY	PAGE NUMBERS
XL2000E.1.3	Import a table from an HTML file (insert, drag and drop - including HTML round tripping)	635
XL2000E.1.4	Export to other applications	635
XL2000E.2	**Using templates**	
XL2000E.2.1	Apply templates	321
XL2000E.2.2	Edit templates	322
XL2000E.2.3	Create templates	323
XL2000E.3	**Using multiple workbooks**	
XL2000E.3.1	Using a workspace	331
XL2000E.3.2	Link workbooks	326
XL2000E.4	**Formatting numbers**	
XL2000E.4.1	Apply number formats (accounting, currency, number)	199
XL2000E.4.2	Create custom number formats	277
XL2000E.4.3	Use conditional formatting	273
XL2000E.5	**Printing workbooks**	
XL2000E.5.1	Print and preview multiple worksheets	223
XL2000E.5.2	Use the Report Manager	353
XL2000E.6	**Working with named ranges**	
XL2000E.6.1	Add and delete a named range	239
XL2000E.6.2	Use a named range in a formula	241
XL2000E.6.3	Use Lookup Functions (Hlookup or Vlookup)	253
XL2000E.7	**Working with toolbars**	
XL2000E.7.1	Hide and display toolbars	270
XL2000E.7.2	Customize a toolbar	271
XL2000E.7.3	Assign a macro to a command button	889
XL2000E.8	**Using macros**	
XL2000E.8.1	Record macros	889
XL2000E.8.2	Run macros	889
XL2000E.8.3	Edit macros	889
XL2000E.9	**Auditing a worksheet**	
XL2000E.9.1	Work with the Auditing Toolbar	319
XL2000E.9.2	Trace errors (find and fix errors)	316
XL2000E.9.3	Trace precedents (find cells referred to in a specific formula)	318
XL2000E.9.4	Trace dependents (find formulas that refer to a specific cell)	318

TABLE A.4: Excel 2000 Expert Activities *(continued)*

STANDARDIZED CODING NUMBER	ACTIVITY	PAGE NUMBERS
XL2000E.10	**Displaying and Formatting Data**	
XL2000E.10.1	Apply conditional formats	273
XL2000E.10.2	Perform single and multi-level sorts	283
XL2000E.10.3	Use grouping and outlines	299
XL2000E.10.4	Use data forms	299
XL2000E.10.5	Use subtotaling	294
XL2000E.10.6	Apply data filters	286
XL2000E.10.7	Extract data	291
XL2000E.10.8	Query databases	296
XL2000E.10.9	Use data validation	313
XL2000E.11	**Using analysis tools**	
XL2000E.11.1	Use PivotTable autoformat	308
XL2000E.11.2	Use Goal Seek	345
XL2000E.11.3	Create pivot chart reports	310, 304
XL2000E.11.4	Work with Scenarios	349
XL2000E.11.5	Use Solver	347
XL2000E.11.6	Use data analysis and PivotTables	304
XL2000E.11.7	Create interactive PivotTables for the Web	749
XL2000E.11.8	Add fields to a PivotTable using the Web browser	751
XL2000E.12	**Collaborating with workgroups**	
XL2000E.12.1	Create, edit and remove a comment	324
XL2000E.12.2	Apply and remove worksheet and workbook protection	339
XL2000E.12.3	Change workbook properties	339
XL2000E.12.4	Apply and remove file passwords	338
XL2000E.12.5	Track changes (highlight, accept, and reject)	335
XL2000E.12.6	Create a shared workbook	333
XL2000E.12.7	Merge workbooks	337

TABLE A.5: PowerPoint 2000 Core Activities

STANDARDIZED CODING NUMBER	ACTIVITY	PAGE NUMBERS
PP2000.1	**Creating a presentation**	
PP2000.1.1	Delete slides	366
PP2000.1.2	Create a specified type of slide	375

TABLE A.5: PowerPoint 2000 Core Activities *(continued)*

STANDARDIZED CODING NUMBER	ACTIVITY	PAGE NUMBERS
PP2000.1.3	Create a presentation from a template and/or a Wizard	373
PP2000.1.4	Navigate among different views (slide, outline, sorter, tri-pane)	361
PP2000.1.5	Create a new presentation from existing slides	372
PP2000.1.6	Copy a slide from one presentation into another	376
PP2000.1.7	Insert headers and footers	383
PP2000.1.8	Create a Blank presentation	373
PP2000.1.9	Create a presentation using the AutoContent Wizard	358
PP2000.1.10	Send a presentation via e-mail	430
PP2000.2	**Modifying a presentation**	
PP2000.2.1	Change the order of slides using Slide Sorter view	367
PP2000.2.2	Find and replace text	364
PP2000.2.3	Change the layout for one or more slides	375
PP2000.2.4	Change slide layout (Modify the Slide Master)	381
PP2000.2.5	Modify slide sequence in the outline -pane	366
PP2000.2.6	Apply a design template	375
PP2000.3	**Working with text**	
PP2000.3.1	Check spelling	364
PP2000.3.2	Change and replace text fonts (individual slide and entire presentation)	388
PP2000.3.3	Enter text in tri-pane view	363
PP2000.3.4	Import Text from Word	378
PP2000.3.5	Change the text alignment	387
PP2000.3.6	Create a text box for entering text	649
PP2000.3.7	Use the Wrap text in TextBox feature	648
PP2000.3.8	Use the Office Clipboard	358
PP2000.3.9	Use the Format Painter	373
PP2000.3.10	Promote and Demote text in slide & outline panes	363
PP2000.4	**Working with visual elements**	
PP2000.4.1	Add a picture from the ClipArt Gallery	393
PP2000.4.2	Add and group shapes using WordArt or the Drawing Toolbar	654
PP2000.4.3	Apply formatting	652
PP2000.4.4	Place text inside a shape using a text box	649
PP2000.4.5	Scale and size an object including ClipArt	394

TABLE A.5: PowerPoint 2000 Core Activities *(continued)*

STANDARDIZED CODING NUMBER	ACTIVITY	PAGE NUMBERS
PP2000.4.6	Create tables within PowerPoint	401
PP2000.4.7	Rotate and fill an object	652
PP2000.5	**Customizing a presentation**	
PP2000.5.1	Add AutoNumber bullets	399
PP2000.5.2	Add speaker notes	369
PP2000.5.3	Add graphical bullets	397
PP2000.5.4	Add slide transitions	406
PP2000.5.5	Animate text and objects	408
PP2000.6	**Creating output**	
PP2000.6.1	Preview presentation in black and white	369
PP2000.6.2	Print slides in a variety of formats	426
PP2000.6.3	Print audience handouts	426
PP2000.6.4	Print speaker notes in a specified format	426
PP2000.7	**Delivering a presentation**	
PP2000.7.1	Start a slide show on any slide	363
PP2000.7.2	Use on screen navigation tools	437
PP2000.7.3	Print a slide as an overhead transparency	427
PP2000.7.4	Use the pen during a presentation	438
PP2000.8	**Managing files**	
PP2000.8.1	Save changes to a presentation	357
PP2000.8.2	Save as a new presentation	357
PP2000.8.3	Publish a presentation to the Web	755
PP2000.8.4	Use Office Assistant	358
PP2000.8.5	Insert hyperlink	421

TABLE A.6: PowerPoint 2000 Expert Activities

STANDARDIZED CODING NUMBER	ACTIVITY	PAGE NUMBERS
PP2000E.1	**Creating a presentation**	
PP2000E.1.1	Automatically create a summary slide	369
PP2000E.1.2	Automatically create an Agenda Slide	433
PP2000E.1.3	Design a template	422
PP2000E.1.4	Format presentations for the web	757

TABLE A.6: PowerPoint 2000 Expert Activities *(continued)*

STANDARDIZED CODING NUMBER	ACTIVITY	PAGE NUMBERS
PP2000E.2	**Modifying a presentation**	
PP2000E.2.1	Change tab formatting	389
PP2000E.2.2	Use the Wrap text in AutoShape feature	648
PP2000E.2.3	Apply a template from another presentation	375
PP2000E.2.4	Customize a color scheme	379
PP2000E.2.5	Apply animation effects	408
PP2000E.2.6	Create a custom background	384
PP2000E.2.7	Add animated GIFs	396
PP2000E.2.8	Add links to slides within the Presentation	421
PP2000E.2.9	Customize clip art and other objects (resize, scale, etc.)	394
PP2000E.2.10	Add a presentation within a presentation	433
PP2000E.2.11	Add an action button	435
PP2000E.2.12	Hide Slides	420
PP2000E.2.13	Set automatic slide timings	431
PP2000E.3	**Working with visual elements**	
PP2000E.3.1	Add textured backgrounds	379
PP2000E.3.2	Apply diagonal borders to a table	392
PP2000E.4	**Using data from other sources**	
PP2000E.4.1	Export an outline to Word	687, 427
PP2000E.4.2	Add a table (from Word)	401
PP2000E.4.3	Insert an Excel Chart	412
PP2000E.4.4	Add sound	400
PP2000E.4.5	Add video	400
PP2000E.5	**Creating output**	
PP2000E.5.1	Save slide as a graphic	429
PP2000E.5.2	Generate meeting notes	438
PP2000E.5.3	Change output format (Page setup)	425
PP2000E.5.4	Export to 35mm slides	429
PP2000E.6	**Delivering a presentation**	
PP2000E.6.1	Save presentation for use on another computer (Pack 'N Go)	439
PP2000E.6.2	Electronically incorporate meeting feedback	438
PP2000E.6.3	View a Presentation on the Web	430
PP2000E.7	**Managing files**	
PP2000E.7.1	Save embedded fonts in presentation	439

TABLE A.6: PowerPoint 2000 Expert Activities *(continued)*

STANDARDIZED CODING NUMBER	ACTIVITY	PAGE NUMBERS
PP2000E.7.2	Save HTML to a specific target browser	757
PP2000E.8	**Working with PowerPoint**	
PP2000E.8.1	Customize the toolbar	386
PP2000E.8.2	Create a toolbar	892
PP2000E.9	**Collaborating with workgroups**	
PP2000E.9.1	Subscribe to a presentation	432
PP2000E.9.2	View a presentation on the Web	430
PP2000E.9.3	Use Net Meeting to schedule a broadcast	433, 762, 766
PP2000E.9.4	Use NetShow to deliver a broadcast	758
PP2000E.10	**Working with charts & Tables**	
P2000E.10.1	Build a chart or graph	413
P2000E.10.2	Modify charts or graphs	413
P2000E.10.3	Build an organization chart	402
P2000E.10.4	Modify an organization chart	402
P2000E.10.5	Modify PowerPoint tables	406

TABLE A.7: Access 2000 Core Activities

STANDARDIZED CODING NUMBER	ACTIVITY	PAGE NUMBERS
AC2000.1	**Planning and designing databases**	
AC2000.1.1	Determine appropriate data inputs for your database	444
AC2000.1.2	Determine appropriate data outputs for your database	443
AC2000.1.3	Create table structure	445
AC2000.1.4	Establish table relationships	460
AC2000.2	**Working with Access**	
AC2000.2.1	Use the Office Assistant	447
AC2000.2.2	Select an object using the Objects Bar	449
AC2000.2.3	Print database objects (tables, forms, reports, queries)	459
AC2000.2.4	Navigate through records in a table, query, or form	457
AC2000.2.5	Create a database (using a Wizard or in Design View)	447
AC2000.3	**Building and modifying tables**	
AC2000.3.1	Create tables by using the Table Wizard	450
AC2000.3.2	Set primary keys	450, 452

TABLE A.7: Access 2000 Core Activities *(continued)*

STANDARDIZED CODING NUMBER	ACTIVITY	PAGE NUMBERS
AC2000.3.3	Modify field properties	453
AC2000.3.4	Use multiple data types	452
AC2000.3.5	Modify tables using Design View	452
AC2000.3.6	Use the Lookup Wizard	461
AC2000.3.7	Use the input mask wizard	454
AC2000.4	**Building and modifying forms**	
AC2000.4.1	Create a form with the Form Wizard	471
AC2000.4.2	Use the Control Toolbox to add controls	477, 514, 480
AC2000.4.3	Modify Format Properties (font, style, font size, color, caption, etc.) of controls	477
AC2000.4.4	Use form sections (headers, footers, detail)	475
AC2000.4.5	Use a Calculated Control on a form	480
AC2000.5	**Viewing and organizing information**	
AC2000.5.1	Use the Office Clipboard	25, 508
AC2000.5.2	Switch between object Views	456
AC2000.5.3	Enter records using a datasheet	456
AC2000.5.4	Enter records using a form	486
AC2000.5.5	Delete records from a table	458
AC2000.5.6	Find a record	487
AC2000.5.7	Sort records	486
AC2000.5.8	Apply and remove filters (filter by form and filter by selection)	486
AC2000.5.9	Specify criteria in a query	494
AC2000.5.10	Display related records in a subdatasheet	468
AC2000.5.11	Create a calculated field	498
AC2000.5.12	Create and modify a multi-table select query	492
AC2000.6	**Defining relationships**	
AC2000.6.1	Establish relationships	463
AC2000.6.2	Enforce referential integrity	466
AC2000.7	**Producing reports**	
AC2000.7.1	Create a report with the Report Wizard	512
AC2000.7.2	Preview and print a report	512
AC2000.7.3	Move and resize a control	516
AC2000.7.4	Modify format properties (font, style, font size, color, caption, etc.)	514
AC2000.7.5	Use the Control Toolbox to add controls	516

TABLE A.7: Access 2000 Core Activities *(continued)*

STANDARDIZED CODING NUMBER	ACTIVITY	PAGE NUMBERS
AC2000.7.6	Use report sections (headers, footers, detail)	513
AC2000.7.7	Use a Calculated Control in a report	516
AC2000.8	**Integrating with other applications**	
AC2000.8.1	Import data to a new table	507
AC2000.8.2	Save a table, query, form as a Web page	767
AC2000.8.3	Add Hyperlinks	769
AC2000.9	**Using Access Tools**	
AC2000.9.1	Print Database Relationships	466
AC2000.9.2	Backup and Restore a database	519
AC2000.9.3	Compact and Repair a database	519

TABLE A.8: Access 2000 Expert Activities

STANDARDIZED CODING NUMBER	ACTIVITY	PAGE NUMBERS
AC2000E.1	**Building and modifying tables**	
AC2000E.1.1	Set validation text	503
AC2000E.1.2	Define data validation criteria	503
AC2000E.1.3	Modify an input mask	454
AC2000E.1.4	Create and modify Lookup Fields	505
AC2000E.1.5	Optimize data type usage (double, long, int, byte, etc.)	504
AC2000E.2	**Building and modifying forms**	
AC2000E.2.1	Create a form in Design View	485
AC2000E.2.2	Insert a graphic on a form	480
AC2000E.2.3	Modify control properties	480
AC2000E.2.4	Customize form sections (headers, footers, detail)	480
AC2000E.2.5	Modify form properties	483
AC2000E.2.6	Use the Subform Control and synchronize forms	482
AC2000E.2.7	Create a Switchboard	524
AC2000E.3	**Refining queries**	
AC2000E.3.1	Apply filters (filter by form and filter by selection) in a query's recordset	486
AC2000E.3.2	Create a totals query	496
AC2000E.3.3	Create a parameter query	495
AC2000E.3.4	Specify criteria in multiple fields (AND vs. OR)	494

TABLE A.8: Access 2000 Expert Activities *(continued)*

STANDARDIZED CODING NUMBER	ACTIVITY	PAGE NUMBERS
AC2000E.3.5	Modify query properties (field formats, caption, input masks, etc.)	499
AC2000E.3.6	Create an action query (update, delete, insert)	500
AC2000E.3.7	Optimize queries using indexes	502
AC2000E.3.8	Specify join properties for relationships	492
AC2000E.4	**Producing reports**	
AC2000E.4.1	Insert a graphic on a report	516
AC2000E.4.2	Modify report properties	513
AC2000E.4.3	Create and modify a report in Design View	513
AC2000E.4.4	Modify control properties	515
AC2000E.4.5	Set section properties	513
AC2000E.4.6	Use the Subreport Control and synchronize reports	517
AC2000E.5	**Defining relationships**	
AC2000E.5.1	Establish one-to-one relationships	465
AC2000E.5.2	Establish many-to-many relationships	465
AC2000E.5.3	Set Cascade Update and Cascade Delete options	467
AC2000E.6	**Utilizing web capabilities**	
AC2000E.6.1	Create hyperlinks	769
AC2000E.6.2	Use the group and sort features of data access pages	773
AC2000E.6.3	Create a data access page	770
AC2000E.7	**Using Access tools**	
AC2000E.7.1	Set and modify a database password	523
AC2000E.7.2	Set startup options	525
AC2000E.7.3	Use Add-ins (Database Splitter, Analyzer, Link Table Manager)	520
AC2000E.7.4	Encrypt and Decrypt a database	523
AC2000E.7.5	Use simple replication (copy for a mobile user)	526
AC2000E.7.6	Run macros using controls	578
AC2000E.7.7	Create a macro using the Macro Builder	520
AC2000E.7.8	Convert database to a previous version	518
AC2000E.8	**Data Integration**	
AC2000E.8.1	Export database records to Excel	508
AC2000E.8.2	Drag and drop tables and queries to Excel	509
AC2000E.8.3	Present information as a chart (MS Graph)	460
AC2000E.8.4	Link to existing data	508

TABLE A.9: Outlook 2000 Core Activities

STANDARDIZED CODING NUMBER	ACTIVITY	PAGE NUMBERS
OL2000.1	**Use Outlook 2000 Mail to communicate with others inside and outside your company**	
OL2000.1.1	Read mail	564
OL2000.1.2	Send mail	558
OL2000.1.3	Compose mail by entering text	551
OL2000.1.4	Print mail	573
OL2000.1.5	Address mail by entering text	551
OL2000.1.6	Use mail features (forward, reply, recall)	563, 566
OL2000.1.7	Use address book to address mail	551
OL2000.1.8	Flag mail messages	559
OL2000.1.9	Navigate within mail	564
OL2000.1.10	Find messages	565
OL2000.1.11	Configure basic mail print options	573
OL2000.1.12	Work with attachments	566
OL2000.1.13	Add a signature to mail	554
OL2000.1.14	Customize the look of mail	553
OL2000.1.15	Use mail templates to compose mail	563
OL2000.1.16	Integrate and use mail with other Outlook components	545, 561, 581
OL2000.1.17	Customize menu and task bars	576
OL2000.2	**Use Outlook 2000 to manage messages**	
OL2000.2.1	Create folders	570
OL2000.2.2	Sort mail	564
OL2000.2.3	Set viewing options	609
OL2000.2.4	Archive mail messages	607
OL2000.2.5	Filter a view	609
OL2000.3	**Use the Outlook 2000 calendar**	
OL2000.3.1	Navigate within the calendar	585
OL2000.3.2	Schedule appointments and events	586
OL2000.3.3	Set reminders	586
OL2000.3.4	Print in calendar	546
OL2000.3.5	Schedule multi-day events	588
OL2000.3.6	Configure calendar print options	595
OL2000.3.7	Customize the calendar view	609

TABLE A.9: Outlook 2000 Core Activities *(continued)*

STANDARDIZED CODING NUMBER	ACTIVITY	PAGE NUMBERS
OL2000.3.8	Schedule recurring appointments	588
OL2000.3.9	Customize menu and task bars	576
OL2000.3.10	Add and remove meeting attendees	589
OL2000.3.11	Plan meetings involving others	589
OL2000.3.12	Save a personal or team calendar as a Web page	594
OL2000.3.13	Book office resources directly (e.g., conference rooms)	593
OL2000.3.14	Integrate calendar with other Outlook components	606
OL2000.4	**Navigate and use Outlook 2000 effectively**	
OL2000.4.1	Use Outlook Help and Office Assistant.	530
OL2000.4.2	Move items between folders	572
OL2000.4.3	Navigate between Outlook components	531
OL2000.4.4	Modify the Outlook Master Categories List	539
OL2000.4.5	Assign items to a category	539, 535
OL2000.4.6	Sort information using categories	609
OL2000.4.7	Use the Office Clipboard	530
OL2000.5	**Use Contacts**	
OL2000.5.1	Create, edit, and delete contacts	537
OL2000.5.2	Send contact information via e-mail	561
OL2000.5.3	Organize contacts by category	536, 535
OL2000.5.4	Manually record an activity in a journal	602
OL2000.5.5	Link activities to a Contacts	601
OL2000.5.6	Sort contacts using fields	642
OL2000.6	**Use Tasks**	
OL2000.6.1	Create and update one-time tasks	577, 581
OL2000.6.2	Accept and decline tasks	582
OL2000.6.3	Organize tasks using categories	609
OL2000.6.4	Assign tasks to others	581
OL2000.6.5	Create tasks from other Outlook components	606
OL2000.6.6	Change the view for tasks	535
OL2000.7	**Integrate Office applications and other applications with Outlook 2000 components**	
OL2000.7.1	Create and use Office documents inside Outlook 2000	544

TABLE A.9: Outlook 2000 Core Activities *(continued)*

STANDARDIZED CODING NUMBER	ACTIVITY	PAGE NUMBERS
OL2000.8	**Use Notes**	
OL2000.8.1	Create and edit notes	604
OL2000.8.2	Organize and view notes	604
OL2000.8.3	Customize notes	604

TABLE A.10: Outlook 2000 Expert Activities

STANDARDIZED CODING NUMBER	ACTIVITY	PAGE NUMBERS
OL2000E.1	**Use Outlook 2000 Mail to communicate with others inside and outside your company**	
OL2000E.1.1	Work off-line or use remote mail	620
OL2000E.1.2	Add a Vcard to a message	556
OL2000E.1.3	Create re-usable mail templates	563
OL2000E.1.4	Use mail with Office applications	628
OL2000E.2	**Use Outlook 2000 to manage messages**	
OL2000E.2.1	Customize the look of mail	553, 557
OL2000E.2.2	Create a personal address book	537
OL2000E.2.3	Customize menu and task bars	535
OL2000E.2.4	Track when mail messages are delivered or read	560
OL2000E.2.5	Create a personal distribution list	561
OL2000E.2.6	Create a Quick Synchronization group	622
OL2000E.2.7	Synchronize by message size	622
OL2000E.2.8	Organize mail using the Rules Wizard	572
OL2000E.3	**Use the Outlook 2000 calendar**	
OL2000E.3.1	Configure calendar options	595
OL2000E.3.2	Share calendar information with other applications over the Internet	595
OL2000E.3.3	Schedule real-time meetings (NetMeeting)	591
OL2000E.3.4	Schedule times to watch broadcasts using NetShow	591
OL2000E.4	**Share folders and files with other Outlook users and with users inside and outside of the company**	
OL2000E.4.1	Use Netfolders and public folders	616
OL2000E.4.2	Grant delegate access	617
OL2000E.4.3	Grant permissions to folders	617

TABLE A.10: Outlook 2000 Expert Activities *(continued)*

STANDARDIZED CODING NUMBER	ACTIVITY	PAGE NUMBERS
OL2000E.5	**Navigate and use Outlook 2000 effectively**	
OL2000E.5.1	Customize and use Outlook Today	548
OL2000E.5.2	Configure time zone information	592
OL2000E.5.3	Manage favorite Web site addresses	598
OL2000E.5.4	Import and export data between Outlook and other mail applications.	537, 572
OL2000E.5.5	Create Outlook forms	611
OL2000E.5.6	Create a shortcut to a file on your Outlook Bar	597
OL2000E.6	**Use Contacts**	
OL2000E.6.1	Flag contacts for follow-up (reminder)	559
OL2000E.6.2	Customize Contacts menu and task bars	535
OL2000E.6.3	Integrate Contacts with other Outlook components	579, 602
OL2000E.6.4	Use Contacts with Office applications	544
OL2000E.7	**Use Tasks**	
OL2000E.7.1	Create and update recurring tasks	579
OL2000E.7.2	Customize menu and task bars	535
OL2000E.7.3	Record tasks for any with Office file with the journal	601
OL2000E.7.4	Set delegate access to share tasks with two or more people.	617
OL2000E.8	**Integrate Office applications and other applications with Outlook 2000 components**	
OL2000E.8.1	Import and export data between Outlook and other Office applications	546
OL2000E.8.2	Use Mail Merge with Word	628
OL2000E.9	**Use the fax service from within Outlook 2000**	
OL2000E.9.1	Receive a fax	569
OL2000E.9.2	Create and send a fax from within Outlook 2000.	568
OL2000E.9.3	Customize a fax	568
OL2000E.10	**Use Newsreader**	
OL2000E.10.1	Send and receive information through Newsreader	575
OL2000E.10.2	Set up Newsreader	575

TABLE A.11: FrontPage 2000 Core Activities

STANDARDIZED CODING NUMBER	ACTIVITY	PAGE NUMBERS
FP2000.1	**Create a new Web site**	
FP2000.1.1	Save a FrontPage Web	792
FP2000.1.2	Create a Web site using a Web wizard	790
FP2000.1.3	Create a Web site using a Web template	790
FP2000.2	**Open and edit an existing FrontPage-based Web site**	
FP2000.2.1	Open an existing FrontPage Web	795, 796
FP2000.2.2	Modify and save changes to the Web site	795
FP2000.3	**Apply and edit a Theme across the entire Web site**	
FP2000.3.1	Apply a Theme to entire Web site	832
FP2000.3.2	Apply a custom Theme across entire Web site	833
FP2000.4	**Add a new Web page**	
FP2000.4.1	Create and Preview a new Web page using a FrontPage page template or wizard	835
FP2000.4.2	Create a new page within Page View	778
FP2000.5	**Open, view and rename Web page**	
FP2000.5.1	View a Web document in Normal, HTML and Preview view	802
FP2000.5.2	Open an Office document in a FrontPage Web	798
FP2000.5.3	Rename page title and change page URL	797
FP2000.6	**Import text and images onto Web page**	
FP2000.6.1	Add or import images into a Web page (automatically converted to GIF/JPEG)	812
FP2000.6.2	Add or import text to a Web page (automatically converted to HTML)	798
FP2000.6.3	Add or import elements from a Web site to a FrontPage Web	799
FP2000.7	**Type and format text and paragraphs and create hyperlinks**	
FP2000.7.1	Type and format text/fonts on a Web page	778
FP2000.7.2	Add multi-level bulleted or numbered lists to Web page	781
FP2000.7.3	Format bulleted or numbered lists	782
FP2000.7.4	Add hyperlinks pointing to: an existing page in the current site, the WWW, or a brand new page	800
FP2000.7.5	Use the Format Painter to apply formats	779
FP2000.7.6	Use the Office Clipboard	780
FP2000.8	**Edit images, apply image effects; create hotspots**	
FP2000.8.1	Rotate, flip, bevel, or resize images on a Web page	817

TABLE A.11: FrontPage 2000 Core Activities *(continued)*

STANDARDIZED CODING NUMBER	ACTIVITY	PAGE NUMBERS
FP2000.8.2	Add text over image	819
FP2000.8.3	Create a hotspot (clickable imagemap)	819
FP2000.9	**Create and edit tables on a Web page**	
FP2000.9.1	Create tables on a Web page	782
FP2000.9.2	Erase or delete table rows or columns	788
FP2000.9.3	Draw or add table rows or columns	787
FP2000.9.4	Resize tables and cells	786
FP2000.9.5	Select and merge table cells	787
FP2000.10	**Insert dynamic, Active Elements and FrontPage components on a Web page**	
FP2000.10.1	Add a Hit Counter to Web page	839
FP2000.10.2	Format Page Transition for Web page	840
FP2000.10.3	Add or edit scrolling Marquee text on a Web page	842
FP2000.10.4	Add a Search Form to Web page	844
FP2000.11	**View and organize Web site documents**	
FP2000.11.1	View a Web site in Reports View, Hyperlinks View, or Folders View	793
FP2000.11.2	View your Web site structure and print it from Navigation View	793, 826
FP2000.11.3	Move and organize files using drag and drop in Folders View and Navigation View	844, 793
FP2000.12	**Manage a Web site (including all files, pages and hyperlinks) and automatically keep contents up-to-date**	
FP2000.12.1	Check spelling on a page or across a Web site	780, 869
FP2000.12.2	Change file name in Folders View and update its hyperlinks	797
FP2000.12.3	Verify hyperlinks	875
FP2000.12.4	Use Global Find and Replace across a Web site	870
FP2000.13	**Manage tasks**	
FP2000.13.1	View task history	866
FP2000.13.2	View and sort tasks in Tasks View	866

TABLE A.12: FrontPage 2000 Expert Activities

STANDARDIZED CODING NUMBER	ACTIVITY	PAGE NUMBERS
FP2000E.1	**Create a FrontPage Web using existing resources**	
FP2000E.1.1	Use Import Wizard to import an existing Web site from a file into FrontPage	799

TABLE A.12: FrontPage 2000 Expert Activities *(continued)*

STANDARDIZED CODING NUMBER	ACTIVITY	PAGE NUMBERS
FP2000E.1.2	Use Import Wizard to import an existing Web site from a URL into FrontPage	799
FP2000E.1.3	Modify HTML tags and verify results using Reveal Tags	803
FP2000E.1.4	Use buttons and drop-down menus to insert code directly in HTML View	804
FP2000E.2	**Apply and change Themes for an entire Web site and individual Web pages**	
FP2000E.2.1	Select a new Theme and apply to an individual Web page	834
FP2000E.2.2	Change attributes (Vivid Colors, Active Graphics, Background Image) for a currently selected site-wide Theme	832
FP2000E.2.3	Create a custom Theme and apply it to an individual Web page	834
FP2000E.3	**Create and organize navigational structure for entire Web site**	
FP2000E.3.1	Rename new pages in Navigation View	827
FP2000E.3.2	Add new pages to Navigation View	827
FP2000E.3.3	Add existing pages to Navigation View	824
FP2000E.3.4	Use drag and drop to organize/re-structure pages in Navigation View	824
FP2000E.4	**Modify the Web page layout**	
FP2000E.4.1	Position graphics on a page	815
FP2000E.4.2	Position text on a page	815
FP2000E.5	**Add or edit Shared Borders across entire site and on individual Web pages**	
FP2000E.5.1	Turn off (deselect) site-wide Shared Borders for the current Web page	830
FP2000E.5.2	Edit content within Shared Borders for an entire Web site	832
FP2000E.5.3	Edit content within Shared Borders for current Web page	832
FP2000E.5.4	Turn on (set) alternate Shared Borders for the current Web page	830
FP2000E.6	**Automatically add navigation bars and page banners to Web pages**	
FP2000E.6.1	Add Navigation Bar to the top of a Web page	827
FP2000E.6.2	Add Page Banner to the top of a Web page	830
FP2000E.6.3	Select/change levels of navigational buttons to include in navigation bar on Web page	827
FP2000E.7	**Add background elements to Web pages**	
FP2000E.7.1	Add a background image on a Web Page	822

TABLE A.12: FrontPage 2000 Expert Activities *(continued)*

STANDARDIZED CODING NUMBER	ACTIVITY	PAGE NUMBERS
FP2000E.8	**Manipulate table contents on a Web page**	
FP2000E.8.1	Center image or text within a table cell	785, 786
FP2000E.8.2	Add a custom background color or image to an entire table and to individual table cells	822
FP2000E.8.3	Add a table within a table	788
FP2000E.9	**Enhance or edit a Web page with custom text/hyperlink styles and formatting**	
FP2000E.9.1	View page Estimated Time to Download	865
FP2000E.9.2	Resample/ Restore image on Web page	814
FP2000E.9.3	Format special styles for fonts, paragraphs, and hyperlinks	805
FP2000E.10	**Customize a Web page with dynamic, Active Elements and FrontPage components**	
FP2000E.10.1	Add Hover Button to Web page	846
FP2000E.10.2	Edit Hover Button transitional effect	846
FP2000E.10.3	Change FrontPage component properties	846
FP2000E.10.4	Insert pre-built and Office Web components into a page	837
FP2000E11	**Build a Web site for user input**	
FP2000E.11.1	Add text boxes, check boxes, radio buttons, drop down pick lists, and push buttons	854
FP2000E.11.2	Save form to file	850
FP2000E.11.3	Add Search Form to a Web page	854
FP2000E.11.4	Save form to email	850
FP2000E.11.5	Create a custom form on a Web page	848
FP2000E.12	**Integrate databases**	
FP2000E.12.1	Create a form that sends data to an Access database	851
FP2000E.12.2	Incorporate data access pages into a Web page	847
FP2000E.12.3	Incorporate database queries using the Database Results Wizard	847, 858
FP2000E.13	**Use collaboration features**	
FP2000E.13.1	Check in and check out FrontPage files	872
FP2000E.13.2	Set rights to a FrontPage Web and sub-Webs	874
FP2000E.14	**Create and edit a Frames Web page**	
FP2000E.14.1	Edit size of existing frames in Frames page using drag and drop of border lines	862
FP2000E.14.2	Edit actual content within a frame on the Frames page	862
FP2000E.14.3	Create an entirely new frame on an existing Frames page by dragging and dropping existing Frames page outside border	862

TABLE A.12: FrontPage 2000 Expert Activities *(continued)*

STANDARDIZED CODING NUMBER	ACTIVITY	PAGE NUMBERS
FP2000E.14.4	Create a new Frames page from template or using Frames Wizard	861
FP2000E.14.5	Add target content within a frame	862
FP2000E.15	**Publish a Web site**	
FP2000E.15.1	Publish a Web from one server to another	878
FP2000E.15.2	Use FrontPage or Microsoft Personal Web Server as appropriate	877
FP2000E.15.3	Set FrontPage/server permissions as appropriate	877

TABLE A.13: PhotoDraw 2000 Core Activities

STANDARDIZED CODING NUMBER	ACTIVITY	PAGE NUMBERS
PD2000.1	**Use PhotoDraw templates**	
PD2000.1.1	Use PhotoDraw templates to create a 3-D Web button	710
PD2000.1.2	Customize a PhotoDraw Web banner template by replacing the template graphic	711
PD2000.2	**Draw and paint in PhotoDraw**	
PD2000.2.1	Modify a line or outline style with Plain, Artistic, and Photo paintbrushes	681
PD2000.2.2	Create an object using Shapes	679
PD2000.2.3	Create an object using Draw and Paint brushes	679, 685
PD2000.2.4	Apply a Negative effect to a PhotoDraw object	693
PD2000.3	**Create text in PhotoDraw**	
PD2000.3.1	Bold and italicize text	703
PD2000.3.2	Change font size and style	703
PD2000.3.3	Create a text object in PhotoDraw	703
PD2000.3.4	Apply 3-D, Bend and designer text effects	704
PD2000.4	**Insert objects in PhotoDraw**	
PD2000.4.1	Use Visual Insert to locate and insert an image in PhotoDraw	666
PD2000.4.2	Insert a graphic file in a PhotoDraw picture	667
PD2000.4.3	Insert a digital image into a PhotoDraw picture	665
PD2000.5	**Arrange objects in PhotoDraw**	
PD2000.5.1	Resize and reposition objects in PhotoDraw	669, 668
PD2000.5.2	Group and ungroup objects in PhotoDraw	671
PD2000.5.3	Order and align objects in PhotoDraw	671
PD2000.5.4	Rotate and flip objects in PhotoDraw	670

TABLE A.13: PhotoDraw 2000 Core Activities *(continued)*

STANDARDIZED CODING NUMBER	ACTIVITY	PAGE NUMBERS
PD2000.6	**Compose and modify graphics in PhotoDraw**	
PD2000.6.1	Crop a photographic object in PhotoDraw	687
PD2000.6.2	Resize objects in PhotoDraw	669
PD2000.6.3	Specify colors for fills, lines, and outlines	679
PD2000.6.4	Apply shadow, transparency and fade out attributes to a PhotoDraw object	697
PD2000.6.5	Apply Designer Effects to a PhotoDraw object	701
PD2000.6.6	Colorize a PhotoDraw object	693
PD2000.6.7	Blur and sharpen objects in PhotoDraw	694
PD2000.6.8	Combine several PhotoDraw objects into one picture	664
PD2000.6.9	Distort effects	700
PD2000.7	**Edit and retouch photographs in PhotoDraw**	
PD2000.7.1	Adjust brightness and contrast attributes of a PhotoDraw object	692
PD2000.7.2	Blur and sharpen pictures in PhotoDraw	697
PD2000.7.3	Adjust the tint attribute of a PhotoDraw object	692
PD2000.7.4	Remove red eye from a photographic object in PhotoDraw	694
PD2000.7.5	Remove dust and spots from a photographic object in PhotoDraw	694
PD2000.7.6	Remove scratches from a photographic object in PhotoDraw	694
PD2000.7.7	Correct the tint of a photographic object in PhotoDraw	692
PD2000.7.8	Adjust hue and saturation attributes of a PhotoDraw object	693
PD2000.7.9	Clone an area of a picture in PhotoDraw	695
PD2000.7.10	Hide portions of a picture in PhotoDraw	687
PD2000.7.11	Change the image Preview	677
PD2000.8	**Save and print in PhotoDraw**	
PD2000.8.1	Print a PhotoDraw picture	675
PD2000.8.2	Use the "Save for Use In" Wizard to save a PhotoDraw picture for use in other Office 2000 applications	672
PD2000.8.3	Save PhotoDraw pictures in MIX, GIF, JPEG, and PNG formats	672
PD2000.8.4	Preview a PhotoDraw picture to determine the amount of time required to download the image from a Web site for a given resolution and file type	675
PD2000.8.5	Fit the PhotoDraw canvas to the object size	662

TABLE A.14: PhotoDraw 2000 Expert Activities

STANDARDIZED CODING NUMBER	ACTIVITY	PAGE NUMBERS
PD2000E.1	**Use PhotoDraw templates**	
PD2000E.1.1	Apply a Designer Edge to a PhotoDraw Web button template	712
PD2000E.1.2	Use Designer Clip Art to create a custom clip art image	712
PD2000E.2	**Create graphic objects in PhotoDraw**	
PD2000E.2.1	Add, delete, and edit points of a shape in PhotoDraw	684
PD2000E.3	**Modify 3-D attributes in PhotoDraw**	
PD2000E.3.1	Change fill settings on a 3-D PhotoDraw object	705
PD2000E.3.2	Change rotate settings on a 3-D PhotoDraw object	706
PD2000E.3.3	Change extrusion settings on a 3-D PhotoDraw object	706, 707
PD2000E.3.4	Change tilt settings on a 3-D PhotoDraw object	705
PD2000E.3.5	Change bevel settings on a 3-D PhotoDraw object	707
PD2000E.3.6	Change lighting settings on 3-D PhotoDraw objects	707
PD2000E.4	**Modify objects in PhotoDraw**	
PD2000E.4.1	Erase an area in a picture	687
PD2000E.4.2	Colorize an object	693
PD2000E.4.3	Apply Designer Effects to objects	701
PD2000E.4.4	Clone an area in a picture	695
PD2000E.4.5	Use a paintbrush to modify, correct or distort an object	681, 700
PD2000E.4.6	Blend edges in a picture	695
PD2000E.4.7	Bulge or shrink an area in picture	700
PD2000E.4.8	Smudge or smear an area in a picture	695, 700
PD2000E.4.9	Modify Designer Effects settings	701
PD2000E.4.10	Skew objects in PhotoDraw	668
PD2000E.4.11	Use custom color palettes	682
PD2000E.4.12	Import/export color palettes	682
PD2000E.4.13	Apply a plug-in effect	700
PD2000E.5	**Retouch photograph objects in PhotoDraw**	
PD2000E.5.1	Correct the brightness and contrast of a photograph in PhotoDraw	692
PD2000E.6	**Populate the Clip Gallery**	
PD2000E.6.1	Create new categories in Clip Gallery	642
PD2000E.6.2	Add keywords to Clip Gallery pictures	642
PD2000E.6.3	Add PhotoDraw content to a picture	667

TABLE A.14: PhotoDraw 2000 Expert Activities *(continued)*

STANDARDIZED CODING NUMBER	ACTIVITY	PAGE NUMBERS
PD2000E.7	**Compose pictures in PhotoDraw**	
PD2000E.7.1	Set gridlines in PhotoDraw	668
PD2000E.7.2	Blend edges in a PhotoDraw picture	695
PD2000E.7.3	Trace, remove, and place an object from within a PhotoDraw picture	689
PD2000E.7.4	Match brightness, contrast, and color in a PhotoDraw picture	692, 682, 683
PD2000E.8	**Save and share pictures in PhotoDraw**	
PD2000E.8.1	Size a PhotoDraw picture output	675, 674
PD2000E.8.2	Save a PhotoDraw picture as a JPEG at specific export size	672
PD2000E.8.3	Save a PhotoDraw picture as a preview in a Clip Gallery category	674
PD2000E.9	**Print pictures from PhotoDraw**	
PD2000E.9.1	Print/re-print a PhotoDraw picture on Avery labels	677

Index

Note to the Reader: Page numbers in **bold** indicate the principal discussion of a topic or the definition of a term. Page numbers in *italic* indicate illustrations.

Numbers

A

B

C

D

E

F

G

H

I

J

K

L

M

N

O

P

S

T

U

V

W

X

Z